S0-BSR-004

HF

Consumer Behavior
Buying, Having, and Being

Michael R. Solomon
Rutgers University

Allyn and Bacon
Boston ▲ London ▲ Toronto ▲ Sydney ▲ Tokyo ▲ Singapore

Editor-in-Chief: Bill Barke
Executive Editor: Rich Wohl
Series Editor: Susan Nelle Barcomb
Series Editorial Assistant: Sarah Carter
Text Designer: Melinda Grosser for *silk*
Cover Administrator: Linda Dickinson
Cover Designer: Susan Slovinsky
Manufacturing Buyer: Megan Cochran
Editorial-Production Supervisor: Elaine Ober
Production Services by BMR Corte Madera, CA

Library of Congress Cataloging-in-Publication Data

Solomon, Michael R.
    Consumer behavior : buying, having, nad being / Michael R.
Solomon.
    p.   cm.
    Includes index.
    ISBN 0-205-13163-8
    1. Consumer behavior.   I. Title
HF5415.32.S6   1991
    658.8'342--dc20   91-41319
                                                   CIP

Printed in the United States of America
10 9 8 7 6 5 4 3 2 1 95 94 93 92 91

To Gail, Amanda, Zachary, and Alex —
my favorite consumers

Contents

CHAPTER 3   MOTIVATION AND INVOLVEMENT   65

CHAPTER 4   LEARNING 99

SECTION II: THE CONSUMER AS A DECISION MAKER AND PRODUCT USER 199

Preface

I wrote this book because I am fascinated by people's everyday behavior—especially their behavior as consumers. Consumer behavior is, to me, the study of how our world is influenced by the actions of marketers. Because I am a consumer myself, I have a selfish interest in learning more about how this process works.

We are, in fact, all consumers. Nearly everyone can relate to the experience of last-minute shopping at the mall, agonizing over an important purchase, celebrating a holiday, or commemorating a landmark event such as a graduation or a wedding. Thus, many of the topics in this book have both personal and professional relevance to the reader, whether he or she is a student, a professor, or a marketing practitioner.

BEYOND FAHRVERGNÜGEN: BUYING, HAVING, AND BEING

As the book's subtitle suggests, my vision of this field embraces buying, having, and being. Consumer behavior is more than the act of buying a Volkswagen: It goes beyond the act of purchase to considerations of how having (or not having) things affects our life; it examines how owning a Volkswagen (or a Chevy) influences the way we feel about ourselves and about each other—our state of being.

A BALANCE OF TRADITIONAL AND EMERGING PERSPECTIVES

The field of consumer behavior is young, dynamic, and in flux; I have tried to express the field's diversity in these pages. As Chapter 1 explains, consumer researchers currently active in the field represent virtually every social science discipline, plus a scattering of people from the liberal arts and physical sciences. This academic "melting pot" has created a healthy mix of research methods and of attitudes about what are and are not appropriate issues for researchers to study.

Two colleagues in adjacent offices may study consumer behavior in opposite ways. The first, in her lab, explores the ways people mentally encode brand information in memory. The second, in the field, videotapes families as they use a microwave. (A third colleague, analyzing the way women are depicted in Japanese versus American car ads, may think they are both on the wrong track!) This plurality is what makes the field so exciting right now.

Despite the frequent debates in the field, I do not believe that one has to choose between the "traditional" perspective on the consumer as an objective decision maker and the "emerging" perspective on the consumer as a subjective, idiosyncratic experiencer of emotions and fantasies. Each perspective has its merits, and each is appropriate for analyzing different consumer behavior issues. I have worked hard to provide a bridge between these two approaches in the hope that you will feel free to cross back and forth as needed.

HOW THIS BOOK IS ORGANIZED

This book is organized in four parts from a "micro" to a "macro" perspective. Section I begins with issues related to the individual consumer at his or her most "micro" level. It examines how an individual receives information from the immediate environment. This first part covers motivation, learning, memory, and the formation of attitudes. Section II explores the ways in which consumers use information to make decisions about buying and having various goods and services. Building on these parts, Section III develops and expands the focus by considering how the consumer functions within a larger social structure. This structure includes the influence of social groups to which the consumer belongs, social class, and also the effects of memberships in subcultures such as ethnic groups, age groups, and place of residence. Finally, Section IV traces marketing's impact on mass culture, which has been considerable. These effects include marketing's relationship to the expression of cultural values and consumers' lifestyle choices; how products and services are related to rituals and cultural myths; and finally the interface between marketing efforts and the creation of art, music, and other forms of popular culture. I hope you will enjoy reading these final chapters as much as I enjoyed writing them.

FEATURES OF THIS BOOK

There are a number of special features and pedagogical tools that are woven into each chapter to make reading and studying consumer behavior a rewarding and fun experience.

OPENING CASE STORY

Each chapter opens with a case story describing a specific consumer engaged in a particular form of consumer behavior. Real products, real companies, and real situations are used to paint a vivid picture.

REAL-WORLD EXAMPLES

Throughout each chapter real-world examples are used to highlight specific behavior. Recognizable products, services, and strategies are used to illustrate principles of consumer behavior.

ART PROGRAM
Various tables, charts, photographs, and advertisements are used throughout the text to highlight important points and make studying the subject more interesting.

MULTICULTURAL DIMENSIONS
These boxes underscore how different cultures respond to various marketing strategies and how marketers use cultural differences to advertise and sell products and services to various cultures and subgroups within a country.

MARKETING OPPORTUNITIES
The book emphasizes the importance of understanding consumers in formulating a marketing strategy. To illustrate the potential of consumer research to strengthen marketing strategy, numerous boxed examples offer specific applications of consumer behavior concepts or windows of opportunity where such concepts could be used. In the text you will find these labeled *Marketing Opportunity*.

MARKETING PITFALLS
This book does *not* assume that everything marketers do is ethically, physically, or socially in the best interests of consumers or of their environment. Likewise, not all consumer behavior is positive. Marketing mistakes or ethically suspect activities are highlighted in boxes designated *Marketing Pitfall*.

CHAPTER SUMMARY
A descriptive chapter summary highlights the main points and provides an easy mechanism for review.

KEY TERMS
Key terms from the chapter are provided for review at the end of each chapter. They are defined in the glossary at the end of the text.

REVIEW QUESTIONS AND DISCUSSION TOPICS
Two kinds of thought-provoking questions are provided at the end of each chapter. The first, Review Questions, are designed to help you master the text material and developing a working knowledge of the subject. The second, Discussion Topics, are designed for lively discussions concerning specific chapter content.

HANDS-ON EXERCISES
These experiential activities follow the review and discussion topics at the end of each chapter. They allow practice and application of consumer behavior chapter content to real-world situations.

END NOTES
End notes give additional references to further studies and articles.

BUYING, HAVING, AND BEING: THE WASHINGTON POST CONSUMER BEHAVIOR COMPANION.

This is a special reader containing over seventy-five articles from The Washington Post's Style section. These current articles offer a wide range of readings to broaden your understanding of consumer behavior issues and to deepen your insight into marketing practices. If your professor has not already ordered this supplement, ask her to do so or contact your campus bookstore.

SUPPLEMENTARY MATERIALS AVAILABLE FOR INSTRUCTORS

Instructor's Annotated Edition

Instructor's Resource Manual with Test Bank and Transparency Masters

Computerized Test Bank

Video: The Consumer Behavior Odyssey

For further information about these supplements, please contact your Allyn and Bacon representative.

Acknowledgements

No undertaking of this magnitude can be done alone, and I certainly had help and encouragement from many people during this long and challenging process. I would like to take this opportunity to thank as many of them as I can.

I have been tremendously impressed by the competence and professionalism of the people at Allyn and Bacon, who have so ably guided me through the treacherous shoals of writing a textbook. Henry Reece and Ellen Mann first approached me with the proposition of writing this book and they shared my vision of what a good consumer text should be. Elaine Ober and Sylvia Dovner created a book plan designed to maximize the reader's understanding and interest; Bill Barke taught me to appreciate the blues; and Susan Nelle Barcomb brought the project to fruition. Thanks to all of them.

I am grateful for the outstanding advice on how to improve this book that was provided by my peer reviewers. Special thanks go to Ishmael Akkah, Wayne State University; Laurel Anderson, Arizona State University–West; Sharon Beatty, University of Alabama at Tuscaloosa; Bettina Cornwell, Memphis State University; Ron Goldsmith, Florida State University; Cathy Goodwin, University of Alaska; Ronald Hill, Villanova University; Carol Kaufman, Rutgers University–Camden; Robert Kleine, Arizona State University; James Leigh, Texas A&M University; Lee Meadow, Salisbury State University; Bruce Newman, DePaul University; Carol Scott, University of California–Los Angeles; Mary Zimmer, University of Georgia; George Zinkhan, University of Houston.

My friends and colleagues at Rutgers have been fantastic since the project began. Without their support and tolerance I would never have been able to sustain the "illusion" that I was still an active Department Chair during this time. I would like to thank the Dean's Office for support and resources, and especially Sakae Hata for making my life easier. My secretary, Carol Gibson, has been remarkably patient and helpful over the last two years; I'm sure she will be relieved when office life returns to what passes for normal. My departmental colleagues have provided nothing but enthusiasm and constructive comments. I am particularly indebted to Beth Hirschman and Basil Englis for this intellectual and emotional support—they personify my image of what good colleagues (and friends) should be. Also, I am grateful to my students, who have been a source of inspiration, examples, and feedback. The satisfaction I have garnered from teaching them about consumer behavior motivated me to write a book that I felt they would like to read.

Last but not least, I would like to thank my family and extended family for standing by me during this hectic period. I send my gratitude and love to my parents, Jackie and Henry, and to my in-laws, Marilyn and Phil. My super children, Amanda, Zachary, and Alexandra, made the sun shine even on grey days. Finally, thanks above all to Gail, my wonderful wife, friend, and partner: I do it all for you.

CONSUMER BEHAVIOR

The Conceptual and Strategic Importance of Consumer Behavior

CHAPTER 1

As the whistle blows at 3:00, Darlene breathes a sigh of relief and rushes outside to grab a smoke. She looks forward to these breaks from the assembly line, when her friends gather to swap the latest stories about their love lives, new clothes, music videos, and other must haves. Darlene feels that she has much in common with her group. They share the same interests, read the same magazines, and they all believe in putting in their forty hours during the week and partying all weekend.

On her way out, Darlene experiences a moment of panic as she remembers that she is out of cigarettes. She runs over to the factory commissary and quickly scans the cigarette rack for Marlboros, the brand she has smoked since high school. Darlene scarcely notices the many other brands competing for her attention. She tried Virginia Slims once, but her friends laughed at her. Since then, only Marlboros will do. As she lights up, Darlene fantasizes about riding on horseback into the sunset with the Marlboro Man— she loves the strong, silent type.

INTRODUCTION TO CONSUMER BEHAVIOR: A DAY IN THE LIFE OF A SMOKER

This book is about everyday people like Darlene. It concerns the products and services they buy and use and the ways in which these fit into their lives. This introductory chapter briefly describes some important aspects of the field of consumer behavior including the topics studied, who studies them, and some different ways in which these issues are approached by consumer researchers. For now, though, let's return to the opening vignette about Darlene, the factory worker. Although not exciting, even this brief story allows us to highlight some aspects of consumer behavior that will be covered in the rest of the book.

- As a consumer, Darlene can be described and compared to other individuals in a number of ways. For some purposes, marketers might find it useful to categorize Darlene in terms of her age, sex, income, or occupation. These are some examples of descriptive characteristics of a population, or *demographics.* In other cases, marketers would rather know something about Darlene's interests in clothing or music or about how she spends her leisure time. This sort of information comes under the category of *psychographics,* which refers to aspects of a person's lifestyle and personality. Knowledge of consumer characteristics plays an extremely important role in many marketing applications, such as defining the market for a product or deciding upon the appropriate techniques to employ to reach that market.
- Darlene's purchasing decisions are heavily influenced by the opinions and behaviors of her friends. A lot of product information, as well as recommendations to use or avoid particular brands, is transmitted through conversations among people rather than through television commercials, magazines, billboards, or other media.

    In the case of Darlene and her friends, *group bonds* are cemented by the common products they use. There is pressure on each group member to buy things that will meet with the group's approval, and often there is a price to pay in the form of group rejection or embarrassment when one does not conform to others' conceptions of what is good or bad, "in" or "out." This group also shares certain patterns of behavior, or *rituals,* such as Darlene's daily cigarette breaks, that involve the consumption of products.
- As members of a large society, such as the United States, people share certain *cultural values,* or strongly held beliefs, about the way the world should be structured. Other values are shared by members of *subcultures,* or smaller groups within the culture. Some examples are Hispanics, teens, Midwesterners, or even "Valley Girls," and "Hell's Angels." Darlene's *reference group,* or people whose opinions matter to her, share the viewpoint that a good job is one that pays the bills and allows a person to do fun things during leisure time.

- When buying cigarettes on her break, Darlene was exposed to many competing brands (there are over 250 brands of cigarettes in the marketplace). Many of the brands did not capture her attention at all; others were noticed and rejected because they did not fit the image with which she identified. Marketing strategies for most brands are *targeted* to specific groups of consumers rather than to everybody—even if this means that untargeted consumers will not be interested or will even deliberately avoid that brand.
- Brands often have clearly defined images or personalities that are formed by product advertising, packaging, and other marketing strategies that *position* a product in a certain way. Consumers often choose products because of desirable images, believing that the qualities represented by the images somehow correspond to their own, or will somehow rub off onto them. Darlene's favorite cigarettes, Marlboros, for example, convey a very powerful image composed of such attributes as ruggedness, freedom, and independence.

  As in the case of Marlboros, brand images are sometimes altered, or repositioned, to gain a larger share of the market. Many people do not realize that when Marlboro cigarettes were introduced in 1924, they were intended to appeal primarily to women and even featured a red "Beauty Tip" to mask lipstick marks. Thirty years later, the company reformulated its strategy to create the brand image represented by the Marlboro Man. Marlboro now accounts for almost one pack of every four sold in the United States.[1]
- Consumers' decisions about products are often affected by their interpretation of physical factors, such as the shape and color of a package. The *perceptual cues* conveyed by the packaging as well as the *symbolism* used in a brand name or advertisement can evoke meaningful associations that are transferred to the product. These interpretations may be influenced by—and often reflect—how a particular group feels people should define themselves at that point in time. For example, Darlene's history with Marlboro's says something about how men and women are viewed within her group, while the Virginia Slims brand rejected by Darlene's friends is more likely to be popular among women who see themselves as liberated ("You've come a long way, baby"), and Capri (with its flowery design printed on the cigarette itself) is more likely to appeal to fashion-conscious women. Many product meanings are hidden below the surface of the packaging and advertising, and this book discusses some of the methods used by marketers and social scientists to discover or apply these meanings.
- Products and services are important sources of consumer *experiences,* which may be both positive and negative. These may range from the relief a dedicated smoker like Darlene feels upon gratifying a harmful habit to a romantic fantasy that she experiences after lighting up. This book highlights both good and bad aspects of consumption and discusses both functional and experiential product benefits.

WHAT IS CONSUMER BEHAVIOR?

As treated in this book, **consumer behavior** covers a lot of ground: It is the study of the *processes involved when individuals or groups select, purchase, use, or dispose of products, services, ideas, or experiences to satisfy needs and desires.* Consumers take many forms, ranging from an eight-year-old child begging her mother for Gummy Bears to an executive in a large corporation deciding on a multimillion-dollar computer system. The objects that are consumed can include anything from canned peas, a massage, democracy, or rap music, to other people (e.g., the images of rock stars). Needs and desires to be satisfied range from hunger and thirst to love, status, or even spiritual fulfillment.

THE PROCESS In its early stages of development, the field was often referred to as *buyer behavior,* reflecting an emphasis on the interaction between consumers and producers at the time of purchase. Marketers now recognize that consumer behavior is an ongoing process, not merely what happens at the moment a consumer hands over money or a credit card and in turn receives some good or service.

The **exchange,** in which two or more organizations or people give and receive something of value, is an integral part of marketing.[3] While exchange remains an important part of consumer behavior, the expanded view emphasizes the entire consumption process, which includes the issues that influence the consumer before, during, and after a purchase. Figure 1-1 illustrates some of the issues that are addressed during each stage of the consumption process.

THE CONSUMERS A consumer is generally thought of as a person who identifies a need or desire, makes a purchase, and then disposes of the product during the three stages in the consumption process. In many

MULTICULTURAL DIMENSIONS

Marketers are divided over whether product meanings can be developed and communicated uniformly to different cultures around the world. Some people advocate a standardized approach to cross-cultural product promotions. This strategy has several advantages. It reduces costs, gives marketers more control over ad content, permits the creation of strong and consistent brand images, and simplifies strategic planning. This approach has been especially popular in Europe, where brands sold in different countries are being standardized to form new "Eurobrands." For example, Mars, Inc., recently changed the name of the Marathon candy bar that sells in Great Britain to Snickers, the name under which it already sells in other countries.

Although the use of a standardized strategy is tempting, marketers must be sensitive to the different interpretations of images that may occur from one culture to another. Even the venerable Marlboro cowboy, who shows up on billboards around the world, ran into trouble in Hong Kong. In that country, a cowboy has the status of a common laborer. The company boosted the standing of its cowboy by taking care to photograph him on a white horse, a symbol of esteem in that culture.[2]

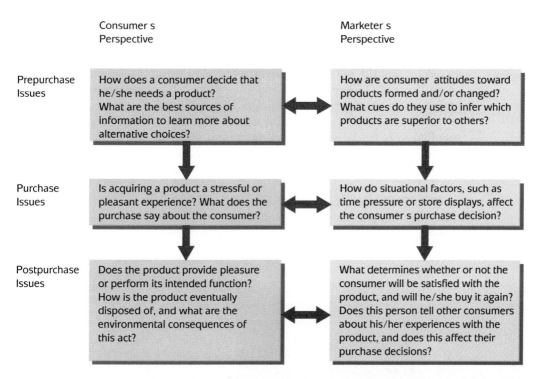

Consumer's Perspective		Marketer's Perspective
Prepurchase Issues	How does a consumer decide that he/she needs a product? What are the best sources of information to learn more about alternative choices?	How are consumer attitudes toward products formed and/or changed? What cues do they use to infer which products are superior to others?
Purchase Issues	Is acquiring a product a stressful or pleasant experience? What does the purchase say about the consumer?	How do situational factors, such as time pressure or store displays, affect the consumer's purchase decision?
Postpurchase Issues	Does the product provide pleasure or perform its intended function? How is the product eventually disposed of, and what are the environmental consequences of this act?	What determines whether or not the consumer will be satisfied with the product, and will he/she buy it again? Does this person tell other consumers about his/her experiences with the product, and does this affect their purchase decisions?

Figure 1-1 Some issues that arise during various stages in the consumption process

cases, however, different people may be involved in the process. The *purchaser* and *user* of a product might not be the same person, as when a parent picks out clothes for a teenager (and makes selections that can result in "fashion suicide" in the view of the teen). In other cases, another person may act as an *influencer,* providing recommendations for or against certain products without actually buying or using them. For example, a friend, rather than a parent, accompanying a teen on a shopping trip, might actually pick out the clothes that the teen decides to purchase.

Finally, consumers may be organizations or groups, in which one person may make the decisions involved in purchasing products that will be used by many, as when a purchasing agent orders the company's office supplies. In other organizational situations, purchase decisions may be made by a large group of people—for example, company accountants, designers, engineers, sales personnel, and others—all of whom will have a say in the various stages of the consumption process.

CONSUMERS AS ROLE PLAYERS The perspective of *role theory,* which this book emphasizes, takes the view that much of consumer behavior resembles actions in a play.[4] As in a play, each consumer has lines, props, costumes, and so on, and makes relevant consumption decisions. Since people act out many different roles, they sometimes alter their consumption decisions depending on the particular "play" they are in at the time. The criteria that they use to evaluate products and services in one of their roles may be quite different from those used in another role.

WHY STUDY CONSUMER BEHAVIOR?

The field of consumer behavior as defined in this book covers many topics. Why should managers, advertisers, and other professionals learn about this field? Very simply, understanding consumer behavior is good business. An elementary marketing concept states that organizations exist to satisfy consumers' wants and needs. These wants and needs can be satisfied only to the extent that marketers *understand* the people or organizations that will use the products and services they are trying to sell and that they do so better than their competitors.

CONSUMERS' IMPACT ON MARKETING STRATEGY

Consumer response is the ultimate test of whether or not a marketing strategy will succeed. Thus, knowledge about consumers is incorporated

This ad for Carrier Furnaces highlights the fact that consumers use different criteria to evaluate products, depending on the role they are playing at the time. The man in the ad is shown in two of his roles: an engineer by day and a homeowner by night. *Courtesy of Carrier Corporation, subsidiary of United Technologies Corporation.*

into virtually every facet of a successful marketing plan. Data about consumers helps marketers to define the market and to identify threats and opportunities in their own and different countries that will affect consumers' receptivity to the product.

TARGETED MARKETING STRATEGY: LISTENING TO CONSUMERS   A **targeted marketing strategy** defines both a market and the tactics used to reach that market. To appreciate the centrality of consumer behavior data in this vital process, consider the steps a company might go through after it decides to produce and market a new product.[5]

1. Define the relevant market. In this step, the market is broadly defined in terms of *product form,* or category, such as toothpaste, diet soda, or cigarettes. The company identifies the number of product users in the country.
2. Analyze characteristics and wants of potential customers. In this analysis, the company utilizes both demographic and psychographic information.
3. Identify bases for segmenting the market. For the company, this process involves the identification of characteristics that could isolate smaller markets existing within the larger market.
4. Define and describe market segments. After identifying appropriate bases for segmentation, the company develops *market segment profiles* for the different groups by describing their unique characteristics and desires.
5. Analyze competitors' positions. Within each segment of interest, the company wants to know how consumers perceive the brands that are already available. It identifies the **determinant attributes** of these brands, or product features that influence the consumers' choices.
6. Evaluate market segments. The cost of developing a new product to meet the needs of each segment is considered as well as the revenue potential if these needs are met.
7. Select market segments. On the basis of its analysis of the segments it has identified, the company decides which segment(s) to target.
8. Finalize the marketing mix. After selecting a target market, the company now decides upon the specific **marketing mix,** or the combination of variables over which marketers have control and which are usually known as the "Four P's": product, place (where the product is sold), price, and promotion. Careful decisions must be made about the new brand's position and how its image will be communicated in terms of pricing, naming, packaging, advertising, and so on.

▼   MARKETING PITFALL

The power of target marketing lies in its ability to fine-tune a product's features and image to make it especially appealing to its intended segment. Although this process occurs all of the time, objections are raised when it encourages consumption of unhealthy products such as cigarettes.

The R. J. Reynolds Company recently introduced a new brand of cigarettes called Dakota in several test markets. The marketing plan, submitted to the company by an outside consulting firm, specifically targets the cigarette to 18 to 24 year-old women like Darlene, with a high school education or less, who work in entry-level factory or service jobs. This segment is one of the few remaining demographic groups in the United States that is exhibiting an increase in smoking rates. Thus, from a purely fiscal point of view, it clearly has market potential.

The brand was developed to appeal to a segment that the company calls the Virile Female. This woman has the following psychographic characteristics: Her favorite pastimes are cruising, partying, and going to hot rod shows and tractor pulls with her boyfriend; her favorite television shows are "Roseanne" and evening soap operas. Her chief aspirations are to get married in her early twenties and to spend time with her boyfriend, doing whatever he does. R. J. Reynolds claims that the brand is aimed at switching current Marlboro smokers, not at attracting new smokers, but over 100 public health officials signed a resolution asking that the product be withdrawn.[6]

MARKET SEGMENTATION Effective market segmentation creates segments whose members are similar to one another in one or more characteristics and different from members of other segments. Depending upon its goals and resources, a company may choose to focus on only one segment or on several, or it may ignore differences among segments by pursuing a mass market strategy.

TABLE 1-1 Variables for market segmentation

Category	Variables	Location of Discussion
Demographic	Age	Chapter 14
	Sex	Chapter 7
	Social class, occupation, income	Chapter 12
	Ethnic group, religion	Chapter 13
	Stage in life	Chapter 9
	Purchaser versus user	Chapter 9
Geographic	Region of the country	Chapter 14
	Type of residence	Chapter 14
Psychographic	Self-concept, personality	Chapter 7
	Lifestyle	Chapter 15
Behavioral	Brand loyalty, extent of usage	Chapters 3, 4, 10
	Usage situation	Chapter 10
	Benefits desired	Chapter 3

At last! A male/female 18-49.

No one would dispute the fact that network television reaches males, females, younger viewers, and older viewers.

Unfortunately, those groups don't come as one person.

So companies selling nail polish reach millions of men. Makers of aftershave reach millions of women.

And cat food manufacturers reach millions of viewers who own pets named Spot.

In reality, the notion of mass marketing has become precisely that: a notion.

With astonishingly few exceptions, there are virtually no more products appropriately targeted to a mass audience. So the vast majority of advertisers on TV are reaching millions of viewers they don't need.

Worse than that, they're paying for them.

Which is why more and more major advertisers are becoming clients of ours. At Whittle Communications we create media that reach only the people our clients need to reach.

Our vehicles deliver messages about toothpaste on dentists' walls; news about baby products in pediatricians' offices; and ads about office equipment in a magazine delivered only to top-level executives.

In case after case, we've created media that deliver our clients' messages with exceptional impact, without competing advertising and without any waste at all.

And because our clients have benefited, so have we. For the past ten years our average annual growth rate has been 36%.

We're currently an $85,000,000 company with a staff of 650 people.

And obviously there isn't a male/female 18-49 among them.

Whittle
communications

© 1987 Whittle Communications L.P. Knoxville/New York

This Whittle Communications ad demonstrates the diversity of market segmentation. Courtesy of Whittle Communications

Segmentation Variables. A variety of *segmentation variables* form the basis for slicing up the market, and a great deal of this book is devoted to exploring the ways marketers describe and characterize different segments within the market. The segmentation variables listed in Table 1-1 are grouped into four categories, and the table indicates where in the book these categories are considered in more depth.

Criteria for Identifying Usable Market Segments. While consumers can be described in many ways, the segmentation process is valid only when the following criteria are met:[7]

- Consumers within the segment are similar to one another in terms of product needs, and these needs are different from consumers in other segments.

- Important differences among segments can be identified.
- The segment is large enough to be profitable.
- Consumers in the segment can be reached by an appropriate marketing mix.
- The consumers in the segment will respond in the desired way to the marketing mix designed for them.

A SEGMENTING EXAMPLE: THE CIGARETTE MARKET A market segment profile of smoking consumers exemplified by Darlene might contain this information:

Segment Name: Macho Woman

Size of Segment: 2 million (in the United States)

Demographic and Geographic Characteristics: female; blue-collar, low-level factory or service job; high school education; income under $25,000; predominantly rural

Psychographic Characteristics: outgoing; not career-oriented; enjoys partying, tractor pulls, and the bar scene; pessimistic about the future; reads *People* and *The National Enquirer;* heroes include Roseanne Barr Arnold and Dolly Parton

Product-Related Characteristics: moderate user, smoking more heavily at night; brand loyal

Favorite Brand(s): Marlboro

After identifying this market segment, a cigarette company thinking about introducing a new brand would examine how smokers in the group perceive the brands that are currently available. It might find, for example, that the two most important dimensions for Darlene's segment are one physical feature—harsh taste versus smooth taste—and one image-related variable—masculine versus feminine. Further consumer research and sensitive probing might show, for instance, that Darlene and her friends would like a cigarette with a somewhat smoother taste than Marlboro's. However, they are uncomfortable with what they perceive to be the frilly image of milder women's cigarettes. They have trouble identifying with the type of women (e.g., successful executives or trendy city types) depicted in advertising for these brands. They would like something a little less overtly masculine and a bit more mellow than the brand symbolized by the Marlboro cowboy.

The company would want to position its brand by setting it apart from the others and to convince consumers that the brand possesses the attributes they desire. It might develop a *product position map,* like the one shown in Figure 1-2, that sorts the perceptions of existing brands along the two dimensions identified as being most important in order to determine the ideal position for a brand aimed at the Macho Woman group.

Following this analysis, the company would further evaluate the potential of the Macho Woman group. It could decide, for example, that Marlboro is so close to the ideal for Darlene's segment that it would not be worth the cost of trying to wean people away from such a powerful

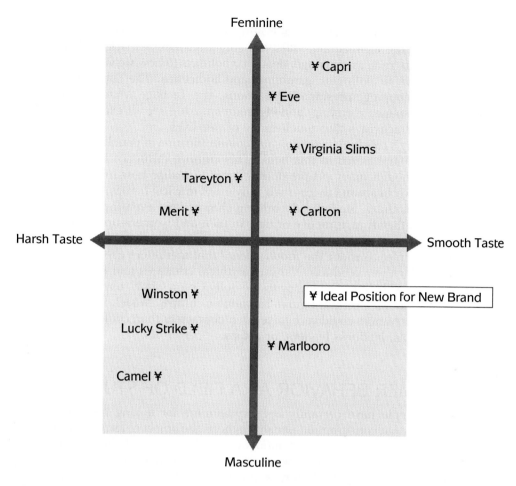

Figure 1-2 Product position map for Macho Woman market segment example

brand. If, on the other hand, the company feels that a new brand targeted to this segment has significant potential, decisions must be made in choosing the appropriate marketing mix.

Based on the company's consumer research, the promotion in the final marketing mix might include a package design, type of woman appearing in ads, and so on, that in fact resembles the controversial Dakota brand described previously. If the company really listened to the feedback from the consumer segment it targeted, it would create a new product that meets the desires of Darlene and her friends and creates loyal customers in the process.

MARKETING'S IMPACT ON CONSUMERS: SOCIAL LIVES AND POPULAR CULTURE

For better or for worse, we all live in a world that is significantly influenced by the actions of marketers. We are surrounded by marketing stimuli in the form of advertisements, stores, brand names, and so on. *Popular culture,* consisting of the music, movies, sports, books, celebrities, and other forms of entertainment consumed by the mass market, is both a product of and inspiration for marketing strategies. Our lives are also affected in more far-reaching ways, ranging from how we acknowledge cultural events such as marriage, death, or holidays to how we view social issues such as air pollution, gambling, and addictions. The Super Bowl, Christmas shopping, presidential elections, the Teenage Mutant Ninja Turtles, newspaper recycling, and cigarette smoking are all examples of products and activities that touch many of our lives.

Marketing's role in the creation and communication of popular culture is especially emphasized in this book. This cultural influence is hard to overlook, although many people do not seem to realize how much their views of the world around them—their movie and musical heroes, the latest fashions in clothing, food and decorating choices, and even the physical features that they find attractive or ugly in men and women—are affected by members of marketing systems.

For example, consider the *product icons* that marketers use to create an identity for their products. Various mythical creatures and personalities—from the Pillsbury Doughboy to the Jolly Green Giant—have been at one time or another central figures in popular culture. In fact, it is likely that more consumers could recognize such characters than could identify past presidents, business leaders, or artists.

CONSUMER BEHAVIOR AS A FIELD OF STUDY

Although people have certainly been consumers for a long time, it is only recently that consumption per se has been the object of formal study. In fact, while many business schools now *require* that marketing majors take a consumer behavior course, most colleges did not even offer such a course until the 1970s. Much of the impetus for the attention now being given to consumer behavior was the realization by many businesspeople that the consumer really *is* the boss. No matter how much time, money, and effort is put into developing and promoting a product, the consumer will not buy it unless it meets some need.

INTERDISCIPLINARY INFLUENCES

Consumer behavior is a very young field, and as it grows, it is being influenced by many different perspectives. Indeed, it is hard to think of a field that is more interdisciplinary: People with training in a very wide range of fields, from psychophysiology to literature, can now be found doing consumer research. Consumer researchers are employed by universities, manufacturers, museums, advertising agencies, and governments. Several professional groups, such as the Association for Consumer Research, have been formed since the mid-1970s.

To gain an idea of the diversity of interests of people who do consumer research, consider the list of professional associations that sponsor the field's major journal, the *Journal of Consumer Research:* American Home Economics Association, American Statistical Association, Association for Consumer Research, Society for Consumer Psychology, International Communication Association, American Sociological Association, The Institute of Management Sciences, American Anthropological Association,

American Marketing Association, Society for Personality and Social Psychology, American Association for Public Opinion Research, and American Economic Association.

LEVELS OF ANALYSIS: THE BLIND MEN AND THE ELEPHANT   You might remember a children's story about the blind men and the elephant. The gist of the story is that each man touched a different part of the animal, and as a result, the descriptions each gave of the elephant were quite different. This analogy applies to consumer research as well. For example, a similar consumer phenomenon can be studied in different ways and at different levels depending on the training and interests of the researchers studying it.

Figure 1-3 provides a glimpse at some of the disciplines working in the field and the level at which each approaches research issues. These diverse disciplines can be roughly characterized in terms of their focus on *micro* versus *macro* consumer behavior. The fields closer to the top of the pyramid concentrate upon the individual consumer (micro issues), while those toward the base are more interested in the *aggregate* activities that occur among larger groups of people, such as consumption patterns shared by members of a culture or subculture (macro issues).

To demonstrate that the same marketing issue can be explored at different levels, Table 1-2 lists research issues that might be of interest to each contributing discipline and provides examples of how these might be applied in the marketing and consumption of Marlboro cigarettes.

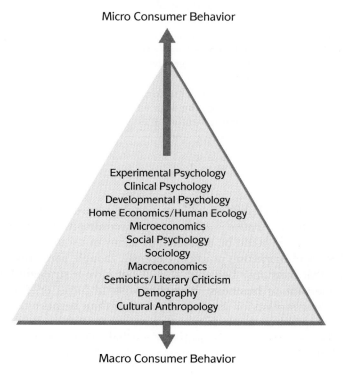

Micro Consumer Behavior

Experimental Psychology
Clinical Psychology
Developmental Psychology
Home Economics/Human Ecology
Microeconomics
Social Psychology
Sociology
Macroeconomics
Semiotics/Literary Criticism
Demography
Cultural Anthropology

Macro Consumer Behavior

Figure 1-3 The pyramid of consumer behavior

TABLE 1-2 Interdisciplinary research issues in consumer behavior and example applications

Discipline/Consumer Behavior Issue	Application to Marlboro Cigarettes
Experimental psychology: Product role in perception, learning, and memory processes	How specific aspects of cigarette brands, such as the name or package design, are recognized and interpreted; what parts of the Marlboro ad are most likely to be noticed and remembered
Clinical psychology: Product role in psychological adjustment	Ways in which smoking satisfies some deepseated psychological need (e.g., oral gratification as a symbolic substitute for a mother figure); how Marlboros help/hinder self-image and efforts to identify with the Marlboro cowboy
Home economics/human ecology: Product role in consumption decisions	Ways in which consumers can be educated about the dangers of smoking; techniques to counteract peer pressure on teenage smokers to smoke Marlboros instead of a lower-nicotine brand
Microeconomics: Product role in allocation of individual or family resources	Factors that influence the amount of money spent on cigarettes; degree to which smokers will expend time and energy to obtain Marlboros over some other brand
Social psychology: Product role in the behavior of individuals as members of social groups	Ways in which cigarette ads affect a consumer's attitudes toward smoking; how being a Marlboro smoker affects people's perceptions of that person
Sociology: Product role in the nature of social institutions and group relationships	Factors that influence the likelihood that consumers in a subculture will be smokers: patterns by which a preference for Marlboros versus other brands spreads through different subcultures
Macroeconomics: Product role in consumers' relations with the marketplace	Effects of unemployment rates on the proportion of smokers: attractiveness of Marlboros versus less expensive brands during periods of high unemployment
Semiotics/literary criticism: Product role in the verbal and visual communication of meaning	Underlying messages communicated by cigarette advertising: the symbolism conveyed by the Marlboro Man to readers of the company's advertising
Demography: Product role in the measurable characteristics of a population	Factors associated with smoking rates in a population (e.g., age, sex, geographic region); degree to which younger women versus older women smoke Marlboros
Cultural anthropology: Product role in a society's beliefs and practices	Ways in which smoking is used to categorize people in a society; the degree to which the choice of Marlboros signifies a smoker's "virility."

THE ISSUE OF STRATEGIC FOCUS Many people regard the field of consumer behavior as an *applied social science*. Accordingly, the value of the knowledge generated should be evaluated in terms of its ability to improve the effectiveness of marketing practice. Recently, though, some researchers have argued that consumer behavior should not have a strategic focus at all or be a servant to business. It should instead focus on the understanding of consumption for its own sake, rather than because the knowledge can be applied by marketers.[8]

This rather extreme view is probably not held by most consumer researchers, but it has encouraged many to expand the scope of their work beyond the field's traditional focus on the purchase of consumer goods such as food, appliances, cars, and so on.

A Trip to the "Darker Side" of Consumer Behavior. This more critical view of consumer research has also led the field to recognize that not all consumer behavior and/or marketing activity is necessarily beneficial to individuals or to society. As a result, current consumer research is likely to include attention to the "darker side" of consumer behavior, such as addiction, prostitution, homelessness, shoplifting, or environmental waste. This activity builds upon the earlier work of researchers who have studied issues related to public policy, ethics, and consumerism.

TWO MAJOR CONSUMER BEHAVIOR PARADIGMS

One general way to group consumer researchers is in terms of the fundamental assumptions they make about what they are studying and how they study it. This set of beliefs is known as a *paradigm.* Like other fields of study, consumer behavior is dominated by a paradigm, but some believe it is in the middle of a paradigm shift, which occurs when a competing paradigm challenges the dominant set of assumptions. Consumer behavior has been strongly influenced by the information-processing paradigm, which views consumers as rational decision makers; but many in the field are now beginning to embrace the experiential paradigm, which stresses the subjective, nonrational aspects of consumption as well as cultural influences on consumer behavior.

Two television commercials for Kool-Aid reflect the divergence of these paradigms. Representing the information-processing paradigm is a 1982 ad that highlights objective attributes of the drink mix as a smiling mother says: "I keep a pitcher ready so they can have those fruity flavors and vitamin C anytime." In contrast, a 1988 commercial for the same product shows several men and women in a kitchen engaged in adult conversation and does not even mention specific product attributes. Notes a company executive, "The idea was to place the brand in the context of people's lives," a concept advertisers call "bonding."[9]

THE INFORMATION-PROCESSING PARADIGM   The **information-processing paradigm** has been the driving force in consumer behavior for the last thirty years. This perspective is concerned with how people receive, store, and use information. Consumers are goal oriented, and their purchase decisions are often (but certainly not always) carefully calculated to provide the greatest amount of benefits received for the money spent. The important early research in the field, beginning in the late 1950s, stemmed from work in economics and psychology and focused primarily on consumers' evaluations of the rewards and costs involved when weighing purchase alternatives.[10]

The *information-processing paradigm* focuses on consumers as rational problem solvers and decision makers who carefully consider the objective features and *functional benefits* of products and services—that is, on the practical purposes they serve. The body of work in this area is heavily influenced by theories and research methods developed in the discipline of cognitive psychology, which seeks to understand how people store, organize, and interpret knowledge. The topics studied span areas of consumer decision making, such as how people decide between the benefits offered by specific brands, how they evaluate the information presented in advertisements, or factors affecting a family's allocation of its money to different product categories. The information- processing perspective remains a dominant influence on the study of consumer behavior.

THE EXPERIENTIAL PARADIGM   The continuing expansion of the boundaries of consumer research has led to new emphases on other topics as well, including fantasy, play, rituals, and popular culture. As researchers from disciplines other than psychology and economics, such as sociology and anthropology, have also moved into the field of consumer behavior, the information-processing paradigm has begun to share the spotlight with other areas of inquiry.

In contrast to an emphasis on the consumer as a rational decision maker, the **experiential paradigm** highlights the subjective, symbolic aspects of consumer behavior and focuses on the *hedonic benefits* of products and services—that is, on the sensory pleasures they provide.[11] There also tends to be more of an emphasis on the rich social and cultural aspects of consumer behavior, which are factors that cannot necessarily be quantified and studied in the laboratory.

THE VALUE OF BOTH APPROACHES   The information-processing and experiential consumer paradigms represent fundamentally different ways of looking at consumers. The perspective taken depends both on the orientation of the researcher and the nature of the problem to be studied. Both paradigms are important. This book incorporates relevant research from both points of view, and in many cases the understanding of a topic is improved when more than one perspective is considered.

THE DUAL GOALS OF CONSUMER RESEARCH

Consumer research can attempt to accomplish one of two goals:

1. to *predict* future consumer behavior from what is already known about how consumers react;
2. to *understand* the behavior for its own sake.

In very general terms, researchers who follow the information-processing paradigm tend to design their research according to a set of assumptions known as **positivism,** in which a single reality is believed to exist independent of what is perceived by individuals. Events in the world can be objectively measured, and the causes of behavior can be identified and manipulated.

In contrast, researchers who emphasize the experiential aspects of consumption tend to adhere to a set of assumptions called **interpretivism,** in which the existence of a single, objective truth is denied. Reality is seen as being subjective, and cause-and-effect aspects of behavior cannot be isolated. Some of the major differences between the two approaches to "doing science" are shown in Table 1-3.

TABLE 1–3 Positivist versus interpretivist approaches to consumer behavior

Assumptions	Positivist Approach	Interpretivist Approach
Nature of reality	Objective, tangible Single	Socially constructed Multiple
Goal	Prediction	Understanding
Knowledge generated	Nomothetic Time free Context independent	Idiographic Time bound Context dependent
View of causality	Real causes exist	Multiple, simultaneous shaping events
Research relationship	Separation between researcher and subject	Interactive, cooperative with researcher being part of phenomenon under study

Source: Adapted from Laurel A. Hudson and Julie L. Ozanne, "Alternative Ways of Seeking Knowledge in Consumer Research," *Journal of Consumer Research* 14 (March 1988): 508–521, 509. Reprinted with the permission of the University of Chicago Press

POSITIVIST CONSUMER RESEARCH

The major goal of positivist inquiry is to predict future behaviors.

DESIGNING POSITIVIST STUDIES Positivists often employ the *scientific method* to study consumer behavior. In controlled studies, variables that are hypothesized to be the causes of an action (called *independent variables*) are isolated and manipulated, often (but not always) in a laboratory setting. The effect of these variables on a subject's responses (called *dependent variables*) can then be assessed, and competing explanations can be ruled out over time. The goal is to identify cause-and-effect sequences, which then allows the researcher to predict that the same response will occur in the future if the subject is exposed to the same stimulus.

Obtaining Generalizable Data. The data obtained from consumer responses should be generalizable to populations other than the consumers who were actually used in the study. This perspective assumes that while there may be some individual variations or effects due to chance, the differences will "wash out" if enough different subjects are studied. The goal is not to predict the behavior of any one person, but rather to predict the typical or average response of people who share certain characteristics. This aggregate emphasis, which focuses on how a phenomenon affects many people rather than on the experiences of a select few, is a *nomothetic* approach to research.

Obtaining Quantifiable Data. The responses obtained from consumers should be quantifiable in some way so that they can easily be compared with each other. To maximize the reliability of the results and make it more likely that the same effect will be observed in future studies, the measures should require little interpretation on the part of the researcher, who is expected to remain an impartial observer. Responses can be physiological (e.g., eye-tracking studies measure eye movements to determine what parts of commercials capture consumers' attention), verbal (e.g., consumers respond to questions about the commercials they have seen), or behavioral (e.g., a company might monitor changes in purchase volume in a market after introducing a special price promotion).

A Positivist Study Example: Cigarette Brand Recognition. Say a researcher wants to know whether consumers' responses to Marlboro advertising are affected by whether or not the ad actually features the brand name (some Marlboro ads do not, because the Marlboro Man motif is so well-known). Smokers might be brought to a laboratory and be shown slides of different ads. Some subjects might view a Marlboro ad with the brand name included,

Figure 1-3 This page from a typical survey form illustrates the detailed information syndicated services collect from consumer panelists regarding their purchasing patterns.

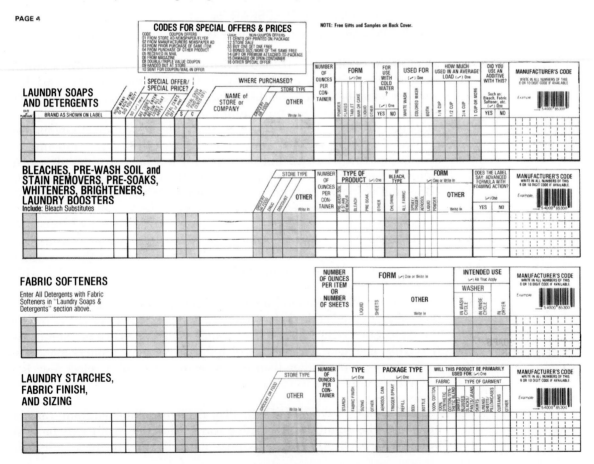

and others would view the same ad with the logo removed. (This variation in exposure would be the independent variable.)

The researcher would then measure the subjects' reactions to various aspects of the ad and the product, perhaps including the degree to which people remembered the ad or their intention to buy that brand the next time they are out of cigarettes. The subjects might even be offered a free pack of cigarettes (of a brand of their choice) at the end of the study, and their choices would be recorded. These measures would constitute the study's dependent variables. If differences were found, on the average, between the responses of the two groups—those who saw the ad with logo versus those who saw only the picture part—the researcher could conclude that including the brand name makes a difference.

COLLECTING POSITIVIST DATA In addition to controlled experiments, positivist studies can include the collection of data in the field in a number of ways. Unlike controlled studies, these types of data do not usually permit inferences about causes and effects, but they do provide valuable descriptive statistics about one or more consumer segments. A primary goal is to *sample* a group of consumers whose responses can be generalized to a larger population.

Surveys may be conducted by phone or mail, door-to-door, or through mall intercepts, in which shoppers are stopped and asked to participate in the survey. One of the largest of these surveys is conducted by the U.S. Census Bureau, which uses a combination of mailed questionnaires and door-to-door interviews to collect valuable information on American consumers.

Syndicated Services. Many syndicated services collect large amounts of consumer data and provide information for a fee to marketers. For example, some services maintain *consumer panels,* which are composed of a group of people intended to be statistically representative of some larger group. Participants respond to detailed questionnaires about their purchasing habits, media usage, and so on.

These procedures used by syndicated services are increasingly going high-tech. Scanning technology, which uses the UPC (universal product code) marking on products bought in stores to collect data on consumers' purchases, allows marketers to track buying patterns and to tailor their promotions to the specific wants and needs of consumers (e.g., by issuing diaper coupons to consumers who purchase baby food).[12]

▼ MARKETING PITFALL

The growing use of sophisticated demographic data bases is not sitting well with many consumers, who are concerned about possible violations of privacy. After receiving 30,000 complaints, Lotus Development Corporation killed plans to sell its MarketPlace: Households data base software, which contained demographic information on 80 million households. At around the same time, New England Telephone

& Telegraph cancelled plans to sell a list of 4.7 million of its customers, and Blockbuster Entertainment Corp. denied its intent to sell information detailing customers' video rental habits.[13]

Unobtrusive Data Collection. Because the accuracy of consumer responses can be distorted due to various biases, such as people's desire to portray themselves in the best possible light, some data collection methods use measures that do not require direct human responses. *Unobtrusive techniques* use various clues to obtain objective data. For example, instead of asking a person to report on the products that are currently in his or her house, the researcher might actually go there and record the products in that person's kitchen. This technique is called a "pantry check."

Another example of an unobtrusive technique is provided by a study of magazine readership that measured exposure to specific pages by placing small glue spots on each page. Researchers could then record which seals had been broken to determine what sections had been skipped over.[14] One innovative research method, called "garbology," involves sifting through people's garbage (after it has been collected and anonymously labeled) to determine product usage. This unobtrusive technique is especially useful when the individual might be reluctant to report his or her usage truthfully, as may be the case for such sensitive products as liquor or contraceptives.[15]

INTERPRETIVE CONSUMER RESEARCH

The interpretive paradigm attempts to understand consumer behavior rather than predict it. Interpretivists argue that reality is "socially constructed," with each person having a version that reflects his or her unique background, personality, and needs.

DESIGNING INTERPRETIVE STUDIES

Interpretivism attempts to generate a "thick description" of the experiences of one or a few people. Interpretive research is an *idiographic* approach, since it attempts to get a lot of in-depth information from relatively few people rather than generalizable, descriptive information from a lot of people. No attempt is made to generalize the experiences to others, although the interpretations of each informant can certainly be compared and contrasted to others' explanations.

Researcher Subjectivity. The interpretive approach stresses that the researcher is also a part of the interpretive process because his or her own beliefs and background influence what is being studied. For example, an interpretivist study may be designed with an overall goal of understanding gift-giving behavior among a certain group, but specific dependent variables—such as what prompts the action of giving a gift—are not established. Thus, in the in-depth interviews conducted with participants, themes emerge that reflect the interpretations of the researchers. Because the interview is not based on a specific set of questions designed to determine specific conclusions, a researcher's questions, as the interview progresses, are based on the conclusions he or she has drawn from the participant's comments.

Context Dependency. In interpretivist studies, consumer behavior cannot be studied apart from the natural context in which it occurs. A consumer's responses in the laboratory cannot be compared to what he or she tells friends or family. This perspective would argue that the simple laboratory experiment on cigarette advertisements described earlier might be invalid, since a subject's "reality" in the laboratory is very different from what he or she experiences while leafing through a magazine at home.

An Interpretivist Study Example: The Social Meaning of Smoking Cigarettes. An interpretive approach to cigarette marketing might consider how the symbols used in Marlboro ads are interpreted by consumers or how the act of smoking is integrated into a person's self-concept. Darlene's fantasy about riding off with the Marlboro Man would be important to an interpretive researcher, who might ask her to elaborate on the role smoking plays in her life and how her feelings of femininity are affected by different brands. This researcher might use a variety of techniques to allow Darlene to *project* her feelings about the brand, such as showing her a picture of the Marlboro Man and asking her to tell a story about him. Darlene's responses would then be interpreted by the researcher, who would also ask Darlene to comment on this interpretation. The researcher might conclude, for example, that women like Darlene grow attached to a strong, independent figure like the Marlboro Man, who compensates for their own inner feelings of powerlessness and relieves their doubts about the negative side effects of smoking.

COLLECTING INTERPRETIVIST DATA The interpretive approach to consumer behavior, while gaining popularity, is still in its infancy in terms of the sophistication of its research methods. Some techniques have been around since the early days of consumer behavior, some are now being borrowed from other fields such as anthropology and literary criticism, and still others are under development.

Ethnography. Much of the methodology for interpretivist studies of consumers in their natural "habitats" is derived from techniques used by anthropologists when studying foreign cultures. A common strategy is *participant observation,* in which the researcher is immersed in the host culture. Although the researcher does not "go native," the aim is to try to understand the people on their own terms. This in-depth study of a specific group's behaviors, social rules, and beliefs is called **ethnography.** Research is usually done in a natural setting, and is reported in the form of a very detailed *case study.*

The ethnographic approach has come to the forefront of the consumer behavior discipline largely as the result of a recent project called the Consumer Behavior Odyssey, in which a team of marketing professors traveled across the United States in a recreational vehicle to interact with consumers in a wide variety of natural settings, ranging from swap meets and festivals to convents and museums.[16] The project yielded enormous quantities of field notes, still photos, and videotapes that documented interviews with many diverse types of consumers. The Odyssey was one of the first systematic attempts by consumer researchers to study consumers in their real environments rather than in controlled or laboratory settings.

Qualitative Research and Marketing Executions. Techniques for conducting *qualitative research,* which relies on the researcher's interpretive skills, are described in detail in chapter 3. For now, it is sufficient to note that marketers are increasingly relying on studies that probe consumers' inner feelings about products to devise marketing and advertising strategy.

The following are a few examples of recent qualitative studies that resulted in concrete marketing changes:

- Schick devised an ad for its razors with a woman gently stroking a man's face after a study of consumer perceptions of rival brands showed that Gillette ads featuring men in rugged, outdoor situations made them feel like "lone wolves," rather than people who like to be touched.[17]
- The cuddly bear used in ads for Snuggle fabric softener was developed to capitalize on animal symbolism. The bear is an ancient symbol of aggression, while consumers interpret the teddy bear to mean that this viciousness has been tamed. This symbolic relationship was applied to communicate the dominant product attribute: Snuggle "tames" the rough texture of clothing.
- A woman out of a group of consumers who were gathered to talk in a *focus group* about tooth care observed that tartar felt "like a wall" on her teeth. This imagery was used in ads for Colgate Tartar Control, in which room-sized teeth were shown covered by walls of tartar.[18]
- American Express redirected its advertising emphasis away from overachievers after its qualitative research indicated that people were intimidated by its approach. One subject, asked to pretend that he was an American Express card come to life, sneered, "You're not really my type—you can't keep up." Later ads instead featured people in laid-back situations, such as spontaneous vacations.[19]
- A Danish firm wanted to introduce a new cigarette brand targeted to blue-collar American males. Unfamiliar with American consumers, it sent researchers to interview men in Arkansas, where the brand was to be test marketed. In-depth interviews found that many potential customers felt sexually frustrated and powerless and that they responded to these deep feelings by getting together with their buddies and smoking cigarettes. The company used an ad depicting a brash confident smoker and challenged these frustrated men to "Make your move."[20]

PLAN OF THE BOOK

This book covers many facets of consumer behavior, and many of the research perspectives briefly described in this chapter will be highlighted in later chapters. The plan of the book is simple: It goes from micro to macro. Think of the book as a sort of photograph album of consumer behavior: Each chapter provides a "snapshot" of consumers, but the lens used to take each picture gets successively wider.

The book begins with issues related to the individual consumer and expands its focus until it eventually considers the behaviors of large groups of people in their social settings. The topics to be covered correspond to the wheel of consumer behavior presented in Figure 1-4, which will be repeated at the beginning of each section.

Figure 1-4 The wheel of consumer behavior

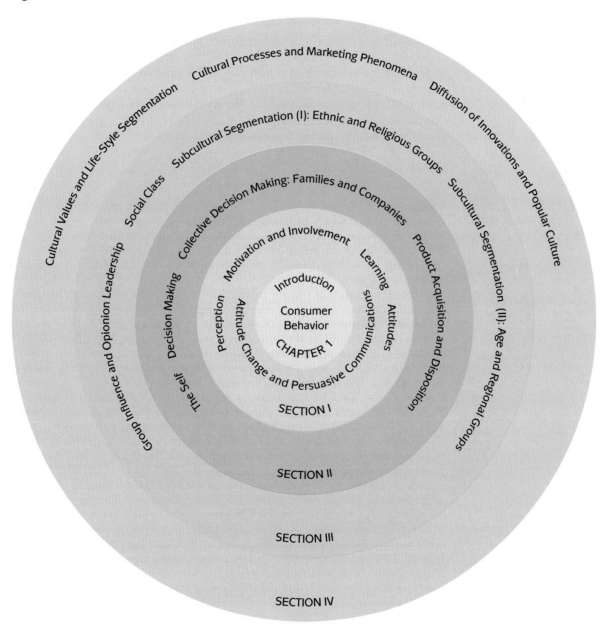

Section I, "The Consumer as an Individual," considers the consumer at his or her most micro level. It examines how the individual receives information from his or her immediate environment and how this material is learned, stored in memory, and used to form and modify individual attitudes. Section II, "The Consumer as a Decision Maker and Product User," explores the ways in which consumers use the information they have acquired to make decisions about consumption activities. Section III, "The Consumer as a Social Entity," expands the focus further by considering how the consumer functions as a part of a larger social structure. This structure includes the influence of social groups to which the consumer belongs, social class, and also the effects of membership in subcultures, such as the person's ethnic group, age group, and place of residence.

Finally, section IV's "The Consumer and Culture," completes the picture as it examines marketing's impact on mass culture. These effects include the relationship of marketing to the expression of cultural values and consumers' lifestyle choices, how products and services are related to rituals and cultural myths, and finally the interface between marketing efforts and the creation of art, music, and other forms of popular culture that are so much a part of our daily lives.

CHAPTER SUMMARY

Consumer behavior is the study of the processes that are involved when individuals or groups select, purchase, use, or dispose of products, services, ideas, or experiences to satisfy needs and desires. This introductory chapter reviews the foundations of consumer behavior, including the topics covered by the discipline, the types of people who study them, and some different approaches to consumer research.

Consumer behavior can be regarded as both a pure and an applied social science. As a pure science, it tries to understand how people are affected by the objects and messages in their world. As an applied discipline, it is used to provide valuable input for the formation of marketing strategy. By understanding consumers, marketers can make decisions about market segmentation, product positioning, and the appropriate marketing mix needed to effectively reach a target market. The chapter points out that many of the dimensions that describe consumers are used by marketers to divide the mass market into segments. These variables fall into such categories as demographics (e.g., age, income, sex, and occupation) and psychographics (e.g., personality and lifestyle).

The chapter also discusses the many different levels of analysis at which consumer behavior phenomena can be approached. These range from the micro level, which stresses the internal thoughts and feelings of the individual consumer, to the macro level, at which the consumer is considered as a member of larger social groups and cultures. Research orientations also vary due to the underlying goals of the researcher. One general way to describe current research activities is to group them as either positivist or interpretivist. Positivist research seeks to describe an objective, single reality in which buying behaviors can be framed in terms of general laws and to then to predict future purchase decisions on this basis. Interpretivist research denies the idea that there is one reality and instead focuses on the unique experiences and interpretations of consumers as they relate to one another in their natural social contexts. The chapter discusses some of the different assumptions, methods, and research topics that arise from these two different perspectives and stresses that each is valuable for addressing certain issues.

The chapter concludes by providing an overview of the book, emphasizing that it will proceed systematically from micro issues to macro issues. The wheel of consumer behavior presented in Figure 1-4 illustrates that all of these levels of analysis are interrelated, stressing the importance of understanding consumer behavior at both the individual and societal levels.

KEY TERMS

Consumer behavior	Information-processing paradigm
Determinant attributes	Interpretivism
Ethnography	Marketing mix
Experiential paradigm	Positivism
Exchange	Targeted marketing strategy

REVIEW QUESTIONS AND DISCUSSION TOPICS

1. This chapter states that people play different roles and that their consumption behaviors may differ depending on the particular role they are playing. State whether you agree or disagree with this perspective, giving examples from your personal life.

2. Some researchers believe that the field of consumer behavior should be a pure, rather than an applied, science. In other words, research issues should be framed in terms of their scientific interest rather than their applicability to immediate marketing problems. Give your views on this issue.

3. Name some products or services that are widely used by your social group. State whether you agree or disagree with the notion that these products help to form the group bonds, supporting your argument with examples from your list of products used by the group.

4. Describe the differences between functional and hedonic product benefits. Name some benefits in both categories that you might desire in a car, and give the criteria that you would use to determine whether a particular car would satisfy your desire for these benefits.

5. Although demographic information on large numbers of consumers is used in many marketing contexts, some people believe that the sale of data on customers' incomes, buying habits, and so on constitutes an invasion of privacy and should be stopped. Comment on this issue from both a consumer's and a marketer's point of view.

6. List the three stages in the consumption process. Describe the issues that you considered in each of these stages when you made a recent important purchase.

7. State the differences between the positivist and interpretivist approaches to consumer research. For each type of inquiry, give examples of product dimensions that would be more usefully explored using that type of research over the other.

8. What aspects of consumer behavior are likely to be of interest to a financial planner? To a university administrator? To a graphic arts designer? To a social worker in a government agency? To a nursing instructor?

9. Use your own words to describe the steps involved in developing a targeted marketing strategy. Give your opinion on which step is most crucial in the success or failure of a strategy planned according to these steps.

10. Critics of targeted marketing strategies argue that this practice is discriminatory and unfair, especially if such a strategy encourages a group of people to buy a product that may be injurious to them or that they cannot afford. On the other hand, The Association of National Advertisers argues that banning targeted marketing constitutes censorship and is thus a violation of the First Amendment. What are your views regarding both sides of this issue?

HANDS-ON EXERCISES

1. Collect a set of product icons from magazines and packages. Prepare a display board of unnamed icons to show to six individual consumers, selecting one male and one female "subject" from each of three different age groups. Determine the level of recognition for each icon, as well as interpretations of how the image represents the brand or company. Prepare a report of your findings.

2. For each category listed in Table 1-1, find an ad containing one or more elements that indicate that the ad was targeted on the basis of some aspect of the category. Comment on each ad relative to its relationship to the category.

3. Select a product and brand that you use frequently, and make a list of what you consider to be the brand's determinant attributes. Without revealing your list, ask a friend who is approximately the same age but of the opposite sex to make a similar list for the same product (although the brand may be different). Compare and contrast the identified attributes and report your findings.

4. Visit the cosmetics department of a large department store and sample eight to ten brands of perfume. Draw a product positioning map for the two dimensions of price and "lightness" of the scent for the brands that you tested. Determine the ideal position for a new perfume, and describe the image characteristics and price for it. Prepare a report on your analysis and conclusions.

5. Arrange to observe shoppers in a busy retail outlet that sells cigarettes. Record the brands selected by thirty people according to their approximate age and sex. Assume that your sample of thirty is representative of the entire smoking population and generalize your findings regarding brand preference by age and sex.

6. Collect ads for five different brands of the same product. Report on the segmentation variables, target markets, and emphasized product attributes in each ad.

7. Review current newspapers and magazines to find a report of a research study conducted in some field of study other than marketing in which consumer behavior played a role. Write a report summarizing the role of consumer behavior relative to the findings of the study.

8. Select a well-known manufacturer of breakfast cereals and two of its products. Write a report comparing and contrasting the strategies used to promote the two different cereals in terms of the "Four P's" in the marketing mix.

NOTES

1. Jeffrey A. Trachtenberg, "Here's One Tough Cowboy," *Forbes* (February 9, 1987)3:108.
2. Richard Tansey, Michael R. Hyman, and George M. Zinkhan, "Cultural Themes in Brazilian and U.S. Auto Ads: A Cross-Cultural Comparison," *Journal of Advertising* 19 (1990)2:30–39.

3. William F. Schoell and Joseph P. Guiltinan, *Marketing: Contemporary Concepts and Practices,* 4th ed., (Boston: Allyn and Bacon, 1990).

4. Erving Goffman, *The Presentation of Self in Everyday Life* (Garden City, N.Y.: Doubleday, 1959); George H. Mead, *Mind, Self, and Society* (Chicago: University of Chicago Press, 1934); Michael R. Soloman, "The Role of Products as Social Stimuli: A Symbolic Interactionism Perspective," *Journal of Consumer Research* 10 (December 1983):319–29.

5. These steps are adapted from a discussion of targeted marketing strategy in Schoell and Guiltinan, *Marketing.*

6. Anthony Ramirez, "New Cigarettes Raising Issue of Target Market," *New York Times* (February 18, 1990):28; Schlossberg, "Segmenting Becomes Constitutional Issue," *Marketing News* (April 16, 1990)2:1.

7. See Schoell and Guiltinan, *Marketing.*

8. Morris B. Holbrook, "The Consumer Researcher Visits Radio City: Dancing in the Dark," in *Advances in Consumer Research,* ed. Elizabeth C. Hirschman and Morris B. Holbrook (Provo, Utah: Association for Consumer Research, 1985),12:28–31.

9. Randall Rothenberg, "Ad Research Shifts from Products to People," *New York Times* (April 6, 1989):D1.

10. Some important early contributions include Robert Ferber and Hugh G. Wales, eds., *Motivation and Market Behavior* (Homewood, Ill.: Richard D. Irwin, 1958); John A. Howard and Jagdish N. Sheth, *The Theory of Buyer Behavior* (New York: John Wiley & Sons, 1969); James F. Engel, David T. Kollat, and Roger D. Blackwell, *Consumer Behavior* (New York: Holt, Rinehart and Winston, 1968); George Katona, *The Powerful Consumer* (New York: McGraw-Hill, 1960).

11. See Morris B. Holbrook and Elizabeth C. Hirschman, "The Experiential Aspects of Consumption: Consumer Fantasies, Feelings, and Fun," *Journal of Consumer Research* 9 (September 1982):132–40.

12. "Scan of the Century," *American Demographics* (March 1989):39.

13. Alan Radding, "Consumer Worry Halts Data Bases," *Advertising Age* (February 11, 1991):28.

14. David A. Aaker and George S. Day, *Marketing Research,* 4th ed. (New York: John Wiley & Sons, 1990).

15. Joseph A. Cote, James McCullough, and Michael D. Reilly, "Effects of Unanticipated Situations on Behavior-Intention Differences: A Garbology Analysis," *Journal of Consumer Research* 12 (September 1985):188–94.

16. Russell W. Belk, Melanie Wallendorf, and John F. Sherry, Jr., "The Sacred and the Profane in Consumer Behavior: Theodicy on the Odyssey," *Journal of Consumer Research* 16 (June 1989):1–38.

17. Ronald Alsop, "Agencies Scrutinize Their Ads for Psychological Symbolism," *The Wall Street Journal* (June 11, 1987):27.

18. Jeffrey F. Durgee, "On Cezanne, Hot Buttons, and Interpreting Consumer Storytelling," *Journal of Consumer Marketing* 5 (Fall 1988):47–51.

19. Bernice Kanner, "Mind Games," *Marketing Insights* (Spring 1989)9:50.

20. Joshua Levine, "Desperately Seeking Jeepness," *Forbes* (May 15, 1989):134; Ramirez, "New Cigarettes Raising Issue of Target Market"; Schlossberg, "Segmenting Becomes Constitutional Issue."

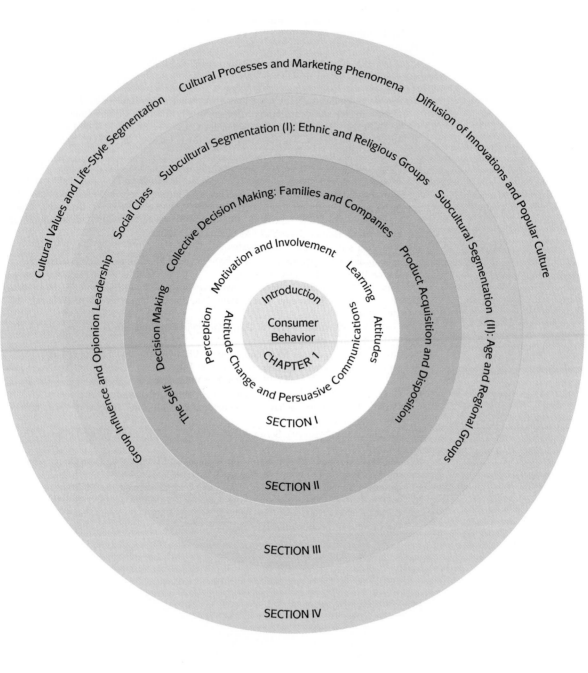

Introduction

Consumer Behavior

CHAPTER 1

Motivation and Involvement

Learning

Attitudes

Perception

Attitude Change and Persuasive Communications

Product Acquisition and Disposition

Decision Making

The Self

SECTION I

Collective Decision Making: Families and Companies

Subcultural Segmentation (I): Ethnic and Religious Groups

Subcultural Segmentation (II): Age and Regional Groups

SECTION II

Group Influence and Opionion Leadership

Social Class

Cultural Values and Life-Style Segmentation

Cultural Processes and Marketing Phenomena

Diffusion of Innovations and Popular Culture

SECTION III

SECTION IV

In this section, we focus on the internal dynamics of consumers. While "no man is an island," each of us is to some degree a self-contained receptor for information from the outside world. We are constantly confronted with advertising messages, products, other people persuading us to buy, and reflections of ourselves. Each chapter in this section will consider a different aspect of the consumer that is invisible to others—sensations, memories, and attitudes. Chapter 2 describes the process of perception, where information from the outside world about products and other people is absorbed by the individual and interpreted. Chapter 3 discusses our reasons or motivations for absorbing this information, and how particular needs influence the way we think about products. Chapter 4 focuses on the ways this information is mentally stored, and how it adds to our existing knowledge about the world as it is learned. Chapters 5 and 6 discuss how attitudes—our evaluations of all these products, ad messages, and so on—are formed and (sometimes) changed by marketers. When all of these "internal" parts are put together, the unique role of each individual consumer as a self-contained agent in the marketplace will be clear.

The Consumer
as an Individual

Perception

Barbara has been invited to dinner at her boss's house for the first time. She's been very nervous about this occasion, and she wants to make a good impression by politely bringing an appropriate gift for the host. Barbara has been so busy that she hasn't had time to get a gift, and now she's running late. Fortunately, on her way to the boss's house she sees a liquor store she's never noticed before, and she stops. Although Barbara is not a wine drinker, she heads straight for the wine section, bypassing hundreds of interesting-looking liqueurs, cases of imported beer, and other varieties of liquor, because she thinks wine would be more appropriate.

Once in the wine section, Barbara does not even look at bottles of inexpensive sweet wines she recognizes (she still remembers getting sick from drinking too much sweet wine in college). Barbara's gaze happens to fall on a group of bottles displayed at eye level; they catch her attention because their labels have distinctive gold lettering on a rich burgundy background.

She picks up one of the bottles and notices approvingly that it is a white wine (she associates white wine with elegant dinners). She also likes the "feel" of the bottle (it's slim and sophisticated). To confirm her hunch that this wine will be acceptable, she sees that

CHAPTER **2**

it costs $18.99 and that the name on the label is French. Glancing at her watch, Barbara takes the bottle to the cash register, confident that her choice will make the desired impression.

INTRODUCTION

We live in a world overflowing with sensations. Wherever we turn, we are bombarded by a symphony of colors, sounds, and odors. Some of the "notes" in this symphony occur naturally, such as the loud barking of a dog, the shades of the evening sky, or the heady smell of a rosebush. Others come from people; the person sitting next to you in class might sport tinted blonde hair, bright pink pants, and enough perfume to make your eyes water.

Marketers certainly contribute to this commotion. Consumers are never far from advertisements, product packages, radio and television commercials, and billboards that clamor for their attention. Each of us copes with this bombardment in a unique way by selectively seeing and hearing only the stimuli that we want to allow into our consciousness. When we do make a decision on a purchase, such as a bottle of wine for the boss, we are responding not only to these influences but to our interpretations of them.

This chapter focuses on the process of perception, in which sensations are absorbed by the consumer and used to interpret the surrounding world. After discussing the stages of this process, the chapter examines how the five senses of sight, smell, sound, touch, and taste affect consumers. It also highlights some interesting ways in which marketers develop products and communications that appeal to the senses.

The chapter emphasizes that the way in which a marketing stimulus is presented plays a role in determining whether the consumer will make sense of it or even notice it in the first place. The techniques and marketing practices that make messages more likely to be noticed are discussed, as is the topic of subliminal persuasion, which includes techniques designed to influence consumers through images and sounds of which they are not aware. Finally, the chapter discusses the process of interpretation, in which the stimuli that are noticed by the consumer are organized and assigned meaning.

THE PERCEPTUAL PROCESS

As you sit in a lecture, you might find your attention shifting. One minute you are concentrating on the instructor's words, and in the next, you catch yourself daydreaming about the upcoming weekend before you realize that you are missing some important points and tune back into the lecture.

Like computers, people undergo stages of *information processing* in which stimuli are input and stored. Unlike computers, though, we do not passively process whatever information happens to be present. In the first place, only a very small number of the stimuli in our environment are ever noticed. Of these, an even smaller amount are attended to. And the stimuli that do enter consciousness might not be processed objectively. The meaning of a stimulus is interpreted by the individual, who is influenced by his or her unique biases, needs, and experiences. The stages involved in selecting and interpreting stimuli are illustrated in Figure 2-1, which provides an overview of the perceptual process.

FROM SENSATION TO PERCEPTION

Sensation is the immediate response of our sensory receptors (e.g., eyes, ears, nose, mouth, fingers) to such basic stimuli as light, color, and sound. **Perception** is the process by which these stimuli are selected, organized, and interpreted. Like a computer, we process raw data (sensation). However, the study of perception focuses on what we add to or take away from these sensations as we assign meaning to them.

The subjective nature of perception is demonstrated by a controversial advertisement developed for Benetton by a French agency. The ad features a black man and a white man handcuffed together. This ad was the target of many complaints about racism after it appeared in magazines and on billboards around the United States, even though the company has a reputation for promoting racial tolerance. People *interpreted* it to depict a black man who had been arrested by a white man.[1] Even though both men are dressed the same, people's prior assumptions distorted the ad's meaning.

Such interpretations or assumptions stem from the **schemas,** or organized collections of beliefs and feelings, that a person has. That is, we tend to group in our memories the objects we see as having similar characteristics, and the schema to which an object is assigned is a crucial determinant of how we choose to evaluate this object at a later time.

The perceptual process is illustrated by Barbara's experience in the example at the beginning of this chapter. Her needs dictated that she would "suddenly" see a liquor store, and her goal of locating a "classy"

Figure 2-1 An Overview of the Perceptual Process

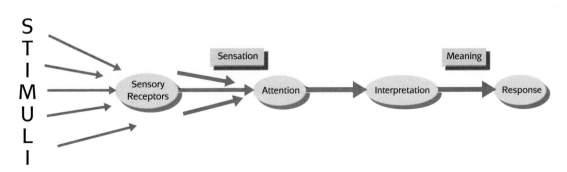

UNITED COLORS
OF BENETTON.

This Benetton ad created controversy because people interpreted it as depicting a black man in the custody of a white man. Is this interpretation justified? Photo by Oliverio Toscani for BENETTON

gift led her to tune out many competing alternatives (e.g., beer). Her memory of a sweet taste and a hangover headache generalized to all sweet wines, so she avoided considering them. The wine that she chose was more likely to be selected because it happened to be in her field of vision.

Barbara used basic sensations, such as the feel of the bottle and the color of the label, to infer the meaning that this variety of wine would be seen as sophisticated. Barbara thus accessed a small portion of the raw data available and then processed it to be consistent with her needs.

Many of the associations that she made from her basic sensations were culturally determined. Although a French person would be equally capable of seeing the burgundy and gold label and feeling the weight of the bottle, he or she would probably rely on very different cues to select an appropriate wine.

STAGES IN THE PERCEPTUAL PROCESS Barbara's perceptual process can be broken down into the following stages:[2]

1. *Primitive categorization,* in which the basic characteristics of a stimulus are isolated. Barbara, needing a gift in a hurry, chooses a liquor store and decides on wine.
2. *Cue check,* in which the characteristics are analyzed in preparation for the selection of a schema. Barbara has her own unique schemas or categories for different types of wine, such as "sweet wine that makes me sick" or "white wine that sophisticated people drink." Barbara uses certain cues, such as the color of the label, to decide in which schema a particular bottle of wine belongs.
3. *Confirmation check,* in which the schema is selected. Barbara decides that the bottle of wine most likely falls into her "sophisticated" schema.
4. *Confirmation completion,* in which a decision is made as to what the stimulus is. Barbara decides this is a good bottle of wine and reinforces this judgment by looking at the foreign label and the relatively high price.

▼ MARKETING PITFALL

A misunderstanding stemming from a marketer's promotional campaign illustrates what can happen when the categorization process goes awry. Sample bottles of Sunlight dishwashing liquid, which contains 10 percent lemon juice, were mailed to consumers. Almost 80 people were treated at poison centers after drinking some of the detergent.[3] These individuals apparently assumed that the product was actually lemon juice, since many of the packaging cues resembled Minute Maid frozen lemon juice.

Among the characteristics of the Sunlight stimulus used during the cue check stage in the perceptual process were the yellow bottle with a prominent picture of a lemon. During confirmation check, a juice schema was selected instead of a dishwashing liquid schema. Consumers found out their mistake the hard way following confirmation completion.[4]

SENSORY SYSTEMS

External stimuli, or *sensory inputs,* can be received on a number of channels. We may see a billboard, hear a jingle, feel the softness of a cashmere sweater, taste a new flavor of ice cream, or smell a leather jacket.

The inputs picked up by our five senses constitute the raw data that generates many types of responses. For example, sensory data emanating from the external environment (e.g., hearing a song on the radio) can generate internal sensory experiences when the song on the radio triggers a young man's memory of his first dance and brings to mind the *smell* of his date's perfume or the *feel* of her hair on his cheek.

Sensory inputs evoke *historic imagery,* in which events that actually occurred are recalled. *Fantasy imagery* is the result when an entirely new, imaginary experience is the response to sensory data. These responses

Many consumers confused samples of Sunlight dishwashing liquid with lemon juice because of the similarity in packaging cues, and some became ill after consuming the dishwashing product.

are an important part of *hedonic consumption*—the multisensory, fantasy, and emotional aspects of consumers' interactions with products.[5] The data that we receive from our sensory systems determine how we respond to products.

◢ MARKETING OPPORTUNITY

Although we usually trust our sensory receptors to give us an accurate picture of the external environment, new technology is making the linkage between our senses and reality more questionable. Computer-simulated environments, known as *virtual reality*, allow surgeons to "cut into" a person without actually drawing blood or an architect to see a building design from different perspectives. This technology, which creates a three-dimensional perceptual environment that the viewer experiences as being virtually real, is already being adapted to more everyday pursuits. The Battletech Center in Chicago features an interactive video game that lets players compete against each other in a simulated 31st century war (at about $7 a chance).[6] Enterprising businesspeople will no doubt continue to find new ways to adapt this technology for consumers' entertainment.

COLOR

Colors are rich in symbolic value and have powerful cultural meanings. The display of red, white, and blue evokes feelings of patriotism in both Americans and the French. Remember how impressed Barbara was by the gold lettering on the wine bottle she selected. Gold is associated with elegance and wealth, and these qualities were transferred to the bottle.

COLOR IN THE MARKETPLACE   The powerful cultural meanings attached to colors make them a central aspect of many marketing strategies. Color choices are made carefully with regard to packaging, advertising, and even store decor.

The expectations created by colors can actually affect consumers' experience of products. Consumers ascribe a sweeter taste to orange drinks as the orange shade of the bottle is darkened. When the background color on Barrelhead Sugar-Free Root Beer was changed from blue to beige, consumers said it tasted more like old-fashioned root beer served in a frosty mug.[7]

Package Design: Telling a Book by Its Cover.   The choice of color is frequently a key issue in package design. These choices used to be made casually. For example, the familiar Campbell's soup can was produced in red and white because a company executive liked the football uniforms at Cornell University! Now, however, color is a serious business, and companies frequently employ consultants to assist in these decisions.

Some color combinations come to be so strongly associated with corporations that these companies are granted exclusive use of these colors through a legal device known as *trade dress*. For example, Eastman Kodak has successfully protected its trade dress of yellow, black, and red in court. As a rule, however, trade dress protection is granted only when consumers might be confused about what they are buying because of similar coloration of a competitor's packages.[8]

Since the number of competing brands has proliferated for many types of products, the color of a package can be a crucial spur to sales. When RJR Nabisco introduced a version of Teddy Grahams (a children's product) for adults, restrained packaging colors were used to reinforce the idea that the new product was for grown-ups. However, after finding that sales were alarmingly low, the company undertook a crash redesign program. One major change was to make the box a bright yellow. This color implied that the product was intended to be a "fun" snack, rather than a "serious" graham cracker. Sales picked up dramatically after the changes.[9]

Marketers know that consumers tend to associate certain qualities with colors. The makers of Microsoft software revamped the old forest green package to red and royal blue after it found that consumers associated green with frozen vegetables and chewing gum but not software.[10] The color black connotes quality and elegance, and is used by Minute Maid, Heinz vinegar, Armour Dinner Classics, and Johnnie Walker Scotch to convey a sophisticated image.

THEORIES ABOUT COLOR   Despite the almost mystical effects that colors seem to have on people, little is known about the degree to which these effects are due to the colors themselves or to the cultural meanings that become attached to them. While it is premature to draw any firm conclusions, some evidence indicates that colors can actually affect us regardless of their cultural connotations.

In one experiment, for example, a phone company painted some of its phone booths yellow and found that people making calls from these booths on the average finished their conversations faster.[11] Exposure to "warm" hues such as red, orange, and yellow appears to raise blood pressure, heart rate, and perspiration, while blue exerts an opposite, calming effect. Researchers have also claimed that rooms painted all pink appear to calm down delinquents and prison inmates, and a Canadian dental clinic used a blue room to relax anxious patients. Some fast-food chains rely on the color orange to stimulate customers' hunger.

PERSONALITY DIFFERENCES AND INDIVIDUAL PREFERENCES   Some people believe that people's preferences for colors are somehow indicative of their personalities. While there is little evidence to support this claim, there are clear differences among consumers in terms of their color preferences. Some of these preferences vary by sex, region, social class, or culture. For example, 25 percent of college women say that their favorite color is purple, but less than 10 percent of college men state this preference.[12]

Some product designers believe that lower-income consumers prefer simple colors—those that can be described in two words, such as "grass green" or "sky blue"—and that these people find complex colors dirty or dull. In contrast, higher-income people are thought to like complex colors such as "grey-green with a hint of blue." Simple colors are said to "declassify" or extend a product's appeal, while others "classify" a product by elevating its perceived status. Forest green and burgundy are the colors preferred by the wealthiest 3 percent of Americans.[13]

THE COLOR INDUSTRY   *Color Forecasting.* In a given year, certain colors appear to be "hot" and to show up over and over in clothing, home furnishings, cars, and so on. These favored colors tend to disappear as fast as they came, to be replaced by another set of "hot" colors the next year or season.

The color choices of many consumers are affected by these trends. One simple reason for this is that consumers' choices are largely limited by the colors available in the stores they patronize. Few people, however, realize the extent to which these "hot" colors result from deliberate choices made by a small group of people. Several trade groups and consulting firms engage in the practice of *color forecasting,* in which a set of experts attempts to estimate what colors will best reflect a season in one year, five years, and sometimes even ten years.

Color Analysis. In the last decade, a number of systems have been marketed to determine the colors that best suit an individual. An entire color analysis industry has been created to meet consumers' demands to "have their colors done." Some of the marketing programs have been quite successful. For example, a self-help book called *Color Me Beautiful* sold over three million copies.[14] Color analysis systems have now been developed to guide not only clothing and cosmetics choices, but also interior decorating decisions and even purchases of stationery, cars, and flowers.

Some practitioners of color analysis have even made mystical claims for the power of colors. One of the originators of this movement, for example, describes color analysis as a deeply spiritual experience and claims the ability to sense a person's "inner vibrations," which in turn dictate that individual's proper colors.[15]

There is no evidence to date that these color systems work.[16] It is unclear how much of an influence color analysis will have on consumer decisions in the future. Nonetheless, the popularity of such systems reflects the interest of many consumers in applying "scientific principles" to their everyday purchase decisions.

ODOR

Odors can stir emotions or create a calming feeling. They can invoke memories or relieve stress. Some of our responses to scents result from early associations with other experiences. As a marketer noted, one example ". . . is a baby-powder scent that is frequently used in fragrances because the smell connotes comfort, warmth, and gratification."[17]

Consumers' love of fragrances has contributed to a very large industry. In 1988, Americans alone spent $2.6 billion on women's perfumes. Because this market is extremely competitive (about thirty to forty new scents are introduced each year) and expensive (it costs an average of $50 million to introduce a new fragrance), manufacturers are scrambling to find new ways to expand the use of scents and odors in our daily lives.[18]

BEYOND PERFUME The effects of smells on consumers' environments extend beyond the use (or misuse) of perfumes and colognes. Perhaps in part because home entertaining has gained in popularity, consumers appear to be placing a greater emphasis on creating a warm and inviting home. They have discovered that this atmosphere can be created through more than the visual channel.

MULTICULTURAL DIMENSIONS

Not everyone is enthusiastic about perfumes. For example, American and European fragrance companies historically have not done well in Japan, where perfume is not part of the cultural tradition. The Japanese value cleanliness and personal privacy and also have a diet that produces less body odor. They feel that fragrances invade other people's space, especially since living spaces in Japan are much smaller than those in the West. Tiffany recently introduced a fragrance in Japan, gambling that the popularity of its name among Japanese women would overcome their resistance to buying perfume. However, in contrast to introductions of new scents in the United States, department store customers in Tokyo will not get spritzed with the scent.[19]

Home fragrance products, consisting primarily of potpourri, room sprays and atomizers, drawer liners, sachets, and scented candles, bring in about $250 million annually.[20] Even cigarette companies are sensitive to improving the smell of their products. One brand, named Chelsea, was touted as ". . . the first cigarette that smells good"—and even featured a scented scratch and sniff to prove it.

Fragrances play an obvious role in interpersonal attraction and feelings about our immediate environments, and other effects that they may have on consumers are now beginning to be explored. An industry group known as the Fragrance Research Fund, for example, supports research on what it has called "aromachology." Fragrances have been used to relieve stress during long, painful medical procedures (such as CAT scans), and the productivity of workers doing mundane tasks was reportedly improved when they received occasional whiffs of peppermint through oxygen masks.[21]

▲ MARKETING OPPORTUNITY

A large Japanese construction company was recently granted a patent on a computerized system for "environmental fragrancing." The system delivers fragrances to large buildings through the ventilation ducts, and is intended to combat "sick building syndrome," a problem in many energy-efficient structures whose windows are sealed to save fuel.

The company found in tests that the error rate of keypunch operators dropped by almost 50 percent following exposure to a lemon scent and almost 80 percent after exposure to lavender. The system is in use in several buildings in Japan, including a retirement complex. Future projects that are under development include casinos, airport terminals, and the interiors of airplanes and trains.[22]

SOUND

Music is an important part of many people's lives. In one survey, respondents were asked what experiences gave them thrills. Musical passages were cited by 96 percent of the respondents, as compared to 70 percent who cited sexual activity and 26 percent who named parades (respondents could list more than one item).[23]

Music and sound are also important to marketers. Consumers buy millions of dollars worth of sound recordings each year, advertising jingles maintain brand awareness, and background music creates desired moods.[24]

Many aspects of sound may affect people's feelings and behaviors. Two areas of research that have widespread applications in consumer contexts are the effects of background music on mood and the influence of speaking rate on attitude change and message comprehension.

THE SOUND OF MUZAK The Muzak Corporation estimates that its recordings are heard by 80 million people every day. This so-called functional music is played in stores, shopping malls, and offices to either relax or stimulate consumers.

Research shows that workers tend to slow down during midmorning and midafternoon, so Muzak uses a system it calls "stimulus progression," in which the tempo increases during those slack times. Muzak has been linked to reductions in absenteeism among factory workers, and even the milk and egg output of cows and chickens is claimed to increase under its influence. Muzak is played in the Pentagon and the White House, and the system went to the moon with the Apollo astronauts.[25]

TIME COMPRESSION *Time compression* is a technique used by broadcasters to manipulate perceptions of sound. It is a way to pack more information into a limited time by speeding up an announcer's voice in commercials. The speaking rate is typically accelerated to about 120 percent to 130 percent of normal. This effect is not detectable by most people; in fact, some tests indicate that consumers prefer a rate of transmission that is slightly faster than the normal speaking rate.[26]

The evidence for the effectiveness of time compression is mixed. It has been shown to increase persuasion in some situations and to reduce it in others. One explanation for a positive effect is that the listener uses a person's speaking rate to infer whether the speaker is confident; people seem to think that fast talkers must know what they are talking about.[27]

Another, more plausible, explanation is that the listener is given less time to elaborate in his or her mind on the assertions made in the commercial. This acceleration disrupts normal cognitive responses to the ad and changes the cues used to form judgments about its content. (Chapter 6 examines the issue of cognitive responses to advertising in detail.) This change can either hinder or facilitate attitude change, depending on other conditions.[28]

TOUCH

Although relatively little research has been done on the effects of tactile stimulation on consumer behavior, common observation tells us that this sensory channel is important. Moods are stimulated or relaxed on the basis of sensations of the skin, whether from a luxurious massage or the bite of a winter wind. Tactile sensations also influence our behavior via the physical messages that products send us. We use tactile sensations to evaluate cars in terms of how they "feel" on the road, and detergents brag about how "baby soft" they will get our clothes. Recall also that Barbara's choice was influenced by the "sophisticated feel" of the wine bottle.

SYMBOLIC MEANING OF TACTILE CLUES: "SMOOTH AS SILK" People associate the textures of fabrics with underlying product qualities. The perceived richness or quality of the material in clothing, bedding, or upholstery is linked to its "feel," whether it is rough or smooth, flexible or inflexible. Silk is equated with luxury, while denim is considered practical and durable.

Some of these tactile/quality associations are summarized in Table 2-1. Fabrics that are composed of scarce materials or that require a high degree of processing to achieve their smoothness or fineness tend to be more expensive, and thus are seen as being higher-class. Similarly, lighter, more delicate textures are assumed to be feminine: Roughness is often positively valued for men, while smoothness is sought by women. When was the last time you saw a commercial in which a man was fretting about "dishpan hands?"

TASTE

Our taste receptors obviously contribute to our experience of many products. Specialized companies called "flavor houses" keep busy trying to develop new tastes to please the changing palates of consumers. Their work has been especially important as consumers continue to demand good-tasting foods that are also low in calories and fat.

When the Quaker Oats Company decided to capitalize on this trend by buying a small rice cake manufacturer, consumers complained that the cakes tasted like styrofoam, and sales were disappointing. A flavor house was hired to develop a rice cake that tasted like buttered popcorn. This new taste was perfected along with several others in recent years. Industry-wide sales of rice cakes now exceed $100 million a year.[29]

TASTE TESTING   Food companies go to great lengths to ensure that their products taste as they should. Consider, for example, the procedures used by Nabisco as it monitors the quality of its cookies. The company uses a group of "sensory panelists" as cookie tasters. These consumers are recruited because they have superior sensory abilities, and they are then given six months of training.

The panelists rate the products of Nabisco and its competitors (the specific types and brands being tested are kept secret) on a number of dimensions. These include "rate of melt," "fracturability and density," "molar packing" (the amount of cookie that sticks to the teeth), and the "notes" of the cookie, such as sweetness, saltiness, or bitterness. A typical evaluation session takes the group eight hours to rate just one sample of cookies.[31]

Blind Taste Tests.   Are blind taste tests worth their salt? While taste tests often provide valuable information, their results can be misleading when it is forgotten that objective taste is only *one* component of product evaluation. The most famous example of this mistake concerns New Coke, Coca-Cola's answer to the Pepsi Challenge.[32]

TABLE 2-1 Tactile oppositions in fabrics

Perception	Male	Female	
			Fine
High Class	Wool	Silk	↑ ↓
Low Class	Denim	Cotton	Coarse
	Heavy ← → Light		

Cultural differences account for many of the variations in taste preferences. Children in Mexico and the Southwest United States begin to eat hot peppers at a very early age and get "conditioned" to the fiery taste, while preferences for raw fish are largely limited to Asian cultures for similar reasons. Nevertheless, consumers' preferences for hot, spicy foods seem to be increasing. Americans alone consume more than 125 million pounds of hot peppers a year.[30]

The new formulation was preferred to Pepsi in *blind taste tests* (in which the products were not identified) by an average of 55 percent to 45 percent in seventeen markets, yet New Coke ran into problems when it replaced the older version. People do not buy a cola for taste alone; they are buying intangibles like brand image as well.

It is one thing for people to prefer a new, anonymous flavor in the laboratory and quite another for them to give up a product like Coca-Cola that they have grown up with. In addition, some subtle factors might have influenced even these objective taste judgments. For example, although Coke avoided any mention of the brand, perhaps it was not coincidental that the aprons worn by the testers and the promotional signage used were "Coca-Cola red."

Sometimes taste test failures can be overcome by repositioning the product, since the reported taste dislikes might be based on the product used in the test. For example, Vernor's ginger ale did poorly in a taste test against leading ginger ales. When the research team instead introduced it as a new type of soft drink with a tangier taste, it won handily. As an executive noted, "People hated it because it didn't meet the preconceived expectations of what a ginger ale should be."[33]

SENSORY THRESHOLDS

If you have ever blown a dog whistle and watched pets respond to a sound you cannot hear, you know that there are some stimuli that people simply are not capable of perceiving. And, of course, some people are better able to perceive things than are others.

The science that focuses on how the physical environment is integrated into our personal, subjective world is known as **psychophysics.** By understanding some of the physical laws that govern what we are capable of responding to, this knowledge can be translated into marketing strategies.

THE ABSOLUTE THRESHOLD

When we define the lowest intensity of a stimulus that can be registered on a sensory channel, we speak of a *threshold* for that receptor. The **absolute threshold** refers to the minimum amount of stimulation that can be detected on a sensory channel. The sound emitted by a dog whistle is too low to be detected by human ears, so this stimulus is below our auditory absolute threshold. Obviously, though, it is not below a dog's auditory threshold.

The absolute threshold is an important consideration in designing marketing stimuli. A billboard might have the most entertaining copy ever written, but this genius is wasted if the print is too small for passing motorists to see it from the highway.

THE DIFFERENTIAL THRESHOLD

The **differential threshold** refers to the ability of a sensory system to detect changes or differences among stimuli. A commercial that is intentionally produced in black-and-white might be noticed on a color television because this decrease in the intensity of color differs from what preceded it. Obviously, the same commercial being watched on a black-and-white television would not be seen as different and might be ignored altogether.

According to the differential threshold, a consumer's ability to detect a difference between two stimuli is relative, not absolute as in the case of the absolute threshold. A whispered conversation that might be unintelligible on a noisy street can suddenly become public and embarrassing knowledge in a quiet library. It is the relative difference between the decibel level of the conversation and its surroundings, rather than the loudness of the conversation itself, that determines whether the stimulus will register.

WANTING (OR NOT WANTING) CONSUMERS TO NOTICE A CHANGE   The issue of when and if a change will be noticed by consumers is relevant to many marketing situations. Sometimes a marketer may want to ensure that a change is noticed, such as when merchandise is offered at a discount. In other situations, the fact that a change has been made is downplayed, as in the case of price increases or when a product is downsized.

The JND and Weber's Law.   The minimum change in a stimulus that can be detected is also known as the **JND,** which stands for *just noticeable difference.* In the nineteenth century, a psychophysicist named Ernst Weber found that the amount of change that is necessary to be noticed is systematically related to the original intensity of the stimulus. The stronger the initial stimulus, the greater the change must be for it to be noticed. This relationship is known as **Weber's Law.** Many companies choose to update their packages periodically, making small changes that will not necessarily be noticed at the time. When a product icon is updated, the manufacturer does not want people to lose their identification with a familiar symbol.

SUBLIMINAL PERSUASION

Most marketers are concerned with creating advertising messages above consumers' thresholds. There is, however, another side to this story. A good number of consumers appear to believe that many advertising messages in fact are designed to be received unconsciously, or below the threshold of recognition. Another word for threshold is *limen,* and stimuli that fall below the limen are termed *subliminal.* **Subliminal perception** thus occurs when the stimulus is below the level of the consumer's awareness.

SUBLIMINAL PERCEPTION

Subliminal perception is a topic that has captivated the public for over thirty years, despite the fact that there is virtually *no proof* that this process has any effect on consumer behavior. In fact, most supposed examples of subliminal perception that have been "discovered" are not subliminal at all; they are quite visible. Remember, if you can see it or hear it, it is *not* subliminal, because the stimulus is above the level of conscious awareness! Nonetheless, the continuing controversy about subliminal persuasion has been important in shaping the public's beliefs about advertising and marketers' ability to manipulate consumers against their will. Because of this influence, the dynamics of subliminal perception are worth discussing.

The public's fear of unconscious manipulation began with a widely popularized experiment that was performed in a New Jersey drive-in movie theater in September 1957. During a showing of the movie *Picnic,* a firm called the Subliminal Projection Company inserted messages that said "Drink Coca-Cola" and "Eat Popcorn" for $\frac{1}{3000}$ second every five seconds. This rate was too fast for viewers to be aware that they had seen the images.

It was claimed that sales of popcorn increased by almost 20 percent and that consumption of Coke grew by almost 60 percent. These claims created an uproar across America as journalists and social critics expressed fears that social scientists would team up with advertisers to invade privacy and control consumers against their will. As one magazine put it at the time, consumers' minds had been "broken and entered."[34]

This experiment was never replicated and has repeatedly been criticized. The design of the study was flawed in that other possible effects on consumption, such as the movie itself, the weather during the showing, and so on, could not be ruled out. Indeed, the executive responsible for the test later admitted that he had *made up* results to revive his failing research firm![35]

Despite the continued failure to provide further support for this phenomenon, other attempts at subliminal persuasion followed. Examples include a Seattle radio station that broadcasted "subaudible" messages such as "TV's a bore" and the police in a midwestern city who tried to capture a murderer by interspersing subliminal frames in television news footage of the murder.[36]

SUBLIMINAL TECHNIQUES

EMBEDS **Embeds** are tiny figures that are inserted into magazine advertising by use of high-speed photography or airbrushing. These hidden figures, usually of a sexual nature, supposedly exert strong but unconscious influences on innocent readers. Ice cubes are a prime culprit for accusations of this type of subliminal persuasion; critics often focus on ambiguous shapes in drinks as evidence for the use of this technique.

ABSOLUT SUBLIMINAL.

TO SEND A GIFT OF ABSOLUT® VODKA (EXCEPT WHERE PROHIBITED BY LAW) CALL 1-800-243-3787.
PRODUCT OF SWEDEN. 40 AND 50% ALC/VOL (80 AND 100 PROOF). 100% GRAIN NEUTRAL SPIRITS. © 1989 CARILLON IMPORTERS, LTD., TEANECK, N.J.

This Absolut ad pokes fun at the belief that advertisers embed messages in pictures of ice cubes Courtesy of Absolut Vodka, imported by Carillon Importers Ltd., Teaneck, NJ.

For instance, one ad presented as evidence for the use of subliminal methods is a Gilbey's Gin ad in which the letters S E X are spelled out in the ice cubes.

AUDITORY MESSAGES In addition to subliminal visual messages, many consumers and marketers seem to be fascinated by the possible effects of messages hidden on sound recordings. An attempt to capitalize on subliminal auditory perception techniques is found in the growing market for self-help cassettes. These tapes, which typically feature the sound of waves crashing or some other natural setting, supposedly contain subliminal messages to help the listener stop smoking, lose weight, gain confidence, and so on.

Despite the rapid growth of this market, there is little evidence that subliminal stimuli transmitted on the auditory channel can bring about desired changes in behavior. Indeed, a recent study that set out to examine this effect reported a surprising finding. The researchers randomly picked some tapes that were on the market and subjected them to sophisticated audiological analyses. They were unable even to find any evidence that embedded messages had been placed on the commercial tapes selected, much less that these messages had any effect.[37]

Along with the interest in hidden self-help messages on recordings, some consumers have become concerned about rumors of satanic messages recorded backward on rock records. The popular press has devoted much attention to such stories, and state legislatures have considered bills requiring warning labels about these messages. These backward messages do indeed appear on some albums, including Led Zeppelin's classic song "Stairway to Heaven," which contains the lyric ". . . there's still time to change." When played in reverse, this phrase sounds like "so here's to my sweet Satan." The novelty of such reversals might help to sell records, but the "evil" messages within have no effect.[38] Humans do not have a speech perception mechanism operating at an unconscious level that is capable of decoding a reversed signal.

LOW-LEVEL AUDITORY STIMULATION: "I WON'T STEAL." One application of subliminal techniques does appear to work. This technique is known as psychoacoustic persuasion. Subtle acoustical messages such as "I am honest. I won't steal. Stealing is dishonest" are broadcast in more than 1000 stores in the United States to prevent shoplifting. Unlike subliminal perception, though, these messages are played at a (barely) audible level, using a technique known as threshold messaging.[39] After a nine-month test period, theft losses in one six-store chain declined almost 40 percent, saving the company $600,000.

Some evidence indicates, however, that these messages are effective only on individuals whose value systems make them predisposed to suggestion. For example, someone who might be thinking about taking something on a dare but who feels guilty about it might be susceptible to these messages, but they will not sway a professional thief or a kleptomaniac.[40]

EVALUATING THE EVIDENCE

While some research by clinical psychologists suggests that people can be influenced by subliminal messages under very specific conditions, it is unlikely that these techniques would be of much use in marketing contexts. For one thing, effective messages must be very specifically tailored to individuals, rather than the mass messages required by advertising.[41] Other discouraging factors include the following issues.

1. There are wide individual differences in threshold levels. In order for a message to avoid conscious detection by consumers who have a low threshold, it would have to be so weak that it would not reach those who have a high threshold.
2. Advertisers lack control over consumers' distance and position from a screen. In a movie theater, for example, only a small portion of the audience would be in exactly the right seats to be exposed to the subliminal message.
3. The consumer must be paying absolute attention to the stimulus. People watching a television program or a movie typically shift their

attention periodically and might not even be looking when the stimulus is presented.

4. Even if the desired effect is induced, it operates only at a very general level. For example, a message might increase a person's thirst, but not necessarily for a specific drink. Because basic drives are affected, marketers could find that after all the bother and expense of creating a subliminal message, demand for competitors' products increases as well!

PERCEPTUAL SELECTION

Although we live in an "information society," we can have too much of a good thing. Consumers are often in a state of sensory overload, exposed to far more information than they are capable of or willing to process. People who have been in the middle of a noisy, crowded bar or party for several hours might feel the need to step outside periodically to take a break. A consumer can experience a similar overwhelmed feeling after being forced to sift through the claims made by hundreds of competing brands.

Because the brain's capacity to process information is limited, consumers are very selective about what they pay attention to. The process of *perceptual selectivity* means that people attend to only a small portion of stimuli to which they are exposed. Consumers practice a form of psychic economy, picking and choosing among stimuli, to avoid being overwhelmed by what has come to be known as **advertising clutter.** This overabundance of advertising stimuli has put emphasis on two important aspects of perceptual selectivity as it relates to consumer behavior: exposure and attention.

FACTORS AFFECTING EXPOSURE

Exposure is the degree to which people notice a stimulus that is within range of their sensory receptors. Consumers concentrate on some stimuli, are unaware of others, and even go out of their way to ignore some messages. An experiment by a Minneapolis bank illustrates consumers' tendencies to miss or ignore information in which they are not interested.

After a state law was passed that required banks to explain details about money transfer in electric banking, the Northwestern National Bank distributed a pamphlet to 120,000 of its customers at considerable cost to provide the required information, which was hardly exciting bedtime reading. In one hundred of the mailings, a section in the middle of the pamphlet offered the reader $10.00 just for finding that paragraph. Not a single person claimed the reward.[42]

SELECTIVE EXPOSURE
Experience, which is the result of acquiring stimulation, is one factor that determines how much exposure to a particular stimulus a person accepts. *Perceptual filters* based on consumers' past experiences tend to operate in response to stimuli. For example, a consumer who has had an unpleasant dental experience is likely to ignore advertising messages for mouthwash products because they call to mind the experience of going to the dentist's office.

If this is happening to your print advertising, call (212)210-0227.

Getting noticed these days is tough enough.

And, if the media you use creates confusion with advertorials, inserts, bingo cards and enough other material designed to discourage all but the most persistent readers, you might as well call it quits even before you begin.

But, before you do, call *Pensions & Investments*.

Because, at *P&I,* we have a commitment to providing an uncluttered environment. Which gives advertisers who run with us a distinct competitive advantage.

And, because *P&I* offers you this environment, it explains why more decision makers from your target audience of financial and investment management executives make *P&I* priority reading over all other publications.

The *P&I* advantage incorporates another important idea, too.

It's simple -- each advertising unit generates an equal amount of additional editorial content. Your advertising dollars are reinvested into editorial, our readers get more news, and you get a more powerful newspaper.

Yet, none of this costs you any more. In fact, *P&I* advertising rates continue to be among the lowest in the business.

So, when you feel overwhelmed by the confusion, chaos and clutter in the publications you use to reach professionals in professional money, give us a call. We're here to help you stand out.

Pensions&Investments
The newspaper of corporate and institutional investing

New York	Chicago	Boston	Los Angeles
(212) 210-0227	(312) 649-5280	(617) 248-6991	(213) 651-3710

This photograph featured in an ad for *Pensions & Investment Age* illustrates how visual stimuli can cause advertising clutter, the sensory overload to which consumers are exposed in the marketplace. Courtesy of *Pensions and Investment Age:* Concept: W. Bisson; Copy: W. Bisson; Design: J. Hunt, Donna Klein.

More positive experiences take many forms, and they are often related to consumers' desires to experience sensations. Some consumers enjoy external sensory stimulation and thrill-seeking, while others prefer safe experiences and quiet times.[43] Advertising stimuli that appeal to these preferences are more likely to be noticed. For example, a young man who likes contact sports will concentrate on a commercial set in a locker room or sports arena but might be unaware of one set in a library or a sunny meadow.

Perceptual vigilance is also a factor in selective exposure. Consumers are more likely to be aware of stimuli that relate to their current needs. These needs may be conscious or unconscious. For example, a consumer who rarely notices car ads will become very much aware of them when in the market for a new car. A newspaper ad for a fast-food place that would otherwise go unnoticed takes on significance when one glances at the paper in the middle of a 5:00 class.

Television Messages: Consumers Take Control. The advent of the VCR has allowed consumers armed with remote control fast-forward buttons to be much more selective about which television messages they are exposed to. By "zapping," viewers fast-forward through commercials while playing recorded tapes of their favorite programs. A VCR marketed by Mitsubishi in Japan even removes the need for zapping. It distinguishes between the different types of TV signals used to broadcast programs and commercials and automatically pauses during ads.[44]

ADAPTATION   Another factor affecting exposure is **adaptation,** the degree to which consumers continue to notice a stimulus over time. The process of adaptation occurs when consumers no longer pay attention to a stimulus because it is so familiar. Almost like drug addiction, a consumer can become "habituated" and require increasingly stronger "doses" of a stimulus for it to continue to be noticed. For example, a consumer en route to work might read a billboard message when it is first installed, but after a few days, it becomes part of the passing scenery that is barely noticed.

NOTHING ATTRACTS LIKE THE IMPORTE

CORIANDER SEEDS FROM MOROCCO   ANGELICA ROOT FROM SAXONY   JUNIPER BERRIES FROM ITALY   CASSIA BARK FROM INDOCHINA   ALMONDS FROM IND

Factors Leading to Adaptation. Generally, several factors can lead to adaptation and thus cause consumers to become habituated to the stimulus:[45]

- *Intensity:* Less intense stimuli (e.g., soft sounds or dim colors) habituate because they have less of a sensory impact.
- *Duration:* Stimuli that require relatively lengthy exposure in order to be processed tend to habituate because they require a long attention span.
- *Discrimination:* Simple stimuli tend to habituate because they do not require attention to detail.
- *Exposure:* Frequently encountered stimuli tend to habituate as the rate of exposure increases, the degree of sensory impact decreases with exposure.
- *Relevance:* Stimuli that are irrelevant or unimportant will habituate for consumers to whom they have no basis for attracting attention.

METHODS OF GETTING ATTENTION

Attention is the degree to which consumers focus on stimuli within their range of exposure. Because consumers are being exposed to so many advertising stimuli, marketers are becoming increasingly creative in their attempts to gain attention for their products.

In pretesting of the original version of this Bombay gin ad, eye-tracking tests showed that consumers tended not to read the copy below the visual portion or see the Bombay bottle on the far right. These results led to the revised ad seen here, in which the bottle size and the copy are given more emphasis. Courtesy of Bombay Gin imported by Carillon Importers Ltd., Teaneck, NJ.

A dynamic package is one way to gain this attention. Recall that Barbara was attracted by a distinctive wine bottle that was placed at eye level, and the package essentially sold the product to her. Some consulting firms have established elaborate procedures to measure package effectiveness, such as an instrument called an *angle meter,* which measures package visibility as a shopper moves down the aisle and views the package from different angles.

Data from *eye tracking* tests, in which consumers' eye movements as they look at packages and ads are followed and measured, can result in subtle but powerful changes that influence their impact. Consider, for example, the ad for Bombay gin shown here. Eye tracking tests on an earlier version of the ad showed that virtually no consumers were reading the copy below the visual portion and that the Bombay bottle on the far right was not seen by nine out of ten readers. The result was low recall scores for the ad. In the revised ad, the bottle's size was increased, and the line "Nothing attracts like the imported taste of Bombay gin" was emphasized. Recall scores for this version were almost 100 percent higher than those for the original.[46]

COUNTERING ADVERTISING CLUTTER   Many marketers are making specific attempts to counter the sensory overload caused by advertising clutter in order to call attention to their products. For example, one expensive strategy involves buying large blocks of advertising space in a medium in order to dominate consumers' attention. Ralph Lauren utilized fifteen consecutive full pages in a single issue of *Vanity Fair* for its ads. Other companies adopting this strategy include The Gap, Benetton, Bass shoes, and Esprit.

Another solution has been to put ads in unconventional places, where there will be less competition for attention. These places include the backs of shopping carts, tunnels, sports stadiums, and even movies.[47] An executive at Campbell's Soup, commenting on the company's decision to place ads in church bulletins, noted, "We have to shake consumers up these days in order to make them take notice. . . . Television alone won't do that. Now we have to hit them with our ads where they shop and play and on their way to work."[48]

CREATING CONTRAST   When many stimuli are competing to be noticed, one will receive attention to the extent that it differs from those around it. Stimuli that fall into *unpredictable patterns* often command a lot of attention. For example, the British Family Planning Association creatively drew consumers' attention to its message by featuring a pregnant male in its ads.

Size and color differences are also powerful ways to achieve contrast. For example, a black-and-white object in a color ad is quite noticeable, as is a block of printed type surrounded by large amounts of white space. Many products rely on contrast to gain attention. For example, a French shoe company uses the color contrast approach in its black-and-white ad of a model with red shoes. The size of the stimulus itself in contrast to the competition is also important as in the case of magazine advertising in which readership of an ad increases in proportion to the size of the ad.[49]

COMBATING ADAPTATION Even highly successful advertisements are prone to the adaptation process. Marketers combat this problem, known as *advertising wear-out,* by periodically updating their ads so that they will be fresh to consumers. One way to keep ads fresh is to create a series of ads revolving around a central theme, such as the classic Benson & Hedges cigarette campaign featuring many different applications of the "silly millimeter longer" theme. Each humorous commercial depicts a smoker who is not used to the longer cigarette and gets the tip stuck in an elevator door or burns a hole in the newspaper. This type of strategy permits a company to maintain a consistent theme while avoiding boredom and adaptation by viewers.

This British Family Planning Association ad gets attention by relying on a stimulus that doesn't follow a familiar or predictable pattern. Family Planning Association, U.K.

Would you be more careful if it was you that got pregnant?

Contraception is one of the facts of life.
Anyone, married or single, can get free advice on contraception from their doctor or family planning clinic.
You can find your local clinic under Family Planning in the telephone directory or Yellow Pages.

The Family Planning Information Service

Presenting images in unexpected situations or paired in unusual ways is another method for overcoming the problem of consumer habituation. This strategy generates attention, and may also encourage the consumer to think about the product in new ways. This approach is especially important for fashion-related products, for which the context of the message can help to create a unique image for the product or its use.

COUNTERACTING TELEVISION "ZAPPING" How big an issue is "zapping," or fast-forwarding commercials by VCR viewers, for marketers?[50] The jury is still out on this question. In one survey, 69 percent of VCR owners said that they had increased their television viewing time, so overall exposure to commercials might actually be increased as people continue to purchase VCRs.

On the other hand, VCRs allow viewers to practice "time shifting," which allows them to watch previously recorded shows whenever they want to. This practice makes risky business of scheduling commercials intended for audiences who are likely to watch TV at certain times of the day. Approximately 70 percent of all recorded programs are not viewed at the time of taping, and about 25 percent of the recordings are never watched at all. By some estimates, 50 percent to 60 percent of the commercial messages in the recorded programs that are watched are zapped.[51]

Zapping has enhanced the need for advertising creativity. Interesting commercials do not get zapped as frequently. Evidence indicates that viewers are willing to stop fast-forwarding to watch an enticing or novel commercial. In addition, longer commercials and those that keep a static figure on the screen (such as a brand name or a logo) appear to counteract the effects of zapping; these executions are not as affected by a speed increase, since the figure remains in place.[52]

Overall, zapping appears to have surprisingly little effect on advertising recall scores. Ironically, the viewer must pay closer attention to a commercial when fast-forwarding in order to stop the process when programming resumes. Indeed, it has been proposed that only three exposures might be sufficient to accomplish the commercial's objectives. The first exposure, if executed properly, creates curiosity. The second exposure generates recognition, and the third exposure prompts a decision about the product being advertised.[53]

INTERPRETATION: ASSIGNING MEANING TO STIMULI

Interpretation is the meaning that people assign to sensory stimuli. Just as people differ in terms of the stimuli that they perceive, the eventual assignment of meanings to these stimuli varies as well. Two people can see or hear the same event, but their interpretation of it can be like night and day.

In a classic experiment, students at Princeton and Dartmouth viewed a movie of a particularly rough football game between the two schools. Although everyone was exposed to the same stimulus, the degree to which students saw infractions and the blame they assigned for those they did see, was quite different depending on which college they attended.[54] As this study demonstrates, the assignment of meaning can be colored by what one expects or hopes it to be.[55]

Consumers assign meaning to stimuli based on the schema, or set of beliefs, to which the stimulus is assigned. Certain properties of a stimulus will more likely evoke a schema than others. (This process is known as *priming.*) For example, a brand name can communicate expectations about product attributes and color consumers' perceptions of product performance by activating an existing schema. When Toro introduced a lightweight snow thrower, it was named the "Snow Pup." Sales were disappointing because the word pup called up a schema for many that grouped small, cuddly things together—not the desirable attributes for a snow thrower. When the product was renamed the "Snow Master," sales went up markedly.[56]

Stimulus ambiguity occurs when a stimulus is not clearly perceived or when it conveys a number of meanings. In such cases, consumers tend to project their own wishes and desires to assign meaning. Although ambiguity in product advertisements is usually undesirable to marketers, it can be used creatively to generate controversy or interest. For example, a recent ad for Benson & Hedges cigarettes featured a group of nicely-dressed people sitting around a dinner table, while a "mystery man" wearing only pajama bottoms stands in the background. This ambiguous character yielded valuable publicity for the company as people competed to explain the meaning of the mysterious man.

STIMULUS ORGANIZATION

People do not perceive a single stimulus in isolation. They tend to view it in terms of relationships with other events, sensations, or images. A number of specific grouping principles describe how stimuli are perceived and organized on the basis of characteristics that are relative to those of other stimuli.

THE GESTALT   These perceptual grouping principles are based on work in **Gestalt psychology,** a school of thought that maintains that people derive meaning from the totality of a set of stimuli, rather than from any individual stimulus. While there is no exact English translation for the German word *gestalt,* it roughly means whole, pattern, or configuration, and this perspective is best summarized by the saying "the whole is greater than the sum of its parts." The importance of a gestalt is underscored when consumers' interpretations are affected by aesthetic, symbolic, or sensory qualities. In such cases, a piecemeal perspective that analyzes each component of the stimulus separately will be unable to capture the total effect. For instance, a "punk" black leather jacket and "preppie" khaki pants might look right separately, but the gestalt created when they are worn together would not be "right." The gestalt perspective provides several principles relating to the way stimuli are organized. Three of these principles, or perceptual tendencies, are illustrated in Figure 2-2.

Closure.   The principle of **closure** implies that consumers tend to perceive an incomplete picture as complete. That is, we tend to fill in the blanks based on our prior experiences. This principle explains why most of us have no trouble reading a neon sign even if one or two of its letters are burned out. The principle of closure is also at work when we hear only part of a jingle or theme.

For many years, consumers heard the jingle, "You can take Salem out of the country, but you can't take the country out of Salem." Some more recent ads for Salem cigarettes have capitalized on this experience by including only the copy "You can take Salem out of the country. . . ."

The closure principle underlies the J&B ad featuring incomplete text of a holiday message. The advertisers know that people will complete the rest of the line on their own. Utilization of the principle of closure in marketing strategies enhances consumer involvement with ads because it encourages audience participation.

Similarity. The **principle of similarity** tells us that consumers tend to group together objects that share similar physical characteristics. That is, they group like items into sets to form an integrated whole. Green Giant, for example, relied upon this principle when the company redesigned the packaging for its line of frozen vegetables. It created a "sea of green" look to unify all of its different offerings.

Figure-Ground. Another important principle is the **figure-ground relationship,** in which one part will dominate (the figure) while other parts recede into the background. This concept is easy to understand if one thinks literally of a photograph with a clear and sharply focused object (the figure) in the center. The figure is dominant, and the eye goes straight to it. The area around the object (the ground) is usually less focused, and because it is perceived as hazy or indistinct, it makes the figure seem even more dominant.

The parts of the configuration that will be perceived as figure or ground can vary depending on the individual consumer as well as other factors. Similarly, in marketing messages that use the figure-ground principle, a stimulus can be made the focal point of the message or merely the context that surrounds the focus. Music provides one example of a figure

Figure 2-2 Principles of Stimulus Organization Derived from Gestalt Psychology

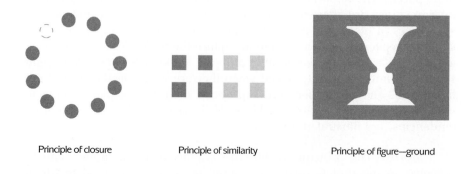

Principle of closure   Principle of similarity   Principle of figure—ground

and ground relationship that can be varied. Soft background music can be used to create an appropriate atmosphere for the spoken and visual images promoting a product. Loud and lively music that dominates the spoken message or visual image and is used to convey the message, however, becomes the figure rather than the ground.

STIMULUS MEANING

Symbols, which may be composed of words, pictures, sounds, or scents, play an important role in the meanings people assign to stimuli. Symbols may be *evocative* in that they evoke emotions, moods, and feelings through actual or culturally learned past experiences and events. For example, a child *learns* that lions are courageous, but may

This J&B ad illustrates use of the principle of closure, in which people participate in the ad by mentally filling in the gaps. Reprinted with permission by THE PADDINGTON CORPORATION ©.

experience the unqualified love given by a puppy. The specific meaning assigned to evocative symbols, such as a lion or a puppy, is consistent with each person's individual background and experiences.

Other types of symbols are more *objective* in that they represent a specific meaning that is agreed upon by members of a group. Language, letters, and numbers are examples of this type of symbolism. For instance, English-speaking people have agreed that the word *cat* and the letters *C A T* are symbols for a particular kind of animal.

▼ MARKETING PITFALL

When agreements about meaning are violated, trouble can arise. This occurs when marketers try to impose a meaning on a culture with a different set of rules regarding verbal or pictorial symbolism. When the Coca-Cola Company was planning to expand into China in the 1920s, a translator developed a group of Chinese characters that phonetically resembled the company name. Since the product was new to the country, people would not recognize the Coca-Cola logo, so they had to rely upon the meaning as conveyed phonetically. Unfortunately, the Chinese characters that sounded like Coca-Cola translated to mean "bite the wax tadpole," and changes had to be made quickly.[57]

SYMBOLOGY IN MARKETING MESSAGES The use of symbols provides a powerful means for marketers to convey product attributes to consumers. Expensive cars, designer fashions, and diamond jewelry—all widely recognized symbols of success—frequently appear in ads promoting personal products. Household products are often ascribed the qualities of clean and fresh in product messages utilizing the lemon symbol in the form of its image, its color, or even its scent. In some cases, product icons and logos have become so well-known that they go beyond merely representing the product to being larger symbols of the attributes of the product. The Coca-Cola logo (the real thing), the Playboy bunny icon (sophisticated man-about-town), and the Mercedes-Benz hood ornament (wealth) are examples.

Whether symbols are used to promote a product or to create identification for it, the interpretation or meaning may not always convey what the marketer intended, or it may limit the consumers who see the association as positive. For example, while the Playboy symbol may be seen positively by some as a symbol of sophistication and affluence, others may view it as representing a crass macho image that is demeaning to women.

Every marketing message has three basic components: an object, a sign or symbol, and an interpretant. The *object is* the product that is the focus of the message (e.g., Marlboro cigarettes). The *sign* or *symbol* is the sensory imagery that represents the intended meanings of the object (e.g., the Marlboro cowboy). The *interpretant* is the meaning derived (e.g., rugged, individualistic, American). This relationship is diagrammed in Figure 2-3.

For assistance in understanding how consumers interpret the meanings of symbols used in these communications, many marketers are turning

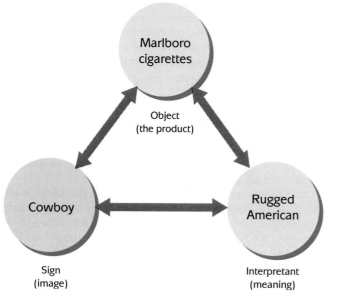

Object
(the product)

Sign
(image)

Interpretant
(meaning)

Figure 2-3 Relationships of Components in Semiotic Analysis of Meaning

to a field of study known as **semiotics,** which examines the correspondence between signs and symbols and their role in the assignment of meaning.[58]

According to semiotician Charles Sanders Peirce, signs are related to objects in one of three ways. Signs and symbols can resemble objects, be connected to them, or be conventionally tied to them.[59] An <u>icon</u> is a sign that resembles the product in some way (e.g., Bell Telephone uses an image of a bell to represent itself). An <u>index</u> is a sign that is connected to a product because they share some property (e.g., the pine tree on some of Spic and Span's cleanser products conveys the shared property of fresh scent). A *symbol* is a sign that is related to a product through either conventional or agreed-upon associations (e.g., the lion in Dreyfus Fund ads provides the conventional association with fearlessness that is carried over to the company's approach to the investments; Hertz utilizes the agreed-upon "Number 1" in its promotions to indicate its rank among competitors).

Carefully crafted marketing messages may contain several signs that together strengthen the intended interpretation.

CHAPTER SUMMARY

Perception is the process by which physical sensations such as sights, sounds, and smells are selected, organized, and interpreted. The eventual interpretation of a stimulus allows it to be assigned meaning. The chapter describes the stages involved as a stimulus moves from sensation to perception.

Marketing stimuli have important sensory qualities. We rely on colors, odors, sounds, tastes, and even the "feel" of products when forming evaluations of them. Some specific applications of sensory marketing are discussed, including color preferences, package design, fragrances, and taste testing.

Not all sensations successfully make their way through the perceptual process. Many stimuli compete for our attention, and the majority are not noticed or accurately comprehended. People have different thresholds of perception. A stimulus must be presented at a certain level of intensity before it can be detected by sensory receptors. In addition, a consumer's ability to detect whether two stimuli are different (the differential threshold) is an important issue in many marketing contexts, such as changing a package design, altering the size of a product, or reducing its price.

Despite the necessity of presenting a stimulus at or above a consumer's threshold of perception, a lot of controversy has been sparked by so-called subliminal persuasion and related techniques, by which people are exposed to visual and audio messages below the threshold. Although evidence that subliminal persuasion is effective is virtually nonexistent, many consumers continue to believe that advertisers use this technique.

Some of the factors that determine which stimuli (above the threshold level) do get perceived are reviewed. These include the amount of exposure to the stimulus, how much attention it generates, and how it is interpreted. In an increasingly crowded stimulus environment, advertising clutter occurs when too many marketing-related messages compete for attention. The chapter reviews some ways in which marketers make it more likely that a message will be attended to.

A stimulus that is attended to is not perceived in isolation. It is classified and organized according to principles of perceptual organization. These principles are guided by a *gestalt,* or overall pattern. Specific grouping principles include closure, similarity, and figure-ground relationships.

The final step in the process of perception is interpretation. Symbols help us to make sense of the world by providing us with an interpretation of a stimulus that is often shared by others. The degree to which the symbolism is consistent with our previous experience affects the meaning we assign to related objects. Every marketing message contains a relationship between the product, the sign or symbol, and the interpretation of meaning. A semiotic analysis involves the correspondence between stimuli and the meaning of signs.

Signs function on several levels. The intended meaning may be literal (e.g., an icon like a street sign with a picture of children playing). The meaning may be indexical; it relies on shared characteristics (e.g., the red in a stop sign means danger). Finally, meaning can be conveyed by a symbol, where an image is given meaning by convention or by agreement by members of a society (e.g., stop signs are octagonal, while yield signs are triangular).

KEY TERMS

Absolute threshold
Adaptation
Advertising clutter
Attention
Closure
Differential threshold
Embeds
Experience
Exposure
Figure-ground relationship
Gestalt psychology

Interpretation
JND
Perception
Psychophysics
Schema
Semiotics
Sensation
Principle of similarity
Stimulus ambiguity
Subliminal perception
Weber's Law

1. Which of the human senses do you think is strongest? Which is weakest? Discuss the implications of your choices for a marketer.
2. Many marketers have been inserting perfumed samples into magazines. Some consumers have objected, claiming the right to determine whether they want to smell the products, and at least one state legislature has considered a proposal requiring such samples be sealed in scent-proof packaging. Evaluate this issue both from a marketing perspective and from the offended consumer's point of view. Should marketers have the right to distribute scented product samples?
3. Discuss the implications of the figure-ground relationship for marketers using print media, radio, and television, respectively. How can this principle help or interfere with communicating the desired message?
4. Evaluate each of the factors that lead to adaptation as given in this chapter. Give examples of particular marketing strategies that you believe have had a habituating effect on you, and explain the reasons.
5. Some consumers have objected to ads for cigarettes and alcoholic beverages being displayed in sports stadiums. What is your view of this marketing practice?
6. Many studies have shown that our sensory detection abilities decline as we grow older. Discuss the implications of the absolute threshold for marketers attempting to appeal to the elderly.
7. Assuming that some forms of subliminal persuasion may have the desired effect of influencing consumers, do you think the use of these techniques is ethical? Explain your answer.
8. Assume that you are a consultant for a marketer who wants to design a package for a new premium chocolate bar targeted to an affluent market. What recommendations would you provide in terms of such package elements as color, symbolism, and graphic design (remembering the grouping principles discussed in the chapter)? Give the reasons for your suggestions.
9. Do you believe that marketers have the right to use any or all public spaces to deliver product messages? Where would you draw the line in terms of places and products that should be restricted?
10. Think of some products for which the new virtual reality technology would be particularly helpful in the marketing process. Explain the benefits of this technique over conventional media for these products.
11. Find one ad that is rich in symbolism and perform a semiotic analysis of it. Identify each type of sign used in the ad and the product qualities being communicated by each. Comment on the effectiveness of the signs that are used to communicate the intended message.

1. Conduct your own Pepsi–Coke blind taste test using Pepsi, New Coke, and Classic Coke. Assess the results and prepare a report of your findings.
2. Using magazines archived in the library, track the packaging of a specific brand over time. Find an example of gradual changes in package design that may have been below the JND.
3. In three separate hours of television viewing, record both the total number of commercials and the number in which music is used as a stimulus. Of the commercials containing music, note the number in which the music is used as a figure or as one of the primary stimulants in the

ad versus the number of those in which it is used solely as background to create a mood. Based on your findings, identify some conditions that seem to determine when and if music is an effective factor in commercials.

4. Collect a set of current ads for one type of product (e.g., personal computers, perfumes, laundry detergents, or athletic shoes) from magazines, and analyze the colors employed. Describe the images conveyed by different colors, and try to identify any consistency across brands in terms of the colors used in product packaging or other aspects of the ads.

5. Collect ads for five different products that feature the product's scent or aroma. Exclude products that are directly scent-related such as perfumes, deodorants, and air fresheners. Report on the emphasis given to scent or aroma relative to the product's primary use in each of the ads.

6. Find three ads for food products that present these products in a particular scene or setting. Report on the symbols used in the setting and how you believe the marketer intended them to be interpreted relative to the food product.

7. Collect ads for several products that are advertised on the basis of tactile sensations. Report on the symbols used to convey each product's feel.

8. Locate several ads for different brands of the same product. Compare and evaluate the symbols the marketers have used in each ad.

9. Look through a current magazine and select one ad that captures your attention over the others. Give the reasons why.

10. Identify a stimulus that is likely to evoke historic imagery for you and your peers. Describe how this stimulus could be used in a marketing campaign targeted to consumers like you.

11. Find ads that utilize the techniques of contrast and novelty. Give your opinion of the effectiveness of each ad and whether the technique is likely to be appropriate for the consumers targeted by the ad.

NOTES

1. Kim Foltz, "Campaign on Harmony Backfires for Benetton," *New York Times* (November 20, 1989):D8.
2. Jerome S. Bruner, "On Perceptual Readiness," *Psychological Review* 64 (March 1957):123–52.
3. "The Lemon Juice That Wasn't," *Newsweek* (August 2, 1982):53.
4. Gail Tom, Teresa Barnett, William Lew, and Jodean Selmants, "Cueing the Consumer: The Role of Salient Cues in Consumer Perception," *Journal of Consumer Marketing* 4 (1987)2:23–27.
5. Elizabeth C. Hirschman and Morris B. Holbrook, "Hedonic Consumption: Emerging Concepts, Methods, and Propositions," *Journal of Marketing* 46 (Summer 1982):92–101.
6. Woody Hochswender, "Battles So Real They Almost Hurt," *New York Times* (August 29, 1990):C1.
7. Ronald Alsop, "Color Grows More Important in Catching Consumers' Eyes," *The Wall Street Journal* (November 29, 1984):37.
8. Alsop, "Color Grows More Important in Catching Consumers' Eyes."
9. Anthony Ramirez, "Lessons in the Cracker Market: Nabisco Saved New Graham Snack," *New York Times* (July 5, 1990):D1.
10. Alsop, "Color Grows More Important in Catching Consumers' Eyes."
11. Kelly Costigan, "How Color Goes to Your Head," *Science Digest* 24 (December 1984)1.
12. Brad Edmondson, "The Color Purple," *American Demographics* 24 (June 1987).
13. Bernice Kanner, "Color Schemes," *New York* (April 3, 1989):22–23.

14. Carole Jackson, *Color Me Beautiful* (New York: Ballantine Books, 1981).
15. Judith Rasband, *Color Crazed* (privately published, 1983).
16. Israel Abramov, "An Analysis of Personal Color Analysis," in *The Psychology of Fashion,* ed. Michael R. Soloman (Lexington, Mass.: Lexington Books, 1985):212–23.
17. Quoted in Cynthia Morris, "The Mystery of Fragrance," *Essence* 71 (May 1988)3:71.
18. Debora Toth, "To Relax or Stay Alert: New Mood-Altering Scents," *New York Times* (September 24, 1989):F15.
19. Wendy Hochswender, "Scents Without Spritz," *New York Times* (May 29, 1990:B9.
20. James LaRossa, Jr., "Home Fragrances Bloom in Wide-Open Field," *Home Textiles* 54 (May 8, 1989)4.
21. "Environmental Fragrancing: The Muzak of the 90s?" *Fragrance Forum* 4 (Fall 1988); Toth, "To Relax or Stay Alert."
22. "Environmental Fragrancing"; Toth, "To Relax or Stay Alert."
23. Anne H. Rosenfeld, "Music, the Beautiful Disturber," *Psychology Today* (December 1985)4:48.
24. Gail Tom, "Marketing with Music," *Journal of Consumer Marketing* 7 (Spring 1990):49–53; J. Vail, "Music as a Marketing Tool," *Advertising Age* (November 4, 1985):24.
25. Otto Friedrich, "Trapped in a Musical Elevator," *Time* 110 (December 10, 1984)3.
26. James MacLachlan and Michael H. Siegel, "Reducing the Costs of Television Commercials by Use of Time Compression," *Journal of Marketing Research* 17 (February 1980):52–57.
27. James MacLachlan, "Listener Perception of Time Compressed Spokespersons," *Journal of Advertising Research* 2 (April/May 1982):47–51.
28. Danny L. Moore, Douglas Hausknecht, and Kanchana Thamodaran, "Time Compression, Response Opportunity, and Persuasion," *Journal of Consumer Research* 13 (June 1986):85–99.
29. Eben Shapiro, "The People Who Are Putting Taste Back on the Table," *New York Times* (July 22, 1990):F5.
30. Beauchamp, Gary K. (1987), "Recent Developments in Flavor Research," *Beverage World* June, 74 (2).
31. Judann Dagnoli, "Cookie Tasters Chip in for Nabisco," *Advertising Age* (August 21, 1989):58.
32. See Tim Davis, "Taste Tests: Are the Blind Leading the Blind?" *Beverage World* (April 1987)5:43.
33. Quoted in Davis, "Taste Tests,"44.
34. *The New Yorker* (September 21, 1957):33.
35. Erv Wolk, "Can Subliminal Ads Work for You?" *Modern Floor Coverings* (June 1986):23.
36. Reported in the *New York Times* (May 18, 1978):C22.
37. Philip M. Merikle, "Subliminal Auditory Messages: An Evaluation," *Psychology & Marketing* 5 (1988)4:355–72.
38. Timothy E. Moore, "The Case Against Subliminal Manipulation," *Psychology & Marketing* 5 (Winter 1988):297–316.
39. Sid C. Dudley, "Subliminal Advertising: What Is the Controversy About?" *Akron Business and Economic Review* 18 (Summer 1987):6–18; "Subliminal Messages: Subtle Crime Stoppers," *Chain Store Age Executive* (July 1987)2:85; "Mind Benders," *Money* (September 1978):24.
40. Moore, "The Case Against Subliminal Manipulation."
41. Joel Saegert, "Why Marketing Should Quit Giving Subliminal Advertising the Benefit of the Doubt," *Psychology & Marketing* 4 (Summer 1987):107–20.
42. "$10 Sure Thing," *Time* (August 4, 1980):51.
43. Marvin Zuckerman, *Sensation Seeking* (Hillsdale, N.J.: Lawrence Erlbaum, 1979).
44. David Kilburn, "Japanese VCR Edits Out the Ads," *Advertising Age* (August 20, 1990):16.
45. James F. Engel, Roger D. Blackwell, and Paul W. Miniard, *Consumer Behavior,* 5th ed. (Chicago: Dryden, 1986).
46. Elliot Young, "Overcoming the Zapping Problem in Magazines: New Learning from Eye Tracking Research," (presented at Copy Research Workshop, Advertising Research Federation, May 3, 1988).

47. "Traffic Now Tuned to Boston's Tunnel Radio," *New York Times* (August 1, 1982); Alison Fahey, "In the Lobby," *Advertising Age* (September 18, 1989); Kim Foltz, "Ads Popping Up All Over," *Newsweek* (August 12, 1985)2:50.

48. Quoted in Foltz, "Ads Popping Up All Over."

49. Roger Barton, *Advertising Media* (New York: McGraw-Hill, 1964).

50. Kate Lewin, "Getting Around Commercial Avoidance," *Marketing and Media Decisions* (December 1988)4:116.

51. Michael G. Harvey and James T. Rothe, "Video Cassette Recorders: Their Impact on Viewers and Advertisers," *Journal of Advertising Research* 25 (December/January 1985)10:19.

52. Craig Reiss, "Fast-Forward Ads Deliver," *Advertising Age* (October 27, 1986)2:3; Steve Sternberg, "VCR's: Impact and Implications," *Marketing and Media Decisions* 22 (December 1987)5:100.

53. Herbert E. Krugman, "Why Three Exposures May Be Enough," *Journal of Advertising Research* 12 (December 1972):11–14.

54. Albert H. Hastorf and Hadley Cantril, "They Saw a Game: A Case Study," *Journal of Abnormal and Social Psychology* 49 (1954):129–34.

55. Roberto Friedmann and Mary R. Zimmer, "The Role of Psychological Meaning in Advertising," *Journal of Advertising* 17 (1988)1:31–40.

56. Tom, et al., "Cueing the Consumer."

57. David A. Ricks, "Products That Crashed the Language Barrier," *Business and Society Review* (Spring 1983):46–50.

58. See David Mick, "Consumer Research and Semiotics: Exploring the Morphology of Signs, Symbols, and Significance," *Journal of Consumer Research* 13 (September 1986):196–213.

59. Arthur Asa Berger, *Signs in Contemporary Culture: An Introduction to Semiotics* (New York: Longman, 1984); Mick, "Consumer Research and Semiotics"; Charles Sanders Peirce, *Collected Papers,* ed. Charles Hartshorne, Paul Weiss, and Arthur W. Burks (Cambridge, Mass.: Harvard University Press, 1931–1958).

Motivation and Involvement

CHAPTER 3

It's Saturday night, and Basil is anxious. He has been trying to get up the nerve for over a month now to ask Lisa, that attractive woman in his Accounting class, for a date and he knows he's running out of time. He can almost feel a physical pain in his chest every time he looks in her direction, and he cannot stop thinking about her. Could this be love? Basil's "spies" have told him that the object of his desire will be at the Cadillac Bar tonight, so the stage is set.

What to wear? As Basil scans his closet, he realizes that he will need every ounce of confidence he can muster. He can't pretend to be some dandy out of *Gentleman's Quarterly;* he has to be himself. There's really no choice. Basil reaches for his "lucky" pants, his Levi's 501s. He imagines himself as his idol, the cult hero James Dean, striding assuredly through the bar and up to Lisa, who falls into his arms. As he slides the jeans on and they mold comfortably to his body, Basil starts to relax. These pants have been with him through thick and thin, and he knows they won't let him down.

INTRODUCTION

Basil is not alone in feeling that his blue jeans play an important part in his life. In a national survey on consumers' attachments to their Levi's 501 jeans, one-quarter of the respondents associated special memories and experiences with a particular pair of jeans. Wearers told fascinating stories about their relationships with their jeans, and some even attributed almost magical properties to them. Many of these associations were of a romantic nature. One consumer reported that "I asked my wife to marry me in 501 jeans," and another said "I wore them on my wedding night."

Consumers' attachments to their jeans can become so intense that they cannot bear to dispose of them after they have become too worn to wear, even as cutoffs. Some people sew the tattered remains into quilts, and others actually mail them to Levi Strauss headquarters, requesting that they be given a decent burial.[1]

The forces that drive people to buy and use products can be straightforward, as when a person purchases a pair of blue jeans to work around the house. As these hard-core Levi's owners demonstrate, however, even the consumption of an everyday product like blue jeans may also be related to deep-seated experiences. Sometimes, people are not even fully aware of the forces that drive them toward some products and away from others.

To understand motivation is to understand *why* consumers do what they do. We do everything for a reason, whether to quench a thirst, kill boredom, or attain some deep spiritual experience. Marketing students are taught from day one that the goal of marketing is to satisfy consumers' needs. However, this insight is useless unless we can discover *what* those needs are and why they exist.

THE MOTIVATION PROCESS

Motivation refers to the processes that cause people to behave as they do. It occurs when a need is aroused that the consumer wishes to satisfy. Once a need has been activated, a state of tension exists that drives the consumer to attempt to reduce or eliminate the need. Marketers try to create products and services that will provide the desired benefits and permit the consumer to reduce this tension.

Figure 3-1 gives an overview of the motivation process. The sections to follow will elaborate on the components in this model, but in general the process works this way: A need is recognized by the consumer. This need may be utilitarian (i.e., a desire to achieve some functional or practical benefit, as when a person requires a pair of durable work pants) or it may be hedonic (i.e., an experiential need, involving emotional responses, fantasies, etc., as when Basil uses his Levi's to bolster his self-confidence and help him to get a date). The desired end state is the consumer's **goal.**

In either case, a discrepancy exists between the consumer's present state and some ideal state. This gulf creates a state of tension. The magnitude of this tension determines the urgency the consumer feels to reduce the tension. This degree of arousal is called a **drive.** A basic need can be

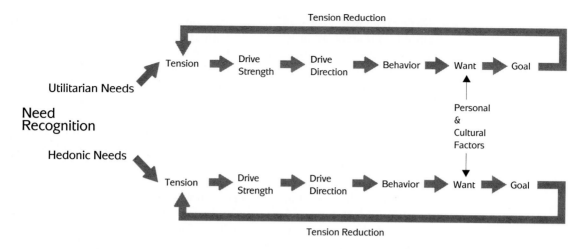

Figure 3-1 An Overview of the Motivation Process

satisfied any number of ways, and the specific path a person chooses is influenced by his or her unique set of experiences, cultural upbringing, and so on.

These factors combine to create a **want,** which is one manifestation of a need. For example, hunger is a basic need that must be satisfied by all; the lack of food creates a tension state that can be reduced by the intake of such products as cheeseburgers, double fudge Oreo cookies, raw fish, or bean sprouts. The specific route to hunger reduction is culturally determined.

Once the goal is attained, tension is reduced and the motivation recedes (for the time being). Motivation can be described in terms of its *strength,* or the pull it exerts on the consumer, and its *direction,* or the particular way the consumer attempts to reduce motivational tension.

MOTIVATIONAL STRENGTH

The degree to which a person is willing to expend energy to reach one goal as opposed to another reflects his or her underlying motivation to attain that goal. Many theories have been advanced to explain why people behave the way they do. Most share the basic idea that people have some finite amount of energy that must be directed toward certain goals.

BIOLOGICAL VERSUS LEARNED NEEDS

Early work on motivation ascribed behavior to *instinct*—innate patterns of behavior that are universal in a species. This view is now largely discredited. For one thing, the existence of an instinct is difficult to prove or disprove. The instinct is inferred from the behavior it is supposed to explain (this type of circular explanation is called a tautology)[2] It is like saying that a consumer buys status symbols because he or she is motivated to attain status—hardly a satisfying explanation.

DRIVE THEORY *Drive theory* focuses on biological needs that produce unpleasant states of arousal (e.g., your stomach grumbles during a morning class). We are motivated to reduce the tension caused by this arousal. Tension reduction has been proposed as a basic mechanism governing human behavior.

In marketing, tension reduction refers to the unpleasant state that exists if a person's need is not fulfilled. A person may be grumpy if he hasn't eaten, or he may be dejected or angry if he cannot afford that new car he wants. This state activates goal-oriented behavior, which attempts to reduce or eliminate this unpleasant state and return to a balanced one termed **homeostasis**.

Those behaviors that are successful in reducing the drive by eliminating the underlying need are strengthened and tend to be repeated (this aspect of the *learning* process will be further discussed in Chapter 4). Your motivation to leave class early in order to grab a snack would be greater if you hadn't eaten in twenty-four hours than if you had eaten only two hours earlier. If you did sneak out and got indigestion after, say, wolfing down a package of Twinkies, this behavior would be less likely to be repeated the next time you wanted a snack. One's degree of motivation, then, depends upon the distance between one's present state and the goal.

Drive theory, however, runs into difficulties when it tries to explain some facets of human behavior that run counter to its predictions. People often do things that *increase* a drive state rather than decrease it. For example, people may delay gratification. If you know you are going out for a lavish dinner, you might decide to forego a snack earlier in the day even though you are hungry at that time. In other cases, people deliberately watch erotic movies, even though these stimuli often increase sexual arousal rather than relieve it.

EXPECTANCY THEORY Most current explanations of motivation focus on cognitive factors rather than biological ones to understand what drives behavior. **Expectancy theory** suggests that behavior is largely pulled by expectations of achieving desirable outcomes—*positive incentives*—rather than pushed from within. We choose one product over another because we expect this choice to have more positive consequences for us. Thus the term drive is used here more loosely to refer to both physical and cognitive processes.

INVOLVEMENT
Involvement refers to "the level of perceived personal importance and/or interest evoked by a stimulus (or stimuli) within a specific situation."[3] This definition implies that aspects of the person, the product, and the situation all combine to determine the consumer's motivation to process product-related information at a given point in time. When consumers are intent on doing what they can to satisfy a need, they will be motivated to pay attention and process any information felt to be relevant to achieving their goals.

On the other hand, a person may not bother to pay any attention to the same information if it is not seen as relevant to satisfying some need. One person who prides himself on his knowledge of stereo equipment may read anything he can find about the subject, spend his spare time in electronics stores, and so on, while his friend may skip over this information without giving it a second thought.

Involvement can be viewed as the motivation to process information.[4] To the degree that there is a perceived linkage between a consumer's needs, goals, or values, and product knowledge, the consumer will be motivated to pay attention to product information, learn about the product, and so on. When relevant knowledge is activated in memory, a motivational state is created that drives behavior (e.g., shopping). This subjective feeling of personal relevance is termed *felt involvement.* As felt involvement with a product increases, people devote more attention to ads related to the product, exert more cognitive effort to understand these ads, and focus their attention on the product-related information in them.[5]

FROM INERTIA TO PASSION   The type of information processing that will occur thus depends upon the consumer's level of involvement. This can range from *simple processing,* where only the basic features of a message are considered, all the way to *elaboration,* where the incoming information is linked to one's preexisting knowledge systems.[6]

Degree of involvement can be conceived as a continuum, ranging from absolute lack of interest in a marketing stimulus at one end to obsession at the other. Consumption at the low end of involvement is characterized by **inertia,** where decisions are made out of habit because the consumer lacks the motivation to consider alternatives.

At the high end of involvement we can expect to find the type of passionate intensity reserved for people and objects that carry great meaning to the individual. Of course, a consumer's involvement level with many products falls somewhere in the middle, and the marketing strategist must determine the relative level of importance to understand how much elaboration of product information will occur.

 ## MARKETING OPPORTUNITY

The passion of some consumers for famous people demonstrates the high end of the involvement continuum. Celebrity worship is evident in activities ranging from autograph collections to the cement shrines at Graumann's Chinese Theatre in Hollywood. Consumers can be described in terms of the intensity of their admiration for a celebrity. At the bottom of this intensity ladder are people who are uninvolved, oblivious, or even hostile to a celebrity.

As identification with a star increases, so does the consumer's degree of passion and desire to accumulate artifacts belonging to that star, or even to make actual contact with him or her. Groupies, for example, are people who follow celebrities, and often attempt to become a part of stars' lives by seducing them or even harassing them.

There are more than 1200 active fan clubs in the United States. These are composed of people who are devoted to an individual, whether a musician, race car driver, or soap opera star. While some clubs are spontaneously created by devoted fans, others are deliberately engineered by the stars themselves to perpetuate their worship. For example, singer Lionel Richie's clubs are run by his wife, and the merchandise purchased by members is subcontracted by the star.[7]

THE MANY FACES OF INVOLVEMENT As defined above, involvement can take many forms. Basil could certainly be said to be involved with his Levi's, since they help to define and bolster his self-concept. This involvement seems to increase at certain times, as when he must prove himself in some situation. Alternatively, the act of *buying* the jeans may be very involving for people who are passionately devoted to shopping. To complicate matters further, advertisements, such as those produced for Levi Strauss, may themselves be involving for some reason (e.g., because they make us laugh or cry).

It seems that involvement is a fuzzy concept, because it overlaps with other things and means different things to different people. Indeed, the consensus appears to be that there are actually several broad types of involvement.

Purchase Involvement. Purchase involvement is related to a consumer's level of interest in the buying process that is triggered by the need to consider a particular purchase. This process is important to such situational factors as store displays and environmental conditions and will be considered at length in Chapter 10.

Message-Response Involvement. Message-response involvement refers to the processing of marketing communications.[8] Involvement with the mass media is mediated by the number of bridging experiences provided— the connections that are made between the viewer and the stimulus.[9]

Television is considered a low-involvement medium, because it requires a passive viewer who exerts relatively little control (remote control "zipping" and "zapping" notwithstanding) over content. In contrast, print is a high-involvement medium. The reader is actively involved in processing the information and is able to pause and reflect on what he or she has read before moving on. The role of message characteristics in changing attitudes is further discussed in Chapter 6.

Ego Involvement. **Ego involvement** (sometimes termed *enduring involvement*) refers to the importance of a product to a consumer's self-concept. This concept implies a high level of *social risk;* the prospect of the product not performing its desired function may result in embarrassment or damage to the consumer's self-concept (Chapter 7 is devoted to the importance of the self-concept for consumer behavior issues). For example, Basil's jeans are clearly an important part of his self-identity (i.e., they are said to have high *sign value*).

This type of involvement is independent of particular purchase situations. It is an ongoing concern related to the self and the person's hedonic experiences (e.g., the emotions he or she feels as a result of using the product).[10]

TABLE 3-1 A scale to measure product involvement

(Insert name of object to be judged)		
important	_: _: _: _: _: _: _:	unimportant*
of no concern	_: _: _: _: _: _: _:	of concern to me
irrelevant	_: _: _: _: _: _: _:	relevant
means a lot to me	_: _: _: _: _: _: _:	means nothing to me*
useless	_: _: _: _: _: _: _:	useful
valuable	_: _: _: _: _: _: _:	worthless*
trivial	_: _: _: _: _: _: _:	fundamental
beneficial	_: _: _: _: _: _: _:	not beneficial*
matters to me	_: _: _: _: _: _: _:	doesn't matter
uninterested	_: _: _: _: _: _: _:	interested
significant	_: _: _: _: _: _: _:	insignificant*
vital	_: _: _: _: _: _: _:	superfluous*
boring	_: _: _: _: _: _: _:	interesting
unexciting	_: _: _: _: _: _: _:	exciting
appealing	_: _: _: _: _: _: _:	unappealing*
mundane	_: _: _: _: _: _: _:	fascinating
essential	_: _: _: _: _: _: _:	nonessential*
undesirable	_: _: _: _: _: _: _:	desirable
wanted	_: _: _: _: _: _: _:	unwanted*
not needed	_: _: _: _: _: _: _:	needed

*Indicates item is reverse scored.
Items on the left are scored (1) low involvement to (7) high involvement on the right.
Totaling the 20 items gives a score from a low of 20 to a high of 140.
Source: Judith Lynne Zaichowsky, "Measuring the Involvement Construct," *Journal of Consumer Research* 12 (December 1985): 350. Reprinted with permission of The University of Chicago Press.

MEASURING INVOLVEMENT   The many conceptualizations of involvement have led to some confusion about the best way to measure the concept. The scale shown in Table 3-1 is one widely used method.

A pair of French researchers argued that no single component of involvement is predominant. Recognizing that consumers can be involved with a product because it is a risky purchase and/or its use reflects upon or affects the self, they advocate the development of an *involvement profile* containing four components:[11]

- importance and risk (the perceived importance of the product and the consequences of a bad purchase)
- the probability of making a bad purchase
- the pleasure value of the product category
- the sign value of the product category

These researchers asked a sample of housewives to rate a set of fourteen product categories on each of the above facets of involvement. The results are shown in Table 3-2. These data indicate that no single component captures consumer involvement, since this quality can occur for different reasons. For example, the purchase of a durable such as a vacuum cleaner is seen as risky, because one is stuck with a bad choice for many years. However, the vacuum cleaner does not provide pleasure (hedonic value), nor is it high in sign value (i.e., its use is not related to the person's self-concept). In contrast, chocolate is high in pleasure value but is not seen as risky or closely related to the self. Dresses and bras, on the other hand, appear to be involving for a combination of reasons.

Segmenting by Involvement Levels. A measurement approach of this nature allows consumer researchers to capture the diversity of the involvement construct, and it also provides the potential to use involvement as a basis for market segmentation. For example, a yogurt manufacturer might find that even though its product is low in sign value for this group of consumers, it might be highly related to the self-concept of another market segment, such as health-food enthusiasts or avid dieters. The company could adapt its strategy to account for the motivation of different segments to process information about the product. These variations are discussed in Chapter 6. Note also that involvement with

TABLE 3-2 Involvement profiles for a set of French consumer products

	Importance of negative consequences	Subjective probability of mispurchase	Pleasure value	Sign value
Dresses	121	112	147	181
Bras	117	115	106	130
Washing machines	118	109	106	111
TV sets	112	100	122	95
Vacuum cleaners	110	112	70	78
Irons	103	95	72	76
Champagne	109	120	125	125
Oil	89	97	65	92
Yogurt	86	83	106	78
Chocolate	80	89	123	75
Shampoo	96	103	90	81
Toothpaste	95	95	94	105
Facial soap	82	90	114	118
Detergents	79	82	56	63

Average product score = 100.

Source: Gilles Laurent and Jean-Noël Kapferer, "Measuring Consumer Involvement Profiles," *Journal of Marketing Research* 22 (February 1: p. 45, Table 3)

a product class may vary across cultures. While this sample of French consumers rated champagne high in both sign value and personal value, the ability of champagne to provide pleasure or be central to self-definition may not transfer to other countries.

▲ MARKETING OPPORTUNITY

A fragrance marketer has come up with an ingenious way to build product involvement by relating the product to users' intimate lives. In a contest sponsored by Dare perfume, women submit details of their most intimate trysts by letter or by phone to radio talk shows. The winning stories are edited into a romance novel published by Bantam Books. These books, in turn, are given away as a gift with the purchase of the perfume.[12]

MOTIVATIONAL DIRECTION

Motives have direction as well as strength. They are goal-oriented in that specific objectives are desired to satisfy a need. Most goals can be reached by a number of routes, and the objective of marketers is to convince consumers that the alternative they offer provides the best chance to attain the goal. For example, a consumer who decides that he needs a pair of jeans to help him reach his goal of being accepted by others or projecting an appropriate image can choose among Levi's, Wranglers, Guess, Calvin Klein, and many other alternatives, each of which promises to deliver certain benefits.

NEEDS VERSUS WANTS

The specific way a need is satisfied depends upon the individual's unique history, learning experiences, and his or her cultural environment. The particular form of consumption used to satisfy a need is termed a *want*. For example, two classmates may feel their stomachs rumbling during a lunchtime lecture. If neither person has eaten since the night before, the strength of their respective needs (hunger) would be about the same. However, the way each person goes about satisfying this need might be quite different. The first person may be a health nut who fantasizes about gulping down a big handful of trail mix, while the second person may be equally aroused by the prospect of a greasy cheeseburger and fries.

This distinction between needs and wants is an important one, because it relates to the issue of whether marketers are actually capable of creating needs. That issue will be considered at the end of the chapter. For now, it is important to note that marketing strategies are more effective when they aim to influence the direction a consumer will take to satisfy a need rather than to create the need itself. Thus, a marketer will likely be more successful in convincing the "junk food junkie" to reach for the trail mix instead of the burger when hunger hits, rather than creating his or her hunger.

INNATE VERSUS ACQUIRED NEEDS

People are born with a need for certain elements necessary to maintain life, such as food, water, air, and shelter. These are called *biogenic needs.* People have many other needs, however, that are not innate. *Psychogenic needs* are acquired in the process of becoming a member of a culture. These include the need for status, power, affiliation, and so on. Psychogenic needs reflect the priorities of a culture, and their effect on behavior will vary in different environments. For example, an American consumer may be driven to devote a good chunk of his income to products that permit him to display his wealth and status, while his Japanese counterpart may work equally hard to ensure that he does not stand out from his group. These differences in cultural values will be discussed in Chapter 15.

TYPES OF NEEDS

As shown in Figure 3-1, consumers can be motivated to satisfy utilitarian or hedonic needs. The satisfaction of utilitarian needs implies that consumers will emphasize the objective, tangible attributes of products, such as miles per gallon in a car; the amount of fat, calories, and protein in a cheeseburger; and the durability of a pair of blue jeans. Hedonic needs are subjective and experiential; consumers may rely on a product to meet their needs for excitement, self-confidence, fantasy, and so on.[14] Of course, consumers may be motivated to purchase a product because it provides *both* types of benefits. For example, a mink coat may be bought because it feels soft and luxurious against the skin *and* because it keeps one warm on a snowy day.

MOTIVATIONAL CONFLICTS

A goal has *valence;* in addition to varying in its strength, it can be positive or negative. A positively valued goal is one toward which consumers direct their behavior; they are motivated to *approach* the goal and will seek out products that will be instrumental in attaining it. In the earlier example,

MULTICULTURAL DIMENSIONS

The American fast food industry satisfies consumers' needs the world over. Foreign outlets of American chains often are among the busiest. The Paris Burger King does more business than any other outlet in the world, and the same is true for the Kentucky Fried Chicken store in Beijing. However, the industry has learned that even though the need for fast, relatively inexpensive food exists almost everywhere, consumers' wants still vary in different cultures, so products must be tailored to local tastes. For example, McDonald's operates in fifty-two countries, but its menu varies. The company serves beer in Germany, wine in France, and sugarcane juice in Malaysia. Japanese customers can buy corn chowder and Teriyaki McBurgers, and McSpaghetti is sold in the Philippines.[13]

Basil used his blue jeans to help him approach Lisa, his goal. However, not all behavior is motivated by the desire to approach a goal. In other cases, consumers are instead motivated to *avoid* a negative outcome. They will structure their purchases or consumption activities to reduce the chances of attaining this end result. For example, many consumers work hard to avoid rejection, a negative goal. They will stay away from products that they associate with social disapproval. Products such as deodorants and mouthwash frequently rely upon consumers' negative motivation by depicting the onerous social consequences of underarm odor or bad breath. Basil would most likely be especially vigilant about using these products as he prepared for his big encounter with Lisa.

Because a purchase decision may involve more than one source of motivation, consumers often find themselves in situations where different motives, both positive and negative, conflict with one another. Since marketers are attempting to satisfy needs, they can also be helpful by providing possible solutions to these dilemmas. Three general types of conflicts can occur: approach-approach, approach-avoidance, and avoidance-avoidance.

APPROACH-APPROACH CONFLICT   Here, a person must choose between two desirable alternatives. A student might be torn between going home for the holidays or going on a skiing trip with friends. Or, he or she might have to choose between two record albums.

Cognitive Dissonance.   The conflict that arises when choosing between two alternatives may be resolved *after* a choice is made through a process of *cognitive dissonance reduction*. The theory of **cognitive dissonance** is based on the premise that people have a need for order and consistency in their lives. A state of tension is created when beliefs or behaviors conflict with one another and people are motivated to reduce this inconsistency (or dissonance) and thus eliminate unpleasant tension.[15]

A state of dissonance occurs when there is a logical inconsistency between two or more beliefs or behaviors. This often occurs when one must make a choice between two products, where both alternatives usually possess both good and bad qualities. By choosing one product and not the other, the person gets the bad qualities of the chosen product and loses out on the good qualities of the unchosen one.

This loss creates an unpleasant, dissonant state that the person is motivated to reduce. People tend to convince themselves after the fact that the choice they made was the smart one by finding additional reasons to support the alternative they chose, or perhaps by "discovering" flaws with the option they did not choose. A marketer can resolve an approach-approach conflict by bundling several benefits together. Miller Lite's claim that it is "less filling" *and* "tastes great" allows the drinker to "have his beer and drink it too."

APPROACH-AVOIDANCE CONFLICT   Many of the products and services we desire have negative consequences attached to them as well. We may feel guilty or ostentatious when buying a status-laden product or feel like a glutton when contemplating a box of Twinkies.

Some solutions to these conflicts include the proliferation of fake furs, which eliminate guilt about harming animals to make a fashion statement, and the success of diet foods, such as Weight Watchers, that promise good food without the calories. Many marketers try to overcome guilt by convincing consumers that they are deserving of luxuries (e.g., when the model for L'Oreal cosmetics claims "Because I'm worth it.").

AVOIDANCE-AVOIDANCE CONFLICT Sometimes consumers find themselves caught "between a rock and a hard place." They may face a choice with two undesirable alternatives. A person may have to cut down on drinking alcohol or face the consequences, or be faced with the option of either throwing more money into an old car or buying a new one. This conflict can be addressed by messages that stress the unforeseen benefits of choosing one option (e.g., the disappearance of a beer belly) or perhaps by the provision of credit or installment plans to ease the pain of payment.

CLASSIFYING CONSUMER NEEDS

Much research has been done on classifying human needs. On the one hand, some psychologists have tried to define a universal inventory of needs that could be traced systematically to explain virtually all behavior. One such effort, developed by Henry Murray, delineates a set of twenty needs that (sometimes in combination) result in specific behaviors. These needs include such dimensions as autonomy (being independent), defendance (defending the self against criticism), and even play (engaging in pleasurable activities).[16]

Others have focused on specific needs (which often are included in general models like Murray's) and their ramifications for behavior. For example, individuals with a high *need for achievement* strongly value personal accomplishment.[17] They place a premium on products and services that signify success because these consumption items provide feedback about their realization of their goals. These consumers are good prospects for products that provide evidence of their achievement. One study of working women found that those who were high in achievement motivation were more likely to choose clothing they considered business-like, and less likely to be interested in apparel that accentuated their femininity.[18] Some other important needs that are relevant to consumer behavior include:

- the need for affiliation (to be in the company of other people).[19] This need is relevant to products and services that are consumed in groups and may alleviate loneliness, such as team sports, bars, and shopping malls.
- the need for power (to control one's environment).[20] Many products and services allow consumers to feel that they have mastery over their surroundings, ranging from "hopped up" muscle cars and loud "boom boxes" (large portable radios) to hotels, restaurants, and resorts that promise to respond to the customer's every whim.

- the need for uniqueness (to assert one's individual identity).[21] This need is satisfied by products that pledge to accentuate a consumer's distinctive qualities. For example, Cachet perfume claims to be "as individual as you are."

MASLOW'S HIERARCHY OF NEEDS   One influential approach to motivation was proposed by the psychologist Abraham Maslow. Maslow's approach is a general one originally developed to understand personal growth and the attainment of "peak experiences."[22] Maslow formulated a *hierarchy of needs,* where levels of motives are specified. A hierarchical approach implies that the order of development is fixed—a certain level must be attained before the next, higher one is activated. This universal approach to motivation has been adapted by marketers because it (indirectly) specifies certain types of product benefits people might be looking for, depending upon the different stages in their development and/or their environmental conditions.

These levels are summarized in Figure 3-2. At each level, different priorities exist in terms of the product benefits a consumer is looking for. Ideally, an individual progresses up the hierarchy until his or her dominant motivation is a focus on "ultimate" goals, such as justice and beauty. Unfortunately, this state is difficult to achieve (at least on a regular basis); most of us have to be satisfied with occasional glimpses, or peak experiences. Examples of product appeals tailored to each level are provided in Table 3-3.[23]

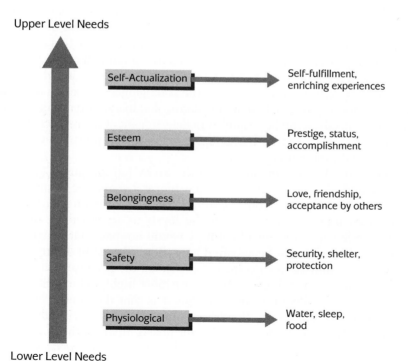

Figure 3-2 Levels of Needs in the Maslow Hierarchy

Upper Level Needs

Self-Actualization → Self-fulfillment, enriching experiences

Esteem → Prestige, status, accomplishment

Belongingness → Love, friendship, acceptance by others

Safety → Security, shelter, protection

Physiological → Water, sleep, food

Lower Level Needs

TABLE 3-3 Maslow's hierarchy and marketing strategies

Level of Hierarchy	Relevant Products	Example
Physiological	Medicines, staple items, generics	Quaker Oat Bran —"It's the right thing to do"
Safety	Insurance, alarm systems, retirement investments	Allstate Insurance — "You're in good hands with Allstate"
Belongingness	Clothing, grooming products, clubs, drinks	Pepsi — "You're in the Pepsi generation"
Esteem	Cars, furniture, credit cards stores, country clubs, liquors	Royal Salute Scotch — "What the rich give the wealthy"
Self-Actualization	Hobbies, travel, education	Club Med: "The antidote for civilization"

Criticisms of the Maslow Hierarchy. The implication of Maslow's hierarchy is that one must first satisfy basic needs before progressing up the ladder (i.e., a starving man is not interested in status symbols, friendship, or self-fulfillment). This hierarchy is not set in stone. Its use in marketing has been somewhat simplistic, especially since the same product or activity can satisfy a number of different needs.

Sex, for example, is characterized as a basic biological drive. While this is true throughout most of the animal kingdom, it is obviously a more complicated phenomenon for humans. Indeed, this activity could conceivably fit into every level of Maslow's hierarchy. A sociobiologist, who approaches human behavior in terms of its biological origins, might argue that reproductive behavior provides security because it ensures continuation of a person's gene pool and the provision of children to care for the person in old age. Sex can also express love and affiliation at the belongingness level. In addition, sex is often used as a vehicle to attain status, domination over another, and to satisfy ego needs; it can be a significant determinant of self-respect. Finally, a sexual experience can be self-actualizing in that it may provide an ecstatic, transcendental experience.

Another problem with taking the hierarchy too literally is that it is culture-bound. The assumptions of the hierarchy may be restricted to Western culture. People in other cultures (or, for that matter, in Western culture) may question the order of the levels as specified. A religious person who has taken a vow of celibacy would not necessarily agree that physiological needs must be satisfied for self-fulfillment to occur.

Similarly, many Eastern cultures operate on the premise that the welfare of the group (belongingness needs) are more highly valued than needs of the individual (esteem needs). The point is that this hierarchy, while widely applied in marketing, should be valued because it reminds us that consumers may have different need priorities at different times (i.e., you have to walk before you can run) rather than because it *exactly* specifies a consumer's progression up the ladder of needs.

HIDDEN MOTIVES: PROBING BENEATH THE SURFACE

A motive is an underlying reason for behavior, and not something researchers can see or easily measure. Furthermore, the same behavior can be caused by a number of different motives. To compound the problem of identifying motives, the consumer may be unaware of the actual need he or she is attempting to satisfy, or alternatively he or she may not be willing to admit that this need exists. Because of these difficulties, motives usually must be *inferred* by the analyst.

Although some consumer needs undoubtedly are utilitarian and fairly straightforward, some researchers feel that a great many purchase decisions are not the result of deliberate, logical decisions. To the contrary, people may do things to satisfy motives of which they are not even aware. These hidden motives cannot be easily assessed by pencil-and-paper questionnaires, telephone interviews, or any of the other quantitative survey techniques discussed in chapter 1. As that chapter noted, a variety of qualitative research methods have been devised to probe beneath the surface of consumers' responses and identify the "deep meanings" of behavior.

CONSUMER BEHAVIOR ON THE COUCH: FREUDIAN THEORY

Sigmund Freud had a profound (if controversial) impact on many basic assumptions of human behavior. His work changed the way we view such topics as adult sexuality, dreams, and psychological adjustment. Freud developed the idea that much of human behavior stems from a fundamental conflict between a person's desire to gratify his or her physical needs and the necessity to function as a responsible member of society. This struggle is carried out in the mind among three systems. (Note: These systems do not refer to physical parts of the brain.)

The **id** is entirely oriented toward immediate gratification—it is the "party animal" of the mind. It operates according to the **pleasure principle;** behavior is guided by the primary desire to maximize pleasure and avoid pain. The id is selfish and illogical. It directs a person's psychic energy toward pleasurable acts without regard for any consequences.

The **superego** is the counterweight to the id. This system is essentially the person's conscience. It internalizes society's rules (especially as communicated by parents) and works to prevent the id from seeking selfish gratification.

Finally, the **ego** is the system that mediates between the id and the superego. It is in a way a referee in the fight between temptation and virtue. The ego tries to balance these two opposing forces according to the **reality principle.** It finds ways to gratify the id that will be acceptable to the outside world. These conflicts occur on an unconscious level, so the person is not necessarily aware of the underlying reasons for behavior.

According to Freudian theory, a person's development hinges on the way these systems interact in childhood. Aspects of Freudian theory are controversial, and his observations are not always accepted literally. For example, the bulk of Freud's insights were based on his own patients, a limited sample composed primarily of affluent Viennese housewives.

It took Freud 38 years to understand it. You have one night.

The psych exam is in 12 hours. And your id wants to party. Your ego wants to conk out. But your superego knows you need to stay awake tonight to cram.

Fortunately, you've got Vivarin. It helps keep you awake and mentally alert for hours. Safely and conveniently. So all your brainpower can focus on understanding the brain.

If Freud had used Vivarin, maybe he could have understood the brain faster, too.

Revive with VIVARIN.®

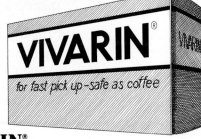

© 1990 Sigmund Freud copyright represented by The Roger Richman Agency, Beverly Hills, CA

© 1990 SmithKline Beecham
Use as directed. Contains caffeine equivalent of two cups of coffee.

This ad for Vivarin stimulants depicts the three components of Freud's perspective on motivation and the unconscious. Licensed by The Roger Richman Agency, Inc., Beverly Hills, CA. Courtesy of Grey Advertising, Inc.

Many feminists object to Freud's assumptions about the inferiority of women, ideas that were widely accepted in his time. Nonetheless, Freud had a profound impact on the fields of psychiatry and clinical psychology.

FREUD AND CONSUMERS   Some of Freud's ideas have also been adapted by consumer researchers. In particular, his work highlights the potential importance of unconscious motives underlying purchases. This implies that consumers cannot necessarily tell us their true motivation for choosing a product, even if we can devise a sensitive way to ask them directly.

The Freudian perspective also hints at the possibility that the ego relies on the symbolism in products to compromise between the demands of the id and the prohibitions of the superego. The person channels his or her unacceptable desire into acceptable outlets by using products that signify these underlying desires. This is the connection between product symbolism and motivation: The product stands for, or represents, a consumer's true goal, which is socially unacceptable or unattainable. By acquiring the product, the person is able to vicariously experience the forbidden fruit.

Sexual Symbolism.   Most Freudian applications in marketing are related to the sexuality of products. For example, some analysts have speculated that a sports car is a substitute for sexual gratification for many men. Indeed, some men do seem inordinately attached to their cars and may spend many hours lovingly washing and polishing them.

Others focus on male-oriented symbolism that appeals to women—so-called phallic symbols. Though Freud himself joked that "sometimes a cigar is just a cigar," many pop applications of Freud's ideas revolve around the use of objects that resemble sex organs (e.g., cigars, trees, or swords for men; tunnels for women). This stems from Freud's analysis of dreams, which were often interpreted as communicating repressed desires through symbols.

MOTIVATIONAL RESEARCH

The first attempts to apply Freudian ideas to understand the deeper meanings of products and advertisements were made in the 1950s as a perspective known as **motivational research** was developed. This approach was largely based on psychoanalytic (Freudian) interpretations, with a heavy emphasis on unconscious motives. A basic assumption is that socially unacceptable needs are channeled into acceptable outlets. Product use or avoidance is motivated by unconscious forces that often are determined in childhood.

This form of research relies on *depth interviews* with individual consumers. Instead of asking many consumers a few general questions about product usage and combining these responses with those of many other consumers in a representative statistical sample, this technique uses relatively few consumers but probes deeply into each person's purchase motivations. A typical depth interview might take one hour or even several hours, and is based on the assumption that the respondent cannot immediately articulate his or her latent, or underlying, motives. These can be derived only after careful questioning and interpretation on the part of a carefully trained interviewer.

This work was pioneered by Ernest Dichter, a psychologist who was trained in Vienna in the early part of the century. Dichter conducted in-depth interview studies on over 230 different products, and many of his findings have been incorporated in actual marketing campaigns.[24] For example, Esso (now Exxon) for many years reminded consumers to "Put a Tiger in Your Tank" after Dichter found that people responded well to this powerful animal symbolism containing vaguely suggestive overtones. A summary of major consumption motivations identified using this approach appears in Table 3-4.

CRITICISMS OF MOTIVATIONAL RESEARCH   Motivational research has been attacked for two quite opposite reasons. Some feel it does not work, while others feel it works *too* well.

On the one hand, social critics reacted much the same way they had to subliminal perception studies (see Chapter 2). They attacked this school

TABLE 3-4 Major motives for consumption as identified by Ernest Dichter

Motive	Associated Products
Power–Masculinity–Virility	Power: Sugary products and large breakfasts (to charge oneself up), bowling, electric trains, hot rods, power tools Masculinity–virility: Coffee, red meat, heavy shoes, toy guns, buying fur coats for women, shaving with a razor.
Security	Ice cream (feel like loved child again, full drawer of neatly ironed shirts, real plaster walls (feel sheltered), home baking, hospital care.
Eroticism	Sweets (require licking), gloves (removed by women as a form of undressing), a man lighting a woman's cigarette (a tension-filled moment culminating in pressure, then relaxation).
Moral Purity–Cleanliness	White bread, cotton fabrics (connote chastity), harsh household cleaning chemicals (make housewives feel moral after using), bathing (Pontius Pilate washed blood from his hands), oatmeal (sacrifice, virtue).
Social Acceptance	Companionship: Ice cream (fun to share), coffee Love and affection: Toys (express love for children), sugar and honey (terms of affection) Acceptance: Soap, beauty products.
Individuality	Gourmet foods, foreign cars, cigarette holders, vodka, perfume, fountain pens.
Status	Scotch, ulcers, heart attacks, and indigestion (because this means one has a high stress, important job!), carpets (one does not live on bare earth like peasants).
Femininity	Cakes and cookies, dolls, silk, tea, household curios (all are light, decorative, and have a heavy tactile component).
Reward	Cigarettes, candy, alcohol, ice cream, cookies.
Mastery Over Environment	Kitchen appliances, boats, sporting goods, cigarette lighters
Disalienation (a desire to feel connectedness to things)	Home decorating, skiing, morning radio broadcasts (to feel "in touch" with the world).
Magic–Mystery	Soups (have healing powers, paints (change the mood of a room), carbonated drinks (magical effervescent property), vodka (romantic history), unwrapping of gifts.

Source: Adapted from Jeffrey J. Durgee, "Interpreting Dichter's Interpretations. An Analysis of Consumption Symbolism in *The Handbook of Consumer Motivations*, paper presented at the Marketing and Semiotics Conference at the Copenhagen School of Economics and Business Administration.

of thought for giving advertisers the power to manipulate consumers.[25] On the other hand, many consumer researchers felt the research lacked sufficient rigor and validity, since interpretations were subjective and indirect.[26] Because conclusions are based on the analyst's own judgment and are derived from discussions with a small number of people, some researchers are dubious as to the degree these results can be generalized to a large market. In addition, because the original motivational researchers were heavily influenced by orthodox Freudian theory, their interpretations usually carried strong sexual overtones. This emphasis tends to overlook other plausible causes for behavior.

THE POSITIVE SIDE OF MOTIVATIONAL RESEARCH Motivation research had great appeal to at least *some* marketers for several reasons, some of which are detailed here.

Cost-Efficiency. Motivational research tends to be less expensive than large-scale, quantitative survey data because interviewing and data processing costs are relatively minimal.

Providing Insights. The knowledge derived from motivation research can possibly help to develop marketing communications that appeal to deep-seated needs and thus provide a more powerful hook to relate a product to consumers. Even if they are not necessarily valid for all consumers in a target market, these insights can be valuable when used in an exploratory way. For example, the rich imagery that may be associated with a product can be used by creatives as a guide when developing advertising copy.

Intuitive Sense. Some of the findings seem intuitively plausible *after the fact.* For example, motivational studies concluded that coffee is associated with companionship, that people avoid prunes because they remind them of old age, and that men fondly equate the first car they owned as an adolescent with the onset of their sexual freedom.

Other interpretations were hard for some people to swallow, such as the observation that to a woman baking a cake symbolizes giving birth, or that men are reluctant to give blood because they feel that their vital fluids are being drained. On the other hand, some people do refer to a pregnant woman as "having a bun in the oven," and Pillsbury claims that "nothing says lovin' like something from the oven." Motivational research for the American Red Cross did find that men (but not women) tend to drastically overestimate the amount of blood that is taken during a donation, and counteracted the fear of loss of virility by symbolically equating the act of giving blood with fertilization: "Give the gift of life." Despite its drawbacks, motivational research continues to be employed as a useful diagnostic tool. Its validity is enhanced, however, when used in conjunction with the other research techniques available to the consumer researcher.

QUALITATIVE RESEARCH TECHNIQUES

A consumer's motivation for purchasing a product does not have to be sexual to be hidden. A product may contain a variety of symbolic qualities, and research techniques are required to allow consumers to express their underlying thoughts and feelings about them. Consumer researchers have developed many qualitative research methods that stress the symbolic benefits of products.

FOCUS GROUPS Of all qualitative research techniques, focus groups are the most widely used.[27] It has been estimated that approximately 140,000 such groups are held each year in the United States alone. **Focus groups** help to gather information from group interaction that is *focused* on a series of topics introduced by a discussion leader or moderator. Each participant is encouraged to express his or her views and to react to the views of others. The group typically consists of five to nine people who have been screened on some basis, often to represent demographic characteristics of the target market of interest. The outcomes from focus groups are often used as input to the development of more structured, quantitative survey instruments.

Focus Group Structure. Focus groups often incorporate some or all of the following elements:[28]

- *exploratory phase:* A series of general questions (e.g., "What comes to mind when I mention bread?") helps to establish the direction of the encounter and let subjects define the issues they consider to be important.
- *probing:* The moderator probes for understanding to more narrowly focus the discussion.
- *tasks:* Group members are given a task, such as writing an advertising slogan.
- *evaluation:* The group may be asked to evaluate such items as product design, logos, or product communications.
- *closing:* A wind-down procedure ensures that respondents have reacted as fully as possible.

Advantages and Disadvantages of Focus Groups. Compared to an individual interview, the group setting may stimulate participants by allowing them to feed off of comments made by others. This makes meaningful comments more likely. It allows the researcher access to useful data with little direct input.

In some situations the security of being in a group may also encourage more candor. This is especially true if other group members share some important characteristic. For example, one project used groups of overweight women to explore their reactions to clothing and shopping. Amongst themselves, members had a tendency to bitterly refer to themselves as "fat ladies." They felt ignored by the rest of society (especially by merchants). This insight allowed the client to develop a strategy that stressed the special attention paid to this group.[29]

Another advantage is that groups representing specific, desired characteristics can be assembled. The client can obtain feedback from representatives of a distinct segment, and can elicit responses from multiple segments. General Motors regularly conducts focus groups among *both* consumers and dealers to identify desirable car features possessed by competitors. These results led them to model their air filter covers after Mazda's, and to follow the example of Saab in putting fuses in the glove box.[30]

A drawback to focus groups is that, while they are easy to conduct, they are not often based in natural settings. As a result, there is always some uncertainty about the accuracy of responses.[31]

Another problem is that individual decision-making processes are not always the same as group processes. For example, the degree to which people accept risk as members of a group tends to differ from when they make a decision alone. Group judgments tend to be polarized (i.e., more extreme) than individual judgments, and under some circumstances this factor leads to riskier decisions by groups (this increased tolerance of risk is known as the "risky shift phenomenon").

Using the Results of Focus Groups. The degree to which results of the focus groups are actionable should be considered in light of at least three points:[32]

1. How close is the sample to the target market?
2. How variable were responses? Some groups leave no doubt about the likely reactions toward a concept, while others display a lot of ambivalence. In the latter case, further research is needed to more precisely define the determinants of positive versus negative attitudes. One study looking at snack foods found unanimous dislike for the aroma of a proposed snack food. Because of this consensus, the client felt no need to follow-up with a larger survey to clarify this reaction.
3. How intense were responses? It is not just what the group members say, but *how* they say it. People might have a lukewarm reaction or decide they like something after some polite hesitation. This positive response is not equivalent to a group's instantaneous, enthusiastic, and genuine affirmation of a concept.

PROJECTIVE TECHNIQUES   A projective stimulus is often used in conjunction with individual, non directed interviews. Projective tests involve the presentation of an ambiguous, unstructured object, activity, or person to which the consumer responds in some way (e.g., explaining the object, telling a story about it, drawing a picture of it, etc.). Projectives are used when it is believed that a consumer will not or cannot respond meaningfully to direct questioning.

Projective techniques allow consumers to respond to neutral situations, where presumably their own feelings are not at issue and they are freer to respond openly. These techniques assume that a person's responses can then be inferred to reflect back to his or her own deep-seated feelings about an issue. Because there are no right or wrong answers, it is hoped that consumers will project their own unconscious feelings into their answers.

An early application of projective research illustrates the value of these procedures.[33] When Saran Wrap was introduced in the 1950s, consumers developed strong negative attitudes toward it because it was very difficult to handle. Depth interviews revealed that this product attribute per se was not responsible for the negative effect.

At that time, women did not have an acceptable outlet to express their dislike of housekeeping. Their frustration with the product was a symbolic reflection of their frustration with the role of homemaker. This deep-seated feeling would not be expressed in a straightforward interview. Acting on these findings, the product was made less clingy, and its non-kitchen uses were stressed in advertising.

The term *projection* was first used by Freud to refer to an ego defense mechanism similar to rationalization or repression. The ego masters threats to the self by distorting reality and attributing anxiety about these threats to the outside world. The basic assumption is that the individual will interpret material to be consistent with his or her value system.[34]

As with all qualitative research, the subjectivity of interpretation is a disadvantage of projectives. On the other hand, respondents tend to react positively to these techniques. They typically are seen as fun and novel and allow people to be creative by imagining themselves in unfamiliar (and sometimes bizarre) situations.

For example, a person might be asked to imagine how she would feel if she were a car or a box of chocolate. It is likely she has never before considered these possibilities! Projectives are useful in concert with other interviewing techniques, either as a way to break the ice or to stimulate responses.

Figure 3-3 A Bubble Drawing Projective Instrument Source: Wendy Gordon and Roy Langmaid, *Qualitative Market Research* (Hants, England: Gower, 1988), 104.

Overcoming Consumers' Resistance to Responding. Projective techniques enable the researcher to penetrate various barriers to response. These barriers include:[35]

- awareness. The respondent may not be aware of an attitude toward a product or activity at a conscious level and thus is unable to respond accurately.
- irrationality. The respondent may have developed elaborate rationalizations for a behavior that would prevent an honest response.
- inadmissibility and self-incrimination. People are disinclined to admit negative things about themselves.
- politeness. The respondent may have negative or unacceptable feelings but will not divulge these to the interviewer for fear of offending him or her.

Pictorial Projectives. Consumers enjoy working with pictures, and a number of projective techniques involve the use of pictorial stimuli. Some techniques are simply useful devices to stimulate associations by presenting a consumer in a situation and assessing reactions to it.

Bubble drawings depict a person in a commonplace situation (e.g., in a supermarket or driving a car) and require respondents to provide a caption or to fill in his or her comments. Alternatively, the consumer could be shown confronting a new situation (e.g., a new product or a change in product packaging) and expressing some apprehension about it—this can be used as a springboard for the respondent's own doubts. The bubble drawing in Figure 3-3 allows the respondent to voice concerns about trying a new product by imagining what the woman in the picture is saying.

The Thematic Apperception Test (TAT) was developed by the psychologist Henry Murray in 1938. The original version contained thirty cards with pictures for which subjects were to make up stories. This technique is very useful as a projective, especially since it provides great flexibility. The pictures used can be modified to fit specific marketing situations of interest.

One study employed a set of TAT pictures specifically designed to assess underlying dimensions of grooming behaviors and rituals.[36] By responding to pictures of people engaged in various activities (e.g., applying make-up), respondents projected their own priorities and fantasies. Some of the resultant grooming themes included the magical and healing qualities attributed to cosmetics (e.g., restoration of youth), their linkage to sexual fortune, the use of grooming products to exhibit maturity and social capability, and the performance of "secret identities" (e.g., homosexual behavior).

Psychodrawing allows the respondent to express his or her perceptions of products or usage situations in a pictorial format. In Figure 3-4, a consumer has projected feelings before, after, and during toothbrushing. In a variation of this technique, an ad agency asked fifty consumers to sketch pictures of people who were likely to buy two brands of cake mixes. As seen in Figure 3-5, many subjects drew Pillsbury users as grandmotherly types, while Duncan Hines customers were younger and more dynamic.[37]

Figure 3-4 A Consumer's Psychodrawing of the Act of Toothbrushing Source: Wendy Gordon and Roy Langmaid, *Qualitative Market Research* (Hants, England: Gower, 1988), 110.

Cleaning Your Teeth: Before

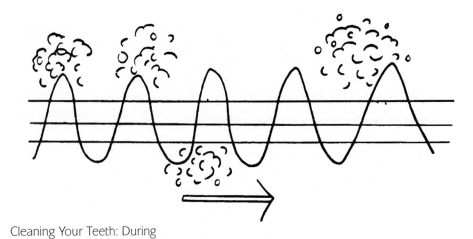

Cleaning Your Teeth: During

Cleaning Your Teeth: After

Who Baked the Cake?

Figure 3-5 Consumers' Sketches of Typical Cake-Mix Users Source: Annetta Miller and Dody Tsiantar, "Psyching Out Consumers," *Newsweek* (February 27, 1989):46–47.

Verbal Projectives. In addition to pictures, researchers also rely on a variety of verbal exercises to allow subjects to project their feelings about products. Some of these techniques are described below.

With a *sentence completion* technique, the respondent is given a sentence and is asked to fill in the missing word(s). In keeping with the intent of projection, sentences should be phrased in the third person. Sentence completion has the advantage of being focused and yielding concise answers. For this reason, it is especially useful in large groups, since it can be administered to more than one person at a time and responses across people can be easily compared. Commonly used examples include "The average person considers television _____" and "Most people feel that men who use cologne _____." Some versions supply a short story and ask people to describe how it ends.

One study employing this technique found that men and women view automobiles differently. When asked to complete the sentence "When you first get a car, . . ." women tended to supply responses like "you would go for a ride," while men responded "you check the engine," "you polish it," and so on. These results imply that women see a car as something to use, while for men it is an object to protect and be responsible for.

In another variation, people are asked how friends or neighbors would react to a product or service. Since these people are similar to the subject, one can assume that responses will be a good indicator of the subject's own real responses without being contaminated by social desirability.

During *word association,* the respondent is given a series of words or phrases and for each is asked to supply the first thing that comes to mind. The stimuli should be administered rapidly so that the respondent is providing gut reactions rather than consciously editing replies.

This technique is especially good for testing reactions to potential brand names and advertising slogans. For example, Bell Telephone found that the theme "The System is the Solution" triggered negative reactions because people tended to associate it with "Big Brother" and authoritarianism.

The *brand personalities* technique asks the respondent to imagine the product as a person, animal, or some other object and to tell a story about it. Women who described a particular cosmetic product as if it was a woman tended to see it as an older person with a boring life—hardly a desirable image. Similarly, consumers might be asked "if a Honda Accord were an animal, what animal would it be?" If the response is a cat, a sparrow, a bull, or whatever, the researcher can probe about the qualities of that particular animal that seem to be manifested in the car.

With a *stereotype* technique, respondents are given a description of a typical family or person and are asked to supply related information. For example, a description of a successful executive might be followed by the request to describe the contents of his wallet. By assessing which credit cards appear there, the researcher can determine which are associated with this social type.

In one of the classic demonstrations of this approach, women in the 1940s were asked to describe two housewives based on their shopping lists.[38] The only difference between the lists was that one included regular coffee, while the other instead specified instant coffee. The "instant coffee housewife" was described as lazy and a poor planner. This response revealed

Figure 3-6 Hidden Life Issues in the Fantasies, Work, and Social Lives of Seven Male Managers Source: Jeffrey F. Durgee, "Depth-Interview Techniques for Creative Advertising," *Journal of Advertising Research* 25 (1986) 6: 36.

	Mgr. No. 1	*Mgr. No. 2*	*Mgr. No. 3*	*Mgr. No. 4*	*Mgr. No. 5*	*Mgr. No. 6*	*Mgr. No. 7*
Fantasies	WWII fighter pilot. Beat the Krauts	18th century France. Fencing master	100 years in future to see the new technologies	Rome Decadence!	1930s grand prix race driver	WWII fight with Patton	Tahiti. Women!
Work lives	Distrust top management	Proud of high IQ level	Main appeal of work: intellectual challenge	Cynical about company and top management	Terrified of failure	Obsessed with getting ahead, Very smart	Turning mid-age. Feels he has to catch up if he will ever get to top
Social lives	Pick and choose friends who can help his career	Like to chase women	Late 30s, unmarried, lonely	Unmarried, like strange friends	Feel uncomfortable holding marriage together	Like to be center of attention in group of guys	Anxious whether women still find him interesting

the concern of women (at that time) for buying time-saving products that would lead their husbands to think they were poor homemakers.

These findings were incorporated directly into marketing strategy. Advertisements for instant coffee were subsequently executed in family settings with the husband's approval clearly communicated. Obviously, this concern would not be present in today's society, where quickness is considered a virtue rather than a vice. Indeed, by 1970 researchers were unable to repeat these findings in a replication study.[39]

The *hidden-issue questioning technique* focuses on the identification of hidden fantasies that are present just below the surface.[40] These fantasies occupy consumers when their attention is not absorbed in work or other daily tasks. They represent a "second life" where everyday shortcomings are removed and the fantasies are driving issues in people's lives. For example, many middle-class women apparently smoke in order to keep their weight down; this may explain the success of cigarettes that stress slimness, such as Virginia Slims or Ultra Thins.

Hidden issues can emerge through open-ended questioning, such as "If you had enough money to live any way you like, what would your life be like?" or "If you could have a different career, what would it be?" Some illustrations of this technique as derived from middle-aged male executives are presented in Figure 3-6.

NEEDS AND WANTS: DO MARKETERS MANIPULATE CONSUMERS?

One of the most common and stinging criticisms of marketing is that marketing techniques (especially advertising) are responsible for convincing consumers that they "need" many material things and that they will be unhappy and somehow inferior people if they do not have these "necessities." The issue is a complex one, and is certainly worth considering: Do marketers give people what they want, or tell people what they *should* want?

Philosophers have approached this question when considering the issue of free will. It has been argued that in order to claim that consumers are acting autonomously in response to ads, the capacity for free will and free action must be present. That is, the consumer must be capable of *independently* deciding what to do and not be prevented from carrying out that decision. This situation is probably true for purely informative advertising, where only the product or store information required to make a rational decision is provided. The case for persuasive advertising, where imagery or underlying motivations are tapped, is not as clear.[41] Three issues related to the complex relationship between marketing practices and consumers' needs are considered here.

MARKETERS CREATE ARTIFICIAL NEEDS
The marketing system has come under fire from both ends of the political spectrum. On the one hand, some members of the religious right believe that advertising contributes to the moral breakdown of society by presenting images of hedonistic pleasure, thus encouraging the pursuit of

secular humanism. On the other hand, some leftists argue that the same deceitful promises of material pleasure function to buy off people who would otherwise be revolutionaries working to change the system.[42] Through advertising, then, the system creates demand that only its products can satisfy.

A Response: A need is a basic biological motive, while a want represents one way that society has taught us that the need can be satisfied. For example, while thirst is biologically based, we are taught to want Coca-Cola to satisfy that thirst rather than, say, goat milk. Thus, the need is already there; marketers simply recommend ways to satisfy it. A basic objective of advertising is to create awareness that these needs exist, rather than to create them. In some circumstances, however, the marketer can engineer an environment to make it more *probable* that a need will be activated. This occurs, for example, when movie theaters sell popcorn and bars supply free peanuts to patrons in order to stimulate thirst.

▼ MARKETING PITFALL

The charge that businesses create artificial needs is relevant in the case of gasoline marketing, where oil companies attempt to convince consumers of the need for premium gasolines. As one automotive engineer noted, "'Oil company advertising has led people to the conclusion that more expensive fuels will make their car start easier, get more gas mileage and last longer, ...' But in most cases this is untrue. . . . 'Your engine has to be designed to use that extra octane. . . .' Otherwise, . . . the extra cost 'is just lining the pockets of the oil companies.'"

An oil industry executive wrote that "'When prices go up a bit, people will come to their senses and premium volumes will diminish. . . . .' But for now, people buy higher-octane fuel for reasons that have nothing to do with car engines; one, he theorized, is 'the use of premium as an expression of self-worth.'"[43] Is the need for higher octane a genuine one, or something manufactured by the oil companies by associating premium gasoline with power, status, manliness, and so on?

ADVERTISING MANIPULATES CONSUMERS AND IS UNNECESSARY

The social critic Vance Packard wrote over thirty years ago that: "Large scale efforts are being made, often with impressive success, to channel our unthinking habits, our purchasing decisions and our thought processes by the use of insights gleaned from psychiatry and the social sciences."[44]

The economist John Kenneth Galbraith felt that radio and television are important tools to accomplish this manipulation of the masses. Since virtually no literacy is required to use these media, they allow repetitive and compelling communications to reach almost everyone.

Goods are arbitrarily linked to desirable social attributes. One influential critic even argued that the problem is that we are not materialistic *enough*—we do not sufficiently value goods for the utilitarian functions they deliver, but instead focus on the irrational value of goods for what

DESPITE WHAT SOME PEOPLE THINK, ADVERTISING CAN'T MAKE YOU BUY SOMETHING YOU DON'T NEED.

Some people would have you believe that you are putty in the hands of every advertiser in the country.

They think that when advertising is put under your nose, your mind turns to oatmeal.

It's mass hypnosis. Subliminal seduction. Brain washing. Mind control. It's advertising.

And you are a pushover for it.

It explains why your kitchen cupboard is full of food you never eat.

Why your garage is full of cars you never drive.

Why your house is full of books you don't read, TV's you don't watch, beds you don't use, and clothes you don't wear.

You don't have a choice. You are forced to buy.

That's why this message is a cleverly disguised advertisement to get you to buy land in the tropics.

Got you again, didn't we? Send in your money.

ADVERTISING
ANOTHER WORD FOR FREEDOM OF CHOICE.
American Association of Advertising Agencies

they symbolize. According to this view, for example, "Beer would be enough for us, without the additional promise that in drinking it we show ourselves to be manly, young at heart, or neighborly. A washing machine would be a useful machine to wash clothes, rather than an indication that we are forward-looking or an object of envy to our neighbors."[45]

A Response: Products are designed to meet existing needs, and advertising only helps to communicate their availability. Marketing overcomes some of the disadvantages of labor specialization, where most consumers are unfamiliar with the characteristics of mass-produced goods.[46] According to the *economics of information* perspective, advertising is an important source of consumer information.[47] This view emphasizes the economic cost of the time spent searching for products. Accordingly, advertising is a service for which consumers are willing to pay, since the information it provides reduces search time.

MARKETERS PROMISE MIRACLES
Consumers are led to believe through advertising that products have magical properties; they will do special and mysterious things for them that will transform their lives. They will be beautiful, have power over others' feelings, be successful, be relieved of all ills, and so on. In this respect, advertising functions like mythology does in primitive societies; it provides simple, anxiety-reducing answers to complex problems.

A Response: The effectiveness of advertising is overstated. There is little evidence that advertising creates patterns of consumption (though it may accelerate them). Instead, the marketing system creates a new way to satisfy an old need.

As an example, consider one analysis of the cigarette industry, which has been accused of using advertising to erode traditional taboos against smoking among women and the young. In the period between 1918 and 1940, the consumption of cigarettes increased steadily, but the overall level of *tobacco consumption* was unchanged. This suggests that the effect of advertising was to make people switch to cigarettes from cigars and pipes.[48] Advertising merely latched onto new consumption patterns, since cigarette smoking is more adaptable to a fast-paced urban lifestyle.

Advertisers simply do not know enough about people to manipulate them. Consider that the failure rate for new products ranges from 40 percent to 80 percent. In testimony before the Federal Trade Commission, one advertising executive observed that while people think that advertisers have an endless source of magical tricks and/or scientific techniques to manipulate people, in reality, the industry is successful when it tries to sell good products and unsuccessful when selling poor ones.[49]

CHAPTER SUMMARY

Marketers try to satisfy consumer needs, but the reasons any product is purchased can vary widely. The identification of consumer motives is an important step in ensuring that the appropriate needs will be met by a product. Traditional approaches to consumer behavior have focused on the abilities of products to satisfy rational needs (utilitarian motives), but hedonic motives (e.g., the need for exploration or for fun) also play a role in many purchase decisions.

As demonstrated by Maslow's hierarchy of needs, the same product can satisfy different needs, depending upon the consumer's state at the time. In addition to his or her objective situation (e.g., have basic physiological needs already been satisfied?), the consumer's degree of involvement with the product must be considered. Since consumers are not necessarily able or willing to communicate their underlying needs to marketers, various techniques such as projective tests can be employed to indirectly assess these. A number of different qualitative approaches to consumer research were reviewed that attempt to tap consumers' hidden motivations.

The chapter also addressed the issue of whether marketers are capable of creating needs for their own purposes rather than merely satisfying existing needs. While marketers do seem to be able to suggest new ways for needs to be satisfied, it is not clear that they have the desire (much less the ability) to actually create underlying needs.

KEY TERMS

Cognitive dissonance	Inertia
Drive	Involvement
Ego	Motivation
Ego involvement	Motivational research
Expectancy theory	Pleasure principle
Focus groups	Projective techniques
Goal	Reality principle
Homeostasis	Superego
Id	Want

REVIEW QUESTIONS AND DISCUSSION TOPICS

1. Describe three types of motivational conflicts, citing an example of each from current marketing campaigns.
2. Should consumer researchers have the ability (and the right) to probe into the consumer's unconscious? Is this a violation of privacy, or just another way to gather deep knowledge of purchase motivations?
3. Describe three barriers to response that can be overcome by projective research techniques.
4. Discuss some factors that would make a marketing manager more or less confident in accepting the results of focus group findings.

HANDS-ON EXERCISES

1. Develop your own projective tests and try them on friends (e.g., "If your perfume or cologne came to life, what kind of person would it be?" What do their responses tell you about the brand images of these products, especially as these correspond to those images the brands are trying to promote?
2. Devise a promotional strategy for a product that stresses each of the levels of Maslow's hierarchy.
3. Conduct a focus group on a topic of your choice. Note how individuals' responses may be facilitated or inhibited by other group members. What are some factors that determine the quality of responses in a focus group?

NOTES

1. Michael R. Solomon, "Deep-Seated Materialism: The Case of Levi's 501 Jeans," in *Advances in Consumer Research* ed. Richard Lutz (Las Vegas, Nev.: Association for Consumer Research, 1986) 13:619–22.

2. Robert A. Baron, *Psychology: The Essential Science* (Needham, Mass.: Allyn & Bacon, 1989).

3. John H. Antil, "Conceptualization and Operationalization of Involvement," in *Advances in Consumer Research,* ed. Thomas C. Kinnear (Provo, Utah: Association for Consumer Research, 1984) 11:203–9. The literature offers numerous approaches to the construct of involvement. See also Peter H. Bloch, "Involvement Beyond the Purchase Process: Conceptual Issues and Empirical Investigation," in *Advances in Consumer Research,* ed. Kent Monroe (Provo, Utah: Association for Consumer Research, 1981) 8:61–65; George S. Day, *Buyer Attitudes and Brand Choice Behavior* (Chicago: Free Press 1970; Michael J. Houston and Michael L. Rothschild, "Conceptual and Methodological Perspectives on Involvement," in *Research Frontiers in Marketing: Dialogues and Directions,* ed. S. C. Jain (Chicago: American Marketing Association, 1978), 184–87; John L. Lastovicka and David Gardner, "Components of Involvement," in *Attitude Research Plays for High Stakes,* ed. John C. Maloney and Bernard Silverman (Chicago: American Marketing Association, 1979), 53–73; Andrew Mitchell, "Involvement: A Potentially Important Mediator of Consumer Behavior," in *Advances in Consumer Research,* ed. William L. Wilkie (Provo, Utah: Association for Consumer Research, 1979), 191–96.

4. Mitchell, "Involvement."

5. Richard L. Celsi and Jerry C. Olson, "The Role of Involvement in Attention and Comprehension Processes," *Journal of Consumer Research* 15 (September 1988): 210–24.

6. Anthony G. Greenwald and Clark Leavitt, "Audience Involvement in Advertising: Four Levels," *Journal of Consumer Research* 11 (June 1984): 581–92.

7. Irving Rein, Philip Kotler, and Martin Stoller, *High Visibility* (New York: Dodd, Mead, 1987).

8. Rajeev Batra and Michael L. Ray, "Operationalizing Involvement as Depth and Quality of Cognitive Responses," in *Advances in Consumer Research,* ed. Alice Tybout and Richard Bagozzi (Ann Arbor, Mich.: Association for Consumer Research, 1983) 10:309–13.

9. Herbert E. Krugman, "The Impact of Television Advertising: Learning Without Involvement," *Public Opinion Quarterly* 29 (Fall 1965), 349–56.

10. Marsha L. Richins and Peter H. Bloch, "After the New Wears Off: The Temporal Context of Product Involvement," *Journal of Consumer Research* 13 (September 1986): 280–85.

11. Gilles Laurent and Jean-Noel Kapferer, "Measuring Consumer Involvement Profiles," *Journal of Marketing Research* 22 (February 1985): 41–53.

12. Freeman, Laurie, "Fragrance Sniffs Out Daring Adventures," *Advertising Age* (November 6, 1989):47.

13. David Kilburn, "In Japan, It's the Teriyaki McBurger," *Advertising Age* (September 11, 1989):16; Calvin Trillin, "Uncivil Liberties: American Fast Food Restaurants Around the World," *The Nation* (April 10, 1989):473.

14. Morris B. Holbrook, and Elizabeth C. Hirschman, "The Experiential Aspects of Consumption: Consumer Fantasies, Feelings, and Fun," *Journal of Consumer Research* 9 (September 1982): 132–40.

15. Leon Festinger, *A Theory of Cognitive Dissonance* Stanford, Calif.: (Stanford University Press, 1957).

16. See Paul T. Costa and Robert R. McCrae, "From Catalog to Classification: Murray's Needs and the Five-Factor Model," *Journal of Personality and Social Psychology* 55 (1988)2:258–65; Calvin S. Hall and Gardner Lindzey, *Theories of Personality,* 2nd ed. (New York: John Wiley, 1970); James U. McNeal and Stephen W. McDaniel, "An Analysis of Need-Appeals in Television Advertising," *Journal of the Academy of Marketing Science* 12 (Spring 1984): 176–90.

17. See David C. McClelland, *Studies in Motivation.* (New York: Appleton-Century-Crofts, 1955).

18. Mary Kay Ericksen and M. Joseph Sirgy, "Achievement Motivation and Clothing Preferences of White-Collar Working Women," in *The Psychology of Fashion,* ed. Michael R. Solomon (Lexington, Mass.: Lexington Books, 1985), 357–69.

19. See Stanley Schachter, *The Psychology of Affiliation* Stanford, Calif.: (Stanford University Press, 1959).

20. Eugene M. Fodor and Terry Smith, "The Power Motive as an Influence on Group Decision Making," *Journal of Personality and Social Psychology* 42, (1982):178-85.

21. C. R. Snyder and Howard L. Fromkin. *Uniqueness: The Human Pursuit of Difference* (New York: Plenum Press, 1980).

22. Abraham H. Maslow, *Motivation and Personality,* 2nd ed. (New York: Harper & Row, 1970).

23. Del Hawkins, Roger J. Best, and Kenneth A. Coney, *Consumer Behavior: Implications for Marketing Strategy,* 4th ed. (Homewood, Ill.: BPI Irwin, 1989).

24. Ernest Dichter, *A Strategy of Desire,* (Garden City, N.Y.: Doubleday, 1960); Ernest Dichter, *The Handbook of Consumer Motivations,* (New York: McGraw-Hill, 1964); Jeffrey J. Durgee, "Interpreting Dichter's Interpretations: An Analysis of Consumption Symbolism in *The Handbook of Consumer Motivations,*" (unpublished manuscript, Rensselaer Polytechnic Institute, 1989); Pierre Martineau, *Motivation in Advertising* (New York: McGraw-Hill, 1957).

25. Vance Packard, *The Hidden Persuaders* (New York: D. McKay, 1957).

26. Harold Kassarjian, "Personality and Consumer Behavior: A Review," *Journal of Marketing Research* 8 (November 1971):409-18.

27. Bobby J. Calder, "Focus Groups and the Nature of Qualitaitive Marketing Research," *Journal of Marketing Research* 14 (1977):353-64.

28. Hy Mariampolski, "The Resurgence of Qualitative Research," *Public Relations Journal* (July 1984):21-23.

29. Judith Langer, "Getting to Know the Consumer Through Qualitative Research," *Management Review* (April 1987): 42-46.

30. David Kiley, "At Long Last, Detroit Gives Consumers the Right of Way," *Adweek* (June 6, 1988): 26-27.

31. Nicholas G. Calo, "Focus Group Data Can Be Used Immediately—But Be Careful," *Marketing News* (October 24, 1988): 24.

32. Calo, "Focus Group Data Can Be Used Immediately."

33. David A. Aaker and George S. Day, *Marketing Research,* 4th ed. (New York: John Wiley & Sons, 1990).

34. Harold H. Kassarjian, "Projective Methods," in *Handbook of Marketing Research,* ed. R. Ferber (New York: McGraw-Hill, 1974), 3-85-3-100.

35. Peter Sampson, "Qualitative Research and Motivation Research," in *Consumer Market Research Handbook,* ed. Robert M. Worcester (London: McGraw-Hill, 1972), 7-27.

36. Dennis W. Rook and Sidney J. Levy, "Psychosocial Themes in Consumer Grooming Rituals," in *Advances in Consumer Research,* ed. R. Bagozzi and A. Tybout (1983)10:328-33.

37. Annetta Miller and Dody Tsiantar, "Psyching Out Consumers," *Newsweek* (February 27, 1989)2:46.

38. Mason Haire, "Projective Techniques in Marketing Research," *Journal of Marketing* 14 (April 1950): 649-50.

39. Frederick E. Webster, Jr., and Fredrick Von Pechmann, "A Replication of the 'Shopping List' Study," *Journal of Marketing* 34 (April 1970): 61-63.

40. Jeffrey F. Durgee, "Depth-Interview Techniques for Creative Advertising," *JAR* 25 (1986)6:29-37.

41. Roger Crisp, "Persuasive Advertising, Autonomy, and the Creation of Desire," *Journal of Business Ethics* 6 (1987):413-18.

42. William Leiss, Stephen Kline, and Sut Jhally, *Social Communication in Advertising: Persons, Products, & Images of Well-Being,* (Toronto: Methuen, 1986); Jerry Mander, *Four Arguments for the Elimination of Television* (New York: William Morrow, 1977).

43. Matthew L. Wald, "Looking for Savings as Gas Prices Rise," *New York Times* (May 27, 1989):48.

44. Packard (1957), page 11, quoted in Leiss, el al., *Social Communication.*

45. Raymond Williams, "Advertising: The Magic System," in *Problems in Materialism and Culture* (London: New Left Books, 1962).

46. Leiss, et al., *Social Communication.*

47. George Stigler, "The Economics of Information," *Journal of Political Economy* (1961):69.

48. Michael Schudson, *Advertising: The Uneasy Persuasion* (New York: Basic Books, 1984).

49. Quoted in Leiss, et al., *Social Communications.*

Learning

As Joe is talking to his old friend Ron in a bar, a curious thing happens. A woman walks by and Joe picks up the strong, distinctive scent of Charlie perfume. "It's funny," he says. "I haven't smelled that scent in a long time. But whenever I do, I start feeling funny, my palms sweat, and my heart pounds. I'm not normally that sensitive to different perfumes. I wonder why I have that reaction?"

C H A P T E R   4

Ron just snickers. "How quickly you forget! Teri, your first girlfriend when we were in college, used to practically bathe in that stuff. Even though she dumped you like a hot potato after a month, you never did get over her."

A flood of memories washes over Joe. Thinking of Teri reminds him of other college experiences and associations he has with Teri, like the time they went to that Rolling Stones concert. . . . Joe learned how to dance by watching Teri and imitating her. Later on, Joe digs out a box of mementos from that era of his life and spends a nostalgic evening going through them, reliving old memories. Even though it's been years, he can't seem to get Teri out of his mind.

THE LEARNING PROCESS

Learning refers to a relatively permanent change in a behavior that is caused by experience. This experience does not have to directly affect the learner; we can learn *vicariously* by observing events that affect others.[1] We also learn even when we are not trying. Consumers recognize many brand names and can hum many product jingles, for example, even for those product categories they themselves do not use. This casual, unintentional acquisition of knowledge is known as *incidental learning*. Like the concepts of perception and motivation discussed in the last two chapters, learning is a process. Our knowledge about the world is constantly being revised as we are exposed to new stimuli and receive ongoing feedback that allows us to modify behavior in other, similar situations.

The concept of learning covers a lot of ground, ranging from a consumer's simple association between a stimulus such as a product logo (e.g., "Coca-Cola") and a response (e.g., "refreshing soft drink") to a complex series of cognitive activities (e.g., writing an essay on learning for a Consumer Behavior exam). Psychologists who study learning have advanced several theories to explain the learning process. These theories range from those focusing on simple stimulus-response connections to perspectives that regard consumers as complex problem-solvers who learn abstract rules and concepts by observing others.

BEHAVIORAL LEARNING THEORIES

Behavioral learning theories assume that learning takes place as the result of responses to external events. Psychologists who subscribe to this viewpoint do not focus on internal thought processes. Instead, they approach the mind as a "black box" and emphasize the observable aspects of behavior, as depicted in Figure 4-1. The observable aspects consist of things that go into the box (*stimuli,* or events perceived from the outside world) and things that come out of the box (*responses,* or reactions to these stimuli).

This view is represented by two major approaches to learning, classical conditioning and instrumental conditioning. Just as Joe learned to associate

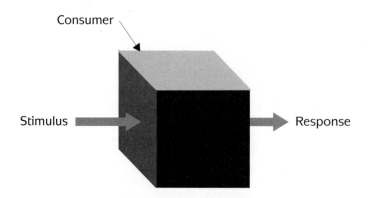

Consumer

Stimulus

Response

Figure 4-1 The Consumer as a "Black Box": A Behaviorist Perspective on Learning

the smell of Charlie perfume with unrequited love, people's experiences are shaped by the feedback they receive as they go through life.

Similarly, consumers respond to brand names, scents, jingles, and other marketing stimuli based upon the learned connections they have formed over time. People also learn that actions they take result in rewards and punishments, and this feedback influences the way they will respond in similar situations in the future. Consumers who receive compliments on a product choice will be more likely to buy that brand again, while those who get food poisoning at a new restaurant will not be likely to patronize it in the future.

CLASSICAL CONDITIONING **Classical conditioning** occurs when a stimulus that elicits a response is paired with another stimulus that initially does not elicit a response on its own. Over time, this second stimulus causes a similar response because it is associated with the first stimulus. This phenomenon was first demonstrated in dogs by Ivan Pavlov, a Russian physiologist doing research on digestion in animals.

Pavlov conducted a number of *conditioning trials* by pairing a neutral stimulus (a bell) with a stimulus known to cause a salivation response in dogs (he squirted dried meat powder into their mouths). The powder was an *unconditioned stimulus* (UCS) because it was naturally capable of causing the response. Over time the bell became a *conditioned stimulus* (CS); it did not initially cause salivation, but the dogs learned to associate the bell with the meat power and began to salivate at the sound of the bell only. The drooling of these canine consumers over a sound, now linked to feeding time, was a *conditioned response* (CR).

Analogously, our friend Joe's reaction to the perfume smell (*conditioned stimulus*) was caused by the repeated pairing of this scent with his old girlfriend, Teri. Teri was an *unconditioned stimulus* who was capable of eliciting Joe's *unconditioned response* of sexual arousal. Even after the initial, unconditioned stimulus was gone, the conditioned stimulus was still capable of causing a response.

This basic form of classical conditioning demonstrated by Pavlov primarily applies to responses controlled by the autonomic (e.g., salivation) and skeletal (e.g., eyeblink) nervous systems. That is, it focuses on visual and olfactory cues that induce hunger, thirst, sexual arousal, and other basic drives discussed in Chapter 3. When these cues are consistently paired with conditioned stimuli such as brand names, consumers may learn to feel hungry, thirsty, or aroused when later exposed to the brand cues.

Classical conditioning can have similar effects for more complex reactions, too. A counselor who works with gambling addicts in Spain, for example, would like to have the bells removed from slot machines. As he notes: "For many addicts, the sound of the music is enough to set them off."[2] Even a credit card becomes a conditioned cue that triggers greater spending, especially since it is a stimulus that is present only in situations where consumers are spending money. People learn they can make larger purchases when using credit cards, and they also have been found to leave larger tips than when using cash.[3] Small wonder that we are reminded, "Don't leave home without it."

Repetition. Conditioning effects are more likely to occur after the conditioned and unconditioned stimuli have been paired a number of times.[4] Repeated exposures increase the strength of stimulus-response associations and prevent the *decay* of these associations in memory.

Many classic advertising campaigns consist of product slogans that have been repeated so many times that they are etched in consumers' minds. The ad shown here brags about the high awareness of the Chiquita banana jingle ("I'm Chiquita banana, and I'm here to say . . . ") and the effect this familiarity has had on sales. Conditioning will not occur or will take longer if the CS is only occasionally presented with the UCS. One result of this lack of association may be *extinction.* This occurs when the effects of prior conditioning are reduced and finally disappear.

Stimulus Generalization. **Stimulus generalization** refers to the tendency of stimuli similar to a CS to evoke similar, conditioned responses.[5] For example, Pavlov noticed in subsequent studies that his dogs would sometimes salivate when they heard noises that only *resembled* a bell (e.g., keys jangling). People react to other, similar stimuli in much the same way they responded to the original stimulus. A drug store's bottle of private brand mouthwash deliberately packaged to resemble Listerine mouthwash may evoke a similar response among consumers, who assume that this "me too" product shares other characteristics of the original.

Stimulus Discrimination. **Stimulus discrimination** occurs when a stimulus similar to a CS is *not* followed by a UCS. When this happens, reactions are weakened and will soon disappear. Part of the learning process involves making a response to some stimuli but not to other, similar stimuli. Manufacturers of well-established brands commonly urge consumers not to buy "cheap imitations," because the results will not be what they expect.

OPERANT CONDITIONING **Operant conditioning,** also known as *instrumental conditioning,* occurs as the individual learns to perform behaviors that produce positive outcomes and to avoid those that yield negative

MULTICULTURAL DIMENSIONS

Many companies work hard to associate their products with high quality. Unfortunately, manufacturers of watches, recording tape, and even contraceptives have encountered a worldwide problem with stimulus discrimination: the proliferation of counterfeit goods bearing well-known brand names. Many of these goods are manufactured in Asia. It is estimated that South Korea alone is responsible for 60 percent to 70 percent of all counterfeited products. In parts of Asia, a fake Rolex watch can be had for $25 (a real one starts at about $1200); a fake Gucci handbag for $12 is a bargain compared to the real price of $120, and Ralph Lauren polo shirts go for $3 instead of $30 to $50.[6]

How strong is the Chiquita® name?
How many banana commercials can you sing?

Most people can't remember the TV commercials they saw last night as well as the Chiquita jingle they first heard in 1944.

In the 32 years since, Chiquita has come to be the first name that comes to mind for 9 out of every 10 consumers who buy bananas. Which is another reason why Chiquitas sell better than bananas.

Chiquita bananas today have a brand awareness of 92%. That's 30% higher than the awareness of the next leading brand…"what'sitsname?"

The Chiquita Banana jingle, largely due to its repetition over a number of years, has helped the product to create a high degree of awareness among consumers.

outcomes. This learning process is most closely associated with the psychologist B. F. Skinner, who demonstrated the effects of instrumental conditioning by teaching animals to dance, play ping-pong, and so on by systematically rewarding them for desired behaviors.

While responses in classical conditioning are involuntary and fairly simple, those in instrumental conditioning are made deliberately to obtain a goal and may be more complex. The desired behavior may be learned over a period of time, as intermediate actions are rewarded in a process called *shaping*. For example, the owner of a new store may award prizes to shoppers just for coming in, hoping that over time they will continue to drop in and eventually buy something.

Also, classical conditioning involves the close pairing of two stimuli. Instrumental learning occurs as a result of a reward received *following* the desired behavior and takes place over a period where a variety of other behaviors are attempted and abandoned because they are not reinforced. A good way to remember the difference is to keep in mind that in instrumental learning, the response is performed because it is *instrumental* to gaining a reward or avoiding a punishment. Consumers over time come to associate with people that reward them, and to choose products that make them feel good or satisfy some need.

Reinforcement. The reinforcers that shape behavior can be distinguished in terms of whether they help to satisfy basic physiological needs or social needs. *Primary reinforcers* are rewards related to basic biological needs, such as the need for a cool drink of water on a hot day. *Conditioned (secondary) reinforcers* are rewards associated with primary reinforcers, but the needs are more abstract. As discussed in chapter 3, these rewards, which include money, status, and praise, are related to social rather than biological needs. For example, teenagers may learn that they will be accepted by their peers if they smoke cigarettes or drink alcohol.

Instrumental learning occurs in one of three ways. When the environment provides **positive reinforcement** in the form of a reward, this strengthens the responses to stimuli so that appropriate behavior is learned. For example, a woman who gets reactions similar to Joe's after wearing Charlie perfume will learn that this product has the desired effect, and she will be more likely to keep buying the product. **Negative reinforcement** occurs when the environment weakens responses to stimuli so that inappropriate behavior is avoided. A perfume company, for example, might run an ad showing a woman sitting home alone on a Saturday night because she did *not* use its fragrance. In contrast to situations where we learn to do certain things in order to *avoid* unpleasantness, *punishment* occurs when a response is followed by unpleasant events (such as being ridiculed by friends for wearing an offensive smelling perfume)—we learn not to repeat these behaviors. The different mechanisms operating to produce instrumental conditioning are summarized in Figure 4-2.

An important factor in operant conditioning is the set of rules by which appropriate reinforcements are given for a behavior. The issue of what is the most effective *reinforcement schedule* to use is important to marketers, because it relates to the amount of effort and resources they must devote to rewarding consumers in order to condition desired behaviors.

- Fixed-interval reinforcement: After a specified time period has passed, the first response that is made brings the reward. Under such conditions, people tend to respond slowly right after being reinforced, but their responses speed up as the time for the next reinforcement looms. For example, consumers may crowd into a store for the last day of its seasonal sale and not reappear again until the next one.
- Variable-interval reinforcement: The time that must pass before reinforcement is delivered varies around some average. Since the person does not know exactly when to expect the reinforcement, responses must be performed at a consistent rate. This is the logic behind retailers' use of so-called *secret shoppers;* people who periodically test for service quality by posing as a customer at unannounced

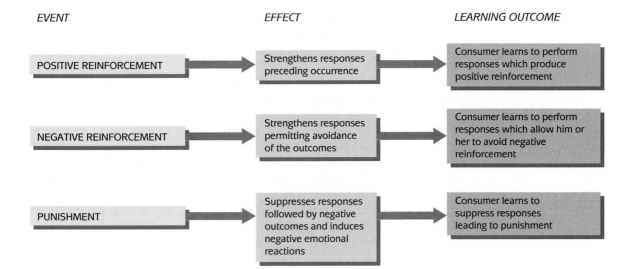

EVENT	EFFECT	LEARNING OUTCOME
POSITIVE REINFORCEMENT	Strengthens responses preceding occurrence	Consumer learns to perform responses which produce positive reinforcement
NEGATIVE REINFORCEMENT	Strengthens responses permitting avoidance of the outcomes	Consumer learns to perform responses which allow him or her to avoid negative reinforcement
PUNISHMENT	Suppresses responses followed by negative outcomes and induces negative emotional reactions	Consumer learns to suppress responses leading to punishment

Figure 4-2 An Overview of Three Types of Reinforcement in Instrumental Conditioning

times. Since store employees never know exactly when to expect a visit, high quality must be constantly maintained.

- Fixed-ratio reinforcement: Reinforcement occurs only after a fixed number of responses. This schedule motivates people to continue performing the same behavior over and over. For example, a consumer might keep buying groceries at the same store in order to earn a prize after collecting fifty books of trading stamps.
- Variable-ratio reinforcement: The person is reinforced after a certain number of responses, but he or she does not know how many responses are required. People in such situations tend to respond at very high and steady rates, and this type of behavior is very difficult to extinguish. This reinforcement schedule is responsible for consumers' attraction to slot machines. They learn that if they keep throwing money into the machine they will eventually win something (if they don't go broke first).

COGNITIVE LEARNING THEORY

Cognitive learning occurs as a result of mental processes. In contrast to behavioral theories of learning, cognitive learning theory stresses the importance of internal mental processes. This perspective views people as problem solvers who actively use information from the world around them to master their environment. Supporters of this viewpoint also stress the role of creativity and insight during the learning process.

THE ISSUE OF CONSCIOUSNESS   A lot of controversy surrounds the issue of whether or when people are aware of their learning processes. While behavioral learning theorists emphasize the routine, automatic nature of conditioning, proponents of cognitive learning argue that even these simple effects are based on cognitive factors: Expectations are created that a stimulus will be followed by a response (the formation of expectations requires mental activity). According to this school of thought, conditioning occurs because subjects develop conscious hypotheses and then act on them.

On the one hand, there is some evidence for the existence of nonconscious procedural knowledge. People apparently do process at least some information in an automatic, passive way—a condition that has been termed *mindlessness*.[7] When we meet someone new or encounter a new product, for example, we have a tendency to respond to the stimulus in terms of existing categories, rather than taking the trouble to formulate different ones. Our reactions are activated by a *trigger feature,* some stimulus that cues us toward a particular pattern. For example, men in one study rated a car in an ad as superior on a variety of characteristics if a seductive woman (the trigger feature) was present. This happened despite the fact that the men did not believe the woman's presence actually had an influence.[8]

Nonetheless, many modern theorists are beginning to regard many instances of conditioning as cognitive processes, where expectations are formed about the linkages between stimuli and responses. Indeed, studies using *masking effects,* where it is difficult for subjects to learn CS/UCS associations, show substantial reductions in conditioning.[9] For example, an adolescent girl may observe that women on television and in real life seem to be rewarded with compliments and attention when they smell nice and wear feminine clothing. She figures out that the probability of these rewards occurring is greater when she wears perfume, and deliberately wears a popular scent to obtain the payoff of social acceptance.

OBSERVATIONAL LEARNING   **Observational learning** occurs when people watch the actions of others and note the reinforcements *they* receive for their behaviors. This type of learning is a complex process;

Figure 4-3 Components of Observational Learning

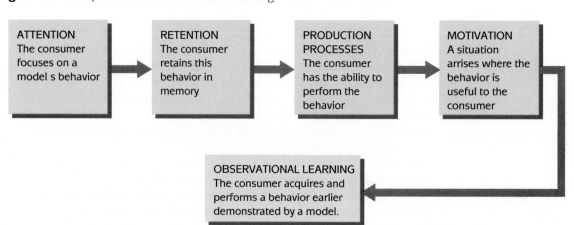

people store these observations in memory as they accumulate knowledge, perhaps using this information at a later point to guide their own behavior. This process of imitating the behavior of others is called *modeling.* For example, a woman shopping for a new kind of perfume may remember the reactions her friend received upon wearing a certain brand several months earlier, and she will base her behavior on her friend's actions.

In order for observational learning in the form of modeling to occur, four conditions must be met.[10] These factors are summarized in Figure 4-3.

1. The consumer's attention must be directed to the appropriate model, who for reasons of attractiveness, competence, status, or similarity is desirable to emulate.
2. The consumer must remember what is said or done by the model.
3. The consumer must convert this information into actions.
4. The consumer must be motivated to perform these actions.

MARKETING APPLICATIONS OF LEARNING PRINCIPLES

Understanding how consumers learn is very important to marketers. After all, many strategic decisions are based on the assumption that consumers are continually accumulating information about products, and that these people can be "taught" to prefer some alternatives over others.

BEHAVIORAL LEARNING APPLICATIONS

Many marketing strategies focus on the establishment of associations between stimuli and responses. Behavioral learning principles apply to many consumer phenomena, ranging from the creation of a distinctive brand image to the perceived linkage between a product and an underlying need.

USING CLASSICAL CONDITIONING The transfer of meaning from an unconditioned stimulus to a conditioned stimulus explains why "made-up" brand names like Marlboro, Coca-Cola, or IBM can exert such powerful effects on consumers. The association between the Marlboro Man and the cigarette is so strong that in some cases the company no longer even bothers to include the brand name in its ad. When nonsense syllables (meaningless sets of letters) are paired with such evaluative words as *beauty* or *success,* the meaning is transferred to the nonsense syllables. This change in the symbolic significance of initially meaningless words shows that complex meanings can be conditioned.[11]

Repetition. One advertising researcher argues that more than three exposures are wasted. The first creates awareness of the product, the second demonstrates its relevance to the consumer, and the third serves as a reminder of the product's benefits.[12] However, even this bare-bones approach implies that repetition is needed to ensure that the consumer is actually exposed to (and processes) the ad at least three times. Marketers attempting to condition an association must ensure that the consumers they have targeted will be exposed to the stimulus a sufficient number of times.

On the other hand, it is possible to have too much of a good thing: Consumers can become so used to hearing or seeing a marketing stimulus that they no longer pay attention to it (see Chapter 2). This problem, known as *advertising wearout,* can be alleviated by varying the way in which the basic message is presented. For example, the tax preparation firm of H&R Block is famous for its long-standing "Another of the seventeen reasons to use H&R Block . . ." campaign.

Conditioning Product Associations. Advertisements often pair a product with a positive stimulus to create a desirable association. Various aspects of a marketing message, such as music, humor, or imagery, can affect conditioning. In one study, for example, subjects who viewed a slide of pens paired with either pleasant or unpleasant music were more likely to later select the pen that appeared with pleasant music.[13]

The order in which the conditioned stimulus and the unconditioned stimulus is presented can affect the likelihood that learning will occur. Generally speaking, the unconditioned stimulus should be presented prior to the conditioned stimulus. The technique of *backward conditioning,* such as playing a jingle (the CS) and then showing a soft drink (the UCS) is generally not effective.[14] Because sequential presentation is desirable for conditioning to occur, classical conditioning is not very effective in static situations, such as in magazine ads, where (in contrast to TV or radio) the marketer cannot control the order in which the CS and the UCS are perceived.

Just as product associations can be formed, they can be *extinguished* as well. Because of the danger of extinction, a classical conditioning strategy may not be as effective for products that are frequently encountered, since there is no guarantee they will be accompanied by the CS. A bottle of Pepsi paired with the refreshing sound of a carbonated beverage being poured over ice may seem like a good example of conditioning. Unfortunately, the product would also be seen in many other contexts where this sound was absent, reducing the effectiveness of the conditioning.

By the same reasoning, a novel tune should be chosen over a popular one to pair with a product, since the popular song might also be heard in many situations where the product is not present.[15] Music videos in particular may serve as effective UCSs because they often have an emotional impact on viewers—this effect may transfer to ads accompanying the video.[16]

Stimulus Generalization. The process of stimulus generalization is often central to branding and packaging decisions that attempt to capitalize on consumers' positive associations with an existing brand or company name, as illustrated by a haircutting establishment called United Hairlines.[17] In one twenty-month period Procter & Gamble introduced almost ninety new products. Not a single one carried a new brand name. In fact, roughly 80 percent of all new products are actually extensions of existing brands or product lines.[18] Strategies based on stimulus generalization include:

- *family branding,* where a variety of products capitalize on the reputation of a company name. Companies such as Campbell's, Heinz, and General Electric rely on their positive corporate images to sell different product lines.
- *product line extensions,* where related products are added to an established brand. Dole, which is associated with fruit, was able to introduce refrigerated juices and juice bars, while Sun Maid went from raisins to raisin bread. Other recent extensions include Woolite Rug Cleaner, Cracker Jack gourmet popping corn, and Ivory shampoo.[19]
- *licensing* where well-known names are "rented" by others. This strategy is increasing in popularity as marketers try to link their products and services with well-established figures. The ad shown here

The images of well-known figures, both real and fictitious, are often licensed for use by advertisers. This trade ad for King Features promotes the characters from the Blondie comic strip to potential licensers. © King Features.

tries to lure licensers by emphasizing the widespread popularity of the Dagwood and Blondie cartoon characters. Companies as diverse as McDonald's and Harley-Davidson have authorized the use of their names on products ranging from clothing to chocolates and cologne. After conducting extensive research, the Murjani clothing company found that people associated the Coca-Cola name with value and quality. They then approached Coca-Cola for permission to license the name and develop a line of Coca-Cola clothing. As one Murjani executive observed: "Because of the advertising Coke had done over the years, it turned out that people had a picture in their minds of what the clothes would look like."[20]

- *look-alike packaging*, where distinctive packaging designs create strong associations with a particular brand. This linkage often is exploited by makers of generic or private-label brands who wish to communicate a quality image by putting their products in very similar packages. As one drug store executive commented, "You want to tell the consumer that it's close to the national brand. . . . You've got to make it look like, within the law, as close {sic} to the national brand. They're at least attracted to the package."[23]

MARKETING PITFALL

For a stimulus-response connection to be maintained, a new product must share some important characteristics with the original. Trouble can result if consumers do not make the connection between a brand and its extension. When Cadillac came out with the smaller Cadillac Cimarron, people who already owned Cadillacs did not regard the new model as a bona fide Cadillac. Arm & Hammer deodorant failed, possibly because consumers identified the product too strongly with something in the back of their refrigerators.[21] An extension even has the potential to weaken the parent brand, as the Carnation Company discovered. The company cancelled plans for "Lady Friskies," a contraceptive dog food, after tests indicated it would reduce sales of regular Friskies.[22]

Stimulus Discrimination. An emphasis on communicating a product's distinctive attributes vis-à-vis its competitors is an important aspect of *positioning,* where consumers learn to differentiate a brand from its competitors (see chapter 2). Companies with a well-established brand image try to encourage stimulus discrimination by promoting the unique attributes of their brand. Thus, the constant reminders for American Express Traveler's Checks: "Ask for them by name. . . ." On the other hand, a brand name that is used so widely that it is no longer distinctive becomes part of the *public domain,* and can be used by competitors. This has been the case for such well-known products as aspirin, cellophane, and kleenex.

USING INSTRUMENTAL CONDITIONING Principles of instrumental conditioning are at work when a consumer is rewarded or punished for a purchase decision. Businesspeople shape behavior by gradually reinforcing consumers for taking appropriate actions. For example, a car dealer might encourage a reluctant buyer to just sit in a floor model, then suggest a test drive, and so on.

Reinforcement of Consumption. Marketers have many ways to reinforce consumers, ranging from a simple "thank you" after a purchase to substantial rebates and follow-up phone calls. For example, a life insurance company obtained a much higher rate of policy renewal among a group of new customers who received a thank you letter after each payment compared to a control group that did not receive any reinforcement.[24]

A popular technique known as *frequency marketing* reinforces regular purchasers by giving them prizes with values that increase along with the amount purchased. This operant learning strategy was pioneered by the airline industry, which introduced "frequent flyer" programs in the early 1980s to reward loyal customers. Well over 20 percent of food stores, for example, now offer trading stamps or some other frequent-buyer promotion.

In some industries, these reinforcers take the form of clubs, including a Luv's Baby Club, a Virginia Slims Club, and a Hilton Hotel Club. Club members usually earn bonus points to apply toward future purchases, and some get such privileges as magazines, toll-free numbers, and sometimes even invitations to exclusive outings. The George Dickel Tennessee Whiskey Water Conservation Society takes the concept a step further. Members pay $4.95 to own a Duel Kit, which allows them to challenge other whiskey drinkers to a taste test. This kit contains two shot glasses, a blindfold, napkins, and a score card.[25]

COGNITIVE LEARNING APPLICATIONS

Consumers' ability to learn vicariously by observing how the behavior of others is reinforced makes the lives of marketers much easier. Because people do not have to be directly reinforced for their actions, marketers do not necessarily have to reward or punish them for purchase behaviors. Instead, they can show what happens to desirable models who use or do not use their products, knowing that consumers will often be motivated to imitate these actions at a later time. For example, a perfume commercial may depict a woman surrounded by a throng of admirers who are providing her with positive reinforcement for using the product. Needless to say, this learning process is more practical than providing the same attention to each woman who actually buys the perfume!

MARKETING PITFALL

The modeling process is a powerful form of learning, and people's tendencies to imitate others' behaviors can have negative effects. Of particular concern is the potential of television shows and movies to teach violence to children. Children may be exposed to new methods of aggression by models (e.g., cartoon heroes) in the shows they watch. At some later point, when the child becomes angry, these behaviors will be available for actual use. A classic study demonstrates the effect of modeling on children's actions. Kids who watched an adult stomp on, knock down, and otherwise torture a large inflated "Bobo doll" repeated these behaviors when later left alone in a room with the doll, in contrast to other children who did not witness these acts.[26] The parallel to violent programming is, unfortunately, clear.

Consumers' evaluations of models go beyond simple stimulus-response connections. For example, a celebrity's image is often more than a simple reflexive response of "good" or "bad."[27] It is a complex combination of many attributes. In general, the degree to which a model will be emulated depends upon his or her social attractiveness. Attractiveness can be based upon several components, including physical appearance, expertise, or similarity to the evaluator.

These factors will be further addressed in chapter 6, which discusses personal characteristics that make a communication's source more or less effective in changing consumers' attitudes. In addition, many applications of consumer problem-solving are related to ways information is represented in memory and recalled at a later date. This aspect of cognitive learning is the focus of the next section.

THE ROLE OF MEMORY IN LEARNING

THE MEMORY PROCESS

As suggested by Joe's experience at the beginning of the chapter, many of our experiences are locked inside our heads, and they may surface years later if prompted by the right cues. Marketers rely on consumers to retain information they have learned about products and services, trusting that it will later be applied in situations where purchase decisions must be made. During the consumer decision-making process, this *internal memory* is combined with *external memory,* which includes all of the product details on packages, in shopping lists, and other marketing stimuli, to permit brand alternatives to be identified and evaluated.[28]

Memory involves a process of acquiring information and storing it over time so that it will be available when needed. Contemporary approaches to the study of memory employ an *information-processing* approach. They assume that the mind is in some ways like a computer; data are input, processed, and output for later use in revised form. In the **encoding** stage, information is entered in a way the system will recognize. In the **storage** stage, this knowledge is integrated with what is already in memory and "warehoused" until needed. During **retrieval,** the person accesses the desired information.[29] The memory process is summarized in Figure 4-4.

ENCODING INFORMATION

The way information is encoded, or mentally programmed, helps to determine how it will be represented in memory. In general, incoming data that are associated with other information already in memory stand a

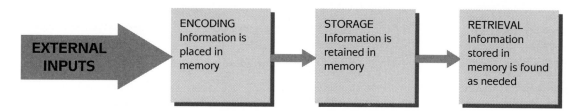

Figure 4-4 The Memory Process

better chance of being retained. For example, brand names that are linked to physical characteristics of a product category (e.g., CoffeeMate creamer or Sani-Flush toilet bowl cleaner) or that are easy to visualize (e.g., Tide detergent or Cougar cars) tend to be more easily retained in memory than more abstract brand names.[30]

TYPES OF MEMORIES   A consumer may process a stimulus simply in terms of its *sensory meaning,* such as its color or shape. When this occurs, the meaning may be activated when the person sees a picture of the stimulus. We may experience a sense of familiarity upon seeing an ad for a new snack food we had recently tasted, for example.

Abstract Meanings.   In many cases, meanings are encoded at a more abstract level. *Semantic meaning* refers to symbolic associations, such as the idea that rich people drink champagne or that fashionable men wear earrings.

Episodic memories are those that relate to events that are personally relevant, such as Joe's memory that was triggered by a whiff of perfume.[31] As a result, a person's motivation to retain these memories will likely be strong. Couples often have "their song" that reminds them of their first date or wedding. The memories that might be triggered upon hearing this song would be quite different and unique for them.

Commercials sometimes attempt to activate episodic memories by focusing on experiences shared by many people (e.g., Woodstock or the dismantling of the Berlin Wall). Recall of the past may have an effect on future behavior. For example, a college fund-raising campaign can get higher donations by evoking pleasant college memories. Some especially vivid associations are called *flashbulb memories.* These are usually related to some highly significant event. For example, many people claim to remember exactly what they were doing when President Kennedy was assassinated in the early 1960s.

MEMORY SYSTEMS   According to the information-processing perspective, there are three distinct memory systems: sensory memory, short-term memory (STM), and long-term memory (LTM). Each plays a role in processing brand-related information. The interrelationships of these memory systems are summarized in Figure 4-5.

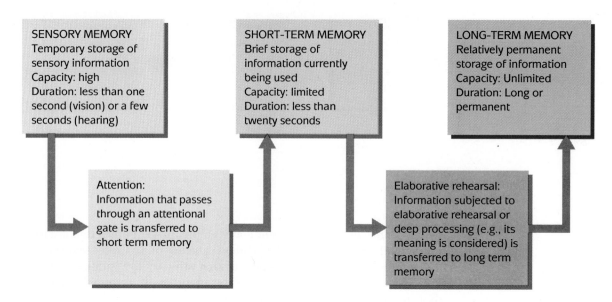

Figure 4-5 Relationships Among Memory Systems

Sensory Memory. **Sensory memory** permits storage of the information we receive from our senses. This storage is very temporary; it lasts a couple of seconds at most. For example, a person might be walking past a donut shop and get a quick, enticing whiff of something baking inside. While this sensation would only last for a few seconds, it would be sufficient to allow the person to determine if he or she should investigate further. If the information is retained for further processing, it passes through an *attentional gate* and is transferred to short-term memory.

Short-Term Memory. **Short-term memory** also stores information for a limited period of time, and its capacity is limited. Similar to a computer, this system can be regarded as *working memory;* it holds the information we are currently processing. Verbal input may be stored *acoustically* (in terms of how it sounds) or *semantically* (in terms of its meaning).[32]

The information is stored by combining small pieces into larger ones in a process known as *chunking.* A chunk is a configuration that is familiar to the person and can be manipulated as a unit. For example, a brand name can be a chunk that summarizes a great deal of detailed information about the brand.

Initially, it was believed that STM was capable of processing between five to nine chunks of information at a time, and for this reason phone numbers were designed to have seven digits.[33] It now appears that three to four chunks is the optimum size for efficient retrieval (seven-digit phone numbers can be remembered because the individual digits are chunked, so we may remember a three-digit exchange as one piece of information).[34]

Long-Term Memory.   **Long-term memory** is the system that allows us to retain information for a long period of time. In order for information to enter into long-term memory from short-term memory, *elaborative rehearsal* is required. This involves thinking about the meaning of a stimulus and relating it to other information already in memory. Marketers sometimes assist in this process by devising catchy slogans or jingles that consumers repeat on their own.

STORING INFORMATION

Relationships among the types of memory are a source of some controversy. The traditional perspective, known as *multiple-store,* assumes that STM and LTM are separate systems. More recent research has moved away from the distinction between the two types of memory, instead emphasizing the interdependence of the systems. This work argues that depending upon the nature of the processing task, different levels of processing occur that *activate* some aspects of memory rather than others. These approaches are called **activation models of memory.**[35] The more effort it takes to process information (so-called "deep processing"), the more likely it is that information will be placed in long-term memory.

ASSOCIATIVE NETWORKS   Activation models propose that an incoming piece of information is stored in an *associative network* containing many bits of related information organized according to some set of relationships. The consumer has organized systems of concepts relating to brands, stores, and so on.

The Structure of Knowledge Structures.   These storage units are known as *knowledge structures,* which can be thought of as complex spider webs filled with pieces of data. This information is placed into *nodes* and *associative links* within these structures. Pieces of information that are seen as similar in some way are chunked together under some more abstract category. New, incoming information is interpreted to be consistent with the structure already in place.[36] According to the *hierarchical processing model,* a message is processed in a bottom-up fashion. Processing begins at a very basic level and is subject to increasingly complex processing operations that require greater cognitive capacity. If processing at one level fails to evoke the next level, processing of the ad is terminated and capacity is allocated to other tasks.[37]

Links form between nodes as an associative network is developed. For example, a consumer might have a network for "perfumes." Each node represents a concept related to the category. This node can be an attribute, a specific brand, a celebrity identified with a perfume, or even a related product. A network for perfumes might include concepts like the names Chanel, Obsession, and Charlie, as well as attributes like sexy and elegant.

When asked to list perfumes, the consumer would recall only those brands contained in the appropriate category. This group is termed the **evoked set.** The task of a new entrant that wants to position itself as a category member (e.g., a new luxury perfume) is to provide cues that facilitate its placement in the appropriate category. A sample network for perfumes is shown in Figure 4-6.

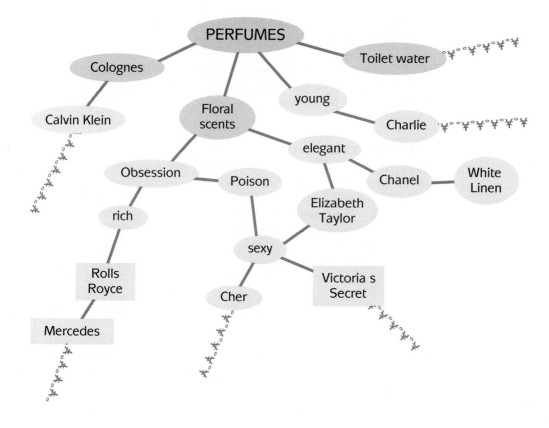

Figure 4-6 An Associative Network for Perfumes

Spreading Activation. A meaning can be activated indirectly; energy spreads across nodes of varying levels of abstraction. As one node is activated, other nodes associated with it also begin to be triggered. Meaning thus spreads across the network, bringing up concepts including competing brands and relevant attributes that are used to form attitudes toward the brand.

This process of *spreading activation* allows consumers to shift back and forth between levels of meaning. The way a piece of information is stored in memory depends upon the type of meaning assigned to it. This meaning type will in turn determine how and when the meaning is activated. For example, the *memory trace* for an ad could be stored in one or more of the following ways:

- brand-specific (e.g., in terms of claims made for the brand)
- ad-specific (in terms of the medium or content of the ad itself)
- brand identification (the brand name)
- product category (i.e., how the product works, where it should be used, or in terms of experiences with the product)
- evaluative reactions (e.g., "that looks like fun")[38]

Levels of Knowledge. Knowledge is coded at different levels of abstraction and complexity. *Meaning concepts* are individual nodes (e.g., elegant). These may be combined into a larger unit, called a *proposition* (also known as a *belief*). A proposition links two nodes together to form a more complex meaning, which can serve as a single chunk of information. For example, a proposition might be that "Chanel is a perfume for elegant women." Propositions are in turn integrated to produce a complex unit known as a *schemata.* A schema is a cognitive framework that is developed through experience. Information that is consistent with an existing schema is encoded more readily.[39] The ability to move up and down among levels of abstraction greatly increases processing flexibility and efficiency. For this reason, young children, who do not yet have well-developed schemata, are not able to make efficient use of purchase information compared to older children.[40]

One type of schema that is relevant to consumer behavior is a *script,* a sequence of procedures that is expected by an individual. For example, consumers learn *service scripts* that guide expectations and purchasing behavior in business settings. Consumers learn to expect a certain sequence of events, and they may become uncomfortable if the service departs from the script. For example, a service script for a visit to the dentist might include such events as (1) drive to the dentist, (2) read old magazines in the waiting room, (3) hear name called and sit in dentist's chair, (4) dentist puts funny substance on my teeth, (5) dentist cleans my teeth, and so on. This desire to follow a script helps to explain why such service innovations as automatic bank machines and self-service gas stations have met with resistance by some consumers, who have trouble adapting to a new sequence of events.[41]

▼ MARKETING PITFALL

Consumers process incoming information to be consistent with existing knowledge structures, and as a result incorrect inferences about a product may be made. In one national survey that examined the miscomprehension of advertisements and editorials, on average more than 20 percent of the material was incorrectly understood, while an additional 15 percent was not learned at all.[42]

The tendency to make inferences paves the way for *misleading advertising,* which occurs when there is a discrepancy between a consumer's beliefs about a product based upon an ad and its performance. For example, people may confuse a *direct assertion,* where a product benefit is stated directly, with a *pragmatic implication,* which indirectly implies a benefit that may not exist.

The mock ad shown in Figure 4-7 was used in a study to test this effect. More than 80 percent of the subjects who read the version that contained a pragmatic implication ("your waist will love it too") believed that eating the product would not make them fatter, even though the ad copy never actually said this.[43]

Do you love chocolate, but it doesn t love you? I m talking about the way your waistline expands every time you eat your favorite chocolate snack. Here s good news for you:

> New CHOCOTRIM, the delicious natural snack that tastes like chocolate, but with fewer waist-expanding calories. Try new CHOCOTRIM alone or in your favorite recipe. Not only will your mouth love it, but

> *CHOCOTRIM will not increase your waistline*
> [direct assertion version]

or

> *your waist will love it too*
> [pragmatic implication version]

Figure 4-7 A Mock Ad Used in a Study on Misleading Advertising Gary J. Gaeth and Timothy E. Heath, "The Cognitive Processing of Misleading Advertising in Young and Old Adults," *Journal of Consumer Research* 14 (June 1987) Reprinted with Permission of The University of Chicago Press.

RETRIEVING INFORMATION

Retrieval is the process whereby information is accessed from long-term memory. As evidenced by the popularity of the game Trivial Pursuit, people have a vast quantity of information stored in their heads that is not necessarily available on demand. Although most of the information entered in long-term memory does not go away, it may be hard or impossible to retrieve unless the appropriate cues are present.

FACTORS INFLUENCING RETRIEVAL Some differences in retrieval ability are physiological. Older adults consistently display inferior recall ability for current items such as prescription information, though events that happened to them when they were younger may be recalled with great clarity.[44]

Other factors are situational, relating to the environment in which the message is delivered. Not surprisingly, recall is enhanced when the consumer pays more attention to the message in the first place. For example, commercials shown during baseball games yield the lowest recall scores among sports programs because the activity is stop and go rather than continuous. Unlike football or basketball, the pacing of baseball gives many opportunities for attention to wander even during play. Similarly, General Electric found that its commercials fared better in television shows with continuous activity, such as stories or dramas, compared to variety shows or talk shows that are punctuated by a series of acts.[45]

State-Dependent Retrieval. In a process termed *state-dependent retrieval,* people are better able to access information if their internal state is the same at the time of recall as when the information was learned. For example, if a student drinks a lot of coffee while studying for an exam, he or she should also drink coffee right before taking it. (Note that merely drinking coffee before an exam will not help recall if one did not also study under the influence of caffeine—the important thing is that the two states should match.)[46]

This phenomenon, called the *mood congruence effect,* underscores the desirability of matching a consumer's mood at the time of purchase when planning exposure to marketing communications. A consumer is more likely to recall an ad, for example, if his or her mood or level of arousal at the time of exposure is similar to that in the purchase environment. By recreating the cues that were present when the information was first presented, recall can be enhanced. For example, Life cereal uses a picture of "Mikey" from its commercial on the cereal box; this should facilitate recall of brand claims and more favorable brand evaluations.[47]

Everybody remembers the '80s.

Trivial Pursuit, a popular board game, tests consumers' memories of cultural happenings. TRIVIAL PURSUIT® is a registered trademark of Horn Abbot Ltd., under exclusive license to Parker Brothers and used with permission.

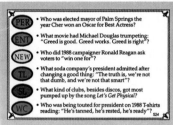

The <u>new</u> 1980's Edition. All new questions, all about the '80s. Cards also sold separately.

148

Familiarity.   As a general rule, prior familiarity with an item enhances its recall. Indeed, this is one of the basic goals of marketers who are trying to create and maintain awareness of their products. The more experience a consumer has with a product, the better use he or she is able to make of product information.[48]

However, there is a possible fly in the ointment: As noted earlier in the chapter, some evidence indicates that extreme familiarity can result in *inferior* learning and/or recall.

When consumers are highly familiar with a brand or an advertisement, they may attend to fewer attributes because they do not believe that any additional effort will yield a gain in knowledge.[49] For example, when consumers are exposed to the technique of *radio replay,* where the audio track from a television ad is replayed on the radio, they do very little critical, evaluative processing and instead mentally replay the video portion of the ad.[50]

Salience.   The *salience* of a brand refers to its prominence or level of activation in memory. As noted in Chapter 2, stimuli that stand out in contrast to their environment are more likely to command attention, and this in turn increases the likelihood they will be recalled. Almost any technique that increases the novelty of a stimulus also improves recall (this is known as the *von Restorff effect*).[51] This effect explains why unusual advertising or distinctive packaging tends to facilitate brand recall.[52]

Pictorial Versus Verbal Cues.   There is some evidence for the superiority of visual memory over verbal memory, but this advantage is unclear because it is more difficult to measure recall of pictures.[53] However, the available data indicate that information presented in picture form is more likely to be recognized later.[54] Certainly, visual aspects of an ad are more likely to grab attention. Eye movement studies indicate that about 90 percent of viewers look at the dominant picture in an ad before they bother to view the copy.[55] Pictorial ads may enhance recall without improving comprehension. Television news items presented with illustrations (still pictures) as a backdrop result in improved recall for details of the news story, though understanding of the story's content does not improve.[56]

 MARKETING OPPORTUNITY

One overlooked factor that contributes to advertising recall is the rhythm and beat of the verbal message. By stressing important words, cognitive overload is avoided because the commercial cues viewers to predict when they should be paying the most attention to the ad content. A technique called the TLK Picture Sort assesses the effect of rhythm on recall. Subjects are given a deck of still pictures from a commercial they have seen, and they sort them into "remember" and "don't remember" piles.

Commercials that score well on recall have an identifiable rhythmic stroke. Typically, the opening frames have an arousing sequence that hooks the viewer, and superior comprehension is found at the close of the commercial because curiosity and involvement build as the communication develops.[57]

FACTORS INFLUENCING FORGETTING Marketers obviously hope that consumers will not forget about their products. However, in a poll of more than 13,000 adults, over half were unable to remember *any* specific ad they had seen, heard, or read in the last thirty days.[58] Forgetting is obviously a problem for marketers.

Decay and Interference. Early memory theorists assumed that memories fade due to the simple passage of time. In a process of **decay,** the structural changes in the brain produced by learning simply go away.

The memorabilia in this ad for First Interstate Bank is intended to invoke a feeling of nostalgia in readers, underscoring the important role played by products in memory for past events. Courtesy of First Interstate Bank.

Forgetting also occurs due to **interference;** as additional information is learned, it displaces the earlier information.

Stimulus-response associations will be forgotten if the consumers subsequently learn new responses to the same or similar stimuli. This is known as *retroactive interference.* Or, prior learning can interfere with new learning, a process termed *proactive interference.* Since pieces of information are stored as nodes in memory that are connected to one another by links, a meaning concept that is connected by a larger number of links is more likely to be retrieved. But, as new responses are learned, a stimulus loses its effectiveness in retrieving the old response.[59]

These interference effects help to explain problems in remembering brand information. Consumers tend to organize attribute information by brand.[60] Additional attribute information regarding a brand or similar brands may limit the person's ability to recall old brand information. Recall may also be inhibited if the brand name is composed of frequently used words. These words cue competing associations and result in less retention of brand information.[61]

In one study, brand evaluations deteriorated more rapidly when ads for the brand appeared with messages for twelve other brands in the *same* category than when the ad was shown with ads for twelve dissimilar products.[62] By increasing the salience of a brand, the recall of other brands can be impaired.[63] On the other hand, calling a competitor by name can result in poorer recall for one's own brand.[64]

 MARKETING OPPORTUNITY

A phenomenon known as the *part-list cueing effect* allows marketers to strategically utilize the interference process. When only a portion of the items in a category are presented to consumers, the omitted items are not as easily recalled. For example, comparative advertising that mentions only a subset of competitors (preferably those that the marketer is not very worried about) may inhibit recall of the *unmentioned* brands with which the product does not favorably compare.[65]

PRODUCTS AS MEMORY MARKERS   Products and ads can themselves serve as powerful retrieval cues. Indeed, the three types of possessions most valued by consumers are furniture, visual art, and photos. The most common explanation for this attachment is the ability of these things to call forth memories of the past.[66] Products are particularly important as markers when our sense of past is threatened, as when a consumer's current identity is challenged due to some change in role caused by divorce, moving, graduation, and so on.[67] Products have *mnemonic* qualities that serve as a form of external memory, prompting consumers to retrieve episodic memories. For example, family photography allows consumers to create their own retrieval cues—the 11 billion amateur photos taken annually form a kind of external memory bank for our culture.

The Power of Nostalgia.   *Nostalgia* has been described as a bitter-sweet emotion, where the past is viewed with both sadness and longing. This feeling was strongly experienced by Joe in the vignette at the beginning of the chapter. A stimulus is at times able to evoke a weakened response much later, an effect known as *spontaneous recovery,* and this reestablished connection may explain consumers' powerful nostalgic reactions to songs or pictures they have not been exposed to in many years. Some marketers are realizing the appeal nostalgia holds for many consumers. They are resurrecting *retro ads,* successful campaigns from the past that have been in retirement, as when Maypo cereal brought back its "I want my Maypo" slogan in the ad shown here. The Coca-Cola Company went so far as to hire a detective agency to track down actors from a commercial made over twenty years earlier who gathered on a hilltop to sing "I'd Like to Buy the World a Coke." The original participants appeared with their children in a highly publicized ad called "Hilltop Reunion."[68]

The McDonald's Corporation is capitalizing on nostalgia in a creative way. The company opened a test restaurant in Hartsville, Tennessee call the Golden Arch Cafe. It resembles a 1950s diner, done in chrome and glass with neon lights. The cafe features spin-seat stools, a jukebox, and an old-fashioned Coke machine. Traditional "American" foods are on the menu, such as Salisbury steak, fried chicken, and country ham, along with pie à la mode. Unlike other McDonald's, the food is delivered to one's table by servers dressed in authentic period clothing.[69]

Maypo cereal brought back its original commercial ("I want my Maypo!") to appeal to consumers' nostalgic memories. Maypo photo courtesy of American Home Food Products.

The souvenir industry depends upon consumers' desires to *tangibilize,* or give physical form to, their experiences as tourists. Indeed, the word souvenir is French for memory. While many opportunities exist to provide consumers with tangible markers of important events, sometimes the end results are in questionable taste. A good case in point was the marketing of the visit of Pope John Paul II to the United States in 1987. The following are samples of some memorabilia that were offered to capitalize on this event:

- T-shirts picturing Budweiser beer mascot Spuds MacKenzie in papal hat and robe. The caption read "The Original Vatican Animal."
- A lawn sprinkler that shoots water from the out-turned palms of a plywood pope. The slogan: "Let Us Spray."
- A company called Popepourri Ltd. sold a papal ring made of gold plastic with red lips. According to the ring's creator, "When you kiss it, it'll kiss you back."[70]

MEASURING MEMORY FOR ADVERTISING   Because advertisers pay so much money to place their messages in front of consumers, they are naturally concerned that people will actually remember these messages at a later point. It seems that they have good reason to be concerned. In one study, less than 40 percent of television viewers made positive links between commercial messages and the corresponding products, only 65 percent noticed the brand name in a commercial, and only 38 percent recognized a connection to an important point.[71]

Even more sadly, only 7 percent of television viewers can recall the product or company featured in the most recent television commercial they watched. This figure represents less than half the recall rate recorded in 1965, and may be attributed to such factors as the increase of thirty and fifteen second commercials and the practice of airing television commercials in clusters rather than in single-sponsor programs.[72] The ad for Whittle Communications highlights this problem.

Recognition Versus Recall.   One indicator of good advertising is, of course, the impression it makes on consumers. But how can this impact be defined and measured? Two basic measures of impact are *recognition* and *recall.* In the typical recognition test, subjects are shown ads one at a time and asked if they have seen them before. In contrast, free recall tests ask consumers to independently produce previously acquired information and then perform a recognition check on it.

Under some conditions, these two memory measures tend to yield the same results, especially when the researchers try to keep the viewers' interest in the ads constant.[73] Generally, though, recognition scores tend to be more reliable and do not decay over time the way recall scores do.[74] Recognition scores are almost always better than recall scores because recognition is a simpler process and more retrieval cues are available to the consumer.

You've been exposed to roughly 5,000 advertising messages in the last 24 hours. Can you remember three?

Two?
One?
Most people can't.
Not even most people in advertising.
And if you find this alarming, you're not alone.
Many advertisers are growing more and more concerned about the extraordinary amount of advertising the ordinary consumer sees.
Or, more accurately, doesn't see.
Approximately 5,000 messages a day.
35,000 a week.
150,000 a month.
Almost two million over the course of a year.
The obvious question is, how do you cut through such overwhelming clutter?

The answer, for more and more advertisers, is the media we provide.
At Whittle Communications, we produce media that range from magazines to video systems.
And we limit the advertising in every one of these.
Usually to only one advertiser per category.
Or, more frequently, to one advertiser, period.
The result is an absence of clutter and a level of impact that have attracted many of the country's largest and most sophisticated advertisers.
And have also helped Whittle Communications become a $100 million company, with a staff of 850 people.
So if you're concerned about the memorability of the ads you're running, may we make a simple suggestion?
Try not to forget this one.

Whittle
communications

© 1987 Whittle Communications L.P. Knoxville/New York

This ad for Whittle Communications points out that consumers' memory for advertising is surprisingly limited. The company tries to circumvent this problem by presenting messages in places where consumers will be more likely to see and process them, including specialized magazines, doctors' waiting rooms, and even in high school video programs. Courtesy of Whittle Communications.

Both types of retrieval play important roles in purchase decisions. Recall tends to be more important in situations where consumers do not have product data at their disposal, and so they must rely upon memory to generate this information.[75] On the other hand, recognition is more likely to be an important factor in a store, where consumers are confronted with thousands of product options and information (i.e., external memory is abundantly available) and the task may simply be to recognize a familiar package. Unfortunately, this process can backfire: For example, frequently used product warning labels may be ignored, since their existence is taken for granted and not really noticed.[76]

The Starch Test. A widely used commercial measure of advertising recall for magazines is called the Starch test, a syndicated service founded in 1932. This service provides scores on a number of aspects of consumers' familiarity with an ad, including such categories as "noted," "associated," and "read most." It also scores the impact of the component parts of an overall ad, giving such information as "seen" for major illustrations and "read some" for a major block of copy.[77] Such factors as the size of the ad, whether it appears toward the front or the back of the magazine, if it is on the right or left page, and the size of illustrations play an important role in affecting the amount of attention given to an ad as determined by Starch scores.

Problems with Memory Measures. While the measurement of an ad's memorability is important, the ability of existing measures to accurately assess these dimensions has been criticized for several reasons:

- Response biases: Results obtained from a measuring instrument are not necessarily due to what is being measured, but rather to something else about the instrument or the respondent. This form of contamination is called a *response bias*. For example, people tend to give yes responses to questions, regardless of what is asked. In addition, consumers often have an eagerness to be "good subjects" by pleasing the experimenter. They will try to give the responses they think he or she is looking for. In some studies, the claimed recognition of bogus ads (ads that have not been seen before) is almost as high as the recognition rate of real ads.[78]
- Memory lapses: Typical problems include *omitting* (leaving facts out), *averaging* (the tendency to "normalize" things and not report extreme cases), and *telescoping* (inaccurate recall of time).[79] These distortions call into question the accuracy of various product usage data bases that rely upon consumers to recall their purchase and consumption of food and household items. In one study, for example, people were asked to describe what portion of various foods—small, medium, or large—they ate in a normal meal. However, different definitions of medium were used (e.g., ¾ cup versus 1½ cups). Regardless of the measurement used, about the same number of people claimed they normally ate medium portions.[80]

Memory Versus Feeling. Although techniques are being developed to increase the accuracy of memory scores, these improvements do not address the more fundamental issue of whether recall is necessary for advertising to have an effect. In particular, some critics argue that these measures do not adequately tap the impact of "feeling" ads where the objective is to arouse strong emotions rather than to convey concrete product benefits. Many ad campaigns, including those for Hallmark cards, Chevrolet, and Pepsi use this approach.[81] An affective strategy relies on a long-term buildup of feeling rather than on a one-shot attempt to convince consumers to buy the product.

Also, it is not clear that recall translates into preference. We may recall the benefits touted in an ad but not *believe* them. Or, the ad may be memorable because it is so obnoxious and the product becomes one we "love to hate." The bottom line: While recall is important, especially for creating brand awareness, it is not necessarily *sufficient* to alter consumer preferences. To accomplish this, more sophisticated attitude-change strategies are needed. These issues will be discussed in the next two chapters.

CHAPTER SUMMARY

Our knowledge about products is acquired through learning. Different aspects of this process can be understood by examining principles of both behavioral learning theory, such as classical and instrumental conditioning, and cognitive learning theory, which stresses the importance of observation and active problem-solving. Learned information, such as that imparted by advertising, is stored in memory. The impact of this information on future product evaluations depends on its accessibility in memory and the way the information is organized vis-à-vis other, competing data. Factors such as the familiarity and salience of the information help to determine if it will be remembered. Techniques for measuring the impact of advertising on memory also were discussed, as was the concept of nostalgia and other social aspects played by memory in the lives of consumers.

KEY TERMS

Activation models of memory
Behavioral learning theories
Classical conditioning
Cognitive learning
Decay
Encoding
Evoked set
Interference
Learning
Long-term memory
Memory

Negative reinforcement
Observational learning
Operant conditioning
Positive reinforcement
Retrieval
Sensory memory
Short-term memory
Stimulus discrimination
Stimulus generalization
Storage

REVIEW QUESTIONS AND DISCUSSION TOPICS

1. List two factors that make classical conditioning effects more likely to occur.
2. Identify three patterns of reinforcement and provide an example of how each is used in a marketing context.
3. Describe the functions of short term and long term memory. What is the apparent relationship between the two?

HANDS-ON EXERCISES

1. Devise a "product jingle memory test." Compile a list of brands that are or have been associated with memorable jingles, such as Chiquita Banana or Alka-Seltzer. Read this list to friends, and see how many jingles are remembered. You may be surprised at the level of recall.

2. Identify some important characteristics for a product with a well-known brand name. Based on these attributes, generate a list of possible brand extension or licensing opportunities, as well as some others that would most likely not be accepted by consumers.
3. Collect some pictures of "classic" products that have high nostalgia value. Show these pictures to consumers, and allow them to free associate. Analyze the types of memories that are evoked, and think about how these associations might be employed in a product's promotional strategy.

NOTES

1. Robert A. Baron, *Psychology: The Essential Science* (Boston: Allyn & Bacon, 1989).
2. Quoted in Alan Riding, "In Spain, Land of Gamblers, Help for Addicts," *New York Times* (May 14, 1989):19.
3. Richard A. Feinberg, "Credit Cards as Spending Facilitating Stimuli: A Conditioning Interpretation," *Journal of Consumer Research* 13 (December 1986): 348–56.
4. R. A. Rescorla, "Pavlovian Conditioning: It's Not What You Think It Is," *American Psychologist* 43 (1988):151–60; Elnora W. Stuart, Terence A. Shimp, and Randall W. Engle, "Classical Conditioning of Consumer Attitudes: Four Experiments in an Advertising Context," *Journal of Consumer Research* 14 (December 1987): 334–39.
5. Baron, *Psychology.*
6. Diane P. Marshall, "Is It the Real Thing?" *Travel-Holiday,* (October 1988):24.
7. Stephen J. Gould, "Hypnosis and Advertising: The Construct of Advertising Suggestion," (unpublished manuscript, Rutgers University 1989); E. J. Langer, *The Psychology of Control* (Beverly Hills, Calif.: Sage, 1983).
8. R. B. Cialdini, *Influence: Science and Practice,* 2nd ed. (New York: William Morrow, 1984).
9. Chris T. Allen and Thomas J. Madden, "A Closer Look at Classical Conditioning," *Journal of Consumer Research* 12 (December 1985): 301–15.
10. Albert Bandura, *Social Foundations of Thought and Action: A Social Cognitive View* (Englewood Cliffs, N.J.: Prentice-Hall, 1986); Baron, *Psychology.*
11. Chris T. Allen and Thomas J. Madden, "A Closer Look at Classical Conditioning"; Chester A. Insko and William F. Oakes, "Awareness and the Conditioning of Attitudes," *Journal of Personality and Social Psychology* 4 (November 1966): 487–96; Carolyn K. Staats and Arthur W. Staats, "Meaning Established by Classical Conditioning," *Journal of Experimental Psychology* 54 (July 1957): 74–80.
12. Herbert Krugman, "Low Recall and High Recognition of Advertising," *Journal of Advertising Research* (February/March 1986): 79–86.
13. Gerald J. Gorn, "The Effects of Music in Advertising on Choice Behavior: A Classical Conditioning Approach," *Journal of Marketing* 46 (Winter 1982): 94–101.
14. Calvin Bierley, Frances K. McSweeney, and Renee Vannieuwkerk, "Classical Conditioning of Preferences for Stimuli," *Journal of Consumer Research* 12 (December 1985): 316–23; James J. Kellaris and Anthony D. Cox, "The Effects of Background Music in Advertising: A Reassessment," *Journal of Consumer Research* 16 (June 1989): 113–18.
15. Frances K. McSweeney and Calvin Bierley, "Recent Developments in Classical Conditioning," *Journal of Consumer Research* 11 (September 1984): 619–31.
16. Basil G. Englis, "The Reinforcement Properties of Music Videos: 'I Want My . . . I Want My . . . I Want My . . . MTV,'" (paper presented at the meetings of the Association for Consumer Research, New Orleans, 1989).
17. "Giving Bad Puns the Business," *Newsweek* (December 11, 1989): 71.
18. Bernice Kanner, "Growing Pains—and Gains: Brand Names Branch Out," *New York* (March 13, 1989):22.
19. Peter H. Farquhar, "Brand Equity," *Marketing Insights* (Summer, 1989): 59.
20. Beth Sherman, "Coca-Cola Finds Murjani Clothes Are It," *Advertising Age* (June 9, 1986): S-4.
21. Kanner, "Growing Pains."
22. Farquhar, "Brand Equity."

23. Quoted in "Look-Alikes Mimic Familiar Packages," *New York Times* (August 9, 1986):D1.
24. Blaise J. Bergiel and Christine Trosclair, "Instrumental Learning: Its Application to Customer Satisfaction," *Journal of Consumer Marketing* 2 (Fall 1985): 23–28.
25. Lisa Towle, "What's New in Frequency Marketing," *New York Times* (December 3, 1989): F13.
26. Bandura, *Social Foundations of Thought and Action.*
27. Terence A. Shimp, "New-Pavlovian Conditioning and Its Implications for Consumer Theory and Research," in *Handbook of Consumer Behavior,* ed. Thomas S. Robertson and Harold H. Kassarjian, (Englewood Cliffs, N.J.: Prentice-Hall, 1991).
28. James R. Bettman, "Memory Factors in Consumer Choice: A Review," *Journal of Marketing* (Spring 1979): 37–53.
29. R.C. Atkinson and R. M. Shiffrin, "Human Memory: A Proposed System and Its Control Processes," in *The Psychology of Learning and Motivation: Advances in Research and Theory,* ed. K. W. Spence and J.T. Spence (New York: Academic Press, 1968) 2: 89–195.
30. Kim Robertson, "Recall and Recognition Effects of Brand Name Imagery," *Psychology & Marketing* 4 (Spring 1987): 3–15.
31. Endel Tulving, "Remembering and Knowing the Past," *American Scientist* 77 (July/August 1989): 361.
32. Baron, *Psychology.*
33. Goerge A. Miller, "The Magical Number Seven, Plus or Minus Two: Some Limits on Our Capacity for Processing Information," *Psychological Review* 63, (1956): 81–97.
34. James N. MacGregor, "Short-Term Memory Capacity: Limitation or Optimization?" *Psychological Review* 94 (1987): 107–8.
35. See Catherine A. Cole and Michael J. Houston, "Encoding and Media Effects on Consumer Learning Deficiencies in the Elderly," *Journal of Marketing Research* 24 (February 1987): 55–64; A. M. Collins and E. F. Loftus, "A Spreading Activation Theory of Semantic Processing," *Psychological Review* 82 (1975): 407–28; Fergus I. M. Craik and Robert S. Lockhart, "Levels of Processing: A Framework for Memory Research," *Journal of Verbal Learning and Verbal Behavior* 11 (1972): 671–84.
36. Walter A. Henry, "The Effect of Information-Processing Ability on Processing Accuracy," *Journal of Consumer Research* 7 (June 1980): 42–48.
37. Anthony G. Greenwald and Clark Leavitt, "Audience Involvement in Advertising: Four Levels," *Journal of Consumer Research* 11 (June 1984): 581–92.
38. Kevin Lane Keller, "Memory Factors in Advertising: The Effect of Advertising Retrieval Cues on Brand Evaluations," *Journal of Consumer Research* 14 (December 1987): 316–33. For a discussion of processing operations that occur during brand choice, see Gabriel Biehal and Dipankar Chakravarti, "Consumers Use of Memory and External Information in Choice: Macro and Micro Perspectives," *Journal of Consumer Research* 12 (March 1986): 382–405.
39. Susan T. Fiske and Shelley E. Taylor, *Social Cognition* (Reading, Mass.: Addison-Wesley, 1984).
40. Deborah Roedder John and John C. Whitney, Jr., "The Development of Consumer Knowledge in Children: A Cognitive Structure Approach," *Journal of Consumer Research* 12 (March 1986): 406–17.
41. Michael R. Solomon, Carol Surprenant, John A. Czepiel, and Evelyn G. Gutman, "A Role Theory Perspective on Dyadic Interactions: The Service Encounter," *Journal of Marketing* 49 (Winter 1985): 99–111.
42. Jacob Jacoby and Wayne D. Hoyer, "The Comprehension-Miscomprehension of Print Communication: Selected Findings," *Journal of Consumer Research* 15 (March 1989): 434–44.
43. Gary J. Gaeth and Timothy B. Heath, "The Cognitive Processing of Misleading Advertising in Young and Old Adults," *Journal of Consumer Research* 14 (June 1987): 43–54.
44. Roger W. Morrell, Denise C. Park, and Leonard W. Poon, "Quality of Instructions on Prescription Drug Labels: Effects on Memory and Comprehension in Young and Old Adults," *The Gerontologist* 29 (1989): 345–54.
45. Herbert E. Krugman, "Low Recall and High Recognition of Advertising," *Journal of Advertising Research* (February/March 1986): 79–86.

46. Baron, *Psychology.*
47. Keller, "Memory Factors in Advertising."
48. Eric J. Johnson and J. Edward Russo, "Product Familiarity and Learning New Information," *Journal of Consumer Research* 11 (June 1984): 542–50.
49. Eric J. Johnson and J. Edward Russo, "Product Familiarity and Learning New Information," in *Advances in Consumer Research,* ed. Kent Monroe (Ann Arbor, Mich.: Association for Consumer Research, 1981)8: 151–55; John G. Lynch and Thomas K. Srull, "Memory and Attentional Factors in Consumer Choice: Concepts and Research Methods," *Journal of Consumer Research* 9 (June 1982): 18–37.
50. Julie A. Edell and Kevin Lane Keller, "The Information Processing of Coordinated Media Campaigns," *Journal of Marketing Research* 26 (May 1989) 26: 149–64.
51. Lynch and Srull, "Memory and Attentional Factors in Consumer Choice."
52. Joseph W. Alba and Amitara Chattopadhyay, "Salience Effects in Brand Recall," *Journal of Marketing Research* 23 (November 1986): 363–70.
53. Elizabeth C. Hirschman and Michael R. Solomon, "Utilitarian, Aesthetic, and Familiarity Responses to Verbal Versus Visual Advertisements," in *Advances in Consumer Research,* ed. Thomas C. Kinnear (Provo, Utah: Association for Consumer Research, 1984):11 426–31.
54. Terry Childers and Michael Houston, "Conditions for a Picture-Superiority Effect on Consumer Memory," *Journal of Consumer Research* 11 (September 1984): 643–54; Terry Childers, Susan Heckler, and Michael Houston, "Memory for the Visual and Verbal Components of Print Advertisements," *Psychology & Marketing* 3 (Fall 1986): 147–50.
55. Werner Krober-Riel, "Effects of Emotional Pictorial Elements in Ads Analyzed by Means of Eye Movement Monitoring," in *Advances in Consumer Research,* ed. Thomas C. Kinnear (Provo, Utah: Association for Consumer Research, 1984)11: 591–96.
56. Hans-Bernd Brosius, "Influence of Presentation Features and News Context on Learning from Television News," *Journal of Broadcasting & Electronic Media* 33 (Winter 1989): 1–14.
57. Charles E. Young and Michael Robinson, "Video Rhythms and Recall," *Journal of Advertising Research* (June/July 1989): 22–25.
58. Raymond R. Burke and Thomas K. Srull, "Competitive Interference and Consumer Memory for Advertising," *Journal of Consumer Research* 15 (June 1988): 55–68.
59. Burke and Srull, "Competitive Interference and Consumer Memory for Advertising."
60. Johnson and Russo, "Product Familiarity and Learning New Information."
61. Joan Meyers-Levy, "The Influence of Brand Name's Association Set Size and Word Frequency on Brand Memory," *Journal of Consumer Research* 16 (September 1989): 197–208.
62. Michael H. Baumgardner, Michael R. Leippe, David L. Ronis, and Anthony G. Greenwald, "In Search of Reliable Persuasion Effects: II. Associative Interference and Persistence of Persuasion in a Message-Dense Environment," *Journal of Personality and Social Psychology* 45 (September 1983): 524–37.
63. Joseph W. Alba and Amitara Chattopadhyay, "Salience Effects in Brand Recall," *Journal of Marketing Research* 23 (November 1986), 363–69.
64. Margaret Henderson Blair, Allan R. Kuse, David H. Furse, and David W. Stewart, "Advertising in a New and Competitive Environment: Persuading Consumers to Buy," *Business Horizons* 30 (November/December 1987): 20.
65. Lynch and Srull, "Memory and Attentional Factors in Consumer Choice."
66. Russell W. Belk, "Possessions and the Extended Self," *Journal of Consumer Research* 15 (September 1988): 139–68.
67. Russell W. Belk, "The Role of Possessions in Constructing and Maintaining a Sense of Past," in *Advances in Consumer Research,* ed. Marvin E. Goldberg, Gerald Gorn, and Richard W. Pollay (Provo, Utah: Association for Consumer Research, 1989)17: 669–78.
68. Marcus Mabry, "Rememberance of Ads Past," *Newsweek* (July 30, 1990): 42.
69. Alan Salomon, "Nostalgia's Free at Golden Arch," *Advertising Age* (September 10, 1990):28.
70. "The Selling of the Pope, American Style," *Newsweek* (June 29, 1987): 48.
71. "Only 38% of T.V. Audience Links Brands with Ads," *Marketing News* (January 6, 1984): 10.

72. "Terminal Television," *American Demographics* (January 1987), 15.

73. Richard P. Bagozzi and Alvin J. Silk, "Recall, Recognition, and the Measurement of Memory for Print Advertisements," *Marketing Science* (1983)2: 95–134.

74. Adam Finn, "Print Ad Recognition Readership Scores: An Information Processing Perspective," *Journal of Marketing Research* 25 (May 1988): 168–77.

75. Bettman, "Memory Factors in Consumer Choice."

76. Mark A. deTurck and Gerald M. Goldhaber, "Effectiveness of Product Warning Labels: Effects of Consumers' Information Processing Objectives," *Journal of Consumer Affairs* 23 (1989)1: 111–25.

77. Finn, "Print Ad Recognition Readership Scores."

78. Surendra N. Singh and Gilbert A. Churchill, Jr., "Response-Bias-Free Recognition Tests to Measure Advertising Effects," *Journal of Advertising Research* (June/July 1987): 23–36.

79. William A. Cook, "Telescoping and Memory's Other Tricks," *Journal of Advertising Research* 27 (February/March 1987): 5–8.

80. "On a Diet? Don't Trust Your Memory," *Psychology Today* (October 1989), 12.

81. Hubert A. Zielske and Walter A. Henry, "Remembering and Forgetting Television Ads," *Journal of Advertising Research* 20 (April 1980): 7–13.

Attitudes

C HAPTER 5

Rocco, a racing veteran, takes two friends with him to the track one Saturday. Rocco immediately buys the *Racing Form* and evaluates the records of all the horses entered in the race. He considers who sired each horse, the jockey "up" on each, how they have performed on wet versus dry tracks, and so on. After weighing all this information, Rocco decides on a horse he likes (number seven) and places a bet on the first race.

Eric views the excursion as a good excuse not to study, but he is not terribly interested in horseracing. He notices that Rocco's pick happens to be his lucky number, and that's good enough for him. Naturally, when number seven wins, he becomes a big fan of the horse.

Robert is very excited to be at the track because he has always loved horses. As the horses are being led out to the starting gate, his attention is caught by one particularly striking filly named "Pride 'N Joy." He likes this name, and the horse reminds him of one he used to ride as a child. She is a beautiful shade of brown, with graceful lines, and just a bit headstrong. Without any further thought, Robert runs to place his bet on "Pride 'N Joy." After the race is over (and "Pride 'N Joy" has lost), Robert figures that her free spirit was too much for the jockey to handle.

THE CONTENTS OF ATTITUDES

Each of the three individuals described above has an attitude about horse racing in general and one horse in particular, even though these attitudes were formed in quite different ways. An attitude is one of the most important concepts in consumer behavior because it affects everything from profound political issues to the brand of bubble gum we buy or how we feel about leisure activities like horse racing.

The term *attitude* is widely used in popular culture. You might be asked, "What is your attitude toward abortion?" A parent might scold, "Young man, I don't like your attitude." Some bars even euphemistically refer to Happy Hour as "an attitude adjustment period."

Consumer researchers use the term a bit differently. Simply put, an **attitude** is a lasting, general evaluation of people (including oneself), objects, or issues.[1] Anything toward which one has an attitude, whether it is tangible such as bubble gum, or intangible as democracy, is called an **attitude object** (or A_o).

An attitude is lasting because it tends to endure over time. It is general because it applies to more than a momentary event like hearing a loud noise, though you might over time develop a negative attitude toward all loud noises. Consumers have attitudes toward very product-specific behaviors (e.g., using Crest toothpaste rather than Colgate) as well as toward more general consumption-related behaviors (e.g, how often one should brush one's teeth). Attitudes help to determine who a person chooses to date, what music he or she listens to, whether he or she will recycle or discard aluminum cans, or whether he or she chooses to become a market researcher for a living.

THE ABC MODEL OF ATTITUDES

Most researchers agree that an attitude has three components: affect, behavior, and cognition. **Affect** refers to the way a consumer feels about an attitude object. **Behavior** involves the person's intentions to *do* something with regard to an attitude object (but, as will be discussed at a later point, an intention does not always result in an actual behavior). **Cognition** refers to the *beliefs* a consumer has about an attitude object.

These three components of an attitude can be remembered as the ABC model of attitudes. This model emphasizes the interrelationships among feeling, knowing, and doing. For example, we cannot necessarily discern consumers' attitudes toward a product just by identifying their beliefs about it. They may "know" that a Magnavox Camcorder has an 8:1 power zoom lens, auto-focus, and a flying erase head, but we do not know if they consider these attributes to be good, bad, or irrelevant. We also would like to find out if, given the right opportunity and circumstances, they would be disposed to buy the Camcorder.

HIERARCHIES OF EFFECTS

While all three components of an attitude are important, their relative importance will vary depending upon a consumer's level of motivation with regard to the attitude object. The differences among the three friends at the track illustrate how these elements can be combined in different ways to create an attitude. Attitude researchers have developed the concept of a **hierarchy of effects** to explain the relative impact of the three components. Each hierarchy specifies that a fixed sequence of steps occurs en route to an attitude. Three different hierarchies are summarized in Figure 5-1.

THE STANDARD LEARNING HIERARCHY   Rocco's approach to betting on horses closely resembles the process by which most attitudes have been assumed to be constructed. A consumer approaches a product decision as a problem-solving process. First, he or she forms beliefs about a product by accumulating knowledge (beliefs) regarding relevant attributes (as Rocco did when he carefully studied the *Racing Form)*. Next, the consumer evaluates these beliefs and forms a feeling about the product (affect). Rocco integrated the information about the competing alternatives and formed a preference for one horse. Finally, based on this evaluation, the consumer engages in a relevant behavior, such as buying the product, avoiding it, or in this case placing a bet on it.

This hierarchy assumes that a consumer is highly *involved* in making a purchase decision.[2] The person is motivated to seek out a lot of information, carefully weigh alternatives, and come to a thoughtful decision. This process is likely to occur if the decision is important to the consumer or in some way central to the consumer's self-concept. Rocco's winnings are very important to him. His betting performance helps to determine how well he will eat in the following week, and his success at "picking the ponies" is an important part of his self-concept. The learning of an attitude is thus likely to be the result of a complex process of cognitive learning.

Figure 5-1 Three Hierarchies of Effects

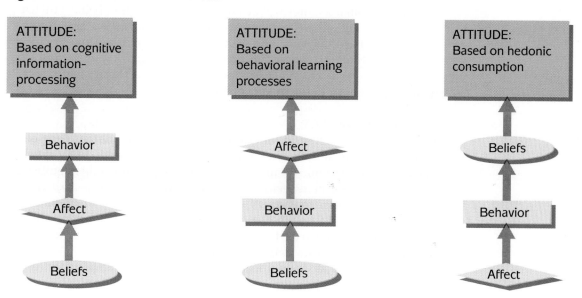

THE LOW INVOLVEMENT HIERARCHY In sharp contrast to Rocco, Eric's interest in the attitude object (horse racing) is at best lukewarm. He collects only a minimal amount of information before acting and has an emotional response only after the race is over. Eric is typical of a consumer who forms an attitude via the *low-involvement hierarchy of effects.* In this sequence, the consumer initially does not have a strong preference for one brand over another. He or she acts on the basis of limited knowledge about the product, and forms an evaluation of it only after the fact.[3] The attitude is likely to come about through behavioral learning, where the consumer's choice is reinforced by good or bad experiences with the product after purchase.

The possibility that consumers simply don't care enough about many decisions to carefully assemble a set of product beliefs and then evaluate them is important, because it implies that all of the concern about influencing beliefs and carefully communicating information about product attributes may largely be a wasted effort. Consumers aren't necessarily going to pay attention anyway. Instead, they are more likely to respond to simple stimulus-response connections when making purchase decisions. For example, a consumer choosing among paper towels might remember that "Bounty is the quicker picker-upper" rather than bothering to systematically compare all of the brands on the grocery shelf.

Managers' Views on Low Involvement. This notion is a bitter pill for some managers to swallow. Who wants to admit that what they market is not very important or involving? A brand manager for, say, a brand of bubble gum or cat food may find it hard to believe that consumers don't put that much thought into purchasing her product since *she* spends many of her waking (and perhaps sleeping) hours thinking about it. This difference in perspective is nicely illustrated in the restaurant ad shown here.

However, future brand managers can cheer up because there is an ironic silver lining to this low-involvement cloud. Under these conditions, consumers are not motivated to process a lot of complex brand-related information. Instead, they will be swayed by principles of behavioral learning, such as the simple responses caused by conditioned brand names, point-of-purchase displays, and so on. The *less* important the product to consumers, the *more* important are many of the marketing stimuli (e.g., packages, jingles) that must be devised to sell it. These factors will be explored at length in the next chapter.

ATTITUDE AS AFFECT

Robert, the third bettor at the track, exemplifies still another perspective on attitudes. His attitude was based on his "gut reaction" to a particular horse. Researchers in recent years have begun to stress the significance of affect as a central aspect of an attitude. According to the *experiential hierarchy of effects,* consumers act on the basis of their emotional reactions to products. Though the factors of beliefs and behavior still are recognized as playing a part, a consumer's overall evaluation of an attitude object is considered by many to be the core of an attitude.

The centrality of visceral feelings to an attitude is emphasized by the *Sports Illustrated* ad shown on page 138. This perspective highlights the

Steak is our life.
All we ask is that you
make it your lunch.

Smith & Wollensky.
The quintessential New York City steakhouse.
49th St. & 3rd Ave. (212) 753-1530.

Winner of The *Wine Spectator's* 1987 Grand Award.

idea that attitudes can be strongly influenced by intangible product attributes, such as package design, and by consumers' reactions toward accompanying stimuli, such as advertising and even the brand name. As discussed in Chapter 3, resulting attitudes will be affected by consumers' hedonic motivations, such as how the product makes them feel or the fun its use will provide.

ARE FEELINGS AND BELIEFS INDEPENDENT? One important debate about the experiential hierarchy concerns the *independence* of cognition and affect. On the one hand, the *cognitive-affective model* argues that an affective judgment is but the last step in a series of cognitive processes. Earlier steps include the sensory registration of stimuli and the retrieval of meaningful information from memory to categorize these stimuli.[4]

The *independence hypothesis* takes the position that affect and cognition involve two separate, partially independent systems; affective responses do

It's cold. You're hurting.
And three rookies
will kill for your job.

How does it feel?

Sports Illustrated

Get the feeling.

Sports Illustrated's emphasis on feelings underscores the importance of affect in forming attitudes. John Iacono/ Sports Illustrated.

not always require prior cognitions.[5] A number one song on the Billboard Top 40 may possess the same attributes as many other songs (e.g., dominant bass guitar, raspy vocals, persistent downbeat), but beliefs about these attributes cannot explain why one song will become a classic while another sharing the same characteristics will wind up in the bargain bin at the local record store.

The independence hypothesis does not *eliminate* the role of cognition in experience. It simply balances this traditional, rational emphasis on calculated decision making by paying more attention to the impact of aesthetic, subjective experience. This type of holistic processing is more likely to occur when the product is perceived as primarily expressive or delivers sensory pleasure rather than utilitarian benefits.[6]

ATTITUDE TOWARD THE ADVERTISEMENT Consumers' affective reactions to a product are influenced by their evaluations of its advertising, over and above their feelings about the product itself. **A$_{ad}$ (attitude toward the advertisement)** is defined as a predisposition to respond in a favorable or unfavorable manner to a particular advertising stimulus during a particular exposure occasion. Determinants of A$_{ad}$ include attitude toward the advertiser, evaluations of the ad execution itself, the mood evoked by the ad, or the degree to which the ad affects viewers' arousal levels.[7] The effects demonstrated by A$_{ad}$ emphasize the importance of an ad's entertainment value on the purchase process—creative advertising is usually also effective advertising.

Feelings Elicited by Advertising. The feelings generated by an ad have the capacity to directly affect brand attitudes. Commercials can evoke a wide range of emotional responses, from disgust to happiness, as illustrated in the ad for an egg substitute shown here. These reactions can in turn influence memory for advertising content.[8] At least three

This ad for EggStrodinaire, an egg substitute, illustrates that ads are capable of communicating negative feelings. Courtesy of Food Service Division, Sandoz Nutrition, Minneapolis, MN 55416.

Until now, your customers have had some definite opinions about healthier eggs.

Introducing EggStro'dnaire. EggStro'dnaire is an incredible alternative to shell eggs that will definitely increase your sales. And revolutionize your breakfast menu. All because they taste exactly like shell eggs. And not like egg substitutes.

EggStro'dnaire will sell. And not just to people with health concerns. But to anyone who likes eggs. And we can prove it.

In numerous scientific taste panels, blind taste tests with executive hotel chefs and restaurant menu tests, EggStro'dnaire's taste, texture and appearance proved to be indistinguishable from shell eggs.

Which isn't surprising since EggStro'dnaire is 98% real egg and 100% natural. With 78% less cholesterol, 67% less fat and 50% fewer calories than shell eggs. There are no artificial ingredients or preservatives. So they taste like the real McCoy.

And they're very convenient. EggStro'dnaire is available frozen in twelve, 16-oz. or six, 5-lb. cartons. Just thaw and use in any egg recipe.

For more information, talk to your distributor sales representative. Find out how EggStro'dnaire can definitely become your bread and butter.

EggStro'dnaire
The healthy egg alternative.

Food Service
SANDOZNUTRITION

© 1989 Sandoz Nutrition

emotional dimensions have been identified in commercials: pleasure, arousal, and intimidation.[9] Specific types of feelings that can be generated by an ad include:[10]

- upbeat feelings (e.g., amused, delighted, playful)
- warm feelings (e.g., affectionate, contemplative, hopeful)
- negative feelings (e.g., critical, defiant, offended)

MARKETING PITFALL

In a study of *irritating advertising*, researchers examined over 500 prime time network commercials that had registered negative reactions by consumers. The most irritating commercials were for feminine hygiene products, hemorrhoid medication or laxatives, and women's underwear. The researchers identified these factors as contributors to irritation:[11]

- A sensitive product is shown, (e.g., hemorrhoid medicine) and its use or package is emphasized.
- The situation is contrived or overdramatized.
- A person is "put down" in terms of appearance, knowledge, or sophistication.
- An important relationship is threatened (e.g., a marriage).
- There is a graphic demonstration of physical discomfort.
- Uncomfortable tension is created by an argument or by an antagonistic character.
- An unattractive or unsympathetic character is portrayed.
- A sexually suggestive scene is included.
- The commercial suffers from poor casting or execution.

FORMING ATTITUDES

Everyone has lots of attitudes, and we don't usually question how we got them. Certainly, a person isn't born with the conviction that, say, Pepsi is better than Coke, or that heavy metal music liberates the soul. Where do these attitudes come from?

As noted earlier, an attitude can form in several different ways, depending upon the particular hierarchy of effects in operation. It can occur because of classical conditioning, where an attitude object such as the Pepsi name is repeatedly paired with a catchy jingle ("You're in the Pepsi Generation . . ."). Or, it can occur through instrumental conditioning, where consumption of the attitude object is reinforced (e.g., Pepsi quenches one's thirst). Or the learning of an attitude can be the outcome of a very complex cognitive process. For example, a teenager may come to model the behavior of friends and media figures who drink Pepsi because she believes that this act will allow her to fit in with the desirable images of the Pepsi Generation.

It is thus important to distinguish among types of attitudes, since not all of are formed the same way.[12] For example, a highly brand loyal consumer has an enduring, deeply held positive attitude toward an attitude object, and this involvement will be difficult to weaken. On the other hand, another consumer may have a mildly positive attitude toward the same brand but be quite willing to abandon it when the winds of fashion shift. Consumers vary in their degree of *commitment* to an attitude, which is related to their level of involvement with the attitude object.[13]

LEVELS OF COMMITMENT TO AN ATTITUDE

COMPLIANCE   At the lowest level of involvement, *compliance,* an attitude is formed because it helps in gaining rewards or avoiding punishments from others. This is a very superficial attitude; it is likely to change when the person's behavior is no longer monitored by others or when another option becomes available. A person may drink Pepsi because this brand is sold in the cafeteria, and it is too much trouble to go elsewhere for a Coca-Cola.

IDENTIFICATION   A process of *identification* occurs when attitudes are formed in order to be similar to another person or group. Advertising that depicts the social consequences of choosing some products over others is relying on the tendency of consumers to imitate the behavior of desirable models.

INTERNALIZATION   At a high level of involvement, deep-seated attitudes are internalized and become part of the person's value system (see Chapter 15). These attitudes are very difficult to change because they are so important to the individual. For example, many consumers had strong attitudes toward Coca-Cola and reacted quite negatively when the company attempted to switch to the New Coke formula. This allegiance to Coke was obviously more than a minor preference for these people; the brand had become intertwined with their social identities, taking on patriotic and nostalgic properties.

CONSISTENCY SHAPES ATTITUDES

Have you ever heard someone say, "Pepsi is my favorite soft drink. It tastes terrible," or "I love my husband. He's the biggest idiot I've ever met"? Probably not too often, because these beliefs or evaluations are not consistent with one another. According to the **principle of cognitive consistency,** consumers value *harmony* among their thoughts, feelings, and behaviors, and they are motivated to maintain uniformity among these elements. This desire means that, if necessary, consumers will *change* their thoughts, feelings, or behaviors to make them consistent with their other experiences. The consistency principle is an important reminder that attitudes are not formed in a vacuum. An important determinant of the way an attitude object will be evaluated is how it fits with other, related attitudes already held by the consumer.

CONSISTENCY AND FREEDOM OF CHOICE   Attitude theories based on the consistency principle assume that consumers are motivated to seek agreement between behaviors and attitudes. Note, however, that these processes primarily operate when the person believes that he or she performed the behavior voluntarily. If not, there is no need for attitudes to fall in line with the behavior.

Reactance theory states that people value their freedom to choose.[14] When they feel they are being deprived of this freedom, the option being prohibited gains in attractiveness. A study on consumer perceptions of phosphate detergents demonstrates this effect. After phosphates were banned in Miami, the attitudes of Miami residents were compared to people living in Tampa (where the products were still allowed). Miami respondents thought phosphates were more effective, presumably because they were deprived of the chance to use them.[15] Another study found that soda ads that put limits on the quantities consumers could buy increased the attractiveness of the brand.[16]

COGNITIVE DISSONANCE THEORY   Cognitive dissonance theory is one of the most influential approaches to attitudes based upon the consistency principle.[17] Dissonance in music refers to harsh sounds that are grating or somehow do not belong together. This word has a similar meaning in the present context; it is intended to describe a feeling of discomfort experienced by people when things do not go together.

Cognitive dissonance theory proposes that, much like hunger or thirst, people are motivated to reduce this negative state by making things fit with one another. The theory focuses on situations where two *cognitive elements* are inconsistent with one another. A cognitive element can be something a person believes about himself, a behavior he performs, or an observation about his surroundings. For example, the two cognitive elements "Smoking cigarettes causes cancer" and "I smoke cigarettes" are *dissonant* with one another. This logical inconsistency creates a feeling of discomfort that the smoker is motivated to reduce. The magnitude of dissonance depends upon both the importance and number of dissonant elements.[18] In other words, the pressure to reduce dissonance is more likely to be observed in high involvement situations, where the elements are more important to the individual.

Dissonance reduction can occur either by eliminating, adding, or changing elements. For example, the person could stop smoking (elimination), or remember great-aunt Sophie, who smoked until the day she died at age ninety (adding). Alternatively, he might question the research that links cancer and smoking (changing), perhaps by believing industry-sponsored studies that try to refute this connection.

Post-Purchase Dissonance.   One application of dissonance theory is that evaluations of a product tend to increase *after* it has been purchased. The cognitive element "I made a stupid decision" is dissonant with the element "I am not a stupid person" so people tend to find even more reasons to like something after it becomes theirs.

Apropos of Rocco and his friends at the track, a field study performed at a horse race demonstrated post-purchase dissonance. Bettors evaluated their chosen horse more highly and were more confident of its success *after* they had placed a bet than before. Since the bettor is financially committed to the choice, he or she reduces dissonance by increasing the attractiveness of the chosen alternative relative to the unchosen ones.[19] One implication of this phenomenon is that consumers actively seek support for their purchase decisions, so marketers should supply them with additional reinforcement to build positive brand attitudes.

SELF-PERCEPTION THEORY   Do attitudes necessarily change following behavior because people are motivated to feel good about their decisions? **Self-perception theory** provides an alternative explanation of dissonance effects.[20] It assumes that people use observations of their own behavior to infer their attitudes. The theory states that we maintain consistency by inferring that we must have a positive attitude toward an object if we have bought or consumed it (assuming that we freely made this choice). In other words, "I guess I must like this brand of beer. I seem to order it a lot."

Self-perception theory is relevant to the *low-involvement hierarchy,* since it involves situations where behaviors are initially performed in the absence of a strong internal attitude. After the fact, the cognitive and affective components of attitude fall into line. Thus, buying a product out of habit may result in a positive attitude toward it *after the fact*—why would I buy it if I didn't like it?

The Foot-in-the-Door Technique.   Self-perception theory helps to explain the effectiveness of a sales strategy called the foot-in-the-door technique, which is based on the observation that a consumer is more likely to comply with a request if he or she has first agreed to comply with a smaller request.[21] The term comes from the practice of door-to-door selling, where salespeople were taught to plant their foot in a door so the prospect could not slam it on them. A good salesperson knows that he or she is more likely to get an order if the customer can be persuaded to open the door and talk. By agreeing to do this, the customer has established that she or he is willing to listen to the salesperson. Placing an order is consistent with this self-perception. This technique is especially useful for inducing consumers to answer surveys or to donate money to charity. Such factors as the time lag between the first and second request, the similarity between the two requests, and whether the same person makes both requests have been found to influence its effectiveness.[22]

SOCIAL JUDGMENT THEORY   **Social judgment theory** also assumes that people assimilate new information about attitude objects in light of what they already know or feel.[23] The initial attitude acts as a *frame of reference,* and new information is categorized in terms of this existing standard. Just as our decision that a box is heavy depends in part on other boxes we have lifted, we develop a subjective standard when making judgments about attitude objects.

Latitudes of Acceptance and Rejection.   One important aspect of the theory is the notion that people differ in terms of the information they will find acceptable or unacceptable. They form *latitudes of acceptance and rejection* around an attitude standard. Ideas that fall within a latitude will be favorably received, while those falling outside of this zone will not. If a woman has a favorable attitude toward wearing furs, she will be likely to be receptive to communications defending the right to do so. If she is opposed to this practice, these messages will probably not be considered.

Assimilation and Contrast. Messages that fall within the latitude of acceptance tend to be seen as *more* consistent with one's position than they actually are. This is called an *assimilation effect.* On the other hand, messages falling in the latitude of rejection tend to be seen as even farther from one's position than they actually are, resulting in a *contrast effect.*

As a person becomes more involved with an attitude object, his or her latitude of acceptance gets smaller. In other words, the consumer accepts fewer ideas that are removed from his or her own position and tends to oppose even mildly divergent positions. This tendency is evident in ads that appeal to discriminating buyers, which claim that knowledgeable people will reject anything but the very best (e.g., "choosy mothers choose Jif"). On the other hand, relatively uninvolved consumers will consider a wider range of alternatives. They are less likely to be brand loyal and will be more likely to be brand switchers.[24]

BALANCE THEORY **Balance theory,** developed by psychologist Fritz Heider, considers relations among *elements* a person might perceive as belonging together.[25] Much of Heider's work involved relations (always from the perceiver's subjective point of view) of three elements, so the resulting attitude structures are called *triads.* Each triad contains: (1) a person and his or her perceptions of, (2) an attitude object, and (3) some other person or object. These perceptions can be either positive or negative. More important, people *alter* these perceptions in order to make relations among them consistent. The theory specifies that people desire relations among elements in a triad to be harmonious, or *balanced.* If they are not, a state of tension will result until somehow perceptions are changed and balance is restored.

In Heider's view, elements can be perceived as going together in one of two ways. They can have either (1) a *unit relation,* where one element is seen as somehow belonging to or being a part of the other (something like a belief) or (2) a *sentiment relation,* where the two elements are linked because one has expressed a preference (or dislike) for the other. A dating couple might be seen as having a positive sentiment relation. Upon getting married, they will have a positive unit relation. The process of divorce is an attempt to sever a unit relation.

To see how balance theory might work, consider the following scenario:

- Noreen would like to date Sal, who is in her Consumer Behavior class. In balance theory terms, Noreen has a positive sentiment relation with Sal.
- One day, Sal shows up in class wearing an earring. Sal has a positive unit relation with the earring. It belongs to him and is literally a part of him.

- Noreen does not like men who wear earrings. She has a negative sentiment relation with men's earrings.

According to balance theory, this is an unbalanced triad, so Noreen will experience pressure to restore balance by altering some aspect of the triad as shown in Figure 5-2. She could, for example, decide that she does not like Sal after all. Or, her liking for Sal could prompt a change in her attitude toward earrings. She might even try to negate the unit relation between Sal and the earring by deciding that he must be only wearing it as part of a fraternity initiation (thus reducing the free choice element). Finally, she could choose to "leave the field" by not thinking any more about Sal and his controversial earring.

Note that while the theory does not specify which of these routes will be taken, it does predict that one or more of Noreen's perceptions will probably change in order to achieve balance. While this is most likely an oversimplified representation of most attitude processes, it helps to explain a number of consumer behavior phenomena.

Applications of Balance Theory. Balance theory reminds us that when perceptions are balanced, attitudes are likely to be stable. On the other hand, when inconsistencies are observed, we are more likely to observe changes in attitudes. Balance theory also helps to explain why

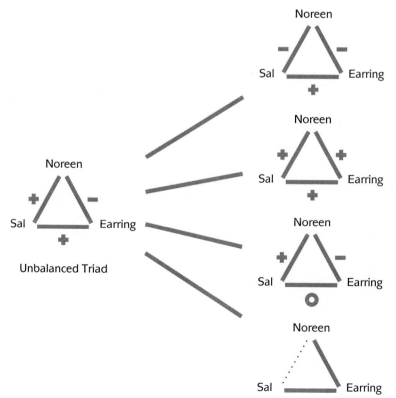

Figure 5-2 Alternative Routes to Restoring Balance in a Triad

consumers like to be associated with positively valued objects. Forming a unit relation with a popular product (e.g., buying and wearing fashionable clothing, driving a flashy car) may improve one's chances of being included as a positive sentiment relation in other people's triads.

Finally, balance theory is useful in accounting for the widespread use of celebrities to endorse products. In cases where a triad is not fully formed (e.g., perceptions about a new product or one about which the consumer does not yet have a well-defined attitude), the marketer can create a positive sentiment relation between the consumer and the product by depicting a positive unit relation between the product and a well-known personality. In other cases, behaviors are discouraged when admired people argue against them, as is the goal when athletes appear in anti-drug public service advertisements.

This balancing act is at the heart of celebrity endorsements, where it is hoped that the star's popularity will transfer to the product. This strategy will be considered at length in the next chapter. For now, it pays to remember that this creation of a unit relation between product and star can backfire if the public's opinion of the celebrity endorser shifts from positive to negative. This happened when Pepsi pulled an ad featuring Madonna after she was associated with a controversial music video involving religion and sex. The strategy can also cause trouble if the star-product unit relation is questioned. This happened when actress Cybill Shepherd, who did promotions for the beef industry, subsequently confessed that she herself did not eat red meat.

 MARKETING OPPORTUNITY

Consumers often like to publicize their connections with successful people or organizations (no matter how tenuous the connection) to enhance their own standing. In balance theory terms, they are attempting to create a unit relation with a positively valued attitude object. This a tactic that has been called "basking in reflected glory."[26]

A series of studies performed at Arizona State University showed how students' desire to identify with a winning image—in this case, ASU's football team—influenced their consumption behaviors. After the team played a game each weekend, observers went around campus and recorded the incidence of school-related items displayed by students (e.g., ASU T-shirts, caps, etc.). The frequency of these behaviors was related to the team's performance. If the team had won, students were more likely to show off their school affiliation (basking in reflected glory) than if the team had lost. This relationship was affected by the *magnitude* of the win—the bigger the point spread, the more likely were observers to note a sea of ASU insignias the following Monday.

Consumers' desires to bask in reflected glory by purchasing products associated with a valued attitude object create marketing opportunities. College bookstores reap over $400 million a year by selling items bearing their school's name and logo, and the total market for collegiate licensing amounts to about $750 million annually. The UCLA bookstore alone sells $5 million worth of Bruin items a year. Many schools now license their names (usually for a 6.5 percent royalty) to get a stake in this market. Because people tend to identify with successful teams, it is not surprising that the most successful licensing universities also happen to have renowned athletic programs, including: Michigan, Ohio State, Florida, Penn State, Texas, Kentucky, Alabama, Florida State, Indiana, and Washington.[27]

CONGRUITY THEORY **Congruity theory** is yet another consistency theory that, like balance theory, specifically addresses how attitudes are affected when a person is linked to an object.[28] Congruity theory can help to answer two questions regarding the effectiveness of this strategy. Assuming that we can measure the appeal (positive or negative) of an endorser and the favorability of a product:

1. How big a boost would a product get by being paired with the endorser?
2. How will the *endorser's* reputation be affected by his or her connection with the product?

Congruity theory predicts that the value of the more negatively valued element will rise (as a company would hope) when linked to a positively valued one such as a popular personality. In addition, though, the positively valued element will be affected: Its ratings will be *diminished* by its association with the first element. This implies that a person or organization that is linked to some other entity does so at some risk. This process helps to explain why some media outlets are careful to select advertisers whose images are congruent with their own. For example, the high-fashion magazine *Mirabella* denies space to such mass market products as Maybelline and Avon cosmetics and Jaclyn Smith clothes for K Mart. As its publisher explained, "We wanted to be perceived as a "department store" magazine. We're talking about Armani or Calvin Klein or Bulgari jewelry—not furnishing your home from Woolworth's."[29]

However, the two elements will not change equally: Change is inversely proportional to degree of *attitude polarization.* In plain English, this means that the more extremely related object will change its value *less* than will the more moderate one. To understand this, suppose that an extremely negative source (say, Saddam Hussein of Iraq) stated publicly that *Penthouse* (rated somewhat positively) was his favorite magazine. The image of *Penthouse* would drop to a greater degree than that of Hussein would rise. The attitude polarization process is depicted in Figure 5-3.

Congruity theory was used to investigate the impact of brand and retailer images on perceptions of quality. One catalyst for this study was the decision by the designer Halston (who had a very upscale image) to create a clothing line for J. C. Penney (a more downscale image). This study found that, consistent with congruity theory predictions, arrangements between stores and brands should be entered into carefully. While a store or brand can boost its image by associating itself with a more prestigious entity, this may happen at the expense of the other party.[30]

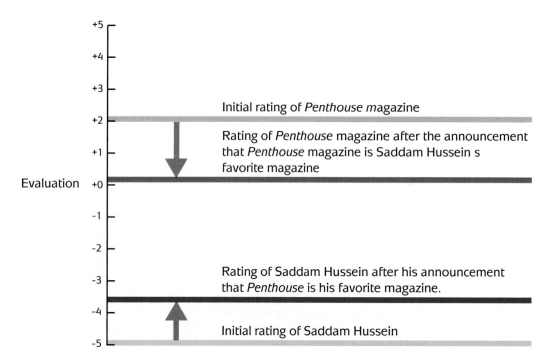

The graph's y-axis is labeled "Evaluation" with markings from +5 down to -5.

- At +2: Initial rating of *Penthouse* magazine
- At +1 to +0: Rating of *Penthouse* magazine after the announcement that *Penthouse* magazine is Saddam Hussein s favorite magazine
- At -3: Rating of Saddam Hussein after his announcement that *Penthouse* is his favorite magazine.
- At -4 to -5: Initial rating of Saddam Hussein

Figure 5-3 A Hypothetical Example of Congruity Theory: A Model of Attitude Polarization

ATTITUDE MODELS

As noted earlier, a consumer's overall evaluation of a product appears to account for the bulk of his or her attitude. When market researchers want to assess attitudes, it is sometimes sufficient for them to simply ask consumers "How do you feel about Budweiser?" or "How satisfied are you with your grocery store?"

ATTITUDE MEASUREMENT TECHNIQUES

Suppose a supermarket chain wanted to measure shoppers' attitudes toward its stores. The firm might administer one of the following types of attitude scales to consumers by mail, phone, or in person (see Chapter 1):[31]

- Single-item scales: For example

  How satisfied are you with your grocery store?

Very satisfied	Satisfied	Somewhat satisfied	Not at all satisfied

- Multiple-item batteries: Many attitude measures assess a set of beliefs about an issue and combine these reactions into an overall score. Two of the most widely used are:

Likert scale:

1. My grocery store has a good selection of produce.

2. My grocery maintains sanitary conditions.
4. I never have trouble finding exotic foods at my grocery store.

| Agree strongly | Agree somewhat | Neither agree nor disagree | Disagree somewhat | Disagree strongly |

Semantic-differential scale:

This type of scale is useful for a describing a person's set of beliefs about a company or brand, and it is also used to compare the images of competing brands. Respondents rate each attribute on a series of rating scales, where each end is anchored by adjectives or phrases, such as:
My grocery store has:

Poor selection   1——2——3——4——5——6——7   Good selection

Semantic-differential scales can be used to construct a *profile analysis* of the competition, where the images of several stores or products can be visually compared by plotting the mean ratings for each object on several attributes of interest. This simple technique can help to pinpoint areas where the product or store diverges sharply from the competitors (in either a positive or a negative way). The fictitious profiles of three different types of grocery stores are shown in Figure 5-4. Based on these findings, the management of the supermarket chain might want to emphasize its low prices and/or try to improve its stores' selection and cleanliness.

Figure 5-4 Hypothetical Profiles of Three Types of Food Stores

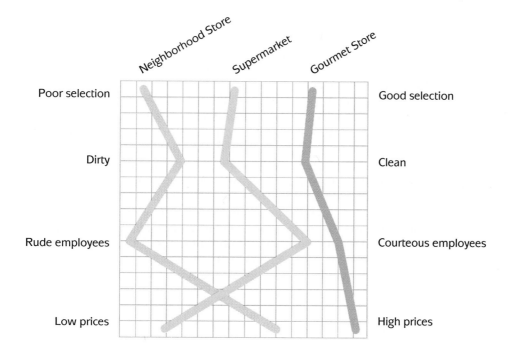

MULTI-ATTRIBUTE ATTITUDE MODELS

A simple response does not always tell us everything we need to know about either *why* the consumer feels a certain way toward a product or about *what* marketers can do to change the consumer's attitude. For this reason, **multi-attribute attitude models** have been extremely popular among marketing researchers. This type of model assumes that a consumer's attitude (evaluation) of an attitude object will depend on the beliefs he or she has about several or many attributes of the object. The use of a multi-attribute model implies that an attitude toward a product or brand can be predicted by identifying these specific beliefs and combining them to derive a measure of the consumer's overall attitude.

Basic multi-attribute models specify three elements:[32]

- *Attributes* are characteristics of the attitude object. Most models assume that the relevant characteristics can be identified. That is, the researcher can include those attributes that consumers take into consideration when evaluating the attitude object. For example, scholarly reputation is an attribute of a university.
- *Beliefs* are cognitions about the specific attitude object (usually relative to others like it). A belief measure assesses the extent to which the consumer perceives that a brand possesses a particular attribute. For example, a student might have a belief that the University of Michigan has a strong academic standing.
- *Importance weights* reflect the relative priority of an attribute to the consumer. Although an attitude object can be considered on a number of attributes, some are likely to be more important than others (i.e., they will be given greater weight). And, these weights are likely to differ across consumers. In the case of universities, for example, one student might stress library resources, while another might weight athletic programs more heavily.

THE FISHBEIN MODEL   The most influential multi-attribute model is called the Fishbein model, after its primary developer.[33] The model measures three components: (1) the *salient beliefs* people have about an attitude object (i.e., those beliefs about the object that are considered during evaluation); (2) *object-attribute linkages,* or the probability that a particular object has an important attribute; and (3) an *evaluation* of each of the important attributes. Note, however, that the model makes some assumptions that may not always be warranted. For example, it assumes that we have been able to adequately specify all of the relevant attributes that a student will use in evaluating his or her choices about which college to attend. The model also assumes that he or she will go through the process (formally or informally) of identifying a set of relevant attributes, weighing them, and summing them. Although this particular decision is likely to be highly involving, it is still possible that his or her attitude will instead be formed by an overall affective response (a process known as *affect-referral*).

COMBINING THE ELEMENTS IN A MULTI-ATTRIBUTE MODEL   By combining these three elements, a consumer's overall attitude toward an object can be computed (we'll see later how this basic equation has been modified to increase its accuracy). The basic formula is:

$$A_{ijk} = B_{ijk}I_{ik}$$

where

i = attribute

j = brand

k = consumer

I = the importance weight given attribute i by consumer k

B = consumer k's belief regarding the extent to which brand j possesses attribute i

A = a particular consumer's (k's) attitude score for brand j

The overall attitude score (A) is obtained by multiplying a consumer's rating of each attribute for all of the brands considered, by the importance rating for that attribute.

To see how this basic multi-attribute model might work, let's suppose we want to predict which college a high school senior is likely to attend. After months of waiting, Saundra has been accepted to four schools. Since she must now decide among these, we would first like to know which attributes Saundra will consider in forming an attitude toward each school.

TABLE 5-1 The basic multiattribute model: Saundra's college decision

Attribute (i)	Importance (I)	Beliefs (B)			
		Smith	Princeton	Rutgers	King County Comm. College
Academic reputation	6	8	9	6	3
All women	7	9	3	3	3
Cost	4	2	2	6	9
Proximity to home	3	2	2	6	9
Athletics	1	1	2	5	1
Party atmosphere	2	1	3	7	9
Library facilities	5	7	9	7	2
Attitude score		163	142	153	131

Note: These hypothetical ratings are scored from 1 to 10, where higher numbers indicate "better" standing on an attribute. This means that higher scores of a negative attribute (e.g., cost) indicate that the school is believed to have "less" of that attribute (i.e., to be cheaper).

A COMPLETE LIST OF THE SURGEON GENERAL'S RECOMMENDATIONS FOR NUTRITIOUS EATING:

CHOOSE FOODS:

1. Low in Fat and Cholesterol
2. Whole Grain and Complex Carbohydrates
3. Not High in Calories
4. Relatively Low in Sodium
5. Rich in Calcium
6. Rich in Iron
7. Low in Sugar

Based on the U.S. Surgeon General's Report on Nutrition and Health.
*Points 5-7 of particular interest to specific population groups. See Wheat Total package back for more information on these recommendations.

S T A R T

© 1990 General Mills, Inc.

We can then ask Saundra to assign a rating regarding how well each school performs on each attribute and also determine the relative importance of the attributes to her. An overall attitude score for each school can then be computed by summing scores on each attribute (after weighing each by its relative importance). These hypothetical ratings are shown in Table 5-1. Based on this analysis, it seems that Saundra has the most favorable attitude toward Smith. She is clearly someone who would like to attend an all-woman's school with a solid academic reputation rather than a school that offers a strong athletic program or a party atmosphere.

STRATEGIC APPLICATIONS OF THE MULTI-ATTRIBUTE MODEL Suppose you were the Director of Marketing for King County Community College, another school Saundra was considering. How might you use the data from this analysis to improve your image?

Capitalize on Relative Advantage. If one's brand is viewed as being superior on a particular attribute, try to convince consumers like Saundra that this is an important attribute.

A COMPLETE LIST OF THE LEADING CEREALS THAT MEET THEM ALL:

1. Whole Wheat Total

EATING HEALTHIER WITH TOTAL.

The ad for Total cereal advises consumers on the product attributes they should look for in a cereal; it also points out the one cereal that (the ad claims) has them all.   Used with the permission of General Mills, Inc.

While Saundra rates King's social atmosphere highly, she does not believe this is a valued aspect for a college. Perhaps you might emphasize the importance of an active social life, varied experiences, or even the development of future business contacts forged through strong college friendships.

Strengthen Perceived Product/Attribute Linkages. A marketer may discover that consumers do not equate his or her brand with a certain attribute. This problem is commonly addressed by campaigns that stress the product's qualities to consumers (e.g., "new and improved"). Saundra apparently does not think much of King's academic quality, athletic programs, or library facilities. You might develop an informational campaign to improve these perceptions (e.g., "little known facts about King").

Add a New Attribute. Product marketers frequently try to create a distinctive position from their competitors by adding a product feature. King Community College might try to emphasize some unique aspect, such as a hands-on internship program for business majors that takes advantage of ties to the local community.

This Chrysler ad is an example of comparative advertising, where the attributes of competitors are specifically considered in the message. © 1989 Chrysler Corporation, used with permission.

Influence Competitors' Ratings. Finally, you might try to decrease the positivity of competitors. This is a rationale for the strategy of *comparative advertising.* One tactic might be to publish tuition rates for a number of area schools, emphasizing the value of King's program. In addition, you could de-emphasize the importance of an attribute where you do not score highly. This can be accomplished, if desired, by running negative ads about colleges that place more emphasis on their basketball teams than on academics.

USING ATTITUDES TO PREDICT BEHAVIOR

Although multi-attribute models like the Fishbein model have been used by consumer researchers for many years, they have been plagued by a major problem: In many cases, knowledge of a person's attitude is *not* a very good predictor of behavior. In a classic demonstration of "do as I say, not as I do," many studies have obtained a very low correlation between a person's reported attitude toward something and his or her actual behavior toward it. Some researchers have been so discouraged that they have questioned whether attitudes are of any use at all in understanding behavior.[34]

THE EXTENDED FISHBEIN MODEL The original Fishbein model, which focused on measuring a consumer's attitude toward a product, has been extended in several ways to improve its predictive ability. The newer version is called the **theory of reasoned action**.[35] This model contains several important additions to the original, and while the model is still not perfect, adoption of this version has improved on its ability to predict relevant behaviors in some cases.[36]

Intentions Versus Behavior. Many factors might interfere with performance of the actual behavior, even if the consumer sincerely intends to carry it out. A person might save up with the intention of buying a stereo system. In the interim, though, any number of things could happen. He or she could lose a job, he or she could get mugged on the way to the store, or he or she might arrive at the store to find that the desired model is out of stock. For this reason, it is not surprising that in some instances past purchase behavior has been found to be a better predictor of future behavior than is a consumer's behavioral intention.[37] The theory of reasoned action aims to measure behavioral intentions, recognizing that certain uncontrollable factors will always inhibit perfect prediction of actual behavior.

Social Pressure. The theory acknowledges the power of other people in influencing behavior. Many of our behaviors are not determined in a vacuum. Much as we may hate to admit it, what we think others would *like* us to do may be more crucial than our own individual preferences.

In the case of Saundra's college choice, note that she was very positive about going to a predominantly female school. However, if she felt that this choice would be unpopular (perhaps her friends would think she was crazy), she might ignore or downgrade this preference when coming to a decision. A new element, the *subjective norm* (SN) was thus added to include the effects of what we believe other people think we should do. The value of SN is arrived at by including two other factors: (1) the intensity of a *normative belief* (NB) that others believe an action should be taken or not taken, and (2) the *motivation to comply* (MC) with that belief (i.e., the degree to which the consumer takes others' anticipated reactions into account when evaluating a course of action or a purchase).

A_{act}. The model now measures attitude toward the act of buying a product, rather than only the attitude toward the product itself. In other words, it focuses on the perceived consequences of a purchase. Knowing about how someone feels about buying or using an object turns out to be more valid than merely knowing the consumer's evaluation of the object itself.[38]

To understand this distinction, consider a problem that might arise when measuring attitudes toward condoms. Although a group of college students might have a positive attitude toward condoms, does this necessarily predict that they will buy and use them? Better prediction would be obtained by asking the students how likely they are to *buy* condoms. While a person might have a positive attitude toward condoms, he or she might have a negative attitude toward the act (A_{act}) of buying them due to embarrassment or the hassle involved.

MULTICULTURAL DIMENSIONS

The theory of reasoned action has primarily been applied in Western settings. Certain assumptions inherent in the model may not necessarily apply to consumers from other cultures. Several cultural roadblocks diminish the universality of the theory of reasoned action:

- The model was developed to predict the performance of any *voluntary act.* Across cultures, however, many consumer activities, ranging from taking exams and entering military service to receiving an inoculation or even choosing a marriage partner, are not necessarily voluntary.
- The relative impact of subjective norms may vary across cultures. For example, Asian cultures tend to value conformity and "face-saving," so it is possible some subjective norms would be even more powerful among these consumers.

- The model measures behavioral intentions, and thus presupposes that consumers are actively thinking ahead and planning future behaviors. The intention concept assumes that consumers have a *linear time sense;* they think in terms of past, present, and future. As will be discussed in chapter 10, this perspective on time is not held by all cultures.
- A consumer who forms an intention is (implicitly) claiming that he or she is in control of his or her actions. Some cultures (e.g., Muslim peoples) tend to be fatalistic and do not necessarily believe in the concept of free will. For example, one recent study comparing students from the United States, Jordan, and Thailand found evidence for cultural differences in assumptions about fatalism and control over the future.[39]

OTHER OBSTACLES TO PREDICTING BEHAVIOR

Despite these improvements to the Fishbein model, problems still arise when it is misapplied. In many cases the model is used in ways for which it was not intended, or where certain assumptions about human behavior may not be warranted.[40] Other obstacles to predicting behavior must be considered by market researchers:

- The model was developed to deal with actual behavior (e.g., taking a diet pill), not with the *outcomes* of behavior that are instead assessed in some studies (e.g., losing weight).
- Some outcomes are beyond the consumer's control, such as when the purchase requires the cooperation of other people. For instance, a woman might *want* to get a mortgage, but this intention will be worthless if she cannot find a banker to give her one.
- The basic assumption that behavior is intentional may be invalid in a variety of cases, including impulsive acts, sudden changes in one's situation, novelty seeking, or even simple repeat buying. One study found that such unexpected events as having guests, changes in the weather, or reading articles about the healthfulness of certain foods exerted a significant effect on actual behaviors.[41]
- Measures of attitude often do not really correspond to the behavior they are supposed to predict, either in terms of the attitude object or when the act will occur. One common problem is a difference in the level of *abstraction* employed. For example, knowing a person's attitude toward sports cars may not predict whether he

or she will purchase a Nissan 300ZX. It is very important to match the *level of specificity* between the attitude and the behavioral intention.

- A similar problem relates to the *time-frame* of the attitude measure. In general, the longer the time between the attitude measurement and the behavior it is supposed to assess, the weaker the relationship will be. For example, predictability would improve markedly by asking consumers the likelihood that they would buy a house in the next week as opposed to within the next five years.

- Attitudes formed by direct, personal experience with an attitude object are stronger and more predictive of behavior than those formed indirectly, such as through advertising.[42] According to the *attitude accessibilty* perspective, behavior is a function of the person's immediate perceptions of the attitude object, in the context of the situation in which it is encountered. An attitude will guide the evaluation of the object, but *only* if it is activated from memory when the object is observed.

When a brand attitude is based on actual trial, attitudes toward the brand have been found to predict behavior very well. This consistency is reduced when the attitude is only based on learning via advertising.[43] Attitudes that are held with more confidence are more predictive than attitudes based upon a single exposure.[44] These findings underscore the importance of strategies that either seek to (1) induce trial by widespread product sampling, encouraging the consumer to try the product at home, or take test-drives, or (2) maximize exposure to marketing communications.

TRACKING ATTITUDES OVER TIME

An attitude survey is like a snapshot taken at a single point in time. While it may tell us a lot about a brand's position at that moment, it does not permit many inferences about progress the brand has made over time or any predictions about possible future changes in consumer attitudes. To accomplish that, it is necessary to develop an *attitude tracking* program. This activity helps to increase the predictability of behavior by allowing researchers to analyze attitude trends over an extended period of time. It is more like a movie than a snapshot.

Attitude tracking involves the administration of an attitude survey at regular intervals. Preferably, the identical methodology is used each time so that results can be reliably compared. Many syndicated services, such as the Gallup Poll or the Yankelovich, Skelley, and White Monitor, track consumer attitudes over time.

This activity can be extremely valuable for many strategic decisions. For example, one firm monitored changes in consumer attitudes toward one-stop financial centers. Although a large number of consumers were warm to the idea when it was first introduced, the number of people who liked the concept did not increase over time despite the millions of dollars invested in advertising to promote the centers. This indicated some problems either with the concept or the way it was being presented to consumers.

Some of the dimensions that can be included in attitude tracking include the following:

- a focus on changes in different age groups. Attitudes tend to change as people age (a *life-cycle effect*). In addition, *cohort effects* occur, where members of a particular generation tend to share certain outlooks (e.g., the yuppie). Also, *historical effects* can be observed as large groups of people are affected by profound cultural changes (such as the Great Depression or the democratization of Eastern Europe).
- scenarios about the future. Consumers are frequently tracked in terms of their future plans, confidence in the economy, and so on. These measures can provide valuable data about future behavior and yield insights for public policy. For example, Americans tend to overestimate how much they will earn after retirement, which is potentially a dangerous miscalculation.
- identification of agents of change. Social phenomena can change people's attitudes toward basic consumption activities over time, as when consumers' willingness to buy fur shifts. Or, consumers' likelihood of desiring a divorce may be affected by such *facilitators* as changes in the legal system that make this action easier, or by *inhibitors,* such as the prevalence of AIDS and the value of two paychecks in today's economy.[45]

CHAPTER SUMMARY

An attitude is a predisposition to evaluate an object positively or negatively. Attitudes are made up of three components: beliefs, affect, and behavioral intentions. Consumers have attitudes toward virtually every product or brand they are aware of, though these will differ in intensity and complexity. Attitude researchers traditionally assumed that attitudes were learned in a fixed sequence, consisting first of the formation of beliefs (cognitions) regarding an attitude object, followed by some evaluation of that object (affect) and then some action (behavior). Depending upon the consumer's level of involvement and the circumstances, though, attitudes can result from other hierarchies of effects as well. A key to attitude formation is the function the attitude plays for the consumer (e.g., is it utilitarian or ego-defensive?). One organizing principle of attitude formation is the importance of consistency among attitudinal components—some parts of an attitude may be altered to be in line with others. Such theoretical approaches to attitudes as cognitive dissonance theory, balance theory, and congruity theory stress the vital role of the need for consistency. The chapter reviews some approaches to identifying and measuring consumers' attitudes toward products. The complexity of attitudes is underscored by multiattribute attitude models, where a set of beliefs and evaluations is identified and combined to predict an overall attitude. Some of the factors that get in the way of accurate prediction of behavior from knowledge of a person's attitudes are discussed, and the ways in which these factors have been integrated into attitude measures, such as the inclusion of subjective norms and the specificity of attitude scales, to improve predictability are reviewed. Also, the importance of other attitude-related measures is stressed.

KEY TERMS

Affect	Congruity theory
Attitude	Hierarchy of effects
Attitude object (A_o)	Multi-attribute attitude models
Attitude toward the advertisement (A_{ad})	Principle of cognitive consistency
Balance theory	Self-perception theory
Behavior	Social judgment theory
Cognition	Theory of reasoned action

REVIEW QUESTIONS AND DISCUSSION TOPICS

1. Contrast the hierarchies of effects outlined in the chapter. How will strategic decisions related to the marketing mix be influenced by which hierarchy is operative among target consumers?
2. List three functions played by attitudes, giving an example of how each function is employed in a marketing situation.
3. Describe three applications of data obtained from a multi-attribute attitude model.

HANDS-ON EXERCISES

1. Ask people to name an aesthetic object that is very special to them (e.g., a favorite song or painting). Then request that they describe the tangible attributes of the object that make it so well liked. Can people identify the specific attributes that affect their attitude toward the object?
2. Think of a behavior someone does that is inconsistent with their attitudes (e.g., attitudes toward cholesterol, drug use, or even buying things to make them stand out or attain status). Ask the person to elaborate on why he or she does the behavior anyway, and try to identify the way the person has resolved dissonant elements.
3. Replicate the study on basking in reflected glory described in the chapter. This can be done by observing people's behaviors before, during, and after important sports events. Devise measures of team identification, such as team-related paraphernalia in evidence, or uses of different pronouns ("we" vs. "they") in describing the team's performance, depending on whether the game was won or lost by the home team.
4. Using a series of semantic differential scales, devise an attitude survey for a set of competing automobiles. Identify areas of competitive advantage or disadvantage for each model you incorporate.
5. Construct a multi-attribute model for a set of local restaurants. Based on your findings, suggest how restaurant managers can improve an establishment's image via the strategies described in the chapter.

NOTES

1. Robert A. Baron and Donn Byrne, *Social Psychology: Understanding Human Interaction,* 5th ed. (Boston: Allyn & Bacon, 1987).
2. Michael Ray, "Marketing Communications and the Hierarchy-of-Effects," in *New Models for Mass Communications,* ed. P. Clarke (Beverly Hills, Calif.: Sage, 1973), 147–76.
3. Herbert Krugman, "The Impact of Television Advertising: Learning Without Involvement," *Public Opinion Quarterly* 29 (Fall 1965): 349–56; Robert Lavidge and Gary

Steiner, "A Model for Predictive Measurements of Advertising Effectiveness," *Journal of Marketing* 25 (October 1961): 59–62.

4. Punam Anand, Morris B. Holbrook, and Debra Stephens, "The Formation of Affective Judgments: The Cognitive-Affective Model Versus the Independence Hypothesis," *Journal of Consumer Research* 15 (December 1988): 386–91; Richard S. Lazarus, "Thoughts on the Relations Between Emotion and Cognition," *American Psychologist* 37 (1982)9: 1019–24.

5. Robert B. Zajonc, "Feeling and Thinking: Preferences Need No Inferences," *American Psychologist* 35 (1980)2: 151–75.

6. Banwari Mittal, "The Role of Affective Choice Mode in the Consumer Purchase of Expressive Products," *Journal of Economic Psychology* 4 (1988)9: 499–524.

7. Scot Burton and Donald R. Lichtenstein, "The Effect of Ad Claims and Ad Context on Attitude Toward the Advertisement," *Journal of Advertising* 17 (1988)1: 3–11; Karen A. Machleit and R. Dale Wilson, "Emotional Feelings and Attitude Toward the Advertisement: The Roles of Brand Familiarity and Repetition," *Journal of Advertising* 17 (1988)3: 27–35; Scott B. Mackenzie and Richard J. Lutz, "An Empirical Examination of the Structural Antecedents of Attitude Toward the Ad in an Advertising Pretesting Context," *Journal of Marketing* 53 (April 1989): 48–65; Scott B. Mackenzie, Richard J. Lutz, and George E. Belch, "The Role of Attitude Toward the Ad as a Mediator of Advertising Effectiveness: A Test of Competing Explanations," *Journal of Marketing Research* 23 (May 1986): 130–43; Darrel D. Muehling and Russell N. Laczniak, "Advertising's Immediate and Delayed Influence on Brand Attitudes: Considerations Across Message-Involvement Levels," *Journal of Advertising* 17 (1988)4: 23–34; Mark A. Pavelchak, Meryl P. Gardner, and V. Carter Broach, "Effect of Ad Pacing and Optimal Level of Arousal on Attitude Toward the Ad," in *Advances in Consumer Research,* ed. Rebecca H. Holman and Michael R. Solomon (Provo, Utah: Association for Consumer Research, 1991)18: 94–99. Some research evidence indicates that a separate atttitude is also formed regarding the brand name itself, see George M. Zinkhan and Claude R. Martin, Jr., "New Brand Names and Inferential Beliefs: Some Insights on Naming New Products," *Journal of Business Research* 15 (1987): 157–72.

8. Basil G. Englis, "Consumer Emotional Reactions to Television Advertising and Their Effects on Message Recall," in *Emotion in Advertising: Theoretical and Practical Explorations,* ed. S. Agres, J. A. Edell, and T. M. Dubitsky (Westport, Conn.: Quorum Books, 1990): 231–54.

9. Morris B. Holbrook and Rajeev Batra, "Assessing the Role of Emotions as Mediators of Consumer Responses to Advertising," *Journal of Consumer Research* 14 (December 1987): 404–20.

10. Marian Burke and Julie Edell, "Ad Reactions Over Time: Capturing Changes in the Real World," *Journal of Consumer Research* 13 (June 1986): 114–18.

11. David A. Aaker and Donald E. Bruzzone, "Causes of Irritation in Advertising," *Journal of Marketing* 49 (Spring 1985): 47–57.

12. Herbert Kelman, "Compliance, Identification, and Internalization: Three Processes of Attitude Change," *Journal of Conflict Resolution* 2, (1958): 51–60.

13. See Sharon E. Beatty and Lynn R. Kahle, "Alternative Hierarchies of the Attitude–Behavior Relationship: The Impact of Brand Commitment and Habit," *Journal of the Academy of Marketing Science* 16 (Summer 1988): 1–10.

14. Jack Brehm, *A Theory of Psychological Reactance* (New York: Academic Press, 1966).

15. Michael B. Mazis, Robert B. Settle, and D.C. Leslie, "Elimination of Phosphate Detergents and Psychological Reactance," *Journal of Marketing Research* 10 (1973): 390–95.

16. Greg J. Lessne and Elaine M. Notarantonio, "The Effect of Limits in Retail Advertisements: A Reactance Theory Perspective," *Psychology & Marketing* 5 (1988)1: 33–44.

17. Leon Festinger, *A Theory of Cognitive Dissonance* (Stanford, Calif.: Stanford University Press, 1957).

18. Chester A. Insko and John Schopler, *Experimental Social Psychology* (New York: Academic Press, 1972).

19. Robert E. Knox and James A. Inkster, "Postdecision Dissonance at Post Time," *Journal of Personality and Social Psychology* 8 (1968)4: 319–23.

20. Daryl J. Bem, "Self-Perception Theory," in *Advances in Experimental Social Psychology,* ed. Leonard Berkowitz (New York: Academic Press, 1972)6: 1–62.

21. Jonathan L. Freedman and Scott C. Fraser, "Compliance Without Pressure: The Foot-in-the-Door Technique," *Journal of Personality and Social Psychology* 4 (August 1966): 195–202; for further consideration of possible explanations for this effect, see William DeJong, "An Examination of Self-Perception Mediation of the Foot-in-the-Door Effect," *Journal of Personality and Social Psychology* 37 (December 1979): 2221–31; Alice M. Tybout, Brian Sternthal, and Bobby J. Calder, "Information Availability as a Determinant of Multiple-Request Effectiveness," *Journal of Marketing Research* 20 (August 1988): 280–90.

22. David H. Furse, David W. Stewart, and David L. Rados, "Effects of Foot-in-the-Door, Cash Incentives and Follow-ups on Survey Response," *Journal of Marketing Research* 18 (November 1981): 473–78; Carol A. Scott, "The Effects of Trial and Incentives on Repeat Purchase Behavior," *Journal of Marketing Research* 13 (August 1976): 263–69.

23. Muzafer Sherif and Carl I. Hovland, *Social Judgment: Assimilation and Contrast Effects in Communication and Attitude Change* (New Haven, Conn.: Yale University Press, 1961).

24. Mark B. Traylor, "Product Involvement and Brand Commitment," *Journal of Advertising Research* (December 1981): 51–56.

25. Fritz Heider, *The Psychology of Interpersonal Relations* (New York: Wiley, 1958).

26. R. B. Cialdini, R. J. Borden, A. Thorne, M. R. Walker, S. Freeman, and L. R. Sloan, "Basking in Reflected Glory: Three (Football) Field Studies," *Journal of Personality and Social Psychology* 34, (1976): 366–75.

27. Howard G. Ruben, "College Stores Cash in on School Logos," *Daily News Record* (May 20, 1987):1.

28. Charles E. Osgood and Percy H. Tannenbaum, "The Principle of Congruity in the Production of Attitude Change," *Psychological Review* 62 (1955): 42–55.

29. Quoted in Karen Springen and Annetta Miller, "When Ads Don't Fit the 'Image,'" *Newsweek* (January 22, 1990):48.

30. Jacob Jacoby and David Mazursky, "Linking Brand and Retailer Images: Do the Potential Risks Outweigh the Potential Benefits?" *Journal of Retailing* 60 (Summer 1984): 105–22.

31. A number of criteria beyond the scope of this book are important in evaluating methods of attitude measurement, including such issues as reliability, validity, and sensitivity. For an excellent treatment of attitude scaling techniques, see David S. Aaker and George S. Day, *Marketing Research,* 4th ed. (New York: Wiley, 1990).

32. William L. Wilkie, *Consumer Behavior* (New York: Wiley, 1986).

33. M. Fishbein, "An Investigation of the Relationships Between Beliefs About an Object and the Attitude Toward that Object," *Human Relations* 16 (1983): 233–40.

34. Allan Wicker, "Attitudes Versus Actions: The Relationship of Verbal and Overt Behavioral Responses to Attitude Objects," *Journal of Social Issues* 25 (Autumn 1969): 65.

35. Icek Ajzen and Martin Fishbein, "Attitude-Behavior Relations: A Theoretical Analysis and Review of Empirical Research," *Psychological Bulletin* 84 (September 1977): 888–918.

36. Morris B. Holbrook and William J. Havlena, "Assessing the Real-to-Artificial Generalizability of Multi-attribute Attitude Models in Tests of New Product Designs," *Journal of Marketing Research* 25 (February 1988): 25–35; Terence A. Shimp and Alican Kavas, "The Theory of Reasoned Action Applied to Coupon Usage," *Journal of Consumer Research* 11 (December 1984): 795–809.

37. Richard P. Bagozzi, Hans Baumgartner, and Youjae Yi, "Coupon Usage and the Theory of Reasoned Action," in *Advances in Consumer Research,* ed. Rebecca H. Holman and Michael R. Solomon (Provo, Utah: Association for Consumer Research, 1991)18: 24–27; Edward F. McQuarrie, "An Alternative to Purchase Intentions: The Role of Prior Behavior in Consumer Expenditure on Computers," *Journal of the Market Research Society* 30 (October 1988): 407–37; Arch G. Woodside and William O. Bearden, "Longitudinal Analysis of Consumer Attitude, Intention, and Behavior Toward Beer Brand Choice," in *Advances in Consumer Research,* ed. William D. Perrault, Jr. (Ann Arbor, Mich.: Association for Consumer Research, 1977)4: 349–56.

38. Michael J. Ryan and Edward H. Bonfield, "The Fishbein Extended Model and Consumer Behavior," *Journal of Consumer Research* 2 (1975): 118–36.

39. Joseph A. Cote and Patriya S. Tanushaj, "Culture Bound Assumptions in Behavior Intention Models," in *Advances in Consumer Research,* ed. Thom Srull (Provo, Utah: Association for Consumer Research, 1989)16: 105–09.

40. Blair H. Sheppard, Jon Hartwick, and Paul R. Warshaw, "The Theory of Reasoned Action: A Meta-Analysis of Past Research with Recommendations for Modifications and Future Research," *Journal of Consumer Research* 15 (December 1988): 325–43.

41. Joseph A. Cote, James McCullough and Michael Reilly, "Effects of Unexpected Situations on Behavior-Intention Differences: A Garbology Analysis," *Journal of Consumer Research* 12 (September 1985), 188–94.

42. Russell H. Fazio, Martha C. Powell, and Carol J. Williams, "The Role of Attitude Accessibility in the Attitude-to-Behavior Process," *Journal of Consumer Research* 16 (December 1989): 280–88.

43. Robert E. Smith and William R. Swinyard, "Attitude-Behavior Consistency: The Impact of Product Trial Versus Advertising," *Journal of Marketing Research* 20 (August 1983): 257–67.

44. Ida E. Berger and Andrew A. Mitchell, "The Effect of Advertising on Attitude Accessibility, Attitude Confidence, and the Attitude-Behavior Relationship," *Journal of Consumer Research* 16 (December 1989): 269–79.

45. Mathew Greenwald and John P. Katosh, "How to Track Changes in Attitudes," *American Demographics* (August 1987):46.

Attitude Change and Persuasive Communications

CHAPTER 6

When Robin got her big promotion, she decided this was the opportunity she'd been waiting for. She has always wanted a fur coat, though she knows that recently this symbol of wealth and luxury has lost some of its appeal as people have become more concerned about animal rights. Just this morning, a newspaper columnist observed that the "... dried, dead, hairy animal skin—or if you insist, luxurious fur coat—has become as passé and vulgarly uncivilized as flogging one's servants."[1]

Robin has also heard about animal rights activists who have made it increasingly difficult to buy, sell, and wear fur. Some furriers have had their store locks glued shut and have received death threats, and in a few cases fur wearers have been doused with red dye intended to resemble animal blood. To add to the controversy, groups such as People for the Ethical Treatment of Animals have run hard-hitting ads to influence consumers' opinions about buying fur. In a parody of the long-running ads for Blackglama furs, which depict famous women wrapped in furs and bear the caption "What Becomes a Legend Most?" one ad featuring Cassandra Petersen (a.k.a. horror-show hostess and cult heroine Elvira) asks, "What Disgraces a Legend Most?

What disgraces a legend most?

FUR IS DEAD

PETA
PEOPLE FOR THE ETHICAL TREATMENT OF ANIMALS
Washington, DC 20015 (301) 770-7444

Model: Cassandra Petersen   Photo: David Goldner

A group called People for the Ethical Treatment of Animals (PETA) is attempting to change consumers' attitudes toward the wearing of fur. In this case, actress Cassandra Petersen is used in a parody of a long-running fur campaign to reduce the social desirability of wearing fur.   Courtesy of People For the Ethical Treatment of Animals (PETA).

Still, Robin wants that coat, and she searches eagerly for reasons to justify her passion. She feels better after reading some information distributed by the Fur Information Council of America, which asks "If fashion isn't about freedom of choice, what is?" Research conducted by the fur industry showed that most consumers felt they were entitled to wear fur, but needed reassurance in the face of the social pressures confronting them. Thus, according to industry claims, the animals, which often kill each other in the wild anyway, are treated humanely. As one industry spokesperson put it, the forces opposing fur believe that if the business were abolished, "animals would all sit around the campfire roasting marshmallows and telling stories . . . like 'Bambi' . . . but it doesn't happen that way. Nature is cruel."[2] After some thought, Robin buys her coat—but she plans to be *really* careful about where she wears it.

CHANGING ATTITUDES THROUGH COMMUNICATION

As consumers, we are constantly bombarded by messages inducing us to change our attitudes. The passionate debate about whether consumers should wear fur illustrates some of the tactics used to change attitudes. These devices range from logical arguments to graphic pictures, and from intimidation by peers to celebrity spokespeople. This chapter will review some of the factors that help to determine the effectiveness of these communication attempts. Of course, much activity by marketing practitioners involves the design and execution of messages that are supposed to affect buying behavior, so many of the topics covered in other chapters bear on this issue as well.

For now, however, the focus will be on some basic aspects of communication that specifically help to determine how and if attitudes will be created or modified. This objective relates to **persuasion,** which refers to an active attempt to change attitudes. Persuasion is the central goal of many marketing communications.

Suppose that a perfume company wants to create an advertising campaign for a new fragrance. As it plans this campaign, it must develop a message that will create desire for the perfume in potential consumers. A number of questions must be answered, such as:

- Who will be depicted as using the scent in an ad? Should it be linked to a glamorous celebrity? A career woman? A rock star? The source of a message helps to determine consumers' acceptance of it as well as their desire to try the product.
- How should the message be constructed? Should it emphasize the negative consequences of smelling badly? Perhaps it should directly compare the fragrance with others already on the market, or maybe present a fantasy where a princess is swept off her feet by a dashing knight after she applies the scent. Product benefits can be expressed in many ways.
- What media should be used to transmit the message? Should it be depicted in a print ad? On television? Sold door-to-door? If a print ad is produced, should it be run in the pages of *Vogue? Good Housekeeping? The National Enquirer?* Sometimes *where* something is said can be as important as *what* is said. Ideally, the attributes of the product should be matched to those of the medium. For example, magazines with high prestige are more effective at communicating messages about overall product image and quality, while specialized, expert magazines do a better job at conveying factual information.[3]
- What characteristics of the target market might influence the ad's acceptance? If targeted users are frustrated in their daily lives, these women might be more receptive to a fantasy appeal. If they don't tend to wear perfume, they may not pay any attention to a traditional perfume ad at all.

THE FUNCTIONS OF ATTITUDES

The **functional theory of attitudes** was initially developed by psychologist Daniel Katz to explain how attitudes facilitate social behavior.[4] According to this pragmatic approach, attitudes exist *because* they serve some function for the person. That is, they are determined by a person's motives. Consumers who expect that they will need to deal with similar information at a future time will be more likely to start forming attitudes in anticipation.[5]

Two people can each have an attitude toward some object for very different reasons. It follows that an advertiser must know *why* an attitude is held before attempting to change it. The following are attitude functions as identified by Katz.

UTILITARIAN FUNCTION   Utilitarian function is related to the basic principles of reward and punishment. We develop some attitudes toward products simply on the basis of whether these products provide pleasure or pain. If a person likes the taste of a cheeseburger, that person will develop a positive attitude toward cheeseburgers. Ads that stress straightforward product benefits (e.g., you should drink Diet Coke "just for the taste of it") appeal to the utilitarian function.

VALUE-EXPRESSIVE FUNCTION   Attitudes that perform a value-expressive function express the consumer's central values or self-concept. A person forms a product attitude not because of objective product benefits, but rather because of what using the product says about him or her as a person (e.g., "What sort of man reads *Playboy?*"). Value-expressive attitudes are highly relevant to life-style analyses, where consumers cultivate a cluster of activities, interests, and opinions to express a particular social identity (as will be further discussed in Chapter 15).

EGO-DEFENSIVE FUNCTION   Attitudes that are formed to protect the person, either from external threats or internal feelings of insecurity, perform an ego-defensive function. An early marketing study indicated that housewives in the 1950s resisted the use of instant coffee because it threatened their conception of themselves as capable homemakers.[6] Products that promise to help a man project a "macho" image (e.g., Marlboro cigarettes) may be appealing to his insecurities about his masculinity. Many deodorant campaigns stress the dire, embarrassing consequences of being caught with underarm odor in public.

KNOWLEDGE FUNCTION   Some attitudes are formed as the result of a need for order, structure, or meaning. This need is often present when a person is in an ambiguous situation or is confronted with a new product (e.g., "Bayer wants you to *know* about pain relievers").

FUNCTIONAL THEORY AND STRATEGIC POSITIONING

An attitude can serve more than one function, but in many cases a particular one will be dominant. Identifying the dominant function served can be helpful to marketers, who can structure ad copy to emphasize it over another. Ads relevant to the function engaged by a product prompt more favorable thoughts about what is being marketed and result in a heightened preference for both the product and the ad.

For example, a recent study determined that for most people coffee serves more of a utilitarian function than a value-expressive function. As a consequence, subjects responded more positively to copy for a (fictitious) coffee that read: "The delicious, hearty flavor and aroma of Sterling Blend coffee comes from a blend of the freshest coffee beans" (utilitarian appeal) than to: "The coffee you drink says something about the type of person you are. It can reveal your rare, discriminating taste" (value-expressive function).[7]

THE COMMUNICATIONS MODEL

The **communications model** specifies that a number of elements are necessary for communication to be achieved. A *source* must choose and encode a message (i.e., initiate the transfer of meaning by choosing appropriate symbolic images that represent that meaning). This meaning must be put in the form of a *message*. There are many ways to say something, and the structure of the message has a big effect on how it is perceived. The message must be transmitted via a *medium*. This could be television, radio, magazines, in person, on a billboard, and so on. The message is then decoded by one or more *receivers,* who interpret the symbols in light of their own experiences. Finally, *feedback* must be received by the source, who uses the reactions of receivers to modify aspects of the message. The communications process is depicted in Figure 6-1.

THE SOURCE

Common sense tells us that the same words uttered by different people can have very different effects. Research on *source effects* has been carried out for over thirty years. By attributing the same message to different sources and measuring the degree of attitude change that occurs after listeners hear it, it is possible to determine what aspects of a communicator will induce attitude change. This change is observed independent of the particular message content.[8]

Figure 6-1 The Communications Model

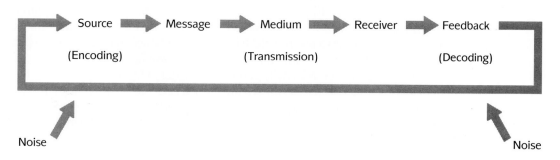

Under most conditions the source of a message can have a big impact on the likelihood the message will be accepted. The choice of a source to maximize attitude change can tap into several dimensions. The source can be chosen because he or she is an expert, attractive, famous, or even a "typical" consumer who is both likable and trustworthy. Two important source characteristics are credibility and attractiveness.[9]

CHOOSING A SOURCE DIMENSION

How do marketing specialists decide which dimension to stress? There should be a match between the needs of the recipient and the potential rewards offered by the source. When this match occurs, the recipient is more motivated to process the message. People who tend to be sensitive about social acceptance and the opinions of others, for example, are more persuaded by an attractive source, while those who are more internally oriented are swayed by an expert source.[10]

The choice may also depend on the type of product. While a positive source can help to reduce risk and increase message acceptance, particular types of sources are more effective at reducing different kinds of risk. Experts are effective at changing attitudes toward utilitarian products that have high *performance risk,* such as vacuums (i.e., they may be complex and not work as expected). Celebrities are more effective when they focus on products such as jewelry and furniture that have high *social risk;* the user of such products is aware of their effect on the impression others have or him or her. Finally, "typical" consumers, who are appealing sources because of their similarity to the recipient, tend to be most effective when endorsing everyday products that are low risk, such as cookies.[11]

THE SLEEPER EFFECT While in general more positive sources tend to increase attitude change, exceptions can occur. Sometimes a source can be obnoxious or disliked and still manage to be effective at getting the product's message across. A case in point is Mr. Whipple, the irritating but well-known television character who for many years scolded customers: "Please don't squeeze the Charmin!"

In some instances the differences in attitude change between positive sources and less positive sources seem to get erased over time. After a while people appear to "forget" about the negative source and wind up changing their attitudes anyway. This is known as the **sleeper effect.**[12]

The explanation for the sleeper effect is a subject of debate, as is the more basic question regarding whether and when it really exists. Initially, the *dissociative cue hypothesis* proposed that over time the message and the source become disassociated in the consumer's mind. The message remains on its own in memory, causing the delayed attitude change termed the sleeper effect.[13] A more recent explanation is the *availability-valence hypothesis,* which emphasizes the selectivity of memory owing to limited capacity.[14] If the associations linked to the negative source are less available than those linked to the message information, the residual impact of the message enhances persuasion. Consistent with this view, the sleeper effect has been obtained only when the message was encoded elaboratively—it had stronger associations in memory than did the source.[15]

CREDIBILITY

Source credibility refers to a source's perceived expertise, objectivity, or trustworthiness. This characteristic relates to consumers' beliefs that a communicator is competent and willing to provide the necessary information to adequately evaluate competing products.

SOURCE BIASES   A consumer's beliefs about a product's attributes can be weakened if the source is perceived to be the victim of *bias* in presenting information.[16] *Knowledge bias* implies that a communicator's knowledge about a topic is not accurate. The politician Dan Quayle encountered trouble swaying opinions because he was not perceived to be as knowledgeable as he could be on important national issues. *Reporting bias* occurs in the situation where a source has the required knowledge, but his or her willingness to convey it accurately is compromised. This might occur, for example, when an expert endorses a product. While his or her credentials might be appropriate, the fact that the expert is perceived as a "hired gun" compromises believability.

MARKETING PITFALL

A television program generally has more credibility than a commercial because the show is assumed to be impartial and thus low in reporting bias. The line between objective programming and commercials, however, is blurring with the proliferation of *informercials* on cable television. These are half-hour or hour commercials that resemble a program but in actuality are intended to sell products like rock-and-roll collections or self-help courses. Producers currently are only required to identify these programs as commercials at the beginning. Since people tend to switch channels frequently, they may not be aware of the show's bias. The Federal Trade Commission is beginning to investigate some of the claims made by these productions.

Some of these shows mimic talk shows or interview programs, while others borrow the format of documentaries. Many have a celebrity host. Samples include:[17]

Dick Clark: "Is There Love After Marriage?"

E. G. Marshall: "A Stop Smoking Breakthrough"

Fran Tarkenton: "Personal Power, Thirty Days to Unlimited Success"

Morgan Brittany: "Morgan Brittany on Beauty"

Brenda Vaccaro: "Light His Fire"

BUILDING CREDIBILITY   Credibility can be enhanced if the source's qualifications are perceived as somehow relevant to the product being endorsed. This linkage can overcome other objections people may have to the endorser or the product. When former baseball pitcher Jim Palmer endorsed Jockey International products, his athleticism was instrumental in reassuring men that it was acceptable for them to wear skimpy underwear in unusual colors.[18] Similarly, Ronald Biggs, whose claim to fame was his 1963 role in the Great Train Robbery in the U.K., is now successfully serving as a spokesman in Brazil for a company that makes door locks—a topic about which he is presumably knowledgeable![19]

ATTRACTIVENESS

A source's attractiveness refers to his or her perceived social value. This quality can emanate from the person's physical appearance, personality, social status, or his or her similarity to the receiver (we like to listen to people who are like us). The latter issues are discussed in chapters 11 and 12, so this chapter will focus exclusively on the role of a source's physical attractiveness in changing consumers' attitudes.

"WHAT IS BEAUTIFUL IS GOOD" Almost everywhere we turn, beautiful people are trying to persuade us to buy or do something. Our society places a very high premium on physical attractiveness, and we tend to assume that people who are good looking are smarter, more "with it," and so on. Such an assumption is called a *halo effect,* which occurs when persons who rank high on one dimension are assumed to excel on others as well. The effect can be explained in terms of the consistency principle discussed in Chapter 5, which states that people are more comfortable when all of their judgments about a person go together. This notion has been termed the "what is beautiful is good" stereotype.[20]

BEAUTY AND ATTITUDE CHANGE A physically attractive source tends to facilitate attitude change. His or her degree of attractiveness exerts at least modest effects on consumers' purchase intentions or product evaluation.[21] How does this happen?

Beauty Gets Our Attention. One explanation is that physical attractiveness functions as a cue that facilitates or modifies information processing by directing consumers' attention to relevant marketing stimuli. Some evidence indicates that consumers pay more attention to ads that contain attractive models, though not necessarily to the ad copy.[22] In other words, an ad with a beautiful person may stand a better chance of getting noticed, but not necessarily *read.* While we may enjoy looking at a beautiful or handsome person, these positive feelings do not necessarily affect product attitudes or purchase intentions.[23]

Beauty as information. The effectiveness of highly attractive spokespeople in ads appears to be largely limited to those situations where the advertised product is overtly related to attractiveness or sexuality.[24] One reason for this effect is that beauty can function as a source of information. The *social adaptation perspective* assumes that information seen to be instrumental in forming an attitude will be more heavily weighted by the perceiver. We filter out irrelevant information to minimize cognitive effort.

Under the right circumstances, an endorser's level of attractiveness constitutes a source of information instrumental to the attitude change process and thus functions as a central, task-relevant cue.[25] An attractive spokesperson, for this reason, is more likely to be an effective source when the product is relevant to attractiveness. For example, attractiveness affects attitudes toward ads about perfume or cologne (where attractiveness is relevant) but not toward coffee ads, where attractiveness is not relevant.[26]

✓CELEBRITIES AS COMMUNICATIONS SOURCES

When used properly, famous or expert spokespeople can be of great value in improving the fortunes of a product. Celebrities increase awareness of a firm's advertising and enhance both company image and brand attitudes—the intent of the L.A. Gear ad shown here featuring rock star Paula Abdul.[27] One reason for this effectiveness is that consumers are better able to identify products that are associated with a spokesperson.[28] The use of celebrity endorsers is an expensive but common strategy. Pepsi's sponsorship of Michael Jackson's tour and his use in commercials reportedly cost $5.5 million.[29] Paul McCartney reportedly received a payment in the seven-digit range for appearing in a Visa card campaign.[30] People now pay up to $175 for celebrity fragrances endorsed by the likes of Sophia Loren, Liz Taylor, Joan Collins, and Julio Iglesias (this perfume is targeted specifically to Hispanics). While a celebrity endorsement strategy is expensive, it can pay off handsomely. When Panasonic sponsored the R&B group Earth, Wind & Fire, for example, its share in the radio/cassette player market rose from last to first in a short time.[31]

THE STRATEGIC VALUE OF CELEBRITIES

One reason for the popularity of celebrity endorsements is that this strategy is viewed as a way to differentiate among similar products. This is especially important when consumers do not perceive many actual differences among competitors, as often occurs when brands are in the mature stage of the product life cycle.

Sodas of the Stars. A good illustration of an extensive reliance on star power is the battle between Coke and Pepsi, two mature products that rely heavily upon celebrity endorsements. As observed by the consultant who designed Coke's logo: "Coke and Pepsi aren't in the product business anymore. . . . They're in the image business, in show business. There is almost no differentiation between Coke and Pepsi, so they have run out of things to say about their products. They have to do it via image."[32] Coca-Cola's stable of endorsers includes such figures as hockey player Wayne Gretzky, George Michael, model Elle MacPherson, Roger Rabbit, and the rap group Run-DMC. Pepsi has employed David Bowie, (ex-vice presidential candidate) Geraldine Ferraro, Michael J. Fox, Dwight Gooden, Madonna, and Tina Turner, among many others.

Coke regularly polls consumers to see how closely they identify the product with a set of 18 attributes, such as young, modern, warm, and

I STILL BURN TOAST.

I STILL GET COLDS.

I STILL LISTEN

TO MY MOM.

BUT NO ONE TELLS ME

HOW TO DANCE.

HOW TO SING.

OR WHAT TO WEAR.

STREET FLASH

In one recent celebrity endorsement campaign, L.A. Gear used singer Paula Abdul to promote its line of jeans. Courtesy of L.A. Gear.

so on. When a dip in ratings on an attribute is detected, ads are created to bolster that image. Coke reacted to one ratings decline by using rock star George Michael in ads to reassure Coke drinkers that Coke is young and modern.

EFFECTIVENESS OF CELEBRITY ENDORSEMENTS   Famous people can be effective because they are credible, attractive, or both—it depends on the reasons for their fame. Henry Kissinger is unlikely to be a "sex symbol," but he may be quite effective at advocating use of a financial product. On the other hand, Vanna White may not be perceived as highly expert (except perhaps at turning letters on game shows), but her perceived physical attractiveness might make her a persuasive source for a message about perfume or clothing.

Wanted: Believable Celebrities.   The effectiveness of celebrities as communications sources often depends upon their perceived credibility. Consumers may not trust a celebrity's motives for endorsing a product, or they may question the star's competence to critically evaluate the product's claims. This "credibility gap" appears to be widening. In a recent one-year period, for example, the number of consumers who find celebrity advertising "less than credible" jumped to 52 percent. The greatest erosion of confidence comes from younger consumers, 64 percent of whom thought that celebrities appeared in ads just for the money.[33]

A lack of credibility is aggravated by incidences where celebrities endorse products that they do not really believe in, or in some cases do not use. In 1978, the situation was so bad that the Federal Trade Commission announced that it would go after celebrities who made false claims in advertising. One casualty of that effort was the singer Pat Boone, who was forced to stop his endorsement of an acne cream. More recent embarrassments stemmed from revelations by highly paid endorsers that they did not use the product. For example, the actress Cybill Shepherd who worked for the beef industry to promote meat consumption revealed that she did not eat meat, and Pepsi-endorser Michael Jackson created a flap when it was discovered that he does not drink soda.

This type of false representation may also hurt the celebrities in the long run. As the country singer Charlie Daniels observed after endorsing Skoal Bandit chewing tobacco: "I can't respect anybody who endorses a product and does not use it. You can definitely jeopardize your integrity by attaching your name to things you don't use. This {Skoal} fits my life style."[34] Some firms get around this problem by using animated characters, such as Garfield the cat or Snoopy. In fact, a large portion of the most memorable television commercials use cartoon characters (e.g., the California Raisins) rather than real people.[35]

Because there is some indication that the public is growing weary of spots using well-known celebrities, some marketers are instead turning to obscure or highly specialized endorsers (who also happen to be cheaper). Dewar's Scotch received a lot of free publicity for its campaign that featured non-celebrities in its famous "Profiles" spots, and Amaretto liqueur uses obscure cultural figures, such as actors who have appeared in low-budget cult movies. As the account executive for Amaretto explained about these ads, "We didn't want established stars. These personalities are saying, 'You don't know who I am, but you should.'"[36]

Testing Celebrity Images.   For celebrity campaigns to be effective, the endorser must have a clear and popular image. Many promotional strategies employing stars fail for this reason, such as unsuccessful attempts to market fragrances by Candice Bergen, Michael Jackson, Marlo Thomas, and even the late artist Salvador Dali.

The images of celebrities are often pre-tested to increase the probability of consumer acceptance. One widely used technique is the *"Q" rating* (Q stands for quality) developed by a market research company. This rating considers two factors in surveys: Consumers' level of familiarity with a name, and the number of respondents who indicate that a person, program, or character is a favorite.

While not the most sophisticated research technique, the Q rating acknowledges that mere *familiarity* with a celebrity's name is not sufficient to gauge popularity since some widely known people are also widely disliked. Celebrities with low Q ratings include athlete Bruce Jenner, Michael Jackson, Gene Simmons, Wayne Newton, Madonna, and Cyndi Lauper. Some with high ratings are Stevie Wonder, Billy Joel, Phil Collins, George Michael, Whitney Houston, Cher, and Dolly Parton.[37]

THE MESSAGE

Characteristics of the message itself help to determine its impact on attitudes. These variables include how the message is said as well as what is said. Some of the issues facing marketers include:

- Should the message be conveyed in words or pictures?
- How often should the message be repeated?
- Should a conclusion be drawn, or should this be left up to the listener?
- Should both sides of an argument be presented?
- Is it effective to explicitly compare one's product to competitors?
- Should a blatant sexual appeal be used?
- Should negative emotions, such as fear, ever be aroused?
- How concrete or vivid should the arguments and imagery be?
- Should the ad be funny?

A major study of over 1000 commercials identified factors that appear to determine whether or not a commercial message will be persuasive. The single most important feature was whether the communications contained a brand-differentiating message. In other words, did the communication

MULTICULTURAL DIMENSIONS

Some celebrities choose to maintain their credibility by endorsing products only in other countries, so these ads will not be seen by consumers in their own land. Many celebrities who do not do many American advertisements appear frequently in Japan. Mel Gibson endorses Asahi beer, Sly Stallone appears for Kirin beer, Sean Connery plugs Ito hams, and the singer Sheena Easton was featured in ads for Shochu liquor—dressed in a kimono and wig. Even the normally reclusive comedian and film director Woody Allen was featured in a campaign for a large Tokyo department store.[38]

stress a unique attribute or benefit of the product? Other good and bad elements are depicted in Table 6-1.[39]

SENDING THE MESSAGE

WORDS VERSUS PICTURES   The saying "one picture is worth a thousand words" captures the idea that visual stimuli can economically deliver big impact, especially when the communicator wants to influence receivers' emotional responses. For this reason, advertisers often place great emphasis on vivid and creative illustrations or photography.[40]

On the other hand, a picture is not always as effective at communicating factual information. Ads that contain the same information, presented in either visual or verbal form, have been found to elicit different reactions. The verbal version affects ratings on the utilitarian aspects of a product, while the visual version affects aesthetic evaluations.[41] Verbal elements are more effective when reinforced by an accompanying picture, especially if the illustration is *framed* (the message in the picture is strongly related to the copy).[42]

Because it requires more effort to process, a verbal message is most appropriate for high-involvement situations, such as in print contexts where the reader is motivated to really pay attention to the advertising. Because verbal material decays more rapidly in memory, more frequent exposures are needed to obtain the desired effect. Visual images, in contrast, allow the receiver to *chunk* information at the time of encoding (see chapter 4 on memory processes). This results in a stronger memory trace that aids retrieval over time.[43]

Visual elements may affect brand attitudes in one of two ways: (1) The consumer may form inferences about the brand and change his or her beliefs because of an illustration's imagery. For example, people who saw

TABLE 6-1 Positive and negative effects of elements in television commercials

Positive Effects	Negative Effects
Showing convenience of use	Extensive information on components, ingredients, or nutrition
Showing new product or improved features	Background cast (people incidental to message)
Indirect comparison to other products	Outdoor setting (message gets lost)
Demonstration of the product in use	Large number of on-screen characters
Demonstration of tangible results (e.g., bouncy hair)	Graphic displays
An actor playing the role of an ordinary person	
No principal character (more time devoted to the product)	

Source: Adapted from David W. Stewart and David H. Furse, "The Effects of Television Advertising Execution on Recall, Comprehension, and Persuasion," *Psychology & Marketing* 2 (Fall 1985): 135–160

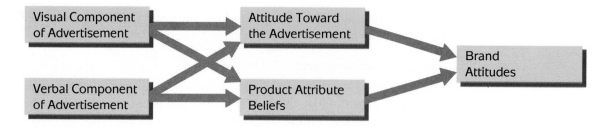

Figure 6-2 Effects of Visual and Verbal Components of Advertisements on Brand Attitudes Source: Andrew A. Mitchell, "The Effect of Verbal and Visual Components of Advertisements on Brand Attitudes and Attitude Toward the Advertisement," *Journal of Consumer Research* 13 (June 1986): 21. The University of Chicago Press.

an ad for a facial tissue accompanied by a photo of a sunset were more likely to believe that the brand came in attractive colors. Or (2) brand attitudes may be affected more directly; if the illustration elicits a strong positive or negative reaction, this will influence the consumer's attitude toward the ad (A_{ad}), which will then affect brand attitudes (A_B). This is the *dual component model* of brand attitudes, as illustrated in Figure 6-2.[44]

Vividness. Both pictures and words can differ in *vividness.* Powerful descriptions or graphics command attention and are more strongly embedded in memory. This may be because they tend to activate mental imagery, while abstract stimuli inhibit this process.[45] Of course, this effect can cut both ways: Negative information presented in a vivid manner may result in more negative evaluations at a later time.[46]

The concrete discussion of a product attribute in ad copy also influences the importance of that attribute, because more attention is drawn to it. For example, the copy for a watch that read "According to industry sources, three out of every four watch breakdowns are due to water getting into the case" was more effective than this version: "According to industry sources, many watch breakdowns are due to water getting into the case."[47]

REPETITION *Repetition Can Be a Two-Edged Sword.* As noted in Chapter 4, multiple exposures to a stimulus are usually required for learning (especially conditioning) to occur. And, contrary to the saying "familiarity breeds contempt," people have a tendency to like things that are more familiar to them, even if they were not that keen on them initially.[48] This is known as the *mere exposure effect.* On the other hand, too much repetition creates habituation, where the consumer no longer pays attention to the stimulus because of fatigue or boredom. Excessive exposure can cause *advertising wear-out,* which can result in negative reactions to an ad after seeing it too much.[49]

Two-Factor Theory. The fine line between familiarity and boredom has been explained by the **two-factor theory,** which proposes that two separate psychological processes are operating when a person is repeatedly exposed to an ad. The positive side of repetition is that it increases familiarity and thus reduces uncertainty about the product. The negative side is that over time boredom increases with each exposure. At some point the amount of boredom incurred begins to exceed the amount of uncertainty reduced, resulting in wear-out. This pattern is depicted in Figure 6-3. Its effect is especially pronounced in cases where each exposure is of a fairly long duration (such as a sixty-second commercial).[50]

The theory implies that advertisers can overcome this problem by either limiting the amount of exposure per repetition (such as using fifteen-second spots), or by maintaining familiarity but alleviating boredom by slightly varying the content of ads over time. This can be accomplished by campaigns that revolve around a common theme, though each spot may be different. For example, H&R Block systematically presents different reasons to use their firm for tax preparation.

CONSTRUCTING THE ARGUMENT

Many marketing messages are similar to debates or trials, where someone presents arguments and tries to convince the receiver to shift his or her opinion accordingly. The way the argument is presented can thus be very important.

ONE- VERSUS TWO-SIDED ARGUMENTS Most messages merely present one or more positive attributes about the product or reasons to buy it.

Figure 6-3 Two-Factor Theory and Advertising Wear-Out Source: Adapted from Arno J. Rathans, John L. Swasy, and Lawrence J. Marks, "Effects of Television Commercial Repetition, Receiver Knowledge," *Journal of Marketing Research* 23 (February 1986), 50–61, Fig. 1, p. 51.

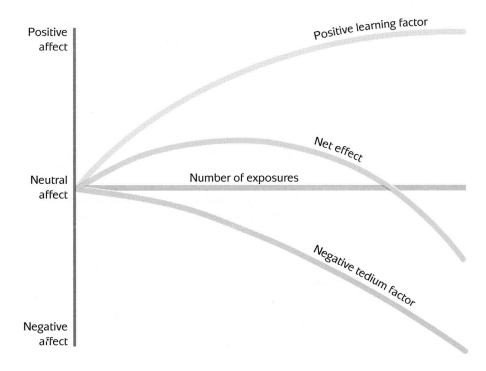

These are known as *supportive* arguments. An alternative is to use a *two-sided message,* where both positive and negative information is presented. Research has indicated that two-sided ads can be quite effective, yet they are not widely used.[51]

Why would a marketer want to devote advertising space to publicizing a product's negative attributes? Under the right circumstances, the use of *refutational arguments* where a negative issue is raised and then dismissed can be quite effective. This approach can increase source credibility by reducing reporting bias. Also, people who are skeptical about the product may be more receptive to a balanced argument instead of a "whitewash."[52] In one novel application, a Chateau Potelle winery ad included both positive and negative reviews of a wine by two experts. The ad suggested that consumers develop their own taste rather than relying on reviews in wine magazines.[53]

This is not to say that the marketer should go overboard in presenting major problems with the product. In the typical refutational strategy, relatively minor attributes are discussed that may present a problem or fall short when compared with competitors. These drawbacks are then refuted by emphasizing positive, important attributes. For example, Avis got a lot of mileage out of claiming to be only "No. 2," while an ad for Volkswagen woefully described one of its cars as a "lemon" because there was a scratch on the glove compartment chrome strip.[54] A two-sided strategy appears to be the most effective when the audience is well educated (and is presumably more impressed by a balanced argument).[55] It is also best to use when receivers are not already loyal to the product; "preaching to the converted" about possible drawbacks may raise doubts unnecessarily.

DRAWING CONCLUSIONS   A related factor is the issue of whether the argument should draw conclusions, or whether the points should merely be presented, permitting the consumer to arrive at his or her own. Should the message only say "Our brand is superior," or should it add "You should buy our brand?" On the one hand, consumers who make their own inferences instead of having them spoon-fed will form stronger, more accessible attitudes. On the other, leaving the conclusion ambiguous increases the chance that the desired attitude will not be formed.

The answer to this question depends upon the consumers' motivation to process the ad and the complexity of the arguments. If the message is personally relevant, people will pay attention to it and spontaneously form inferences. However, if the arguments are hard to follow or consumers' motivation to follow them is lacking, it is safer for the ad to draw conclusions.[56]

COMPARATIVE ADVERTISING   In 1971, the FTC issued guidelines that encouraged advertisers to name competing brands in their ads. This action was taken to improve the information available to consumers.[57] **Comparative advertising** refers to a strategy where a message compares two or more specifically named or recognizably presented brands and makes a comparison of them in terms of one or more specific attributes.[58] For example, Schering-Plough claimed that "New Ocu-Clear relieves three times longer than Visine," and Bristol-Myers stated that "New Liquid Vanish really does clean tough rust stains below the water line better than Lysol."

This strategy has yielded mixed results. While some comparative ads result in desired attitude change or positive A_{ad}, they have also been found to be lower in believability and may result in more source derogation (i.e., the consumer may doubt the credibility of a biased presentation).[59]

Comparative ads do appear to be effective in the case of new products. Here, they are superior in anchoring a new brand closer to a dominant one and in building a clear brand image. However, if the aim is to compare the new brand with the market leader in terms of specific product attributes, merely saying it is as good or better than the leader is not sufficient. For example, the use of the claim "Spring has the same fluoride as Crest" in a study resulted in attitude change for the fictitious product, while the more global statement "Preferred by Europeans in comparison with Crest" did not.[60]

▼ MARKETING PITFALL

When a marketer makes a specific comparative claim, he or she must be prepared to defend that claim. The risks of expensive litigation are high, and many companies get involved in complex lawsuits after using this approach. As one judge who was involved in a ten-year court battle being fought between two makers of rival analgesics noted: "Small nations have fought for their very survival with less resources."[61]

The disparaged brand may sue, even if it is not directly named in the ad. For example, if the maker of a soft drink said "Brand X is the most preferred," Brand Y is entitled to sue. Alberto-Culver sued Gillette about a hair rinse commercial on this basis. However, the advertiser is under no obligation to prove the claim in court. The plaintiff must prove it false.

The process of proving or disproving a claim often results in intense debate about the results of market research, and especially about whether research studies were properly designed, conducted or interpreted. One problem can occur if the company "cherry picks" results by selecting only those data in a study that support its position.

In one case, Triumph cigarettes claimed that a majority of respondents in a survey rated its brand, compared to Winston Lights, higher on "preference" and "better taste." However, the brand did not score higher on "amount of taste" or "satisfying quality," and so the company chose to use only the first two claims in its ad.

Illustrations can also be used to misrepresent a product. Tropicana Premium Pack orange juice claimed that unlike other leading brands it was not made from concentrate. The ad showed athlete Bruce Jenner squeezing an orange into a carton. Coca-Cola (makers of Minute Maid) disputed this claim. The company sued and won the case because the visual sequence shown in the ad was false: The orange juice is not squeezed directly into the carton. It is first pasteurized and in some cases frozen.[62]

TYPES OF MESSAGE APPEALS

EMOTIONAL VERSUS RATIONAL APPEALS In 1989, both Toyota and Nissan made bold advances into a segment of the car market they had not yet entered. Each introduced a large luxury car that sold for over $40,000. The two companies chose very different ways to communicate their product's attributes, as seen in the ads shown here. Toyota's advertising for its Lexus model used a rational appeal, with ads concentrating on the large number of technical advancements incorporated in the car's design. Print ads were dominated by copy describing these engineering features.

In sharp contrast, Nissan's controversial campaign for its Infiniti used an emotional appeal. The new model was introduced with a series of print and television ads that did not even discuss the car at all. The ads instead focused on the Zen-like experience of driving and featured long shots of serene landscapes. As one executive involved with the campaign explained, "We're not selling the skin of the car; we're selling the spirit."[63] While these ads were innovative, American consumers had trouble grasping the Japanese conception of luxury. Later ads for the Infiniti emphasized functional features of the car to compensate for this initial confusion.

The goal of an emotional appeal is to establish a connection between the product and the consumer, a strategy known as *bonding*.[64] Emotional appeals have the potential to increase the chance the message will be perceived, they may be more likely to be retained in memory, and they can also increase the consumer's involvement with the product. Although Nissan's gamble on emphasizing the aesthetic aspects of its product did not pay off in this case, other emotional appeals are quite effective. Many companies turned to this strategy after realizing that consumers do not find many differences among brands, especially those in well-established, mature categories. Ads for products ranging from cars (Lincoln Mercury) to cards (Hallmark) focus instead on emotional aspects. Mercury's capitalization on emotional attachments to old rock songs succeeded in lowering the median age of their consumers for some models by ten years.[65]

The precise effects of rational versus emotional appeals are hard to gauge. Though recall of ad contents tends to be better for "thinking" ads than for "feeling" ads, conventional measures of advertising effectiveness (e.g., day-after recall) may not be adequate to assess the cumulative effects of emotional ads. These open-ended measures are oriented toward cognitive responses, and feeling ads may be penalized because these reactions are not as easy to articulate.[66]

While they can make a strong impression, emotional appeals also run the risk of not getting across an adequate amount of product-related information. This potential problem is reminding some advertisers that the arousal of emotions is functional only to the extent that it sells the product. Procter & Gamble's original ads for Bounce fabric softener showed a happy young couple dancing to the song "Jump," with the message that Bounce is for clothes "you can't wait to jump into." In more recent spots, a woman discusses why the product makes her clothes feel and smell better. It is still somewhat emotional and experiential, but the main selling point of "softness without static cling" is driven home.[67]

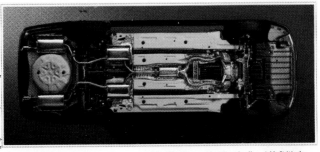

When Car and Driver magazine remarked that Lexus "has left no luxury sedan stone unturned," little did they know we also overturned the luxury sedan itself.

You see, wind traveling under a car is just as capable of creating drag as wind that travels over it.

To understand the full significance of this, you've only to take a cursory glance beneath the average car.

However smooth and aerodynamic it may look from above, the

When Car and Driver Said Lexus Left No Stone Unturned, They Had No Idea How Right They Were.

same can hardly be said of the numerous components underneath, the things that actually make the car work.

Now, one school of thought says that if you install a big

enough front spoiler, the problem goes away.

But this solution was hardly conducive to what Toyota was trying to create in Lexus: a true, high-performance luxury

sedan, not a race car.

So while they were painstakingly smoothing and refining the upper part of the car to achieve the most beautifully aerodynamic body shape, they were taking

equal pains to achieve similar results underneath.

This involved a phenomenal amount of wind-tunnel testing, but the result was also phenomenal.

A coefficient of drag so low, it makes the LS 400 one of the most

aerodynamic luxury sedans sold in America.

Its cabin is astoundingly quiet. (Characteristically, our engineers went as far as to bury microphones in their clay models so they could monitor wind noise.)

And, for all its high performance and luxury, the LS 400 is projected to be efficient enough to avoid the Gas-Guzzler tax.

What's most remarkable, though, is that aerodynamic law points to the perfect car being shaped like a jellybean.

And that's a law Lexus has just overturned.

LEXUS
The Relentless Pursuit Of Perfection.

The LS 400. Coming September 1. For more information, call 800-USA-LEXUS.

Lexus, A Division Of Toyota. © 1989 Toyota Motor Sales, U.S.A., Inc. Lexus reminds you to wear seat belts and obey all speed laws.

UNDER-PROMISE.
OVER-DELIVER.

If it's possible to capsulize the values that shape the philosophy of Infiniti, the words 'under-promise and over-deliver' come closest.

It means promise to do one thing, on time and well.

Then deliver two things, well done and early.

It means living by your word and then doing more than you said you would.

To an Infiniti engineer, it means setting the standard at "best of class" and then delivering a standard that exceeds the best in the class.

At the assembly plant, it means that an Infiniti car can be sent back or rejected for even the most ambiguous reason, such as: "It doesn't feel right."

At Infiniti headquarters it means an open checkbook to designers, researchers and development teams and an order to spend

what it costs to do the job right.

It means years are spent on the touch of a button. The pull of a door handle. The feel of the leathers. The sound of the radio.

And at the dealership, it means designing a space that's more like a contemporary art gallery than an automobile showroom. It means the customer is king. It means surprising—even heroic—levels of service. It means spending a portion of each day following up on customers, checking in, calling up if only to ask: "How are you enjoying the car? What more can we do for you?"

Few dealers can live up to the simple commitment of 'under-promise, over-deliver.'

The few that can are Infiniti dealers.

And by the way, it was a pleasure seeing all of our friends and colleagues who joined us at the recent NADA convention.

Thank you.

INFINITI.
created by Nissan

The rational versus the mysterious: While ads for Lexus automobiles (top) emphasize design and engineering, the initial ads for rival Infiniti (bottom) did not even show the car. Courtesy of Lexus. Courtesy of INFINITI®, A division of Nissan Motor Corporation, USA.

SEX APPEALS Under the assumption that "sex sells," campaigns for everything from perfumes to auto mechanics feature a heavy dose of erotic suggestion, ranging from subtle hints to blatant displays of skin. Perhaps not surprisingly, female nudity in print ads generates negative feelings and tension among female consumers, while men's reactions are more positive.[68]

Does Sex Work? Although the use of sex does appear to draw attention to an ad, its use may actually be counterproductive to the marketer.

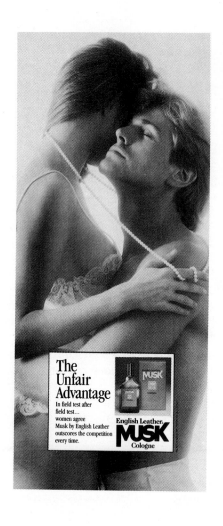

This ad for English Leather musk cologne relies on a sexual appeal. Since the product itself is intended to enhance interpersonal attraction, is this an appropriate use of sexuality in advertising?
Courtesy of MEM Company, Inc.

Ironically, a provocative picture can be *too* effective. It attracts so much attention that it hinders processing and recall of the ad's contents. Sexual appeals appear to be ineffective when used merely as a "trick" to grab attention. They do, however, appear to work when the product is *itself* sexually related.

HUMOROUS APPEALS   The use of humor can be tricky, particularly since what is funny to one person may be offensive or incomprehensible to another. Specific cultures may have different senses of humor and also use funny material in diverse ways. For example, commercials in the U.K. are more likely to use puns and satire than in the United States.[69]

Does humor work?   Overall, humorous advertisements do get attention. One study found that recognition scores for humorous liquor ads were better than average, particularly among white males. However, the verdict is mixed as to whether humor affects recall or product attitudes in a significant way.[70] One function it may play is to provide a source of *distraction*. A funny ad inhibits the consumer from counterarguing, thereby increasing the likelihood of message acceptance.[71]

Humor is more likely to be effective when the brand is clearly identified and the funny material does not "swamp" the message. This danger is similar to that of beautiful models diverting attention from copy points. Subtle humor is usually better, as is humor that does not make fun of the potential consumer. Finally, humor should be appropriate to the product's image. An undertaker or a bank might want to avoid humor, while other products adapt to it quite well. Sunsweet prunes quadrupled sales based on their claim "Today the pits, tomorrow the wrinkles."[72]

FEAR APPEALS   Fear appeals highlight the negative consequences that can occur unless the consumer changes a behavior or an attitude. This strategy is widespread; fear appeals are used in over 15 percent of all television ads.[73] The arousal of fear is a common tactic for public policy issues, such as convincing consumers to stop smoking or to drive safely (i.e., to reduce physical risk). It can also be applied to social risk issues by threatening one's success with the opposite sex, career, and so on. This tactic has been half-jokingly called "slice of death."

One early application of this tactic was in AT&T's "True Confessions" campaign, where consumers faced the dire consequences of a bad choice of phone systems. In one commercial, two young executives meet in the executive washroom. One expresses anxiety about selecting an obsolete phone system and worries that as a result he may be obsolete as well.[74]

Does Fear Work?   Fear appeals are usually most effective when only a moderate amount of fear is induced. The relationship between fear and attitude change is *nonmonotonic*.75 As shown in Figure 6-4, this means that increasing levels of fear do *not* result in increased change; the relationship instead resembles a U-shaped curve.

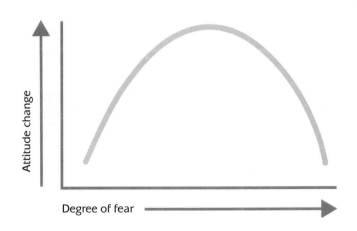

Figure 6-4 The Relationship Between Fear and Attitude Change

If the threat is too great, the audience tends to deny that it exists as a way to rationalize the danger. A study that manipulated subjects' degree of anxiety about AIDS, for example, found that condom ads were evaluated most positively when a moderate amount of fear was induced. In this context, copy that promoted the use of the condom because "Sex is a risky business" (moderate fear) resulted in more attitude change than either a low fear appeal that instead emphasized the product's sensitivity or a high fear appeal that discussed the certainty of death from AIDS.[76] Similarly, scare tactics have not been as effective as hoped in getting teen-agers to decrease their use of alcohol or drugs. Teens simply tune out the message or deny its relevance to them.[77]

Some of the most effective fear appeals try to convey a moral lesson by creating a powerful character who demonstrates how to avoid negative outcomes. For example General Motors' Mr. Goodwrench personifies the concept of "good car-maintenance," appealing to the desire to avoid an accident or death by properly maintaining one's car. Mr. Goodwrench's enemy is consumer inertia (not getting one's car serviced regularly). By embodying struggles or other evil forces in made-up characters, some threatening aspects are softer than they would be if a real person were used.[78]

Fear appeals appear to be most effective when the consumer is already afraid of the problem discussed in the ad. The threats should not be excessive, and a solution to the problem should be presented (otherwise, consumers will tune out the ad since they can do nothing to solve the problem).[79] This technique is at work in the ad shown here, where the actress Cher advises readers about doing breast self-examinations. Appeals also work better when source credibility is high.[80]

THE MESSAGE AS ART FORM: METAPHORS BE WITH YOU

Many advertisements take the form of short stories or poems that rely heavily on the use of imagery, fantasy, and the like. Marketers may be thought of as storytellers who supply visions of reality similar to those provided by authors, poets, and artists. These communications take the form of stories because the product benefits they describe are intangible and must be given tangible meaning by expressing them in a form that is concrete and visible. Advertising creatives rely (consciously or not) on various literary devices to communicate these meanings.

For example, a product or service might be *personified* by a character such as Mr. Goodwrench, the Jolly Green Giant, or the California Raisins. Many ads take the form of an *allegory,* where a story is told about an abstract trait or concept that has been personified as a person, animal, vegetable, and so on. Some modern allegories include the "marriage" of two neighboring area codes in a New York Telephone ad or the use of a character named "Rusty" by Rusty Jones to teach consumers about the proper way to protect their cars from dirt and rust.

A *metaphor* involves the use of an explicit comparison, where the reader is told A is B (e.g., "United Airlines is your friend in faraway places"). The term was even used literally by Reebok to equate the shoe with comfort, as seen in their ad. Metaphors allow the marketer to activate meaningful images and apply them to everyday events. In the stock market

I never shower alone.

And neither should you. Because simply by hanging this free card in your shower, you could save your own life.

You see, this shower card will show you how to do monthly breast self-examination. And remind you to do it. This is vitally important. Because even though 1 in 10 women will develop breast cancer, 90% of those cancers are controllable if detected early.

So send for your free Coors/High Priority Shower Card today. Then put it in your shower and use it. And if you're over 35, ask your doctor about getting a mammogram. Because in the fight against cancer, we're not alone.

HIGH PRIORITY
Breast Cancer Research/Information Network of the AMC Cancer Research Center

Coors

© 1987 Adolph Coors Company, Golden, Colorado 80401
Brewer of Fine Quality Beers Since 1873.

For your free Coors/High Priority Shower Card, send this coupon to the AMC Cancer Research Center at: Shower Card, Box 1987, Denver, CO 80201.

NAME
ADDRESS
CITY   STATE   ZIP   CO
One card per coupon. Offer good while supplies last.

Cher, High Priority Charter Member

Fear appeals have a greater chance of being effective if they also provide consumers with a possible solution to the problem. Here, celebrity Cher gives concrete advice about breast self-examinations. Courtesy of Coors Brewing Company and AMC Cancer Research Center.

"white knights" battle "hostile raiders" using "poison pills," while Tony the Tiger allows us to equate cereal with strength and the Merrill Lynch bull sends the message that the company is "a breed apart."[81]

FORMS OF STORY PRESENTATION   Just as a story can be told in words or pictures, the way the audience is addressed can also make a difference. Commercials are structured like other art forms, borrowing conventions from literature and art as they communicate their messages.[82]

One important distinction is between a *drama* and a *lecture*.[83] A lecture is like a speech where the source speaks directly to the audience in an attempt to inform them about a product or persuade them to buy it. Because a lecture clearly implies an attempt at persuasion, the audience will regard it as such. Assuming listeners are motivated to do so, the merits of the message will be weighed, along with the credibility of the source.

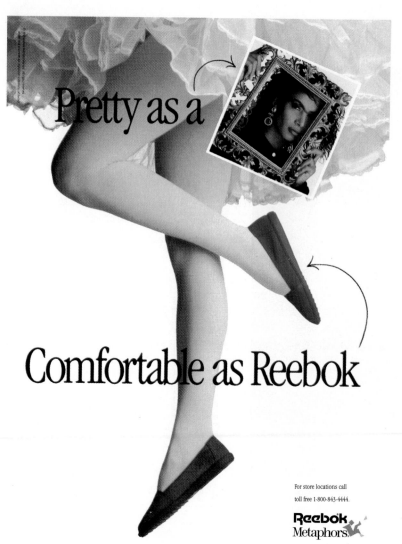

Pretty as a

Comfortable as Reebok

For store locations call
toll free 1-800-843-4444.

Reebok
Metaphors

Reebok uses the metaphor "Pretty as a picture" to promote its line of Metaphors shoes. Reprinted by permission of Reebok International Ltd.

Cognitive responses, such as counterargumentation, will occur. The appeal will be accepted to the extent that it overcomes objections and is congruent with a person's beliefs.

In contrast, a drama is similar to a play or movie. While an argument holds the viewer at arm's length, a drama draws the viewer into the action. The characters only indirectly address the audience; they interact with each other about a product or service in an imaginary setting. Dramas attempt to be experiential—to involve the audience emotionally. In *transformational advertising*, the consumer associates the experience of product usage with some subjective sensation. Thus, ads for the Infiniti attempted to transform the "driving experience" into a mystical, spiritual event.

THE SOURCE VERSUS THE MESSAGE: SELL THE STEAK OR THE SIZZLE?

Two major components of the communications model, the source and the message, have been reviewed. Which aspect has the most impact on persuading consumers to change their attitudes? Should marketers worry more about *what* is said, or *how* it's said and *who* says it?

The answer is, it depends. Variations in a consumer's level of involvement, as discussed in Chapter 3, result in the activation of very different cognitive processes when a message is received. Research indicates that this level of involvement will determine which aspects of a communication are processed. The situation appears to resemble a traveler who comes to a fork in the road: One or the other path is chosen, and this path has a big impact on the factors that will make a difference in persuasion attempts.

THE ELABORATION LIKELIHOOD MODEL

The **elaboration likelihood model** (ELM) assumes that once a consumer receives a message he or she begins to process it.[84] Depending upon the personal relevance of this information, one of two *routes* to persuasion will be followed. Under conditions of high involvement, the consumer takes the *central route to persuasion.* Under conditions of low involvement, a *peripheral route* is taken instead. This model is diagrammed in Figure 6-5.

THE CENTRAL ROUTE TO PERSUASION When the consumer finds the information in a persuasive message to be relevant or somehow interesting, he or she will carefully attend to the message content. The person is likely to actively think about the arguments presented and generate *cognitive*

Figure 6-5 The Elaboration Likelihood Model of Persuasion

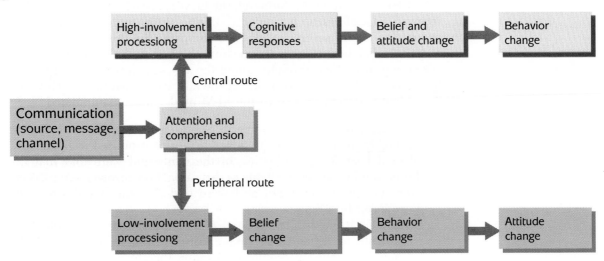

responses to these arguments. Upon hearing a radio message warning about drinking while pregnant, an expectant mother might say to herself, "She's right. I really should stop drinking alcohol now that I'm pregnant." Or, she might offer *counterarguments,* such as "That's a bunch of baloney. My mother had a cocktail every night when she was pregnant with me, and I turned out fine." If a person generates counterarguments in response to a message, it is less likely that he or she will yield to the message, while the generation of further supporting arguments increases the probability of compliance.[85]

The central route to persuasion is likely to involve the traditional hierarchy of effects, as discussed in Chapter 5. Beliefs are carefully formed and evaluated and strong attitudes are then formed that will be likely to guide behavior. This implies that message factors, such as the quality of arguments presented, will be important in determining attitude change. Prior knowledge about a topic results in more thoughts about the message and also increases the number of counterarguments.[86]

THE PERIPHERAL ROUTE TO PERSUASION   In contrast, the peripheral route is taken when the person is not motivated to really think about the arguments presented. Instead, the consumer is likely to use other cues in deciding on the suitability of the message. These cues might include the product's package, the attractiveness of the source, or the context in which the message is presented. Sources of information extraneous to the actual message content are called *peripheral* cues because they surround the actual message.

The peripheral route to persuasion highlights the irony about low involvement alluded to in Chapter 5: When consumers do not care about a product, the stimuli associated with it *increase* in importance. This implies that low-involvement products may be purchased chiefly because the marketer has done a good job in designing a "sexy" package, choosing a popular spokesperson, or perhaps just creating a pleasant shopping environment.

SUPPORT FOR THE ELM   Although the ELM approach is fairly new, it has received a lot of research support.[87] In one study, undergraduates were exposed to one of several mock advertisements for Break, a new brand of low-alcohol beer. Using the technique of *thought-listing,* they were asked to provide their thoughts about the ads, which were later analyzed by the researchers. Two versions of the ads are shown here.[88] Three independent variables crucial to the ELM model were manipulated.

1. Message-processing involvement. Some subjects were motivated to be highly involved with the ads. They were promised a gift of low-alcohol beer for participating in the study and were told that the brand would soon be available in their area. Low-involvement subjects were not promised a gift and were told that the brand would be introduced in a distant area.
2. Argument strength. One version of the ad used strong, compelling arguments to drink Break (e.g., "Break contains one-half of the amount of alcohol of regular beers, and therefore, has less calories

Introducing the new breakthrough in beer.

There are times when you want the taste and refreshment that only beer can provide, without the alcohol content of regular beer-- now you have that choice with **BREAK** beer.

●Break contains one-half the amount of alcohol of regular beers, and therefore, has less calories than regular beer-- both important in today's health conscious world.

●Unlike regular beer, Break's lower alcohol and lower calorie content allow you to have a great tasting beer while keeping physically and mentally fit.

●Break is a smart choice for those times when you want to relax without becoming intoxicated.

●If you're thinking about switching from regular beer, Break is the one to try.

●So enjoy yourself with Break, a great tasting beer that won't slow you down.

John and Becky Fitzgerald enjoying the great taste of Break.
EDUCATION: *recent graduates of a major university.*
PROFESSION:
  John, orthopedic surgeon.
  Becky, corporate lawyer.
HOBBIES: *running, raquetball, photography, and travel.*

For the good times, without the bad times.

Introducing the new breakthrough in beer.

There are times when you want the taste and refreshment that only beer can provide, without the alcohol content of regular beer-- now you have that choice with **BREAK** beer.

●Break is just as good as any other regular beer.

●You really can't tell the difference between Break and regular beer.

●Break has been designed with the beer drinker in mind.

●If desired, one can obtain the full strength effect of a regular beer by drinking a few more Break beers than one would normally drink.

●So enjoy yourself with Break, the beer of the future.

John and Becky Fitzgerald enjoying the great taste of Break.
EDUCATION: *high school graduates.*
PROFESSION:
  John, sales clerk for a department store.
  Becky, toll booth operator.
HOBBIES: *bowling, TV, movies, and stock-car races.*

For the good times, without the bad times.

These mock ads were used in a study on the elaboration likelihood model. The one on the left contains strong, logical arguments and socially attractive sources. The one on the right employs weak arguments with pictures of the same people now depicted as relatively unattractive. Consistent with the model, the attitudes of high-involvement experimental subjects were more likely to be swayed by powerful arguments, while the attitudes of low-involvement subjects were more likely to be influenced by attractive sources. Source: J. Craig Andrews and Terence A. Shimp, "Effects of Involvement, Argument Strength, and Source Characteristics on Central and Peripheral Processing in Advertising," *Psychology & Marketing* 7 (Fall 1990): 195–214.

than regular beer . . .") while the other listed only weak arguments (e.g., "Break is just as good as any other regular beer").

3. Source characteristics. While both ads contained a photo of a couple drinking the beer, their relative social attractiveness was varied by their dress, posture and nonverbal expressions, and the background information given about their educational achievements and occupations.

Consistent with the ELM model, high-involvement subjects had more thoughts related to the ad messages than did low-involvement subjects, who devoted more cognitive activity to the sources used in the ad. The attitudes of high-involvement subjects were more likely to be swayed by powerful arguments, while the attitudes of low-involvement subjects were more likely to be influenced by the ad version using attractive sources. The results of this study, paired with others, indicate that the relative effectiveness of a strong message and a favorable source depends upon consumers' level of involvement with the product being advertised.

These results, typical of such studies, underscore the basic idea that highly involved consumers look for the "steak" (e.g., strong, rational arguments). Those who are less-involved are more affected by the "sizzle" (e.g., the colors and images used in packaging, endorsements by famous people, and so on). It is important to remember, however, that the *same* communications variable can be both a central and a peripheral cue, depending upon its relation to the attitude object. For example, the physical attractiveness of a model might serve as a peripheral cue in a car commercial. However, her beauty might be a central cue for a beauty-related product such as shampoo, where the product's benefits are directly tied to enhancing attractiveness.[89]

SOCIAL MARKETING

The power of persuasive communications to shape consumer behavior can be harnessed to promote health and social well-being. Frequently this involves the *de-marketing* of negative behaviors or lifestyles, where consumption of harmful products is discouraged. **Social marketing** involves the promotions of causes and ideas (called *social products)*, such as energy conservation, museums, population control, and so on.[90] For example, a major campaign to combat drug use was undertaken by the Partnership for a Drug-Free America, a group organized by the American Association of Advertising Agencies. This campaign was the largest *pro bono* effort (meaning the ad agencies involved donated their services) in history. As one involved executive noted, "We are approaching the problem posed by the $110 billion illegal drug industry from a marketing point of view. What we're doing is competing with drug pushers for market share of *non-users*."[91]

PUBLIC-SERVICE ADVERTISING

Many government and private groups rely on *public-service advertising* to promote changes in drug usage, sexual practices, smoking, and so on. The British Government, for example, is that country's third largest advertiser. It uses advertising to "sell" its social policies, including promotion of small business activity, and anti-drug and AIDS messages.[92]

Ads that attempt to de-market must be high impact, because no one can guarantee their frequency or placement to the target audience. If executed properly, these efforts can be highly effective. A recent major study by the Advertising Research Foundation demonstrated under tightly controlled conditions that the number of men in four test markets who asked their doctors about colon cancer more than doubled after they were exposed to a year-long television ad campaign.[93]

 MARKETING OPPORTUNITY

Consumers' attitudes can also be influenced by the behaviors of media role models, who act as communications sources even when not explicitly endorsing a product. The behavior of television characters often encourages irresponsible behavior by glamorizing greed, promiscuity, excessive alcohol and drug use, and so on. For example, the depiction of sexual activity on television is increasing, but the consequences of these acts in terms of unwanted pregnancies, venereal diseases and AIDS are rarely mentioned.[94]

Some social marketers are turning their attention to the possibility that attitudes can be changed more effectively by influencing the consumption activities depicted in popular media. As observed by the creator of the popular television show "L.A. Law," "If you put a cigarette in a character's hand, you are announcing that he smells bad and doesn't take care of himself. And if you are going to give them a drink, it better be wine with a fancy, multiple name."[95]

The power of television to mold behavior was used successfully by a public service campaign called the Harvard Alcohol Project. This was the first attempt to change consumer behavior by coordinating the subtle messages conveyed by a number of popular television shows. To promote the use of designated drivers by people who are out drinking, the scripts of prime-time shows like "Cheers" were deliberately written to include mentions of designated drivers. Within one year, the project reported a 10 percent increase in the proportion of consumers who claimed to have used a designated driver.[96]

CHAPTER SUMMARY

Marketers fight a constant battle to persuade consumers. Attitude change strategies can take many forms, some of which are more or less effective depending upon the structure of a persuasive communication, who delivers it, and how motivated the consumer is to attend to it. The elaboration likelihood model stipulates two possible routes to persuasion, depending upon the consumer's level of involvement with the attitude object. If the consumer is highly involved, the central route will be more effective. This means that the quality of the arguments themselves will be carefully considered and the consumer will generate cognitive responses to them. If, on the other hand, the consumer is not sufficiently motivated to process these arguments, the peripheral route to persuasion will be more effective. This route emphasizes the persuasive role of other characteristics of the message, such as the source of the communication. This chapter reviews aspects of the communications model, including the nature of the message source, the medium, and the structure of the communication. Such factors as source credibility, source attractiveness, emotional versus rational appeals, and the effectiveness of sex and humor in changing attitudes are discussed.

KEY TERMS

Communications model

Comparative advertising

Elaboration likelihood model

Functional theory of attitudes

Persuasion

Sleeper effect

Social marketing

Source credibility

Two-factor theory

REVIEW QUESTIONS AND DISCUSSION TOPICS

1. A Government agency wants to encourage the use of designated drivers by people who have been drinking. What advice could you give the organization about constructing persuasive communications? Discuss some factors that might be important, including the structure of the communications, where they should appear, and who should deliver them. Should fear appeals be used, and if so, how?
2. Compare and contrast knowledge bias and reporting bias. Which is the bigger problem for marketers?
3. Are informercials ethical? Should marketers be allowed to use any format they want to present product-related information?
4. Discuss some conditions where it would be advisable to use a comparative advertising strategy.
5. Why would a marketer consider saying *negative* things about his or her product? When is it feasible to do this? Can you find any current examples of this strategy?
6. Although a competing company may sue a marketer who makes false claims about its products, the burden of proof is on the challenger. Why, then, should a marketer be careful about making such claims?
7. A marketer must decide whether to incorporate rational or emotional appeals in its communications strategy. Describe conditions that are more favorable to using one or the other.
8. Discuss the case for and against the use of repetition in advertising.

HANDS-ON EXERCISES

1. Collect ads that rely on sex appeal to sell products. How often are benefits of the actual product communicated to the reader?
2. To observe the process of counterargumentation in action, ask a friend to talk out loud while watching or reading a commercial or ad. Ask him or her to respond to each of the points in the ad, or to write down reactions to the claims made. How much skepticism regarding what is claimed in the ad can you detect?
3. Make a log of all the commercials shown on one network television channel over a six-hour period. Categorize each according to product category, and whether they are presented as drama or argument. Describe the types of messages used (e.g., two-sided arguments), and keep track of the types of spokespeople (e.g., television actors, famous people, animated characters). Based on these observations, what can you conclude about the dominant forms of persuasive tactics currently employed by marketers?

NOTES

1. Quoted in Cyndee Miller, "The Fur Flies as Fashion Foes Pelt It Out Over Animal Rights," *Marketing News* 2 (December 4, 1989):2.
2. Quoted in Miller, "The Fur Flies as Fashion Foes Pelt It Out Over Animal Rights,".
3. Gert Assmus, "An Empirical Investigation into the Perception of Vehicle Source Effects," *Journal of Advertising* 7 (Winter 1978): 4-10; for a more thorough discussion of the pros and cons of different media, see Stephen Baker, *Systematic Approach to Advertising Creativity* (New York: McGraw-Hill, 1979).
4. Daniel Katz, "The Functional Approach to the Study of Attitudes," *Public Opinion Quarterly* 24 (Summer 1960): 163-204; Richard J. Lutz, "Changing Brand Attitudes through Modification of Cognitive Structure," *Journal of Consumer Research* 1 (March 1975): 49-59.

5. Russell H. Fazio, T. M. Lenn, and E. A. Effrein, "Spontaneous Attitude Formation," *Social Cognition* 2 (1984): 214–34.

6. Mason Haire, "Projective Techniques in Marketing Research," *Journal of Marketing* 14 (April 1950): 649–56.

7. Sharon Shavitt, "The Role of Attitude Objects in Attitude Functions," *Journal of Experimental Social Psychology* 26 (1990): 124–48.

8. Carl I. Hovland and W. Weiss, "The Influence of Source Credibility on Communication Effectiveness," *Public Opinion Quarterly* 15 (1952): 635–50.

9. Herbert Kelman, "Processes of Opinion Change," *Public Opinion Quarterly* 25 (Spring 1961): 57–78; Susan M. Petroshuis and Kenneth E. Crocker, "An Empirical Analysis of Spokesperson Characteristics on Advertisement and Product Evaluations," *Journal of the Academy of Marketing Science* 17 (Summer 1989): 217–26.

10. Kenneth G. DeBono and Richard J. Harnish, "Source Expertise, Source Attractiveness, and the Processing of Persuasive Information: A Functional Approach," *Journal of Personality and Social Psychology* 55 (1988)4: 541–46.

11. Hershey H. Friedman and Linda Friedman, "Endorser Effectiveness by Product Type," *Journal of Advertising Research* 19 (1979)5: 63–71.

12. Anthony R. Pratkanis, Anthony G. Greenwald, Michael R. Leippe, and Michael H. Baumgardner, "In Search of Reliable Persuasion Effects: III. The Sleeper Effect Is Dead. Long Live the Sleeper Effect," *Journal of Personality and Social Psychology* 54 (1988)2: 203–18.

13. Herbert C. Kelman and Carl I. Hovland, "Reinstatement of the Communication in Delayed Measurement of Opinion Change," *Journal of Abnormal Psychology* 4, 48 (1953)3: 327–35.

14. Darlene Hannah and Brian Sternthal, "Detecting and Explaining the Sleeper Effect," *Journal of Consumer Research* (September 1984)11: 632–42.

15. David Mazursky and Yaacov Schul, "The Effects of Advertisement Encoding on the Failure to Discount Information: Implications for the Sleeper Effect," *Journal of Consumer Research* 15 (June 1988): 24–36.

16. Alice H. Eagly, Andy Wood and Shelly Chaiken, "Causal Inferences About Communicators and Their Effect in Opinion Change," *Journal of Personality and Social Psychology* 36 (1978)4: 424–35.

17. Barry Meier, "TV Commercials That Go On and On," *New York Times* (January 27, 1990): 54.

18. "Jim Palmer Pitches 'Style' for Jockey," *New York Times* (August 29, 1982).

19. "Robber Makes it Biggs in Ad," *Advertising Age* (May 29, 1989): 26.

20. Karen K. Dion, "What is Beautiful is Good," *Journal of Personality and Social Psychology* 24 (December 1972): 285–90.

21. Michael J. Baker and Gilbert A. Churchill, Jr., "The Impact of Physically Attractive Models on Advertising Evaluations," *Journal of Marketing Research* 14 (November 1977): 538–55; Marjorie J. Caballero and William M. Pride, "Selected Effects of Salesperson Sex and Attractiveness in Direct Mail Advertisements," *Journal of Marketing* 48 (January 1984): 94–100; W. Benoy Joseph, "The Credibility of Physically Attractive Communicators: A Review," *Journal of Advertising* 11 (1982)3: 15–24; Lynn R. Kahle and Pamela M. Homer, "Physical Attractiveness of the Celebrity Endorser: A Social Adaptation Perspective," *Journal of Consumer Research* 11 (1985)4: 954–61; Judson Mills and Eliot Aronson, "Opinion Change as a Function of Communicator's Attractiveness and Desire to Influence," *Journal of Personality and Social Psychology* 1 (1965): 173–77.

22. Leonard N. Reid and Lawrence C. Soley, "Decorative Models and the Readership of Magazine Ads," *Journal of Advertising Research* 23 (1983)2: 27–32.

23. Marjorie J. Caballero, James R. Lumpkin and Charles S. Madden, "Using Physical Attractiveness as an Advertising Tool: An Empirical Test of the Attraction Phenomenon," *Journal of Advertising Research* (August/September 1989): 16–22.

24. Baker and Churchill, Jr., "The Impact of Physically Attractive Models on Advertising Evaluations"; George E. Belch, Michael A. Belch, and Angelina Villareal, "Effects of Advertising Communications: Review of Research," *Research in Marketing* (Greenwich, Conn.: JAI Press, 1987)9: 59–117; A. E. Courtney and T. W. Whipple, *Sex Stereotyping in Advertising* (Lexington, Mass.: Lexington Books, 1983).

25. Kahle and Homer, "Physical Attractiveness of the Celebrity Endorser."

26. Baker and Churchill, "The Impact of Physically Attractive Models on Advertising Evaluations."

27. Michael A. Kamins, "Celebrity and Noncelebrity Advertising in a Two-Sided Context," *Journal of Advertising Research* 29 (June-July 1989): 34; Joseph M. Kamen, A. C. Azhari and J. R. Kragh, "What a Spokesman Does for a Sponsor," *Journal of Advertising Research* 15 (1975)2: 17-24; Lynn Langmeyer and Mary Walker, "A First Step to Identify the Meaning in Celebrity Endorsers," in *Advances in Consumer Research,* ed. Rebecca H. Holman and Michael R. Solomon (Provo, Utah: Association for Consumer Research, 1991)18: 364-71.

28. Jeffrey Burroughs and Richard A. Feinberg, "Using Response Latency to Assess Spokesperson Effectiveness," *Journal of Consumer Research* 14 (September 1987): 295-99.

29. Pamela G. Hollie, "A Rush for Singers to Promote Goods," *New York Times* (May 14, 1984):D1

30. Judith Graham, "Sponsors Line Up for Rockin' Role," *Advertising Age* (December 11, 1989):50.

31. Hollie, "A Rush for Singers to Promote Goods."

32. Quoted in Douglas C. McGill, "Star Wars in Cola Advertising," *New York Times* (March 22, 1989):D1.

33. Thomas R. King, "Credibility Gap: More Consumers Find Celebrity Ads Unpersuasive," *The Wall Street Journal* (July 5, 1989): B5.

34. Michael J. Specter, "Rock Puts on a Three-Piece Suit," *New York Times* (October 2, 1983).

35. Joanne Lipman, "When It's Commercial Time, TV Viewers Prefer Cartoons to Celebrities Any Day," *The Wall Street Journal* (February 16, 1990): B1.

36. Quoted in Barbara Kallen, "Who Cares What Eszter Balint Drinks?" *Forbes* (November 2, 1987): 192-93.

37. Bruce Haring, "Company Totes Up Popularity Quotients," *Billboard Magazine* 101 (1989): 12.

38. Marie Okabe, "Fading Yen for Foreign Stars in Ads," *Singapore Straits-Times* (1986).

39. David W. Stewart and David H. Furse, "The Effects of Television Advertising Execution on Recall, Comprehension, and Persuasion," *Psychology & Marketing* 2 (Fall 1985): 135-60.

40. R. C. Grass and W. H. Wallace, "Advertising Communication: Print Vs. TV," *Journal of Advertising Research* 14, (1974) 19-23.

41. Elizabeth C. Hirschman and Michael R. Solomon, "Utilitarian, Aesthetic, and Familiarity Responses to Verbal Versus Visual Advertisements," in *Advances in Consumer Research,* ed. Thomas C. Kinnear (Provo, Utah: Association for Consumer Research, 1984), 426-31.

42. Andrew A. Mitchell and Jerry C. Olson, "Are Product Attribute Beliefs the Only Mediator of Advertising Effects on Brand Attitude?" *Journal of Marketing Research* 18 (1981)3: 318-32.

43. Terry L. Childers and Michael J. Houston, "Conditions for a Picture-Superiority Effect on Consumer Memory," *Journal of Consumer Research* 11 (September 1984) 643-54.

44. Andrew A. Mitchell, "The Effect of Verbal and Visual Components of Advertisements on Brand Attitudes and Attitude Toward the Advertisement," *Journal of Consumer Research* 13 (June 1986): 12-24.

45. John R. Rossiter and Larry Percy, "Attitude Change Through Visual Imagery in Advertising," *Journal of Advertising Research* 9 (1980)2: 10-16.

46. Jolita Kiselius and Brian Sternthal, "Examining the Vividness Controversy: An Availability-Valence Interpretation," *Journal of Consumer Research* 12 (March 1986): 418-31.

47. Scott B. Mackenzie, "The Role of Attention in Mediating the Effect of Advertising on Attribute Importance," *Journal of Consumer Research* 13 (September 1986): 174-95.

48. Robert B. Zajonc, "Attitudinal Effects of Mere Exposure," *Journal of Personality and Social Psychology* 8 (Monograph, 1968): 1-29.

49. George E. Belch, "The Effects of Television Commercial Repetition on Cognitive Response and Message Acceptance," *Journal of Consumer Research* 9 (June 1982): 56-65; Marian Burke and Julie Edell, "Ad Reactions Over Time: Capturing Changes in the Real World," *Journal of Consumer Research* 13 (June 1986): 114-18; Herbert

Krugman, "Why Three Exposures May Be Enough," *Journal of Advertising Research* 12 (December 1972): 11–14.

50. Robert F. Bornstein, "Exposure and Affect: Overview and Meta-Analysis of Research, 1968-1987," *Psychological Bulletin* 106 (1989)2: 265–89; Arno Rethans, John Swasy, and Lawrence Marks, "Effects of Television Commercial Repetition, Receiver Knowledge, and Commercial Length: A Test of the Two-Factor Model," *Journal of Marketing Research* 23 (February 1986): 50–61.

51. Linda L. Golden and Mark I. Alpert, "Comparative Analysis of the Relative Effectiveness of One- and Two-Sided Communication for Contrasting Products," *Journal of Advertising* 16 (1987); Kamins, "Celebrity and Noncelebrity Advertising in a Two-Sided Context"; Robert B. Settle and Linda L. Golden, "Attribution Theory and Advertiser Credibility," *Journal of Marketing Research* 11 (May 1974): 181–85.

52. See Alan G. Sawyer, "The Effects of Repetition of Refutational and Supportive Advertising Appeals," *Journal of Marketing Research* 10 (February 1973): 23–33; George J. Szybillo and Richard Heslin, "Resistance to Persuasion: Inoculation Theory in a Marketing Context," *Journal of Marketing Research* 10 (November 1973): 396–403.

53. Lawrence M. Fisher, "Winery's Answer to Critics: Print Good and Bad Reviews," *New York Times* (January 9, 1991): D5.

54. Golden and Alpert, "Comparative Analysis of the Relative Effectiveness of One- and Two-Sided Communication for Contrasting Products."

55. Belch, et al., "Effects of Advertising Communications."

56. Frank R. Kardes, "Spontaneous Inference Processes in Advertising: The Effects of Conclusion Omission and Involvement on Persuasion," *Journal of Consumer Research* 15 (September 1988): 225–33.

57. Belch, et al., "Effects of Advertising Communications."

58. C. Dröge and R. Y. Darmon, "Associative Positioning Strategies Through Comparative Advertising: Attribute vs. Overall Similarity Approaches," *Journal of Marketing Research* 24 (1987):377–89; D. Muehling and N. Kangun, "The Multidimensionality of Comparative Advertising: Implications for the FTC," *Journal of Public Policy and Marketing* (1985): 112–28; Beth A. Walker and Helen H. Anderson, "Reconceptualizing Comparative Advertising: A Framework and Theory of Effects," in *Advances in Consumer Research,* ed. Rebecca H. Holman and Michael R. Solomon (Provo, Utah: Association for Consumer Research, 1991)18: 342–47; William L. Wilkie and Paul W. Farris, "Comparison Advertising: Problems and Potential," *Journal of Marketing* 39 (October 1975): 7–15; R. G. Wyckham, "Implied Superiority Claims," *Journal of Advertising Research* (Feburary/March 1987): 54–63.

59. Stephen A. Goodwin and Michael Etgar, "An Experimental Investigation of Comparative Advertising: Impact of Message Appeal, Information Load, and Utility of Product Class," *Journal of Marketing Research* 17 (May 1980): 187–202; Gerald J. Gorn and Charles B. Weinberg, "The Impact of Comparative Advertising on Perception and Attitude: Some Positive Findings," *Journal of Consumer Research* 11 (September 1984): 719–27; Terence A. Shimp and David C. Dyer, "The Effects of Comparative Advertising Mediated by Market Position of Sponsoring Brand," *Journal of Advertising* 3 (Summer 1978): 13–19; R. Dale Wilson, "An Empirical Evaluation of Comparative Advertising Messages: Subjects' Responses to Perceptual Dimensions," in *Advances in Consumer Research,* ed. B. B. Anderson (Ann Arbor, Mich.: Association for Consumer Research, 1976)3: 53–57.

60. Cornelia Droge and Rene Y. Darmon, "Associative Positioning Strategies Through Comparative Advertising: Attribute Versus Overall Similarity Approaches," *Journal of Marketing Research* 24 (November 1987): 377–88.

61. Quoted in Bruce Buchanan and Doron Goldman, "Us Vs. Them: The Minefield of Comparative Ads," *Harvard Business Review* 38 (May-June 1989)7: 50.

62. Buchanan and Goldman, "Us Vs. Them."

63. Michael Lev, "For Car Buyers, Technology or Zen," *New York Times* (May 22, 1989):D1.

64. "Connecting Consumer and Product," *New York Times* (January 18, 1990):D19.

65. Edward F. Cone, "Image and Reality," *Forbes* (December 14, 1987): 226.

66. H. Zielske, "Does Day-After Recall Penalize 'Feeling' Ads?" *Journal of Advertising Research* 22 (1982): 19–22.

67. Cone, "Image and Reality."

68. Belch, et al., "Effects of Advertising Communications"; Courtney and Whipple, "Sex Stereotyping in Advertising"; Michael S. LaTour, "Female Nudity in Print Advertising: An Analysis of Gender Differences in Arousal and Ad Response," *Psychology & Marketing* 7 (1990)1: 65–81; B. G. Yovovich, "Sex in Advertising—The Power and the Perils," *Advertising Age* (May 2, 1983):M4-M5.

69. Marc G. Weinberger and Harlan E. Spotts, "Humor in U.S. Versus U.K. TV Commercials: A Comparison," *Journal of Advertising* 18 (1989)2: 39–44.

70. Thomas J. Madden, "Humor in Advertising: An Experimental Analysis," (Working Paper No. 83-27, University of Massachusetts, 1984); Thomas J. Madden and Marc G. Weinberger, "The Effects of Humor on Attention in Magazine Advertising," *Journal of Advertising* 11 (1982)3: 8–14; Weinberger and Spotts, "Humor in U.S. Versus U.K. TV Commercials."

71. David Gardner, "The Distraction Hypothesis in Marketing," *Journal of Advertising Research* 10, (1970): 25–30.

72. "Funny Ads Provide Welcome Relief During These Gloom and Doom Days," *Marketing News* (April 17, 1981):3.

73. Lynette S. Unger and James M. Stearns, "The Use of Fear and Guilt Messages in Television Advertising: Issues and Evidence," in *1983 AMA Educators' Proceedings,* ed. Patrick E. Murphy, et al., Chicago: American Marketing Association, 1983), 16–20.

74. Lynn Coleman, "Advertisers Put Fear Into the Hearts of Their Prospects," *Marketing News* (August 15, 1988): 1.

75. Michael L. Ray and William L. Wilkie, "Fear: The Potential of an Appeal Neglected by Marketing," *Journal of Marketing* 34 (1970)1: 54–62.

76. Ronald Paul Hill, "An Exploration of the Relationship Between AIDS-Related Anxiety and the Evaluation of Condom Advertisements," *Journal of Advertising* 17 (1988)4: 35–42.

77. Randall Rothenberg, "Talking Too Tough on Life's Risks?" *New York Times* (February 16, 1990):D1.

78. Barbara B. Stern, "Medieval Allegory: Roots of Advertising Strategy for the Mass Market," *Journal of Marketing* 52 (July 1988): 84–94.

79. Judith Waldrop, "They're Coming to Take You Away (Fear as a Form of Persuasion)," *American Demographics* (June 15, 1988)2.

80. Brian Sternthal and C. Samuel Craig, "Fear Appeals: Revisited and Revised," *Journal of Consumer Research* 1 (December 1974): 22–34.

81. Stern, "Medieval Allegory."

82. See Linda M. Scott, "The Troupe: Celebrities as *Dramatis Personae* in Advertisements," in *Advances in Consumer Research,* ed. Rebecca H. Holman and Michael R. Solomon (Provo, Utah: Association for Consumer Research, 1991)18: 355–63; Barbara Stern, (1989), "Literary Criticism and Consumer Research: Overview and Illustrative Analysis," *Journal of Consumer Research* 16 (1989): 322–34; Judith Williamson, *Decoding Advertisements* (Boston: Marion Boyars, 1978).

83. John Deighton, Daniel Romer and Josh McQueen, "Using Drama to Persuade," *Journal of Consumer Research* 16 (December 1989): 335–43.

84. Richard E. Petty, John T. Cacioppo and David Schumann, "Central and Peripheral Routes to Advertising Effectiveness: The Moderating Role of Involvement," *Journal of Consumer Research* 10 (1983)2: 135–46.

85. Jerry C. Olson, Daniel R. Toy, and Philip A. Dover, "Do Cognitive Responses Mediate the Effects of Advertising Content on Cognitive Structure?" *Journal of Consumer Research* 9 (1982)3: 245–62.

86. Julie A. Edell and Andrew A. Mitchell, "An Information Processing Approach to Cognitive Responses," in *Research Frontiers in Marketing: Dialogues and Directions,* ed. S. C. Jain (Chicago: American Marketing Association, 1978).

87. See Mary Jo Bitner and Carl Obermiller, "The Elaboration Likelihood Model: Limitations and Extensions in Marketing," in *Advances in Consumer Research,* ed. Elizabeth C. Hirschman and Morris B. Holbrook (Provo, Utah: Association for Consumer Research, 1985)12: 420–25; Meryl P. Gardner, "Does Attitude Toward the Ad Affect Brand Attitude Under a Brand Evaluation Set?" *Journal of Marketing Research* 22 (1985): 192–98; C. W. Park and S.M. Young, "Consumer Response to Television Commercials: The Impact of Involvement and Background Music on

Brand Attitude Formation," *Journal of Marketing Research* 23 (1986): 11–24; Richard E. Petty, John T. Cacioppo, and David Schumann, "Central and Peripheral Routes to Advertising Effectiveness: The Moderating Role of Involvement," *Journal of Consumer Research* 10 (1983): 135–46; for a discussion of how different kinds of involvement interact with the ELM, see Robin A. Higie, Lawrence F. Feick, and Linda L. Price, "The Importance of Peripheral Cues in Attitude Formation for Enduring and Task-Involved Individuals," in *Advances in Consumer Research,* ed. Rebecca H. Holman and Michael R. Solomon (Provo, Utah: Association for Consumer Research, 1991)18: 187–93.

88. J. Craig Andrews and Terence A. Shimp, "Effects of Involvement, Argument Strength, and Source Characteristics on Central and Peripheral Processing in Advertising," *Psychology & Marketing* 7 (Fall 1990): 195–214.

89. Richard E. Petty, John T. Cacioppo, Constantine Sedikides, and Alan J. Strathman, "Affect and Persuasion: A Contemporary Perspective," *American Behavioral Scientist* 31 (1988)3: 355–71.

90. Seymour H. Fine, *Social Marketing: Promoting the Causes of Public and Nonprofit Agencies* (Boston: Allyn & Bacon, 1990).

91. Quoted in Cecelia Reed, "Partners for Life," *Advertising Age* (November 9, 1988): 122.

92. Steve Lohr, "Major British Advertiser: Government," *New York Times* (May 23, 1989):D1.

93. Randall Rothenberg, "Study Shows Power of Public-Service Ads," *New York Times* (April 8, 1991):D8.

94. Dennis T. Lowry and David E. Towles, "Prime Time TV Portrayals of Sex, Contraception and Venereal Diseases," *Journalism Quarterly* 86 (Summer 1989): 347–52.

95. Quoted in Molly O'Neill, "Words to Survive Life With: None of This, None of That," *New York Times* (May 27, 1990):1.

96. Bill Carter, "A Message on Drinking is Seen and Heard," *New York Times* (September 11, 1989):D11.

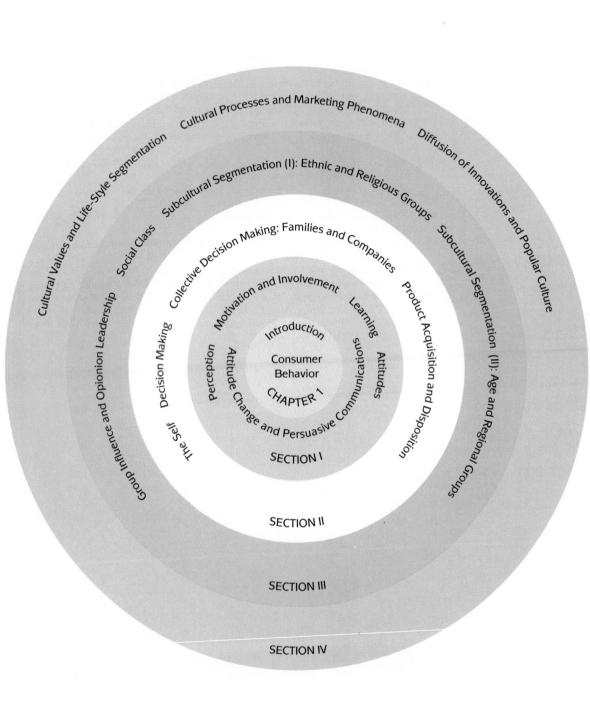

Cultural Processes and Marketing Phenomena

Diffusion of Innovations and Popular Culture

Cultural Values and Life-Style Segmentation

Subcultural Segmentation (I): Ethnic and Religious Groups

Social Class

Collective Decision Making: Families and Companies

Subcultural Segmentation (II): Age and Regional Groups

Group Influence and Opionion Leadership

Motivation and Involvement

Learning

Product Acquisition and Disposition

Decision Making

Introduction

Attitudes

Perception

Consumer Behavior

Communications

The Self

Attitude Change and Persuasive Communications

CHAPTER 1

SECTION I

SECTION II

SECTION III

SECTION IV

This section looks at consumers as they use products in everyday life. Consumer researchers and marketers try to understand how people decide what to buy and what to do with things after they are purchased. The section begins with an in-depth view of the self in Chapter 7, which examines how products are used to modify our images of ourselves and how marketers help to affect the way we feel about ourselves. Chapter 8 focuses on steps in the decision-making process, as the consumer becomes aware of a need and tries to satisfy this need by evaluating and selecting products and services he or she believes will provide the best solution. However, many purchase decisions are not solely in the hands of one person; they may be made by several people, or on behalf of others. Chapter 9 considers collective decisions, in both companies and families, where some degree of negotiation among two or more people often is required before a decision is made. The section ends with Chapter 10, which discusses important factors affecting consumer decisions at the time of purchase and examines what people do with products after they have finished with them.

The Consumer as a Decision Maker and Product User

The Self

Gail, a thirty-year-old insurance executive, is in a rut. She's been working so hard that she's starting to feel like she was born wearing a mannish tailored suit. Even though she's doing well professionally, it's been months since she had a date with a decent guy. Feeling unattractive and depressed, Gail decides to go shopping on her lunch hour. On a whim, she ducks into Victoria's Secret and buys herself a pair of black silk pantyhose and a frilly camisole, which she slips on underneath her suit. On her way back to the office, Gail feels more feminine and attractive than she has in a long time. Is it her imagination, or did Robert in Accounting look at her differently when she returned from the mall?

Many female consumers purchase fantasy products to enhance their femininity. Stores such as Victoria's Secret, which sell sensual lingerie in a "non-tacky" atmosphere, have benefited from this trend. They appeal to women who like to buy such products for themselves, marking a shift from the time when these items were bought by men for women as a way to play out *their* fantasies.

A California store called Fireworks exemplifies this new attitude. Located in a former firehouse, the store is dominated by a huge brass bed with a mannequin on her hands and knees. All sorts of G-strings, teddies, and related items are strewn over the bed. One theme featured in the store's windows was domestic bliss. The displays consisted of mannequins wearing black lace bras and bikini panties, flipping pancakes over stoves. The owner, a former chorus girl, noted: "I merchandise with high fantasy in mind, and I have a fantasy building. Women want to feel beautiful and feminine, and I dress them from the inside out."[1]

PERSPECTIVES ON THE SELF

Some of the most important attitudes consumers have are those regarding themselves. Many products, from cars to cologne, are bought because the person is trying to highlight or hide some aspect of the self. As in the case of women buying intimate apparel, these self-expressions are performed publicly and privately. This chapter will focus on the self, and discuss how consumers' feelings about themselves shape their consumption practices.

The 1980s were called the "Me Decade" because for many this time was marked by an absorption with the self. While it seems natural to think about each consumer having a self, this concept is actually a relatively new way of regarding people and their relationship to society.

The idea that each single human life is unique, rather than a part of a group, only developed in late medieval times (between the eleventh and fifteenth centuries). The notion that the self is an object to be pampered is even more recent. In addition, the emphasis on the unique nature of the self is much greater in Western societies.[2] Many Eastern cultures instead stress the importance of a "collective self," where the person's identity is derived in large measure from his or her social group.

The self can be understood from many different theoretical vantage points. From a psychoanalytic, or Freudian, perspective, the self is a system of competing forces riddled with conflict (see Chapter 3). Behaviorists tend to regard the self as a collection of conditioned responses. From a cognitive orientation the self is an information processing system, an organizing force that serves as a nucleus around which new information is processed.[3]

SELF-CONCEPT

Self-concept refers to the attitude a person holds toward him- or herself. Just as a consumer has an attitude toward Pepsi or democracy, the self is also a subject of evaluation. While an overall self-attitude is frequently positive, this is not always the case; there are certainly parts of the self that are evaluated more positively than others. For example, Gail felt better about her professional side than she did about her feminine side.

COMPONENTS OF THE SELF-CONCEPT   Compared to other attitudes, the self-concept is a very complex structure. It is composed of many attributes, some of which are given greater emphasis in determining the overall self-attitude. Attributes of self-concept can be described along such dimensions as their content (e.g., facial attractiveness versus mental aptitude), positivity or negativity (i.e., self-esteem), intensity, stability over time, and accuracy (i.e., the degree to which one's self-assessment corresponds to reality).[4] As will be seen later in the chapter, consumers' self-asessments can be quite distorted, especially with regard to their physical appearance.

PERSONALITY

Some theorists focus on the concept of **personality** to understand the nature of the self. This refers to a person's unique psychological makeup, and how these features consistently influence the way a person will respond to his or her environment.

In recent years the nature of the personality construct has been hotly debated. Many studies have found that people tend to not behave that consistently across different situations; they do not seem to exhibit stable personalities. In fact, some researchers feel that personality does not really exist at all; it is merely a convenient way to describe the behavior of other people.

This argument is a bit hard to accept intuitively, possibly because we tend to see others in a limited range of situations and so to us people do act consistently. On the other hand, we each know that we are not all that consistent; we may be "wild and crazy" at times and "the model of respectability" at others. While certainly not all psychologists have abandoned the idea of personality, many now recognize that a person's underlying characteristics are but one part of the puzzle—situational factors often play a very large role in determining behavior.[5] (This realization underscores the potential importance of segmenting according to situations, a concept discussed in Chapter 10.)

TRAIT THEORY One approach to personality is to focus on the quantitative measurement of *traits,* or identifiable characteristics that define a person. For example, people can be distinguished by the degree to which they are socially outgoing (the trait of extraversion). Some specific traits that are relevant to consumer behavior include: innovativeness (the degree to which a person likes to try new things); materialism (amount of emphasis placed on acquiring and owning products); and self-consciousness (the degree to which a person deliberately monitors and controls the image of the self projected to others).[6]

Problems with Trait Theory. Since large numbers of consumers can be categorized in terms of their standing on various traits, these approaches can in theory be used for segmentation purposes. If a car manufacturer, for example, could determine that drivers who fit a trait profile are more likely to prefer a car with certain features, this match could be used to great advantage. That assumption is evident in an ad for a Danish shampoo, which tells consumers to "Be good to your hair. It's part of your personality."

The notion that consumers buy products that are extensions of their personalities makes intuitive sense. This idea is endorsed by many marketing managers, who try to create *brand personalities* that will appeal to different types of consumers. Indeed, as will be seen in an upcoming section, there is some support for the contention that people make some purchases that are consistent with their selves.

However, the use of standard personality trait measurements to predict these choices has met with mixed success at best. In general marketing researchers have simply not been able to predict consumers' behaviors on the basis of their measured traits. A number of explanations have been offered for these equivocal results:

- The scales are not sufficiently valid or reliable—they do not adequately measure what they are supposed to measure, and their results may not be stable over time.
- Personality tests are often developed for specific populations (e.g., mental patients); these tests are then "borrowed" and applied to the general population where their relevance is questionable.
- The tests often are not administered under the appropriate conditions; they may be given in a classroom or over a kitchen table by people who are not properly trained.
- Researchers often make changes in the instruments to adapt them to their own situations, in the process deleting or adding items and renaming variables.
- Many trait scales are intended to measure gross, overall tendencies (e.g., emotional stability or introversion); these results are then used to make predictions about purchases of specific brands of toothpaste, car wax, and so on.
- In many cases a number of scales are given with no advance thought about how these measures should be related to consumer behavior. The researchers then use a "shotgun approach," following up on anything that happens to look interesting.[7]

SELF-CONSCIOUSNESS

There are times when people seem to be painfully aware of themselves. If you have ever walked into a class in the middle of a lecture and noticed that all eyes were on you, you can understand this feeling of self-consciousness. In contrast, consumers sometimes behave with little self-consciousness. For example, people may do things in a stadium, a riot, or a fraternity party that they would never do if they were highly conscious of their behavior.[8]

CHRONIC SELF-CONSCIOUSNESS   Some people appear to possess the personality trait of self-consciousness; they are more likely to be sensitive to the image they communicate to others. This heightened concern also results in more concern about the social appropriateness of products and consumption activities.

Several measures have been devised to measure this trait. Consumers who score high on the trait of *public self-consciousness,* for example, are more interested in clothing, and are heavier users of cosmetics.[9] A similar measure is *self-monitoring*. High self-monitors are more attuned to how they present themselves in their social environments, and their product choices are influenced by their estimate of how these items will be perceived by others.[10] Self-monitoring is assessed by consumers' extent of agreement with such items as "I guess I put on a show to impress or entertain others," or "I would probably make a good actor."[11]

SELF-ESTEEM

Self-esteem refers to the positivity of one's attitude toward oneself. People with low self-esteem do not expect that they will perform very well, and they will try to avoid embarrassment, failure, or rejection. In developing a new line of snack cakes, for example, Sara Lee found that consumers low in self-esteem preferred portion-controlled snack items because they felt they lacked self-control.[12]

On the other hand, people with high self-esteem expect to be successful, will take more risks, and are more willing to be the center of attention.[13] Self-esteem often is related to acceptance by others. For example, high school students who hang out in high-status "crowds" have higher self-esteem than their classmates.[14]

SELF-ESTEEM ADVERTISING   *Self-esteem advertising* attempts to change product attitudes by stimulating positive feelings about the self.[15] One way to do this is to challenge the consumer's self-esteem, then show a linkage to a product. The Marines do this when they use the theme "If you have what it takes. . . ."

Another strategy is to flatter the consumer, as when Virginia Slims says "You've come a long way, baby." Sometimes such compliments are derived by comparing the consumer to others. For instance, many consumers are socialized to consider body odors repulsive and are motivated to protect their self-image by denying the existence of these odors in themselves. This explains the success of the theme "Aren't you glad you use Dial, don't you wish everyone did?"[16] Other examples of self-esteem appeals appear in Table 7-1.

REAL AND IDEAL SELVES   Self-esteem is influenced by a process where the consumer compares his or her actual standing on some attribute to some ideal. For example, a consumer might ask himself, "Am I as attractive as I would like to be?" "Do I make as much money as I should?" and so on.

The *ideal self* is a person's conception of how he or she would like to be. This ideal self is partly molded by elements of the consumer's culture, such as heroes or people depicted in advertising, who serve as models of achievement, appearance, and so on.[17] Products may be purchased because they are believed to be instrumental in helping us achieve these goals. As will be seen shortly, some products are chosen because they are perceived to be consistent with the consumer's actual self, while others are used to help in reaching the standard set by the ideal self.

Fantasy: Bridging the Gap.   While most people experience a discrepancy between their real and ideal selves, for some consumers this gap is larger than for others. These people are especially good targets for *fantasy appeals.*[18] A **fantasy** or daydream is a self-induced shift in consciousness,

TABLE 7-1 Examples of self-esteem appeals in advertising

Product	Ad Theme
Virginia Slims cigarettes	"You've come a long way, baby."
Clairol shampoo	"You're not getting older, you're getting better."
Michelob beer	"You know where you're going."
Budweiser beer	"For all you do, this Bud's for you."
Pepsi Cola	"You're feeling good about yourself and you're drinking Diet Pepsi —and it shows."
McDonald's	"You deserve a break today."
Salem cigarettes	"You've got what it takes."
Republic airlines	"Perks; you've earned them."

Source: Adapted from Jeffrey F. Durgee, "Self-Esteem Advertising," *Journal of Advertising* 14 (1986)4: 21.

which is sometimes a way of compensating for a lack of external stimulation or coping with problems in the real world.[19]

Many products and services are successful because they appeal to a fantasy element. They allow us to extend our vision of the self by placing us in unfamiliar, exciting situations or by permitting us to "try on" interesting or provocative roles. From Benihana restaurants to the Disney Corporation, marketers cater to the desire for experience and fantasy. Nissan played on this theme in its commercials for the 240SX model. In one ad, a male driver imagines that his girlfriend is with him in the car instead of his dog. He then makes a more unlikely substitution by fantasizing that model Christie Brinkley has taken her place.

MARKETING OPPORTUNITY

The aging of the population and the market saturation of material goods for many affluent consumers is fueling a demand for fantasy experiences. People with ample disposable income appear to be running out of material things to buy, so their attention is instead turning inward to experiential consumption. "Experience vacations," as they are called in the travel industry, combine physical and mental exertion and often have a large sensory component. Popular examples include mountain climbing, safaris, and exploring primitive countries. These trips now account for between 5 percent and 10 percent of the money spent by Americans on travel. The typical adventure traveler is an affluent male approaching middle age.[20]

A number of hotels and resorts now cater to the emerging fantasy market. The new Hyatt Regency Waikaloa in Hawaii offers man-made

If I had a Nissan 240SX ... It would be a red coupe.

Wait! A silver fastback. And I'd go for a spin up Route 7, the twisty part.

Just me and Astro ...

no Amy.

Heck, Christy Brinkley!

Wow! Yeah me and Christy

In my silver – no red 240SX ... driving into the sunset.

Many products appeal to fantasy by placing the consumers in unfamiliar, exciting situations or by permitting them to "try on" interesting or provocative roles. In this storyboard for a Nissan 240SX ad, a male driver imagines that his girlfriend is with him in the car instead of his dog. He then makes a more unlikely substitution by fantasizing that model Christie Brinkley has taken her place. Reprinted by permission of Nissan Motor Corporation USA and Christie Brinkley.

islands, lagoons, and waterfalls, as well as gondola transportation and deer, exotic birds, and porpoises. A seven-story floating resort is opening on the Great Barrier Reef off the coast of Australia. Jules' Undersea Lodge in Florida is a luxury hotel built into the shell of a former underwater sea lab.[21]

MULTIPLE SELVES

In a way, each consumer is really a number of different people. We have as many selves as we do different social roles. Depending upon the situation, we act differently, use different products and services, and even vary in terms of how much we like ourselves. For example, a student who quietly sits in the back of a classroom taking notes may turn into a "party animal" on the weekend.

Each self may require a different set of products to play a desired role: She may choose a sedate, understated perfume when she is being her "professional self," but splash on something more provocative on Saturday night as she becomes her "femme fatale self." The *dramaturgical perspective* on consumer behavior views people much like actors who play different roles. We each play many roles, and each has its own script, props, and costumes.[22] The Sony Walkman ad shown here reflects this perspective.

Depending on the characteristics of a situation and the other people with whom one is interacting, different roles are played. The self can be thought of as having different components or *role identities,* and only some of these are active at any given time. Some identities (e.g., husband, boss, student) are more central to the self than others, but other identities (e.g., stamp collector, dancer, or advocate for the homeless) may be dominant in specific situations.

SYMBOLIC INTERACTIONISM   If each person potentially has many social selves, how does each develop, and how do we decide which self to "activate" at any point in time? The sociological tradition of **symbolic interactionism** stresses that relationships with other people play a large part in forming the self.[23] This perspective maintains that people exist in a symbolic environment and the meaning attached to any situation or object is determined by the interpretation of these symbols. As members of society, we learn to agree on shared meanings. Thus, we "know" that a red light means stop, the "golden arches" means fast food, and "blondes have more fun."

Like other social objects, the meanings of consumers themselves are defined by social consensus. The consumer interprets his or her own identity, and this assessment is continually evolving as he or she encounters new situations and people. In symbolic interactionist terms, we "negotiate" these meanings over time. Essentially the consumer poses the question: "Who am I in this situation?" The answer to this question is greatly influenced by those around us—"Who do other people think I am?" We tend to pattern our behavior on the perceived expectations of others in a form of *self-fulfilling prophecy.*

Sony Walkman® Personal Stereo.
Now Available In 41 Personalities.

"Just call me the Decathalon Man."

"Despite my youthful appearance, I'm actually quite sophisticated."

"Sure I'm rugged, but I'm sensitive, too."

"I'll only accept one thing. The best."

"I run to the beat of a different Walkman."

"I love fishing. But not for my favorite station."

"My parents gave me a lot of self-esteem. But I deserve it."

"Mega-Bass for the Mega-Boss."

"I may be small, but I'm powerful."

Sony celebrates all the sides of your personality with 41 different Walkman personal stereos to keep by your side. With innovative features like digital tuning, Mega Bass, wired remote control—and, of course, Sony's legendary sound quality. Will Sony stop here? Don't count on it. After all, we invented the original Walkman personal stereo—so stopping now isn't exactly in our personality.

SONY.

Sony Walkman. The Only Walkman.™

The Sony Walkman is associated in this ad with a variety of personality types. Courtesy of Sony Corporation of America.

✓ *The Looking-Glass Self.* This process of imagining the reactions of others toward us is known as "taking the role of the other," or the "looking-glass self."[24] According to this view, a process of *reflexive evaluation* occurs when the individual attempts to define the self. This operates as a sort of psychological sonar: We take readings of our own identity by "bouncing" signals off of others.

The looking-glass image we receive will differ depending upon whose views we are considering. Like the distorted mirrors in a funhouse, our appraisal of who we are can vary, depending upon whose perspective we are taking. A confident career woman like Gail who is treated with respect in the office environment may sit morosely at a bar or discotheque, imagining that others see her as an unattractive, aging woman with little sex appeal (whether these perceptions are true or not).

CONSUMPTION AND SELF-CONCEPT

The psychologist William James greatly influenced modern ideas about the self. As illustrated in Figure 7-1, James distinguished between the self as an active agent (known as the *I*) and the self as an object of reflection (known as the Me). The Me is composed of *everything* the individual can call his or her own. This includes attitudes, personality traits, and inner experiences. The importance of consumer activities in defining the self is highlighted by James' emphasis on the *Material self,* which includes our bodies, things we own, and places we live.

By extending the dramaturgical perspective a bit further, it is easy to see how the consumption of products and services contributes to the Material self. For an actor to play a role convincingly, he or she needs the correct props, stage setting, and so on. Consumers learn that different roles are accompanied by *constellations* of products and activities that help to define these roles and, in a symbolic interactionist sense, negotiate the

Figure 7-1 The Components of the Self

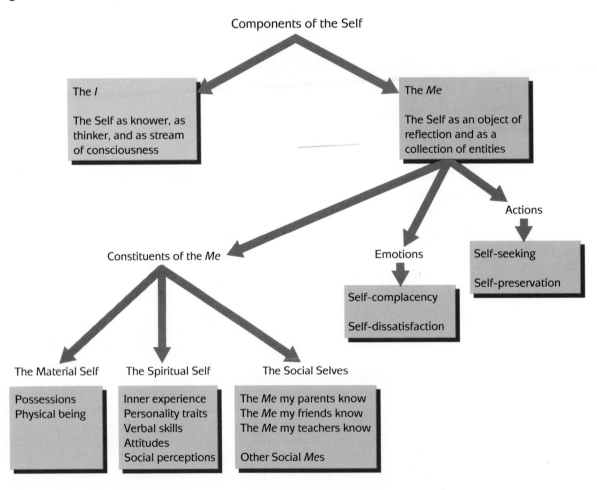

desired meaning.[25] Some "props" are so important to the roles we play that they can be viewed as a part of the *extended self,* a concept to be discussed shortly.

PRODUCTS SHAPE THE SELF: YOU ARE WHAT YOU CONSUME

The reflected self helps to shape self-concept, which implies that people see themselves as they imagine others see them. Since what others see includes a person's clothing, jewelry, furniture, car, and so on, it stands to reason that these products also help to determine the perceived self. A consumer's products place him or her into a social role, which helps to answer the question "Who am I now?"

People use an individual's consumption behaviors to help them make judgments about who that person is. In addition to considering a person's clothes, grooming habits, and so on, we make inferences about personality based on a person's choice of leisure activities (e.g., squash versus bowling), food preferences (e.g., vegetarians versus "steak and potatoes" people), cars, home decorating choices, and so on. People who are shown pictures of someone's living room, for example, are able to make surprisingly accurate guesses about that consumer's personality.[26] In the same way that a consumer's use of products influences others' perceptions, the same products can help to determine his or her *own* self-concept.[27]

Objects can act as a sort of security blanket by reinforcing our identities, especially in unfamiliar situations. For example, students who decorate their dorm rooms with personal items are less likely to drop out of college. This coping process may protect the self from being diluted in a strange environment.[28]

The use of consumption information to define the self is especially important when an identity is yet to be adequately formed, as occurs when a consumer plays a new or unfamiliar role. **Symbolic self-completion theory** predicts that people who have an incomplete self-definition will strive to complete this identity by acquiring symbols associated with it.[29] For example, adolescent boys use "macho" products like cars and cigarettes to bolster their developing masculinity—these products are a sort of "social crutch" to be leaned upon during a period of uncertainty. As is discussed in Chapter 12, the "nouveau riche" tend to demonstrate their new-found status by the ostentatious display of luxury products, while "old money" consumers who are comfortable in this role tend to avoid such "flashy" purchases.

Loss of Self. The contribution of possessions to self-identity is perhaps most apparent when these treasured objects are lost or stolen. One of the first acts performed by institutions that want to repress individuality and encourage group identity, such as prisons or convents, is to confiscate personal possessions.[30] Victims of burglaries and natural disasters commonly report feelings of alienation, depression, or of being "violated." One consumer's comment after being robbed is typical: "It's the next worse thing to being bereaved; it's like being raped."[31] Burglary victims exhibit a diminished sense of community, less feelings of privacy, and less pride in their houses' appearance than do their neighbors.[32]

SELF-PRODUCT CONGRUENCE

Because many consumption activities are related to self-definition, it is not surprising to learn that consumers demonstrate consistency between their values and attitudes and the things they buy.[33] **Self-image congruence models** predict that products will be chosen when their attributes match some aspect of the self.[34] These models assume a process of cognitive matching between these attributes and the consumer's self-image.[35]

While results are somewhat mixed, the ideal self appears to be more relevant as a comparison standard for highly expressive social products such as perfume. In contrast, actual self is more relevant for everyday, functional products. These standards are also likely to vary by usage situation. A consumer might want a functional, reliable car to commute to work, but something with more "zing" when going out on a date in the evening.

Research tends to support the idea of congruence between product usage and self-image. For example, one of the earliest studies to examine this process found that car owners' ratings of themselves tended to match their perceptions of their cars—Pontiac drivers saw themselves as more active and flashier than did Volkswagen drivers.[36] Congruity also has been found between consumers and their most-preferred brands of beer, soap, toothpaste, and cigarettes relative to their least-preferred brands, as well as between consumers' self-images and their favorite stores.[37] Some specific attributes that have been found to be useful in describing matches between consumers and products include rugged/delicate, excitable/calm, rational/emotional, and formal/informal.[38]

PROBLEMS WITH THE CONGRUENCE CONCEPT While these findings make some intuitive sense, we cannot blithely assume that consumers will always buy products whose "personality" characteristics match their own. It is not clear that consumers really see aspects of themselves in down-to-earth, functional products that don't have very complex or humanlike images. It is one thing to consider a brand personality for an expressive, image-oriented product like perfume, and quite another to impute human characteristics to a toaster.

Another problem is the old "chicken-and-egg" question: Do people buy products because they are seen as similar to the self, or do they *assume* that these products must be similar because they have bought them? The similarity between a person's self-image and the images of products purchased does tend to increase with ownership, so this explanation cannot be ruled out.

Self-Congruity Theory. According to *self-congruity theory,* the matching process can be explained in terms of self-evaluation. Consumers, when judging the suitability of a product, do not evaluate the product per se. Instead, they construct a mental image of themselves using the product, and then decide if they like this image. This imaginary process most likely occurs in the case of socially visible products and for those that are not commonly used (i.e., it is more likely to occur for the selection of living room furniture than for a bar of soap).

THE EXTENDED SELF

As noted earlier, many of the props and settings consumers use to define their social roles in a sense become a part of their selves. Those external objects that we consider a part of us comprise the **extended self.** In some cultures, people literally incorporate objects into the self—they lick new possessions, take the name of conquered enemies (or in some cases eat them), or bury the dead with their possessions.[39]

Ranging from personal possessions and pets to national monuments or landmarks, there are many things that help to form a consumer's identity even though they are outside of his or her body. Just about everyone can name a valued object that has a lot of the self "wrapped up" in it, whether this object is a treasured photograph, a trophy, an old shirt, a car, or a cat. As the psychologist William James wrote, "We feel and act about certain things that are ours very much as we feel and act about ourselves."[40]

In one study on the extended self, people were given a list, ranging from electronic items, facial tissue, and television programs to parents, body parts, and favorite clothes. They were asked to rate each in terms of its closeness to the self. Objects were more likely to be considered a part of extended self if "psychic energy" was invested in them by expending effort to obtain them or because they were personalized and kept for a long time. Items rated very close to the self included feelings, childhood memories, favorite travel experiences, and occupation, while politicians, shampoo, toothpaste, and favorite movie stars ranked near the bottom of the list.[41]

LEVELS OF THE EXTENDED SELF   At least four levels of the extended self are used by consumers to define themselves. These range from very personal objects to places and things that allow people to feel like they are rooted in their environments.[42]

The Individual Level. Consumers include many of their personal possessions in self-definition. These products can include jewelry, cars, clothing, and so on. The saying "You are what you wear" reflects the belief that one's things are a part of what one is.

The Family Level. This part of the extended self includes a consumer's residence and the furnishings in it. The house can be thought of as a symbolic body for the family and is often a central aspect of identity.

The Community Level. It is common for consumers to describe themselves in terms of the neighborhood or town from which they come (e.g., Brooklyn boys). For farm families or residents with close ties to a community, this sense of belonging is very important.

The Group Level. Our attachments to certain social groups also can be considered a part of self (see section III). A consumer may feel that landmarks, monuments, or sports teams are a part of the extended self.

SEX ROLES

Sexual identity is a very important component of a consumer's self-concept, as Gail's lingerie purchase showed. People often conform to their culture's expectations about what those of their sex should do. Of course, these guidelines change over time, and they can differ radically across societies. This ad for Paco Rabanne illustrates one marketer's contribution to these changing norms; it blurs the boundaries between the sexes and promotes an emphasis on sensuality.

GENDER DIFFERENCES IN SOCIALIZATION

A society's assumptions about the proper roles of men and women is communicated in terms of the ideal behaviors that are stressed for each sex. For example, an activity such as Christmas shopping is widely regarded as "women's work."[43] In many societies, males are controlled by

Hello?
You snore.
And you steal all the covers. What time did you leave?
Six-thirty. You looked like a toppled Greek statue lying there. Only some tourist had swiped your fig leaf. I was tempted to wake you up.
I miss you already.
You're going to miss something else. Have you looked in the bathroom yet?
Why?
I took your bottle of Paco Rabanne cologne.
What on earth are you going to do with it...give it to a secret lover you've got stashed away in San Francisco?
I'm going to take some and rub it on my body when I go to bed tonight. And then I'm going to remember every little thing about you... and last night.
Do you know what your voice is doing to me?
*You aren't the only one with imagination. I've got to go; they're calling my flight. I'll be back Tuesday.
Can I bring you anything?*
My Paco Rabanne. And a fig leaf.

Paco Rabanne.
A cologne for men.
What is remembered is up to you.

© 1980 Par Parfums Ltd.

Sexual identity is a very important component of a consumer's self-concept. This Paco Rabanne ad illustrates that norms are changing with regard to the sexual frankness that is acceptable in our society.
Courtesy of Ogilvy & Mather New York.

COLGATE-PALMOLIVE

TITLE: "BEDROOM"
COMM. NO.: CLCX 4083
PRODUCT: CURAD
LENGTH: 30 SECONDS
DATE: JUNE, 1984

(MUSIC Throughout)

ANNCR (VO): A Curad Bandage brings out the mother in all of us.

Especially a

Curad Flexible Bandage.

It's soft...Comforting...

and it stays in place...Even on a bending place.

And Curad is the Ouchless Bandage.

It sticks to the skin not the sore.

So the next time...

you have to mother someone...

mother 'em with a Curad.

This ad for Curad is designed to appeal to women's maternal instincts. Courtesy of CURAD Bandages.

agentic goals, which stress self-assertion and mastery. Females, on the other hand, are taught to value *communal goals,* such as affiliation and the fostering of harmonious relations.[44] Assumptions about sex roles are deeply engrained in marketing communications. Consider, for example, the Curad ad shown here, which appeals to women's maternal instinct: One would not expect to see the parallel phrase "*Father* 'em with a Curad."

MACHO MARKETERS? The field of marketing has been largely defined by men, so it tends to be dominated by male values. Competition rather than cooperation is stressed, and the language of warfare and domination is often used. Strategists often use distinctly masculine concepts; "market penetration" or "competitive thrusts" are but two examples.

Academic marketing articles also place a strong emphasis on agentic rather than communal goals. The most pervasive theme is power and control over others. Other themes include instrumentality (manipulating people for the good of an organization) and competition. This bias may diminish to some extent in coming years, as more marketing researchers begin to stress such factors as emotions and aesthetics in purchase decisions.[45]

GENDER VERSUS SEXUALITY

Sex role identity is a state of mind as well as body. A person's biological gender (i.e., male or female) does not totally determine if he or she will exhibit **sex-typed traits**—characteristics that are stereotypically associated with one sex or the other. A consumer's subjective feelings about his or her sexuality are crucial as well. Unlike maleness and femaleness, masculinity and femininity are *not* biological characteristics. A behavior that would be considered masculine in one culture may not necessarily be as such in another. For example, the norm in the United States is that males should be "strong" and repress tender feelings—"real men don't eat quiche." Male friends avoid touching each other (except in "safe" situations such as on the football field). In some Latin and European cultures, however, it is a common sight to see men hugging one another. Each society determines what "real" men and women should and should not do.

SEX-TYPED PRODUCTS   Many products (other than quiche) also are *sex-typed;* they take on masculine or feminine attributes, and consumers often associate them with one sex or another.[46] The car, for example, has long been thought of as a masculine product. The sex-typing of products is often created or perpetuated by marketers (e.g., Princess telephones, boys' and girls' toys, and Luvs color-coded diapers). Some sex-typed products are listed in Table 7-2.

TABLE 7-2 Sex-Typed Products

Masculine	Feminine
pocket knife	scarf
tool kit	baby oil
shaving cream	bedroom slippers
briefcase	hand lotion
35 mm camera	clothes dryer
stereo system	food processor
scotch	wine
IRA account	long distance phone service
wall paint	facial tissue

Source: Adapted from Kathleen Debevec and Easwar Iyer, "Sex Roles and Consumer Perceptions of Promotions, Products, and Self: What Do We Know and Where Should We Be Headed," in *Advances in Consumer Research*, Ed. Richard J. Lutz (Provo, Utah: Association for Consumer Research, 1986)13: 210–14.

ANDROGYNY Masculinity and femininity are not opposite ends of the same dimension. **Androgyny** refers to the possession of both masculine and feminine traits.[47] Researchers make a distinction between sex-typed people, who are stereotypically masculine or feminine, and androgynous people, whose mixture of characteristics allows them to function well in a variety of social situations.

Differences in sex-role orientation can influence responses to marketing stimuli, though evidence for the strength of this factor is unclear.[48] For example, women with a relatively strong masculine component in their sex-role identity prefer ad portrayals that include non-traditional women.[49] Some research indicates that sex-typed people are more sensitive to the sex-role depictions of characters in advertising, though women appear to be more sensitive to gender role relationships than are men.[50] Sex-typed people in general are more concerned with ensuring that their behavior is consistent with their culture's definition of gender appropriateness.

FEMALE SEX ROLES

Sex roles for women are changing rapidly. Social changes, such as the dramatic increase in the proportion of women working outside of the home, have created an upheaval in the way women are regarded by men, the way they regard themselves, and in the products they choose to buy. Modern women now play a greater role in decisions regarding traditionally male purchases. For example, women now buy approximately 40 percent of all condoms sold.[51]

▼ MARKETING PITFALL

Even gun manufacturers are capitalizing on women's changing roles. At least three manufacturers have introduced guns for women. One company makes a .32 magnum model called "Bonnie," to go with its .38 "Clyde" for his-and-hers shooting. Smith & Wesson introduced the Lady-Smith, a revolver with a slimmed-down grip.[52] The company's ads have been criticized for preying on the fears of women.

SEGMENTING WOMEN In the 1949 movie "Adam's Rib," Katharine Hepburn played a stylish and competent lawyer. This film was one of the first to show that a woman can have a successful career and still be happily married. In reality, women have always worked outside of the home, especially during wartime, as the WWII poster of Rosie the Riveter shows. However, the presence of women in positions of authority is a fairly recent phenomenon. The evolution of a new managerial class of women has forced marketers to change their traditional assumptions about women as they target this growing market.

Sub-Segments of Working Women. Ironically, it seems that in some cases marketers have overcompensated for their former emphasis on women as housewives. Many attempts to target the vast female working market tend to depict all working women in glamorous, executive positions. This ignores the fact that the majority of working women do not hold such jobs, and that many work because they have to, rather than for self-fulfillment.[53] For example, over 95 percent of all secretaries are women, as are the very large majority of bookkeepers, nursing aides, and cashiers.[54] This diversity means that all women should not be expected to respond to marketing campaigns that stress professional achievement or the glamour of the working life. Adult women can be segmented into four distinct groups:

√ 1. Housewives who do not plan to work outside of the home.
2. Housewives who plan to work at some point. They may be temporarily staying at home until small children grow old enough to enter school,

The character of Rosie the Riveter was created during World War II to symbolize the efforts of American women to take the place of men on factory production lines.

Some countries are redefining the role of women at a faster pace than others. This process tends to reflect the rate at which women are working outside of the home. For example, the percentage of active women (defined as those not in school, retired, or disabled), who are in the workforce is approximately 65 percent in the United States, and 50 percent in the U.K. In contrast, only 43 percent of Italian women are employed, and only 37 percent work in Venezuela.[56]

Many cultures appear to be undecided about accepting an updated version of the female sex role. For example, while it is not unusual for Russian women to work as physicians, pilots, or scientists, the ideal of women as anchor of the family is still dominant in that culture. When a female cosmonaut landed at the Salyut-7 space station, the flight engineer greeted her by saying "We've got an apron ready for you, Sveta. It's as if you've come home. Of course, we have a kitchen for you; that'll be where you work."[57]

One of the most marked changes in sex roles is occurring in Japan. Traditionally, Japanese wives stay home and care for children while their husbands work late and entertain clients. The good Japanese wife is expected to walk two paces behind her husband. However, these attitudes are changing as women are less willing to live vicariously through their husbands.[58] More than half of Japanese women aged 25 to 29 are either working or looking for a job.[59] Japanese marketers and advertisers are beginning to depict women in professional situations (though still usually in subservient roles) and even to develop female market segments for such traditionally male products as automobiles.

and they should not be lumped together with housewives who have voluntarily chosen a domestic lifestyle.

3. Career-oriented working women who value professional success and the trappings of achievement.
4. "Just-a-job" women who work primarily because they need the money.[55]

Appealing to independence and mobility. Whether or not they work outside of the home, many women have come to value greater independence and respond positively to marketing campaigns that stress the freedom to make their own lifestyle decisions. The American Express Company has been targeting women for a long time, but the company found that its "Do you know me?" campaign did not appeal to women as much as to men. A campaign aimed specifically at women instead features confident women using their American Express cards. By depicting women in active situations, the company greatly increased its share of the woman's credit card market.[60]

The desire for independence by women has also affected the car market. While men traditionally were primarily responsible for choosing and purchasing cars, this situation is changing radically and car makers are scrambling to keep up with it. While most car advertising is still male-oriented, women are increasingly depicted as serious buyers. In 1987, women bought 45 percent of the new cars sold in the United States, up from 23 percent in 1970. More than six in ten of new car buyers under the age of 50 are female.[61] Furthermore, women exert a significant influence on 80 percent of new car purchases.

Women also are more sensitive to the aesthetics of the car showroom. They are more likely to notice and be turned off if the selling floor is dirty, and they are more likely to shop more dealers before buying. Hyundai has responded to this difference by designing car dealerships to resemble shopping malls, emphasizing a light and airy atmosphere.[62]

THE DEPICTION OF WOMEN IN ADVERTISING   As implied by the ads for Virginia Slims cigarettes that state "You've come a long way, baby," attitudes about the female sex role have changed remarkably in this century. Still, women continue to be depicted by advertisers and the media in stereotypical ways. Analyses of ads in such magazines as *Time, Newsweek, Playboy,* and even *Ms,* have shown that the large majority of women included were presented as sex objects or in traditional roles.[63] Similar findings have been obtained in the U.K.[64] One of the biggest culprits may be rock videos, which tend to reinforce traditional women's roles. The women portrayed in these videos are usually submissive, and their primary attribute is high physical attractiveness. Recent evidence indicates an increase in the amount of lingerie and nudity contained in rock videos.[65]

Our culture's expectations about appropriate sex role behavior are often communicated through advertising. Ads may (unintentionally) reinforce negative stereotypes. Women often are portrayed as stupid, submissive, temperamental, or as sexual objects who exist solely for the pleasure of men. Sometimes the messages are blatant, as was the case for a promotion for the "Dynasty" television show, which featured the pictures of three of the aggressive women leads. The caption above them: "Bitch, Bitch, Bitch." These messages can also be transmitted more subtly. A recent ad for Newport cigarettes illustrates how the theme of female submission may be perpetuated. The copy "Alive with pleasure!" is accompanied by a photo of a woman in the woods, playfully hanging from a pole being carried by two men. The underlying message may be interpreted as two men bringing home their captured prey.[66]

Updated Images.   Although women continue to be depicted in traditional roles, this situation is changing as advertisers scramble to catch up with reality. Women are now as likely as men to be central characters in television commercials. Still, while males increasingly are depicted as spouses and parents, women are still more likely than men to be seen in domestic settings. Also, about 90 percent of all narrators in commercials are male. The deeper male voice apparently is perceived as more authoritative and credible.[67]

Prompted by concerns about how advertising portrayed women, The National Advertising Review Board in 1975 issued a checklist for advertisers to consider when creating or approving an ad. These guidelines caution against perpetuating sexual stereotypes, such as portraying women as weak, over-emotional, or subservient to men.[68] Marketers by and large have responded to this challenge, though with mixed success. Note that even Virginia Slims, which bases its campaign on women's progress, still says "You've come a long way, *baby!*"

Many modern ads now feature role-reversal, where women occupy traditional men's roles. In other cases, women are portrayed in romantic situations, but they tend to be more sexually dominant. Ironically, current advertising is more free to emphasize traditional female traits now that sexual equality is becoming more of an accepted fact. This freedom is demonstrated in a German poster for a women's magazine. The caption reads "Today's women can sometimes show weakness, because they are strong."

MARKETING PITFALL

The R. J. Reynolds Tobacco Co. created controversy with its highly successful "Smooth Character" campaign for Camel cigarettes. Designed to update the brand's image for a younger audience, ads feature "Old Joe," the company's traditional spokescamel, who presents tips on how to become a "smooth character." One tip suggested a way to impress a person at the beach: ". . . run into the water, grab someone and drag her back to shore. . . . The more she kicks and screams, the better." Several women's rights groups complained, and the ad was pulled.[69]

MALE SEX ROLES

While the traditional conception of the ideal male as a tough, aggressive, muscular man who enjoys "manly" sports and activities is not dead, society's definition of the male role is also evolving. Men are allowed to be more compassionate, and to have close friendships with other men. In contrast to the depiction of "macho" men who do not show their feelings, some marketers are promoting men's "sensitive" side. An emphasis on male bonding has been the centerpiece of many ad campaigns, most notably for beer companies.[70]

The prototype of the "new man" was expressed in the positioning statement for Paco Rabanne Pour Homme, a cologne that attempted to focus on this new lifestyle: "Paco Rabanne Pour Homme is a prestige men's fragrance for the male who is not a cliched stereotype, the man who understands and accepts the fluidity of male/female relationships." The ideal personality of the target consumer for the cologne was described by the company with adjectives like confident, independent, romantic, tender, and playful.[71]

MARKETING OPPORTUNITY

As sex roles for males and females evolve, some cosmetics companies are attempting to expand their markets by targeting men. Estee Lauder, for example, sells four different male skin-care lines. Men are somewhat resistant to the concept of skin care, and cosmetics marketers cannot use the same appeals they might employ when communicating to female consumers. As one industry consultant noted, "If you tell a man that a product makes his razor burn feel better, or it makes him look healthier, he's more likely to respond. The cosmeticky language doesn't work."

So far the most profitable products are treatments for baldness, but some companies are trying to move beyond this problem. Lancome sells an Anti-Wrinkle Creme and an Anti-Aging Eye Balm for men. One turn-off to men appears to be multi-step skin-care systems. Men just aren't used to thinking that way about grooming. Despite only marginal success, companies are hoping that in the long run a new generation of younger men will be more open to products traditionally designed for women.[72]

The Joys of Fatherhood. Males' lifestyles are changing to allow greater freedom of expression in clothing choices, hobbies such as cooking, and so on. Men also are taking on more domestic duties to compensate for the increasing numbers of working women. For example, over 75 percent of American men go on a major shopping trip in a four-

week period, and men account for about 40 percent of food shopping dollars. Most men expect their sons to shop as much as their daughters do, and these attitudes do not seem to be affected by income or education. Men who shop view themselves as considerate, contemporary people to a greater degree than do those who don't.[73]

Men also are getting more involved in parenting, and advertising campaigns for such companies as Kodak, Omega watches, and Pioneer electronics stress the theme of fatherhood. The European campaign for the Ford Fiesta emphasized this father/child bond, as seen in the ad shown here.[74] Still, this change is coming slowly. A commercial for 7-Eleven stores showed two men out for a walk, each pushing a stroller. As they near a 7-Eleven, they begin to push their strollers faster until they are racing. As the campaign's creative director explained, "We showed them engaged in

This ice cream ad illustrates the father/child bond now being emphasized by many advertisers Courtesy of H.P. Hood.

ood

Vanilla FLAVORED

You can feel good about **Hood**

a competition to make it easier for men to accept the concept of taking care of children."[75]

WHAT'S GOOD FOR THE GOOSE . . . ?   Men as well as women often are depicted in a negative fashion in advertising. They frequently come across as helpless or bumbling. As one advertising executive put it, "The woman's movement raised consciousness in the ad business as to how women can be depicted. The thought now is, if we can't have women in these old-fashioned traditional roles, at least we can have men being dummies."[76] An organization called Men's Rights Inc. identifies ads that demean men by depicting them as incompetent, panicked, smelling bad, and so on.[77]

From Cheesecake to Beefcake.   In a twist on traditional portrayals, advertising increasingly depicts men as sex objects. This is known in the trade as "beefcake."[78] A recent campaign for Sansabelt trousers has the theme "What women look for in men's pants." Ads feature a woman who confides, "I always lower my eyes when a man passes {pause} to see if he's worth following." One female executive commented, ". . . turnabout is fair play. . . . If we can't put a stop to sexism in advertising . . . at least we can have some fun with it and do a little leering of our own."[79]

BODY IMAGE

A person's physical appearance is a large part of his or her self-concept. **Body image** refers to a consumer's subjective evaluation of his or her physical self. This image is not necessarily accurate. A man may think of himself as being more muscular than he really is, or a woman may feel she appears fatter than is the case. In fact, it is not uncommon to find marketing strategies that exploit consumers' tendencies to distort their body images by preying upon insecurities about appearance. This creates a gap between the real and ideal physical self and, consequently, the desire to purchase products and services to narrow that gap.

BODY CATHEXIS
A person's feelings about his or her body can be described in terms of **body cathexis.** Cathexis refers to the emotional significance of some object or idea to a person, and some parts of the body are more central to self-concept than are others. One study of young adults' feelings about their bodies found that these respondents were the most satisfied with their hair and eyes and had the least positive feelings about their waists. These feelings also were related to usage of grooming products. Consumers who were more satisfied with their bodies were more frequent users of such "preening" products as hair conditioner, blower dryers, cologne, facial bronzer, tooth polish, and pumice soap.[80]

IDEALS OF BEAUTY
A person's satisfaction with the physical image he or she presents to others is affected by how closely that image corresponds to the image valued by his or her culture. An **ideal of beauty** is a particular model,

or exemplar, of appearance. Female ideals of beauty are especially easy to identify; they include physical features (e.g., large lips or small lips, big breasts or small breasts) as well as such aspects as clothing styles, cosmetics, hairstyles, skin tone (pale vs. tan), and musculature (petite, athletic, voluptuous). These ideals often are summed up in a sort of cultural shorthand. We may talk about a "vamp," a "girl-next-door," or an "ice queen," or we may refer to specific women who have come to embody an ideal, such as Cher, Marilyn Monroe, or Princess Grace.

An ideal of beauty functions as a sort of cultural yardstick. Consumers compare themselves to some standard and are dissatisfied with their appearance to the extent that they don't match up to it. Ideals of beauty, however, vary radically across cultures, and even over time within the same society. Because a society defines what is beautiful and what is not, then, beauty really *is* in the eye of the beholder.[81] The women in the Benetton ad exemplify some current ideals of beauty in different cultures.

IDEALS OF BEAUTY OVER TIME   While beauty may be only skin deep, throughout history women in particular have worked very hard to attain it. They have starved themselves, painfully bound their feet, inserted plates into their lips, spent countless hours under hairdryers, in front of mirrors, and beneath tanning lights, and have undergone breast reduction or enlargement operations to alter their appearance and meet their society's expectations of what a beautiful woman should look like.

In much of the nineteenth century, the desirable waistline for American women was eighteen inches, a circumference that required the use of corsets pulled so tight that they routinely caused headaches, fainting

As suggested by this Benetton ad, a global perspective on ideals of beauty is resulting in more ways to be considered attractive.   Photo by Oliviero Toscani for Benetton.

spells, and possibly even the uterine and spinal disorders common among women of the time. While modern women are not quite as "straightlaced," many still endure such indignities as high heels, body waxing, eye-lifts, and liposuction. In addition to the millions spent on cosmetics, clothing, health clubs, and fashion magazines, these practices remind us that— rightly or wrongly—the desire to conform to current standards of beauty is alive and well.

In retrospect, periods of history tend to be characterized by a specific "look," or ideal of beauty. American history can be described in terms of a succession of dominant ideals. For example, in sharp contrast to today's emphasis on health and vigor, in the early 1800s it was fashionable to appear delicate to the point of looking ill. The poet Keats described the ideal woman of that time as "a milk white lamb that bleats for man's protection."

Other looks have included the voluptuous, lusty woman as epito- mized by Lillian Russell, the athletic Gibson Girl of the 1890s, and the small, boyish flapper of the 1920s as exemplified by Clara Bow. In modern times, we have experienced the pinup girl of the 1940s, the buxom Marilyn Monroe ideal of the 1950s, and even the emaciated look of the early 1960s popularized by the model Twiggy.[82] The ad for *Allure* magazine demonstrates how radically our conceptions of a beautiful body have changed.

The ideal body type of Western women has changed radically over time. This has resulted in a realignment of *sexual dimorphic markers*— those aspects of the body that distinguish between the sexes. For example, analyses of the measurements of *Playboy* centerfolds over a twenty-year period from 1958 to 1978 show that these "ideals" got thinner and more muscular. For example, the average hip measurement went from 36" in 1958 to just over 34" in 1978. Average bust size shrunk from almost 37" in 1958 to about 35" in 1978.[83] More recently, the pendulum seems to be shifting back a bit, as the more buxom, "hourglass figure" popular in the 1950s (exemplified by the Marilyn Monroe ideal) has reappeared.[84]

WORKING ON THE BODY

Because many consumers are motivated to match up to some ideal of appearance, they often go to great lengths to change aspects of their physical selves. From cosmetics to plastic surgery, tanning salons to diet drinks, a multitude of products and services are directed toward altering or maintaining aspects of the physical self in order to present a desirable appearance. It is difficult to overstate the importance of the physical self- concept (and the desire by consumers to improve their appearance) to many marketing activities.

FATTISM As reflected in the expression, "you can never be too thin or too rich," our society has an obsession with weight. Even elementary school children perceive obesity as worse than being handicapped or disabled.[85] The pressure to be slim is continually reinforced both by advertising and by peers. Americans in particular are preoccupied by what they weigh. We are continually bombarded by images of thin, happy people.

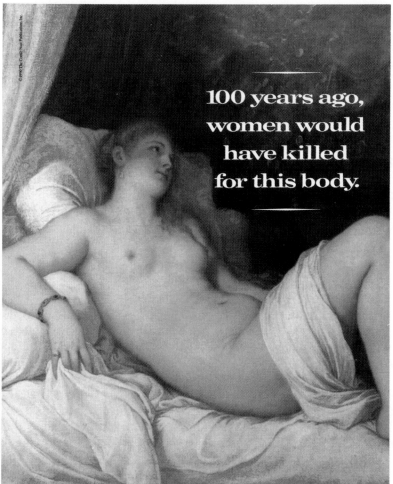

100 years ago,
women would
have killed
for this body.

Beauty changes. Every century, every decade, every month. And Allure magazine will be there. With straight-forward reporting. And the latest news about skin care and fitness, fragrance and fashion, travel and trends. Beginning in March. For information call Diane Wichard, Advertising Director, 212-880-5554.

allure
The shape of things to come.

This ad for *Allure* magazine illustrates how a culture's ideals of beauty change over time. Reprinted by permission of Allure Magazine. Copyright 1990 The Conde Nast Publications Inc.

Diet and Exercise. The desire to be thin has had a big impact on consumers' lifestyles and eating habits. The mania for dieting has been accepted as a fact of life by many. Ironically, the number of adults who said they were on a diet *dropped* 26 percent in a two-year period. This is because many consumers no longer view the act of "going on a diet" as a special activity. It is now a fact of life.

Almost 100 million Americans regularly consume lo-cal foods and beverages (double the number in 1980). A number of companies specifically target the weight-conscious: Weight Watchers International, the largest weight-loss company, developed a new program called Quick Success that recognizes the new lifestyle of busy working women. This program includes eating guidelines for working lunches and cocktail parties.[86] Weight-loss related products are expected to produce retail sales of more than $50 billion by 1995.[87]

Unrealistic Standards. Many consumers focus on attaining an un-realistic ideal weight, sometimes by relying upon height and weight charts that show what one should weigh. These charts are often outdated, be-cause they don't take into account today's larger body frames or such factors as muscularity, age, or activity level.[88] Indeed, only 12 percent of blacks, and 21 percent of whites (but 43 percent of Hispanics) weigh within the recommended range.[89] American women believe that the "ideal" body size is a 7, an unrealistic goal for most.[90] Even women who are at their best medical weight want on average to be eight pounds ligh-ter.[91] These expectations are communicated in subtle ways. Even fashion dolls, such as the ubiquitous Barbie, reinforce the ideal of thinness. The dimensions of these dolls, when extrapolated to average female body sizes, are unnaturally long and thin.[92]

◢ MARKETING OPPORTUNITY

Many businesses have recently prospered by paying attention to the needs of larger women, as designers are starting to acknowledge that most consumers cannot wear a size 7 (the average American woman weights 146 pounds and wears a size 12/14). More than 100 specialty stores now cater to bigger women, and large-size clothing sales have grown from $2 billion to $10 billion over the last ten years. When the Spiegel Co. introduced a fashion videocassette featuring clothing in size 16 and larger, it sold 2000 copies in the first month. Realizing that overweight women may be intimidated by public exercise programs, a chain of exercise clubs called Women at Large was opened specifically for this group in Washington state to provide an embarrassment-free environment.[93]

Eating Disorders. While many people perceive a strong link between self-esteem and appearance, some consumers unfortunately exaggerate this connection even more and sacrifice greatly to attain what they con-sider to be a desirable body image. Women tend to be taught to a greater degree than men that the quality of their bodies reflects their self-worth, so it is not surprising that most major distortions of body image occur among females.

Men do not tend to differ in ratings of their current figure, their ideal figure, and the figure they think is most attractive to women. In contrast, women rate both the figure they think is most attractive to men and their ideal figure as much thinner than their actual figure.[94] In one survey, ⅔ of college women admitted resorting to unhealthy behavior to control weight. Advertising messages that convey an image of slimness help to reinforce these activities by arousing insecurities about weight.[95]

Two (related) eating disorders are common. People with *anorexia* al-ways see themselves as fat and virtually starve themselves in the quest for thinness. This condition often results in *bulimia,* which involves two stages: First, binge eating occurs (usually in private), where more than

5000 calories may be consumed at one time. This is followed by induced vomiting, abuse of laxatives, fasting, and/or overly strenuous exercise—a "purging" process that reasserts the woman's sense of control.

Most eating disorders are found in white, upper-middle class teenage and college-age girls. Victims often have brothers or fathers who are hypercritical of their weight, and these disorders are also associated with a history of sexual abuse.[96] In addition, binge eating can be encouraged by one's peers. Groups such as athletic teams, cheerleading squads, and sororities may develop positive norms regarding binge eating. In one study of a college sorority, members' popularity within the group increased the more they binged.[97]

Exercise Addiction. Eating disorders have also been documented in men. They are common among male athletes who must also conform to various weight requirements, such as jockeys, boxers, and male models.[98] In general, though, most men who have distorted body images consider themselves to be too light rather than too heavy—society has taught them that they must be muscular to be masculine. Men are more likely than women to express their insecurities about their bodies by becoming addicted to exercise. In fact, striking similarities have been found between male compulsive runners and female anorexics. These include a commitment to diet and exercise as a central part of one's identity and susceptibility to body-image distortions.[99]

COSMETIC SURGERY   Consumers are increasingly electing to have cosmetic surgery to change a poor body image.[100] More than half a million cosmetic surgeries are performed in the United States every year, and this number continues to grow.[101] There is no longer much (if any) of a psychological stigma associated with having this type of operation; it is commonplace and accepted among many segments of consumers.[102]

Many women turn to surgery either to reduce weight or to increase sexual desirability. The use of the liposuction procedure, where fat is removed from the thighs with a vacuum-like device, has almost doubled since it was introduced in the United States in 1982.[103] Some women feel that larger breasts will increase their allure and undergo breast augmentation procedures. In more traditional areas of the country, such as the Sun Belt, this procedure is more likely to be selected.[104] The implication that larger breasts somehow result in a more "fulfilled" woman is plain in the ad shown here.

The importance of breast size to self-concept resulted in an interesting and successful marketing strategy undertaken by an underwear company. While conducting focus groups on bras, an analyst noted that small-chested women typically reacted with hostility when discussing the subject. They would unconsciously cover their chests with their arms as they spoke, and felt that their needs were ignored by the fashion industry. To meet this overlooked need, the company introduced a line of A-cup bras called "A-OK" and depicted wearers in a positive light. A new market segment was born.

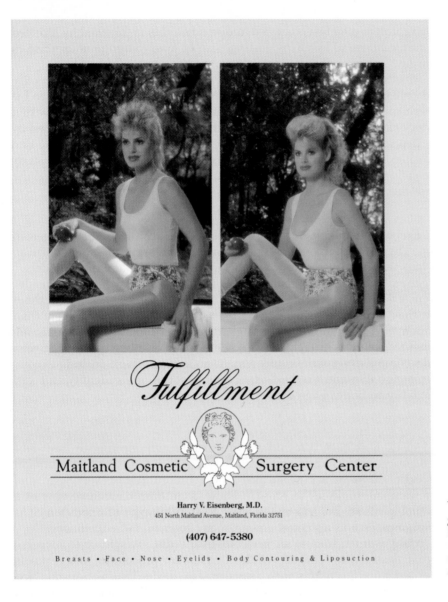

The Maitland Cosmetic Surgery Center ad implies that larger breasts will result in "fulfillment." Do you agree? Courtesy of Harry V. Eisenberg, MD, Maitland Cosmetic Surgery Center.

BODY DECORATION AND MUTILATION   The body is adorned or altered in some way in every culture. Decorating the self serves a number of purposes, including:[105]

- Separating group members from nonmembers. The Chinook Indians of North America pressed the head of a newborn between two boards for a year, permanently altering its shape. In our society, teens go out of their way to adopt distinctive hair and clothing styles that will separate them from adults.
- Placing the individual in the social organization. Many cultures engage in puberty rites, where the boy symbolically becomes a man. Young men in Ghana paint their bodies with white stripes to

resemble skeletons to symbolize the death of their child status. In Western culture, this rite may involve some form of mild self-mutilation or engaging in dangerous activities.

- Placing the person in a gender category. The Tchikrin Indians of South America insert a string of beads in a boy's lip to enlarge it. Western women wear lipstick to enhance femininity. At the turn of the century, small lips were fashionable because they represented women's submissive role at that time.[106] Today, big, red lips are provocative and indicate an aggressive sexuality. Some women, including a number of famous actresses and models, receive collagen injections or lip inserts to create large, pouting lips (known in the modeling industry as "liver lips").[107]

  Other body parts also may be "mutilated" to enhance sex-role identification. Consider the traditional Oriental practice of foot-binding, or the modern use of high heels, which podiatrists agree are a prime cause of knee and hip problems, backaches, and fatigue. As one doctor observed, "When they {women} get home they can't get their high heeled shoes off fast enough. But every doctor in the world could yell from now until Doomsday, and women would still wear them."[108]

- Indicating desired social conduct. The Suya of South America wear ear ornaments to emphasize the importance placed in their culture on listening and obedience. In Western society gay men may wear an earring to signal how they expect to be treated.

- Indicating high status or rank. The Hidates Indians of North America wear feather ornaments that indicate how many people they have killed. In our society, some people wear glasses with clear lenses, even though they do not have eye problems, to increase their perceived status.

- Providing a sense of security. Consumers often wear lucky charms, amulets, rabbits' feet, and so on to protect them from the "evil eye." A modern woman may wear a "mugger whistle" around her neck for the same reason.

Tattoos. Tattoos are one popular form of body adornment. This body art can be used to communicate aspects of the self to onlookers and may serve some of the same functions that other kinds of body painting do in primitive cultures. Tattoos (from the Tahitian *ta-tu*) have deep roots in folk art. Until recently the images were crude and were primarily either death symbols (e.g., a skull), animals (especially panthers, eagles, and snakes), pinup women, or military designs. More current influences include science-fiction themes, Japanese symbolism, and tribal designs.

A tattoo may be viewed as a fairly risk-free way of expressing an adventurous side of the self. Tattoos have a long history of association with people who are socially disvalued. For example, the faces and arms of criminals in sixth-century Japan were tattooed as a means to identify them, as were Massachusetts prison inmates in the nineteenth century. These emblems are often used by marginal groups, such as bikers or Japanese yakuze (gang members) to express group identity and solidarity.

More recently, tattooing is being chosen by women. One newly developed technique called Accents involves etching a circle around a woman's eyes, resulting in a permanent eyeliner. The procedure takes about thirty minutes and costs about $9000.[109] More than 5000 women have undergone this process.

CHAPTER SUMMARY

Consumers' self-concepts are reflections of their attitudes toward themselves. Whether these attitudes are positive or negative, they will help to guide many purchase decisions; products can be used to bolster self-esteem or to "reward" the self.

Many product choices are dictated by the consumer's perceived similarity between his or her personality and attributes of the product. The symbolic interactionist perspective on the self implies that each of us actually has many selves, and a different set of products is required as "props" to play each. Self-identity is largely a product of the real or imagined appraisals of those around us. Many things other than the body can also be viewed as part of the self. Valued objects, car, homes, and even attachments to sports teams or national monuments are used to define the self, when these are incorporated into the extended self.

A person's sex-role identity is a major component of self-definition. Conceptions about masculinity and femininity, largely shaped by society, guide the acquisition of "sex-typed" products and services. Advertising and other media play an important role in socializing consumers to be male and female. While traditional women's roles have often been perpetuated in advertising depictions, this is changing somewhat. The media do not always portray men accurately either.

A person's conception of his or her body also provides feedback to self-image. A culture communicates certain ideals of beauty, and consumers go to great lengths to attain these. Many consumer activities involve manipulating the body, whether through dieting, cosmetic surgery, tattooing, or so forth. Sometimes these activities are carried to an extreme, as people try too hard to live up to cultural ideals. One example is found in eating disorders, where women in particular become obsessed with thinness.

KEY TERMS

Androgyny	Personality
Body cathexis	Self-concept
Body image	Self-image congruence models
Extended self	Sex-typed traits
Fantasy	Symbolic interactionism
Ideal of beauty	Symbolic self-completion theory

REVIEW QUESTIONS AND DISCUSSION TOPICS

1. How might the creation of a self-conscious state be related to consumers who are trying on clothing in dressing rooms? Does the act of preening in front of a mirror change the dynamics by which people evaluate their product choices? Why?
2. Is it ethical for marketers to encourage infatuation with the self?
3. List three dimensions by which the self-concept can be described.

4. What are the three components of the looking-glass self?
5. Describe how the process of reflexive evaluation might work for a consumer who is trying on a new bathing suit in a store dressing room.
6. Compare and contrast the real versus the ideal self. List three products for which each type of self is likely to be used as a reference point when a purchase is considered.

HANDS-ON EXERCISES

1. Find examples of self-esteem advertising. How might this strategy transfer to positive attitudes toward a product?
2. Watch a set of ads featuring men and women on television. Try to imagine the characters with reversed roles (i.e., the male parts played by women and vice versa). Can you see any differences in assumptions about sex-typed behavior?

NOTES

1. Quoted in Steve Ginsberg, "Fireworks' Fantasy Approach," *Women's Wear Daily* (February 26, 1987):14.
2. Harry C. Triandis, "The Self and Social Behavior in Differing Cultural Contexts," *Psychological Review* 96 (1989)3: 506–20.
3. Anthony G. Greenwald and Mahzarin R. Banaji, "The Self as a Memory System: Powerful, But Ordinary," *Journal of Personality and Social Psychology* 57 (1989)1: 41–54; Hazel Markus, "Self-Schemata and Processing Information About the Self," *Journal of Personality and Social Psychology* 35, (1977): 63–78.
4. Morris Rosenberg, *Conceiving the Self* (New York: Basic Books, 1979; M. Joseph Sirgy, "Self-Concept in Consumer Behavior: A Critical Review," *Journal of Consumer Research* 9 (December 1982).
5. See J. Aronoff and J. P. Wilson, *Personality in the Social Process* (Hillsdale, N.J.: Erlbaum, 1985); Walter Mischel, *Personality and Assessment* (New York: Wiley, 1968).
6. Linda L. Price and Nancy Ridgway, "Development of a Scale to Measure Innovativeness," in *Advances in Consumer Research,* ed. Richard P. Bagozzi and Alice M. Tybout, (Ann Arbor, Mich.: Association for Consumer Research, 1983)10: 679–84; Russell W. Belk, "Three Scales to Measure Constructs Related to Materialism: Reliability, Validity, and Relationships to Measures of Happiness," in *Advances in Consumer Research,* ed. Thomas C. Kinnear, (Ann Arbor, Mich.: Association for Consumer Research, 1984)11: 291; Mark Snyder, "Self-Monitoring Processes," in *Advances in Experimental Social Psychology,* ed. Leonard Berkowitz, (New York: Academic Press, 1979)12: 85–128.
7. Jacob Jacoby, "Personality and Consumer Behavior: How Not to Find Relationships," (Purdue Papers in Consumer Psychology, No. 102, Lafayette, Ind.: Purdue University, 1969); Harold H. Kassarjian and Mary Jane Sheffet, "Personality and Consumer Behavior: An Update," in *Perspectives in Consumer Behavior,* ed. Harold H. Kassarjian and Thomas S. Robertson, (Glenview, Ill.: Scott, Foresman and Company, 1981): 160–80; John Lastovicka and Erich Joachimsthaler, "Improving the Detection of Personality Behavior Relationships in Consumer Research," *Journal of Consumer Research* 14 (March 1988): 583–87.
8. J. G. Hull and A. S. Levy, "The Organizational Functions of the Self: An Alternative to the Duval and Wicklund Model of Self-Awareness," *Journal of Personality and Social Psychology* 37 (1979): 756–68; Jay G. Hull, Ronald R. Van Treuren, Susan J. Ashford, Pamela Propsom, and Bruce W. Andrus, "Self-Consciousness and the Processing of Self-Relevant Information," *Journal of Personality and Social Psychology* 54 (1988)3: 452–65.
9. Arnold W. Buss, *Self-Consciousness and Social Anxiety* (San Francisco: W.H. Freeman, 1980); Lynn Carol Miller and Cathryn Leigh Cox, "Public Self-Conscious-

ness and Makeup Use," *Personality and Social Psychology Bulletin* 8 (1982)4: 748–51; Michael R. Solomon and John Schopler, "Self-Consciousness and Clothing," *Personality and Social Psychology Bulletin* 8 (1982)3: 508–14.

10. Morris B. Holbrook, Michael R. Solomon, and Stephen Bell, "A Re-Examination of Self-Monitoring and Judgments of Furniture Designs," *Home Economics Research Journal* 19 (September 1990): 6–16; Snyder, "Self-Monitoring Processes."

11. Mark Snyder and Steve Gangestad, "On the Nature of Self-Monitoring: Matters of Assessment, Matters of Validity," *Journal of Personality and Social Psychology* 51 (1986): 125–39.

12. Emily Yoffe, "You Are What You Buy," *Newsweek* (June 4, 1990): 59.

13. Roy F. Baumeister, Dianne M. Tice, and Debra G. Hutton, "Self-Presentational Motivations and Personality Differences in Self-Esteem," *Journal of Personality* 57 (September 1989): 547–75.

14. B. Bradford Brown and Mary Jane Lohr, "Peer-Group Affiliation and Adolescent Self-Esteem: An Integration of Ego-Identity and Symbolic-Interaction Theories," *Journal of Personality and Social Psychology* 52 (1987)1: 47–55.

15. Jeffrey F. Durgee, "Self-Esteem Advertising," *Journal of Advertising* 14 (1986)4: 21.

16. Ernest Dichter, *Handbook of Consumer Motivations* (New York: McGraw-Hill, 1964).

17. Sigmund Freud, *New Introductory Lectures in Psychoanalysis* (New York: Norton, 1965).

18. Harrison G. Gough, Mario Fioravanti, and Renato Lazzari, "Some Implications of Self Versus Ideal-Self Congruence on the Revised Adjective Check List," *Journal of Personality and Social Psychology* 44 (1983)6: 1214–20.

19. Steven Jay Lynn and Judith W. Rhue, "Daydream Believers," *Psychology Today* (September 1985): 14.

20. Blayne Cutler, "Anything For A Thrill," *American Demographics* (August, 1988):38.

21. Frank G. Wells, "Travel and Tourism 1983 to the Year 2003," *Vital Speeches of the Day* (delivered Reno, Nev., October 29, 1987).

22. Erving Goffman, *The Presentation of Self in Everyday LIfe* (Garden City, N.Y.: Doubleday, 1959).

23. George H. Mead, *Mind, Self and Society* (Chicago: University of Chicago Press, 1934).

24. Charles H. Cooley, *Human Nature and the Social Order* (New York: Scribner's, 1902).

25. Michael R. Solomon and Henry Assael, "The Forest or the Trees?: A Gestalt Approach to Symbolic Consumption," in *Marketing and Semiotics: New Directions in the Study of Signs for Sale,* ed. Jean Umiker-Sebeok (Berlin: Mouton de Gruyter, 1987): 189–218.

26. Jack L. Nasar, "Symbolic Meanings of House Styles," *Environment and Behavior* 21 (May 1989): 235–57; E.K. Sadalla, B. Verschure, and J. Burroughs, "Identity Symblism in Housing," *Environment and Behavior* 19 (1987): 599–87.

27. Michael R. Solomon, "The Role of Products as Social Stimuli: A Symbolic Interactionism Perspective," *Journal of Consumer Research* 10 (December 1983): 319–28.

28. William B. Hansen and Irwin Altman, "Decorating Personal Places: A Descriptive Analysis," *Environment and Behavior* 8 (December 1976): 491–504.

29. R. A. Wicklund and P. M. Gollwitzer, *Symbolic Self-Completion* (Hillsdale, N.J.: Lawrence Erlbaum, 1982).

30. Erving Goffman, *Asylums* (New York: Doubleday, 1961).

31. Quoted in Floyd Rudmin, "Property Crime Victimization Impact on Self, on Attachment, and on Territorial Dominance," *CPA Highlights,* Victims of Crime Supplement 9 (1987)2: 4–7.

32. Barbara B. Brown, "House and Block as Territory," (Paper presented at the 1982 Conference of the Association for Consumer Research, San Francisco, Ca).

33. Deborah A. Prentice, "Psychological Correspondence of Possessions, Attitudes, and Values," *Journal of Personality and Social Psychology* 53 (1987)6: 993–1002.

34. Sak Onkvisit and John Shaw, "Self-Concept and Image Congruence: Some Research and Managerial Implications," *The Journal of Consumer Marketing* 4 (Winter 1987): 13–24. For a related treatment of congruence between advertising appeals and self-concept, see George M. Zinkhan and Jae W. Hong, "Self-Concept and Advertising Effectiveness: A Conceptual Model of Congruency, Conspicuousness, and Response

Mode," in *Advances in Consumer Research,* ed. Rebecca H. Holman and Michael R. Solomon, (Provo, Utah: Association for Consumer Research, 1991)18: 348–54.

35. C. B. Claiborne and M. Joseph Sirgy, "Self-Image Congruence as a Model of Consumer Attitude Formation and Behavior: A Conceptual Review and Guide for Further Research," (Paper presented at the Academy of Marketing Science Conference, New Orleans, 1990).

36. Al E. Birdwell, "A Study of Influence of Image Congruence on Consumer Choice," *Journal of Business* 41 (January 1964): 76–88; Edward L. Grubb and Gregg Hupp, "Perception of Self, Generalized Stereotypes, and Brand Selection," *Journal of Marketing Research* 5 (February 1986): 58–63.

37. Ira J. Dolich, "Congruence Relationship Between Self-Image and Product Brands," *Journal of Marketing Research* 6 (February 1969): 80–84; Danny N. Bellenger, Earle Steinberg, and Wilbur W. Stanton, "The Congruence of Store Image and Self Image as It Relates to Store Loyalty," *Journal of Retailing* 52 (1976)1: 17–32; Ronald J. Dornoff and Ronald L. Tatham, "Congruence Between Personal Image and Store Image," *Journal of the Market Research Society* 14 (1972)1: 45–52.

38. Naresh K. Malhotra, "A Scale to Measure Self-Concepts, Person Concepts, and Product Concepts," *Journal of Marketing Research* 18 (November 1981): 456–64.

39. Ernest Beaglehole, *Property: A Study in Social Psychology* (New York: MacMillan, 1932).

40. William James, *The Principles of Psychology* (New York: Henry Holt, 1890), 291.

41. M. Csikszentmihalyi and Eugene Rochberg-Halton, *The Meaning of Things: Domestic Symbols and the Self* (Cambridge, Mass.: Cambridge University Press, 1981).

42. Russell W. Belk, "Possessions and the Extended Self," *Journal of Consumer Research* 15 (September 1988): 139–68.

43. Eileen Fischer and Stephen J. Arnold, "More than a Labor of Love: Gender Roles and Christmas Gift Shopping," *Journal of Consumer Resesarch* 17 (December 1990): 333–45.

44. Joan Meyers-Levy, "The Influence of Sex Roles on Judgment," *Journal of Consumer Research* 14 (March 1988): 522–30.

45. Elizabeth C. Hirschman, "A Feminist Critique of Marketing Theory: Toward Agentic-Communal Balance," (Working paper, School of Business, Rutgers University, New Brunswick, N.J.).

46. Kathleen Debevec and Easwar Iyer, "Sex Roles and Consumer Perceptions of Promotions, Products, and Self: What Do We Know and Where Should We Be Headed," in *Advances in Consumer Research,* ed. Richard J. Lutz , (Provo, Utah: Association for Consumer Research, 1986)13: 210–14.

47. Sandra L. Bem, "The Measurement of Psychological Androgyny," *Journal of Consulting and Clinical Psychology* 42 (1974): 155–62; Deborah E. S. Frable, "Sex Typing and Gender Ideology: Two Facets of the Individual's Gender Psychology That Go Together," *Journal of Personality and Social Psychology* 56 (1989)1: 95–108.

48. See D. Bruce Carter and Gary D. Levy, "Cognitive Aspects of Early Sex-Role Development: The Influence of Gender Schemas on Preschoolers' Memories and Preferences for Sex-Typed Toys and Activities," *Child Development* 59 (1988): 782–92; Bernd H. Schmitt, France Le Clerc, and Laurette Dube-Rioux, "Sex Typing and Consumer Behavior: A Test of Gender Schema Theory," *Journal of Consumer Research* 15 (June 1988): 122–27.

49. Lynn J. Jaffe and Paul D. Berger, "Impact on Purchase Intent of Sex-Role Identity and Product Positioning," *Psychology & Marketing* (Fall 1988): 259–71.

50. Sandra L. Bem, "Gender Schema Theory: A Cognitive Account of Sex Typing," *Psychological Review* 88 (July 1981): 354–64; Keren A. Johnson, Mary R. Zimmer, and Linda L. Golden, "Object Relations Theory: Male and Female Differences in Visual Information Precessing," in *Advances in Consumer Research,* ed. Melanie Wallendorf and Paul Anderson, (Provo, Utah: Association for Consumer Research, 1986)14: 83–87.

51. Blayne Cutler, "Condom Mania," *American Demographics* (June 1989): 17.

52. "A Drive to Woo Women—And Invigorate Sales," *New York Times* (April 2, 1989): F12.

53. "A Drive to Woo Women"

54. "Women's Occupations," *American Demographics* (December 1987):14.

55. Rena Bartos, "Marketing to Women: The Quiet Revolution," *Marketing Insights* (June 1989): 61.

56. Denise Rusoff, "British Women Get the Jobs," *American Demographics* (December 1987): 54; Rena Bartos, "Marketing to Women."

57. John F. Burns, "An Apron For Soviet Woman in Space," *New York Times* (August 28, 1982): D1.

58. Laurel Anderson and Marsha Wadkins, "The New Breed in Japan: Consumer Culture," (Unpublished manuscript, Arizona State University, 1990).

59. Doris L. Walsh, "A Familiar Story," *American Demographics* (June 1987): 64.

60. B. Abrams, "American Express is Gearing New Ad Campaign to Women," *The Wall Street Journal* (August 4, 1983): 23.

61. Julie Candler, "Woman Car Buyer—Don't Call Her a Niche Anymore," *Advertising Age* (January 21, 1991):S-8.

62. Frieda Curtindale, "Marketing Cars to Women," *American Demographics* (November 1988): 28.

63. "Ads' Portrayal of Women Today is Hardly Innovative," *Marketing News* (November 6, 1989):12; Jill Hicks Ferguson, Peggy J. Kreshel, and Spencer F. Tinkham, "In the Pages of Ms.: Sex Role Portrayals of Women in Advertising," *Journal of Advertising* 19 (1990)1: 40–51.

64. Sonia Livingstone and Gloria Greene, "Television Advertisements and the Portrayal of Gender," *British Journal of Social Psychology* 25 (1986): 149–54; L. Z. McArthur and B. G. Resko, "The Portrayal of Men and Women in American Television Commercials," *Journal of Social Psychology* 97 (1975): 209–20.

65. Richard C. Vincent, "Clio's Consciousness Raised? Portrayal of Women in Rock Videos, Re-examined," *Journalism Quarterly* 66 (1989): 155.

66. Richard Edel, "American Dream Vendors," *Advertising Age* (November 9, 1988): 153.

67. Daniel J. Brett and Joanne Cantor, "The Portrayal of Men and Women in U.S. Television Commercials: A Recent Content Analysis and Trends Over 15 Years," *Sex Roles* 18 (9/10 1988): 595–609.

68. *Advertising and Women: A Report on Advertising Portraying or Directed to Women* (New York: The National Advertising Review Board, 1975): 15–19.

69. Judann Dagnoli, "Groups Smoking Over Camel Ad," *Advertising Age* (July 17, 1989): 49.

70. Gordon Sumner, "Tribal Rites of the American Male," *Marketing Insights* (Summer 1989): 13.

71. Margaret G. Maples, "Beefcake Marketing: The "Sexy" Sell, *Marketing Communications* (April 1983): 21–25.

72. Linda Wells, "Flirting With Men," *New York Times Magazine* (April 9, 1989): 64.

73. "Do Real Men Shop?," *American Demographics* (May 1987): 13.

74. "Changing Conceptions of Fatherhood," *USA Today* (May 1988):10.

75. Quoted in Kim Foltz, "In Ads, Men's Image Becomes Softer," *New York Times* (March 26, 1990): D12.

76. Quoted in Jennifer Foote, "The Ad World's New Bimbos," *Newsweek* (January 25, 1988): 44.

77. Mary Jung, "Watchdog Group Lashes Out At Ads That Demean Men," *Marketing News* (March 27, 1989): 2.

78. Maples, "Beefcake Marketing."

79. Quoted in Lynn G. Coleman, "What Do People Really Lust After in Ads?" *Marketing News* (November 6, 1989): 12.

80. Dennis W. Rook, "Body Cathexis and Market Segmentation," in *The Psychology of Fashion*, ed. Michael R. Solomon, (Lexington, Mass.: Lexington Books, 1985): 233–41.

81. Michael R. Solomon and Richard Ashmore, "The Language of Beauty," (Paper presented at the International Institute on Marketing Meaning, Indianapolis, Ind., 1989).

82. Lois W. Banner, *American Beauty* (Chicago: The University of Chicago Press, 1980).

83. David M. Garner, Paul E. Garfinkel, Donald Schwartz, and Michael Thompson, "Cultural Expectations of Thinness in Women," *Psychological Reports* 47 (1980): 483–91.

84. Kathleen Boyes, "The New Grip of Girdles is Lightened by Lycra," *USA Today* (April 25, 1991): 6D.

85. "Girls at 7, Think Thin, Study Finds," *New York Times* (February 11, 1988): B9.

86. Jennifer Stoffel, "What's New in Weight Control," *New York Times* (November 26, 1989): F17.

87. Stoffel, "What's New in Weight Control."

88. "How Much is *Too* Fat?," *USA Today* (February 1989): 8.

89. *American Demographics* (May 1987): 56.

90. Deborah Marquardt, "A Thinly Disguised Message," *Ms.* 15 (May 1987): 33.

91. Vincent Bozzi, "The Body in Question," *Psychology Today* 22 (February 1988): 10.

92. Elaine L. Pedersen and Nancy L. Markee, "Fashion Dolls: Communicators of Ideals of Beauty and Fashion," (Paper presented at the International Conference on Marketing Meaning, Indianapolis, Ind., 1989); Dalma Heyn, "Body Hate," *Ms.* (August 1989): 34.

93. "Big Women, Big Profits," *Newsweek* (February 25, 1991): 48; Monica Gonzales, "Fashionably Large," *American Demographics* (August 1988): 18.

94. Debra A. Zellner, Debra F. Harner, and Robbie I. Adler, "Effects of Eating Abnormalities and Gender on Perceptions of Desirable Body Shape," *Journal of Abnormal Psychology* 98 (February 1989): 93–96.

95. Robin T. Peterson, "Bulimia and Anorexia in an Advertising Context," *Journal of Business Ethics* 6 (1987): 495–504.

96. Jane E. Brody, "Personal Health," *New York Times* (February 22, 1990): B9.

97. Christian S. Crandall, "Social Contagion of Binge Eating," *Journal of Personality and Social Psychology* 55 (1988): 588–98.

98. Judy Folkenberg, "Bulimia: Not For Women Only," *Psychology Today* (March 1984): 10.

99. Eleanor Grant, "The Exercise Fix: What Happens When Fitness Fanatics Just Can't Say No?," *Psychology Today* 22 (February 1988): 24.

100. John W. Schouten, "Selves in Transition: Symbolic Consumption in Personal Rites of Passage and Identity Reconstruction," *Journal of Consumer Research* 17 (March 1991): 412–25.

101. Monica Gonzalez, "Want a Lift?," *American Demographics* (February 1988): 20.

102. Annette C. Hamburger and Holly Hall, "Beauty Quest," *Psychology Today* (May 1988): 28.

103. Keith Greenberg, "What's Hot: Cosmetic Surgery," *Public Relations Journal* (June 1988): 23.

104. Jerry Adler, "New Bodies For Sale," *Newsweek* (May 27, 1985): 64.

105. Ruth P. Rubinstein, "Color, Circumcision, Tatoos, and Scars," in *The Psychology of Fashion,* ed. Michael R. Solomon, (Lexington, Mass.: Lexington Books, 1985): 243–54.

106. Sondra Farganis, "Lip Service: The Evolution of Pouting, Pursing, and Painting Lips Red," *Health* (November 1988): 48–51.

107. Michael Gross, "Those Lips, Those Eyebrows; New Face of 1989 (New Look of Fashion Models)," *New York* (February 13, 1989): 24.

108. Quoted in "High Heels: Ecstasy's Worth the Agony," *New York Post* (December 31, 1981).

109. "The Eyes That Always Have It," *Changing Times* (October 26, 1985).

Decision Making

Billy Sherman dropped by to visit his old friend Rob Chan, who had recently moved back to town. While they were talking over old times, Rob said, "Wait a minute. Let me play an album that's a real 'blast from the past.' I bet you haven't heard this in years."

As the sounds of Pink Floyd's *Dark Side of the Moon* flooded the room, Billy remarked, "Wo! Did you get new speakers or something? I'm hearing things on here I've never heard before!"

Rob laughed. "No, didn't I tell you? I finally bit the bullet and bought myself a CD player. What did it was when I heard that the entire Beatles collection was being reissued on CD. It really makes a difference, doesn't it? Another nice thing about it is that it's programmable, so that you can hear whatever tracks you want, in any order you want."

Billy couldn't believe the difference in sound quality. When he got home, he pulled out his old copy of *Dark Side of the Moon*. After listening to Rob's CD version, he found that he could barely stand to listen to his own album, even though he had never noticed all those scratches before. Billy immediately decided that he must buy a CD player to catch up on what he had been missing. But what kind to buy?

Billy knew that Rob's CD player was a Prime Wave, which he recognized as a well-known brand. He had also heard another friend say something about Precision CD players being good. He also remembered the name Technomatic, but couldn't remember if it was recommended.

That afternoon, Billy dropped by a local electronics store. He went straight to the area where cassette players were displayed because he assumed that CD players would be close by. Since this wasn't one of those huge, warehouse-type stores, he knew that the prices would probably be a bit higher but that the people who worked there would be more likely to know what they were talking about. Billy browsed through a couple of brochures and then asked the salesperson which Prime Wave and Precision units he would recommend.

When the salesman reeled off different features that were available, such as a disc stabilizer and a digital filter, Billy remarked, "The only thing I'm really interested in is one that is programmable and built to last." The salesman narrowed down Billy 's choices to two similar models, one a Prime Wave and one a Precision. At $249.99, the Prime Wave was slightly more expensive, but Billy figured that probably meant it was a little better made. By that evening, Billy was sitting happily in his living room, listening to Pink Floyd as they were *meant* to be heard.

CONSUMERS AS PROBLEM SOLVERS

Billy's situation is similar to that encountered by consumers virtually every day of their lives. He realized (rather suddenly, in this case) that he wanted to make a purchase, and he had to go through a series of steps to do this. In short, he had to make a *decision*. These steps can be described as (1) problem recognition, (2) information search, and (3) evaluation of alternatives. Of course, after a decision has been made, the quality of that decision will in turn affect future decisions, as learning occurs based upon the good or bad outcomes of the consumer's choice. An overview of the decision-making process appears in Figure 8-1.

A consumer decision is a response to a problem. Some problems are more important than others, so the amount of effort we put into each differs. Sometimes the problem-solving process is done almost automatically; we seem to make snap judgments based on very little information. At other times coming to a purchase decision begins to resemble a full-time job. A person may literally spend days or weeks thinking about the purchase, and may even lie awake at night mulling it over. The occasional sleeplessness caused by consumer decision making is depicted in the insurance ad shown here.

PERSPECTIVES ON DECISION MAKING

Traditionally, consumer researchers have approached decision makers from a **rational perspective.** In this view, people calmly and carefully integrate as much information as possible with what they already know

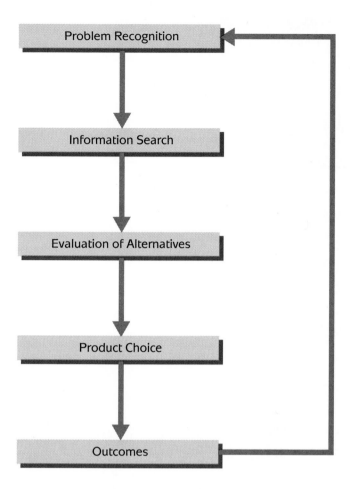

Figure 8-1 Stages in Consumer Decision Making

about a product, painstakingly weigh the pluses and minuses of each alternative, and arrive at a satisfactory decision.

This process implies that steps in decision making should be carefully studied by managers to understand how information is obtained, how beliefs are formed, and what product choice criteria are specified by consumers. Products can then be developed that emphasize appropriate attributes, and promotional strategies can be tailored to deliver the types of information most likely to be desired, in the most effective formats.[1]

While this meticulous process does occur for some purchase decisions, it is not an accurate portrayal of many others.[2] Consumers simply do not go through this elaborate sequence for every decision. If they did, their entire lives would be spent making such decisions, leaving them very little time to enjoy the things they eventually decide to buy.

Some decisions are made under conditions of *low involvement,* as discussed in Chapter 3. In many of these situations, the consumer's decision is a learned response to environmental cues (see Chapter 4), as when a person decides to buy something on impulse that is promoted as a

As this ad for CNA Insurance suggests, some purchase decisions are so important that consumers lose sleep thinking about them. Courtesy of CNA Insurance Companies; Advertisement by: Frank C. Nahser, Inc./Advertising 1990; Photography by: Tony D'Orio.

"surprise special" in a store. A concentration on these types of decisions can be described as the **behavioral influence perspective.** Under these circumstances, managers must concentrate on assessing the characteristics of the environment, such as physical surroundings and product placement, that influence members of a target market.[3]

In other cases, consumers are highly involved in a decision, but it may not lend itself to the rational approach. For example, the traditional approach is hard-pressed to explain a person's choice of art, music, or even a spouse. In these cases, no single quality may be the determining factor. Instead, the **experiential perspective** stresses the *gestalt* or totality of the product or service. Marketers in these areas should focus on measuring consumers' affective responses to products or services, and develop offerings that elicit appropriate subjective reactions and employ effective symbolism.

TYPES OF CONSUMER DECISIONS

One helpful way to characterize the decision-making process is to consider the amount of effort that goes into the decision each time it must be made. Consumer researchers have found it convenient to think in terms of a continuum, which is anchored on one end by **habitual decision making** and at the other extreme by **extended problem solving.** Many decisions fall somewhere in the middle and are characterized by **limited problem solving.**[4] This continuum is presented in Figure 8-2.

EXTENDED PROBLEM SOLVING Decisions involving extended problem solving correspond most closely to the traditional decision-making perspective. The problem-solving process is usually initiated by a motive that is fairly central to the self-concept (see Chapter 7). In addition, the eventual decision will be perceived to carry a fair degree of risk.

For this reason, the consumer will probably try to collect as much information as possible, both from memory (internal search) and from outside sources (external search). Based on the importance of the decision, each product alternative will be carefully evaluated. This is often done by considering the attributes of one brand at a time and seeing how brand attributes shape up to some set of desired characteristics.

LIMITED PROBLEM SOLVING Limited problem solving is usually more straightforward and simple. Buyers are not as motivated to search for information or to rigorously evaluate each alternative. People instead use simple *decision rules* to choose among alternatives. These cognitive shortcuts enable them to fall back on general guidelines instead of having to start from scratch every time a decision is to be made. Some general differences between these modes of problem solving are shown in Table 8-1.

HABITUAL DECISION MAKING Both extended and limited problem-solving modes involve some degree of information search and deliberation among product alternatives; they vary in the *degree* to which these activities are

Figure 8-2 A Continuum of Buying Decision Behavior

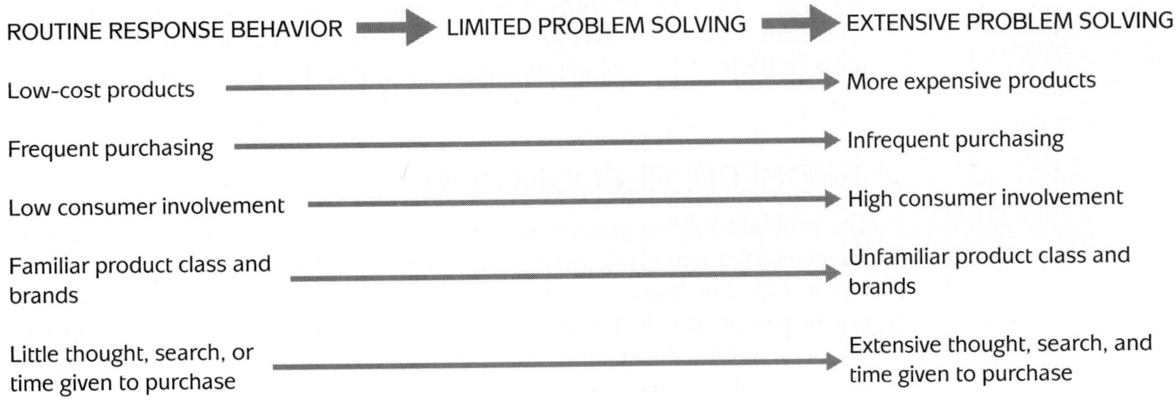

ROUTINE RESPONSE BEHAVIOR ➡ LIMITED PROBLEM SOLVING ➡ EXTENSIVE PROBLEM SOLVING

Low-cost products ➞ More expensive products

Frequent purchasing ➞ Infrequent purchasing

Low consumer involvement ➞ High consumer involvement

Familiar product class and brands ➞ Unfamiliar product class and brands

Little thought, search, or time given to purchase ➞ Extensive thought, search, and time given to purchase

TABLE 8-1 Characteristics of limited versus extended problem solving

Limited Problem Solving	Extended Problem Solving
Motivation	
Low risk and involvement	High risk and involvement
Information Search	
Little search	Extensive search
Information processed passively	Information processed actively
In-store decision making likely	Multiple sources consulted prior to store visits
Alternative Evaluation	
Weakly held beliefs	Strongly held beliefs
Only most prominent criteria used	Many criteria used
Alternatives perceived as basically similar	Significant differences perceived among alternatives
Noncompensatory strategy used	Compensatory strategy used
Purchase	
Limited shopping time; may prefer self-service	Many outlets shopped if needed
Choice often influenced by in-store displays	Communication with store personnel often desirable

Source: Adapted from James F. Engel, Roger D. Blackwell, and Paul W. Miniard, *Consumer Behavior* 6th ed. (Chicago: The Dryden Press, 1990).

undertaken. At the other end of the choice continuum, however, are decisions that are made with little to no conscious effort.

Many of our purchase decisions are so routinized that we may not even realize we've made them until after we look in our shopping carts. Choices characterized by *automaticity* are performed with minimal effort and without conscious control.[5] While on the one hand this kind of thoughtless activity may seem dangerous or at best stupid, in many cases it is actually an efficient way to operate. The development of habitual, repetitive behavior is one way for consumers to minimize the time and energy they must spend on mundane purchase decisions. This strategy allows them to save their real effort for important decisions requiring more careful scrutiny.

✓ PROBLEM RECOGNITION

The problem-solving process known as decision making can only begin when the consumer perceives there is a problem to be solved. Consumer problems can be small or large, simple or complex. A person who unexpectedly runs out of gas on the highway has a problem, as does the same person who gets a new job and becomes dissatisfied with the image of her or his car, even though there is nothing mechanically wrong with it.

✓ **Problem recognition** occurs whenever the consumer sees a significant difference between his or her current state of affairs and some desired or ideal state. Although the quality of Billy's sound system had not changed, for example, his evaluation of its quality had. Because his standard of comparison was altered, Billy was confronted with a need he did not have prior to visiting his friend Rob. As their ad demonstrates, Arm & Hammer has been particularly successful in identifying a succession of new problems its product can solve.

PROBLEM CREATION

Figure 8-3 shows that a problem can arise in one of two ways. As in the case of the person running out of gas, the quality of the consumer's actual state can move downward (*need recognition*). On the other hand, as in the case of the person who craves a newer, flashier car, the

Arm & Hammer prompts consumers to find new uses for an existing product. By permission of Church & Dwight Co., Inc.

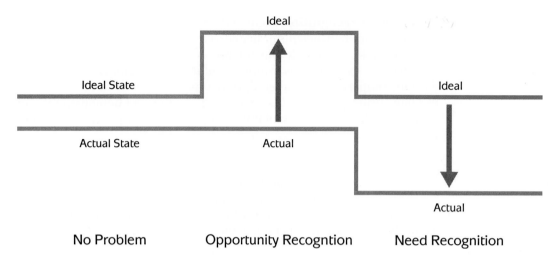

Figure 8-3 Problem Recognition: Shifts in Actual or Ideal States

consumer's ideal state can move upward (*opportunity recognition*). Either way, a gulf will occur between the actual state and the ideal state.[6] In Billy's case, a problem was perceived as a result of opportunity recognition; his ideal state in terms of sound quality was altered.

Need recognition can occur in several ways. The quality of the person's actual state can be diminished simply by running out of a product, by buying a product that turns out not to adequately satisfy needs, or by creating new needs (e.g., the addition of a baby). Opportunity recognition often occurs when a consumer is exposed to different or better quality products. This often happens because the person's circumstances have somehow changed, as when an individual goes to college or gets a new job. Suddenly, the person's frame of reference shifts and a variety of purchases must be made to adapt to a new environment.

MARKETERS' CONTRIBUTIONS TO PROBLEM CREATION   While problem recognition can and does occur naturally, this process is often spurred by marketing efforts. Communications may make consumers aware that they have a problem and then (conveniently) provide a solution.

Building Primary Versus Secondary Demand. In some cases, marketers attempt to create *primary demand,* where consumers are encouraged to use a product or service regardless of the brand they choose (this need often exists in the early stages of a product's life cycle, as when microwave ovens were first introduced). Secondary demand, where consumers are prompted to prefer a specific brand over others, can occur only if primary demand already exists. At this point, marketers must convince consumers that their problem can best be solved by choosing their brand over others in a category.

A common structure for advertisements is to present a person who has a physical or social problem and then "miraculously" show how the product will resolve it. Some marketers go so far as to *invent* a problem, then offer a remedy for it. In the 1940s, the Talon zipper was touted as a cure for "gaposis"; the horrifying condition that develops when puckers appear around the buttons on a woman's skirt. Listerine, which was originally sold to fight dandruff, carried warnings about "bottle bacillus," which caused "infectious dandruff." Geritol gave us "tired blood," and Wisk detergent drew our attention to the shame of "ring around the collar."[7]

Even when a real problem is depicted, the solutions offered may be overly simplistic, implying that the problem will disappear if the product is used. One analysis of over 1000 television ads found that about eight in ten ads suggest that the problem will be resolved within seconds or minutes after using the product. In addition, 75 percent of the ads make definite claims that the product will solve the problem, and over 75 percent imply that this solution is a one-step process. All the consumer needs to do is to buy the product, and the problem will go away.[8]

INFORMATION SEARCH

Once a problem has been recognized, consumers need adequate information to resolve it. This often means that the consumer must engage in **information search,** where the consumer surveys his or her environment for appropriate data to make a reasonable decision. The *Bride's* magazine ad featuring an engaged couple demonstrates the often intensive information search undergone by consumers once a new set of needs has been activated.

A consumer may explicitly search the marketplace for specific information after a need has been recognized, a process called *prepurchase search*. On the other hand, many consumers (especially veteran shoppers) enjoy hunting for information and keeping track of developments just for the fun of it (i.e., *browsing*) or because they like to maintain current information for future use. They engage in *ongoing search*.[9] Some differences between these two search modes are described in Table 8-2.

SEGMENTING BY SEARCH EFFORT

Markets can be segmented in terms of how much information search consumers are likely to do prior to purchase. While some people search extensively, others often are pre-sold. They may already have set preferences regarding manufacturers, retailers, or both, as a result of past experiences or ongoing interest in the product category. For example, one study examined differences among car buyers who had established preferences prior to purchase versus those who had not made a decision before searching. Those who were pre-sold tended to have a lot of prior knowledge about cars but did not tend to consult many consumer information sources. In contrast, those buyers who had no preconceived preferences lacked confidence in

THEY'LL WALK DOWN HUNDREDS OF AISLES BEFORE THEY GET TO THE ALTAR.

Like other important events, planning a wedding generates many product needs requiring extensive information search. *Bride's* magazine is a specialized information source to help meet these needs. Advertisement prepared by Sacks & Rosen, New York.

their ability to judge cars and tended to use consumer information sources to a greater degree.[10]

INTERNAL VERSUS EXTERNAL SEARCH
Information sources can be roughly broken down into two kinds: internal and external. As a result of prior experience and simply living in a consumer culture, each of us often has some degree of knowledge about many products already in memory. When confronted with a purchase decision, we may engage in *internal search* by scanning our own memory banks to assemble information about different product alternatives (see Chapter 4).

DELIBERATE VERSUS "ACCIDENTAL" SEARCH
Our existing knowledge of a product may be the result of *directed learning,* where on a previous

occasion we had already searched for relevant information or experienced some of the alternatives. A parent who bought a birthday cake for one child last month, for example, probably has a good idea of the best kind to buy for another child this month.

Alternatively, we may have acquired information in a more passive manner. Even though a product may not have been of interest before, our exposure to advertising, packaging, and sales promotion activities may result in *incidental learning*. Mere exposure over time to conditioned stimuli and observations of others results in the learning of much material that may not be needed for some time after the fact, if ever. This is one benefit of steady, "low-dose" advertising: Product associations are established and maintained until the time they are needed.[11]

In some cases, we may be so expert about a product category (or at least believe we are) that no additional search is undertaken. Frequently, however, our own existing state of knowledge is not satisfactory to make an adequate decision. This means that we must go outside of ourselves for more information. The ad for *Nation's Business* highlights the important role of media during information search. The sources we consult for advice may be impersonal and marketer-dominated, such as retailers and

TABLE 8-2 A framework for consumer information search

	Prepurchase Search	**Ongoing Search**
Determinants	Involvement in the purchase Market environment Situational factors	Involvement with the product Market environment Situational factors
Motives	To make better purchase decisions	Build a bank of information for future use Experience fun and pleasure
Outcomes	Increased product and market knowledge Better purchase decisions Increased satisfaction with the purchase outcome	Increased product and market knowledge leading to: —future buying efficiencies —personal influence Increased impulse buying Increased satisfaction from search and other outcomes

Source: Peter H. Bloch, Daniel L. Sherrell, and Nancy M. Ridgway, "Consumer Search: An Extended Framework," *Journal of Consumer Research* 13 (June 1986): 120. Reprinted with permission by The University of Chicago Press.

This ad for *Nation's Business* magazine underscores the high involvement often associated with print media that provide needed information. Reprinted by permission, *Nation's Business Magazine*.

catalogs; they may be friends and family members; or perhaps unbiased third parties such as *Consumer Reports*.[12]

THE ECONOMICS OF INFORMATION

The traditional decision-making perspective incorporates the *economics of information* approach to search; it assumes that consumers will gather as much data as is needed to make an informed decision. Consumers form expectations of the value of additional information and continue to search to the extent that the rewards of doing this (i.e., the *utility*) exceed the costs.

This utilitarian assumption also implies that the most valuable units of information will be collected first. Additional pieces will be absorbed only to the extent they are seen as adding to what is already known.[13] In other words, people will put themselves out to collect as much information as possible, as long as the process of gathering it is not too onerous or time-consuming.[14]

DO CONSUMERS ALWAYS SEARCH RATIONALLY? This assumption of rational search is not always supported, however. The amount of external search for most products is surprisingly small, even when additional information would most likely benefit the consumer. For example, lower-income shoppers, who have more to lose by making a bad purchase, actually search *less* prior to buying than do more affluent people.[15] Like our friend Billy, consumers typically visit only one or two stores and rarely seek out unbiased information sources prior to making a purchase decision, especially when little time is available to do so.[16] This pattern is especially prevalent for decisions regarding durables, even when these products represent significant investments. One study of Australian car buyers found that more than a third had made only two or fewer trips to inspect cars prior to buying one.[17]

This tendency to avoid external search is less prevalent when consumers consider the purchase of symbolic items, such as clothing. In those cases, not surprisingly, people tend to do a fair amount of external search, though most of it involves seeking the opinions of peers.[18] While the stakes may be lower financially, these self-expressive decisions may be seen as having dire social consequences if the wrong choice is made. The level of perceived risk, a concept to be discussed shortly, is high.

MEASURING SEARCH ACTIVITY   One widely used device to study the search process in the laboratory is the Information Display Board (IDB). This board is a brand x attribute matrix that allows subjects to access product information in any order they would like prior to making a choice (almost like the game show *Concentration*). Researchers can trace the order of subjects' choices and assess the quality of their eventual decisions to better understand how much information provides optimal decisions and how this information should best be presented.

This technique does have some drawbacks, as the choice situations are somewhat artificial. Also, a structure is imposed on the subjects that they may not necessarily use in real life, where all of the brands and attributes to choose from are not neatly laid out. Nonetheless, the IDB has been an important tool for consumer researchers and policy makers who are concerned with maximizing the quality of product information available to consumers.[19]

DETERMINANTS OF EXTERNAL INFORMATION SEARCH

As a general rule, search activity is greater when the purchase is important, when there is a need to learn more about the purchase, and when the relevant information is easily obtained and utilized.[20] Consumers differ in the amount of search they tend to undertake, regardless of the product category in question. All things being equal, younger, better-educated people who enjoy the shopping/fact-finding process tend to conduct more information search. Women are more inclined to search than are men, as are those who place greater value on style and the image they present.[21]

THE CONSUMER'S PRIOR EXPERTISE Should prior product knowledge make it more or less likely that consumers will engage in search? Products experts and novices use very different procedures during decision making. Novices who know little about a product should be the most motivated to find out more about it. However, experts are more familiar with the product category, so they should be able to better understand the meaning of any new product information they might acquire.

Amount of Search. So, who searches more? The answer is neither: search tends to be greatest among those consumers who are *moderately* knowledgeable about the product. There is an inverted-U relationship between knowledge and external search effort, as shown in Figure 8-4. People with very limited expertise may not feel they are capable of searching extensively. In fact, they may not even know where to start. Billy, who did not spend a lot of time researching his purchase, is representative of this situation. He visited one store, and only looked at brands with which he was already familiar. In addition, he focused on only a small number of product features. On the other hand, people who are extremely knowledgeable in the area can rely heavily on their own memories for information (internal search), so they may not search very much either.[22]

Type of Search. The type of search undertaken by people with varying levels of expertise differs as well. Because experts have a better sense of what information is relevant to the decision, they tend to engage in *selective search,* which means their efforts are more focused and efficient. In contrast, novices are more likely to rely upon the opinions of others and to rely upon "nonfunctional" attributes, such as brand name and price, to distinguish among alternatives. They may also process information in a "top-down" rather than a "bottom-up" manner, focusing less on details than on the big picture. For instance, they may be more impressed by the sheer amount of technical information presented in an ad than by the actual significance of the claims made.[23]

Figure 8-4 The Relationship Between Amount of Information Search and Product Knowledge

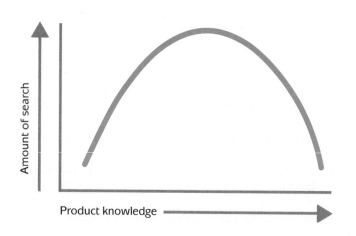

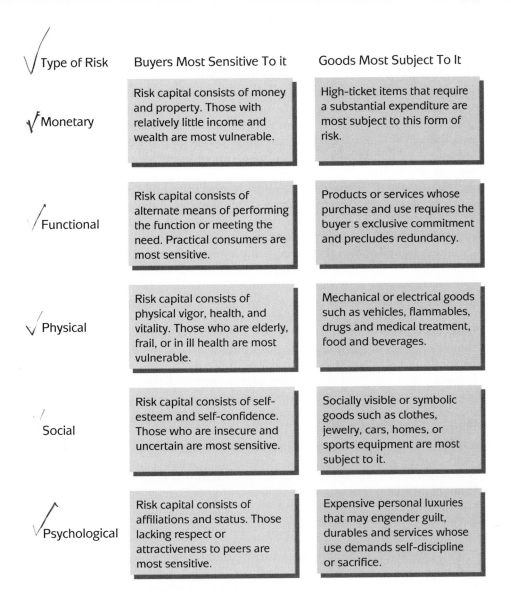

Type of Risk	Buyers Most Sensitive To it	Goods Most Subject To It
Monetary	Risk capital consists of money and property. Those with relatively little income and wealth are most vulnerable.	High-ticket items that require a substantial expenditure are most subject to this form of risk.
Functional	Risk capital consists of alternate means of performing the function or meeting the need. Practical consumers are most sensitive.	Products or services whose purchase and use requires the buyer s exclusive commitment and precludes redundancy.
Physical	Risk capital consists of physical vigor, health, and vitality. Those who are elderly, frail, or in ill health are most vulnerable.	Mechanical or electrical goods such as vehicles, flammables, drugs and medical treatment, food and beverages.
Social	Risk capital consists of self-esteem and self-confidence. Those who are insecure and uncertain are most sensitive.	Socially visible or symbolic goods such as clothes, jewelry, cars, homes, or sports equipment are most subject to it.
Psychological	Risk capital consists of affiliations and status. Those lacking respect or attractiveness to peers are most sensitive.	Expensive personal luxuries that may engender guilt, durables and services whose use demands self-discipline or sacrifice.

Figure 8-5 Five Forms of Buyer Risk

PERCEIVED RISK   As a rule, purchase decisions that involve some kind of **perceived risk** will result in more extensive search. Risk comes in many forms. It may be present if the product is expensive or is complex and hard to understand. Alternatively, perceived risk can be a factor even if a product choice is simply visible to others and we run the risk of embarrassment if the "wrong" choice is made.

Figure 8-5 lists five basic kinds of risk, including both objective (e.g., physical danger) and subjective factors (e.g., social embarrassment). As this figure notes, consumers with greater "risk capital" are less affected by risk. For example, a highly self-confident person would be less worried about the social risk inherent in a product, while a more vulnerable, insecure consumer might be reluctant to take a chance on a product that might not be accepted by peers.

EVALUATION OF ALTERNATIVES

Much of the effort that goes into a purchase decision occurs at the stage where a choice must be made from the available alternatives. After all, modern consumer society abounds with choices. In some cases, there may literally be hundreds of different brands (as in cigarettes) or different variations of the same brand (as in shades of lipstick), each screaming for our attention.

How do we decide what criteria are important, and how do we narrow down product alternatives to an acceptable number and eventually choose one over the others? The answer varies depending upon the decision-making process used. A consumer engaged in extended problem solving may carefully evaluate several brands, while someone making an habitual decision may not consider *any* alternatives to their normal brand.

IDENTIFYING ALTERNATIVES

Just for fun, ask a friend to name all of the brands of perfume she can think of. The odds are she will reel off three to five names rather quickly, then stop and think awhile before coming up with a few more. It is likely that the first set of brands are those with which she is highly familiar, and she probably wears one or more of these. The list may also contain one or two brands that she does not like and would perhaps like to forget. Note also that there are many, many more brands on the market she did not name at all.

If your friend were to go to the store to buy perfume, it is likely that she would consider buying some or most of the brands she listed initially. She might also consider a few more possibilities if these were forcefully brought to her attention while at the store. This may happen if she is "ambushed" by an employee who is spraying scent samples on shoppers, a common occurrence in some department stores.

THE EVOKED SET   The alternatives actively considered during a consumer's choice process are his or her **evoked set.** The evoked set is composed of those products already in memory (the *retrieval set*), plus those prominent in the retail environment. For example, recall that Billy did not know much about the CD product category, and he had only a few major brands in memory. Of these, two were acceptable possibilities and one was not. Those alternatives which the consumer is aware of but would not consider buying are his or her *inept set,* while those not entering the game at all comprise the *inert set*. These categories are depicted in Figure 8-6.

As already noted, consumers usually choose among a limited set of alternatives. One study combined results from several large-scale investigations of consumer choice sets and found that the number considered overall is fairly small, though there are some marked variations by product category and across countries. For example, the average set size for American beer consumers was less than three, while Canadian consumers typically considered seven. In contrast, while auto buyers in Norway studied two alternatives, American consumers looked at more than eight.[24]

For obvious reasons, a marketer who finds that her or his brand is not in the evoked set of many consumers in the target market has cause

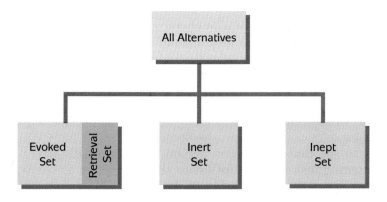

Figure 8-6 The Evoked Set: Getting in the Game

to worry. As people in the lottery industry like to say, "You can't win if you don't play." It is especially difficult to place a product into the evoked set after it has been considered and rejected. Indeed, a new brand is more likely to be added to the evoked set than is an existing brand that was previously considered but passed over, even after additional positive information has been provided for that brand.[25]

PRODUCT CATEGORIZATION

Remember that when consumers process product information, they do not do so in a vacuum. Instead, a product stimulus is evaluated in terms of what people already know about a product or those things it is similar to. A person evaluating a particular 35mm camera will most likely compare it to other 35mm cameras rather than to a Polaroid camera, and the consumer would certainly not compare it to a slide projector or VCR. This means that the category in which a product is placed will be a crucial determinant of how it is evaluated, since this determines the other products it will be compared to. For example, recall that Billy assumed CD players were basically equivalent to cassette players. He grouped them together under the same overall category, which implies that he would use the same criteria to evaluate CD players as he would cassette players.

The products in a consumer's evoked set are likely to be those that share some similar features. It is important to understand how this knowledge is represented in a consumer's **cognitive structure,** which refers to a set of factual knowledge about products (i.e., beliefs) and the way these beliefs are organized.[26] One reason is that marketers want to ensure that their products are correctly grouped. For example, when Toyota and Nissan introduced their expensive Lexus and Infiniti sports cars, they intended them to be compared with other sports cars, rather than to be in people's evoked set when they thought of "cheap but reliable Japanese cars."

LEVELS OF CATEGORIZATION People not only group things into categories, but these groupings occur at different levels of specificity. Typically, a product is represented in a cognitive structure at one of three levels. To understand this, consider how someone might categorize an ice cream cone. What other products share similar characteristics, and which would be considered as alternatives to eating a cone?

This question may be more complex than it first appears. At one level, a cone is similar to an apple, because both could be eaten as a dessert. At another level, a cone is similar to a piece of pie, since both are eaten for dessert and both are fattening. At still another level, a cone is similar to an ice cream sundae. Both are eaten for dessert, are made of ice cream, and are fattening.

It is easy to see that the items a person associates with, say, the category "fattening dessert" will influence the choices he or she will make for what to eat after dinner. The middle level, known as a *basic level category,* is typically the most useful in classifying products, since items grouped together tend to have a lot in common with each other but still permit a range of alternatives to be considered. The broader *superordinate category* is more abstract, while the more specific *subordinate category* often includes individual brands.[27] These three levels are depicted in Figure 8-7. Of course, not all items fit equally well into a category. In the current illustration, apple pie is a better example of the subordinate category pie than is rhubarb pie, though both are legitimate kinds of pies. Apple pie is thus more *prototypical* and would tend to be learned first, especially by category novices. In contrast, pie experts will tend to have knowledge about both typical and atypical category examples.[28]

STRATEGIC IMPLICATIONS OF PRODUCT CATEGORIZATION   Product categorization has many strategic implications. The way a product is grouped with others has very important ramifications for determining both its competitors for adoption and what criteria will be used to make this choice.

Positioning and Repositioning.   The success of a positioning strategy often hinges on the marketer's ability to convince the consumer that his or her product should be considered within a given category. For example, the orange juice industry tried to reposition orange juice as a drink that

Figure 8-7 Levels of Abstraction in Dessert Categories

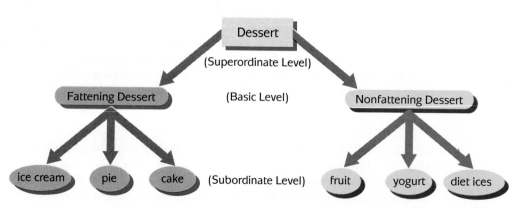

could be enjoyed all day long ("It's not just for breakfast anymore"). On the other hand, soft drink companies are now attempting the opposite by portraying sodas as suitable for breakfast consumption. They are trying to force their way into consumers' "breakfast drink" category, along with orange juice, grapefruit juice, coffee, and so on. The Sunkist ad shown here positions lemon juice as an alternative to salt.

Defining Competitors. At the abstract, superordinate level, many different product forms compete for membership. Both bowling and the ballet may be considered as subcategories of "Entertainment" by some people, but many would not necessarily consider the substitution of one of these activities for the other.

Products and services that on the surface are quite different, actually compete with each other at a broad level, often for consumers' discretionary dollars. While bowling or ballet may not be a likely tradeoff for many people, it is feasible, for example, that a symphony might try to lure away season ticket holders to the ballet by positioning itself as an equivalent member of the category "cultural event."[29]

Consumers are often faced with choices between noncomparable categories, where a number of attributes exist that cannot be directly related to one another: the old problem of counting apples and oranges. The comparison process is easier when consumers can derive an overlapping category that encompasses both items (e.g., entertainment, value, usefulness) and then rate each alternative in terms of that superordinate category.[30]

Prototypicality. If a product is a really good example of a category, it is more familiar to consumers, and as a result is more easily recognized

Sunkist lemon juice is attempting to position itself as a salt substitute—a new product category. Courtesy of Sunkist Growers, Inc.

and recalled.[31] Judgments about category attributes tend to be disproportionately influenced by the characteristics of category exemplars.[32] In a sense, brands that are strongly associated with a category get to "call the shots" by defining the evaluative criteria that should be used to evaluate all category members. Tide, a leader in the detergent category, does this in the ad shown here.

Stimulating Interest.   Being a bit less than prototypical is not necessarily a bad thing. Products that are moderately unusual within their product category may stimulate more information processing and positive evaluations, since they are neither so familiar that they will be taken for granted, or so discrepant that they will be dismissed.[33] A brand that is strongly discrepant may occupy a unique niche position, while those that are moderately discrepant remain in a differentiated position within the general category.[34]

Some dominant brands define the criteria that should be used to evaluate all category members, as Tide detergent does in this ad.   © The Procter & Gamble Company. Used with permission.

Locating Products. Product categorization can also affect consumers' expectations regarding the places they can locate a desired product. For example, Billy's categorization process led him to assume that CD players would be found next to cassette decks rather than, say, personal computers. Sometimes products do not clearly fit into categories (e.g., is a rug furniture?). This may affect consumers' ability to find them or make sense of them. For instance, a frozen dog food that had to be thawed and cooked failed in the market, partly because people could not adapt to the idea of buying dog food in the frozen foods section.

CHOOSING AMONG ALTERNATIVES

Once the relevant options from a category have been assembled, a choice must be made among them. Recall that the decision rules that guide choice can range from very simple and quick strategies to complicated processes requiring a lot of attention and cognitive processing.

EVALUATIVE CRITERIA When Billy was looking at different CD players, recall that he chose to focus on one or two product features and that several others were completely ignored. He narrowed down his choices by only considering two specific brand names, and from the Prime Wave and Precision models he chose one that was programmable and slightly higher priced.

The **evaluative criteria** Billy chose were the dimensions he used to judge the merits of competing options. Any number of criteria can be used to compare alternatives, ranging from very functional attributes (is this CD programmable?) to experiential ones (does this CD's sound reproduction make me imagine I'm in a concert hall?).

Another important point is that criteria on which products *differ* carry more weight in the decision process. If all brands being considered rate equally well on one attribute (e.g., if all CDs are programmable), consumers will have to find other attributes to make a choice. Those attributes that are actually used to differentiate among choices are *determinant attributes.*

NONCOMPENSATORY DECISION RULES One way to differentiate among decision rules is to divide them into those that are **compensatory** versus those that are **noncompensatory.** Consumers consider sets of product attributes by using different rules, depending upon the complexity of the decision, their involvement in it, and so on. To aid the discussion of some of these rules, look at the attributes of CD players considered by Billy, which are summarized in Table 8-3.

Simple rules are noncompensatory; a product with a low standing on one attribute cannot make up for this by being better on another attribute. In other words, people simply eliminate all options that do not meet some basic standards. A consumer like Billy who uses the decision rule "Only buy well-known brand names" would not consider a new brand, even if it was equal or superior to existing ones. When people are less familiar with a product category or not very motivated to process complex information, they tend to use simpler, noncompensatory rules.[35] Specific noncompensatory rules are described below.

TABLE 8-3 Hypothetical alternatives for a CD player

Attribute	Importance Ranking	Brand Ratings			
		Prime Wave	Precision	Technomatic	Store Brand
Brand Reputation	1	Excellent	Excellent	Fair	Poor
Programmable	2	Good	Good	Fair	Good
Quality of Construction	3	Excellent	Good	Fair	Excellent
Disc Stabilizer	4	Poor	Good	Poor	Good
Digital Filter	5	Poor	Poor	Poor	Good

The Lexicographic Rule. When the *lexicographic rule* is used, the brand that is the best on the most important attribute is selected. If two or more brands are seen as being equally good on that attribute, the consumer then compares them on the second most important attribute. This goes on until the tie is broken. In Billy 's case, since both the Prime Wave and Precision models were tied on his two most important attributes, the Prime Wave was chosen because it was superior on quality of construction.

The Elimination by Aspects Rule. Again, brands are evaluated on the most important attribute under the *elimination by aspects* rule. In this case, though, specific cutoffs are imposed. For example, if Billy had been more interested in having a disc stabilizer on his CD player (i.e., if it had a higher importance ranking), he might have stipulated that his choice "must have a disc stabilizer." Since the Precision model had one and the Prime Wave did not, the Precision would have been chosen.

The Conjunctive Rule. While the two former rules involve processing by attribute, the *conjunctive rule* entails processing by brand. As with the elimination by aspects procedure, cutoffs are established for each attribute. A brand is chosen if it meets all of the cutoffs, while failure to meet any one cutoff means it will be rejected. If none of the brands meet all of the cutoffs, the choice may be delayed, the decision rule may be changed, or the cutoffs themselves may be modified.

If Billy had stipulated that all attributes had to be rated "good" or better, he would not have been able to choose any of the options. He might then have modified his decision rule, conceding that it was not possible to attain these high standards in the price range he was considering. Billy could perhaps decide that it was not so important to have a stabilizer and a filter, so his first two choices could again be considered.

COMPENSATORY DECISION RULES Unlike the decision rules discussed above, compensatory rules give a product a chance to make up for its shortcomings. Consumers who employ these rules tend to be more involved in the purchase and thus are willing to exert the effort to consider the entire picture in a more exacting way. The willingness to let good and bad product qualities balance out can result in quite different choices. For example, if Billy were not adamant about buying a brand name, he would notice that the store's private label brand might be worth a look. But because this brand scored poorly on his first-ranked attribute, it would never stand a chance when he uses a noncompensatory rule.

Simple and Complex Compensation. Two basic types of compensatory rules have been identified. When using the *simple additive rule,* the consumer merely chooses the alternative having the largest number of positive attributes. This is most likely to occur when his or her ability or motivation to process information is limited.

One drawback to this approach for the consumer is that some of these attributes may not be very meaningful or important. An ad containing a long list of product benefits may be persuasive, despite the fact that many of the benefits included are actually standard within the product class.[36]

The more complex version is known as the *weighted additive rule.* When using this rule, the consumer also takes into account the relative importance of positively rated attributes, essentially multiplying brand ratings by importance weights. If this process sounds familiar, it should. The calculation process strongly resembles the multi-attribute attitude model described in Chapter 5.

HEURISTICS: THE POWER OF MENTAL SHORTCUTS

Instead of carefully calculating importance weights, consumers often employ decision rules that allow them to use some dimensions as substitutes for others. Especially where limited problem solving occurs prior to making a choice, consumers often fall back upon **heuristics,** mental rules of thumb that lead to a speedy decision. These rules range from the very general, (e.g., "Higher-priced products are higher quality products" or "Buy the same brand I bought last time") to the very specific (e.g., "Buy Domino, the brand of sugar my mother always bought").[37] For example, Billy relied on certain assumptions as substitutes for prolonged information search. He inferred that he would get expert service at a smaller store, so he was more confident in the salesperson's recommendations. He also assumed that a higher-priced product was better. These inferences served as "shortcuts" to more extensive information processing.[38] Two such shortcuts include the following.

THE REPRESENTATIVENESS HEURISTIC
An object is judged in terms of its resemblance to a typical member of its category. This shortcut allows people to overlook information about *base rates,* the relative frequency with which events occur. For example, a person who hears an employee of an advertising agency described as being rather shy and good with numbers might infer that the employee is a research analyst rather than an account executive, even if the company has twenty times more account execs than analysts.

THE AVAILABILITY HEURISTIC We may judge the frequency of events in terms of the vividness with which they come to mind. People tend to overestimate the incidence of violent crimes or natural disasters because these are remembered so easily. By the same token, a professor's grading may be influenced by the impression a particularly talkative student makes in class.

This bias can affect consumers' evaluations of product performance. For example, even though a particular car model may have an excellent repair record overall, you may overlook this if you personally know one or two people who have had problems with that make.[39] Similarly, a product with an unusual name makes experiences with that product—good and bad—even more distinctive.[40]

MARKET BELIEFS In addition to these general cognitive biases that may affect purchasing behavior, consumers often form specific beliefs about relationships in the marketplace. These beliefs then guide their decisions, whether or not they are accurate.[45] Our friend Billy's decisions were influenced by his **market beliefs.** Recall, for instance, that he chose to shop at a small, local store rather than an "electronics supermarket" because he assumed the service would be better (though the prices would be correspondingly higher). A large number of market beliefs have been identified. Some of these are listed in Table 8-4. How many do you share?

Relying on a Product Signal. One shortcut directly related to consumer behavior is to infer hidden dimensions of products from observable attributes. The aspect of the product that is visible acts as a *signal* of some underlying quality. This explains why someone trying to sell a

MULTICULTURAL DIMENSIONS

Modern consumers choose among products made in many countries. Americans may buy Brazilian shoes, Japanese cars, clothing imported from Taiwan, or microwave ovens built in South Korea. Total imports into the United States have been increasing at an annual rate of 39 percent.[41]

Consumers' reactions to these imports are mixed. In some cases, people have come to assume that a product made overseas is of better quality (e.g., cameras, cars), while in other cases the knowledge that a product has been imported tends to lower perceptions of product quality (e.g., for apparel).[42] In general, people tend to rate their own country's products more favorably than do foreigners, and products from industrialized countries are better rated than are those from developing countries.

A product's origin, then, is often used as a signal of quality. Certain items are strongly associated with specific countries, and products from those countries often attempt to benefit from these linkages. In some cases, country-of-origin information may even be more weighted more heavily than the brand name of the product.[43] Recent evidence indicates that learning of a product's country-of-origin is not necessarily good or bad. Instead, it has the effect of stimulating the consumer's interest in the product to a greater degree. The purchaser thinks more extensively about the product and evaluates it more carefully.[44]

TABLE 8-4 Common market beliefs

Brand

All brands are basically the same.

Generic products are just name brands sold under a different label at a lower price.

A brand's quality is the most important determinant of its success. Bad brands just don't survive.

The best brands are the ones that are purchased the most.

When in doubt, a national brand is always a safe bet.

In established product categories, brands that have been around the longest are the most dependable.

Store

Specialty stores are a great place to familiarize yourself with the best brands. But once you figure out what you want, it's cheaper to buy it at a discount outlet.

A store's character is reflected in its window displays.

Sales people in specialty stores are more knowledgeable than other sales personnel.

Larger stores offer better prices than small stores.

Stores that sell on a volume basis can afford to charge less for their merchandise.

Locally owned stores give the best service.

A store that offers a good value on one of its products probably offers good values on all of its items.

Credit and return policies are most lenient at large department stores.

Stores that have just opened usually charge attractive prices.

Prices/Discounts/Sales

Better products cost more to make. That's why higher prices usually indicate better quality.

Sales are typically run to get rid of slow moving merchandise.

Stores that are constantly having sales don't really save you any money.

Within a given store, higher prices generally indicate higher quality.

Sales that do not specify pre-sale price levels do not offer any real savings.

Advertising and Sales Promotion

I associate "hard sell" advertising with low quality products.

The most heavily advertised brands are normally among the best brands.

Stores that advertise a lot have overpriced merchandise.

Items tied to "giveaways" are not a good value (even with the freebee).

Coupons represent real savings for customers because they are not offered by the store.

When you buy heavily advertised products, you are paying for the label, not higher quality.

Product/Packaging

Largest sized containers are almost always cheaper per unit than smaller sizes.

New products are more expensive when they're first introduced. Prices tend to settle down as time goes by.

When you are not sure what you need in a product, it's a good idea to invest in the extra features. You'll probably wish you had them later.

Items that come in fancy packages are not a good value.

In general, synthetic goods are lower in quality than goods made of natural materials.

It's advisable to stay away from products when they are new to the market. It usually takes the manufacturer a little time to work the bugs out.

Required Search

The more information you have, the better.

Once you find a good brand, it pays to stick with it.

It takes time to make a smart purchase.

Source: Adapted from Calvin P. Duncan, "Consumer Market Beliefs: A Review of the Literature and an Agenda for Future Research," in *Advances in Consumer Research,* ed. Marvin E. Goldberg, Gerald Gorn, and Richard W Pollay (Provo, Utah: Association for Consumer Research, 1990)17: 729–35.

used car takes great pains to be sure the car's exterior is clean and shiny: Potential buyers often judge the vehicle's mechanical condition by its appearance.[46]

When product information is incomplete, judgments are often based upon inferences, which in turn are derived from beliefs about *covariation,* or associations among events.[47] For example, a consumer may form an association between product quality and the length of time a manufacturer has been in business. Other signals or attributes assumed to co-exist with good or bad products include well-known brand names, country of origin, price, and the retail outlets that carry the product.

Unfortunately, consumers tend to be poor estimators of covariation. Their beliefs persist despite evidence to the contrary. Similar to the consistency principle discussed in Chapter 5, people tend to see what they are looking for. They will look for product information that confirms their guesses. In one experiment, consumers sampled four sets of products to determine if price and quality were related. Those who believed in this relationship prior to the study elected to sample higher-priced products, thus creating a sort of self-fulfilling prophecy.[48]

Price as a Heuristic.   Recall that Billy chose the higher-priced CD, because higher prices mean higher quality, don't they? The assumption of a *price-quality relationship* is one of the most pervasive market beliefs.[49] Novice consumers may in fact consider price as the only relevant product attribute.

Experts also consider this information, though in these cases price tends to be used for its informational value, especially for products (e.g., virgin wool) that are known to have wide quality variations in the marketplace. When this quality level is more standard or strictly regulated (e.g., Harris Tweed sportcoats), experts do not weigh price in their decisions. For the most part, this belief is justified; you do tend to get what you pay for. However, let the buyer beware—the price/quality relationship is not always justified.[50]

Brand Names as a Heuristic.   Branding is a marketing strategy that often functions as a heuristic. People form preferences for a favorite brand, and then may literally never change their minds in the course of a lifetime. In a study of the market leaders in thirty product categories by the Boston Consulting Group, it was found that *twenty-seven* of the brands that were number one in 1930 are still number one today. These brands include such perennial favorites as Ivory soap, Campbell's soup, and Gold Medal flour.[51]

A brand that exhibits that kind of staying power is treasured by marketers, and for good reason. Brands that dominate their markets are as much as 50 percent more profitable than their nearest competitors.[52] A survey of 3000 consumers on brand power in Japan, Europe, and the United States combined awareness and esteem scores to produce the following list of the most positively regarded brand names around the world:[53]

1. Coca-Cola
2. IBM
3. Sony
4. Porsche
5. McDonald's
6. Disney
7. Honda
8. Toyota
9. Seiko
10. BMW

Consumers' attachments to certain brands, such as Marlboro, Coca-Cola, Gerber, and Levi's, are so powerful that this loyalty is often considered as a positive product attribute in and of itself. Brand equity can actually be quantified in terms of *goodwill,* defined as the difference between the market value and the book value of a brand. Recently, the British company Grand Metropolitan actually decided to record brand names it had acquired on its balance sheets, including these intangible assets in its financial reports to shareholders.[54]

Many people tend to buy the same brand just about every time they go to the store. This consistent pattern is often due to **inertia,** where a brand is bought out of habit merely because this takes less effort. If another product comes along that is for some reason easier to buy (e.g., it is cheaper or the original product is out-of-stock), the consumer will not hesitate to do so. A competitor who is trying to change a buying pattern based on inertia often can do so rather easily, because little resistance to brand switching will be encountered if some reason to do so is apparent. Since there is little to no underlying commitment to the product, such promotional tools as point-of-purchase displays, extensive couponing, or noticeable price reductions may be sufficient to "unfreeze" a consumer's habitual pattern.

This kind of fickleness will not occur if true **brand loyalty** exists. In contrast to inertia, brand loyalty is a form of repeat purchasing behavior reflecting a conscious decision to continue buying the same brand. This concept thus refers to a pattern of purchases over time where actual decision making occurs.[55] For loyalty to exist, a pattern of repeat purchase must be accompanied by an underlying positive attitude toward the brand. Brand loyalty may be initiated by customer preference based on objective reasons, but after the brand has been around for a long time and is heavily advertised it can also create an emotional attachment, either by being incorporated into the consumer's self-image or because it is associated with prior experiences.[56]

Compared to an inertia situation where the consumer passively accepts a brand, a brand loyal consumer is actively (sometimes passionately) involved with his or her favorite. Because of the emotional bonds that can be created between brand loyal consumers and products, "true-blue" users react more vehemently when these products are altered, redesigned, or eliminated.[57] Recall, for example, the national call-in campaigns, boycotts, and other protests when Coca-Cola replaced its tried-and-true formula with New Coke.

Though brand loyalty is alive and well for some well-known products, its power seems to be on the decline. Marketers increasingly are struggling with the problem of *brand parity,* which refers to consumers' beliefs that there are no significant differences among brands. For example, more than one-half of consumers worldwide consider all brands of beer and cigarettes to be about the same, and more than 70 percent believe that all paper towels, soaps, and snack chips are alike.[58]

The *Wall Street Journal*'s survey of American consumers reported that most consumers switch brands for many of the products they use. Twelve percent of consumers surveyed said they were not brand loyal in *any* of the twenty-five product categories included, while only 2 percent are loyal in sixteen or more categories. Specifics are provided in Figure 8-8. Brand loyalty was particularly low for such products as canned vegetables and athletic shoes and tended to be highest for categories such as ketchup and cigarettes that have distinctive flavors. The comments of one thirty-one-year-old homemaker are typical, "The only . . . thing I'm really loyal to is my Virginia Slims cigarettes. Coke and Pepsi are all the same to me, and I usually buy whatever brand of coffee happens to be on sale."[59]

This erosion is due to a number of factors, including an increase in the volume of short-term promotions and the flood of new products that have hit the market in recent years. Also, many people simply are not that knowledgeable about even well-known brand alternatives, especially for very expensive products that they buy infrequently, if at all. In one large survey, consumers were asked to name the "finest, most elegant" brand in a number of categories. The response "don't know" topped the list in several, including men's and women's clothing designers and perfumes.[60]

GETTING HELP WITH DECISIONS Consumers in America suffer from an embarrassment of riches: The marketplace simply offers too many choices. As anyone who has spent an afternoon in a shopping mall can attest, the available options have become so vast that some simplifying strategies are often required to process the available information. In addition, many purchase decisions hold such serious consequences that consumers may be reluctant to rely solely upon personal judgment. They may "subcontract" their decision making, such as when they rely upon recommendations to choose a product or service instead of personally collecting information about the choices themselves.[61] The strategy of seeking outside help is in itself a sort of heuristic: "Let someone better qualified make the decision."

Buyer-Helping Businesses. The need to seek help in making purchase decisions underlies many *buyer-helping businesses,* including such diverse services as financial planners, nutrition consultants, interior decorators, and even psychotherapists and gurus. A person who is paid to help in decision making has been termed a *surrogate consumer.*[62] In general, buyer-helping businesses can be categorized as:[63]

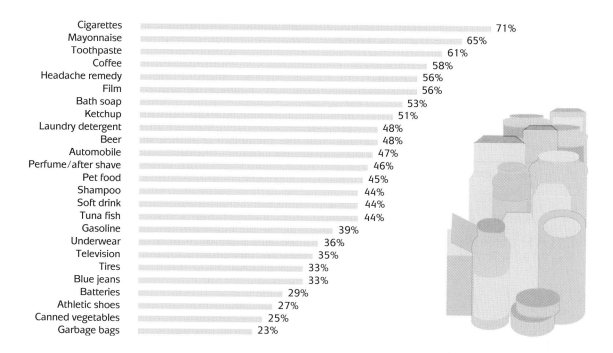

Cigarettes	71%
Mayonnaise	65%
Toothpaste	61%
Coffee	58%
Headache remedy	56%
Film	56%
Bath soap	53%
Ketchup	51%
Laundry detergent	48%
Beer	48%
Automobile	47%
Perfume/after shave	46%
Pet food	45%
Shampoo	44%
Soft drink	44%
Tuna fish	44%
Gasoline	39%
Underwear	36%
Television	35%
Tires	33%
Blue jeans	33%
Batteries	29%
Athletic shoes	27%
Canned vegetables	25%
Garbage bags	23%

Figure 8-8 Faithful or Fickle? Brand Loyalty Across Product Categories   Source: Ronald Alsop, "Brand Loyalty is Rarely Blind Loyalty," *The Wall Street Journal* (October 19, 1989): B2.

- evaluators and appraisers (e.g., critics, the Good Housekeeping Seal, *Consumer Reports*)
- diagnosticians and recommenders (e.g., physicians, architects)
- service locating agencies (e.g., travel agents, Ticketron)
- product finding agencies (e.g., retailers)

MARKETING OPPORTUNITY

CLOTHES ENCOUNTERS: THE WARDROBE CONSULTANT

"I have a lawyer, why not a clothes expert?"

—testimonial from a consultant's brochure

While the role of interior decorators or financial planners as surrogate consumers is well established, other forms of personal counselors are evolving to meet the consumer's need for guidance in the marketplace. One relatively new and growing area is wardrobe and image consultation: Individuals in the United States, Canada, Europe, and Australia have proclaimed themselves dress consultants, image counselors, and even "wardrobe architects." Almost one-fifth of the female executives polled in one national survey in the United States reported that they had employed the services of a wardrobe consultant.[64]

In many instances, the wardrobe consultant is retained to increase the client's chances of success in the interpersonal marketplace. The typical advertisement or brochure for this service emphasizes the crucial nature of appearance for success in the business world, and often provides graphic examples of careers torpedoed by inappropriate dress. As one consultant noted, "You (the businessperson) are a product yourself. People view you like a package of cheese."[65] Whether or not that is an accurate statement, it seems clear that the desire of at least some segments of consumers for guidance in clothing purchases is growing.

CHAPTER SUMMARY

Consumers are faced with the need to make decisions about products all of the time. Some of these decisions are very important and entail great effort, while others are made on a virtually automatic basis. Perspectives on decision making range from a focus on habits that people develop over time to novel situations involving a great deal of risk, where consumers must carefully collect and analyze information prior to making a choice. Even if a brand is consistently purchased over time, this pattern may be due to true brand loyalty, or simply to inertia—it's the easiest thing to do.

A typical decision process involves several steps. These include problem recognition, where the consumer first realizes that some action must be taken. This realization may be prompted in a variety of ways, ranging from the actual malfunction of a current purchase to a desire for new things based on exposure to different circumstances or advertising that provides a glimpse into what is needed to "live the good life."

Once a problem has been recognized and is seen as sufficiently important to warrant some action, information search begins. This search may range from simply scanning memory to determine what has been done to resolve the problem in the past to extensive fieldwork where the person consults a variety of sources to amass as much information as possible. In many cases, however, people engage in surprisingly little search. Instead, they rely upon various mental shortcuts, such as brand names or price, or they may simply imitate others. The product alternatives that are considered comprise the individual's evoked set. Members of the evoked set usually share some characteristics; they are categorized similarly. The way products are mentally grouped influences which alternatives will be considered, and some brands are more strongly associated with these categories than are others (i.e., they are more prototypical). The chapter discusses some of the reasons why this categorization process is so important to marketers.

When the consumer eventually must make a choice among alternatives, a number of decision rules may be used. These range from the simple to the complex, depending upon the person's motivation and knowledge. Non-compensatory rules eliminate alternatives that are deficient on any of the criteria the consumer has chosen to use. Compensatory rules, which are more likely to be applied in high-involvement situations, allow the decision maker to consider each alternative's good and bad points more carefully to arrive at the overall best choice. Very often, heuristics, or mental rules of thumb are used to simplify decision making. In particular, people develop many market beliefs over time. While not necessarily accurate, these beliefs may be applied to guide decisions. One of the most common beliefs is that price is positively related to quality.

KEY TERMS

Behavioral influence perspective	Heuristics
Brand loyalty	Inertia
Cognitive structure	Information search
Compensatory decision rules	Limited problem solving
Evaluative criteria	Market beliefs
Evoked set	Noncompensatory decision rules
Experiential perspective	Perceived risk
Extended problem solving	Problem recognition
Habitual decision making	Rational perspective

REVIEW QUESTIONS AND DISCUSSION TOPICS

1. If people are not always rational decision makers, is it worth the effort to study how these decisions are made? What techniques might be employed to understand experiential consumption and to translate this knowledge into marketing strategy?
2. Compare and contrast the different kinds of information search discussed in the chapter.
3. List three product attributes that can be used as quality signals, and provide an example of each.
4. Why is it difficult to place a product in a consumer's evoked set after it has already been rejected? What strategies might be attempted to accomplish this?
5. Define the three levels of product categorization described in the chapter. Diagram these levels for a health club.
6. Discuss two different noncompensatory decision rules, and highlight the difference(s) between them. How might the use of one rule versus another result in a different product choice?

HANDS-ON EXERCISES

1. Choose a friend or parent who grocery shops on a regular basis, and keep a log of their purchases of common consumer products over the semester. Can you detect any evidence of brand loyalty in any categories based upon consistency of purchases? If so, talk to the person about these purchases. Try to determine if his or her choices are based upon true brand loyalty or based on inertia. What techniques might you use to differentiate between the two?
2. Form a group of three. Pick a product and develop a marketing plan based upon each of the three approaches to consumer decision making: rational, experiential, and behavioral influence. What are the major differences in emphasis among the three perspectives? Which is the most likely type of problem-solving activity for the product you have selected? What characteristics of the product make this so?
3. Locate a person who is about to make a major purchase. Ask that person to make a chronological list of all the information sources consulted prior to making a decision. How would you characterize the types of sources used (i.e., internal versus external, media versus personal, etc.)? Which sources appeared to have the most impact on the person's decision?
4. Perform a survey of country-of-origin stereotypes. Compile a list of five countries and ask people what products they associate with each. What

are their evaluations of the products and likely attributes of these different products? The power of a country stereotype can also be demonstrated in another way. Prepare a brief description of a product, including a list of features, and ask people to rate it in terms of quality, likelihood of purchase, and so on. Make several versions of the description, varying only the country from which it comes. Do ratings change as a function of the country-of-origin?

5. Ask a friend to "talk through" the process he or she used to choose one brand over others during a recent purchase. Based on this description, can you identify the decision rule that was most likely employed?

NOTES

1. John C. Mowen, "Beyond Consumer Decision Making," *Journal of Consumer Marketing* 5 (1988)1: 15–25.
2. Richard W. Olshavsky and Donald H. Granbois, "Consumer Decision Making—Fact or Fiction," *Journal of Consumer Research* 6 (September 1979): 93–100.
3. Mowen, "Beyond Consumer Decision Making."
4. James F. Engel, Roger D. Blackwell, and Paul W. Miniard, *Consumer Behavior,* 6th Ed. (Chicago: Dryden, 1990).
5. Joseph W. Alba and J. Wesley Hutchinson, "Dimensions of Consumer Expertise," *Journal of Consumer Research* 13 (March 1987): 411–54.
6. Gordon C. Bruner III and Richard J. Pomazal, "Problem Recognition: The Crucial First Stage of the Consumer Decision Process," *Journal of Consumer Marketing* 5 (1988)1: 53–63.
7. Ross K. Baker, "Textually Transmitted Diseases," *American Demographics* (December 1987): 64.
8. Julia Marlowe, Gary Selnow, and Lois Blosser, "A Content Analysis of Problem–Resolution Appeals in Television Commercials," *The Journal of Consumer Affairs* 23 (1989)1: 175–94.
9. Peter H. Bloch, Daniel L. Sherrell, and Nancy M. Ridgway (1986), "Consumer Search: An Extended Framework," *Journal of Consumer Research* 13 (June 1986): 119–26.
10. Girish Punj, "Presearch Decision Making in Consumer Durable Purchases," *Journal of Consumer Marketing* 4 (Winter 1987): 71–82.
11. Punj, (1987), "Presearch Decision Making in Consumer Durable Purchases."
12. H. Beales, M. B. Jagis, S. C. Salop, and R. Staelin, "Consumer Search and Public Policy," *Journal of Consumer Research* 8 (June 1981): 11–22.
13. Itamar Simonson, Joel Huber, and John Payne, "The Relationship Between Prior Brand Knowledge and Information Acquisition Order," *Journal of Consumer Research* 14 (March 1988): 566–78.
14. George J. Stigler, "The Economics of Information," *Journal of Political Economy* 69 (June 1961): 213–25.
15. Cathy J. Cobb and Wayne D. Hoyer, "Direct Observation of Search Behavior," *Psychology & Marketing* 2 (Fall 1985): 161–79.
16. Sharon E. Beatty and Scott M. Smith, "External Search Effort: An Investigation Across Several Product Categories," *Journal of Consumer Research* 14 (June 1987): 83–95; William L. Moore and Donald R. Lehmann, "Individual Differences in Search Behavior for a Nondurable," *Journal of Consumer Research* 7 (December 1980): 296–307.
17. Geoffrey C. Kiel and Roger A. Layton, "Dimensions of Consumer Information Seeking Behavior," *Journal of Marketing Research* 28 (May 1981): 233–39.
18. David F. Midgley, "Patterns of Intepersonal Information Seeking for the Purchase of a Symbolic Product," *Journal of Marketing Research* 20 (February 1983): 74–83.
19. Jacob Jacoby, Robert W. Chestnut, Karl C. Weigl, and William Fisher, "Pre–Purchase Information Acquisition: Description of a Process Methodology, Research

Paradigm and Pilot Investigation," in *Advances in Consumer Research,* ed. Beverlee B. Anderson, (Ann Arbor, Mich.: Association for Consumer Research, 1976)3: 306–14; Charles M. Schaninger and Donald Sciglimpaglia, "The Influence of Cognitive Personality Traits and Demographics on Consumer Information Acquisition," *Journal of Consumer Research* 8 (September 1981): 208–16; Merrie Brucks, "The Effects of Product Class Knowledge on Information Search Behavior," *Journal of Consumer Research* 12 (June 1985): 1–16.

20. Girish N. Punj and Richard Staelin, "A Model of Consumer Search Behavior for New Automobiles," *Journal of Consumer Research* 9 (March 1983): 366–80.

21. Cobb and Hoyer, "Direct Observation of Search Behavior"; Moore and Lehmann, "Individual Differences in Search Behavior for a Nondurable"; Punj and Staelin, "A Model of Consumer Search Behavior for New Automobiles."

22. James R. Bettman and C. Whan Park, "Effects of Prior Knowledge and Experience and Phase of the Choice Process on Consumer Decision Processes: A Protocol Analysis," *Journal of Consumer Research* 7 (December 1980): 234–48.

23. Joseph W. Alba and J. Wesley Hutchinson, "Dimensions of Consumer Expertise," *Journal of Consumer Research* 13 (March 1987): 411–54; Bettman and Park, "Effects of Prior Knowledge and Experience and Phase of the Choice Process on Consumer Decision Processes"; Merrie Brucks, "The Effects of Product Class Knowledge on Information Search Behavior"; Joel E. Urbany, Peter R. Dickson, and William L. Wilkie, "Buyer Uncertainty and Information Search," *Journal of Consumer Research* 16 (September 1989): 208–15.

24. John R. Hauser and Birger Wernerfelt, "An Evaluation Cost Model of Consideration Sets," *Journal of Consumer Research* 16 (March 1990): 393–408.

25. Robert J. Sutton, "Using Empirical Data to Investigate the Likelihood of Brands Being Admitted or Readmitted Into an Established Evoked Set," *Journal of the Academy of Marketing Science* 15 (Fall 1987): 82.

26. Alba and Hutchison, "Dimensions of Consumer Expertise"; Joel B. Cohen and Kunal Basu "Alternative Models of Categorization: Toward a Contingent Processing Framework," *Journal of Consumer Research* 13 (March 1987): 455–72.

27. Eleanor Rosch, "Principles of Categorization," in *Recognition and Categorization,* ed. E. Rosch and B. B. Lloyd (Hillsdale, N.J.: Lawrence Erlbaum, 1978).

28. Michael R. Solomon, "Mapping Product Constellations: A Social Categorization Approach to Symbolic Consumption," *Psychology & Marketing* 5 (1988)3: 233–58.

29. Elizabeth C. Hirschman and Michael R. Solomon, "Competition and Cooperation Among Culture Production Systems," in *Marketing Theory: Philosophy of Science Perspectives,* ed. Ronald F. Bush and Shelby D. Hunt (Chicago: American Marketing Association, 1982), 269–72.

30. Michael D. Johnson, "The Differential Processing of Product Category and Noncomparable Choice Alternatives," *Journal of Consumer Research* 16 (December 1989): 300–09.

31. Mita Sujan, "Consumer Knowledge: Effects on Evaluation Strategies Mediating Consumer Judgments," *Journal of Consumer Research* 12 (June 1985): 31–46.

32. Rosch, "Principles of Categorization."

33. Joan Meyers-Levy and Alice M. Tybout, "Schema Congruity as a Basis for Product Evaluation," *Journal of Consumer Research* 16 (June 1989): 39–55.

34. Mita Sujan and James R. Bettman, "The Effects of Brand Positioning Strategies on Consumers' Brand and Category Perceptions: Some Insights from Schema Research," *Journal of Marketing Research* 26 (November 1989): 454–67.

35. C. Whan Park, "The Effect of Individual and Situation-Related Factors on Consumer Selection of Judgmental Models," *Journal of Marketing Research* vol. XIII (May 1976): 144–51.

36. Joseph W. Alba and Howard Marmorstein, "The Effects of Frequency Knowledge on Consumer Decision Making," *Journal of Consumer Research* 14 (June 1987): 14–25.

37. Wayne D. Hoyer, "An Examination of Consumer Decision Making for a Common Repeat Purchase Product," *Journal of Consumer Research* 11 (December 1984): 822–29; Calvin P. Duncan, "Consumer Market Beliefs: A Review of the Literature and an Agenda for Future Research," in *Advances in Consumer Research,* ed. Marvin E. Goldberg, Gerald Gorn, and Richard W. Pollay (Provo, Utah: Association for Consumer Research, 1990)17: 729–35.

38. Robert A. Baron, *Psychology: The Essential Science* (Boston: Allyn & Bacon, 1989); Valerie S. Folkes, "The Availability Heuristic and Perceived Risk," *Journal of Consumer Research* 15 (June 1989): 13–23; Daniel Kahneman and Amos Tversky, "Prospect Theory: An Analysis of Decision Under Risk," *Econometrica* 47 (1979): 263–91.

39. Michael R. Solomon, Sarah Drenan, and Chester A. Insko, "Popular Induction: When is Consensus Information Informative?" *Journal of Personality* 49 (1981)2: 212–24.

40. Folkes, "The Availability Heuristic and Perceived Risk."

41. Barbara C. Garland and Marti J. Rhea, "American Consumers: Profile of an Import Preference Segment," *Akron Business and Economic Review* 19 (Summer 1988): 20–29.

42. Richard Ettenson, Janet Wagner, and Gary Gaeth, "Evaluating the Effect of Country of Origin and the 'Made in the U.S.A.' Campaign: A Conjoint Approach," *Journal of Retailing* 64 (Spring 1988): 85–100; C. Min Han and Vern Terpstra, "Country-of-Origin Effects for Uni-National & Bi-National Products," *Journal of International Business* 19 (Summer 1988): 235–55; Michelle A. Morganosky and Michelle M. Lazarde, "Foreign-Made Apparel: Influences on Consumers' Perceptions of Brand and Store Quality," *International Journal of Advertising* 6 (Fall 1987): 339–48.

43. Gary M. Erickson, Johny K. Johansson, and Paul Chao, "Image Variables in Multi-Attribute Product Evaluations: Country-of-Origin Effects," *Journal of Consumer Research* 11 (September 1984): 694–99.

44. Sung-Tai Hong and Robert S. Wyer, Jr., "Effects of Country-of-Origin and Product–Attribute Information on Product Evaluation: An Information Processing Perspective," *Journal of Consumer Research* 16 (September 1989): 175–87.

45. Duncan, "Consumer Market Beliefs."

46. Beales, et al., "Consumer Search and Public Policy."

47. Gary T. Ford and Ruth Ann Smith, "Inferential Beliefs in Consumer Evaluations: An Assessment of Alternative Processing Strategies," *Journal of Consumer Research* 14 (December 1987): 363–71; Deborah Roedder John, Carol A. Scott, and James R. Bettman, "Sampling Data For Covariation Assessment: The Effects of Prior Beliefs on Search Patterns," *Journal of Consumer Research* 13 (June 1986): 38–47; Gary L. Sullivan and Kenneth J. Berger, "An Investigation of the Determinants of Cue Utilization," *Psychology & Marketing* 4 (Spring 1987): 63–74.

48. John, et al., "Sampling Data for Covariation Assessment."

49. Chr. Hjorth-Andersen, "Price as a Risk Indicator," *Journal of Consumer Policy* 10 (1987): 267–81.

50. David M. Gardner, "Is There a Generalized Price-Quality Relationship?" *Journal of Marketing Research* 8 (May 1971): 241–43; Kent B. Monroe, "Buyers' Subjective Perceptions of Price," *Journal of Marketing Research* 10 (1973): 70–80.

51. Richard W. Stevenson, "The Brands With Billion-Dollar Names," *New York Times* (October 28, 1988): A1.

52. Ronald Alsop, "Enduring Brands Hold Their Allure by Sticking Close to Their Roots," *The Wall Street Journal* (Centennial Edition, 1989): B4.

53. Laura Clark, "Porsche Top Auto Brand Name; Honda, Toyota, BMW Follow in U.S., Japan, Europe Survey," *Automotive News* (December 12, 1988): 62.

54. "What's in a Name?" *The Economist* (August 27, 1988): 62.

55. Jacob Jacoby and Robert Chestnut, *Brand Loyalty: Measurement and Management* (New York: Wiley, 1978).

56. Anne B. Fisher, "Coke's Brand Loyalty Lesson," *Fortune* (August 5, 1985): 44.

57. Jacoby and Chestnut, "Brand Loyalty."

58. Ronald Alsop, "Brand Loyalty is Rarely Blind Loyalty," *The Wall Street Journal* (October 19, 1989): B1.

59. Alsop, "Brand Loyalty is Rarely Blind Loyalty."

60. Dennis Kneale, "Glitzy Brands Make Small Impressions: in Fragrances, Fashion, Many Favor Familiar," *The Wall Street Journal* (December 15, 1989): B1.

61. Dennis L. Rosen and Richard W. Olshavsky, "A Protocol Analysis of Brand Choice Strategies Involving Recommendations," *Journal of Consumer Research* 14 (December 1987): 440–44.

62. Michael R. Solomon, "The Missing Link: Surrogate Consumers in the Marketing Chain," *Journal of Marketing* 50 (October 1986): 208–18.

63. Stanley Hollander, "Buyer-Helping Businesses . . . and Some Not-So-Helpful Ones," *MSU Business Topics* 22 (Summer 1974): 52–68.

64. Michael R. Solomon and Susan P. Douglas, "Diversity in Product Symbolism: The Case of Female Executive Clothing," *Psychology & Marketing* 4 (Fall 1987): 189–212; see also Michael R. Solomon, "The Wardrobe Consultant: Exploring the Role of a New Retailing Partner," *Journal of Retailing* 63 (Summer 1987): 110–28; Joseph Z. Wisenblit, "Person Positioning: Empirical Evidence and a New Paradigm," *Journal of Professional Services Marketing* 4 (1989)2: 51–82.
65. "Designs on Your Appearance," *The Philadelphia Inquirer* (December 11, 1980).

Collective Decision Making: Families and Companies

CHAPTER 9

During dinner, Bob Simpson remarks, "It's time to start thinking about our family vacation."

Steve, 14, groans to himself. Last year, he lost a heated debate for a week-long camping trip when the family decided once again to make the Mouseketeer pilgrimage to Disney World. While Steve had been as big a fan of Mickey's as any kid, he now feels old enough to really promote a change for the family—especially one that is more to his liking.

"Dad, I've been thinking. Maybe this is the year we should try something different. I'll bet there are other places we'll like as much as Disney World."

When Mom asks him what he has in mind, Steve responds, "Well, my friend Paul's family just got back from Club Med, and they really liked it a lot. His Mom really needed to relax after the divorce, and his little brother learned how to swing on a trapeze!"

Bob Simpson snorts, "Club Med! I went to one of those when I got out of college, just before I met your mother. That place is wild, and certainly no place to take a family. Someday when you're older, I'll tell you about it."

Steve retorts, "Come on, Dad. You know Paul's Mom wouldn't take her kids anywhere that wasn't good for families. I'll tell you what, if I check it out, can we at least talk about it?"

The next day, Paul's mother lends Steve a Club Med brochure showing the wide selection of activities to suit everyone's tastes. He sees that the Club Med organization has changed with the times and is now aimed at the growing family market.

Steve discovers that kids can find plenty of things to do. For teens and adults there seem to be all kinds of sports, craft classes, discos, and at some of the clubs, even topless bathing, although Steve decides not to emphasize this point. At dinnertime all the next week, Steve lobbies for his choice, emphasizing the Mini Club for kids aged 2 to 11, which his nine-year-old sister decides she wants to join.

Finally, Steve convinces the family to give it a try. A month later, they are frolicking on the beach at Paradise Island—with no mouse ears in sight.

The Simpsons' choice of a family vacation experience illustrates that many decisions are shared by two or more people. A decision-making unit may be a husband and wife, a family, or executives in a corporation. The decision-making steps outlined in Chapter 8 are in fact often performed by several people, each with his or her own agenda and a certain degree of influence, or power, over others in the group.[1]

THE ORGANIZATIONAL CONSUMER

Many employees of corporations or other organizations make purchase decisions on a daily basis. Industrial buyers must decide on which vendors they want to do business with and what specific items they require from these suppliers. The items considered can range in price and significance from paper clips for the secretarial pool to a multi-million dollar computer system. Obviously there is a lot at stake in understanding how these special and important decisions are made.

INFLUENCING FACTORS

Many factors have been identified to distinguish organizational and industrial purchase decisions from consumer decisions, where a product is purchased for personal use. Some of these factors are as follows:[2]

- Purchase decisions made by companies frequently involve a great number of people, including both those who do the actual buying and those who directly or indirectly influence this decision.
- Organizational and industrial products often are bought according to precise, technical specifications, requiring rational criteria and knowledge about the product category.
- Impulse buying is rare (industrial buyers do not suddenly get an "urge to splurge" on lead pipe or silicon chips). Because buyers

As illustrated by this *Business Week* ad, many marketers try to reach the executives who make important purchase decisions on behalf of their companies. *Courtesy of Business Week.*

are professionals, their decisions are based on past experience and careful weighing of alternatives.

- Decisions often are high risk, especially in the sense that a buyer's career may be riding on his or her demonstration of good judgment.
- Companies are usually part of a narrow customer base, and the dollar volume of purchases is often substantial, dwarfing most individual consumer grocery bills or even mortgage payments. One hundred to 250 organizational customers often account for more than half of a supplier's sales volume, which gives buyers a fairly high degree of influence over the supplier.

- The organizational buyer's perception of the purchase situation is influenced by a number of factors. These include his or her *expectations* of the supplier (e.g., product quality, the competence and behavior of the firm's employees, and prior experiences in dealing with that supplier), the *organizational climate* of his or her own company (i.e., perceptions regarding how the company rewards performance and what it values), and the buyer's own assessment of his or her own performance (e.g., whether he or she believes in taking risks).[3]

PURCHASING STRATEGIES

Factors such as buyers' extent of experience with the organization and the perceived importance of the purchase to the company help to determine the strategy a buyer will use in making a purchase decision. The strategies used by buyers tend to be directly related to the amount of time and effort required. For example, reliance on a fixed set of suppliers for routine purchases is one strategy that greatly reduces the information search and communication that would otherwise be required.[4]

THE BUYCLASS FRAMEWORK   The **buyclass theory of purchasing** uses three decision-making dimensions to describe the purchasing strategies of an organizational buyer:[5]

1. The level of information that must be gathered prior to making a decision.
2. The seriousness with which all possible alternatives must be considered.
3. The degree to which the buyer is familiar with the purchase.

In practice, these three dimensions relate to how much cognitive effort will be expended in making a purchase decision. Three types of "buyclasses," strategies based on these dimensions, encompass most organizational decision situations. The three categories are a *straight rebuy,* a *modified rebuy,* and a *new task.*[6] These strategies are summarized in Table 9-1.

ORGANIZATIONAL CONSUMERS VERSUS "CIVILIANS": THE ILLUSION OF DIFFERENCE?

Are organizational purchase decisions different from the buying choices civilian consumers make? There are actually more similarities between organizational buyers and ordinary consumers than many people seem to believe. Organizational purchase decisions do tend to have a higher economic or functional component relative to individual consumer choices, but the issue is one of degree more than an absolute difference. For example, while organizational buyers appear to the outsider to be models of rationality, their decisions are sometimes guided by brand loyalty, by long-term relationships they have established with particular suppliers, or even by aesthetic concerns.

TABLE 9-1 Buying strategy decision grid

Buying Situation	Newness of the Problem	Consideration of New Alternatives	Strategy
Straight rebuy	Low	None	Repeat price decision
Modified rebuy	Medium	Limited	Consider new suppliers, but minimize risk
New task	High	Many	Extensive information search; others involved in the decision

Source: Adapted from Patrick J. Robinson, Charles W. Faris, and Yoram Wind, *Industrial Buying and Creative Marketing* (Boston: Allyn & Bacon, 1967).

DEFINING THE MODERN FAMILY

The **extended family** was once the most common family unit. It consisted of three generations living together and often included not only grandparents, but aunts, uncles, and cousins. As evidenced by the Cleavers of "Leave It To Beaver" and other television families of the 1950s, the **nuclear family**—a mother and a father and one or more children (perhaps with a sheepdog thrown in for good measure)—became the model family unit over time. However, many changes have occurred since the days of Beaver Cleaver. Though people may continue to conjure up an image of the typical American family based on old shows like "Leave it to Beaver," "Father Knows Best," or "Ozzie and Harriet," demographic data show that this ideal image of the family is no longer a realistic picture.

Demographics are statistics that measure a population's characteristics, such as birth rate, age distribution, income, and so on. The U.S. Census Bureau is a major source of demographic data on families, but many private firms gather additional data on specific population groups. The changes and trends revealed in demographic studies are of great interest to marketers, because the data can be used to locate and predict the size of markets for many products, ranging from home mortgages to brooms and can openers. In addition, changes in consumers' family structures, such as the upheaval caused by divorce, often represent opportunities for marketers as normal purchasing patterns become unfrozen and people make new choices about products and brands.[7]

DESCRIBING THE FAMILY

In taking the national census every ten years, the U.S. Census Bureau regards *any* occupied housing unit as a *household,* regardless of the relationships among people living there. A **family household,** as defined by the Census Bureau, contains at least two people who are related by blood or marriage. While the Census Bureau and other survey firms compile a massive amount of data on family households, certain categories are of particular interest to marketers.

GROWTH AND DISTRIBUTION OF FAMILY HOUSEHOLDS The last half of this century has seen a major shift in where Americans live. Historically, the population was concentrated in northeastern and midwestern urban areas. In more recent times, though, consumers have migrated. Largely through the widespread availability of automobiles, suburban areas grew dramatically.

More recently, people have been pushing out even farther beyond cities. *Exurbs,* smaller towns ringing suburbs, have grown the most rapidly. Consumers are still reporting a greater desire to live in towns and villages than in cities, and some experts predict that this trend will continue.[8] This growth has been concentrated in the southern and western United States, which have accounted for about 90 percent of population growth since 1980 as the population migrates from the North and Midwest.[9]

AGE OF THE FAMILY *Married Couples Are Aging.* Since 1980, the under-25, married couple age group declined by one-third, while the 65+ couples group increased by about 15 percent.[10] Overall, consumers between 35 and 44 were responsible for the largest increase in the number of households, growing by almost 40 percent since 1980.[11] People are waiting longer to get married; according to the U.S. Census Bureau, the average age of marriage is now 24 for women and 26 for men. This trend has implications for businesses ranging from catering to cutlery.

Children in the Family. Worldwide, surveys show that almost all women want smaller families than they did a decade ago. Family size is dependent on such factors as educational level, the availability of birth control, and religion.[12]

Approximately 3.8 million babies are born annually in the United States. This number peaked in 1988, ending a rising trend that began in 1977. Marketers keep a close eye on the population's *birth rate* (also called *fertility)* to gauge how the pattern of births will affect demand for products in the future.

The *fertility rate* is determined by the number of births per year per 1000 women of child-bearing age. The U.S. fertility rate increased dramatically in the late 1950s and early 1960s, the period of the so-called baby boomers. It declined in the 1970s, and began to climb again in the 1980s as baby boomers began to have their own children in a "baby boomlet."

The current figure is about sixty-six babies born annually for every 1000 women between the ages of 15 and 44, a rate almost half that during the baby boom period. Demographers predict that the fertility rate will continue to decline in this decade, even though the number of fertile women between 15 and 44 will grow.[13] Despite the fact that half of American women between the ages of 18 and 34 expect to have children, births will fall because most women are on the older edge of this age group.[14]

Nine million pre-schoolers are involved in child-care programs, most of them in the 600,000 licensed facilities now in operation in the United States. However, the number of families using day care has been projected to be only half of what the market can bear. It has been estimated that the day-care business will grow 21 percent a year over the next seven years and that parents will spend $48 billion annually on day care by 1995. Furthermore, for-profit businesses will provide half of all day care by 1995.[15]

In recent years large numbers of women have entered the workforce (even among married couples, about 50 percent of mothers work outside of the home).[16] Due to this trend and other changes in the family, fewer adult caretakers are available to supervise children. These factors have created a generation of "latchkey children," who come home to a locked, empty home after school and who can be identified by the key worn on a chain around the neck so it won't get lost. It is estimated that almost 10 percent of American kids aged 5 to 13 qualify as latchkey kids.[17]

Whether or not children are supervised, they are being given more responsibility for purchase activities, food preparation, and so on, which increases the importance of this segment to marketers.[18] Children's consumerism, as well as the role of children in family consumer decisions, are discussed later in this chapter.

SEX OF THE FAMILY HEAD   Family households headed by a single person have grown by over 25 percent in the last decade.[19] Well over 1 million couples divorce in a typical year. About one in every five families is headed by a woman.[20] Partly as a result of the divorce rate, the proportion of U.S. households headed by men with no wife present is expected to rise to 18 percent by the turn of the century. Unlike many of their single female counterparts who live with their children and other relatives though, about 80 percent of these men will live with only their children or with the addition of nonrelatives.[21]

Single men and women are quite different markets. More than half of single men are under the age of 35, while more than half of single women are over 65. Despite single males' greater incomes, single women dominate many markets because of their spending patterns and they are being targeted by many marketers. Single women are more likely to own a home and spend more on housing-related items and furniture. Single men, in contrast, spend more in restaurants and on cars.[22]

COMPOSITION OF FAMILY HOUSEHOLDS   In contrast to the "Ozzie and Harriet" stereotype, only *6 percent* of American families now consist of an employed father, a mother who works at home, and two or more kids under the age of 18.[23] Even when a married couple does live with kids, families are shrinking. The average household size decreased from 2.8 to 2.6 persons in the last decade. The number of U.S. families with three or more children under age 18 living at home has fallen to 20 percent of families. Still, large families are good marketing prospects. They use a lot of cleaning products, are more likely to have pets, and typically spend more than average on games, toys, and garments.[24]

The Sandwich Generation. In many cases the nuclear family is being transformed to resemble the old-fashion extended family. Many adults are being forced to care for parents as well as children. In fact, Americans on average spend seventeen years caring for children, but eighteen years assisting aged parents.[25] Middle-aged people have been termed "the sandwich generation," because they must attend to those above and below them in age.

Boomerang Kids. In addition to dealing with live-in parents, many adults are surprised to find that their children are living with them longer, or in some cases moving back in, well after their "lease" has expired.[26] These returnees have been termed *boomerang kids* by demographers. The number of children between 18 and 34 living at home has grown by one-third in the last fifteen years. If this trend continues, it will affect a variety of markets as boomerang kids spend less on housing and staples and more on discretionary purchases like entertainment.

ALTERNATIVE FAMILY STRUCTURES

The Census Bureau regards any occupied housing unit as a household, regardless of the relationships among people living there. Thus, one person living alone, three roommates, or two lovers, all constitute households. The latter arrangement is somewhat euphemistically referred to as *POSSLQ*, which stands for Persons of Opposite Sex Sharing Living Quarters.

Less traditional households will rapidly increase in this decade if trends persist. For example, non-married households headed by men with children under the age of 18 increased by a third between 1981 and 1990.[27] The U.S. Census forecasts a decline in the number of family households and children and an increase in the number of people living alone in the 1990s. By the year 2000, the Census says families will decline 71 percent, married couples will shrink by 3 percent, and families with children will decrease from 25 percent to 20 percent of all families.[28]

KEEPING UP WITH THE CHANGES Families worldwide are becoming smaller and less traditional. Though Scandinavian countries are pacesetters in developing nontraditional forms of family living, the United States has the highest incidence of divorce and single-parent households of any country.[29] To account for the rapid changes in the way families are structured, the U.S. Census included three new categories of family members for its 1990 survey: (1) Natural-born or adopted child, (2) foster child, and (3) unmarried partner. The first two classifications are intended to distinguish stepchildren from other children, and the latter category identifies cohabitating couples such as unmarried heterosexuals and gay or lesbian couples.[30]

GAY CO-HABITATORS Gay people living together constitute an increasingly important alternative family structure. The gay community is in many ways a highly desirable market segment. It numbers at least 25 million people and consists of many consumers who are affluent, highly educated, and brand-loyal. One survey of readers of urban gay newspapers found their average income to be almost $37,000—three times the national average. Nearly 60 percent had a college education (compared to 18 percent of the national population).

Homosexuals are still largely ignored by marketers, with a few exceptions. Remy Martin, for example, advertises its cognac in local gay media with great success. Stolichnaya vodka also recently began to advertise in these media. Experts believe more mainstream companies will jump on board once they realize the market potential of this group.[31]

MAN'S BEST FRIEND: A FAMILY MEMBER?

Many people are extremely attached to pets, to the point where domestic animals might be considered part of the family. They are often an important part of the "extended self" discussed in Chapter 7. U.S. households possess about 51 million dogs, 52 million cats, 14 million birds, 95 million fish, and 9 million other animals. Each year Americans spend $4 billion on pet food, and $3.5 billion on veterinary care.[32] Dog food on average accounts for 6 percent of a dog owner's total grocery bill.[33]

In France, there are twice as many dogs and cats as children. The French are so passionate about their pets that according to a French anthropologist, the danger ". . . is when we get to a point where we place some animals above men."[34] A television show about animals, featuring former actress Brigitte Bardot, who is now the country's leading animal advocate, recently ran against a show about children. The animal show pulled 17 percent of the national audience, as against the 5 percent who watched the children show. Ms. Bardot's love of animals, incidentally, is so intense that until recently she kept a cow in her living room.

MARKETING OPPORTUNITY

The inclusion of pets as family members creates many marketing opportunities, ranging from bejeweled leashes to professional dog-walkers. Listed below are samples of some recent attempts to cater to people's pet attachments:

- Macy's department store opened a Petigree shop for dogs and cats. Says one employee, "You can put your dog in a pink satin party dress or a 20s flapper dress with fringe." Other items include a wedding dress for dogs (for $100, and the veil is extra), a $48 black dinner jacket, and a $30 trench coat.[35]
- Nabisco introduced Milk-Bone T.C. (tartar control) biscuits and rawhide strips. The company claims that 75 percent of dogs have periodontal problems.[36]
- A veterinarian in Maryland offers holistic medicine for pets. He features natural foods, acupuncture, and chiropractic massages. The doctor also sells the Rodeo Drive Fragrance Collection, a set of spray colognes for dogs.[37]

- A twenty-five-minute video, titled "Doggie Adventure," was produced for dogs. Shot with a camera balanced two feet off the ground, it takes viewers on a a romp from a dog's perspective.[38]
- Pet accessories for sale include a pet safety belt for the car and a heated water bed. The Pet Set, a store in Atlanta, offers mink coats, marble feeding bowls, brass beds, jogging suits, and toothpaste for consumers' furry friends.[39]

THE FAMILY IN THE MARKETPLACE

Although the "Leave It to Beaver" ideal of the American family is no longer an accurate picture of consumers' real lives, marketers recognize that families and other household units still tend to function according to the traditional pattern of mom, dad, and kids. For example, the kitchen, where food and household products are often shown, is usually dominated by a mother figure (not necessarily a woman), who dispenses love and food and maintains the home. The den is reserved for a father figure who is the source of wise counsel and advice. Bedrooms are usually used as personal space (often of children), where comforting reassurances are given and confidential problems are resolved.[40]

TARGETING THE FAMILY

Many marketers have focused on the renewed interest in family life brought about by the more flexible definitions of what constitutes a family.[41] While families were indeed out of fashion in the 1960s and 1970s, being seen by some as an infringement on personal freedom, 90 percent of the respondents in one recent survey confirmed that family life was one of the most important things to them.[42] As Steve Simpson discovered, the Club Med organization is one marketer that has changed with the times. More than half a million Club members are married, and members' median age is 37. Many Club Meds now have Mini Clubs for kids aged 2 to 11 and switched in the 1980s from havens for "swinging singles" to family destinations. Some clubs even have a staff to warm bottles and take care of babies as young as four months old.[43]

 MARKETING OPPORTUNITY

The renewed priority on the family and other changes such as increasing birth and marriage rates have been emphasized by direct mail strategists. For example, Kimberly-Clark purchases a list of new parents from a vendor that scans local birth announcements. Every three months these consumers are mailed a free magazine explaining changes in infant behavior, along with coupons for Huggies diapers.

Lamaze, the most widely used program of childbirth preparation for prospective parents, has begun a program that allows other companies to use its consumer base. For a fee, a product can now be featured in Lamaze tapes and brochures, and the company can also get access to the organization's list of program participants, which includes approximately 80 percent of new parents in the United States.[44]

Other advertisers are also climbing on the bandwagon. Companies ranging from Heinz and Polycell (in the U.K.) to Gitano jeans and Johnson outboard motors are revamping their campaigns.[45] Gitano, for example, traditionally positioned as jeans for seductive women, is spending $3 million on its "Spirit of Family" campaign, which depicts an all-American family image. As a company executive explains, "Even though the Gitano ads of the past have been of a self-confident, sexy woman, they've updated with the times. Now, we see that the family is what is important."[46]

Gitano is one company that has revamped its image to stress the family. The ad on the top reflects a typical focus on young, single adults. The more recent ad on the bottom incorporates the company's newer family theme. Courtesy of THE AD GROUP, New York, New York, in-house agency: The Gitano Group, Inc.

EFFECTS OF FAMILY STRUCTURE ON CONSUMPTION

Family structure can affect consumer behavior in a variety of ways. A family's needs and expenditures will vary depending upon such factors as the number of people (children and adults) in the family, their ages, and whether one, two, or more adults are employed outside of the home.

Two important factors that determine how a couple spends time and money are whether they have children and whether the woman works. Couples with children generally have higher expenses (ranging from food to utility bills).[47] In addition, a recently married couple makes very different expenditures than one with young children, who in turn are quite different from a couple with children in college, and so on. Families with working mothers also must often make allowances for such expenses as day care and a work wardrobe for the woman.

THE FAMILY LIFE CYCLE   Recognizing that family needs and expenditures change over time, the concept of the **family life cycle** (FLC) has been widely used by marketers. This form of classification combines trends in income and family composition with the changes in demands placed upon this income. As we age, our preferences for products and activities tend to change. In many cases, our income levels tend to rise (at least until retirement), so that we can afford more as well. In addition, many purchases that must be made at an early age do not have to be repeated very often. For example, we tend to accumulate durable goods, such as large appliances, and only replace these as necessary.

This focus on longitudinal changes in priorities is particularly valuable in predicting demand for specific product categories over time—the money spent by a couple with no children on dinners out and vacations will probably be diverted for quite different purchases after the birth of a child. The family life cycle traditionally includes the following eight categories, each of which describes the head of a household.[48]

The Young Single Stage.   This group is composed of people who are younger than 45 years of age and have never been married. These people tend to have lower incomes, as they are just starting out in life, but they also have fewer financial responsibilities than many other adults. As a result, they have more money to spend on entertainment and other discretionary items.

The Newly Married Stage.   The head of the household is younger than 45 and is married with no children. While this group is relatively small in numbers, their buying activity is substantial. This is the stage where major purchases must be made to establish a household, so this group is a major market for furniture, dishes, appliances, and so on.

The Full Nest I Stage.   At this point the couple has begun to have children, and the youngest one is below the age of 6. Many families begin to feel the financial squeeze during this stage, especially if the woman leaves her job to care for the child. The emphasis is on such necessities as insurance, medical expenses, and baby furniture.

The Full Nest II Stage. The youngest child is now older than 6. In many cases the woman has returned to work so finances are a bit less pressed. Expenditures lean toward the fulfillment of the needs of growing children, such as music lessons and sports equipment.

The Full Nest III Stage. This stage is characterized by a family with teenagers. In some cases children are beginning to contribute to family income. The expenditure emphasis is on replacing durables or purchasing additional products, such as cars and stereos. The family will also begin to explore vacation and travel options (as the Simpsons did in the beginning of the chapter).

The Empty Nest I Stage. The children are no longer living at home and are no longer dependent on the parents for support. This new "freedom" permits consumers in this stage to focus on travel, hobbies, and home improvements.

The Empty Nest II Stage. The couple has retired and consequently is experiencing a significant decline in income. They may move to a smaller home or retirement community and will have greater medical expenses.

The Solitary Survivor Stage. The head of the household (often a woman) is now widowed. These people have low incomes and high medical needs. Their emphasis will be on companionship and restricted, secure activities.

LIMITATIONS OF THE FLC   The FLC has been useful to marketers because family-related expenditures account for substantial purchases in many product categories. However, this traditional perspective has been criticized on several grounds. For one, the stages are highly related to income levels, so it is not always clear how much a stage in the life cycle adds to predictions of expenditures after income has been considered. Also, it is obvious that the eight categories described above exclude many consumers who do not fall neatly into any one of them. More recent modifications to the FLC have added categories to account for divorced people, childless marriages, and non-married couples living together.[49]

DECISION MAKERS IN THE FAMILY

Traditionally, some buying decisions, termed **autocratic decisions,** were usually made by one or the other spouse. Men, for instance, often had sole responsibility for selecting a car, while most decorating choices fell to women. Other decisions, such as vacation destinations, were made jointly; these are known as **syncratic decisions.**

It is important for marketers to know the nature of decision making within their particular product category so that they know whom to target and whether or not they need to reach both spouses to influence a decision. Sometimes this process may be surprising. For example, when market research in the 1950s indicated that women were playing a larger role in household purchasing decisions, lawn mower manufacturers began to emphasize the rotary mower over other power mowers. Rotary mowers, which conceal the cutting blades and engine, were often depicted being used by young women and smiling grandmothers to downplay fears of injuries.[50]

Four factors appear to determine the degree to which decisions will be made jointly or by one or the other spouse:[51]

1. Sex-role stereotypes. Couples who believe in traditional sex-role stereotypes tend to make individual decisions for sex-typed products (i.e., those considered to be "masculine" or "feminine").
2. Spousal resources. The spouse who contributes more resources to the family has the greater influence.
3. Experience. Individual decisions are made more frequently when the couple has gained experience as a decision-making unit.
4. Socio-economic status. Joint decisions are made more by middle-class families than in either higher- or lower-class families.

SEX ROLES AND DECISION-MAKING RESPONSIBILITIES

With many women now working outside of the home, men are participating more in nurturing, family-related activities. Overall, the degree to which a couple adheres to traditional sex-role norms determines how much their allocation of responsibilities will fall along familiar lines and how their consumer decision-making responsibilities will be allocated.

In traditional families (and especially those with low educational levels), women are primarily responsible for family financial management—the man makes it, and the woman spends it.[52] Each spouse "specializes" in certain activities.[53] The pattern is different among families where spouses adhere to more modern sex-role norms. These couples believe that there should be more shared participation in family maintenance activities. In these cases, husbands assume more responsibility for laundering, housecleaning, grocery shopping, and so on, in addition to such traditionally "male" tasks as home maintenance and garbage removal.[54]

MAINTAINING THE KIN NETWORK Despite recent changes in decision-making responsibilities, women still are primarily responsible for the continuation of the family's *kin-network system*. They perform the rituals intended to maintain ties among family members, both immediate and extended. This function includes such activities as coordinating visits among relatives, calling and writing family members, sending greeting cards, making social engagements, and so on.[55] This organizing role means that women often make important decisions about the family's leisure activities, choices regarding whom to see and where to see them, and so on.

SPOUSAL INFLUENCE

In terms of family decision making, the **synoptic ideal** calls for the husband and wife to take a common view and act as joint decision makers. According to this ideal, they would very thoughtfully weigh alternatives, assign one another well-defined roles, and calmly make mutually beneficial consumer

MULTICULTURAL DIMENSIONS

Cultures holds differing expectations regarding which spouse "wears the pants in the family." These expectations are related to the level of a society's economic development. Those that are less developed tend to exhibit more traditional sex-role allocations of responsibility. Differences in marital power relations across societies have been described in terms of the following four "ideal culture types.[56]

1. *Patriarchy*—characterized by highly traditional societies where men hold virtually all power, regardless of social class of the couple. These countries are among the least developed.
2. *Modified Patriarchy*—similar to traditional societies, but tending toward equality for the sexes in the upper strata of society. This pattern tends to be found in modernizing nations.
3. *Transitional Equalitarianism*—less traditional societies where equality between the sexes is largely based upon such factors as education and in-come. Women who have these advantages are accorded more decision-making responsibility.
4. *Equalitarianism*—societies characterized by a very high level of husband and wife sharing. This pattern is most prevalent in some Scandinavian countries (e.g., Denmark and Sweden).

A five-nation study on spousal decision making generally supported these distinctions. The countries were selected to represent a range of economic development. They included Venezuela, the United States, France, Holland, and the African nation of Gabon. Figure 9-1 indicates some of the interesting differences across the countries in terms of responsibilities for purchasing decisions. Consistent with the classification presented above, it was generally found that more joint decision making occurred in developed nations.[57] Decisions were more likely to be made jointly in the United States, France, and Holland, while the husband was given more authority in Gabon and Venezuela.

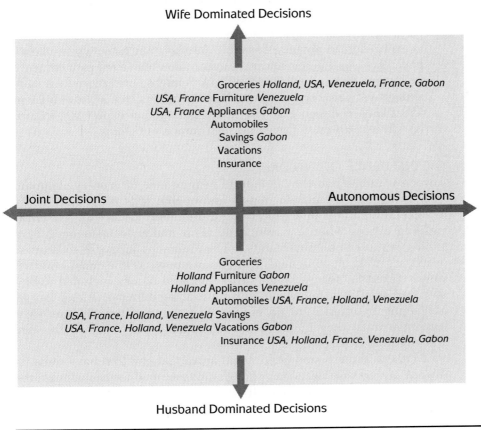

Figure 9-1 Cross-Cultural Spousal Purchasing Decisions: The United States, France, Holland, Venezuela, and Gabon. Source: Adapted from Robert T. Green, Jean-Paul Leonardi, Jean-Louis Chandon, Isabella C. M. Cunningham, Bronis Verhage, and Alain Strazzieri, "Societal Development and Family Purchasing Roles: A Cross-National Study," *Journal of Consumer Research* 9 (March 1983): 440. Reprinted with permission by The University of Chicago Press.

decisions. The couple would act rationally, analytically, and use as much information as possible to maximize joint utility.

In reality, however, spousal decision making is often characterized by the use of influence or methods that are likely to reduce conflict. A couple "reaches" rather than "makes" a decision. This process has been described as "muddling through."[58] One common technique for avoiding conflict is the use of heuristics (see Chapter 8). Some decision-making patterns frequently observed when a couple makes decisions in buying a new house illustrate the use of heuristics.

1. The couple's areas of common preference are based upon salient, objective dimensions rather than more subtle, hard-to-define cues. For example, a couple may easily agree on the number of bedrooms they need in the new home, but will have more difficulty achieving a common view of how the home should look.

2. The couple agrees on a system of task specialization, where each is responsible for certain duties or decision areas and does not interfere on the other's "turf." For many couples, these assignments are likely to be influenced by their perceived sex-roles. For example, the wife may scout out houses in advance that meet their requirements, while the husband determines whether the couple can obtain a mortgage.

3. Concessions are based on the intensity of each spouse's preferences. One spouse will yield to the influence of the other in many cases simply because his or her level of preference for a certain attribute is not particularly intense, where in other situations he or she will be willing to exert effort to obtain a favorable decision.[59] In cases where intense preferences for different attributes exist, rather than attempt to influence each other, spouses will "trade off" a less intense preference for a more strongly felt one. For example, a husband who is somewhat indifferent about kitchen design may give in to his wife, but expect that in turn he will be allowed to design his own garage workshop.

THE INFLUENCE OF CHILDREN

Anyone who has had the "delightful" experience of grocery shopping with one or more children in tow knows that kids often have a say in what their parents buy, especially for products like cereal.[60] **Parental yielding** occurs when a parental decision maker is influenced by a child's request and "surrenders." The strategies kids use to request purchases were documented in a recent study. While most children simply asked for things, some other common tactics included saying they had seen it on television, saying that a sibling or friend has it, bargaining by offering to do chores, and so on. Other actions were less innocuous; they included directly placing the object in the cart and continuous pleading.[61]

Mothers, fathers, and children all agree that children have some influence in purchase decisions, though children tend to overestimate the amount of influence they actually have. A comparison of parent's and children's self-reports of influence is presented in Table 9-2. From the adult decision maker's perspective, children's influence was greatest for

TABLE 9-2 Kid Power Over Family Purchases

Ages 6-17	Parents saying they were influenced by child (percent)	Children reporting influence over parent (percent)
Breakfast cereal	78	60
Clothing	72	83
Toys	68	48
Ice cream	58	54
Soft drinks	56	58
Video movies	48	53
Toothpaste	44	26
Personal computers	10	9
Automobile	8	18

Source: Patricia Sellers, "The ABC's of Marketing to Kids," *Fortune* (May 8, 1989): 115.

less expensive products and those designed for the child's personal use.[62] As might be expected, kids' influence tends to increase as they get older (remember Steve Simpson's Club Med "victory").

THE INTIMATE CORPORATION: FAMILY DECISION MAKING

The decision process within a household unit in some ways resembles a business conference. Certain matters are put on the table for discussion, different members may have different priorities and agendas, and there may be some jockeying for position or power struggles to rival any tale of corporate intrigue. In just about every living situation, whether a conventional family, students sharing a sorority house or apartment, or some other nontraditional arrangement, group members seem to take on different roles just as purchasing agents, engineers, account executives, and others do within a company.

HOUSEHOLD DECISION ROLES

A number of specific roles are played when a decision must be made by either a private household or some other decision-making unit, such as the buying center in a large company. Depending on the decision, some or all of the group members may be involved, and one person may play any number (or even all) of these roles. Indeed, a person living alone may be thought of as a "corporation of one." He or she makes the "executive" decision to initiate a project and is also responsible for information collection and making a purchase.

The roles that may be played are similar to those enacted by industrial purchasers.[63] These roles are described below, in the context of the family decision-making scenario at the beginning of the chapter.

- *Initiator*—the person who brings up the idea or need (Mr. Simpson reminded the family about their vacation).
- *Gatekeeper(s)*—the person(s) who conducts the information search and controls the flow of information available to the group. In this case, Steve sought out appropriate Club Med information. By strategically suppressing the small matter of topless bathing, Steve was better able to support his case.
- *Influencer(s)*—the person(s) who tries to sway the outcome of the decision. Some people may be more motivated to get involved, and participants also differ in terms of the amount of power they have to convince others of their choice. While all of the Simpson family was involved in vacation planning, Steve was able to exert influence because he had a strong preference. This degree of influence had increased over past years; his parents gave more weight to his input as he got older.
- *Buyer(s)*—the person(s) who actually makes the purchase. The buyer may or may not actually use the product. This person may pay for the item, actually procure it, or both. Steve's mother was the one with the credit card, so she booked the vacation for the entire family.
- *User(s)*—the person(s) who winds up using the product or service. All of the Simpsons "consumed" Club Med, but in many cases the eventual user is a different person. An industrial purchaser buys machine parts on behalf of assembly workers, and mothers buy clothes to be worn by their children.

DECISION-MAKING DYNAMICS

As the Simpsons' deliberations suggest, family decisions often involve a fair degree of lobbying and intrigue as each member maneuvers to have his or her preferences recognized. The process often resembles politics. Different "representatives" may form coalitions or voting blocs (as did Steve and his sister), and trading may occur, where individuals agree to compromise on their choices in return for greater say in other decisions.

PURCHASING STRATEGIES AND TYPES OF DECISIONS   Just as purchasing strategies in business organizations vary depending upon the nature of the task, the dynamics of family decision making depend upon how complicated or risky the purchase is. The nature of the buying situation will determine the degree to which family members get involved in seeking out product information, weighing alternatives, lobbying for one option over another, and so on. The *buyclass* decision framework discussed earlier can also be applied to family decision making.

Straight Rebuys. Many household purchases are quite routine and require little input from family members. The family shopping list, for example, may be primarily comprised of standard items that are purchased during every trip to the grocery store.

Modified Rebuys. Other family needs may require a bit more thought and input. If, say, the kitchen coffee maker stops working properly, different family members may consider replacing it with another model. Alternatively, they may decide after doing some limited information search to replace the machine with the same, familiar brand so as to reduce risk.

New Task Decisions. The Simpsons' vacation debate exemplifies a new task decision. Because of the importance of the vacation to the family, the risk of making a bad choice is high. Family members may have strongly held opinions about good and bad choices, and they will probably be more willing to expend the effort to fight for their preference. Also, the criteria for choosing among alternatives are not clear (e.g., sports, organized kids' activities, resort atmosphere, etc.), and this ambiguity means that more information sources must be consulted and the process will be longer and more complicated.

SOURCES OF CONFLICT   Conflict occurs when there is not complete correspondence in family members' needs and preferences. Some specific factors determining the degree of family decision conflict include:[64]

- Interpersonal need (a person's level of investment in the group). A child in a family situation may care more about what his or her family buys for the house than will a college student who is temporarily rooming with an acquaintance.
- Product involvement and utility (the degree to which the product in question will be used or will satisfy a need). A family member who is an avid coffee drinker will obviously be more interested in the purchase of a new coffee maker to replace a malfunctioning one than a similar expenditure for some other item.
- Responsibility for procurement, maintenance, payment, and so on. People are more likely to have disagreements about a decision if it entails long-term consequences and commitments. For example, a family decision about getting a dog may involve conflict regarding who will be responsible for walking it and feeding it.
- Power (or the degree to which one family member exerts influence over the others in making decisions). In traditional families, the husband tends to have more power than the wife, who in turn has more than the oldest child, and so on. In family decisions, conflict can arise when one person continually uses the power he or she has within the group to satisfy his or her priorities. For example, if Steve Simpson believed that his life would end if he did not get to Club Med, he might be more willing to resort to extreme tactics to influence his parents, perhaps by throwing a tantrum or refusing to participate in family chores.

In general, decisions will involve conflict among family members to the extent that they are somehow important or novel and/or if individuals have strong opinions about good and bad alternatives. The degree to which these factors generate conflict determines the type of decision the family will make.

TYPES OF DECISIONS Two basic types of decisions are made by families in new task purchase situations.[65] In a *consensual purchase decision,* the group agrees on the desired purchase, differing only in terms of how it will be achieved. In these circumstances, the family will most likely engage in problem solving and consider alternatives until the means for satisfying the group's goal is found. For example, a household considering adding a dog to the family but concerned about who will take care of it might draw up a chart assigning individuals to specific duties.

In other cases, life is not so easy. In an *accommodative purchase decision,* group members have different preferences or priorities and cannot agree on a purchase that will satisfy the minimum expectations of all involved. It is here that bargaining, coercion, compromise, and the wielding of power are all likely be used to achieve the primary goal of agreement on the purchase itself. Family decisions often are characterized by an accommodative rather than a consensual decision. For example, Steve Simpson might have persuaded his family to try Club Med for one year by promising to babysit for his younger sister and giving up a camping trip he had planned to take with his friends.

DEVELOPMENT OF CHILDREN: CONSUMERS-IN-TRAINING

As has been seen, children often play important roles in family consumer decision making, and they are gaining responsibility as consumers in their own right. They continue to support the toy and candy industries, of course, but now they also buy and/or influence the purchase of many other products as well.

For better or for worse, the new generation is, as the bumper sticker proclaims, "Born to Shop." Shopping now ranks among the top seven interests and activities of America's children.[66] Over 80 percent of young respondents in one survey said their primary wish was to have more money to buy things.[67]

CONSUMER SOCIALIZATION SOURCES Children do not spring from the womb with consumer skills already in memory. Learning the dos and don'ts of being a consumer involves a long and complex process with many influences lending a hand. **Consumer socialization** has been defined as the process ". . . by which young people acquire skills, knowledge, and attitudes relevant to their functioning in the marketplace."[68]

Where does this knowledge come from? Friends and teachers certainly participate in this process; For instance, children talk to one another about consumer products, and this tendency increases with age.[69] Especially for young children, though, the two primary socialization sources are the family and the media.

FAMILY INFLUENCE Parents' influences in consumer socialization are both direct and indirect. They deliberately try to instill their own values about consumption in their children ("you're going to learn the value of a dollar"). Parents also determine the degree that their children will be exposed to other information sources, such as television, salespeople, and peers.[70]

Parents serve as significant models for observational learning (see Chapter 4). Children learn about consumption by watching their parents' behavior and imitating it. This modeling is facilitated by marketers who package adult products in child versions.

Parental Style. Three dimensions combine to produce different "segments" of parental styles. Parents characterized by certain styles have been found to socialize their children differently. For example, "authoritarian parents," who are hostile, restrictive, and emotionally uninvolved, do not have warm relationships with their children, but are more active in filtering the types of media to which their children are exposed and tend to have negative views about advertising. "Neglecting parents" also do not have warm relationships, but they are more detached from their children and do not exercise much control over what their children do. In contrast, "indulgent parents" communicate more with their children about consumption-related matters and are less restrictive. They believe that children should be allowed to learn about the marketplace without much interference.

LEARNING FROM TELEVISION It's no secret that kids watch a lot of television. As a result, they are constantly bombarded with messages about consumption, both contained in commercials and in the shows themselves.

According to **cultivation theory,** the media teaches people about a culture's values and myths. The more a child is exposed to television, whether the show is "Dynasty" or "Teenage Mutant Ninja Turtles" the more he or she will accept the images depicted there as real.[71]

In addition to the large volume of programming targeted directly to children, kids also are exposed to idealized images of what it is like to be an adult. Since children over the age of 6 do about a quarter of their television viewing during prime time, they are affected by programs and commercials targeted to adults. For example, young girls exposed to adult lipstick commercials learn to associate lipstick with beauty.[72]

SEX ROLE REINFORCEMENT
Children pick up on the concept of gender identity (see Chapter 7) at an earlier age than was previously believed—perhaps as young as age 1 or 2. By the age of 3 most children categorize driving a truck as masculine and cooking and cleaning as feminine.[73] Even cartoon characters who are portrayed as helpless are more likely to wear frilly or ruffled dresses.[74]

CHILD'S PLAY One function of child's play is to rehearse for adulthood. Children "act out" different roles they might assume later in life and learn about the expectations others have of them. The toy industry provides the props children use to perform these roles.[75] Often "traditional" sex-roles are stressed; the same product may be designed and positioned differently for boys and girls.

Many companies, such as Guess, design clothing for children that differs little from adult versions. Courtesy of GUESS; Art Director: Paul Marciano; Photographer: Dominick Guiwmot.

Huffy, for example, manufactures bicycles for both boys and girls. The boys' versions have names like "Sigma" and "Vortex," and are described as having ". . . maxed-out features that'll pump your pulse." The girls' version is more sedate. It is called "Sweet Style," and it comes in pink or purple. As a company executive described it in contrast to the boys' bikes, this ". . . is a fashion bike. It's not built for racing or jumping—just the look."[76]

COGNITIVE DEVELOPMENT
The ability of children to make mature, "adult" consumer decisions obviously increases with age (not that grownups always make mature decisions).

Kids can be segmented by age in terms of their stage of **cognitive development,** or ability to comprehend concepts of increasing complexity.

PIAGETIAN STAGES OF DEVELOPMENT   The foremost proponent of the idea that children pass through distinct stages of cognitive development was the Swiss psychologist Jean Piaget, who believed that each stage is characterized by a certain cognitive structure the child uses to handle information.[77]

Piaget identified several developmental stages. For example, in the *preoperational stage* (ages 2–7), the child's cognitive structure is poorly organized and only the plainly visible aspects of a stimulus are the focus of attention. In contrast, children in the *formal operations stage* (ages 11 and older) have the ability to think abstractly and can thus make more sophisticated inferences about a stimulus. These concepts have relevance to consumer contexts. For example, unlike their older counterparts, children in the preoperational stage expect a package to determine the size of the object within, and they do not understand that the size of the package purchased should be related to the consumption need.[78]

AN ALTERNATIVE TO PIAGET   An alternative approach regards children as differing in *information-processing capability,* or ability to store and retrieve information from memory (see Chapter 4). Three segments have been identified in this approach:[79]

1. *Limited.* Below the age of 6, children do not employ storage and retrieval strategies.
2. *Cued.* Children between the ages of 6 and 12 employ these strategies, but only when prompted.
3. *Strategic.* Those 12 and older spontaneously employ storage and retrieval strategies.

This sequence of development underscores the notion that children do not think like adults, and they cannot be expected to use information the same way. It also reminds us that they do not necessarily form the same conclusions as adults do when presented with product information. For example, kids are not as likely to realize that something they see on television is not "real," and as a result they are more vulnerable to persuasive messages.

CHILDREN IN THE MARKETPLACE

Kids are a "dream target" to some marketers because they are brand conscious and they are not price-sensitive.[80] They are also spending more than pennies. The average weekly allowance for young children is $3.00 per week. This doesn't sound like a fortune, but it adds up—to more than $150.00 a year. That figure in turn amounts to $4.7 billion a year spent by children, and this figure does not include the money given to children to buy household necessities. The types of products children buy with their own money are shown in Figure 9-2.

Most children also possess a surprisingly high degree of knowledge about products and brands, and they attribute positive and negative characteristics

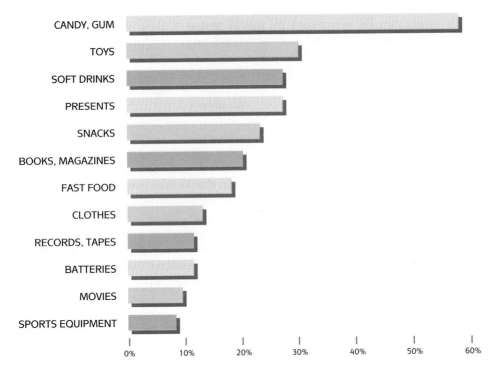

Figure 9-2 What Children Buy. Percent of children aged 6 to 11 who spend their own money on a category in a two- to three-week period.

to others depending upon their product usage. Stereotypes about adults who own different styles of cars and houses are almost fully developed by the sixth grade.[81] Elementary school children also make judgments about other kids depending on the brand of jeans they wear (e.g., Calvin Klein vs. Sears) or even the types of video games they own.[82]

To kids, even the lunch box means more than a container for a bologna sandwich. As one collector put it, "When you're a kid, it's not what you drive, it's what you carry that gives you status in the blackboard jungle."[83] A lunch box is a fashion item. The characters depicted on it express a child's grasp of what is "in." Carrying a box with outdated figures or babyish ones may contribute to social suicide, and the choice of the right lunch box to buy is frequently the source of conflict between parents and children. The trend for young sophisticates is toward what might be thought of as the "anti-lunch box," mini-coolers with no characters on them at all.[84] One Midwest company is offering "Kool Bags," which it calls the "lunch bag of the future." Each pack has 20 different bags adorned with comic strips and jokes.[85]

TARGETING CHILDREN: MORE THAN CHILD'S PLAY

Although three product categories—toys, cereals, and candy or snacks—account for more than three-quarters of all ads on Saturday morning television, marketers are promoting children's versions of products ranging from personal stereos (Sony) to tissues (Scott Paper).[86] While numerous groups have objected to both the products and strategies used in targeting children, four out of five adults have no objections to ads for clothing or toys directed to kids, and a majority also accept the concept of directly advertising such products as cereals, shampoo, pet foods, movies (G-rated), and records.[87]

More than a third of girls aged 9 to 11 are regular users of deodorant, perfume, and nail polish. What's more, almost a third of boys and girls in the same age bracket use hair mousse! Mattel sells stick-on painted fingernails, and Maybelline features bubblegum flavored lip gloss. As one Maybelline market researcher explained the company's strategy, "They start out playing with lip gloss and nail color. Then they move into blusher and eye shadow."[88]

A number of perfumes also are now targeted to children. Prince Matchabelli makes Night Rhythms, MEM sells Wild, and Revlon is touting Electric Youth. Ptisenbon even sells fragrance to be used for children below the age of 2, at $32.00 a bottle.[89] And, boys are starting to get equal time: Gregory, a $15 cologne for future hunks under the age of 10, is now available in over 100 boutiques.[90]

GETTING A HEAD START ON BRAND LOYALTY While marketers' interest in kids has a lot to do what they are able to buy now, in many cases they are as or more interested in what they will spend *later*. Forward-looking companies are realizing that brand loyalties form at an early age, and are devising strategies to cement bonds with their future markets.

The McDonald's Corporation was a pioneer of this concept. The company regards children as three markets in one. First, they appeal directly to kids by offering meal kits, parties, playgrounds, and so on. Second, they realize the child's role as an influencer in family decision making, so advertising often encourages family trips to their restaurants. Finally, they regard children as their future market, realizing that today's kids will someday be bringing *their* children to the Golden Arches.[91]

Other marketers also are trying to cultivate this future market. This is why the Army, Marines, and Air Force advertise in *Boys' Life* magazine and why Levi Strauss & Co. entered the children's market with My First Levi's (a line of corduroy and denim diaper covers, pants, and shirts) when sales of adult jeans began to slump.[92]

MARKET RESEARCH AND CHILDREN Despite their buying power, relatively little real data on children's preferences or influences on spending patterns is available. Compared to adults, kids are difficult subjects for market researchers. They tend to be undependable reporters of their own behavior, they have poor recall, and they often do not understand abstract questions.[93] This problem is compounded in Europe, where some countries restrict marketers' ability to interview children.

Still, market research can pay off, and many companies, as well as a number of specialized firms, have been successful researching some aspects of this segment.[94] After interviewing elementary school kids, Campbell's Soup discovered that kids like soup, but are afraid to admit it, because they associate it with "nerds." The company decided to

This L'eggs ad shows how some companies begin to cultivate future customers at an early age. Courtesy of SARA LEE HOSIERY.

reintroduce the Campbell kids in its advertising after a prolonged absence, but they are now slimmed-down and more athletic to reflect an updated, "un-nerdy" image.[95]

Product Testing. A particularly helpful type of research with children is product testing. Young subjects can provide a valuable perspective on what products will succeed with other kids. One candy company has a Candy Tasters Club, composed of 1200 kids aged 6 to 16, that evaluates its product ideas. For example, the group nixed the idea of a Batman lollipop, claiming that the superhero was too macho to be a sucker.[96] The Fisher-Price Company maintains a nursery known as the Playlab. Children are chosen from a waiting list of 4000 to play with new toys, while staff members watch from behind a one-way mirror.[97]

ADVERTISING TO CHILDREN

Since children differ in their abilities to process product-related informa-tion, many serious ethical issues are raised when advertisers try to appeal directly to them.[98] Kids tend to accept what they see on television as real, and they do not necessarily understand the persuasive intent of commercials. While adults may discount a persuasive communication if they know it is a paid advertisement (see Chapter 6), preschool children may not have the ability to make any distinctions between programming and commercials.

Kids' cognitive defenses are not yet sufficiently developed to filter out commercial appeals, so in a sense altering their brand preferences may be likened to "shooting fish in a barrel," as one critic put it.[99] Though some ads include a *disclaimer,* which is a disclosure intended to clarify a potentially misleading or deceptive statement, the evidence suggests that young children do not adequately understand these either.[100]

Fisher-Price conducts extensive product-testing on children. These toy testers are immersed in their work at the company's Playlab. Joe Traver/GAMMA LIAISON.

Is It a Program or a Commercial?   The problem with children's processing of commercials has been exacerbated by television programming that essentially showcases toys (e.g., Jem, G.I. Joe, Transformers). This format has been the target of a lot of criticism because it blurs the line between programming and commercials (much like "infomercials" for adults, as described in Chapter 6).[101] Parents' groups object to such shows because, as one mother put it, the ". . . whole show is one big commercial."[102]

MEASURING COMPREHENSION   Children's level of understanding is especially hard to assess, since preschoolers are not very good at verbal responses. One way around this problem is to show children pictures of kids in different scenarios, and ask them to point to which sketch corresponds to what a commercial is trying to get them to do.

In the example shown in Figure 9-3, a child who points to sketch 1 after seeing a cereal commercial (depicting the act of buying the product) as opposed to, say, sketches 2 or 3 (where children are eating the cereal or sharing it with friends) would be said to understand the underlying intent of the commercial. Sketch 1 was in fact selected by only 7.5 percent of four-year-olds, but 20 percent of five-year-olds.[103]

Protective Measures.   It has been suggested that children should be better-educated as to how advertising works and encouraged to question what they see on television, perhaps through public-service advertising.[104] Of some help is *Penny Power,* a kids' version of *Consumer Reports* aimed at 9- to 14-year olds. It has been estimated that 20 percent of the advertising complaints received come from children, most of whom read *Penny Power.*[105]

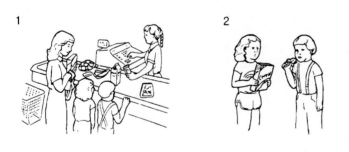

Figure 9-3 Sketches to Measure Children's Perceptions of the Intent of Commercials Source: M. Carole Macklin, "Preschoolers' Understanding of the Informational Function of Television Advertising," *Journal of Consumer Research* 14 (September 1987): 234. Reprinted with permission by The University of Chicago Press.

In addition, the Children's Advertising Review Unit (CARU) of the Council of Better Business Bureaus, Inc. maintains industry guidelines in such areas as product claims, (e.g., is it clear how the toy actually looks and works?), the use of fantasy elements (e.g., are they clearly "just pretend?"), such sales pressure techniques as suggesting that the child will be better than others if he or she owns the product, endorsements by program characters, and disclosures and disclaimers (i.e., "you or your parents have to put it together" versus "assembly required").[106]

ETHICAL ISSUES IN ADVERTISING TO CHILDREN *Are Advertising Tactics Unfair?* Consumers Union has accused major marketers of launching an "unfair advertising assault" on children. Among other issues, the consumer advocate group cited tactics used in schools. These include hidden advertising messages, samples, sponsorship of teaching materials, and donation of equipment in exchange for product labels.

The Response: Marketers claim that their participation in school programs is responsible and appropriate, noting that their contributions are welcomed by parents, teachers, and students.[107]

Is Television Advertising Unfair? The Federal Trade Commission provided one view on this issue in a recent report by noting the unfair state that occurs when the brand loyalty of a gullible eight-year-old child is being courted by the considerable professional and monetary resources devoted to television commercials, including sound effects and lighting specialists, psychological analysts, scriptwriters, and so on.[108]

The Response: Some observers argue that most children (at least those over the age of seven) do recognize the selling intent of commercials and have the right to receive (tasteful) advertising information.

Does Advertising Encourage Poor Product Choices? According to the Federal Trade Commission, many people are concerned, for example, that food advertising distorts nutritional habits, negating any nutrition education imparted by the schools or parents through its heavy emphasis on sugared cereals, snacks, and drinks that account for over half of all products advertised.[109]

The Response: Supporters of children's advertising argue that it helps children to make informed decisions. Also, they feel that it is up to parents to decide which products are inappropriate for their children. Paralleling recent debates about cigarette advertising, they feel it is the products that should be banned, not the advertising.

Does Advertising Create Parent-Child Conflict? According to critics, "The child is unwittingly turned into an 'assistant salesman.' He sells, he nags, until he breaks down the sales resistance of his parent."[110]

The Response: Supporters point to the low level of complaints received from parents about advertising. They feel that children's product requests are a natural part of the parent-child relationship, and according to one industry source, often provide an opportunity for parent-child discussions.[111]

Does Advertising Contribute to Undesirable Socialization? Critics argue that advertising teaches the virtues of materialism, impulsive choice, and immediate gratification.

The Response: Supporters counter that advertising actually *helps* children prepare for the real world. Indeed, the CARU Guidelines recommend that: "Advertisers are urged to capitalize on the potential of advertising to influence social behavior by developing advertising that addresses itself to social standards generally regarded as positive and beneficial."[112]

CHAPTER SUMMARY

This chapter is concerned with the many situations where the process of consumer decision making is performed by two or more people. This situation is quite common in both organizations (e.g., corporations, government, universities) and families. It is commonly assumed that industrial and consumer purchasing decisions are two separate phenomena, but the chapter describes both differences and similarities between the decisions faced by organizations and family members. In both cases, for example, a decision can be framed in turns of the demands of the purchasing situation, where the task can be very simple (as in reordering parts or compiling a basic shopping list) or complex (as when an organization buys a new computer system or a family debates where to go on vacation).

The chapter then explores the modern concepts of the family and discusses ways in which this basic consumer unit has changed. After describing some important changes in family structure, such as the increase in the number of households headed by single adults, some alternatives to the traditional family unit (e.g., gay couples), are considered. The chapter goes on to explore some of the ways marketers are adapting to these new forms of families. The dynamics of household decisions are reviewed, including the roles played by different decision makers within the family and the concept of the amount of power wielded by family members. Discussion then moves on to consider children as consumers. The socialization process, where children learn to be consumers, is reviewed, and the influence of parents and the media on children's brand preferences is considered. In the process, a variety of marketing strategies designed to tap this important market are presented. Some of these strategies have been controversial, because they may take advantage of children's reduced capacity to distinguish between reality and advertising claims. The chapter closes by considering some of the major objections to advertising to children, such as whether it creates conflict between parents and their children, or whether it encourages children to make unsafe or unhealthy product choices.

KEY TERMS

Autocratic decisions

Buyclass theory of purchasing

Cognitive development

Consumer socialization

Cultivation theory

Demographics

Extended family

Family household

Family life cycle

Nuclear family

Parental yielding

Syncratic decisions

Synoptic ideal

1. Do you think market research should be performed on children? Give the reasons for your answer.
2. What do you think of the practice of companies and survey firms collecting public data (e.g., from marriage licenses, birth records, or even death announcements) to compile targeted mailing lists? State your opinion from both a consumer's and marketer's perspective.
3. Do you agree that organizational purchases have a lot in common with everyday consumer decisions? Provide examples to support your answer.
4. Marketers have been criticized for donating products and services to educational institutions in exchange for free promotion. Is this a fair exchange, in your opinion, or should corporations be prohibited from attempting to influence youngsters in school?
5. For each of the following five product categories—groceries, automobiles, vacations, furniture, and appliances—describe the ways in which you believe a married couple's choices would be affected if they had children.
6. In married couples, do you think certain products should be purchased by the husband and others purchased by the wife? If so, what type of products would each be responsible for? If not, what criteria should be used in determining the decision maker for specific products?
7. In identifying and targeting newly divorced couples, do you think marketers are exploiting these couples' situations? Are there instances where you think marketers may actually be helpful to them? Support your answers with examples.
8. In your opinion, what are the benefits and disadvantages of both the extended family and the nuclear family? Consider both social and personal issues in your answer.
9. What is your interpretation of the differences between absolute power and usable power? Use examples from your own living situation to illustrate your points.
10. How might communications about a children's product be varied according to the child's level of cognitive development or information processing capability?
11. In making a family decision, do you think the person who will use the product or the person who pays for it should have a greater say in the purchase? Give examples to support your answer.

1. Arrange to interview two married couples, one younger and one older. Prepare a response form listing five product categories—groceries, furniture, appliances, vacations, and automobiles—and ask each spouse to indicate, without consulting the other, whether purchases in each category are made by joint or unilateral decisions and to indicate whether the unilateral decisions are made by the husband or the wife. Compare each couples' responses for agreement between husbands and wives relative to who makes the decisions and compare both couples' overall responses for differences relative to the number of joint versus unilateral decisions. Report your findings and conclusions.
2. Use library resources to research categories of demographic data available from the U.S. Census Bureau. Prepare a report on the usefulness of the various types of data to marketers.
3. Collect ads for three different product categories in which the family is targeted. Find another set of ads for different brands of the same items

in which the family is not featured. Prepare a report on the effectiveness of the approaches.

4. Observe the interactions between parents and children in the cereal section of a local grocery store. Prepare a report on the number of children who expressed preferences, how they expressed their preferences, and how parents responded, including the number who purchased the child's choice.

5. Watch three hours of children's programming on commercial television stations and evaluate the marketing techniques used in the commercials in terms of the ethical issues raised in the final section of this chapter. Report your findings and conclusions.

6. Analyze the characters in current television sitcoms featuring non-family groups. Select a situation from one of the shows in which the characters play out traditional family roles and prepare an analysis on how the behavior of each character in the situation might be interpreted to resemble that of a particular family member.

7. Interview a salesperson at a local jewelry store about the types of customers who make purchases there. Use the information to outline the store's market segments and how they might be targeted.

8. Use the buyclass framework to categorize some of the purchases you have made over the past year. Provide two examples of purchases for each category in the framework and tell how your purchase related to the buyclass strategy.

9. Diagram the power structure in your own living situation. Describe a recent decision-making incident and assign the decision roles outlined in this chapter to the participants.

10. Assume you are in the business of compiling mailing lists for direct mail advertisers. Review the Sunday newspaper for news articles and features that could be the source of names, and identify the market segments that might be targeted for particular products by your clients.

11. Select a product category, and using the life cycle stages given in the chapter, list the variables that will affect a purchase decision for the product by consumers in each stage of the cycle.

12. Consider three important changes in modern family structure. For each, find an example of a marketer who has attempted to be conscious of this change as reflected in product communications, retailing innovations, or other aspects of the marketing mix. If possible, also try to find examples of marketers who have failed to keep up with these developments.

NOTES

1. Gerald Zaltman and Melanie Wallendorf, *Consumer Behavior: Basic Findings and Management Implications* (New York: Wiley, 1979).

2. B. Charles Ames and James D. Hlaracek, *Managerial Marketing for Industrial Firms* (New York: Random House Business Division, 1984; Edward F. Fern and James R. Brown, "The Industrial/Consumer Marketing Dichotomy: A Case of Insufficient Justification," *Journal of Marketing* 48 (Spring 1984): 68–77.

3. See J. Joseph Cronin, Jr., and Michael H. Morris, "Satisfying Customer Expectations; the Effect on Conflict and Repurchase Intentions in Industrial Marketing Channels," *Journal of the Academy of Marketing Science* 17 (Winter 1989): 41–49; Thomas W. Leigh and Patrick F. McGraw, "Mapping the Procedural Knowledge of Industrial Sales Personnel: A Script-Theoretic Investigation," *Journal of Marketing* 53 (January 1989): 16–34; William J. Qualls and Christopher P. Puto, "Organizational Climate and Decision Framing: An Integrated Approach to Analyzing Industrial Buying," *Journal of Marketing Research* 26 (May 1989): 179–92.

4. Daniel H. McQuiston, "Novelty, Complexity, and Importance as Causal Determinants of Industrial Buyer Behavior," *Journal of Marketing* 53 (April 1989): 66–79.
5. Patrick J. Robinson, Charles W. Faris, and Yoram Wind, *Industrial Buying and Creative Marketing* (Boston: Allyn & Bacon, 1967).
6. Erin Anderson, Wujin Chu, and Barton Weitz, "Industrial Purchasing: An Empirical Examination of the Buyclass Framework," *Journal of Marketing* 51 (July 1987): 71–86.
7. Alan R. Andreasen, "Life Status Changes and Changes in Consumer Preferences and Satisfaction," *Journal of Consumer Research* 11 (December 1984): 784–94.
8. Cheryl Russell, "Bright Lights, Big City," *American Demographics* (August 1988): 13.
9. Judith Waldrop and Thomas Exter, "What the 1990 Census Will Show," *American Demographics* (January 1990): 20; Judith Waldrop and Thomas Exter, "Fast-Track States," *American Demographics* (January 1990): 24.
10. Judith Waldrop, "The Fashionable Family," *American Demographics* (March 1988): 22.
11. "The Big Picture," *American Demographics* (March 1989): 22–27.
12. Karen Hardee-Cleaveland, "Is Eight Enough?" *American Demographics* (June 1989): 60.
13. Thomas Exter, "Peak-a-boo (Recent Baby Boomlet)," *American Demographics* (December 1988): 63.
14. Cheryl Russell, "Is Big Back?" *American Demographics* (May 1988): 15.
15. Blayne Cutler, "McChild Care," *American Demographics* (September 1989): 20.
16. Judith Waldrop, "A Lesson in Home Economics," *American Demographics* (August 1989): 26.
17. Mary Lou Padilla and Garry L. Landreth, "Latchkey Children: A Review of the Literature," *Child Welfare* 68 (July/August 1989): 445.
18. Ellen Graham, "Children's Hour: As Kids Gain Power of Purse, Marketing Takes Aim at Them," *Wall Street Journal* (January 19, 1988): 1.
19. Judith Waldrop and Thomas Exter, "Lone Lifestyle," *American Demographics* (January 1990): 27.
20. Joe Schwartz, "After School," *American Demographics* (June 1987): 60.
21. "Men on Their Own," *American Demographics* (July 1987): 62.
22. Stephanie Shipp, "How Singles Spend," *American Demographics* (April 1988): 22–27.
23. Joe Schwartz, "Family Traditions: Although Radically Changed, the American Family Is as Strong as Ever," *American Demographics* (March 1987): 9.
24. Diane Crispell, "Three's a Crowd," *American Demographics* (January 1989): 34.
25. "Mothers Bearing a Second Burden," *New York Times* (May 14, 1989): 26.
26. Thomas Exter, "Disappearing Act," *American Demographics* (January 1989): 78.
27. "The Big Picture," *American Demographics* (October 1989): 18.
28. Cheryl Russell, "Throw Out the Script," *American Demographics* (September 1990): 2.
29. Constance Sorrentino, "The Changing Family in International Perspective," *Monthly Labor Review* (March 1990): 41.
30. Martha Farnsworth Riche, "Somebody's Baby," *American Demographics* (February 1988): 10.
31. Anne O'Malley, "The Gay Nineties," *The Marketer* (1990): 12.
32. Clinton R. Sanders, "The Animal 'Other': Self Definition, Social Identity, and Companion Animals," in *Advances in Consumer Research,* ed. Marvin E. Goldberg, Gerald Gorn, and Richard W. Pollay, (Provo, Utah: Association for Consumer Research, 1989).
33. Jeffrey P. Rosenfeld, "Barking Up the Right Tree," *American Demographics* (May 1987): 40.
34. Quoted in Youssef M. Ibrahim, "French Love for Animals: Too Fervent?" *New York Times* (February 2, 1990): A5.
35. Woody Hochswender, "The Cat's Meow," *New York Times* (May 16, 1989): B7.
36. Judann Dagnoli, "Toothcare for Terriers," *Advertising Age* (November 20, 1989): 8.
37. "For Fido, Broccoli and Yogurt," *New York Times* (April 16, 1989).
38. Bob Geiger, "Dogged Persistence," *Advertising Age* (November 27, 1989): 8.
39. N.R. Kleinfeld, "Limos and Fine Food: Ah, It's a Dog's Life," *New York Times* (May 3, 1990): C1.
40. Robert Passikoff and Rebecca H. Holman, "The Semiotics of Possession and Commercial Communication," in *Marketing and Semiotics: New Directions in the Study of Signs for Sale,* ed. Jean Umiker-Sebeok (Berlin: Mouton de Guyter, 1987): 375–90.

41. David Cheal, "The Ritualization of Family Ties," *American Behavioral Scientist* 31 (July/August 1988): 632.
42. "Families Come First," *Psychology Today* (September 1988): 11.
43. "Club Med in a Family Way," *American Demographics* (January 1987): 25.
44. Alison Fahey, "Lamaze Testing 'Seal': Program Delivers America's Newest Parents," *Advertising Age* (March 26, 1990): 4.
45. "Connecting Consumer and Product," *New York Times* (January 18, 1990): D19; Maryellen Gordon, "Gitano's New Ad Campaign to Emphasize Family Spirit," *Woman's Wear Daily* (August 16, 1989): 11; David Reed, "Heinz and Polycell Get in the Family Way," *Marketing* (October 27, 1988): 9.
46. Gordon, "Gitano's New Ad Campaign to Emphasize Family Spirit."
47. Waldrop, "A Lesson in Home Economics."
48. Janet Wagner and Sherman Hanna, "The Effectiveness of Family Life Cycle Variables in Consumer Expenditure Research," *Journal of Consumer Research* 10 (December 1983): 281–91; William D. Wells and George Gubar, "Life Cycle Concept in Marketing Research," *Journal of Marketing Research* 3 (November 1966): 355–63; William L. Wilkie, *Consumer Behavior* (New York: Wiley, 1986).
49. Mary C. Gilly and Ben M. Enis, "Recycling the Family Life Cycle: A Proposal for Redefinition," in *Advances in Consumer Research,* ed. Andrew Mitchell, (Ann Arbor, Mich.: Association for Consumer Research, 1982): 271–76; Patrick E. Murphy and William A. Staples, "A Modernized Family Life Cycle," *Journal of Consumer Research* (June 1979): 12–22.
50. Thomas Hine, *Populuxe* (New York: Alfred A. Knopf, 1986).
51. Gary L. Sullivan and P. J. O'Connor, "The Family Purchase Decision Process: A Cross-Cultural Review and Framework for Research," *Southwest Journal of Business & Economics* (Fall 1988): 43.
52. Dennis L. Rosen and Donald H. Granbois, "Determinants of Role Structure in Family Financial Management," *Journal of Consumer Research* 10 (September 1983): 253–58.
53. Robert F. Bales, *Interaction Process Analysis: A Method for the Study of Small Groups* (Reading, Mass.: Addison-Wesley, 1950).
54. Alma S. Baron, "Working Parents: Shifting Traditional Roles," *Business* 37 (Jan./March 1987): 36; William J. Qualls, "Household Decision Behavior: The Impact of Husbands' and Wives' Sex Role Orientation," *Journal of Consumer Research* 14 (September 1987): 264–79; Charles M. Schaninger and W. Christian Buss, "The Relationship of Sex-Role Norms to Household Task Allocation," *Psychology & Marketing* 2 (Summer 1985): 93–104.
55. Micaela DiLeonardo, "The Female World of Cards and Holidays: Women, Families, and the Work of Kinship," *Signs* 12 (Spring 1942): 440–53.
56. Hyman Rodman, "Marital Power and the Theory of Resources in Cross-Cultural Context," *Journal of Comparative Family Studies* 1 (1972): 50–67.
57. Robert T. Green, Jean-Paul Leonardi, Jean-Louis Chandon, Isabella C. M. Cunningham, Bronis Verhage, and Alain Strazzieri, "Societal Development and Family Purchasing Roles: A Cross-National Study," *Journal of Consumer Research* 9 (March 1983): 436–42.
58. C. Whan Park, "Joint Decisions in Home Purchasing: A Muddling-Through Process," *Journal of Consumer Research* 9 (September 1982): 151–62.
59. Kim P. Corfman and Donald R. Lehmann, "Models of Cooperative Group Decision-Making and Relative Influence: An Experimental Investigation of Family Purchase Decisions," *Journal of Consumer Research* 14 (June 1987): 1–13.
60. Charles Atkin, "Observation of Parent-Child Interaction in Supermarket Decision-Making," *Journal of Marketing* 42 (October 1978): 41–45.
61. Leslie Isler, Edward T. Popper and Scott Ward, "Children's Purchase Requests and Parental Responses: Results From a Diary Study," *Journal of Advertising Research* 27 (October/November 1987): 28–39.
62. Ellen R. Foxman, Patriya S. Tanshuaj, and Karin M. Ekstrom, "Family Members' Perceptions of Adolescents' Influence in Family Decision Making," *Journal of Consumer Research* 15 (March 1989): 482–91.
63. Fred E. Webster and Yoram Wind, *Organizational Buying Behavior* (New York: Prentice-Hall, 1972).

64. Daniel Seymour and Greg Lessne, "Spousal Conflict Arousal: Scale Development," *Journal of Consumer Research* 11 (December 1984): 810:21.

65. Harry L. Davis, "Decision Making Within the Household," *Journal of Consumer Research* 2 (March 1972): 241–60; Michael B. Menasco and David J. Curry, "Utility and Choice: An Empirical Study of Wife/Husband Decision Making," *Journal of Consumer Research* 16 (June 1989): 87–97.

66. Horst H. Stipp, "Children as Consumers," *American Demographics* (February 1988): 27.

67. Melissa Turner, "Kids' Marketing Clout Man-Sized," *Atlanta Journal* (February 18, 1988): E10.

68. Scott Ward, "Consumer Socialization," in *Perspectives in Consumer Behavior,* ed. Harold H. Kassarjian and Thomas S. Robertson (Glenville, Ill.: Scott, Foresman, 1980): 380.

69. Thomas Lipscomb, "Indicators of Materialism in Children's Free Speech: Age and Gender Comparisons," *Journal of Consumer Marketing* (Fall 1988): 41–46.

70. George P. Moschis, "The Role of Family Communication in Consumer Socialization of Children and Adolescents," *Journal of Consumer Research* 11 (March 1985): 898–913.

71. See Patricia M. Greenfield, Emily Yut, Mabel Chung, Deborah Land, Holly Kreider, Maurice Pantoja, and Kris Horsley, "The Program-Length Commercial: A Study of the Effects of Television/Toy Tie-Ins on Imaginative Play," *Psychology & Marketing* 7 (Winter 1990): 237–56 for a study on the effects of commercial programming on creative play.

72. Gerald J. Gorn and Renee Florsheim, "The Effects of Commercials for Adult Products on Children," *Journal of Consumer Research* 11 (March 1985): 962–67.

73. Glenn Collins, "New Studies on 'Girl Toys' and 'Boy Toys,'" *New York Times* (February 13, 1984): D1.

74. Susan B. Kaiser, "Clothing and the Social Organization of Gender Perception: A Developmental Approach," *Clothing and Textiles Research Journal* 7 (Winter 1989): 46–56.

75. Lori Schwartz and William Markham, "Sex Stereotyping in Children's Toy Advertisements," *Sex Roles* 12 (January 1985): 157–70.

76. Brad Edmondson, "Snakes, Snails, and Puppy Dogs' Tails," *American Demographics* (October 1987): 18.

77. Jean Piaget, "The Child and Modern Physics," *Scientific American* 196 (1957)3: 46–51.

78. Kenneth D. Bahn, "How and When Do Brand Perceptions and Preferences First Form? A Cognitive Developmental Investigation," *Journal of Consumer Research* 13 (December 1986): 382–93; Gary Soldow, "Ability of Children to Understand the Product Package," *Journal of Public Policy and Marketing* (1985): 55–68.

79. Deborah L. Roedder, "Age Differences in Children's Responses to Television Advertising: An Information-Processing Approach," *Journal of Consumer Research* 8 (September 1981): 144–53.

80. Turner, "Kids' Marketing Clout Man-Sized."

81. Russell W. Belk, Kenneth D. Bahn, and Robert N. Mayer, "Developmental Recognition of Consumption Symbolism," *Journal of Consumer Research* 9 (June 1982): 4–17.

82. Robert N. Mayer and Russell W. Belk, "Fashion and Impression Formation Among Children," in *The Psychology of Fashion,* ed. Michael R. Solomon (Lexington, Mass.: Lexington Books, 1985): 293–308.

83. Quoted in N. R. Kleinfeld, "Another August Under the 'Whine Sign'," *New York Times* (August 6, 1989): D1.

84. Kleinfeld, "Another August Under the 'Whine Sign'."

85. Judann Dagnoli and Julie Liesse, "Kids Foods Flood Market," *Advertising Age* (May 21, 1990): 19.

86. Patricia Sellers, "The ABC's of Marketing to Kids," *Fortune* (May 8, 1989): 114; Turner, "Kids' Marketing Clout Man-Sized."

87. Edmondson, "Snakes, Snails and Puppy Dogs' Tails.".
Quoted in Wells, Linda (1989), "Babes in Makeup Land," *New York Times Magazine* (August 13, 1989): 46.

89. Pat Sloan, "Kids Smell Sweet to Fragrance Marketers," *Advertising Age* (July 10, 1989): 50.

90. Graham, "Children's Hour."

91. Joe Agnew, "Children Come of Age as Consumers," *Marketing News* (December 4, 1987): 8.
92. Agnew, "Children Come of Age as Consumers"; Janet Simons, "Youth Marketing: Children's Clothes Follow the Latest Fashion," *Advertising Age* (February 14, 1985): 16.
93. Stipp, "Children as Consumers"; See Laura A. Peracchio, "Designing Research to Reveal the Young Child's Emerging Competence," *Psychology & Marketing* 7 (Winter 1990): 257–76, for details regarding the design of research on children.
94. "Kid Power," *Forbes* (March 30, 1987): 9–10.
95. Sellers, "The ABC's of Marketing to Kids."
96. Dena Kleiman, "Candy to Frighten Your Parents With," *New York Times* (August 23, 1989): C1.
97. Laura Shapiro, "Where Little Boys Can Play with Nail Polish," *Newsweek* (May 28, 1990): 62.
98. Gary Armstrong and Merrie Brucks, "Dealing with Children's Advertising: Public Policy Issues and Alternatives," *Journal of Public Policy and Marketing* 7 (1988): 98–113.
99. Bonnie Reece, "Children and Shopping: Some Public Policy Questions," *Journal of Public Policy and Marketing* (1986): 185–94.
100. Mary Ann Stutts and Garland G. Hunnicutt, "Can Young Children Understand Disclaimers in Television Commercials," *Journal of Advertising* 16 (Winter 1987): 41–46.
101. Steve Weinstein, "Fight Heats Up Against Kids' TV 'Commershows'," *Marketing News* (October 9, 1989): 2.
102. Alan Bunce, "Are TV Ads Turning Kids Into Consumers?" *Christian Science Monitor* (August 11, 1988): 1.
103. M. Carole Macklin, "Preschoolers' Understanding of the Informational Function of Television Advertising," *Journal of Consumer Research* 14 (September 1987): 229–39.
104. Merrie Brucks, Gary M. Armstrong, and Marvin E. Goldberg, "Children's Use of Cognitive Defenses Against Television Advertising: A Cognitive Response Approach," *Journal of Consumer Research* 14 (March 1988): 471–82.
105. Michael deCourcy Hines, "Young Consumers: Perils and Power," *New York Times* (February 11, 1989): 52; Oscar Suris, "Selling to Savvy Young Buyers," *Orlando Sentinel* (September 10, 1989): F8.
106. Rita Weisskoff, "Current Trends in Children's Advertising," *Journal of Advertising Research* (February/March 1985): 12–14.
107. Judann Dagnoli, "Consumers Union Hits Kids Advertising," *Advertising Age* (July 23, 1990): 4.
108. Federal Trade Commission, "FTC Staff Report on Television Advertising to Children," (Washington, D.C., 1979).
109. Federal Trade Commission, "FTC Staff Report on Television Advertising to Children," (1978), cited in Armstrong and Brucks, "Dealing with Children's Advertising."
110. Federal Trade Commission, "FTC Staff Report on Television Advertising to Children," quoted in Armstrong and Brucks, "Dealing with Children's Advertising."
111. Television Information Office (1986), 8, quoted in Armstrong and Brucks, "Dealing with Children's Advertising."
112. Children's Advertising Review Unit (1983), 5, quoted in Armstrong and Brucks, "Dealing with Children's Advertising."

Product Acquisition and Disposition

CHAPTER 10

After aimlessly flicking through television channels on a boring Saturday afternoon—and even considering the radical move of starting a school assignment ahead of schedule—Mark is suddenly saved as his friend Jan pulls up outside and honks his horn. This timely arrival can only mean one thing: Time to cruise the mall! Soon Mark is happily playing pinball, eating a burger, checking out the girls (and, hopefully, being checked out in return), and rummaging through the stores he already knows so well.

With a few minutes to kill before they have to leave, the two friends hit the record store, a lively place decorated with rock posters. Mark and Jan like to drop in to rap with a few of the salesmen, college guys who are really into the latest music. As they enter, they are bombarded by the amplified beat of the new song by Absolute Threshold, as well as a huge display of T-shirts, pictures, and other paraphernalia from the band's latest tour. As a faithful collector of heavy metal memorabilia with limited resources, Mark has been torn between buying either this band's new tape and other material or the new one by Fingers of Death.

Once in the store, though, Mark is really into "the Hold"—but his wallet isn't. He has just about decided to come back next week with more money when the assistant manager mentions that they are almost out of the Hold tape. His friend Jan doesn't help matters by saying, "Hey, like, it's only money. Go for it! But make it quick, we've got to get home." That did it for Mark. He grabs the tape and lays out the last of his cash for the week (throwing in an official band button while at the register). As soon as he gets home, he runs to his room and plays the tape full blast. Though he had been wavering at the store, Mark thinks the album is even better than he had expected. He is now convinced that he has made the right choice between Absolute Threshold and Fingers of Death—this will round out his collection nicely.

THE SHOPPING EXPERIENCE

We see bumper stickers and T-shirts everywhere: "Shop 'til you drop." "When the going gets tough, the tough go shopping." "Born to shop." Like it or not, shopping is a dominant activity for many consumers. On the average, Americans spend about 6 percent of their waking hours shopping. Only half of this time is devoted to shopping for groceries and other basics.[1]

SHOPPING MOTIVES

As Mark's experience indicates, people often shop even though they do not necessarily intend to buy anything at all. Shopping is a way to acquire needed products and services, but social motives for shopping also are important. Shopping motives can include:[2]

- Social experiences. The shopping center or department store has replaced the traditional town square or county fair as a community gathering place. Like Mark, many people (especially in suburban or rural areas) may have no place else to go to spend their leisure time.
- Sharing of common interests. Stores frequently offer specialized goods that allow people with shared interests to communicate. Mark, for example, relied upon the record store employees for word about new music releases.
- Interpersonal attraction. Shopping centers are a natural place to congregate. The shopping mall has become a central "hangout" for teenagers like Mark, and it provides a cost-efficient way of girl- or boy-watching. It also represents a controlled, secure environment for other groups, such as the elderly.
- Instant status. As every salesperson knows, some people savor the experience of being waited on, even though they may not necessarily buy anything. By playing the role of "store customer," this treatment is often provided. One men's clothing salesman offered this advice: ". . . remember their size, remember what you sold them last time. Make them feel important! If you can make people feel important, they are going to come back. Everybody likes to feel important!"[3]

- "The thrill of the chase." Some people pride themselves on their knowledge of the marketplace. They may relish the process of haggling and bargaining, viewing it almost as a sport.

SHOPPING ORIENTATIONS Many people seem to be falling out of love with shopping. In 1987, a survey done for Neiman-Marcus and American Express found that half of the respondents liked shopping as much as they liked watching television, and 17 percent found it as pleasurable as romance! Just two years later, though, more than half of the respondents in another survey said they hated browsing in stores as much as they loathed housework.[4]

Which way is it? Do people hate to shop or love it? It depends. Consumers can be segmented in terms of their **shopping orientation,** or general attitudes about shopping. These orientations may vary depending on the particular product categories and store types considered. Mark loves to shop for records, but he may have nightmares about buying furniture. Some orientations that have been identified are:[5]

- The economic consumer: a rational, goal-oriented shopper who is primarily interested in maximizing the value of his or her money.
- The personalized consumer: a shopper who tends to form strong attachments to store personnel ("I shop where they know my name").
- The ethical consumer: a shopper who likes to help out the underdog and will support locally owned stores against big chains.
- The apathetic consumer: one who does not like to shop and sees it as a necessary but unpleasant chore.
- The recreational shopper: a person who views shopping as a fun, social activity—it is a preferred way to spend leisure time.

INFLUENCES ON OUTLET SELECTION

Competition for shoppers is getting rougher. Between 1974 and 1984, total retail square footage in the United States grew by 80 percent, but the population grew by only 12 percent. About 200 million square feet of shopping mall space is added every year.[6] Retailers must now offer something extra to lure shoppers, whether that something is excitement or just plain bargains.[7]

MARKETING PITFALL

In 1988, 12.4 billion catalogs were mailed, twice the number sent in 1980. This figure amounts to fifty catalogs for every man, woman, and child in the United States. While $30 billion worth of merchandise was ordered as a result, there are signs that this market is reaching the saturation point as more retailers jump on the direct marketing bandwagon. In addition to increasing competition, rising postal costs have elevated mailing expenses by as much as 30 percent. To economize, many mailers are abandoning their scattershot approach by developing more targeted mailing lists or producing different editions, each catering to a specialized group. L. L. Bean, for example, distributes twenty-two separate catalogs, including one just for fly fishermen.[8]

NON-STORE SHOPPING   The disenchantment with shopping, coupled with consumers' time poverty (to be discussed later in the chapter) has also opened the door for catalog sales, television shopping networks, and other forms of non-store shopping. One popular technique to make shopping easier is to bring retail services to the home. This can be accomplished by having a salesperson actually make house calls (e.g., the Avon lady). Increasingly, though, in-home shopping is being done electronically. For example, France's Minitel System, which was introduced in 1981, offers about 8000 information services and is connected to more than 3.7 million home terminals.[9]

Another emerging trend is to bring retailing to the office, as demonstrated by the Spiegel ad. This makes sense, because people are working longer hours and earning more money but are leaving themselves less free time in which to spend it. Finding that many of its female customers are no longer home during the day, even Avon has expanded its distribution network to the office, where representatives make presentations during lunch and coffee breaks. Similarly, Tupperware features "rush-hour parties" at the end of the workday, and now finds that about 20 percent of its sales are made outside of homes. An employee of Mary Kay cosmetics, another company adapting this strategy, offered another explanation for its success: "Working women buy more in the office because they are not looking at the wall paper that needs replacing. They feel richer away from home."[10]

STORE LOYALTY   **Store loyal** consumers are prized by retailers. They will routinely visit a small set of stores without considering others or doing much in the way of comparative pre-purchase search. However, consumers now have an abundance of choices regarding where to shop, including the non-store alternatives just discussed. For this reason, people do not tend to be as store loyal as they once were.[11]

RETAILING AS THEATER   Shopping malls have tried to gain the loyalty of shoppers by appealing to their social motives as well as providing access to desired goods. The mall is often a focal point in a community. In the United States, 94 percent of adults visit a mall at least once a month. More than half of all retail purchases (excluding autos and gasoline) are made in a mall.

Malls are becoming giant entertainment centers, almost to the point where their traditional retail occupants seem like an afterthought. It is now typical to find such features as carousels, miniature golf, or batting cages in a suburban mall. As one retailing executive put it, "Malls are becoming the new mini-amusement parks."[12]

The importance of creating a positive, vibrant, and interesting image has led innovative marketers to blur the line between shopping and theater. Both shopping malls and individual stores must create environments that stimulate people and allow them to shop and be entertained simultaneously.[13]

The Bill Blass Swimsuit.
Now Available In Offices.

Thanks to Spiegel, the corner office is now a more convenient place to shop than the corner department store. Our Spring Catalog features the latest designs from Ralph Lauren, Gloria Sachs, Adrienne Vittadini, Mikasa, Braun and others. To receive your copy for only $3, simply call (toll-free) 1-800-345-4500 and ask for Catalog 512.

Spiegel

Recognizing that modern women have many time pressures, Spiegel brings retailing to the office. © Copyright 1991, Spiegel, Inc.

- Bloomingdale's department store is noted for its elaborate store-wide promotions, often based upon the culture of a selected country. During these events the entire store is transformed, with each department featuring unusual merchandise from the country. These promotions are accompanied by lavish parties, food, and entertainment associated with that country.
- L. L. Bean's retail operation reflects its "outdoorsy" image, including sound effects, live plants, and stocked trout ponds.
- Babyland (the home of Cabbage Patch dolls) does not have a sales staff. Instead, the company offers "doctors," "nurses," and "adoption officers." Dolls are never "sold," they are "adopted." Every fifteen minutes, Bunny Bees hover over the cabbage patch

and inseminate the cabbages. These cabbages quiver, and the leaves open, displaying a newborn Cabbage Patch baby.

- Ralph Lauren's Madison Avenue store is in a refurbished mansion, and the decor is consistent with the company's image of aristocratic gentility and the good life. The store is furnished with expensive antiques and tapestries, and cocktails and canapés are served in the evening. Even cleaning supplies are carried by maintenance staff in Lauren shopping bags.

STORE IMAGE   With so many stores competing for customers, how do consumers pick one over another? Like products, stores may be thought of as having "personalities." Some stores have very clearly defined images (either good or bad). Others tend to blend into the crowd. They may not have anything distinctive about them and may be overlooked for this reason. This personality, or **store image,** is composed of many different factors. Store features, coupled with such consumer characteristics as shopping orientation, help to predict which outlets people will prefer.[14] Some of the important dimensions of a store's profile are location, merchandise suitability, and the knowledge and congeniality of the sales staff.[15]

Store Gestalt.   When shoppers think about stores, they may not say, "Well, that place is fairly good in terms of convenience, the salespeople are acceptable, and services are good." They are more likely to say "That place gives me the creeps" or "I always enjoy shopping there." Consumers evaluate stores both in terms of both their specific attributes *and* a global evaluation, or *gestalt* (see Chapter 2).[16] This overall feeling may have more to do with such intangibles as interior design and the types of people one finds in the store than with such aspects as return policies or credit availability. As a result, some stores are likely to consistently be in consumers' evoked sets, while others will never be considered.[17]

Atmospherics.   Because a store's gestalt is now recognized to be a very important aspect of the retailing mix, attention is increasingly paid to **atmospherics,** or the "conscious designing of space and its various dimensions to evoke certain effects in buyers."[18] These dimensions include colors, scents, and sounds.

Many elements of store design can be cleverly controlled to attract customers and produce desired effects once consumers have been lured into the store. Light colors impart a feeling of spaciousness and serenity, and signs in bright colors create excitement. In one subtle but effective application, fashion designer Norma Kamali replaced fluorescent lights with pink ones in department store dressing rooms. This had the effect of flattering the face and banishing wrinkles, making female customers more willing to try on (and buy) the company's bathing suits.[19]

In addition to visual stimuli, all sorts of cues can influence behaviors.[20] For example, patrons of country-and-western bars drink more when the jukebox music is slower. According to a researcher, "Hard drinkers prefer listening to slower paced, wailing, lonesome, self-pitying music. . . ."[21] Similarly, music can affect eating habits. Another study found that diners who listened to loud, fast music ate more food. In contrast, those who listened to Mozart or Brahms ate less and more slowly. The researchers concluded that diners who choose soothing music at mealtimes can increase weight loss by at least five pounds a month![22]

INFLUENCES ON IN-STORE PURCHASES

Despite all their efforts to "pre-sell" consumers through advertising, marketers increasingly are recognizing the significant degree to which many purchases are influenced by the store environment. It has been estimated that about two out of every three supermarket purchases are decided in the aisles. The proportion of unplanned purchases is even higher for some product categories. It is estimated that 85 percent of candy and gum, almost 70 percent of cosmetics, and 75 percent of oral hygiene purchases are unplanned.[23] Despite all the talk about rational, planning consumers, most enter the store relatively unprepared. Approximately 90 percent of shoppers do *not* use store circulars, 80 percent do without coupons, and 70 percent do not even bother with a shopping list.[24]

SPONTANEOUS SHOPPING   When a shopper is prompted to buy something while in the store, one of two different processes may be at work.

Unplanned Buying.   Unplanned buying may occur when a person is unfamiliar with a store's layout or perhaps when under some time pressure. Or, a person may be reminded to buy something by seeing it on a store shelf. About one-third of unplanned buying has been attributed to the recognition of new needs while within the store.[25]

Impulse Buying.   In contrast, **impulse buying** occurs when the person experiences a sudden urge that he or she cannot resist, as when Mark grabbed for a band button displayed near the register while paying for his tape.[26] This is why so-called impulse items such as candy and gum are conveniently placed near the checkout. Similarly, many supermarkets have installed wider aisles to encourage browsing, and the widest tend to contain products with the highest margin. Low mark-up items that are purchased regularly tend to be stacked high in narrower aisles, to allow shopping carts to speed through.[27]

Planning Versus Impulse Shopping.   Shoppers can be categorized in terms of how much advance planning they do. *Planners* tend to know what products and specific brands they will buy beforehand, *partial planners* know they need certain products, but do not decide on specific brands until they are in the store, and *impulse purchasers* do no advance planning whatsoever.[28] Figure 10-1 was drawn by a consumer, participating in a study on consumers' shopping experiences, who was asked to sketch a typical impulse purchaser.[29]

Cents-off coupons and rebates are widely used by manufacturers and retailers to induce consumers to switch brands.[30] While coupons are an important aspect of many promotional mixes, evidence regarding their effectiveness at luring *new* customers is mixed. Households that already use the couponed brand are more likely to redeem the coupon, and most customers revert to their original brand after a coupon promotion.[31] As a result, a company that adopts a couponing strategy intended to attract brand switchers may find itself "preaching to the converted."

Similarly, consumers may become frustrated by rebate offers for several reasons, including: (1) a short expiration date, (2) a requirement to purchase a greater quantity than is needed, and (3) difficulty in finding or removing the proof-of-purchase seal.[32]

POINT-OF-PURCHASE STIMULI   Because so much decision making apparently occurs while the shopper is in the purchasing environment, retailers are beginning to pay more attention to the amount of information in their stores, as well as to the way it is presented. Each year, U.S. companies

Figure 10-1 One Consumer's Image of an Impulse Buyer Source: Dennis Rook, "Is 'Impulse Buying' (Yet) a Useful Marketing Concept?" (unpublished manuscript, 1990 fig. 7-A). Reprinted with permission by The University of Chicago Press.

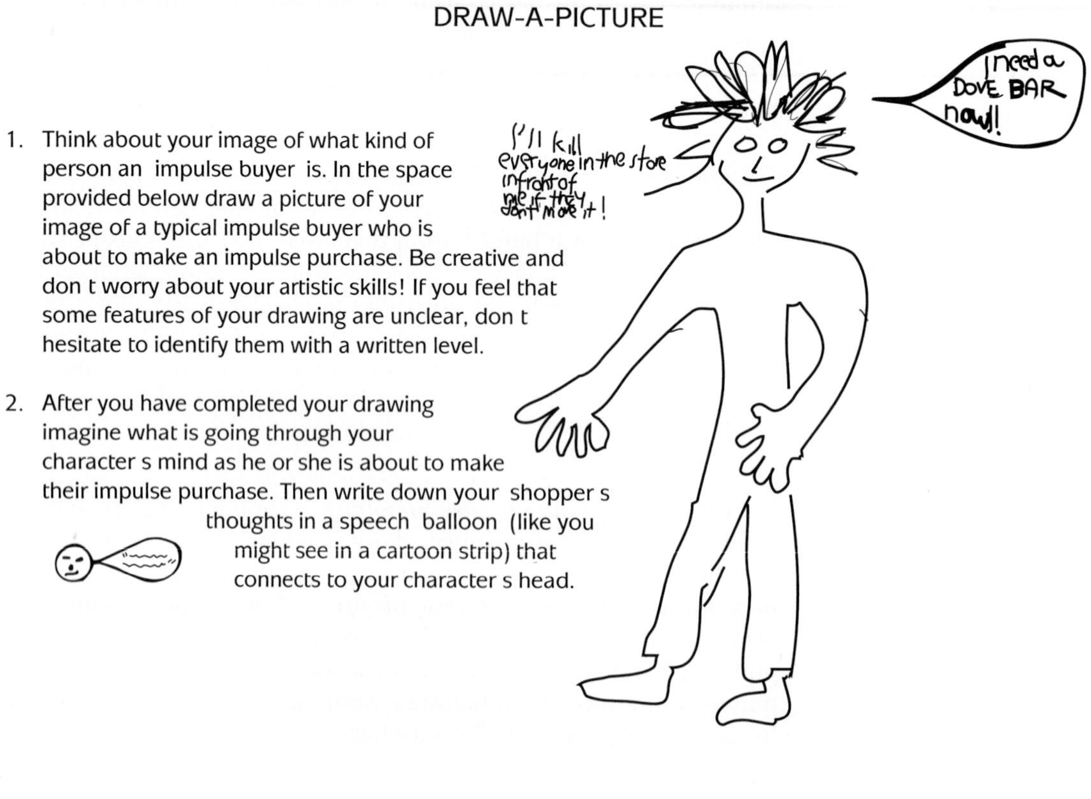

DRAW-A-PICTURE

1. Think about your image of what kind of person an impulse buyer is. In the space provided below draw a picture of your image of a typical impulse buyer who is about to make an impulse purchase. Be creative and don t worry about your artistic skills! If you feel that some features of your drawing are unclear, don t hesitate to identify them with a written level.

2. After you have completed your drawing imagine what is going through your character s mind as he or she is about to make their impulse purchase. Then write down your shopper s thoughts in a speech balloon (like you might see in a cartoon strip) that connects to your character s head.

spend more than $13 billion on **point-of-purchase stimuli (POP).** Some of this money has been diverted from conventional advertising expenditures. This in-store emphasis has made the concept of "retailing as theater" even more important. It has been estimated that impulse purchases increase by 10 percent when appropriate displays are used.

▼ MARKETING PITFALL

Although POP techniques can potentially aid consumers by providing them with more helpful information about nutrition and product safety, so far this promise has not been fulfilled. Research conducted in over 300 supermarkets indicates that POP nutritional signage had no effect on the purchase behavior of customers. One positive aspect for participating outlets: The sheer presence of the signs did improve their store image among customers.[33]

Sampling. One trend has been toward increased sampling in the store. The state-of-the-art Tesco food store in the U.K., for example, has a Food Demonstration Centre in the middle. Surrounded by overhead television monitors, eight home economists dispense 6000 food samples a week from a circular counter.[34]

Displays. The first elaborate (and highly successful) point-of-purchase display was developed for L'eggs pantyhose. This company now has even more sophisticated displays, as shown in the photo. In the newest version, L'eggs even allows other brands to be stocked in its display. The company believes that this strategy builds impulse traffic even more.[35] Some other recently introduced dramatic displays include:[36]

- Timex: A still-ticking watch sits in the bottom of a filled aquarium.
- Elizabeth Arden: In 1984, the company introduced "Elizabeth," a computer and video makeover system. This allows customers to test out their images with different shades of makeup, without having to actually apply the products first. Similarly, the Novell Corporation's line of Clarion cosmetics features a computer to help women select the right shades for them.[37]
- Tower Records: A music sampler allows customers to hear records before buying them and to custom-design their own recordings by mixing and matching singles from assorted artists.
- Nabisco: A display for the company's Fruit Wheats cereal emits the scent of fresh raspberries.
- Trifari: This company offers paper punch-out versions of its jewelry so that customers can "try on" the pieces at home.
- Charmin: Building on the familiar "Please don't squeeze the Charmin" theme, the company now deploys the Charmin Squeeze Squad. Employees hide behind stacks of the toilet tissue, and jump out and blow horns at any "squeezers" they catch in the aisles.

The L'eggs display (inset) is one of the best known and earliest point-of-purchase displays. The newer version also shown here includes other brands as well. *Courtesy of SARA LEE HOSIERY.*

- The Farnam Co.: As somber music plays in the background, a huge plastic rat draped in a black shroud lies next to a tombstone to promote the company's Just One Bite rat poison.

▲ MARKETING OPPORTUNITY

Much of the growth in point-of-purchasing activity has been in new electronic technologies.[38] Some stores feature talking posters that contain a human body sensor that speaks up when a shopper approaches. The Point-of-Purchase Radio Corp. offers in-store radio networks that are now used by about sixty grocery chains.[39] Video shopping carts have a small screen that displays advertising, which is keyed to the specific areas of the store through which the cart is wheeled.[40] In-store video allows advertisers to reinforce major media campaigns at the point of purchase.[41]

Some of the most interesting innovations can be found in state-of-the-art vending machines, which now dispense everything from Hormel's microwaveable chili and beef stew and Ore-Ida french fries to software. French consumers can even purchase Levi's jeans from a machine called

"Libre Service," which offers the pants in ten different sizes. The customer uses a seatbelt to find his or her size, and the jeans sell for about $10 less than the same versions sold in more-conventional stores.

THE SALESPERSON   One of the most important in-store factors is the salesperson, who attempts to influence the buying behavior of the customer.[42] This influence can be understood in terms of *exchange theory,* which stresses that every interaction involves an exchange of value. Each participant gives something to the other and hopes to receive something in return.[43]

Resource Exchange.   What "value" does the customer look for in a sales interaction? There are a variety of resources a salesperson might offer. He or she, for example, might offer expertise about the product to make the shopper's choice easier. Alternatively, the customer may be reassured

The Pitch.   The Follow-through.

This trade ad for Shoppers' Video illustrates that the same product message can span the gap between the consumer's home environment and the purchase situation by the creative use of video and other point-of-purchase stimuli. Courtesy of Advertising Graphics Network, NY, NY.

Now that you've put millions of dollars into advertising your brands on T.V., here's your chance to bring it on home.

Shoppers' Video bridges the gap between the excitement of television and the impact of in-store display, at the very place consumers make 80% of their purchasing decisions—the supermarket.

With Shoppers' Video, your brands will appear on more than 20 monitors throughout the supermarket simultaneously. And your message will be repeated every 10 minutes, on 15-second computer graphic spots.

This exciting new medium is not only a part of an agency's commissionable media mix, it's a way to make that mix more impactful. And more efficient.

Even though it's new, Shoppers' Video has quite a winning percentage. In research tests, Yankelovich Clancy Shulman determined that in most categories Shoppers' Video heightened total product awareness. And it's not just the tests that are proving it. The advertisers who have signed on with us are, too. Where we've begun to roll out, leading packaged goods brands are experiencing dramatic sales increases from their participation in this system.

To find out more, give us a call at 1(800)252-5646. And we'll show you how to score big for your team.

© 1990 Shoppers' Video. Advertising Graphics Network. Diet Pepsi, Caffeine Free Diet Pepsi and The Right Ones are trademarks of PepsiCo, Inc.

because the salesperson is an admired or likable person whose tastes are similar and is seen as someone who can be trusted.[44] Mark's music purchases, for example, were strongly influenced by the expertise of the store's college student employees, who served as role models for him.

The Sales Interaction. A buyer/seller situation is like many other dyadic encounters (two-person groups); it is a relationship where some agreement must be reached about the roles of each participant: A process of *identity negotiation* occurs.[45] For example, if Karen, a salesperson, immediately establishes herself as an all-knowing expert (and the customer accepts this) she is likely to have more influence over the buyer through the course of the relationship. Some of the factors that help to determine a salesperson's role (and relative effectiveness) are his or her age, appearance, educational level, and motivation to sell.[46]

In addition, more effective salespersons usually know their customers' traits and preferences better than do ineffective salespersons, since this knowledge allows them to adapt their approach to meet the needs of the specific customer.[47] The ability to be adaptable is especially vital when customers and salespeople differ in terms of their *interaction styles.*[48] Consumers, for example, vary in the degree of assertiveness they bring to interactions. At one extreme, nonassertive people believe that complaining is not socially acceptable and may be intimidated in sales situations. Assertive people are more likely to stand up for themselves in a firm but nonthreatening way, while aggressives may resort to rudeness and threats if they do not get their way.[49]

Relational Marketing. The strategic perspective that stresses the long-term, human side of buyer/seller interactions is called **relational marketing.** This view recognizes that ". . . the sale merely consummates the courtship. Then the marriage begins. How good the marriage is depends on how well the relationship is managed by the seller."[50] Like a romantic involvement, this long-term sales relationship characteristically goes through five phases.[51]

1. *Awareness.* The buyer enters the market, perhaps becoming aware of local brands.
2. *Exploration.* The buyer undergoes search and trial. A minimal investment is made in the relationship. Norms and expectations begin to develop.
3. *Expansion.* The buyer and seller start to become more interdependent as the relationship becomes solidified.
4. *Commitment.* A pledge is made (this may be done implicitly) to continue the relationship (e.g., a customer may come to refer to someone as "my hairdresser").
5. *Dissolution.* The relationship will dissolve, unless steps are taken to keep it together. One way for the seller to prevent this is to construct *exit barriers,* making it difficult for the buyer to separate. Examples of exit barriers include delayed rebates (customers must accumulate proof-of-purchase seals over time), frequent flier programs (which make it less tempting to switch airlines), or rental deposits.

SERVICES: MARKETING WHAT ISN'T THERE

One of the distinguishing characteristics of a service is its intangibility. Whether an airplane ride or a visit to a lawyer, a service cannot be seen or felt. For this reason, the cues, or **physical evidence,** associated with a service are particularly crucial.[52] As a general rule, the more intangible the service, the more important is the role played by physical evidence. A recent study that examined how the environment influenced consumers' perceptions of service quality illustrates this point. When people were shown the picture of an "organized" travel agency, as seen here, and told of a breakdown in service, they were not as likely to expect such a problem to occur in the future as when they were shown the picture of the "disorganized" agency.[53]

SERVICE IMAGES   The realization that customers' experiences while receiving a service are as important as the service itself has prompted many managers to redouble their efforts to provide quality service.[54] In the realm of services, consumers usually give supermarkets and banks the highest ratings, while auto repair, local government, real estate, and public transportation do not fare very well.[55] Service quality can be assessed on such dimensions as facilities and appearance of personnel (tangibles), reliability, responsiveness, and the knowledge, courtesy, and responsiveness of service personnel.[56]

The Role of Service Providers.   Another characteristic of services is that they tend to be labor-intensive, which means that consumers' images of a service business often depend upon the person who actually delivers the service. An airline may invest millions of dollars in providing top quality planes, devising efficient route systems, training pilots, and so on, but a passenger's experience with the company will be soured (perhaps permanently) by one nasty encounter with a rude ticket clerk.[57]

Because a service company's image is only as good as the image communicated by its people, management must use all available means to ensure that the service provider communicates the company's attributes. This is one reason that many companies are concerned with correctly *packaging* their employees.[58] Company uniforms, for example, can be an important part of the service mix. In addition to such traditional users as nurses, policemen, and the airline industry, large companies such as Hertz, McDonald's, and Coca-Cola have initiated extensive career apparel programs.

MARKETING OPPORTUNITY

Consumers' desires for individualized attention are being met by many businesses that feature personalized service, where the product is tailored to each person's unique needs. Weyerhauser installs computers in home repair stores that allow shoppers to custom design their own home decks. After deciding how they would like the deck to look, customers receive a computer printout, complete with a list of the required materials and their costs.[59] A company called the Perfumer's Workshop custom blends fragrances for its clients (at $130 to $350 each). The person answers a series of twenty questions to reveal preferences about tastes in art, music, and literature. According to the owner, the answers ". . . reveal personality, essence, soul, which are then translated into a secret formula."[60]

SERVICES AS THEATER   Like retail settings that come to resemble a theatrical production, each service encounter is in a sense a performance.

Customers' perceptions of a business are affected by physical cues, as demonstrated by responses to two versions of a travel agency created by a researcher to study this issue. Reprinted courtesy of M. J. Bitner.

As suggested by role theory (see Chapter 7), every participant has a part to play, complete with props and costumes. Think, for example, of the activities that occur in a fancy restaurant, where a fine meal is "presented." Like drama, a number of components of a performance can be isolated.[61]

The Performance. Any activity that takes place before an audience can be considered a performance. Waiters, wine stewards, and so on "perform" for diners by reciting daily specials, opening bottles with a flourish, or perhaps even bringing flaming delicacies to the table without burning down the establishment.

The Performance Team. The actors who are mutually responsible for making sure the "show" goes on make up the performance team. In a restaurant, this troupe would include the maitre d', waiters, chefs, busboys, and even the parking valets.

Regions of Performance. The performance can be divided into areas, primarily distinguishing between the *front* and *backstage*. The front is the setting for the performance that the customer sees. The restaurant will take great care to ensure that tables are clean and elegantly set, appropriate music is playing in the background, and so on.

Backstage is where the props (e.g., the food) are actually produced. The behavior of actors in this region may be quite different. The elegant waiter with the French accent in the front may slip back into the kitchen to grab a smoke, make jokes about the diners, and maybe even revert back into his "real" accent. Many service managers stress the importance of separating regions to produce the appropriate image for clients or customers (the kitchens of even elegant restaurants often exhibit horrifying sights that are better avoided by diners).

◭ MARKETING OPPORTUNITY

Because of rising costs, time pressures, and the inferior quality of service in some situations, many consumers are accepting the idea of self-service. This trend has delighted many businesspeople, since customers are a form of cheap labor. In the United States, about 80 percent of gasoline is pumped by drivers. The Mervyn's chain has introduced self-service in its women's shoe department, and some florists have been successful in placing vending machines at airports. Even restaurants are getting into the act with salad and dessert bars.[62]

The acceptance of such innovations partly depends upon convincing the consumer to be a willing partner. Citibank found this out the hard way a few years ago, when it introduced a policy mandating that customers with accounts less than $5000 use ATMs rather than tellers. This change antagonized customers and resulted in a storm of negative publicity. Citibank quickly eliminated the policy.[63]

SITUATIONAL EFFECTS ON CONSUMER BEHAVIOR

A situation is defined by factors over and above characteristics of the person and of the product. The act of shopping is one important situational variable relating to the conditions under which something is purchased. Other variables, however, relate to the consumer's context at the time a product is to be consumed. In general, situational effects can be behavioral (e.g., entertaining friends) or perceptual (e.g., being depressed, or feeling pressed for time).[64] Common sense tells us that people tailor their purchases to specific occasions or that the way we feel at a specific point in time affects what we feel like buying or doing.

One reason for this variability is that the role a person plays at any time is partly determined by his or her *situational self-image:* "Who am I right now?" (see Chapter 7).[65] Someone trying to impress his date by playing the role of "man-about-town" may spend more lavishly, order champagne instead of beer, and buy flowers—purchases he would never consider when he is hanging out with his friends, slurping beer, and playing the role of "one of the boys." As this example demonstrates, knowledge of what consumers are doing at the time a product is consumed can improve predictions of brand choice.[66]

SITUATIONAL SEGMENTATION   By systematically identifying important usage situations, market segmentation strategies can be developed to position products that will meet the specific needs arising from these situations. Many product categories are amenable to this form of segmentation. For example, consumers' furniture choices are often tailored to specific settings. We prefer different styles for a city apartment, beach house, or an executive suite. Similarly, motorcycles can be distinguished in terms of what riders use them for, including commuting, riding them as dirt bikes, using them on a farm versus highway travel, and so on.[67] This South African ad for Volkswagen emphasizes the versatility of the Volkswagen bus for different situations.

CONSTRUCTING A SITUATIONAL SEGMENTATION MATRIX   Table 10-1 gives one example of how situations can be used to fine-tune a segmentation strategy. By listing the major contexts where a product is used (e.g., snow skiing and sunbathing for a suntan lotion) and the different users of the product, a matrix can be constructed that identifies specific product features that should be emphasized for each situation. For example, a lotion manufacturer might promote the fact that the bottle floats and is hard to lose during the summer, but tout its antifreeze formula during the winter season.

PHYSICAL AND SOCIAL SURROUNDINGS
A consumer's physical and social environment can make a big difference in motives for product usage, as well as affecting how the product is evaluated. Important cues include the person's physical surroundings, as well as the amount and type of other consumers also present in that situation.

Volkswagen announces a Bus you really can take anywhere.

In the early sixties, thousands of surfers, campers and fishermen discovered a strange-looking box on wheels.

The VW Bus.

It wasn't long before it became a part of the South African way of life.

Then, the Bus grew up.

We swopped our old air-cooled engine for a new water-cooled one and added a few modcons like air conditioning and power steering.

Fuel injection followed and soon Bus became a favourite with families too.

Now Bus is poised to take another step forward into the nineties.

With the new all wheel drive Bus Syncro.

The new Bus offers you permanent 4-wheel-drive in a way that doesn't just give you great off-road abilities, it also improves your handling and safety on the road.

As soon as wheels start slipping because of the road condition, power is immediately transferred to the front axle via a viscous coupling.

In extreme off-road conditions, diff-locks transfer drive to either the front or rear wheels, or both, and you don't have to stop the Bus to use them, because the controls are dash mounted.

The new Syncro is an advance in 4-wheel-drive technology – the Bus does all the thinking for you, so there's less chance of driver error.

The result is superb roadholding and traction and a go-anywhere capability that makes the Bus twice as much fun as ever before.

Come to think of it though, isn't that what you'd expect from Volkswagen?

New all wheel drive Bus Syncro.

THE SYNCRO ALL WHEEL DRIVE SYSTEM IS AVAILABLE ON THE 2.1i MICROBUS AND THE 2.1i CARAVELLE.

This South African ad for Volkswagen emphasizes that brand criteria can differ depending upon the situation in which the product will be used. Courtesy of Volkswagen of South Africa.

▼ MARKETING PITFALL

Some marketers will stop at nothing to be sure that consumers are constantly exposed to promotional materials. About one-third of consumers report that they like to read in the bathroom. Top media choices are *True Story, Seventeen,* and *Time.* To capture this audience, enter the *Bathroom Journal.* The magazine, with a signature color of pink, so it won't look out of place, features ads for health and beauty aids and bathroom fixtures. Purchasers of a one-year subscription receive a free wall rack.[68]

CO-CONSUMERS As will be seen in the next chapter, many of a consumer's purchase decisions are significantly affected by the groups or social settings in which these occur. In some cases, the sheer presence or absence of other patrons ("co-consumers") in a setting can be a determinant attribute (see Chapter 8), such as when an exclusive resort or boutique promises to provide privacy to privileged customers. At other

TABLE 10-1 A person situation segmentation matrix for suntan lotion

Persons / Situations	Young Children — Fair Skin	Young Children — Dark Skin	Teenagers — Fair Skin	Teenagers — Dark Skin	Adult Women — Fair Skin	Adult Women — Dark Skin	Adult Men — Fair Skin	Adult Men — Dark Skin	Situation Benefits/Features
beach/boat sunbathing	combined insect repellent				summer perfume				a. windburn protection b. formula and container can stand heat c. container floats and is distinctive (not easily lost)
home-poolside sunbathing					combined moisturizer				a. large pump dispenser b. won't stain wood, concrete, or furnishings
sunlamp bathing					combined moisturizer and massage oil				a. designed specifically for type of lamp b. artificial tanning ingredient
snow skiing					winter perfume				a. special protection from special light rays and weather b. antifreeze formula
person benefit/features	special protection		special protection		special protection		special protection		
person benefit/features	a. protection critical b. non-poisonous		a. fit in jean pocket b. used by opinion leaders		female perfume		male perfume		

Source: Peter R. Dickson, "Person-Situation: Segmentation's Missing Link," *Journal of Marketing* 46 (Fall 1982): 62.

times, the presence of others can have positive value. A sparsely attended ball game or an empty bar can be depressing sights.

The presence of large numbers of people in a consumer environment increases arousal levels, so a consumer's subjective experience of a setting tends to be more intense. This polarization, however, can be both positive and negative. While the presence of other people creates a state of arousal, the consumer's actual experience depends upon his or her *interpretation* of this arousal. It is important to distinguish between *density* and *crowding* for this reason. The former term refers to the actual number of people occupying a space, while the psychological state of crowding exists only if a negative affective state occurs as a result of this density.[69] For example, 100 students packed into a classroom designed for 75 may be unpleasant for all concerned, but the same number of people jammed together at a party occupying a room of the same size might just make for a great party.

In addition, the type of consumers who patronize a store or service can serve as a store attribute. We may infer something about a store's image by examining the image projected by its customers. This is one reason why some restaurants require men to wear a jacket for dinner (and supply one if they don't) or why bouncers of some "hot" nightspots hand-pick patrons they will admit based on whether they have the right "look" for the club. To paraphrase the comedian Groucho Marx, "I would never join a club that would have me for a member."

MARKETING OPPORTUNITY

Developments in the coin-operated laundry business illustrate how a traditionally depressing, isolated service can be repositioned as a fun, social event. Many laundries have taken to installing bars, tanning salons, and exercise machines to encourage customers to look forward to doing their laundry. The Videotown Laundrette in Manhattan features a 6000 title videocassette library, and Suds & Duds in Greensboro, North Carolina has a snack bar, pool hall, and big-screen television.[70]

TEMPORAL FACTORS

Time is one of consumers' most limiting resources. We talk about "making time," or "spending time," and we are reminded that "time is money." Our perspectives on time can affect many stages of decision making and consumption, such as needs that are stimulated, the amount of information search we undertake, and so on. Common sense tells us that more careful information search and deliberation occurs when we have the luxury of taking our time. A meticulous shopper who would normally price an item at three different stores before buying it might be found running through the mall at 9 p.m. on Christmas Eve, furiously scooping up anything left on the shelves that might serve as a last-minute gift.

ECONOMIC TIME   Time is an economic variable; it is a resource that must be divided among activities.[71] Consumers try to maximize satisfaction by allocating time to the appropriate combination of tasks. According to this perspective, time has four components: work, necessities, home-work, and leisure. Of course, people's allocation decisions differ; we all know people who seem to play all of the time, and others who are workaholics. An individual's priorities determine his or her *timestyle*.[72] A model of this time allocation process, which includes the many factors influencing temporal decisions, is presented in Figure 10-2.

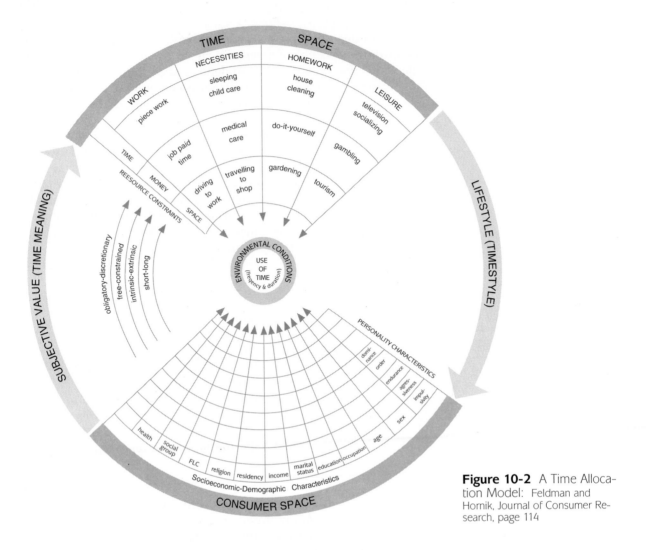

Figure 10-2 A Time Allocation Model: Feldman and Hornik, Journal of Consumer Research, page 114

Time Poverty. Many consumers believe they are more pressed for time than ever before. This feeling may, however, be due more to perception than to fact. People may just have more options for spending their time and feel pressured by the weight of all of these choices. The average working day at the turn of the century was ten hours (six days per week), and women did twenty-seven hours of housework per week, compared to under five hours weekly in the 1980s. Of course, one reason for this difference is that men are sharing these burdens more.[73] Still, about a third of Americans report always feeling rushed, up from 25 percent of the population in 1964.[74]

This sense of time poverty has made consumers very responsive to marketing innovations that allow them to save time. As an executive at Campbell's Soup observed, "Time will be the currency of the 1990s."[75] This priority has created new opportunities for services as diverse as photograph processing, optometrists, and car repair, where speed of delivery has become an important attribute.[76] To cater to this need, a Chicago funeral home even offers drive-through service, where viewers can see a loved one on a screen without taking the time to leave their cars. The owner notes, "The working person doesn't have time to come in. They want to see the body but they don't want to wait."[77]

MARKETING PITFALL

An emphasis on speed resulted in some serious public relations problems for Domino's Pizza, which guarantees delivery within thirty minutes. Critics claimed that this policy encouraged reckless driving and backed up this charge with some damaging statistics. In 1989, more than a dozen lawsuits were filed stemming from death or serious injuries caused by delivery people rushing to make the half-hour deadline. The employee death rate was 50 per 100,000—equal to that suffered in the mining industry.[78] The company now qualifies its claim by stipulating that safety factors must be considered during delivery.

Time poverty has drastically affected eating habits. The market for take-out food doubled in the 1980s, and now accounts for about 25 percent of all restaurant sales. About 40 percent of consumers aged 25 to 44 take out or eat out at least once or twice a week.[79] In the words of a food industry executive, "You are what you *heat.*"[80] Products that require very little time and effort, such as Kraft's Zap-a-Pack cheese spread that heats in the microwave in one minute, are changing consumers' perspectives on food preparation.

Products that are now considered indispensable are most likely to be time savers. As a Kraft executive noted, "It's gotten to the point where it is too burdensome to open a can of soup."[81] To underscore this emphasis on speed and convenience, about a quarter of consumers now report they could not live without a microwave oven, and the average home preparation time of a frozen pizza has shrunk from fifty minutes in 1975 to four minutes now.[82] The time crunch also brings changes in shopping patterns, as retailers who cater to consumers' busy schedules come out ahead. For instance, about one in five shoppers are now most likely to do their grocery shopping between 5:00 and 8:00 at night.[83]

Polychronicity. With the increase in time poverty, researchers also are noting a rise in *polychronic activity,* where consumers do more than one thing at a time.[84] One area where this is especially prevalent is eating patterns. Consumers often do not allocate a specific time to dining, but instead eat "on the run." In a recent poll, 64 percent of respondents said they usually do something else while eating. As one food industry executive commented, "We've moved beyond grazing and into gulping."[85]

PSYCHOLOGICAL TIME The psychological dimension of time, or how it is experienced, is an important factor in *queuing theory,* the mathematical study of waiting lines. A consumer's experience of waiting can radically influence his or her perceptions of service quality. Although we assume that something must be pretty good if we have to wait for it, the negative feelings aroused by long waits can quickly turn off customers.

Marketers have adopted a variety of "tricks" to minimize psychological waiting time. These techniques range from altering customers' perceptions of a line's length to providing distractions that divert attention away from waiting.[86] For example:

- One hotel chain, after receiving excessive complaints about the wait for elevators, installed mirrors near the elevator banks. People's natural tendency to check their appearance reduced complaints, even though the actual waiting time was unchanged.
- Waiting time in restaurants can be managed by turning the waiting area into a bar, or providing posters, reading material, or adult "toys" to distract customers.
- Airline passengers often complain of the time they must wait to claim their baggage. In one airport, they would walk one minute from the plane to the baggage carousel and then wait seven minutes for their luggage. By changing the layout so that the walk to the carousel took six minutes and bags arrived two minutes after that, complaints were almost entirely eliminated.
- McDonald's uses a multiple-line system, where each server deals with a separate line of people. In contrast, Wendy's uses a multi-stage system, where the first server takes orders, the second prepares burgers, the third pours drinks, and so on. While Wendy's lines are longer, customers move continuously through stages, so signs of progress can be seen and psychological time is reduced. Similarly, Disneyland often disguises the length of its lines by bending them around corners so that customers are prevented from judging the actual waiting time.

Time-of-Day. Some products and services are believed to be appropriate for certain times and not for others. One study of fast food preferences found that consumers were more likely to choose Wendy's over other fast food outlets for an evening meal when not rushed than when they were pressed for time.[89] Also, we may be more receptive to advertising messages at certain times (who wants to hear a beer commercial at 7:00 in the morning?). There is some evidence that consumers' arousal levels are lower in the morning than in the evening, which affects their style and quality of information processing.[90]

Numerous marketing themes reflect the idea that a certain time is related to the desire for a particular product. Miller beer, for instance, trains consumers to reach for its brew when "It's Miller time" (sorry, the "Night Belongs to Michelob Light"), and we also are told that orange juice is "not just for breakfast anymore." The coffee industry is trying to bolster lagging sales by inducing members of the college market who are not yet hooked on coffee to switch from soft drinks to iced cappuccino during the day. Similarly, Nestle S.A. of Switzerland has an iced coffee drink, called Nescafe Frappe, which is popular in the U.K, and Coca-Cola's Georgia Coffee brand of iced coffee is already a hit in Japan. Ironically, the soft-drink industry is threatening in turn to capture morning coffee drinkers

ULTICULTURAL DIMENSIONS

To most Western consumers, time is a neatly compartmentalized thing: We wake up in the morning, go to school or work, come home, eat dinner, go out, go to sleep . . . wake up and do it all over again. This perspective is called *linear separable time* (or Christian time); events proceed in an orderly sequence and different times are well-defined: "There's a time and a place for everything." There is a clear sense of past, present, and future. Many activities are performed as the means to some end that will occur later, as when people "save for a rainy day."

This conception of time is not universal. Large cultural differences exist in terms of people's time perspectives.[87] Some cultures run on *procedural time* and ignore the clock completely. People decide to do something "when the time is right." Alternatively, in *circular* or cyclic time, people are governed by natural cycles, such as the regular occurrence of the seasons (a perspective found in many Latino cultures). To these consumers, the notion of the future does not make sense, because that time will be much like the present. Since the concept of future value does not exist, these consumers often prefer to buy an inferior product that is available now to waiting for a better one that may be available later. Also, it is hard to convince people who function on circular time to buy insurance or save for the future when they do not endorse this concept.

When groups of college students were asked to draw a picture of time, the resulting sketches in Figure 10-3 illustrate some of these different temporal perspectives.[88] The drawing at the top represents procedural time; there is lack of direction from left to right and little sense of past, present, and future. The two drawings in the middle denote cyclical time, with regular cycles designated by markers. The bottom drawing represents linear time, with a segmented time line moving from left to right in a well-defined sequence.

Figure 10-3 Drawings of Time Esther S. Page-Wood, Carol J. Kaufman, and Paul M. Lane, "The Art of Time," *Proceedings of the Academy of Marketing Science,* 1990 (cf Endnote 88).

by convincing them to substitute soda for their morning "caffeine fix." The Coca-Cola Co. has its "Coke in the morning" campaign, and Pepsi-Cola is testing its Pepsi A.M. drink (with more caffeine than regular Pepsi).[91]

TASK DEFINITION

The specific reason for a purchase or the occasion for which it is intended to be consumed can change behavioral patterns. One important class of tasks is gift giving, which will be discussed in Chapter 16. Consumers' decision-making processes and product choices tend to be quite different when buying a gift for someone else than when buying for themselves. People may also buy different versions of the same product for different occasions. This tendency has been noted with exasperation by marketers of premium liquors. Some customers only bring out "the good stuff" for company, while continuing to drink "Old Tennis Shoes" on a daily basis.

ANTECEDENT STATES

A person's mood or physiological condition active at the time of purchase can have a big impact on what is bought and can also affect how products are evaluated.[92] One reason is that behavior is directed toward certain goal states, as was discussed in Chapter 3. People spend more in the grocery store if they have not eaten for a while because food is a priority at that time. In addition, the particular social identity, or role that is being played at a given time will be influential.[93] For example, one aspect of situational role is the degree to which a consumer's ethnic identity, or *felt ethnicity,* is activated during a purchase situation. When people are reminded of this connection (which will be further discussed in Chapter 13), they are more likely to tailor their product choices along ethnic lines.[94]

MOOD   A consumer's mood can have a big impact on purchase decisions. For example, stress can impair information processing and problem-solving abilities.[95] Two dimensions determine if a shopper will react positively or negatively to a store environment. These are *pleasure* and *arousal.* A person can enjoy or not enjoy a situation, and he or she can feel stimulated or not. As Figure 10-4 indicates, these two dimensions interact with each other, and a state of heightened arousal is not always desirable. We have all been in unpleasant situations that make us tense or nervous—we just can't wait to get out of there. On the other hand, we might feel really "up" and energized and want to stay in a place as long as possible. Maintaining this feeling is one factor behind the success of theme parks like Disney World, which try to provide constant stimulation in a positive way.[96]

A specific mood is some combination of these two factors. For example, the state of happiness is high in pleasantness and moderate in arousal, while elation would be high on both dimensions.[97] In general, a mood state (either positive or negative) biases judgments of products and service in that direction.[98] Put simply, consumers like things better when they are in a good mood. When in positive moods, consumers process ads with less elaboration. They pay less attention to specifics of the message and rely more on heuristic processing (see Chapter 8).[99]

Moods can be affected by store atmospherics, the weather, or other factors specific to the consumer. In addition, television programming and music

Figure 10-4 Dimensions of Emotional States Russell & Pratt (1980), "A description of the Affective Quality Attributed to Environment" *Journal of Personality and Social Psychology* 38 (Aug.), 311–372

can affect mood, which has important consequences for the commercials that follow a show.[100] When consumers watch happy programs, they have more positive reactions to commercials, especially to emotional messages.[101]

CONSUMER SATISFACTION

Consumer satisfaction or dissatisfaction (CS/D) is determined by the overall feelings, or attitude, a person has about a product after it has been purchased. Consumers are engaged in a constant process of evaluating the things they buy as these products are integrated into their daily consumption activities.[102]

PERCEPTIONS OF PRODUCT QUALITY

Just what do consumers look for in products? That's easy: They want quality and value. Especially because of foreign competition, claims of product quality have become strategically crucial to maintaining a competitive advantage.[103] Consumers use a number of cues to infer quality, including brand name, price, and even their own estimates of how much money has been put into a new product's advertising campaign.[104] These cues, as well as others such as product warranties and follow-up letters from the company, are often used by consumers to relieve perceived risk and assure themselves that they have made smart purchase decisions.[105]

While everyone wants quality, it is not clear exactly what this means. Certainly, many manufacturers claim to provide it. Consider, for example, the following claims that have been made at one time or another by car manufacturers:[106]

Ford: "*Quality* is job 1"

Lincoln-Mercury: ". . . the highest *quality* cars of any major American car company"

Chrysler: "*Quality* engineered to be the best"

GMC trucks: "*Quality* built yet economical"

Oldsmobile: "Fulfilling the . . . *quality* needs of American drivers"

Audi: "*Quality* backed by our outstanding new warranty"

WHAT IS QUALITY? In the book *Zen and the Art of Motorcycle Maintenance,* a cult hero of college students in an earlier generation literally went crazy trying to figure out the meaning of quality.[107] Marketers appear to use the word quality as a catchall term for "good." Because of its wide and imprecise usage, the attribute of "quality" threatens to become a meaningless claim. If everyone has it, what good is it?

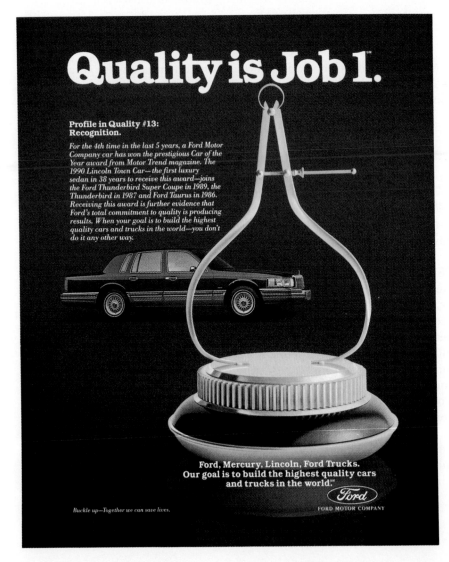

This ad for Ford relies on a common claim about "quality." Courtesy of Ford Motor Company.

THE IMPORTANCE OF EXPECTATIONS Satisfaction or dissatisfaction is more than a reaction to the actual performance quality of a product or service. It is influenced by prior expectations regarding the level of quality. According to the **expectancy disconfirmation model,** consumers form beliefs about product performance based upon prior experience with the product and/or communications about the product that imply a certain level of quality.[108] When something performs the way we thought it would, we may not think much about it. If, on the other hand, it fails to live to expectations, negative affect may result. And, if performance happens to exceed our expectations, we are satisfied and pleased.

To understand this, think once again about different types of restaurants. People expect to be provided with sparkling clear glassware at fancy restaurants, and they might become upset if they discover a grimy glass. On the other hand, we may not be surprised to find fingerprints on our beer mug at a local greasy spoon; this may even be shrugged off because it contributes to the place's "charm." An important lesson emerges from this perspective: Don't overpromise.[109]

Quality and Product Failures. The power of quality claims is most evident when they are not fulfilled, as when a company's product fails in some way. Here, consumers' expectations are dashed, and dissatisfaction results. When this occurs, immediate steps must be taken to reassure customers. If the company confronts the problem truthfully, consumers often are willing to forgive and forget. This was the case for Tylenol (product tampering), Chrysler (disconnecting odometers on executives' cars and reselling them as new), or Perrier (traces of benzene found in the water). When the company appears to be dragging its heels or covering up, on the other hand, consumer resentment will grow. This occurred during Union Carbide's chemical disaster in India and with Exxon following the massive Alaskan oil spill caused by its tanker, the *Exxon Valdez.*

ACTING ON DISSATISFACTION If a person is not happy with a product or service, what can be done? There are essentially three different courses of action that can be taken by a consumer (note that more than one can be taken).[110]

1. *Voice responses.* The consumer can appeal directly to the retailer for redress (e.g., a refund).
2. *Private responses.* Express dissatisfaction about the store or product to friends and/or boycott the store. As will be discussed in Chapter 11, negative word of mouth (WOM) can be very damaging to a store's reputation.
3. *Third party responses.* The consumer can take legal action against the merchant, register a complaint with the Better Business Bureau, or perhaps write a letter to the newspaper.

A number of factors influence which route is eventually taken. The consumer may in general be an assertive or a meek person. Action is more likely to be taken for expensive products such as household durables, cars, and clothing than for inexpensive products.[111] Also, if the consumer does not believe that the store will respond well to a complaint, the person will be more likely to simply switch brands than fight.[112]

PRODUCT DISPOSITION

Because people often do form strong attachments to products, the decision to dispose of something may be a very painful one. One function performed by possessions is to serve as anchors for our identities: Our past lives on in our things.[113] This attachment is exemplified by the Japanese, who ritually "retire" worn-out sewing needles, chopsticks, and even computer chips by burning them as thanks for good service.[114]

Although some people have more trouble than others in discarding things, even a "pack rat" does not keep everything. Consumers must often dispose of things, either because they have fulfilled their designated functions, or possibly because they no longer fit with consumers' view of themselves. Concern about the environment coupled with a need for convenience has made ease of product disposal a key attribute in categories from razors to diapers.

ENVIRONMENTAL ISSUES

The issue of product disposition is doubly vital because of its enormous public policy implications. We live in a throw-away society, which creates problems for the environment and also results in a great deal of unfortunate waste. For instance, it has been estimated that U.S. consumers discard $4.5 billion worth of food every year.[115] Training consumers to recycle has become a priority in many countries. The United States alone puts about three-quarters of the 100 million tons of solid waste it generates into landfills, more than half of which will be full by the mid-1990s.[116] This problem is not unique to the United States. Tokyo is expected to run out of landfill space by 1995, and the Japanese stress the social value of recycling. Most citizens comply and are encouraged by garbage trucks that periodically rumble through the streets playing classical music or children's songs.[117]

DISPOSAL OPTIONS When a consumer decides that a product is no longer of use, several choices are available. The person can either (1) keep the item, (2) temporarily dispose of it, or (3) permanently dispose of it. In many cases, a new product is acquired even though the old one still functions. Some reasons for this replacement include a desire for new features, a change in the person's environment (e.g., a refrigerator is the wrong color for a freshly painted kitchen), or a change in the person's role or self-image.[118] Figure 10-5 provides an overview of consumers' disposal options.

LATERAL CYCLING: JUNK OR "JUNQUE"?

Interesting consumer processes occur during **lateral cycling,** where already-purchased objects are sold to others or exchanged for still other things. Many purchases are made second-hand, rather than new. The reuse of other people's things is especially important in our throw-away society because, as one researcher put it, ". . . there is no longer an 'away' to throw things to."[119]

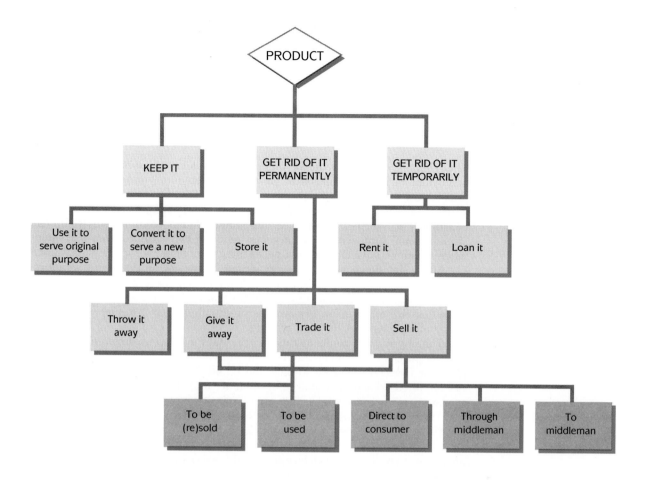

Figure 10-5 Consumers' Disposal Options Source: Jacob Jacoby, Carol K. Berning, and Thomas F. Dietvorst, "What About Disposition?" *Journal of Marketing* 41 (April 1977): 23.

Flea markets, garage sales, classified advertisements, bartering for services, hand-me-downs, and the black market all represent important alternative marketing systems that operate in addition to the formal marketplace. For example, the number of used-merchandise retail establishments has grown at about ten times the rate of other stores.[120] While traditional marketers have not paid much attention to used-product sellers, factors such as concern about the environment, demands for quality, and cost and fashion consciousness are conspiring to make these "secondary" markets more important.[121] Interest in antiques, period accessories, and specialty magazines catering to this niche is increasing. Other growth areas include student markets for used computers and textbooks or ski swaps, where millions of dollars of used ski equipment is exchanged.

Activities such as flea markets and swap meets in some ways resemble shopping malls in that they too provide many benefits other than the acquisition of bargains and "junque." They are also a form of entertainment for many consumers. One flea market patron summed up some differences between more formal shopping settings and flea markets: "The flea market is not as *sterile* as a mall. . . . It's an *event* to go to the flea market. I make a big production of it. I get friends together and spend an entire day. . . . Going to the mall is a chore."[122]

CHAPTER SUMMARY

This chapter reviewed some of the many complex processes underlying the acquisition, use, and disposal of goods. Shopping is an important activity in popular culture, and this behavior is often prompted by social motives as well as being a way to simply satisfy needs. Because shopping is viewed by many consumers as a form of experience, store atmospherics are increasingly emphasized by retail strategists. In some cases, retailing has become a sort of theater, where customers participate in a performance.

Many situational variables exert strong influences on decision making at the time of purchase. A consumer's situational self-image helps to determine the particular array of products and services that may be considered. The chapter identified five other major dimensions of situations that are important in understanding consumer decision making.

The physical environment can be important in shaping preferences or motivating purchases. Point-of-purchase stimuli can remind the person of certain needs or induce the person to pick one brand over another if preferences are not solidified prior to that time (they often are not). These stimuli may facilitate unplanned or impulse purchasing.

The social environment (interpersonal factors) can create feelings of crowding, depression, or positive arousal. In particular, salespeople can play a significant role in buying decisions. While such factors as age, education, and appearance are important determinants of a salesperson's effectiveness, an additional consideration is flexibility—the person's ability to identify a consumer's needs and tailor his or her sales presentation accordingly.

The quality of information search and the types of products bought are affected by the presence or absence of time pressure. Time is an important resource, and many products are valued because of their ability to save time. Conceptions of time vary across cultures; Western values related to the assumption that time is linear—with a clearly defined past, present, and future—may not be valid when marketing in other cultures.

The particular task or usage situation for which a product is bought is another situational variable. A product may be bought as a gift or intended for a very specific purpose or location. These different purposes can be used for segmentation purposes, as product features and promotional messages are tailored to each situation.

A consumer's antecedent state—what he or she brings to the purchase situation—is another consideration. Physiological conditions (e.g., hunger) can drive purchases, and mood states help to determine both what a person is interested in buying as well as his or her evaluation of what has been bought.

Compared to consumer decision-making processes, relatively little attention has been paid to what consumers do with products after purchase, how they evaluate them, and how they get rid of them. The chapter discussed some determinants of consumer satisfaction or dissatisfaction, especially the importance of prior expectations on evaluations. Finally, some aspects of product disposition were examined, and the importance of lateral cycling (e.g., flea markets, used car dealers) to consumption activities was emphasized.

KEY TERMS

Atmospherics

Consumer satisfaction or dissatisfaction (CS/D)

Expectancy disconfirmation model

Impulse buying

Lateral cycling

Physical evidence

Point-of-purchase stimuli (POP)

Relational marketing

Shopping orientation

Store image

Store loyalty

REVIEW QUESTIONS AND DISCUSSION TOPICS

1. Discuss some of the motivations for shopping as described in the chapter. How might a retailer adjust his or her strategy to accommodate these motivations?

2. A number of court cases in recent years have attempted to prohibit special interest groups from distributing literature in shopping malls. Mall management claims that these centers are private property. On the other hand, these groups argue that the mall is the modern-day version of the town square, and as such is a public forum. Find some recent court cases involving this free-speech issue, and examine the arguments pro and con. What is the current status of the mall as a public forum? Do you agree with this concept?

3. What are some positive and negative aspects of requiring employees who interact with customers to wear some kind of uniform or to mandate a dress code in the office?

4. Think about exceptionally good and bad salespeople you have encountered in the past. What qualities seem to differentiate them?

5. What is the difference between true service personalization and cosmetic personalization? Can you point to your own examples of this difference?

6. List the five stages of a long-term service relationship. How can a practitioner of relational marketing incorporate each stage into his or her strategy?

7. Sometimes the expectations of both participants in a service encounter are not consistent with one another. Can you generate some examples of this situation from your own experience? What were the consequences?

8. Can you think of any other products whose consumption is related to time?

9. Discuss the concept of "timestyle." How might consumers be segmented in terms of their timestyles?

10. Compare and contrast different cultures' conceptions of time. What are some implications for marketing strategy within each of these frameworks?

11. Elaborate on the idea that knowing the objective level of service or product quality is not sufficient to predict consumer satisfaction, as proposed by the expectancy disconfirmation model.

12. Why is it accurate to say that marketers and retailers like it when consumers complain?

13. The movement away from a "disposable consumer society" toward one that emphasizes creative recycling creates many opportunities for marketers. Can you identify some?

HANDS-ON EXERCISES

1. Conduct naturalistic observation at a local mall. Sit in a central location and observe the activities of mall employees and patrons. Keep a log of the non-retailing activity you observe (e.g., special performances, exhibits, socializing, etc.). Does this activity enhance or detract from business conducted at the mall?

2. Select three competing clothing stores in your area and conduct a store image study for them. Ask a group of consumers to rate each store on a set of attributes and plot these ratings on the same graph. Based on your findings, are there any areas of competitive advantage or disadvantage you could bring to the attention of store management?

3. Compare and contrast different retailers' use of atmospherics as a marketing tool. For the same type of store, identify one that "feels right" and one that doesn't, and try to delineate how these feelings are achieved.

4. Using Table 10-1 as a model, construct a person/situation segmentation matrix for a brand of perfume.

5. The chapter discusses a restaurant as a service performance. Visit a different service and apply the same dramatic concepts (e.g., regions, performance teams) to understand how this service functions. Can you see any relationships between service satisfaction and aspects of the performance?

6. What applications of queuing theory can you find employed among local services? Interview consumers who are waiting on lines to determine how (if at all) this experience affects their satisfaction with the service.

NOTES

1. John P. Robinson, "When the Going Gets Tough," *Advertising Age* (February 1989): 50.

2. Edward M. Tauber, "Why Do People Shop?" *Journal of Marketing* 36 (October 1972): 47–48.

3. Quoted in Robert C. Prus, *Making Sales: Influence as Interpersonal Accomplishment* (Sage Library of Social Research, Newbury Park, L.A.: Sage Publications, Inc., 1989): 225.

4. Francine Schwadel, "Shoppers' Blues: The Thrill is Gone; Depositors Cite Poor Service, Tight Schedules," *The Wall Street Journal* (October 13, 1989): B1; "Passionate Shopping: The End of the Affair," *Asbury Park Press* (March 18, 1990): D4.

5. Gregory P. Stone, "City Shoppers and Urban Identification: Observations on the Social Psychology of City Life," *American Journal of Sociology* 60 (1954): 36–45; Danny Bellenger and Pradeep K. Korgaonkar, "Profiling the Recreational Shopper," *Journal of Retailing* 56 (1980)3: 77–92.

6. Isabel Wilkerson, "Megamall, A New Fix for Future Shopping Addicts," *New York Times* (June 9, 1989): A14.

7. Nina Gruen, "The Retail Battleground: Solutions for Today's Shifting Marketplace," *Journal of Property Management* (July–August 1989): 14.

8. Wayne Curtis, "Struggling to Hook Shoppers—and Keep Them," *New York Times* (May 14, 1989): F15.

9. William J. Cook, "Reach Out and Touch Everyone; Can Shopping Be as Easy as a Home-Computer Keystroke?" *U.S. News & World Report* (October 10, 1988): 49.

10. Quoted in Kate Ballen, "Get Ready for Shopping at Work," *Fortune* (February 15, 1988): 95.

11. Arieh Goldman, "The Shopping Style Explanation for Store Loyalty," *Journal of Retailing* 53 (Winter 1977–78): 33–46, 94; Robert B. Settle and Pamela L. Alreck, "Hyperchoice Shapes the Marketplace," *Marketing Communications* (May 1988): 15.

12. Quoted in Jacquelyn Bivins, "Fun and Mall Games," *Stores* (August 1989): 35.

13. Sallie Hook, "All the Retail World's a Stage: Consumers Conditioned to Entertainment in Shopping Environment," *Marketing News* 21 (July 31, 1987): 16.

14. Susan Spiggle and Murphy A. Sewall, "A Choice Sets Model of Retail Selection," *Journal of Marketing* 51 (April 1987): 97–111.

15. Most measures of store image are quite similar to other attitude measures, as discussed in Chapter 5. For an excellent bibliography of store image studies, see Mary R. Zimmer and Linda L. Golden, "Impressions of Retail Stores: A Content Analysis of Consumer Images," *Journal of Retailing* 64 (Fall 1988): 265–93.

16. Zimmer and Golden, "Impressions of Retail Stores."

17. Spiggle and Sewall, "A Choice Sets Model of Retail Selection."

18. Philip Kotler, "Atmospherics as a Marketing Tool," *Journal of Retailing* (Winter 1973–74): 48–64, 50.

19. Deborah Blumenthal, "Scenic Design for In-Store Try-Ons," *New York Times* (April 9, 1988).

20. Judy I. Alpert and Mark I. Alpert, "Music Influences on Mood and Purchase Intentions," *Psychology & Marketing* 7 (Summer 1990): 109–34.

21. Quoted in "Slow Music Makes Fast Drinkers," *Psychology Today* (March 1989): 18.

22. Brad Edmondson, "Pass the Meat Loaf," *American Demographics* (January 1989): 19.

23. Marianne Meyer, "Attention Shoppers!" *Marketing and Media Decisions* 23 (May 1988): 67.

24. Donald R. Lichtenstein, Richard G. Netemeyer, and Scot Burton, "Using a Theoretical Perspective to Examine the Psychological Construct of Coupon Proneness," in *Advances in Consumer Research,* ed. Rebecca H. Holman and Michael R. Solomon, (Provo, Utah: Association for Consumer Research, 1991)18: 501–8; Meyer, "Attention Shoppers!"

25. Easwar S. Iyer, "Unplanned Purchasing: Knowledge of Shopping Environment and Time Pressure," *Journal of Retailing* 65 (Spring 1989): 40–57; C. Whan Park, Easwar S. Iyer, and Daniel C. Smith, "The Effects of Situational Factors on In-Store Grocery Shopping," *Journal of Consumer Research* 15 (March 1989): 422–33.

26. Francis Piron, "Defining Impulse Purchasing," in *Advances in Consumer Research,* ed. Rebecca H. Holman and Michael R. Solomon, (Provo, Utah: Association for Consumer Research, 1991)18: 509–14; Dennis W. Rook, "The Buying Impulse," *Journal of Consumer Research* 14 (September 1987): 189–99.

27. Michael Wahl, "Eye POPping Persuasion," *Marketing Insights* (June 1989): 130.

28. Cathy J. Cobb and Wayne D. Hoyer, "Planned Versus Impulse Purchase Behavior," *Journal of Retailing* 62 (Winter 1986): 384–409; Easwar S. Iyer and Sucheta S. Ahlawat, "Deviations from a Shopping Plan: When and Why Do Consumers Not Buy as Planned," in *Advances in Consumer Research,* ed. Melanie Wallendorf and Paul Anderson, (Provo, Utah: Association for Consumer Research, 1987)14: 246–49.

29. Excerpted from Dennis Rook, "Is 'Impulse Buying' (Yet) a Useful Marketing Concept?" (unpublished manuscript, fig. 7-A).

30. See Aradhna Krishna, Imran S. Currim, and Robert W. Shoemaker, "Consumer Perceptions of Promotional Activity," *Journal of Marketing* 55 (April 1991): 4–16.

31. Kapil Bawa and Robert W. Shoemaker, "The Effects of a Direct Mail Coupon on Brand Choice Behavior," *Journal of Marketing Research* 24 (November 1987): 370–76.

32. Peter Tat, William A. Cunningham III, and Emin Babakus, "Consumer Perceptions of Rebates," *Journal of Advertising Research* 28 (August–September 1988): 45–50.

33. Dale D. Achabal, Cherryl H. Bell, Shelby H. McIntyre, and Nancy Tucker, "The Effect of Nutrition P-O-P Signs on Consumer Attitudes and Behavior," *Journal of Retailing* 63 (Spring 1987): 9.

34. Wahl, "Eye POPping Persuasion."

35. Wahl, "Eye POPping Persuasion."

36. Bernice Kanner, "Trolling in the Aisles," *New York* (January 16, 1989): 12.

37. Holloway McCandless, "Automating the Personal Shopper," *Working Woman* (November 1987): 78.

38. William Keenan, Jr., "Point-of-Purchase: From Clutter to Technoclutter," *Sales and Marketing Management* 141 (April 1989): 96.

39. Meyer, "Attention Shoppers!"

40. Cyndee Miller, "Videocart Spruces Up for New Tests," *Marketing News* (February 19, 1990) 19; William E. Sheeline, "User-Friendly Shopping Carts," *Fortune* (December 5, 1988): 9.

41. Paco Underhill, "In-Store Video Ads Can Reinforce Media Campaigns," *Marketing News* (May 1989): 5.

42. See Robert B. Cialdini, *Influence: Science and Practice,* 2nd. ed. (Glenview, Ill.: Scott, Foresman and Company, 1988).

43. Richard P. Bagozzi, "Marketing as Exchange," *Journal of Marketing* 39 (October 1975): 32–39; Peter M. Blau, *Exchange and Power in Social Life* (New York: Wiley, 1964); Marjorie Caballero and Alan J. Resnik, "The Attraction Paradigm in Dyadic Exchange," *Psychology & Marketing* 3 (1986)1 17–34; George C. Homans, "Social Behavior as Exchange," *American Journal of Sociology* 63 (1958): 597–606; Paul H. Schurr and Julie L. Ozanne, "Influences on Exchange Processes: Buyers' Preconceptions of a Seller's Trustworthiness and Bargaining Toughness," *Journal of Consumer Research* 11 (March 1985): 939–53; Arch G. Woodside and J. W. Davenport, "The Effect of Salesman Similarity and Expertise on Consumer Purchasing Behavior," *Journal of Marketing Research* 8 (1974): 433–36.

44. Paul Busch and David T. Wilson, "An Experimental Analysis of a Salesman's Expert and Referent Bases of Social Power in the Buyer-Seller Dyad," *Journal of Marketing Research* 13 (February 1976): 3–11; John E. Swan, Fred Trawick, Jr., David R. Rink, and Jenny J. Roberts, "Measuring Dimensions of Purchaser Trust of Industrial Salespeople," *Journal of Personal Selling and Sales Management* 8 (May 1988): 1.

45. Mary Jo Bitner, Bernard H. Booms, and Mary Stansfield Tetreault, "The Service Encounter: Diagnosing Favorable and Unfavorable Incidents," *Journal of Marketing* 54 (January 1990): 7–84; Robert C. Prus, *Making Sales* (Newbury Park, Ca.: Sage, 1989); Arch G. Woodside and James L. Taylor, "Identity Negotiations in Buyer-Seller Interactions," in *Advances in Consumer Research,* ed. Elizabeth C. Hirschman and Morris B. Holbrook (Provo, Utah: Association for Consumer Research, 1985)12: 443–49.

46. Gilbert A. Churchill, Jr., Neil M. Ford, Steven W. Hartley, and Orville C. Walker, Jr., "The Determinants of Salesperson Performance: A Meta-Analysis," *Journal of Marketing Research* 22 (May 1985): 103–18.

47. Siew Meng Leong, Paul S. Busch, and Deborah Roedder John, "Knowledge Bases and Salesperson Effectiveness: A Script-Theoretic Analysis," *Journal of Marketing Research* 26 (May 1989): 164; Harish Sujan, Mita Sujan, and James R. Bettman, "Knowledge Structure Differences Between More Effective and Less Effective Salespeople," *Journal of Marketing Research* 25 (February 1988): 81–86; Robert Saxe and Barton Weitz, "The SOCCO Scale: A Measure of the Customer Orientation of Salespeople," *Journal of Marketing Research* 19 (August 1982): 343–51; David M. Szymanski, "Determinants of Selling Effectiveness: The Importance of Declarative Knowledge to the Personal Selling Concept," *Journal of Marketing* 52 (January 1988): 64–77; Barton A. Weitz, "Effectiveness in Sales Interactions: A Contingency Framework," *Journal of Marketing* 45 (Winter 1981): 85–103.

48. Jagdish M. Sheth, "Buyer-Seller Interaction: A Conceptual Framework," in *Advances in Consumer Research* (Cincinatti, Ohio: Association for Consumer Research, 1976): 382–86; Kaylene C. Williams and Rosann L. Spiro, "Communication Style in the Salesperson-Customer Dyad," *Journal of Marketing Research* 22 (November 1985): 434–42.

49. Marsha L. Richins, "An Analysis of Consumer Interaction Styles in the Marketplace," *Journal of Consumer Research* 10 (June 1983): 73–82.

50. Theodore Levitt, *The Marketing Imagination* (New York: The Free Press, 1983): 111.

51. Robert F. Dwyer, Paul H. Schurr, and Sejo Oh, "Developing Buyer-Seller Relationships," *Journal of Marketing* 51 (April 1987): 11–27.

52. G. Lynn Shostack, "Human Evidence: A New Part of the Marketing Mix," *Bank Marketing* (March 1977): 32–34.

53. Mary Jo Bitner, "Evaluating Service Encounters: The Effects of Physical Surrounding and Employee Responses," *Journal of Marketing* 54 (April 1990): 69–82.

54. Michael R. Solomon, Carol Surprenant, John A. Czepiel, and Evelyn G. Gutman, "A Role Theory Perspective on Dyadic Interactions: The Service Encounter," *Journal of Marketing* 49 (Winter 1985): 99–111; Teresa A. Swartz and Stephen W. Brown, "Consumer and Provider Expectations and Experiences in Evaluating Professional Service Quality," *Journal of the Academy of Marketing Science* 17 (Spring 1989): 189–95; Valerie A. Zeithaml, "Consumer Perceptions of Price, Quality, and Value: A Means-End Model and Synthesis of Evidence," *Journal of Marketing* 52 (July 1988): 2–22.

55. "Groceries' Services Rated High," *New York Times* (March 10, 1986).
56. A. Parasumaran, Valarie A. Zeithaml, and Leonard L. Berry, "SERVQUAL: A Multiple-Item Scale for Measuring Consumer Perceptions of Service Quality," *Journal of Retailing* 64 (Spring 1988): 12–40.
57. See John A. Czepiel, Michael R. Solomon, and Carol F. Surprenant, eds., *The Service Encounter: Managing Employee/Customer Interaction in Services Businesses* (Lexington, Mass.: Lexington, 1985).
58. M. R. Solomon, "Packaging the Service Provider," *The Service Industries Journal* 5 (March 1985): 64–72.
59. "Weyerhauser Installs Computer Design Centers in Home Repair Outlets," *Marketing News* (May 22, 1989): 32.
60. Quoted in Ron Alexander, "For $350, Capture Your Personality in a Little Bottle and Call it Perfume," *New York Times* (March 4, 1990): 38.
61. Erving Goffman, *The Presentation of Self in Everyday Life* (New York: Doubleday and Co., 1959); Stephen J. Grove and Raymond P. Fisk, "The Dramaturgy of Services Exchange: An Analytical Framework for Services Marketing," in *Emerging Perspectives on Services Marketing,* ed. Leonard L. Berry, G. Lynn Shostack, and Gregory D. Upah (Chicago: American Marketing Association, 1983): 45–49; Solomon, Surprenant, Czepiel, and Gutman, "A Role Theory Perspective on Dyadic Interactions."
62. Claudia H. Deutsch, "The Powerful Push for Self-Service," *New York Times* (April 9, 1989): F1.
63. R. B. Plunkett, Jr., "Customers' Ire Moves Citibank," *New York Daily News* (May 17, 1983): 42.
64. Pradeep Kakkar and Richard J. Lutz, "Situational Influence on Consumer Behavior: A Review," in *Perspectives in Consumer Behavior,* ed. Harold H. Kassarjian and Thomas S. Robertson, 3rd ed. (Glenview, Ill.: Scott, Foresman and Company, 1981): 204–14.
65. Carolyn Turner Schenk and Rebecca H. Holman, "A Sociological Approach to Brand Choice: The Concept of Situational Self-Image," in *Advances in Consumer Research,* ed. Jerry C. Olson (Ann Arbor, Mich.: Association for Consumer Research, 1980)7: 610–14.
66. Russell W. Belk, "An Exploratory Assessment of Situational Effects in Buyer Behavior," *Journal of Marketing Research* 11 (May 1974): 156–63; U. N. Umesh and Joseph A. Cote, "Influence of Situational Variables on Brand-Choice Models," *Journal of Business Research* 16 (1988)2: 91–99.
67. Peter R. Dickson, "Person-Situation: Segmentation's Missing Link," *Journal of Marketing* 46 (Fall 1982): 56–64.
68. "Roll Out Privy Periodical," *Marketing News* (August 1986): 29.
69. Daniel Stokols, "On the Distinction Between Density and Crowding: Some Implications for Future Research," *Psychological Review* 79 (1972): 275–77.
70. Keith Bradsher, "There's More to Coin Laundries Than Just Getting the Wash Done," *New York Times* (January 7, 1990): 38.
71. Paul M. Lane and Carol J. Kaufman, "The Standardization of Time," in *Marketing: Positioning for the 1990s,* ed. Robert L. King (Proceedings of the 1989 Southern Marketing Association Conference, 1989): 1–5.
72. Laurence P. Feldman and Jacob Hornik, "The Use of Time: An Integrated Conceptual Model," *Journal of Consumer Research* 7 (March 1981): 407–19; See also Michelle M. Bergadaa, "The Role of Time in the Action of the Consumer," *Journal of Consumer Research* 17 (December 1990): 289–302.
73. Robert J. Samuelson, "Rediscovering the Rat Race," *Newsweek* (May 15, 1989): 57.
74. John P. Robinson, "Time Squeeze," *Advertising Age* (February 1990): 30–33.
75. Quoted in Judann Dagnoli, "Time—The Currency of the 90's," *Advertising Age* (November 13, 1989): S-2.
76. Leonard L. Berry, "Market to the Perception," *American Demographics* (February 1990: 32.
77. Quoted in Isabel Wilkerson, "New Funeral Options for Those in a Rush," *New York Times* (February 25, 1989): A16.
78. Eric N. Berg, "Fight on Quick Pizza Delivery Grows," *New York Times* (August 29, 1989): D6.
79. "Taking to Take-Out," *Advertising Age* (March 1987): 13.

80. Quoted in Dagnoli, "Time," italics added.

81. Quoted in Dena Kleiman, "Fast Food? It Just Isn't Fast Enough Anymore," *New York Times* (December 6, 1989): A1, C12.

82. Alison Leigh Cowan, "Favorite Things: Timesavers, All," *New York Times* (May 10, 1989): C1; Kleiman, "Fast Food?"

83. Doris Walsh, "The Heart is in the Deli," *Advertising Age* (August 1988): 13.

84. Lane and Kaufman, "Standardization of Time."

85. Quoted in Kleiman, "Fast Food?" C12.

86. David H. Maister, "The Psychology of Waiting Lines," in *The Service Encounter: Managing Employee/Customer Interaction in Service Businesses,* ed. John A. Czepiel, Michael R. Solomon, and Carol F. Surprenant, (Lexington, Mass.: Lexington Books, 1985): 113–24.

87. Robert J. Graham, "The Role of Perception of Time in Consumer Research," *Journal of Consumer Research* 7 (March 1981): 335–42.

88. Esther S. Page-Wood, Carol J. Kaufman, and Paul M. Lane, "The Art of Time," *Proceedings of the Academy of Marketing Science* (1990).

89. Kenneth E. Miller and James L. Ginter, "An Investigation of Situational Variation in Brand Choice Behavior and Attitude," *Journal of Marketing Research* 16 (February 1979): 111–23.

90. Jacob Hornik, "Diurnal Variation in Consumer Response," *Journal of Consumer Research* 14 (March 1988): 588–91.

91. N. R. Kleinfeld, "A Cold War Over Coffee," *New York Times* (October 29, 1989): 57; Patricia Winters, "Cola Companies are All Abuzz Over 'Cold Caffeine' Products," *Advertising Age* (September 4, 1989): 3.

92. Laurette Dube and Bernd H. Schmitt, "The Processing of Emotional and Cognitive Aspects of Product Usage in Satisfaction Judgments," in *Advances in Consumer Research,* ed. Rebecca H. Holman and Michael R. Solomon (Provo, Utah: Association for Consumer Research, 1991)18: 52–56; Lalita A. Manrai and Meryl P. Gardner, "The Influence of Affect on Attributions for Product Failure," in *Advances in Consumer Research,* ed. Rebecca H. Holman and Michael R. Solomon, (Provo, Utah: Association for Consumer Research, 1991)18: 249–54.

93. Peter J. Burke and Stephen L. Franzoi, "Studying Situations and Identities Using Experimental Sampling Methodology," *American Sociological Review* 53 (August 1988): 559–68.

94. Douglas M. Stayman and Rohit Deshpande, "Situational Ethnicity and Consumer Behavior," *Journal of Consumer Research* 16 (December 1989): 361–71.

95. Kevin G. Celuch and Linda S. Showers, "It's Time To Stress *Stress:* The Stress–Purchase/Consumption Relationship," in *Advances in Consumer Research,* ed. Rebecca H. Holman and Michael R. Solomon, (Provo, Utah: Association for Consumer Research, 1991)18: 284–89; Lawrence R. Lepisto, J. Kathleen Stuenkel, and Linda K. Anglin, "Stress: An Ignored Situational Influence," in *Advances in Consumer Research,* ed. Rebecca H. Holman and Michael R. Solomon, (Provo, Utah: Association for Consumer Research, 1991)18: 296–302

96. See Eben Shapiro, "Need a Little Fantasy? A Bevy of New Companies Can Help," *New York Times* (March 10, 1991): F4.

97. John D. Mayer and Yvonne N. Gaschke, "The Experience and Meta-Experience of Mood," *Journal of Personality and Social Psychology* 55 (July 1988): 102–11.

98. Meryl Paula Gardner, "Mood States and Consumer Behavior: A Critical Review," *Journal of Consumer Research* 12 (December 1985): 281–300.

99. Rajeev Batra and Douglas M. Stayman, "The Role of Mood in Advertising Effectiveness," *Journal of Consumer Research* 17 (September 1990): 203.

100. Gordon C. Bruner, "Music, Mood, and Marketing," *Journal of Marketing* 54 (October 1990): 94–104; Basil G. Englis, "Music Television and Its Influences on Consumers, Consumer Culture, and the Transmission of Consumption Messages," in *Advances in Consumer Research,* ed. Rebecca H. Holman and Michael R. Solomon, (Provo, Utah: Association for Consumer Research, 1991)18.

101. Marvin E. Goldberg and Gerald J. Gorn, "Happy and Sad TV Programs: How They Affect Reactions to Commercials," *Journal of Consumer Research* 14 (December 1987): 387–403.

102. Rama Jayanti and Anita Jackson, "Service Satisfaction: Investigation of Three Models," in *Advances in Consumer Research,* ed. Rebecca H. Holman and Michael R. Solomon, (Provo, Utah: Association for Consumer Research, 1991)18: 603–10; David K. Tse, Franco M. Nicosia, and Peter C. Wilton, "Consumer Satisfaction as a Process," *Psychology & Marketing* 7 (Fall 1990): 177–93.

103. Robert Jacobson and David A. Aaker, "The Strategic Role of Product Quality," *Journal of Marketing* 51 (October 1987): 31–44.

104. Anna Kirmani and Peter Wright, "Money Talks: Perceived Advertising Expense and Expected Product Quality," *Journal of Consumer Research* 16 (December 1989): 344–53; Donald R. Lichtenstein and Scot Burton, "The Relationship Between Perceived and Objective Price-Quality," *Journal of Marketing Research* 26 (November 1989): 429–43; Akshay R. Rao and Kent B. Monroe, "The Effect of Price, Brand Name, and Store Name on Buyers' Perceptions of Product Quality: An Integrative Review," *Journal of Marketing Research* 26 (August 1989): 351–57.

105. Shelby Hunt, "Post-Transactional Communication and Dissonance Reduction," *Journal of Marketing* 34 (January 1970): 46–51; Daniel E. Innis and H. Rao Unnava, "The Usefulness of Product Warranties for Reputable and New Brands," in *Advances in Consumer Research,* ed. Rebecca H. Holman and Michael R. Solomon, (Provo, Utah: Association for Consumer Research, 1991)18: 317–22; Terence A. Shimp and William O. Bearden, "Warranty and Other Extrinsic Cue Effects on Consumers' Risk Perceptions," *Journal of Consumer Research* 9 (June 1982): 38–46.

106. Morris B. Holbrook and Kim P. Corfman, "Quality and Value in the Consumption Experience: Phaedrus Rides Again," in *Perceived Quality: How Consumers View Stores and Merchandise,* ed. Jacob Jacoby and Jerry C. Olson (Lexington, Mass.: Lexington Books, 1985): 31–58.

107. Holbrook and Corfman, "Quality and Value in the Consumption Experience"; Robert M. Pirsig, *Zen and the Art of Motorcycle Maintenance: An Inquiry Into Values* (New York: Bantam Books, 1974).

108. Gilbert A. Churchill, Jr. and Carol F. Surprenant, "An Investigation into the Determinants of Customer Satisfaction," *Journal of Marketing Research* 19 (November 1983): 491–504; John E. Swan and I. Frederick Trawick, "Disconfirmation of Expectations and Satisfaction With a Retail Service," *Journal of Retailing* 57 (Fall 1981): 49–67; Peter C. Wilton and David K. Tse, "Models of Consumer Satisfaction Formation: An Extension," *Journal of Marketing Research* 25 (May 1988): 204–12.

109. John W. Gamble, "The Expectations Paradox: The More You Offer Customer, Closer You are to Failure," *Marketing News* (March 14, 1988): 38.

110. Mary C. Gilly and Betsy D. Gelb, "Post-Purchase Consumer Processes and the Complaining Consumer," *Journal of Consumer Research* 9 (December 1982): 323–28; Diane Halstead and Cornelia Dröge, "Consumer Attitudes Toward Complaining and the Prediction of Multiple Complaint Responses," in *Advances in Consumer Research,* ed. Rebecca H. Holman and Michael R. Solomon, (Provo, Utah: Association for Consumer Research, 1991)18: 210–16; Jagdip Singh, "Consumer Complaint Intentions and Behavior: Definitional and Taxonomical Issues," *Journal of Marketing* 52 (January 1988): 93–107.

111. Alan Andreasen and Arthur Best, "Consumers Complain—Does Business Respond?" *Harvard Business Review* 55 (July–August 1977): 93–101.

112. Ingrid Martin, "Expert-Novice Differences in Complaint Scripts," in *Advances in Consumer Research,* ed. Rebecca H. Holman and Michael R. Solomon, (Provo, Utah: Association for Consumer Research, 1991)18: 225–31; Marsha L. Richins, "A Multivariate Analysis of Responses to Dissatisfaction," *Journal of the Academy of Marketing Science* 15 (Fall 1987): 24–31.

113. Russell W. Belk, "The Role of Possessions in Constructing and Maintaining a Sense of Past," in *Advances in Consumer Research,* ed. Marvin E. Goldberg, Gerald Gorn, and Richard W. Pollay, (Provo, Utah: Association for Consumer Research, 1989)17: 669–76.

114. David E. Sanger, "For a Job Well Done, Japanese Enshrine the Chip," *New York Times* (December 11, 1990): A4.

115. James W. Hanson, "A Proposed Paradigm for Consumer Product Disposition Processes," *The Journal of Consumer Affairs* 14 (Summer 1980): 49–67.

116. Vicky Cahan, "Waste Not, Want Not? Not Necessarily," *Business Week* (July 17, 1989): 116.

117. Mike Tharp, "Tchaikovsky and Toilet Paper," *U.S. News and World Report* (December 1987): 62.
118. Jacob Jacoby, Carol K. Berning, and Thomas F. Dietvorst, "What About Disposition?" *Journal of Marketing* 41 (April 1977): 22–28.
119. John F. Sherry, Jr., "A Sociocultural Analysis of a Midwestern American Flea Market," *Journal of Consumer Research* 17 (June 1990): 13–30.
120. Diane Crispell, "Collecting Memories," *American Demographics* (November 1988): 38–42.
121. Allan J. Magrath, "If Used Product Sellers Ever Get Organized, Watch Out," *Marketing News* (June 25, 1990): 9; Kevin McCrohan and James D. Smith, "Consumer Participation in the Informal Economy," *Journal of the Academy of Marketing Science* 15 (Winter 1990), 62.
122. Quoted in Sherry, "A Sociocultural Analysis of a Midwestern American Flea Market."

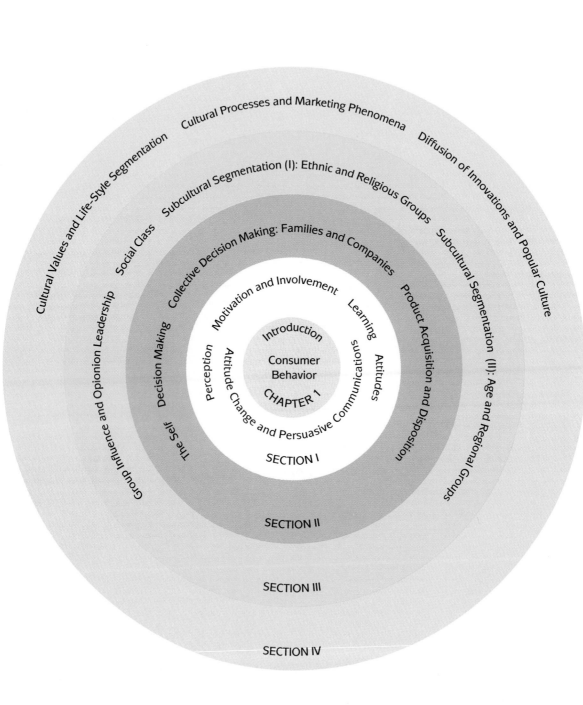

CHAPTER 1

Consumer Behavior

Introduction

SECTION I

Motivation and Involvement

Perception

Learning

Attitudes

Attitude Change and Persuasive Communications

The Self

SECTION II

Decision Making

Collective Decision Making: Families and Companies

Product Acquisition and Disposition

SECTION III

Group Influence and Opinion Leadership

Social Class

Subcultural Segmentation (I): Ethnic and Religious Groups

Subcultural Segmentation (II): Age and Regional Groups

SECTION IV

Cultural Values and Life-Style Segmentation

Cultural Processes and Marketing Phenomena

Diffusion of Innovations and Popular Culture

Although every person is an individual, he or she also is a member of many different groups. The bonds we form with others are an integral part of how we define ourselves. Our group memberships exert a big influence on how we think of ourselves and how we choose to live our lives. People truly are social animals, and many of our consumption decisions are best understood by looking at the types of collective identities that dictate what we buy, with whom we socialize, how we spend our leisure time, where we live, and so on.

In this section, we will explore the types of groups that determine our social identities. Chapter 11 provides an overview of groups and the reasons we are motivated to act in accord with group expectations. The chapter will also discuss how product information is conveyed through our social networks. The remaining three chapters in the section look at some specific ways we divide ourselves into social groups. Chapter 12 deals with social class and status; the kind of identification that results from income, education, and

The Consumer as a Social Entity

occupation. Chapters 13 and 14 consider the ways that our religious and ethnic backgrounds help to stamp our social identities and also how similar rites such as common ages or places of residence unite us. While each chapter "slices consumers up" in a different way, all of them taken together underscore the complex ways we forge common identities with those around us.

Group Influence and
Opinion Leadership

CHAPTER **11**

As soon as Zachary arrived on campus, he could pick out the fraternity men. Most of them stuck together, dressed a certain way, and even seemed to drive the same cars and drink the same beer. Not knowing exactly how to act, Zachary figured these guys must be good models to follow if he wanted to have a successful social life. As Zachary went through fraternity rush, he tried very hard to fit in at the houses that were considering him. He studied the brothers in each house carefully, and wherever possible he mimicked their product choices. When Zachary was accepted into Mu Delt, he was ecstatic. The only thing he wasn't too happy about was the prospect of Hell Week, where new inductees were pelted with eggs, covered with molasses and corn flakes, made to chug warm beer and jog for three miles . . . and that was just the parts he'd heard about. Still, Zachary was willing to endure even these indignities; he knew that those who survived the experience would be bonded for life.

The popularity of college fraternities is increasing. Fraternity membership in the United States rose from 151,000 in 1972 to over 400,000 in 1988. As Zachary knew, students often have to undergo elaborate, degrading, and sometimes dangerous rituals to join these groups. Fraternity hazing has been responsible for at least fifty deaths in the last ten years. To earn the privilege of joining a select group, students have been beaten, branded, buried, stabbed, shot, drowned, and frozen, usually while drunk.[1] On the other hand, the National Intrafraternity Conference announced plans in 1989 to start a campaign to eliminate hazing. According to the group's executive director, "Hazing has no place in the fraternity experience. . . . It is a dangerous form of intimidation that makes a mockery of fraternal love. . . ."[2]

REFERENCE GROUPS

Humans are social animals. We all belong to groups, try to please others, and take cues about how to behave by observing the actions of those around us. In fact, our desire to "fit in" or to identify with desirable individuals or groups is the primary motivation for many of our purchases and activities. As the fraternity hazing experience vividly illustrates, we will often go to great lengths to please the members of a group whose acceptance we covet.[3]

A **reference group** is ". . . an actual or imaginary individual or group conceived of having significant relevance upon an individual's evaluations, aspirations, or behavior."[4] Reference groups influence consumers in three ways. These influences, *informational, utilitarian,* and *value-expressive,* are described in Table 11-1.

TYPES OF REFERENCE GROUPS

Although two or more people are normally required to constitute a group, the term reference group often is used a bit more loosely to describe *any* external influence that provides social cues.[5] The referent may be a cultural figure and have an impact on many people (e.g., Martin Luther King, Jr.) or a person or group whose influence is confined to the consumer's immediate environment (e.g., the local bridge club or a favorite uncle). Reference groups that affect consumption may be parents, a girlfriend or boyfriend, the Communist party, or even the Chicago Bears, Elizabeth Taylor, or the Rolling Stones.

Obviously, some groups and individuals will exert a greater influence than others and for a broader range of consumption decisions. Our parents may play a pivotal role in forming our values toward many important issues, such as attitudes about marriage or where to go to college. This is **normative influence,** where a reference group helps to set and enforce fundamental standards of conduct. In contrast, a rock star like Madonna might exert **comparative influence,** where decisions about specific brands or activities are affected.[6]

FORMAL VERSUS INFORMAL GROUPS A reference group can take the form of a large, formal organization that has a recognized structure, complete with a charter, regular meeting times, and officers. Or it can be

TABLE 11-1 Three forms of reference group influence

1. Informational Influence	The individual seeks information about various brands of the product from an association of professionals or independent group of experts.
	The individual seeks information from those who work with the product as a profession.
	The individual seeks brand-related knowledge and experience (such as how Brand A's performance compares to Brand B's) from those friends, neighbors, relatives, or work associates who have reliable information about the brands.
	The brand the individual selects is influenced by observing a seal of approval of an independent testing agency (such as *Good Housekeeping*).
	The individual's observation of what experts do influences his or her choice of a brand (such as observing the type of car that police drive or the brand of television that repairmen buy).
2. Utilitarian Influence	To satisfy the expectations of fellow work associates, the individual's decision to purchase a particular brand is influenced by their preferences.
	The individual's decision to purchase a particular brand is influenced by the preferences of people with whom he or she has social interaction.
	The individual's decision to purchase a particular brand is influenced by the preferences of family members.
	The desire to satisfy the expectations that others have of him or her has an impact on the individual's brand choice.
3. Value-Expressive Influence	The individual feels that the purchase or use of a particular brand will enhance the image others have of him or her.
	The individual feels that those who purchase or use a particular brand possess the characteristics that he or she would like to have.
	The individual sometimes feels that it would be nice to be like the type of person that advertisements show using a particular brand.
	The individual feels that the people who purchase a particular brand are admired or respected by others.
	The individual feels that the purchase of a particular brand would help show others what he or she is or would like to be (such as an athlete, successful business person, good parent, etc.).

Source: Adapted from C. Whan Park and V. Parker Lessig, "Students and Housewives: Differences in Succeptibility to Reference Group Influence," *Journal of Consumer Research* 4 (September 1977): 102. Reprinted with permission by The University of Chicago Press.

small and informal, such as a group of friends or students living in a dormitory. Marketers tend to be more successful at influencing formal groups because they are more easily identifiable and accessible.

In general, small, informal groups are more powerful with individual consumers. These groups tend to be more involved in our day-to-day lives and to be more important to us, because they are high in *normative influence*. Larger, formal groups tend to be more product- or activity-specific, and thus are high in *comparative influence*.

MEMBERSHIP VERSUS ASPIRATIONAL REFERENCE GROUPS While some reference groups consist of people the consumer actually knows, others are composed either of people the consumer can *identify* with or admire. Not surprisingly, many marketing efforts that specifically adopt a reference group appeal concentrate on highly visible, widely admired figures (such as well-known athletes or performers).

Identificational Reference Groups. Since people tend to compare themselves to others who are similar, they often are swayed by knowing how people like them conduct their lives. For this reason, many promotional strategies include "ordinary" people whose consumption activities provide informational social influence. Recently, for example, MasterCard shifted the focus of its advertising away from glamorous, affluent professionals; the credit card company now highlights relatively ordinary activities—like a young man furnishing his first apartment (and, of course, using his MasterCard to pay for it). The campaign's slogan is "For the Way We Really Live."[7]

These "common man" or "slice-of-life" depictions, which highlight "real" people, are more realistic and thus more credible. While we admire perfect people, it can be frustrating to compare ourselves to them. By including people who are successful but not perfect, consumers' identification with them will be enhanced. This strategy has been successfully employed in the classic "Dewar's Profiles," a series of ads describing the lifestyles of non-celebrity high achievers who happen to drink Dewar's Scotch. A Spanish version is shown here.

The likelihood that people will become part of a consumer's identificational reference group is affected by several factors, including the following:

- *Propinquity.* As physical distance between people decreases and opportunities for interaction increase, relationships are more

Dewar's has successfully used non-celebrities as endorsers in its "Profiles" campaign. The campaign is now being adapted to other countries, as this Spanish ad illustrates. Courtesy of Schenley Industries Inc.

likely to form. Physical nearness is called *propinquity*. An early study on friendship patterns in a housing complex showed this factor's strong effects: Residents were much more likely to be friends with the people next door than with those who lived only two doors away. And, people who lived next to a staircase had more friends than those at the ends of a hall (presumably, they were more likely to "bump into" people using the stairs).[8] Physical structure has a lot to do with who we get to know and how popular we are.

- *Mere exposure.* We come to like persons or things simply as a result of seeing them more often. This is known as the *mere exposure phenomenon.*[9] Greater frequency of contact, even if unintentional, may help to determine one's set of local referents. The same effect holds when evaluating works of art, or even political candidates.[10] One study predicted 83 percent of the winners of political primaries solely by the amount of media exposure given to candidates.[11]

- *Group cohesiveness. Cohesiveness* refers to the degree that members of a group are attracted to each other and value their group membership. As the value of the group to the individual increases, so too does the likelihood that the group will guide consumption decisions. Smaller groups tend to be more cohesive, because it is more difficult to relate to larger groups of people. By the same token, groups often try to restrict membership to a select few. This increases the value of membership to those who are admitted. Exclusivity of membership is a benefit often touted by credit card companies, book clubs, and so on, even though the actual membership base might be fairly large.

Aspirational Reference Groups. The Mastercard campaign noted previously is taking a bit of a risk, since most credit card advertising is "aspirational." As one executive noted, "In this industry, you market to who you want to be, rather than who you are."[12]

Some reference groups are composed of idealized figures such as successful businesspeople, athletes, or performers. While the consumer may have no direct contact with them, these *aspirational reference groups* can have powerful influences on his or her tastes and preferences, because they provide guidance as to the types of products used by admired people.[13] For example, one study that included business students who aspired to the "Executive" role found a strong relationship between products they associated with their *ideal selves* (see Chapter 7) and those they assumed would be owned or used by executives.[14] This appeal to the ideal self is illustrated in the Hart, Schaffner & Marx ad.

POSITIVE VERSUS NEGATIVE REFERENCE GROUPS Reference groups may exert *either* a positive or a negative influence on consumption behaviors. In most cases, consumers model their behavior to be consistent with what they think the group expects of them. In some cases, though, a consumer may try to distance him- or herself from other people or groups that function as *avoidance groups*. He or she may carefully study the dress or mannerisms of a disliked group (e.g., "nerds," "druggies," or "preppies")

For many consumers, the successful executive is an aspirational role. This ad for Hart, Schaffner & Marx suits relies on the desire to emulate such role models by showing a real executive rather than a model wearing the company's clothing.   Courtesy of Hart, Schaffner & Marx.

and scrupulously avoid buying anything that might identify him or her with that group. For example, rebellious adolescents often resent parental influence and may deliberately do the opposite of what their parents would like as a way of making a statement about their independence. As Romeo and Juliet discovered, nothing makes a dating partner more attractive than a little parental opposition.

WHEN REFERENCE GROUPS ARE IMPORTANT

Reference group influences are not equally powerful for all types of products and consumption activities. For example, products that are not very complex, are low in perceived risk, and that can be tried prior to purchase, are less susceptible to personal influence.[15]

The specific impact of reference groups may vary. At times they may determine the use of certain products rather than others (e.g., owning or not owning a computer, eating junk food versus health food), while at other times they may have specific effects on brand decisions within a product category (e.g., wearing Levi's jeans versus Calvin Klein jeans, or smoking Marlboro cigarettes rather than Virginia Slims).

Two dimensions that influence the degree to which reference groups are important are whether the purchase is to be consumed publicly or privately and whether it is a luxury or a necessity. As a rule, reference group effects are more robust for purchases that are (1) luxuries rather than necessities (e.g., sailboats), since products that are purchased with discretionary income are subject to individual tastes and preferences, while necessities do not offer this range of choices; and (2) socially conspicuous or visible to others (e.g., living room furniture or clothing) since consumers do not tend to be swayed as much by the opinions of others if their purchases will never be observed by anyone but themselves.[16]

▲ MARKETING OPPORTUNITY

One of the most recent and widespread applications of reference group influences to consumer behavior is **affinity marketing.** This strategy allows consumers to underscore their identification with some organization by attaching the group's identification to aspects of their personal life.

In its most common form, banks promote special credit cards known as *affinity cards,* which can be tied to a membership group, such as a church or college alumni organization, or to a symbolic group, like an NFL team or a rock group.[17] Even priests and nuns have been targeted to adopt the Caritas card, issued by Catholic charities.[18] Use of these cards has surged since 1985, when rules regarding what could be pictured on a credit card were relaxed. It is estimated that there are over 2700 different affinity cards available, and they are carried by over 26 million people.[19] Even Elvis has appeared on a card.

THE POWER OF REFERENCE GROUPS
Social power refers to ". . . the capacity to alter the actions of others."[20] To the degree that you are able to make someone else do something, whether they do it willingly or not, you have power over that person. And, this power translates directly into consumption. The reasons for this power differ, however. Social power can be distinguished on several dimensions, including the following: (1) whether the action was done voluntarily (*private agreement*) and (2) whether the action would still be taken if the more powerful person or group was not present to monitor the situation (*surveillance*).

A classification of *power bases* will help us to distinguish among the reasons a person can exert power over another, the degree to which the desired behavior is done voluntarily, and whether this influence will continue to have an effect in the absence of the powerful person.[21] These types of power can be summarized as follows:

Referent Power. If a person admires the qualities of a person or a group, he or she will try to imitate those qualities by copying the referent's behaviors (e.g., choice of clothing, cars, leisure activities) as a guide to forming consumption preferences. Prominent people in all walks of life can affect people's consumption behaviors by virtue of product endorsements (e.g., Michael Jordan for Air Nike), distinctive fashion statements (e.g., Madonna's use of lingerie as outerwear), or championing causes (e.g., Jerry Lewis' work for muscular dystrophy). Referent power is important to many marketing strategies because consumers voluntarily change behaviors to please or identify with a referent and surveillance is not needed.

Information Power. A person can have power simply because he or she knows something others would like to know. Editors of trade publications such as *Women's Wear Daily* often possess a lot of power due to their ability to compile and disseminate information that can make or break individual designers or companies.

Legitimate Power. Sometimes people are granted power by virtue of social agreements, such as the power given to policemen and professors. The legitimate power conferred by a uniform is recognized in many consumer contexts, including teaching hospitals, where medical students don white coats to enhance their aura of authority with patients, and banks, where tellers' uniforms communicate trustworthiness.[22]

Expert Power. Expert power is derived from possessing a specific knowledge or skill. This power base underlies the ad for the television show shown here.

▲ MARKETING OPPORTUNITY

The power of celebrity experts can be measured by their visibility on talk shows, lecture circuits, and so on. Prominent economists, for example, can receive between $5000 and $20,000 for a speech, depending on their level of perceived expertise. One analysis of economist "superstars" noted these requirements for success:

- Affiliation with an elite university, think tank, or investment house
- Author of a slim, easy-reading book that yields a vision of the future
- An advisory relationship with at least one presidential candidate.[23]

The need to provide evidence of expert power creates other marketing opportunities, ranging from the provision of certificates and diplomas to coaching for licensing exams. A number of industries where the criteria for expertise are poorly defined are grappling with the need for *credentialing,* or defining what knowledge and experience is necessary to make a person an expert and providing a mechanism to weed out people who do not meet these criteria. Hitting close to home, the American Marketing Association periodically debates the need for licensing of its members as a way to boost the perceived professionalism of marketing research as a discipline.

This ad for the McLaughlin show appeals to viewers' appreciation of expert power. Courtesy of CNBC.

Reward Power. When a person or group has the means to provide *positive reinforcement* (see Chapter 4), that entity will have power over a consumer to the extent that this reinforcement is valued or desired. The reward may be tangible, as occurs when an employee is given a raise. Or, the reward may be intangible: Social approval or acceptance is often what is exchanged in return for molding one's behavior to a group or buying the products expected of group members. The Everlast ad pokes fun at reward power.

Coercive Power. A threatened individual may comply. While coercive power often is effective in the short-term, it does not tend to produce permanent attitudinal or behavioral change. Surveillance of some sort is usually required to make people do something they do not wish to do.

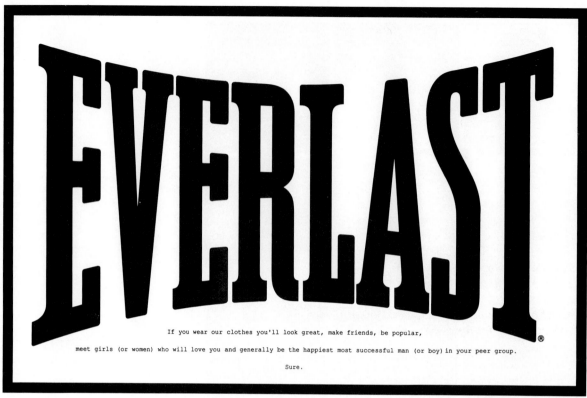

If you wear our clothes you'll look great, make friends, be popular,

meet girls (or women) who will love you and generally be the happiest most successful man (or boy) in your peer group.

Sure.

ACTIVEWEAR BY U.S.A. CLASSIC, INC.

Everlast apparel pokes fun at clothing's ability to make people popular. Courtesy of Goldsmith/Jeffrey, Inc., NY.

Fortunately, coercive power is rarely employed in marketing situations. However, elements of this power base are evident in fear appeals, intimidation in personal selling, and some campaigns that emphasize the negative consequences that might occur if people do not use a product.

CONFORMITY

In order for a society to function, its members develop **norms,** or informal rules that govern behavior. If such a system of agreements did not evolve, chaos would result. Imagine the confusion if a simple norm such as "stop for a red traffic light" did not exist. While norms change slowly over time, there is general agreement within a society about which ones should be obeyed.

As Zachary's experience attests, these unspoken rules govern many aspects of consumption. In addition to norms regarding appropriate use of clothing and other personal items, these include gift giving (we expect birthday presents from loved ones and get upset if they do not materialize), sex roles (men often are expected to pick up the check on a first date), and personal hygiene (we are expected to do laundry every so often and to shower regularly).

TYPES OF SOCIAL INFLUENCE

Just as the bases for social power can vary, the process of social influence operates in several ways.[24] Sometimes a person is motivated to model the behavior of others because this mimicry is believed to yield rewards such as social approval or money. At other times, the social influence process occurs simply because the person honestly does not *know* the correct way to respond, and is using the behavior of the other person or group as a cue to ensure that he or she is responding correctly.[25] **Normative social influence** occurs when a person conforms to meet the expectations of a person or group.

In contrast, **informational social influence** refers to conformity that occurs because the group's behavior is taken as *evidence* about reality: If other people respond in a certain way in an ambiguous situation, we may mimic their behavior because this appears to be the correct thing to do.[26] While Zachary undoubtedly valued the social approval of his fraternity, he also relied on the guidelines provided by the brothers' consumption patterns as a form of informational social influence.

REASONS FOR CONFORMITY   Conformity is not an automatic process, and many factors contribute to the likelihood that consumers will pattern their behavior after others.[27] Some of the factors that affect the likelihood of conformity include:

Cultural Pressures.   Different cultures encourage conformity to a greater or lesser degree. The American slogan "Do your own thing" in the 1960s reflected a movement away from conformity and toward individualism. In contrast, Japanese society is characterized by the dominance of collective well-being and group loyalty over individuals' needs.

Fear of Deviance.   The individual may have reason to believe that the group will apply *sanctions* to punish behavior that differs from the group's. It is not unusual to observe adolescents shunning a peer who is "different" or a corporation passing over a person for promotion because he or she is not a "team player."

Commitment.   The more a person is dedicated to a group and values membership in it, the more motivated he or she will be to follow the dictates of the group. Rock groupies and followers of television evangelists may do anything that is asked of them, and terrorists may be willing to die for the good of their cause. According to the *Principle of Least Interest,* the person or group that is least committed to staying in a relationship has the most power.[28]

Group Unanimity, Size, and Expertise.   As groups gain in power, compliance increases. It is often harder to resist the demands of a large number of people than just a few, and this difficulty is compounded when the group members are perceived to know what they are talking about.

Sex Differences. It has often been assumed that women are more susceptible than men to interpersonal influence, since they are more sensitive to social cues and tend to be more group-oriented and cooperative in nature. However, recent indications show this reasoning as flawed: Both men and women who possess feminine personality traits tend to conform more (see Chapter 7).[29]

SOCIAL COMPARISON: "HOW'M I DOING?"

Informational social influence implies that sometimes we look to the behavior of others to provide a yardstick about reality. **Social comparison theory** asserts that this process occurs as a way to increase the stability of one's self-evaluation, especially when physical evidence is unavailable.[30] Social comparison even applies to choices for which there is no objectively correct answer. Such stylistic decisions as tastes in music and art are assumed to be a matter of individual choice, yet people often assume that some types are "better" or more "correct" than others.[31] If you have ever been responsible for choosing the music to play at a party, you can probably appreciate the social pressure involved in choosing the right "mix."

CHOOSING COMPARISON GROUPS Though people often like to compare their judgments and actions to others', they tend to be selective about precisely whom they will use as benchmarks. Similarity between the consumer and others used for social comparison boosts confidence that the information is accurate and relevant (though we may find it more threatening to be outperformed by someone similar to ourselves).[32] We tend to value the views of obviously dissimilar others only when we are reasonably certain of our own.[33]

Birds of a Feather. In general people tend to choose a *co-oriented peer,* or a person of equivalent standing, when undergoing social comparison. For example, a study of adult cosmetics users found that women were more likely to seek information about product choices from similar friends to reduce uncertainty and to trust the judgments of similar others.[34] The same effects have been found for evaluations of products as diverse as men's suits and coffee.[35]

COMPLIANCE AND OBEDIENCE

The discussion of persuasive communications in Chapter 6 indicated that source and message characteristics have a big impact on the likelihood of influence. Influencers have been found to be more successful at gaining compliance if they are perceived to be confident or expert.[36] In addition, the way a request is phrased can influence the likelihood of compliance.

TACTICAL REQUESTS The way a request for compliance is phrased or structured can make a difference. One well-known sales tactic is known as the *foot-in-the-door technique,* where the consumer is first asked a small request and then is hit up for something bigger.[37] This term is adapted from door-to-door selling. Experienced salespeople know that they are much more likely to make a sale if they first convince a customer to let them in the house to deliver a sales pitch. Once the person has agreed to this small request, it is more difficult to refuse a larger one, since the consumer has legitimized the salesperson's presence by entering into a dialogue. He or she is no longer a threatening stranger at the door.

Other variations on this strategy include the *low-ball technique,* where a person is asked for a small favor and is informed after agreeing to it that it will be very costly, or the *door-in-the-face technique,* where a person is first asked to do something extreme (a request that is usually refused), and then is asked to do something smaller. People tend to go along with the smaller request, possibly because they feel guilty about denying the larger one.[38]

GROUP EFFECTS ON INDIVIDUAL BEHAVIOR With more people in a group, it becomes less likely any one member will be singled out for attention. People in larger groups or those in situations where they are likely to be unidentified tend to focus less attention on themselves, so normal restraints on behavior are reduced. You may have observed that people sometimes behave more wildly at costume parties or on Halloween night than they do normally. This phenomenon is known as **deindividuation,** where individual identities get submerged within a group. The deindividuating qualities of Halloween costumes may be a reason for their immense popularity (see Chapter 16).

Shopping Patterns. Shopping behavior changes when people do it in groups. For example, people who shop with at least one other person tend to make more unplanned purchases, buy more, and cover more areas of a store than those who go alone.[39] These effects are due to both normative and informational social influence. Group members may be convinced to buy something to gain the approval of the others, or they may simply be exposed to more products and stores by pooling information with the group. For these reasons, retailers would be well advised to encourage group shopping activities.

Social Loafing. *Social loafing* refers to the fact that people do not devote as much to a task when their contribution is part of a larger group effort.[40] Waitresses are painfully aware of social loafing: People who eat in groups tend to tip less per person than when they are eating alone.[41] This explains why many restaurants automatically tack on a fixed gratuity for groups of six or more.

The Risky Shift. There is some evidence that decisions made by groups differ from those that would be made by each individual. In many cases, group members show a greater willingness to consider riskier alternatives following group discussion than they would if each member made his or her own decision with no discussion. This is known as the *risky shift.*[42]

Several explanations have been advanced to explain this increased riskiness. One possibility is that something similar to social loafing occurs. As more people are involved in a decision, each individual is less accountable for the outcome, so *diffusion of responsibility* occurs.[43] Another explanation is termed the *value hypothesis.* Riskiness is a culturally valued characteristic, and social pressures operate on individuals to conform to attributes valued by society.[44]

Evidence for the risky shift is mixed. A more general effect appears to be that group discussion tends to increase **decision polarization.** Whichever direction the group members were leaning before discussion began, toward a risky choice or toward a conservative choice, becomes even more extreme in that direction after discussion. Group discussions regarding product purchases tend to create a risky shift for low-risk items, but they yield even more conservative group decisions for high-risk products.[45]

MARKETING OPPORTUNITY

Home shopping parties, as epitomized by the Tupperware Party, capitalize on group pressures to boost sales.[46] A company representative makes a sales presentation to a group of people who have gathered in the home of a friend or acquaintance. This format is effective because of informational social influence: Participants model the behavior of others who can provide them with information about how to use certain products, especially since the home party is likely to be attended by a relatively homogeneous group (e.g., neighborhood housewives) that serves as a valuable benchmark. Normative social influence also operates because actions are publicly observed. Pressures to conform may be particularly intense and may escalate as more and more group members begin to "cave in" (this is sometimes termed the *bandwagon effect*). In addition, deindividuation and/or the risky shift may be activated: As consumers get caught up in the group, they may find themselves willing to try new products they would not normally consider.

An updated, more risqué version of the home party is performed by the UndercoverWear company, whose 35,000 agents assemble groups of women in homes to demonstrate their wares. The company features lingerie and related items for men and women with names such as "French Kiss" and "Girls Just Want to Have Fun." Agents rely on the deindividuation process to overcome normal inhibitions about such intimate purchases. They break the ice with a "Sensuality Test" containing questions about participants' sex lives. The "winner" receives a "Good in Bed" necklace.[47]

RESISTANCE TO INFLUENCE

Many people pride themselves on their independence, unique style, or ability to resist the best efforts of salespeople and advertisers to buy products.[48] Indeed, individuality should be encouraged by the marketing system: Innovation creates change and demand for new products and styles, as demonstrated by the car sound system ad shown on page 367.

ANTICONFORMITY VERSUS INDEPENDENCE   It is important to distinguish between *independence* and *anticonformity,* where defiance of the group

He's a non-conformist, loves music and drives a Ford JBL Audio System.

He is not the kind of person who would be comfortable as a part of the in-crowd. In fact, he avoids crowds altogether, preferring the excitement of wide open spaces and wide open sound. That's why he drives a Ford JBL Audio System in the all new 1991 Ford Explorer. The result of a joint design effort by Ford and JBL that has created a premier high performance automotive sound system. Hear it for yourself at your Ford or Lincoln-Mercury dealer. The optional Ford JBL Audio System, the Sound of Quality in selected Ford, Mercury, and Lincoln vehicles.

AUDIO SYSTEMS
The Sound of Quality

This ad for Ford audio systems appeals to non-conformists by depicting a "loner" who prefers the wide open spaces to groups of people. Courtesy of Ford Motor Company.

is the actual object of behavior.[49] You may know people who will go out of their way *not* to buy whatever happens to be "in" at the moment. Indeed, they may spend a lot of time and effort to ensure that they will not be caught in style. This behavior is a bit of a paradox, since in order to be vigilant about not doing what is expected, one must always be aware of what *is* expected. In contrast, truly independent people are oblivious to what is expected; they "march to their own drummers."

In a sense, the anticonformist is also conforming, since his or her behaviors are directly influenced by the expectations of a group, but in the opposite direction. And, this form of "anti-fashion" often becomes the fashion when entire groups of consumers deliberately structure their consumption to counter current trends. Some examples of this phenomenon include the mass adoption of the "hippie" uniform in the 1960s and the exodus from designer goods with prominent logos in the late 1980s.

The Need for Freedom. People have a deep-seated need to pre-serve freedom of choice. When they are threatened with a loss of this freedom, they try to overcome this loss. This negative emotional state is termed **reactance.**[50]

Efforts to censor books, television shows, or rock music because some people find the content objectionable may result in an *increased* desire for these products by the public.[51] Similarly, extremely overbearing promotions that tell consumers they must or should use a product may wind up losing more customers in the long run, even those who were already loyal to the advertised brand! Reactance is more likely to occur when the perceived threat to one's freedom increases and as the threatened behavior's importance to the consumer also increases.

The Need for Uniqueness. If you have ever shown up at a party wearing the same outfit as someone else, you know how upsetting this can be. Some psychologists believe this reaction is a result of a need for uniqueness.[52] Consumers who have been led to believe they are not unique are more likely to try to compensate by increasing their creativity, or even to engage in unusual experiences. In fact, this could be one explanation for the purchase of relatively obscure brands. People may try to establish a unique identity by deliberately *not* buying market leaders.

WORD-OF-MOUTH COMMUNICATION

Despite the abundance of formal means of communication (such as newspapers, magazines, and television), much information about the world actually is conveyed by individuals on an informal basis. If you think carefully about the content of your own conversations in the course of a normal day, you will probably agree that much of what you discuss with friends, family members, or co-workers is product-related: Whether you compliment someone on her dress and ask her where she bought it, recommend a new restaurant to a friend, or complain to your neighbor about the shoddy treatment you got at the bank, you are engaging in **word-of-mouth communication.**

Information obtained from those we know or talk with directly tends to be more reliable and trustworthy than that received through more formal channels, and unlike advertising, it is often backed up by social pressure to conform with these recommendations.[53] The importance of personal, informal product communication to marketers is underscored by one advertising executive, who stated "Today, 80 percent of all buying decisions are influenced by someone's direct recommendations."[54]

THE DOMINANCE OF WORD-OF-MOUTH COMMUNICATION
Communications theorists began in the 1950s to challenge the assumption that advertising is the primary determinant of purchases: It is now generally accepted that advertising is more effective at reinforcing existing product preferences than at creating new ones.[55] Studies in both industrial and consumer purchase settings underscore the idea that while information from impersonal sources is important for creating brand awareness, word-

of-mouth is relied upon in the later stages of evaluation and adoption.[56] The more positive information a consumer gets about a product from peers, the more likely he or she will adopt the product.[57] The influence of others' opinions is at times even more powerful than one's own perceptions. In one study of furniture choices, for example, consumers' estimates of how much their friends would like the furniture was a better predictor of purchase than their *own* evaluations.[58]

FACTORS INITIATING WORD-OF-MOUTH Product-related conversations can be motivated by a number of factors.[59]

- A person might be highly involved with a type of product or activity and get pleasure in talking about it. Computer hackers, avid birdwatchers, and "fashion plates" seem to share the ability to steer a conversation toward their particular interest.
- A person might be knowledgeable about a product and use conversations as a way to let others know it. Thus, word-of-mouth communication sometimes enhances the ego of the individual who wants to impress others with his or her expertise.
- A person might initiate such a discussion out of a genuine concern for someone else. We often are motivated to ensure that people we care about buy what is good for them, do not waste their money, and so on.
- One way to reduce uncertainty about the wisdom of a purchase is to talk about it. This gives the consumer an opportunity to generate more supporting arguments for the purchase and garner support for this decision from others.

EFFICIENCY OF WORD-OF-MOUTH Interpersonal transmissions can be quite rapid. The producers of the movie *Batman* showed a trailer to 300 Batman fans months prior to its release to counteract widespread anger about the casting of Michael Keaton as the star. The filmmakers attribute the film's eventual huge success to the positive word-of-mouth that quickly spread following the screening.[60]

Word-of-mouth is especially powerful in cases where the consumer is relatively unfamiliar with the product category. Such a situation would be expected in cases where the product is new (e.g., medications to prevent hair loss) or is technologically complex (e.g., CD players). As one example, the strongest predictor of a person's intention to buy a residential solar water heating system was found to be the number of solar heating users the person knows.[61]

NEGATIVE WORD-OF-MOUTH AND RUMOR TRANSMISSION

Word-of-mouth is a two-edged sword that can cut both ways for marketers. Informal discussions among consumers can make or break a product or store. And, negative word-of-mouth is weighted *more* heavily by consumers than are positive comments. Especially when making a decision about trying a product innovation, the consumer is more likely to pay attention to negative information than positive information—and to relate news of this experience to others.[62]

In general, people have been shown to prefer transmitting good news rather than bad, perhaps because they like to avoid unpleasantness or arousing hostility. This is known as the *MUM Effect*.[64] However, this reluctance does not appear to hold when companies are the topic of conversation. Corporations such as Procter & Gamble and McDonald's have been the subjects of rumors about their products, sometimes with noticeable effects on sales.

Rumors are thought to reveal the underlying fears of a society. For example, one rumor regarding snakes coming out of teddy bears imported from the Orient was interpreted to signify Western consumers' apprehensions about Asian influences. While rumors sometimes die out by themselves, in other instances a company may take direct action to counteract them. A French margarine was rumored to contain contaminants, and the company addressed this in its advertising by referring to the story as "The rumor that costs you dearly."[65]

Several marketers in Indonesia, including Nestlé, recently have been hurt by rumors that their foods contain pork, which is prohibited to the 160 million Moslem consumers in that country. Islamic preachers, or mullahs, responded to these rumors by warning consumers not to buy products that might be tainted with pork fat. Nestlé has already spent $250,000 on an ad campaign to counteract the rumors, and a noodle manufacturer plans to spend up to $500,000 to salvage its brand.[66]

DISTORTION IN THE WORD-OF-MOUTH PROCESS In the 1930s, "professional rumor mongers" were hired to organize word-of-mouth campaigns to promote clients' products and criticize those of competitors'.[63] A rumor, even if it has no basis in fact, can be a very dangerous thing. As information is transmitted among consumers, it tends to change. The resulting message usually does not at all resemble the original.

Social scientists who study rumors have examined the process by which information gets distorted. The British psychologist Frederic Bartlett used the method of *serial reproduction* to examine this phenomenon. As in the game of "Telephone," a subject is asked to reproduce a stimulus, such as a drawing or a story. Another subject is given this reproduction and asked to copy that, and so on. This technique is shown in Figure 11-1.

Bartlett found that distortions almost inevitably follow a pattern: They tend to change from ambiguous forms to more conventional ones as subjects try to make them consistent with pre-existing schemas. This process, known as *assimilation,* is characterized by *leveling,* where details are omitted to simplify the structure, or *sharpening,* where prominent details are accentuated.

OPINION LEADERSHIP

Though consumers get information from personal sources, they do not tend to ask just *anyone* for advice about purchases. If you decide to buy a new stereo, you will most likely seek advice from a friend who knows a lot about sound systems. This friend may own a sophisticated system, or he or she may subscribe to specialized magazines like *Stereo Review,* and spend free time browsing through electronics stores. On the other hand, you may have another friend who has a reputation for being stylish and who spends *his* free time reading *Gentlemen's Quarterly* and shopping at trendy boutiques. While you might not bring up your stereo problem with him, you may take him with you to shop for a new fall wardrobe.

THE NATURE OF OPINION LEADERS

Everyone knows people who are knowledgeable about products and whose advice is taken seriously by others. These individuals are **opinion leaders.** An opinion leader is a person who is frequently able to influence others' attitudes or behaviors.[67] Opinion leaders are extremely valuable information sources for a number of reasons.

1. They are technically competent and thus are convincing because they possess expert power.[68]

Figure 11-1 The Transmission of Misinformation. This is a classic example of the distortions that can occur as information is transmitted from person to person. As each participant reproduces the figure, it gradually changes from an owl to a cat. Source: Kenneth J. Gergen and Mary Gergen, *Social Psychology* (New York: Harcourt Brace Jovanovich, 1981), 365, fig. 10-3 (adapted from F. C. Bartlett, *Remembering* (Cambridge, England: Cambridge University Press, 1932).

2. They have prescreened, evaluated, and synthesized product information in an unbiased way, so they possess knowledge power.[69] Unlike commercial endorsers, opinion leaders do not actually represent the interests of one company. They are more credible because they have no "axe to grind."

3. Opinion leaders tend to be socially active and highly interconnected in their community.[70] They are likely to hold office in community groups and clubs and to be active outside of the home. As a result, opinion leaders often have legitimate power by virtue of their social standing.

4. They tend to be similar to the consumer in terms of their values and beliefs, so they possess referent power.
   While opinion leaders are set apart by their interest or expertise in a product category, they are more convincing to the extent that they are *homophilous* rather than *heterophilous. Homophily* refers to the degree that a pair of individuals is similar in terms of education, social status, and beliefs.[71] Effective opinion leaders tend to be slightly higher than those they influence in terms of status and educational attainment but not so high as to be in a different social class.

5. Opinion leaders often are among the first to buy new products, so they absorb much of the risk. This experience reduces uncertainty for others who are not as courageous. And, while company-sponsored communications tend to focus exclusively on the positive aspects of a product, this hands-on experience makes opinion leaders more likely to impart *both* positive and negative information about product performance.

THE EXTENT OF AN OPINION LEADER'S INFLUENCE When marketers and social scientists initially developed the concept of the opinion leader, it was assumed that certain influential people in a community would exert an overall impact on group members' attitudes. Later work, however, began to question the assumption that there is such a thing as a *generalized opinion leader,* somebody whose recommendations are sought for all types of purchases.

Very few people are capable of being expert in a number of fields. Sociologists distinguish between those who are *monomorphic,* or experts in a limited field, and those who are *polymorphic,* or experts in several fields.[72] Even opinion leaders who are polymorphic tend to concentrate on one broad domain, such as electronics or fashion.

Research on opinion leadership generally indicates that while opinion leaders do exist for multiple product categories, expertise tends to overlap across similar categories. It is rare to find a generalized opinion leader. An opinion leader for home appliances is likely to serve a similar function for home cleaners, but not for cosmetics. In contrast, a *fashion opinion leader* whose primary influence is on clothing choices may also be consulted for recommendations on cosmetics purchases, but not necessarily on microwave ovens.[73]

OPINION LEADERS VERSUS OTHER CONSUMER TYPES Early conceptions of the opinion leader role also assumed a static process: The opinion leader absorbs information from the mass media, and in turn transmits these data to opinion receivers. This has turned out to be an overly simplified view of the communication process; it confuses the functions of several different types of consumers.

Innovative Communicators. Opinion leaders may or may not be purchasers of the products they recommend. Early purchasers are known as innovators. Opinion leaders who are also early purchasers have been termed *innovative communicators.*

One study identified a number of characteristics of college men who were innovative communicators for fashion products. These men were among the first to buy new fashions, and their fashion opinions were incorporated by other students in their own clothing decisions. They could be described as follows:

- They were socially active.
- They were appearance-conscious and narcissistic (i.e., they were quite fond of themselves and self-centered).
- They were involved in rock culture.
- They were heavy magazine readers, including *Playboy* and *Sports Illustrated.*
- They were likely to own more clothing, and a broader range of styles, than other students.
- Their intellectual interests were relatively limited.[74]

Opinion Seekers. Opinion leaders also are likely to be *opinion seekers.* They are generally more involved in a product category and actively search for information. As a result, they are more likely to talk about products with others and to solicit others' opinions as well.

Contrary to the static view of opinion leadership, most product-related conversation does not take place in a "lecture" format, where one person does all of the talking. A lot of product-related conversation is prompted by the situation and occurs in the context of a casual interaction rather than as formal instruction.[75] One study, which found that opinion seeking is especially high for food products, revealed that two-thirds of opinion seekers also view themselves as opinion leaders.[76] This updated view of interpersonal product communication is contrasted with the traditional view in Figure 11-2.

Marketing Mavens. Consumers who are expert in a product category may not actively communicate with others, while other consumers may have a more general interest in being involved in product discussions. A consumer category called the *marketing maven* has been proposed to describe people who are actively involved in diffusing marketplace information of all types.[77]

Marketing mavens are not necessarily interested in certain products and may not necessarily be early purchasers of products. They come closer to the function of a generalized opinion leader because they tend to have a solid overall knowledge of how and where to procure products. Table 11-2 compares mavens with opinion leaders and early purchasers in terms of their potential for being reached by marketing efforts.

IDENTIFYING OPINION LEADERS

Because opinion leaders are so central to consumer decision making, marketers are quite interested in identifying influential people for a product category. In fact, many ads are intended to reach these influentials rather than the average consumer. This is especially true of ads that contain a lot of technical information. The average television purchaser probably would not be excited by an ad for a Pioneer projection television that claims to have a lens with a "maximum bore of 160 mm" and a "new high-voltage stabilizing circuit."[78] On the other hand, an electronics buff might be quite impressed by this information, and in turn take it into consideration when recommending a projection television to a more naive friend.

Unfortunately, since most opinion leaders are everyday consumers and are not formally included in marketing efforts, they are harder to find. A celebrity or an influential industry executive is by definition easy to locate. He or she has national or at least regional visibility or may be listed in published directories. In contrast, opinion leaders tend to operate at the local level and may influence five to ten consumers rather than an entire market segment. In some cases, companies have been known to identify influentials and involve them directly in their marketing efforts, hoping to create a "ripple effect" as these consumers sing the company's praises to their friends. Many department stores, for example, have fashion "panels," usually composed of adolescent girls, who provide input into fashion trends, participate in fashion shows, and so on.

Figure 11-2 Perspectives on the Communications Process

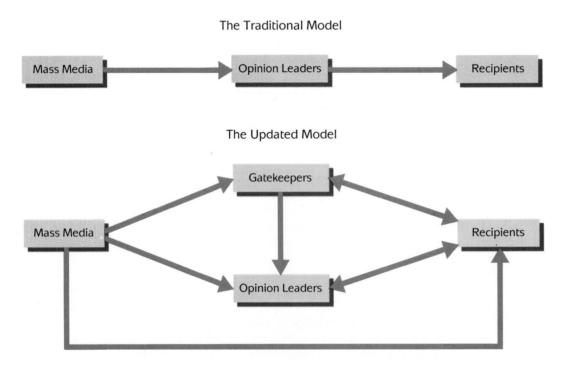

TABLE 11-2 A comparison of three types of influential consumers

Best Prospect Characteristics	Market Mavens	Opinion Leaders	Early Purchasers
1. Knowledge about many different goods & services.	• •	• •	•
2. Knowledge about shopping strategies and the marketplace generally.	• •	•	•
3. Important sources of information in finding out about new products:			
A. Broadcast Media	• •	•	• •
B. Print Media	• •	•	• •
C. Interpersonal Sources	• •	•	•
D. Browsing Shopping	• •	•	• •
4. Early knowers of new goods and services.	• •	•	• •
5. Early triers of new goods and services.	•	•	• •
6. Proactive in giving information and advice to others about goods and services and shopping strategies.	• •	•	•
7. Likely to influence other consumers.	• •	• •	•

Source: Adapted from Lawrence F. Feick and Linda L. Price, "The Market Maven," *Managing* (July 1985): 13.

MARKETING PITFALL

The power of opinion leadership has been exploited in the athletic shoe market. Athletic shoes are very much a fashion statement and a phenomena largely fueled by inner city kids, despite price tags of $100 and more.

Many of the sneaker styles originate in the inner city and then spread outward by word-of-mouth. As one marketer noted, "The urban kid stands for hard-core experience. . . . That, to a youth in the suburbs, represents authenticity." Manufacturers pay close attention to inner-city trend-setters and try to woo them to "endorse" their styles. Nike flew over twenty owners of sporting goods stores in urban areas to Chicago to find out how to influence inner-city kids. Converse spent a year talking to groups of kids in cities before rolling out its "Bold" line, and Avia tests its models on inner-city focus groups before going national. Reebok does its part by repaving basketball courts to curry favor with young opinion leaders.

In addition to paying a few major athletes to endorse shoes (Michael Jordan earns about $1.6 million a year to endorse Nike's Air Jordans), sneaker companies pay many high school and college coaches to outfit team players with their footwear, since this provides exposure and credibility when other kids see their role models wearing a certain type of shoe. A coach can earn as much as $200,000 a year to participate in this kind of promotional arrangement.[79]

Because of the difficulties involved in identifying specific opinion leaders in a large market, most attempts to do so instead focus on exploratory studies where the characteristics of representative opinion leaders can be identified and then generalized to the larger market. This knowledge helps marketers to target their product-related information to appropriate settings and media. For example, one attempt to identify *financial opinion leaders* found that these consumers were more likely to be involved in managing their own finances and tended to use a computer to do so. They also were more likely to follow their investments on a daily basis and to read books and watch television shows devoted to financial issues.[80]

THE SELF-DESIGNATING METHOD The most commonly used technique to identify opinion leaders is simply to ask individual consumers whether they consider themselves to be opinion leaders. A typical measurement scale used for this purpose is shown in Figure 11-3.

Figure 11-3 Opinion Leadership Scale King, Charles W. and John O. Summers (1970), "Overlap of Opinion Leadership Across Consumer Product Categories," *Journal of Marketing Research*, 7 (February), 43-50.

1) In general, do you like to talk about _____ with your friends?

    Yes___ −1   No___ −2

2) Would you say *you give very little information, an average amount of information,* or *a great deal of information* about _____ to your friends?

    You give very little information   ___ −1

    You give an average amount of information   ___ −2

    You give a great deal of information   ___ −3

3) During the *past six months,* have *you told anyone* about some _____?

    Yes___ −1   No___ −2

4) Compared with your circle of friends, are you *less likely, about as likely,* or *more likely* to be asked for advice about _____?

    Less likely to be asked   ___ −1

    About as likely to be asked   ___ −2

    More likely to be asked   ___ −3

5) If you and your friends were to discuss _____, what part would you be most likely to play? Would you *mainly listen* to your friends' ideas or would *you try to convince them* of your ideas?

    You mainly listen to your friends' ideas   ___ −1

    You try to convince them of your ideas   ___ −2

6) Which of these happens more often? Do *you tell your* friends about some _____, or do *they tell you* about some _____?

    You tell them about _____ ___ −1

    They tell you about some _____ ___ −2

7) Do you have the feeling that you are generally regarded by your friends and neighbors as a good source of advice about _____?

    Yes___ −1   No___ −2

Problems with Self-Designation. While respondents who report a greater degree of interest in a product category are more likely to be opinion leaders, results must be viewed with some skepticism, since some people have a tendency to inflate their own importance and influence, while others who really are influential might not admit to this quality.[81]

Just because we transmit advice about products does not mean other people *take* that advice. For someone to be considered a bona fide opinion leader, his or her advice must actually be heard and heeded by opinion seekers. While the self-designating method therefore is not as reliable as a more systematic analysis (where individual claims of influence can be verified by asking others whether the person is really influential), it does have the advantage of being easy to administer to a large group of potential opinion leaders. In some cases not all members of a community are surveyed. An alternative is to select certain group members (*key informants*) who in turn are asked to identify opinion leaders. The success of this approach hinges on locating those who have accurate knowledge of the group and on minimizing their response biases (e.g., the tendency to inflate one's own influence on the choices of others).

SOCIOMETRY *Sociometric methods,* which trace communication patterns among group members, allow researchers to systematically map out the interactions that take place among group members. By interviewing participants and asking them who they go to for product information, those who tend to be sources of product-related information can be identified. While this method is the most precise, it is very hard and expensive to implement, since it involves very close study of interaction patterns in small groups. For this reason, sociometric techniques are best applied in a closed, self-contained social setting where members are largely isolated from other social networks—good prospects include hospitals, prisons, and army bases.

Tracing Referrals. Many professionals and services marketers depend primarily upon word-of-mouth to generate business. In many cases consumers recommend a service provider to a friend or coworker, and in other cases other businesspeople will make recommendations to their customers. For example, only 0.2 percent of respondents in one study reported choosing a physician based on advertising. Advice from family and friends was the most widely used criterion.[82] This crucial referral process is depicted in the bank ad shown here.

Sociometric analyses can be used to better understand *referral behavior* and to locate strengths and weaknesses in terms of how one's reputation is communicated through a community. *Network analysis* focuses on communication in social systems, considers the relations among people in a *referral network,* and measures the *tie strength* among them. Tie strength refers to the nature of the bond between people. It can range from strong primary (e.g., one's spouse) to weak secondary (e.g., an acquaintance that one rarely sees). A strong tie relationship may be thought of as a primary reference group; interactions are frequent and important to the individual.

This ad for Chemical Bank implies that many purchase decisions are made on the basis of personal recommendations, rather than because of persuasive advertising. Reprinted by Permission of Chemical Bank, New York. Copyright 1990 Chemical Bank.

While strong ties are important, weak ties can provide a *bridging function.* This type of connection allows a consumer access between subgroups. For example, you might have a regular group of friends who serve as a primary reference group (strong ties). If you have an interest in tennis, say, one of these friends might introduce you to a group of people in her dorm who play on the tennis team. As a result, you gain access to their valuable expertise through this bridging function. This referral process demonstrates "the strength of weak ties."

One study using this method examined similarities in brand choice among members of a college sorority. The researchers found evidence that subgroups, or *cliques,* within the sorority were likely to share preferences for various products. In some cases, even choices of "private" (i.e., socially inconspicuous products) were shared, possibly because of structural variables such as sharing bathrooms in the sorority house.[83]

A recent study analyzed the referral networks of a services marketer (in this case, a piano tuner) to demonstrate how referral patterns can be better understood. The researchers contacted all of the piano tuner's customers and asked them how they found out about him (referral paths). Through a series of steps, the paths were identified, and the researchers were able to describe where business was being generated (whether through friends, business contacts, etc.) and also to pinpoint opinion leaders in the system (i.e., people who were a referral source for more than one customer).[84] This technique could conceivably be applied by many service providers to identify those customers who are responsible for generating a lot of business.

CHAPTER SUMMARY

Consumers belong to or admire many different groups and are often influenced in their purchase decisions by a desire to be accepted by others. Individuals have influence in a group to the extent that they possess social power; types of power include information power, referent power, legitimate power, expert power, reward power, and coercive power.

We conform to the desires of others for one of two basic reasons. People who model their behavior after others because they take others' behavior as evidence of the correct way to act are conforming because of informational social influence. Those who conform to satisfy the expectations of others and/or to be accepted by the group are affected by normative social influence. Group members often do things they would not do as individuals because their identities become merged with the group; they become deindividuated.

Individuals or groups whose opinions or behavior are particularly important to consumers are reference groups. Both formal and informal groups influence the individual's purchase decisions, though the impact of reference group influence is affected by such factors as the conspicuousness of the product and the relevance of the reference group for a particular purchase. In particular, opinion leaders who are knowledgeable about a product and whose opinions are highly regarded tend to influence others' choices. Specific opinion leaders are somewhat hard to identify, but marketers who know their general characteristics can try to target them in their media and promotional strategies.

Much of what we know about products comes about through word-of-mouth communication rather than formal advertising. Product-related information tends to be exchanged in casual conversations. While this process often is helpful for making consumers aware of products, it can also hurt companies when damaging product rumors or negative word-of-mouth occur.

KEY TERMS

Affinity marketing	**Norms**
Comparative influence	**Opinion leaders**
Decision polarization	**Reactance**
Deindividuation	**Reference group**
Informational social influence	**Social comparison theory**
Normative influence	**Social power**
Normative social influence	**Word-of-mouth communication**

1. Compare and contrast the five bases of power described in the text. Which are most likely to be relevant for marketing efforts?
2. Why is referent power an especially potent force for marketing appeals? What are factors that help to predict whether reference groups will or will not be a powerful influence on a person's purchase decisions?
3. Evaluate the strategic soundness of the concept of affinity marketing. For what type of linkages is this strategy most likely to be a success?
4. Discuss some factors that determine the amount of conformity likely to be observed among consumers.
5. Under what conditions are we more likely to engage in social comparison with dissimilar others versus similar others? How might this dimension be used in the design of marketing appeals?
6. Discuss some reasons for the effectiveness of home shopping parties as a selling tool. What factors might reduce the power of this strategy?
7. Discuss some factors that influence whether or not membership groups will have a significant influence on a person's behavior.
8. Why is word-of-mouth communication often more persuasive than advertising?
9. Is there such a thing as a generalized opinion leader? What is likely to determine if an opinion leader will be influential with regard to a specific product category?
10. The adoption of a certain brand of shoe or apparel by athletes can be a powerful influence on students and other fans. Should high school and college coaches be paid to determine what brand of athletic equipment their players will wear?

1. The power of unspoken social norms often becomes obvious only when these norms are violated. To witness this first hand, try one of the following:
   - stand facing the back wall in an elevator
   - serve dessert before the main course
   - offer to pay cash for dinner at a friend's home
   - wear pajamas to class
   - tell someone *not* to have a nice day
2. Find examples of advertising that use "slice-of-life" depictions. How effective are these ads in inducing compliance with the ad's message? Are these appeals more effective when they exactly mirror how people are in reality, or should they present a somewhat unrealistic view of "real people?"
3. Identify a set of avoidance groups for your peers. Can you identify any consumption decisions that are made with this group in mind?
4. Construct sales pitches or persuasive arguments using the foot-in-the-door technique, and try this approach on friends. What factors seem to determine if this strategy will be successful?
5. Locate a product or service that emphasizes exclusivity as an important attribute. How is this communicated to consumers? Is it successful?
6. Identify fashion opinion leaders on your campus. Do they fit the profile discussed in the chapter?
7. Conduct a sociometric analysis within your dormitory or neighborhood. For a product category such as music or cars, ask each individual to identify *other* individuals with whom they share information. Systematically trace all

of these avenues of communication, and identify opinion leaders by locating individuals who are repeatedly named as providing helpful information.

NOTES

1. Jason DeParle, "About Men, About Cold Beer, Willing Women, Hazing, Conformity—About Fraternities," *Washington Monthly* (November 1988): 38.
2. "Omega to Hazing Sought," *New York Times* (September 3, 1989): 50.
3. Joel B. Cohen and Ellen Golden, "Informational Social Influence and Product Evaluation," *Journal of Applied Psychology* 56 (February 1972): 54–59; Robert E. Burnkrant and Alain Cousineau, "Informational and Normative Social Influence in Buyer Behavior," *Journal of Consumer Research* 2 (December 1975): 206–15; Peter H. Reingen, "Test of a List Procedure for Inducing Compliance with a Request to Donate Money," *Journal of Applied Psychology* 67 (1982): 110–18.
4. C. Whan Park and V. Parker Lessig, "Students and Housewives: Differences in Susceptibility to Reference Group Influence," *Journal of Consumer Research* 4 (September 1977): 102–10.
5. Kenneth J. Gergen and Mary Gergen, *Social Psychology* (New York: Harcourt Brace Jovanovich, 1981).
6. Harold H. Kelley, "Two Functions of Reference Groups," in *Basic Studies in Social Psychology,* ed. Harold Proshansky and Bernard Siedenberg (New York: Holt, Rinehart and Winston, 1965): 210–14.
7. Anthony Ramirez, "Mastercard's Shift from Glamour," *New York Times* (April 9, 1990): D1.
8. L. Festinger, S. Schachter, and K. Back, *Social Pressures in Informal Groups: A Study of Human Factors in Housing* (New York: Harper, 1950).
9. R. B. Zajonc, H. M. Markus, and W. Wilson, "Exposure Effects and Associative Learning," *Journal of Experimental Social Psychology* 10 (1974): 248–63.
10. D. J. Stang, "Methodological Factors in Mere Exposure Research," *Psychological Bulletin* 81 (1974): 1014–25; R. B. Zajonc, P. Shaver, C. Tavris, and D. Van Kreveid, "Exposure, Satiation and Stimulus Discriminability," *Journal of Personality and Social Psychology* 21 (1972): 270–80.
11. J. E. Grush, K. L. McKeogh, and R. F. Ahlering, "Extrapolating Laboratory Exposure Research to Actual Political Elections," *Journal of Personality and Social Psychology* 36 (1978): 257–70.
12. Ramirez, "Mastercard's Shift from Glamour."
13. A. Benton Cocanougher and Grady D. Bruce, "Socially Distant Reference Groups and Consumer Aspirations," *Journal of Marketing Research* 8 (August 1971): 79–81; James E. Stafford, "Effects of Group Influences on Consumer Brand Preferences," *Journal of Marketing Research* 3 (February 1966): 68–75.
14. Cocanougher and Bruce, "Socially Distant Reference Groups and Consumer Aspirations."
15. Jeffrey D. Ford and Elwood A. Ellis, "A Re-examination of Group Influence on Member Brand Preference," *Journal of Marketing Research* 17 (February 1980): 125–32; Thomas S. Robertson, *Innovative Behavior and Communication* (New York: Holt, Rinehart and Winston, Inc., 1980), Chapter 8.
16. William O. Bearden and Michael J. Etzel, "Reference Group Influence on Product and Brand Purchase Decisions," *Journal of Consumer Research* 9 (1982)2: 183–94.
17. Judith Waldrop, "Plastic Wars," *American Demographics* (November 1988): 6.
18. Elaine Santoro, "Catholic Charities Credit Card Unveiled," *Fund Raising Management* 20 (April 1989): 10.
19. Judith Graham, "Affinity Card Clutter: Number of Tie-Ins Raises Doubts About Continued Use," (Special Report: Financial Services Marketing) *Advertising Age* (November 14, 1988): S1; Waldrop, "Plastic Wars."
20. Gergen and Gergen, *Social Psychology,* 312.
21. J. R. P. French, Jr. and B. Raven, "The Bases of Social Power," in *Studies in Social Power,* ed. D. Cartwright (Ann Arbor, Mich.: Institute for Social Research, 1959): 150–67.

22. Michael R. Solomon, "Packaging the Service Provider," *The Service Industries Journal* 5 (March 1985): 64–72.
23. Augustin Hedberg, "Lights! Camera! Economists!" (celebrity economists), *Money* (October 1987): 118.
24. See Robert B. Cialdini, *Influence: Science and Practice,* 2nd ed. (New York: Scott, Foresman, 1988), for an excellent and entertaining treatment of this process.
25. For the seminal work on conformity and social influence, see Solomon E. Asch, "Effects of Group Pressure Upon the Modification and Distortion of Judgments," in *Group Dynamics,* ed. D. Cartwright and A. Zander (New York: Harper and Row, 1953); Richard S. Crutchfield, "Conformity and Character," *American Psychologist* 10 (1955): 191–98; Muzafer Sherif, "A Study of Some Social Factors in Perception," *Archives of Psychology* 27 (1935): 187.
26. Burnkrant and Cousineau, "Informational and Normative Social Influence in Buyer Behavior."
27. For a recent attempt to measure individual differences in proclivity to conformity, see William O. Bearden, Richard G. Netemeyer, and Jesse E. Teel, "Measurement of Consumer Susceptibility to Interpersonal Influence," *Journal of Consumer Research* 15 (March 1989): 473–81.
28. John W. Thibaut and Harold H. Kelley, *The Social Psychology of Groups* (New York: John Wiley, 1959); W. W. Waller and R. Hill, *The Family, a Dynamic Interpretation* (New York: Dryden, 1951).
29. Sandra L. Bem, "Sex Role Adaptability: One Consequence of Psychological Androgyny," *Journal of Personality and Social Psychology* 31 (1975): 634–43.
30. Leon Festinger, "A Theory of Social Comparison Processes," *Human Relations* 7 (May 1954): 117–40.
31. Chester A. Insko, Sarah Drenan, Michael R. Solomon, Richard Smith, and Terry J. Wade, "Conformity as a Function of the Consistency of Positive Self-Evaluation with Being Liked and Being Right," *Journal of Experimental Social Psychology* 19 (1983): 341–58.
32. Abraham Tesser, Murray Millar, and Janet Moore, "Some Affective Consequences of Social Comparison and Reflection Processes: The Pain and Pleasure of Being Close," *Journal of Personality and Social Psychology* 54 (1988)1: 49–61.
33. L. Wheeler, K. G. Shaver, R. A. Jones, G. R. Goethals, J. Cooper, J. E. Robinson, C. L. Gruder, and K. W. Butzine, "Factors Determining the Choice of a Comparison Other," *Journal of Experimental Social Psychology* 5 (1969): 219–32.
34. George P. Moschis, "Social Comparison and Informal Group Influence," *Journal of Marketing Research* 13 (August 1976): 237–44.
35. Burnkrant and Cousineau, "Informational and Normative Social Influence in Buyer Behavior."; M. Venkatesan, "Experimental Study of Consumer Behavior Conformity and Independence," *Journal of Marketing Research* 3 (November 1966): 384–87.
36. Harvey London, *Psychology of the Persuader* (Morristown, N.J.: Silver Burdett/General Learning Press, 1973); William J. McGuire, "The Nature of Attitudes and Attitude Change," in *The Handbook of Social Psychology,* ed. G. Lindzey and E. Aronson (Reading, Mass.: Addison-Wesley, 1968)3; N. Miller, G. Naruyama, R. J. Baebert, and K. Valone, "Speed of Speech and Persuasion," *Journal of Personality and Social Psychology* 34 (1976): 615–24.
37. J. L. Freedman and S. Fraser, "Compliance Without Pressure: the Foot-in-the-Door Technique," *Journal of Personality and Social Psychology* 4 (1966): 195–202.
38. R. B. Cialdini, J. E. Vincent, S. K. Lewis, J. Catalan, D. Wheeler, and B. L. Darby, "Reciprocal Concessions Procedure for Inducing Compliance: The Door-in-the-Face Effect," *Journal of Personality and Social Psychology* 31 (1975): 200–15.
39. Donald H. Granbois, "Improving the Study of Customer In-Store Behavior," *Journal of Marketing* 32 (October 1968): 28–32.
40. B. Latane, K. Williams, and S. Harkins, "Many Hands Make Light the Work: The Causes and Consequences of Social Loafing," *Journal of Personality and Social Psychology* 37 (1979): 822–32.
41. S. Freeman, M. Walker, R. Borden, and B. Latane, "Diffusion of Responsibility and Restaurant Tipping: Cheaper by the Bunch," *Personality and Social Psychology Bulletin* 1 (1978): 584–87.

42. Nathan Kogan and Michael A. Wallach, "Risky Shift Phenomenon in Small Decision-Making Groups: A Test of the Information Exchange Hypothesis," *Journal of Experimental Social Psychology* 3 (January 1967): 75–84; Nathan Kogan and Michael A. Wallach, *Risk Taking* (New York: Holt, Rinehart and Winston, 1964); Arch G. Woodside and M. Wayne DeLozier, "Effects of Word-of-Mouth Advertising on Consumer Risk Taking," *Journal of Advertising* (Fall 1976): 12–19.

43. Kogan and Wallach, *Risk Taking*.

44. Roger Brown, *Social Psychology* (New York: The Free Press, 1965).

45. David L. Johnson and I. R. Andrews, "Risky Shift Phenomenon Tested with Consumer Product Stimuli," *Journal of Personality and Social Psychology* 20 (1971): 382–85.

46. Len Strazewski, "Tupperware Locks in New Strategy" (direct-response campaign, new party formats), *Advertising Age* (February 8, 1988): 30.

47. Peter Wilkinson, "For Your Eyes Only," *Savvy Woman* (January 1989): 68.

48. Gergen and Gergen, *Social Psychology*.

49. L. J. Strickland, S. Messick, and D. N. Jackson, "Conformity, Anticonformity and Independence: Their Dimensionality and Generality," *Journal of Personality and Social Psychology* 16 (1970): 494–507.

50. Jack W. Brehm, *A Theory of Psychological Reactance* (New York: Academic Press, 1966).

51. R. D. Ashmore, V. Ramchandra, and R. Jones, "Censorship as an Attitude Change Induction," (paper presented at the meetings of the Eastern Psychological Association, New York, 1971); R.A. Wicklund and J. Brehm, *Perspectives on Cognitive Dissonance* (Hillsdale, N.J.: Lawrence Erlbaum, 1976).

52. C.R. Snyder and H.L. Fromkin, *Uniqueness: The Human Pursuit of Difference* (New York: Plenum Press, 1980).

53. Johan Arndt, "Role of Product-Related Conversations in the Diffusion of a New Product," *Journal of Marketing Research* 4 (August 1967): 291–95.

54. Quoted in Barbara B. Stern and Stephen J. Gould, "The Consumer as Financial Opinion Leader," *Journal of Retail Banking* 10 (Summer 1988): 43–52.

55. Elihu Katz and Paul F. Lazarsfeld, *Personal Influence* (Glencoe, Ill.: Free Press, 1955).

56. John A. Martilla, "Word-of-Mouth Communication in the Industrial Adoption Process," *Journal of Marketing Research* 8 (March 1971): 173–78; see also Marsha L. Richins, "Negative Word-of-Mouth by Dissatisfied Consumers: A Pilot Study," *Journal of Marketing* 47 (Winter 1983): 68–78.

57. Arndt, "Role of Product-Related Conversations in the Diffusion of a New Product."

58. James H. Myers and Thomas S. Robertson, "Dimensions of Opinion Leadership," *Journal of Marketing Research* 9 (February 1972): 41–46.

59. James F. Engel, Robert J. Kegerreis, and Roger D. Blackwell, "Word of Mouth Communication by the Innovator," *Journal of Marketing* 33 (July 1969): 15–19.

60. Bill Barol, "Batmania," *Newsweek* (June 26, 1989): 70.

61. Dorothy Leonard-Barton, "Experts as Negative Opinion Leaders in the Diffusion of a Technological Innovation," *Journal of Consumer Research* 11 (March 1985): 914–26.

62. Richard J. Lutz, "Changing Brand Attitudes through Modification of Cognitive Structure," *Journal of Consumer Research* 1 (March 1975): 49–59.

63. Charles W. King and John O. Summers, "Overlap of Opinion Leadership Across Consumer Product Categories," *Journal of Marketing Research* 7 (February 1970): 43–50.

64. A. Tesser and S. Rosen, "The Reluctance to Transmit Bad News," in *Advances in Experimental Social Psychology,* ed. L. Berkowitz (New York: Academic Press, 1975): 8.

65. John Leo, "Psst! Wait 'Till You Hear This: A Scholar Says Rumors Reveal Our Fears and Desires," *Time* (March 16, 1987): 76.

66. Sid Astbury, "Pork Rumors vex Indonesia," *Advertising Age* (February 16, 1989): 36.

67. Everett M. Rogers, *Diffusion of Innovations,* 3rd ed. (New York: Free Press, 1983).

68. Leonard-Barton, "Experts as Negative Opinion Leaders in the Diffusion of a Technological Innovation"; Rogers, *Diffusion of Innovations*.

69. Herbert Menzel, "Interpersonal and Unplanned Communications: Indispensable or Obsolete?" *Biomedical Innovation* (Cambridge, Mass.: MIT Press, 1981): 155–63.

70. Meera P. Venkatraman, "Opinion Leaders, Adopters, and Communicative Adopters: A Role Analysis," *Psychology & Marketing* 6 (Spring 1989): 51–68.

71. Rogers, *Diffusion of Innovations.*

72. Robert Merton, *Social Theory and Social Structure,* (Glencoe, Ill.: Free Press, 1957).

73. King and Summers, "Overlap of Opinion Leadership Across Consumer Product Categories."

74. Steven A. Baumgarten, "The Innovative Communicator in the Diffusion Process," *Journal of Marketing Research* 12 (February 1975): 12–18.

75. Russell W. Belk, "Occurrence of Word-of-Mouth Buyer Behavior as a Function of Situation and Advertising Stimuli," in *Combined Proceedings of the American Marketing Association, Series No. 33, e*d. Fred C. Allvine (Chicago: American Marketing Association, 1971): 419–22.

76. Lawrence F. Feick, Linda L. Price, and Robin A. Higie, "People Who Use People: The Other Side of Opinion Leadership," in *Advances in Consumer Research, e*d. Richard J. Lutz (Provo, Utah: Association for Consumer Research, 1986)13: 301–05.

77. Lawrence F. Feick and Linda L. Price, "The Market Maven," *Managing* (July 1985): 10.

78. Willim R. Greer, "The Influentials: Power Brokers to Consumers," *New York Times* (December 4, 1986): C1.

79. Gerald Eskenazi, "Once a Canvas Shoe, Now a Big-Time Player," *New York Times* (March 11, 1990): 1.

80. Stern and Gould, "The Consumer as Financial Opinion Leader."

81. William R. Darden and Fred D. Reynolds, "Predicting Opinion Leadership for Men's Apparel Fashions," *Journal of Marketing Research* 1 (August 1972): 324–28.

82. "Referrals Top Ads as Influence on Patients' Doctor Selections," *Marketing News* (January 30, 1987): 22.

83. Peter H. Reingen, Brian L. Foster, Jacqueline Johnson Brown, and Stephen B. Seidman, "Brand Congruence in Interpersonal Relations: A Social Network Analysis," *Journal of Consumer Research* 11 (December 1984): 771–83; see also James C. Ward and Peter H. Reingen, "Sociocognitive Analysis of Group Decision Making Among Consumers," *Journal of Consumer Research* 17 (December 1990): 245–62.

84. Peter H. Reingen and Jerome B. Kernan, "Analysis of Referral Networks in Marketing: Methods and Illustration," *Journal of Marketing Research* 23 (November 1986): 370–78.

Social Class

One Saturday, Phil decided to take off early from his construction job and treat Marilyn and the kids to an afternoon at the Boat Show. Phil's dream is to buy himself a little boat someday and spend his retirement on the lake reeling in bass. After looking longingly at small boats, the family wanders over to the yacht section to "see how the other half lives."

The show is featuring a photo exhibit of the Trump Princess, one of the world's most luxurious private yachts. The boat was purchased by wealthy real-estate developer Donald Trump, who admitted at the time that he wasn't even that crazy about boats. The Princess' eleven guest suites feature gold-plated bathroom fixtures, and the boat also sports a cinema, a small waterfall, and a disco. Marilyn really can't believe the master bedroom suite, with its ceiling panel that opens to the sky and a wall panel that drops down to reveal a huge television screen. To top it all off, the bathroom has a mirror that slides down to expose a barber chair, a shower stall cut from one solid piece of onyx, and a sauna.[1]

Though the couple are suitably impressed by the boat, they know that they will never have a chance to experience that kind of luxury unless they hit the lottery. Phil is content to return to the small boat section. He can almost see himself out on that lake, tying flies and sucking down cold beer.

CHAPTER 12

SOCIAL CLASS AND CONSUMPTION

The United States is a place where ". . . all men are created equal," but (as the description above implies), some are more equal than others. All societies, regardless of their political systems, can be roughly divided into the "haves" and the "have-nots" (though sometimes having is a question of degree).

CLASS IS UNIVERSAL

In many animal species, a social organization is developed whereby the most assertive or aggressive animals exert control over the others and have the first pick of food, living space, and even mating partners. Chickens, for example, develop a clearly defined dominance-submission hierarchy; each hen has a position in which she is submissive to all of the hens above her and dominates the ones below her (this is the origin of the term *pecking order*).[2]

People are no different. They also develop a "pecking order" where they are ranked in terms of their relative standing in society. This standing determines their access to such resources as education, housing, and consumer goods. And they try to improve their ranking by moving up in the social order whenever possible. This desire to improve one's lot in life—and to let others know one has done so—is at the core of many marketing strategies.

SOCIAL CLASS AND SOCIAL CONTROL   Just as marketers try to carve society into groups for segmentation purposes, sociologists have developed ways to describe meaningful divisions of society in terms of people's relative social and economic resources. Some of these divisions involve political power, while others revolve around purely economic distinctions. Karl Marx felt that position in a society was determined by one's relationship to the *means of production*. Some people (the haves) control resources, and they use the labor of others to preserve their privileged positions. The have-nots lack control and depend on their own labor for survival, so these people have the most to gain by changing the system. Distinctions among people that entitle some to more than others are perpetuated by those who will benefit by doing so.[3]

The sociologist Max Weber showed that the rankings people develop are not one-dimensional. Some involve prestige or "social honor" (he called these *status groups*), some rankings focus on power (or *party*), and some revolve around wealth and property (*class*).[4]

Social Standing.   The term **social class** is now used more generally to describe the overall rank of people in a society. People who are grouped within the same social class are approximately equal in terms of their social standing in the community. They work in roughly similar occupations, and they tend to have similar lifestyles by virtue of their income levels and common tastes. These people tend to socialize with one another and share many ideas and values regarding the way life should be lived.[5]

Social class is as much a state of being as it is of having: Class is also a question of what one *does* with one's money and how one defines his or her role in society. Though people may not like the idea that some members of society are better off or "different" than others, most consumers appear to acknowledge the existence of different classes and the effect of class membership on consumption. As one wealthy woman observed when asked to define social class:

> I would suppose social class means where you went to school and how far. Your intelligence. Where you live. . . . Where you send your children to school. The hobbies you have. Skiing, for example, is higher than the snowmobile. . . . It can't be {just} money, because nobody ever knows that about you for sure.[6]

Does Class Drive Consumption? A consumer's social class can be a *cause* of consumption, since consumers in different classes often have very different preferences about how to spend their money and time. Social class also can be an *effect* of consumption, because we infer others'

Us magazine appeals to consumers' desires to distance themselves from the lower classes by avoiding an association with sensationalistic tabloids. By *US Magazine* from *Ad Age* (7/24/89), By Straight Arrow Publishers, Inc. © 1989.

social class by their consumption choices. Whether its influence is that of cause or of effect, social class is fundamentally related to consumer behavior and the ways products are marketed.

One indication of the social class connotations of different brands is given in Table 12-1, which shows how one group of consumers associated specific products with social classes. Michelob and Heineken beers, for example, clearly have more "snob" appeal to these people than do market leaders Budweiser and Miller. Mass-merchandisers Sears and K-Mart, not surprisingly, have a lower class image than do "elite" (Midwestern) department stores Marshall Field and Carson Pirie Scott.[7]

TABLE 12-1 Social class perceptions of branded goods and services

Product/Service	Upper/ Upper Middle	Middle	Lower Middle	Upper Lower/ Lower	All	Don't Know	Total
a) Beer							
Coors	22	54	16	2	3	3	100
Budweiser	4	46	37	7	4	2	100
Miller	14	50	22	6	6	2	100
Michelob	67	23	4	1	2	3	100
Old Style*	3	33	36	22	1	2	100
Bud Light	22	53	14	3	5	3	100
Heineken	88	9	1	-	1	1	100
*local beer on tap							
b) Stores							
Sears	3	40	44	10	3	-	100
Kmart	-	7	32	57	1	3	100
Marshall Field	87	10	-	-	-	3	100
Montgomery Ward	1	35	42	15	1	6	100
Carson Pirie Scott	59	33	3	1	1	3	100
c) Restaurants							
Burger King	3	49	21	10	15	2	100
Denny's	2	49	39	7	2	1	100
Wendy's	8	61	15	2	10	4	100

n=(163)

Source: Kjell Gronhaus and Paul S. Trapp, "Perceived Social Class Appeals of Branded Goods," *Journal of Consumer Marketing* 5 (Fall 1988): 27.

J. C. Penney found out the hard way about class identification. This retailer traditionally had a very strong identification with the lower-middle class, and these consumers felt great loyalty to the store. In recent years the company tried to go upscale, but was not successful in convincing wealthier consumers of this change. Penney's is now returning to its roots, with promotions featuring "priced-right" apparel instead of designer goods.[8]

SOCIAL STRATIFICATION

In school, it always seems that some kids are more popular. They have access to many resources, such as special privileges, fancy cars, large allowances, or dates with other popular classmates. At work, some people are put on the fast track and are promoted to high-prestige jobs, given higher salaries, and perhaps such perks as a parking space, a large office, or the keys to the executive washroom.

In virtually every context, some people seem to be ranked higher than others. Patterns of social arrangements evolve whereby some members get more resources than others by virtue of their relative standing, power, and/or control in the group.[9] The phenomenon of **social stratification** refers to this creation of artificial divisions in a society: ". . . those processes in a social system by which scarce and valuable resources are distributed unequally to status positions that become more or less permanently ranked in terms of the share of valuable resources each receives."[10]

ACHIEVED VERSUS ASCRIBED STATUS

If you think back to groups you've belonged to, both large and small, you'll probably agree that in many instances some members seem to get more than their fair share of goodies, while other individuals are not so lucky. Some of these resources may have gone to people who earned them through hard work or diligent study. This allocation is due to *achieved status*. Other rewards may have been obtained because the person was lucky enough to be born rich or beautiful. Such good fortune is *ascribed status*. Whether rewards go to "the best and the brightest" or to someone who happens to be related to the boss, allocations are rarely equal within a social group. Most groups exhibit structures, or **status hierarchies.** Some members are somehow better off than others, have more authority or power, or are simply better liked or respected.

CULTURAL DIFFERENCES IN SOCIAL HIERARCHIES While every culture has its social hierarchies, variations in terms of how explicit these distinctions are can be observed. Stratification of one sort or another is universal, even in societies that officially disdain such a process. For example, in China, a supposedly classless society, many Chinese are irritated by the children of top party officials, who are called *gaoganzidi*.

These offspring have a reputation for laziness, enjoying material pleasures, and getting the best jobs by virtue of their family connections. They are thus a privileged class in a classless society.[11]

Japan. In Japan a person's status is a major determinant of how he or she will be treated. Japanese of unequal status usually do not sit together during meetings. The Japanese language contains expressions to be used only when addressing those of higher status (European languages also contain different forms of address for persons of different status). While Americans prefer to spend time with those on the same social rung, the Japanese prefer to socialize with those one or two steps higher on the organizational ladder.[12]

The U.K. England is an extremely class-conscious country, and at least until recently consumption patterns were preordained in terms of one's inherited position and family background. Members of the upper class were educated at schools like Eton and Oxford and spoke like Henry Higgins in *My Fair Lady*. This rigid class structure can still be found. "Hooray Henrys" (wealthy young men) play polo at Windsor, and hereditary peers still dominate the House of Lords.

However, the dominance of inherited wealth appears to be fading in Britain's traditionally aristocratic society. According to a recent survey, 86 of the 200 wealthiest people in England made their money the old–fashioned way: They earned it. Even the sanctity of the Royal Family, which epitomizes the aristocracy, has been diluted because of tabloid exposure and the antics of younger family members who have been transformed into celebrities more like rock stars than royalty. As one observer put it, ". . . the royal family has gone down-market . . . to the point that it sometimes resembles soap opera as much as grand opera."[13]

The United States. The United States supposedly does not have a rigid, objectively defined class system. Nevertheless, America has tended to maintain a stable class structure in terms of income distribution. Unlike other countries, however, what does change are the groups (ethnic, racial, and religious) that have occupied different positions within this structure at different times.[14]

The most influential and earliest attempt to describe American class structure was proposed by W. Lloyd Warner in 1941. Warner identified six social classes:[15]

1. Upper Upper
2. Lower Upper
3. Upper Middle
4. Lower Middle
5. Upper Lower
6. Lower Lower

Note that these classifications imply a *status hierarchy*. They indicate (in ascending order) some judgment of desirability in terms of access to such resources as money, education, and luxury goods. Variations on this system have been proposed over the years, but these six levels summarize fairly well the way social scientists think about class. A more current view of the American status structure is provided in Figure 12-1.

COMPONENTS OF SOCIAL CLASS

When we make estimates about a person's social class, there are a number of pieces of information we may consider. The three major ones are income, education, and occupation.

INCOME AND EDUCATION   A person's income is given the most weight in these judgments. This information counts for about two-thirds of the judgment, while educational level and a person's job split the remainder. This tendency to weigh income heavily has led to the conclusion that it ". . . is of overwhelming importance in how Americans think about social standing."[16]

Income Distribution.   The distribution of wealth is of great interest to social scientists and to marketers, as it determines what groups have the greatest buying power and market potential. Wealth is by no means distributed evenly across the classes. The top fifth of the population controls about 75 percent of all assets.[17]

The Relationship Between Income and Social Class.   Though consumers tend to equate money with class, the precise relationship between social class and income is not clear and has been the subject of debate among social scientists.[18] The two are by no means synonymous, which is why many people with a lot of money try to use it to upgrade their social class (i.e., the "nouveau riches"). One problem is that even if a family increases household income by adding wage-earners, each additional job is likely to be

---

Upper Americans

Upper-Upper (0.3%)–The "capital S society" world of inherited wealth

Lower-Upper (1.2%)–The newer social elite, drawn from current professionals

Upper-Middle (12.5%)–The rest of college graduate managers and professionals; life style centers on private clubs, causes, and the arts

Middle Americans

Middle Class (32%)–Average pay white-collar workers and their blue-collar friends; live on "the better side of town," try to "do the proper things"

Working Class (38%)–Average pay blue-collar workers; lead "working class life style" whatever the income, school, background, and job

Lower Americans

"A lower group of people, but not the lowest" (9%)–Working, not on welfare; living standard is just above poverty; behavior judged "crude," "trashy"

"Real Lower-Lower" (7%)–On welfare, visibly poverty-stricken, usually out of work (or have "the dirtiest jobs"); "bums," "common criminals"

Figure 12-1 A Contemporary View of the American Class Structure: Richard P. Coleman, "The Continuing Significance of Social Class to Marketing," *Journal of Consumer Research* 10 (December 1983): 265–80. Reprinted with permission of The University of Chicago Press

of lower status. For example, a housewife who gets a part-time job is not as likely to get one that is of equal or greater status than the primary wage-earner's. In addition, the extra money earned often is not pooled toward the common good of the family. It is instead used by the individual for his or her own personal spending. More money does not then result in increased status or changes in consumption patterns, since it tends to be devoted to buying *more* of the usual rather than upgrading to higher-status products.[19]

The following general conclusions can be made regarding the relative value of social class versus income in predicting consumer behavior:

- Social class appears to be a better predictor of purchases that have symbolic aspects, but low to moderate prices (e.g., cosmetics, liquor).
- Income is a better predictor of major expenditures that do not have status or symbolic aspects (e.g., major appliances).
- Both social class and income data are needed to predict purchases of expensive, symbolic products (e.g., cars, homes).

OCCUPATIONAL PRESTIGE   In a system where (like it or not) a consumer is defined to a great extent by what he or she does for a living, *occupational prestige* is another way to evaluate the "worth" of people. Hierarchies of occupational prestige tend to be quite stable over time, and they also tend to be similar in different societies. Similarities in occupational prestige have been found in countries as diverse as Brazil, Ghana, Guam, Japan, and Turkey.[20] A typical ranking includes a variety of professional and business occupations at the top (e.g., CEO of a large corporation, physician, and even college professor), while those jobs hovering near the bottom include shoe shiner, ditchdigger, and garbage collector.

MEASUREMENT OF SOCIAL CLASS

Because social class is a complex concept that depends on a number of factors, not surprisingly it has proven difficult to measure. Early measures included the Index of Status Characteristics developed in the 1940s and the Index of Social Position developed in the 1950s.[21] These indices used various combinations of individual characteristics (e.g., income, type of housing) to arrive at a label of class standing.

PROBLEMS WITH MEASURES OF SOCIAL CLASS   Market researchers were among the first to propose that people from different social classes can be distinguished from each other in important ways. While some of these dimensions still exist, others have changed.[22] Unfortunately, many of these measures are badly dated and are not as valid today for a variety of reasons.[23]

TRADITIONAL FAMILY STRUCTURE   Most measures of social class were designed to accommodate the traditional nuclear family, with a male wage-earner in the middle of his career and a female full-time homemaker. Such measures have trouble accounting for two-income families, young singles living alone, or households headed by women that are so prevalent in today's society (see Chapter 9).

ANONYMITY   Another problem with measuring social class is attributable to the increasing anonymity of our society. Earlier studies relied on the *reputational method,* where extensive interviewing was done within a community to determine the reputations and backgrounds of individuals (see the discussion of sociometry in Chapter 11). This information, coupled with the tracing of interaction patterns among people, provided a very comprehensive view of social standing within a community.

Unfortunately, this approach is virtually impossible to implement in most communities today. One compromise is to interview individuals to obtain demographic data and to combine these data with the subjective impressions of the interviewer regarding the person's possessions and standard of living. Such an approach is represented in the Status Index presented in Figure 12-2. Note that the accuracy of this questionnaire relies largely on the interviewer's judgment, especially regarding the quality of the respondent's neighborhood. These impressions are in danger of being biased by the interviewer's own circumstances, which may affect his or her standard of comparison. This potential problem highlights the need for adequate training of interviewers, as well as for some attempt to cross-validate such data, possibly by employing multiple judges to rate the same area.

Status Inconsistency.   One problem with assigning people to a social class is that they may not be equal in their standing on all of the relevant dimensions. A person might come from a low-status ethnic group but have a high-status job, while another may live in a fancy part of town but did not finish high school. The concept of **status crystallization** was developed to assess the impact of inconsistency on the self and social behavior.[24] It was thought that since the rewards from each part of such an "unbalanced" person's life would be variable and unpredictable, stress would result.

A related problem occurs when a person's social class standing creates expectations that are not met. Some people find themselves in the not-unhappy position of making more money than is expected of those in their social class. This is known as an *overprivileged* condition and is usually defined as an income that is at least 25 percent to 30 percent over the median for one's class.[25] In contrast, *underprivileged* consumers, who earn at least 15 percent less than the median, must often devote their consumption priorities to sacrificing in order to maintain the appearance of living up to class expectations.

MARKETING PITFALL

Lottery winners are good examples of consumers who become overprivileged virtually overnight. As attractive as winning is to many people, it has its problems. Consumers with a certain standard of living and level of expectations may have trouble adapting to sudden affluence and engage in flamboyant and irresponsible displays of wealth. Ironically, it is not unusual for lottery winners to report feelings of depression in the

Figure 12-2 Example of A Computerized Status Index: Richard P. Coleman, "The Continuing Significance of Social Class to Marketing," *Journal of Consumer Research* 10 (December 1983): 267. Reprinted with permission of The University of Chicago Press

Interviewer circles code numbers (for the computer) which in his/her judgment best fit the respondent and family. Interviewer asks for detail on occupation, then makes rating. Interviewer often asks the respondent to describe neighborhood in own words. Interviewer asks respondent to specify income—a card is presented the respondent showing the eight brackets—and records R's response. If interviewer feels this is over-statement or under, a "better-judgment" estimate should be given, along with explanation.

	Respondent	Respondent's Spouse
EDUCATION:		
Grammar school (8 yrs or less)	-1	-1
Some high school (9 to 11 yrs)	-2 R's	-2 Spouse's'
Graduated high school (12 yrs)	-3 Age	-3 Age
Some post high school (business, nursing, technical, 1 yr college)	-4 ___	-4 ___
Two, three years of college—possibly Associate of Arts degree	-5	-5
Graduated four-year college (B.A./B.S.)	-7	-7
Master's or five-year professional degree	-8	-8
Ph.D. or six/seven-year professional degree	-9	-9

OCCUPATION PRESTIGE LEVEL OF HOUSEHOLD HEAD: Interviewer's judgment of how head-of-household
 rates in occupational status.
 (Respondent's description—asks for previous occupation if retired, or if R. is widow, ask husband's:_____)

Chronically unemployed—"day" laborers, unskilled; on welfare .... -0

Steadily employed but in marginal semi-skilled jobs; custodians, minimum pay factory help,
 service workers (gas attendants, etc.) .... -1

Average-skill assembly-line workers, bus and truck drivers, police and firefighters, route
 deliverymen, carpenters, brickmasons .... -2

Skilled craftsmen (electricians), small contractors, factory foremen, low-pay salesclerks,
 office workers, postal employees .... -3

Owners of very small firms (2-4 employees), technicians, salespeople, office workers, civil
 servants with average level salaries .... -4

Middle management, teachers, social workers, lesser professionals .... -5

Lesser corporate officials, owners of middle-sized businesses (10-20 employees), moderate-
 success professionals (dentists, engineers, etc.) .... -7

Top corporate executives, "big successes" in the professional world (leading doctors and lawyers),
 "rich" business owners .... -9

AREA OF RESIDENCE: Interviewer's impressions of the immediate neighborhood in terms of its reputation in the
 eyes of the community.

Slum area: people on relief, common laborers .... -1

Strictly working class: not slummy but some very poor housing .... -2

Predominantly blue-collar with some office workers .... -3

Predominantly white-collar with some well-paid blue-collar .... -4

Better white-collar area: not many executives, but hardly any blue-collar either .... -5

Excellent area: professionals and well-paid managers .... -7

"Wealthy" or "society"-type neighborhood .... -9

TOTAL SCORE_____

TOTAL FAMILY INCOME PER YEAR:

Under $5,000	-1	$20,000 to 24,999	-5	
$5,000 to $9,999	-2	$25,000 to $34,999	-6	
$10,000 to 14,999	-3	$35,000 to 49,999	-7	
$15,000 to $19,999	-4	$50,000 and over	-8	Estimated Status_____

(Interviewer's estimate:_____ and explanation _____)
R's MARITAL STATUS: Married____ Divorced/Separated___ Widowed___ Single___ (CODE:_____)

months after cashing in. They may have trouble adjusting to an unfamiliar world and feel pressure from friends, relatives, and businesspeople to "share the wealth."

One New York winner who was featured prominently in the media is a case in point. He was employed as a mail porter until winning $5 million. After winning the lottery, he divorced his wife and married his girlfriend. She wore a $13,000 gown to the ceremony and the couple arrived in a horse-drawn carriage. Other purchases included a Cadillac with a Rolls Royce grill and a $5,000 car phone. This individual now denies rumors that he is heavily in debt due to his extravagant spending.[26]

CONSUMERS' SELF-DESIGNATIONS OF SOCIAL CLASS   American consumers generally have little difficulty placing themselves in either the working or middle classes. Also, the number who reject the idea that such categories exist is rather small.[27] As Table 12-2 shows, the proportion of consumers identifying themselves as working-class tended to rise until about 1960 and has been declining since.

Blue-collar workers with relatively high prestige jobs still tend to view themselves as working-class, even though their income levels may be equivalent to many white-collar workers.[28] This reinforces the idea that the labels of "working-class" or "middle-class" are very subjective. Their meanings say at least as much about self-identity as they do about economic well-being.

SOCIAL MOBILITY

To what degree do people tend to change their social classes? In some societies, such as India, one's social class is very difficult to change, but America is known as a country where "any man (or woman?) can grow

TABLE 12-2 Class identification in the United States, employed white males, 1945–75

Class Identification	Year						
	1945	1952	1956	1960	1964	1968	1975
Upper	3%	1%	%	%	%	%	3%
Middle	43	35	39	33	43	45	49
Working	51	61	58	65	53	52	46
Lower	1	1	2	2	1	1	-
Rejects Classes	1	1	2	2	1	1	-
Don't Know	1	-	1	-	2	2	-
	100%	100%	100%	100%	100%	100%	100%

Source: Leonard Beeghley, **Social Stratification in America:** *A Critical Analysis of Theory and Research* (Santa Monica, Ca.: Goodyear, 1978), 13.

up to be President." **Social mobility** refers to the ". . . passage of individuals from one social class to another. . . ."[29]

DIRECTION OF MOVEMENT   This passage can be upward, downward, or even horizontal. Horizontal mobility refers to movement from one position to another roughly equivalent in social status, like becoming a nurse instead of an elementary school teacher. Downward mobility is, of course, not very desirable, but this pattern is unfortunately quite evident in recent years as farmers and other displaced workers have been forced to go on welfare rolls or have joined the ranks of the homeless. A conservative estimate is that 600,000 Americans are homeless on a given day.[30]

Despite that discouraging trend, there is in fact a fair amount of upward mobility in our society. Simple demographics decree that there must be upward mobility. The middle and upper classes reproduce less than the lower classes (an effect known as *differential fertility*), and they even tend to restrict family size below replacement level. This means that positions of higher status over time must be filled by those of lower status.[31] Overall, though, the offspring of blue-collar consumers tend also to be blue-collar while the offspring of white-collar consumers also tend to wind up as white-collars.[32] People tend to improve their positions over time, but these increases are not usually dramatic enough to catapult them from one social class to another.

WOMEN AND SOCIAL CLASS   The traditional assumption is that husbands define a family's social class, while wives must live it. Women "borrow" their social status from their husbands. This assumption is termed the *postulate of equivalent evaluation*.[33] Indeed, the evidence indicates that physically attractive women tend to "marry up" in social class to a greater extent than attractive men. Women trade the resource of sexual appeal, which historically has been one of the few assets they were allowed to possess, for the economic resources of men.[34]

Nonetheless, the accuracy of this assumption in today's world obviously must be questioned. Many women now contribute equally to the family's well-being and work in positions of comparable or even greater status than their spouses. A woman's magazine recently offered this revelation: "Women who've become liberated enough to marry any man they please, regardless of his social position, report how much more fun and spontaneous their relationships with men have become now that they no longer view men only in terms of their power symbols."[35]

Employed women tend to average both their own and their husband's respective positions when estimating their own subjective status.[36] Nevertheless, a prospective spouse's social class is often an important "product attribute" when evaluating alternatives in the interpersonal marketplace. The same women's magazine discussed the following dilemma, implying that social class differences are still an issue in the dating game:

> You've met the (almost) perfect man. You both adore Dashiell Hammett thrillers, Mozart, and *Doonesbury*. He taught you to jet ski; you taught him the virtues of tofu. . . . The glitch? You're an executive earning ninety-thousand dollars a year. He's a taxi driver. . . . [37]

SOCIAL CLASS CONSUMPTION DIFFERENCES

Different products and stores are perceived by consumers to be appropriate for certain social classes.[38] Working-class consumers tend to evaluate products in more utilitarian terms such as sturdiness or comfort rather than style or fashionability. They are less likely to experiment with new products or styles, such as modern furniture or colored appliances.[39] Consumption differences often reflect underlying differences in priorities. For example, more affluent people living in the suburbs tend to be concerned about appearance and body-image, so they are more avid consumers of diet foods and drinks compared to people in more downscale small towns. These differences mean that the cola market, for example, can be segmented by social class.[40]

CLASS DIFFERENCES IN WORLDVIEW

A major social class difference involves the worldview of consumers. The world of the working-class (i.e., the lower-middle class) is more intimate and constricted. For example, working-class men are likely to name local sports figures as heroes and are less likely to take long vacation trips to out-of-the way places.[41] Immediate needs tend to dictate buying behavior for these consumers, while the higher classes tend to focus on more long-term goals.[42]

This ad for a glass manufacturer implies that there are social class differences in leisure activities and preferred beverages. Courtesy of Libbey Glass Inc.

Whatever your customers love to do for fun, Libbey refreshes them along the way. Libbey offers glasses to fit any lifestyle and specific taste.☐You can satisfy your customers' preferences and reflect your store's distinctiveness, too.☐Contact your Libbey representative today for a personal viewing. We will come out to see you with so many choices, we know it will be very refreshing indeed.

Libbey
America's Glassmaker™

"Peach cooler, please."

"Gimme a brew."

Working-class consumers depend heavily on relatives for emotional support and tend to orient themselves in terms of the community rather than the world-at-large. They are more likely to be conservative and family-oriented. Maintaining the appearance of one's home and property is a priority, regardless of the size of the house.

While they would like to have more in the way of material goods, working-class people do not necessarily envy those who rank above them in social standing.[43] The maintenance of a high-status lifestyle is sometimes not seen as worth the effort. As one blue-collar consumer commented: "Life is very hectic for those people. There are more breakdowns and alcoholism. It must be very hard to sustain the status, the clothes, the parties that are expected. I don't think I'd want to take their place."[44]

▼ ## MARKETING PITFALL

The consumer quoted above may be right. While good things appear to go hand-in-hand with higher status and wealth, the picture is not that clear. The social scientist Emile Durkheim observed that suicide rates are much higher among the wealthy, and wrote in 1897, ". . . the possessors of most comfort suffer most."[45] The quest for riches has the potential to result in depression, deviant behavior, and ruin. In fact, a recent survey of affluent consumers (they made an average of $176,000 a year) supports this notion. Though these people are in the top 2.5 percent income bracket in America, only 14 percent said they are very well off.[46]

TASTE CULTURES The concept of **taste cultures,** which differentiates people in terms of their aesthetic and intellectual preferences, is helpful in understanding the important yet subtle distinctions in consumption choices among the social classes. Taste cultures largely reflect education (and are also obviously income-related):[47] A distinction is often made between low culture and high culture groups (and is discussed in more detail in Chapter 17).

While such perspectives have met with criticism due to the implicit value judgments involved, they are valuable because they recognize the existence of groupings based on shared tastes in literature, art, home decoration, and so on. In one of the classic studies of social differences in taste, researchers cataloged homeowners' possessions while asking more typical questions about income, occupation, and so on.

Clusters of furnishings and decorative items that seemed to appear together with some regularity were identified, and different clusters were found depending upon the consumer's social status (see Figure 12-3). For example, religious objects, artificial flowers, and still-life portraits tended to be found together in relatively lower-class living rooms, while a cluster containing abstract paintings, sculptures, and modern furniture was more likely to appear in a higher-status home.[48]

Codes and Class. A semiotic approach to social class focuses on differences in the types of *codes* (the ways meanings are expressed and

interpreted by consumers) used within different social strata. Discovery of these codes is valuable to marketers, since this knowledge allows us to communicate to markets using concepts and terms most likely to be understood and appreciated by specific consumers.

The nature of these codes varies among social classes. *Restricted codes* are dominant among the working class, while *elaborated codes* tend to be used by the middle and upper classes. Restricted codes focus on the content of objects, not on relationships among objects. Elaborated codes, in contrast, are more complex and depend upon a more sophisticated world orientation. Some differences between these two general types of codes are provided in Table 12-3. As this table indicates, these code differences extend to the way consumers approach such basic concepts as time, social relationships, and objects.

Marketing appeals that are constructed with these differences in mind will result in quite different messages. For example, a life insurance ad targeted to a lower-class person might depict in simple, straightforward terms a hard-working family man who feels good immediately after purchasing a policy. A more upscale appeal might emphasize the satisfaction that comes from planning for the future and highlight the benefits of a whole-life insurance policy over other kinds of financial investments.

inence. This must be accompanied by a family history of public service and philanthropy, which is often manifested in tangible markers that enable these donors to achieve a kind of immortality (e.g., Rockefeller University, or the Whitney Museum).[51] "Old money" consumers tend to make distinctions among themselves in terms of ancestry and lineage rather than wealth.[52] The Jaguar ad illustrates how the elusive quality of "breeding" can be incorporated as a product attribute and selling point.

"Old money" consumers are often hard to identify. One commentator has called this group ". . . the class in hiding."[53] Following the Great Depression of the 1930s, monied families became more discreet about exhibiting their wealth, fleeing from mansions such as those found in Manhattan to hideaways in Virginia, Connecticut, and so on.

Old money people are secure in their status. In a sense, they have been trained their whole lives to be rich. As a result, this group does not

Bred to move swiftly and surely, the XJ6 reflects over a half-century of Jaguar experience on the road and track.

Jaguar's legendary double overhead cam engines first found fame at the 24 Hours of Le Mans endurance races. Now a 3.6 liter DOHC powers today's XJ6. With an engine of cast aluminum alloy for lighter weight and better cooling and with four valves per cylinder for improved breathing, this is one of the quickest Jaguar sedans ever built.

Ride and handling are two other areas for which Jaguars are well known. Although the classic goals of a smooth ride and agile, athletic handling are inherently in opposition, Jaguar engineers have achieved both in one automobile. One part of Jaguar's unique solution is found in its four-wheel independent suspension. Patented pendulum isolation and computer-controlled self-leveling also help produce Jaguar's luxurious ride and excellent road holding characteristics. Up front, Jaguar's power-assisted, rack-and-pinion steering provides the driver with quick, positive response with a remarkable degree of road feel.

Rich in comfort, convenience and Old World craftsmanship, the XJ6 cabin is graced with hand-polished burl walnut fascia, console and door inserts. The seats are faced with the finest leather. A computerized climate control system maintains the cabin temperature and incoming humidity to your liking. An 80-watt, six-speaker stereo receiver and tape deck with Dolby® provide a quality of sound that rivals a live performance.

To test drive this latest refinement of the breed and for information on Jaguar's extensive three-year/36,000-mile warranty, see your dealer. He can provide details of this limited warranty, applicable in the USA and Canada, and Jaguar's uniquely comprehensive Service-On-Site℠ Roadside Assistance Plan. For the name of the dealer nearest you, call toll-free: 1-800-4-JAGUAR. Jaguar Cars Inc., Leonia, NJ 07605.

ENJOY TOMORROW. BUCKLE UP TODAY.

This Jaguar ad appeals to people who aspire to the "old money" class. Note the emphasis on English "breeding." *Courtesy of Jaguar Cars Inc.*

Whether it's a swift horse, a smart hound or an agile car, the English have long known the importance of good breeding.

JAGUAR

tend to be very interested in prominent displays of wealth: They can afford not to be. Surveys of "upper-affluent" Americans show that the wealthy downplay the importance of material goals and status. Less than 10 percent think owning a luxury car, antiques, or art is important, and only 7 percent believe that belonging to a prestigious club is worthwhile.[54] In addition, almost three-quarters describe themselves as thrifty and claim to shop at stores where a particular brand is cheapest.[55]

THE NOUVEAU RICHES   The Horatio Alger myth, where a person goes from "rags to riches" through hard work and a bit of luck is still a powerful one in American society. Although many people do in fact become "self-made millionaires," they often encounter a problem after they have become wealthy and have changed their social status: They do not know how to be rich. Consumers who have relatively recently become members of upper social classes are known as the *nouveau riches,* a term that is sometimes used in a derogatory manner to describe newcomers to the world of wealth.

▲ MARKETING OPPORTUNITY

A California builder has a clear understanding of the needs of the nouveau riches. He helps them to look like "old money." His company offers luxury homes that are completely furnished and outfitted to represent an idealized version of "the rich look." The Tudor homes come complete with furniture, linens, and even stocked refrigerators. A description of these "packages" observed: ". . . it is not just convenience {the builder} has to offer, it is security, the security that comes from knowing that the myriad inanimate objects that surround {the buyers} . . . —from the Lenox china to the . . . Braun coffee makers—are unmistakably appropriate to their place and station in the world." "People don't trust their own taste," says the builder, and they are too impatient to wait three generations for taste to develop.[56]

Status Anxiety.   Many nouveau riches are plagued by *status anxiety.* They monitor the cultural environment to ensure that they are doing the "right" thing, being seen at the "right" places, using the "right" caterer, and so on.[57] Flamboyant consumption can thus be viewed as a form of symbolic self-completion, where the excessive display of symbols thought to denote "class" is used to make up for an internal lack of assurance about the "correct" way to behave (see Chapter 7). Advertising directed to this group often plays on these insecurities by emphasizing the importance of "looking the part." Clever merchandising supplies these consumers with the props necessary to masquerade by playing the role of old money people. For example, ads for *Colonial Homes* magazine feature consumers who " . . . have worked very hard to make it look like they never had to."

THE "GET SET"   While the possession of wealth is clearly an important dimension of affluence, this quality may be as much determined by attitudes toward consumption as it is by level of income. Some marketers have identified a consumer segment composed of well-off, but not rich, people who desire the best products and services, even though they may have to be more selective about those items they are able to buy. These consumers are realistic about what they can afford and prefer to sacrifice in some areas so that they can have the best in others. Various advertising and marketing research agencies have labeled this segment with such terms as *Influentials,* the *New Grown-Ups,* and the *Get Set.* This group has been estimated to represent up to almost 70 percent of U.S. buying power.

While many upper-class brands tried in the past to downscale themselves to attract the mass market, there are some indications that this strategy is reversing. Because of the Get Set's emphasis on quality, one scenario is that marketers will encourage the masses to "buy up" into products associated with the upper classes, even if they are forced to buy less. A print campaign for Waterford Crystal exemplifies this approach. The theme line is "Steadfast in a world of wavering standards," and is calculated to appeal to consumers who desire authenticity and lasting value.[58]

PROBLEMS WITH SOCIAL CLASS SEGMENTATION

Social class remains an important way to categorize consumers. Many marketing strategies do target different social classes. However, marketers have failed to use social class information as effectively as they could for the following reasons:

- They have ignored status inconsistency.
- They have ignored intergenerational mobility.
- They have ignored subjective social class (i.e., the class a consumer identifies with rather than the one he or she objectively belongs to).
- They have ignored consumers' aspirations to change their class standing.
- They have ignored the social status of working wives.

STATUS SYMBOLS

People have a deep-seated tendency to evaluate themselves, their professional accomplishments, their material well-being, and so on, relative to others. The popular phrase "keeping up with the Joneses" (in Japan it's "keeping up with the Satos") refers to the comparison between one's standard of living and one's neighbors.

Satisfaction is a relative concept, however. We hold ourselves to a standard defined by others that is constantly changing. Unfortunately, a major motivation for the purchase and display of products is not to enjoy them, but rather to let others know that we can afford them. In other words, these products function as **status symbols.** The desire to accumulate these "badges of achievement" is summarized by the popular bumper sticker slogan: "He who dies with the most toys, wins."

Japan is a highly status-conscious society, where upscale, designer labels are quite popular, and new forms of status are always being sought. The quest for new symbols has reached the point where owning a traditional rock garden, formerly a vehicle for leisure and tranquility, has become a sought-after item. Possession of a rock garden implies the presence of old money, since aristocrats traditionally were patrons of the arts. In addition, considerable assets are required to afford the required land in a country where real estate is extraordinarily costly.

This also helps to explain why the Japanese are fanatic golfers: Since a golf course takes up so much space, membership in a golf club is extremely valuable.[59]

Japanese consumers also place a high priority on the "snob appeal" of American and European products. For example, the status attached to acquiring the first taste of beaujolais nouveau wine from France each year has become a national obsession.[60] The frenzy to acquire expensive merchandise and Western culture has been dubbed the "prawns and Pavarotti phenomenon."[61]

CONSPICUOUS CONSUMPTION

The motivation to consume for the sake of consuming was first discussed by the social analyst Thorstein Veblen at the turn of the century. Veblen felt that a major role of products was for *invidious distinction*—they are used to inspire envy in others through display of wealth or power. Veblen coined the term **conspicuous consumption** to refer to people's desire to provide prominent visible evidence of their ability to afford luxury goods.

Veblen's work was motivated by the excesses of his time. He wrote in the era of the robber barons, where the likes of J. P. Morgan, Henry Clay Frick, William Vanderbilt, and others were building massive financial empires and flaunting their wealth by throwing lavish parties. Some of these events of excess became legendary, as described in this account:

> . . . there were tales, repeated in the newspapers, of dinners on horseback; of banquets for pet dogs; of hundred-dollar bills folded into guests' dinner napkins; of a hostess who attracted attention by seating a chimpanzee at her table; of centerpieces in which lightly clad living maidens swam in glass tanks, or emerged from huge pies; of parties at which cigars were ceremoniously lighted with flaming banknotes of large denominations.[62]

This flaunting of one's possessions even extended to wives: Veblen criticized the "decorative" role women were often forced to play as they were bestowed with expensive clothes, pretentious homes, and a life of leisure as a way to advertise the wealth of their husbands, a sort of "walking billboard." Such fashions as high-heeled shoes, tight corsets, billowing trains on dresses, and elaborate hairstyles all conspired to ensure that wealthy women could barely move without assistance, much less perform manual labor. Similarly, the Chinese practice of foot binding turned women into cripples, who had to be carried from place to place.

THE MODERN POTLACH Veblen was inspired by anthropological studies of the Kwakiutl Indians, who lived in the Pacific Northwest. These Indians had a ceremony called a *potlach,* a feast where the host showed off his wealth and gave extravagant presents to the guests. The more one gave away, the better one looked to the others. Sometimes, the host would use an even more radical strategy to flaunt his wealth. He would publicly destroy some of his property to demonstrate how much he had.

This ritual was also used as a social weapon: Since guests were expected to reciprocate, a poorer rival could be humiliated by inviting him to a lavish potlach. The need to give away as much as the host, even though he could not afford it, would essentially force the hapless guest into bankruptcy. If this practice sounds "primitive," think for a moment about many modern weddings. Parents commonly invest huge sums of money to throw a lavish party and compete with others for the distinction of giving their daughter the "best" or most extravagant wedding, even if they have to save for twenty years to do it.

The Leisure Class. This process of conspicuous consumption was, for Veblen, most evident among the *leisure class,* people for whom productive work is taboo. In Marxist terms, this reflects a desire to link oneself to ownership or control of the means of production, rather than to the production itself. Any evidence that one actually has to labor for a living is to be shunned, as suggested by the term "the idle rich."

Like the potlach ritual, the desire to convince others that one has a surplus of resources creates the need for evidence of this abundance. According to this argument, then, priority is given to consumption activities that are pursued with the goals of using up as many resources as possible in non-constructive pursuits. This *conspicuous waste* in turn shows others that one has the assets to spare. Veblen noted that ". . . we are told of certain Polynesian chiefs, who, under the stress of good form, preferred to starve rather than carry their food to their mouths with their own hands."[63]

Many modern consumption practices can be analyzed in terms of conspicuous consumption. For example, speculation on the origin of the lawn has its roots in Veblen's analysis. While we (especially children of the suburbs) take it for granted that a house should be surrounded by a wide expanse of green grass, this is actually a relatively new concept. Homes, especially those of the working class, traditionally were surrounded by "useful" plants bearing fruits, vegetables, and so on for the family to consume. By planting grass instead, the homeowner may be saying symbolically that he or she can afford to waste this valuable space and devote it strictly to decoration. The almost fanatic devotion to lawn maintenance displayed by many Americans is as much an attempt to maintain property values and status as it is an expression of gardening or aesthetic appreciation.[64]

The concept of conspicuous consumption can also be applied to understand how cultural ideals regarding skin color evolve. Despite medical warnings about skin cancer, the popularity of tanning products and the willingness of many to subject themselves to hours under ultraviolet lamps attests to the cultural desirability of a deep, dark tan. In fact, though, it is only recently that a tan has been valued, especially among women. Historically, women in Europe and America tried very hard to *avoid* any semblance of a tan: In the mid-1800s they went so far as to paint their faces white![65]

Why the change? One explanation is that a tan results from excessive time spent outside. Traditionally the people who had to spend a lot of time out-of-doors were peasants toiling in the fields. A tan, therefore, was the sign of someone who worked for a living and was thus avoided by those who did not. In the modern era, this trend is reversed. Since most people work inside, a tanned person is also saying "I have the leisure time to sit outside and sun myself." Thus, a tan may be considered a form of conspicuous waste, since it is linked to sun-drenched beaches, trendy resorts, and so on. In our culture, then, a tan is in a sense a memento or souvenir of resources spent on leisure or non-constructive activity. Indeed, the tanning salon industry may be said to owe its success to consumers' desires to pay for the illusion that they have idle time to soak up the sun.

ARE STATUS SYMBOLS DEAD?

The use of material objects to display status is necessary in a large, anonymous society where reputation alone is insufficient to let people know who one is.[66] However, the ability of products to communicate status depends on their exclusivity. If too many people display the symbols, they lose their meaning. Indeed, a *need for uniqueness* is one important motivation for product choice (see Chapters 11 and 17).[67]

FRAUDULENT SYMBOLISM Symbols that become too diffused are said to be **fraudulent,** and their value becomes depleted,[68] which creates a vacuum as new symbols are needed to differentiate the "in crowd" from the "masses." This problem helps to explain the demise of "designer" products in the early to mid-1980s. While *signature goods* (e.g., designer jeans with someone's name written prominently on the rear end) were quite the rage for several years, their popularity eventually diminished because everyone wore them. They became exclusive clothing for the masses, a contradiction that could not last. For example, the designer Pierre Cardin alone has had more than 800 products licensed with his name.[69] As one consumer put it, "No more designer initials. Initials are in poor taste. Initials are tacky. The new thing is the uncluttered look. Dull, dull, dull, but chic, chic, chic."[70]

A 1985 survey by Grey Advertising categorized about 15 percent of the population as "UltraConsumers," people with a strong desire for ". . . luxury goods, go-go and glitz."[71] By 1987, almost 60 percent of consumers fit into this category. More recent trends, however, indicate that people are, at least for now, satiated with status symbols. A later survey by a different agency found the three most popular status symbols to be running one's own business, international pleasure travel, and being the trustee of a cultural institution. This trend is illustrated by the tagline in the Halston ad shown here, which boasts of being "The one label you don't have to see to know it's there."

PARODY DISPLAY As the competition to accumulate status symbols escalates, sometimes the best tactic is to switch gears and go in reverse. One way to do this is to deliberately *avoid* status symbols; to seek status by mocking it. This is a sophisticated form of conspicuous consumption that has been termed **parody display.**[72] A good example of parody display

CONSPICUOUS SUBTLETY

One of the special fabrics that distinguishes Halston as being fashion conscious yet impeccably sensible clothing is Country Silk.™

Loomed in Scotland along the river Tweed this exclusive fabric is a unique blending of high quality wool and the best of silk.

Great weight, great feel, great looks and the perfect update of a classic sport coat by none other than Halston.

THE ONE LABEL YOU DON'T HAVE TO SEE TO KNOW IT'S THERE.

HALSTON
FOR MEN
1290 AVENUE OF THE AMERICAS, NEW YORK, N.Y. 10104 (212) 581 • 6510

FINE FABRICS WOVEN IN SCOTLAND

In a twist on conspicuous consumption, this ad for Ultrasuede by Halston appeals to people who want to avoid the blatant display of status symbols. *Courtesy of Halston For Men Tailored Clothing.*

is the home-furnishing style known as High Tech, which was in vogue a few years ago. This motif incorporated the use of industrial equipment (e.g., floors were covered with plates used on the decks of destroyers), and pipes and support beams were deliberately exposed.[73]

This decorating strategy is intended to show that one is so witty and "in the know" that status symbols aren't necessary. Hence the popularity of old, ripped blue jeans, and "utility" vehicles such as Jeeps among the middle and upper classes. Thus, "true" status is shown by the adoption of product symbolism that is deliberately not fashionable.

Since the products and activities that connote high status are always changing, a significant amount of marketing effort goes into educating consumers as to what specific symbols they should be displaying, and to ensuring that a product is accepted in the pantheon of status symbols.

The need to display the "right" symbols has been a boon to such industries as publishing, where a variety of "how-to" books, magazines, and videos are available to school willing students of status. The concept of "dressing for success," where detailed instructions are provided to allow people to dress as if they are members of the upper middle-class (at least the authors' versions of this) was one popular example. This guidance has now spread to other areas of consumption, including "power lunching," (e.g., order "steak tartare" to intimidate your partner, since raw meat is a power food), office furnishings, and home decoration.

CHAPTER SUMMARY

Virtually all groups make distinctions among members in terms of relative superiority, power, and access to valued resources. This social stratification creates a status hierarchy, where some goods are preferred over others and are used to categorize their owners' social class. A consumer's social class is determined by a number of factors, including education and occupation. At least in the United States, income is a primary indicator of social class, though the relationship is far from perfect, since social class is as much a state of mind as it is of wallet. As a result, purchase decisions are sometimes influenced by the desire to "buy up" to a higher social class or to engage in the process of conspicuous consumption, where one's status is flaunted by the deliberate and non-constructive use of valuable resources. This is a characteristic of the nouveau riches, whose relatively recent acquisition of income, rather than ancestry or breeding, is responsible for their increased social mobility. Products often are used as status symbols to communicate real or desired social class.

KEY TERMS

Conspicuous consumption

Fraudulent symbols

Parody display

Social class

Social mobility

Social stratification

Status crystallization

Status hierarchy

Status symbols

Taste cultures

REVIEW QUESTIONS AND DISCUSSION TOPICS

1. People always seem to find ways to rank others on various dimensions. What are some of the dimensions primarily used to develop these rankings?

2. Sears, J. C. Penney, and to a lesser degree K-Mart, have made concerted efforts in recent years to upgrade their images and appeal to

higher-class consumers. How successful have these efforts been? Do you believe this is a wise strategy?

3. What are some of the obstacles to measuring social class in today's society? Discuss some ways to get around these obstacles.
4. What consumption differences might you expect to observe between a family characterized as underprivileged versus one whose income is average for its social class?
5. When is social class likely to be a better predictor of consumer behavior than mere knowledge of a person's income?
6. What factors might contribute to changes in rankings of occupational prestige, especially for professionals and businesspeople? Can marketing efforts contribute to these changes in positive and/or negative ways?
7. How do you assign people to social classes—or do you? What consumption cues would you use (e.g., clothing, speech, cars, etc.) to determine social standing?
8. Thorstein Veblen argued that women were often used as a vehicle to display their husbands' wealth. Is this argument still valid today?
9. Given present environmental conditions and dwindling resources, what is the future of "conspicuous waste?" Can the desire to impress others with affluence ever be eliminated? If not, can it take on a less dangerous form?
10. Some people argue that status symbols are dead. Do you agree?
11. How much correspondence is there between the "directions" provided in so-called status guides and the sets of products used by high-status people in real life?
12. What are current examples of parody display? Are consumers who adopt this strategy aware of what they are doing?

HANDS-ON EXERCISES

1. Using the Status Index presented in Figure 12-2, compute a social class score for people you know, including their parents if possible. Ask several friends (preferably from different places) to do this as well. How closely do your answers compare? If you find differences, how can you explain this?
2. Compile a list of occupations, and ask a sample of students in a variety of majors (both business and non-business) to rank the prestige of these jobs. Can you detect any differences in these rankings as a function of students' majors?
3. Compile a list of cultural categories and conduct an informal survey to fill in specific practices assumed to characterize different taste groups. How much agreement is there among respondents? Do these responses vary by *their* social class? Where do these social class stereotypes originate? For one clue, compile a collection of ads that depict consumers of different social classes. What generalizations can you make about the reality of these ads and about the media in which they appear?
4. Using Table 12-3 as a guide, construct alternative messages for the same product using restricted versus elaborated codes.
5. Identify a current set of "fraudulent" status symbols, and construct profiles of consumers who are wearing or using these products. Are these profiles consistent with the images portrayed in each product's promotional messages?

NOTES

1. Bill Barol, "Trump Ahoy," *Newsweek* (July 18, 1988): 62–63.
2. Floyd L. Ruch and Philip G. Zimbardo, *Psychology and Life,* 8th ed. (Glenview, Ill.: Scott, Foresman, 1971).
3. Jonathan H. Turner, "Sociology: Studying the Human System," 2nd ed. (Santa Monica, Ca.: Goodyear, 1981).
4. Turner, "Sociology."
5. Richard P. Coleman, "The Continuing Significance of Social Class to Marketing," *Journal of Consumer Research* 10 (December 1983): 265–80; Turner, "Sociology."
6. Quoted by Richard P. Coleman and Lee Rainwater, *Standing in America: New Dimensions of Class* (New York: Basic Books, 1978): 89.
7. Kjell Gronhaus and Paul S. Trapp, "Perceived Social Class Appeals of Branded Goods," *Journal of Consumer Marketing* 5 (Fall 1988): 25–30.
8. Jil Curry, "One Year Later at J. C. Penney" *Chain Store Age—General Merchandise Trends* 63 (February 1987): 35.
9. Coleman and Rainwater, *Standing in America.*
10. Turner, "Sociology."
11. Louise Do Rosario, "Privilege in China's Classless Society," *World Press Review* 33 (December 1986): 58.
12. "Social Class in the Workplace: the United States Versus Japan," *Society* (Jan.–Feb. 1987): 2.
13. Robin Knight, "Just You Move Over, 'Enry 'Iggins; A New Regard for Profits and Talent Cracks Britain's Old Class System," *U.S. News & World Report* 106 (April 24, 1989): 40.
14. James Fallows, "A Talent for Disorder (Class Structure)," *U.S. News & World Report* (February 1, 1988): 83.
15. Coleman, "The Continuing Significance of Social Class to Marketing"; W. Lloyd Warner with Paul S. Lunt, *The Social Life of a Modern Community* (New Haven, Conn.: Yale University Press, 1941).
16. Coleman and Rainwater, *Standing in America,* 220.
17. Turner, "Sociology."
18. See Coleman "The Continuing Significance of Social Class to Marketing"; Charles M. Schaninger, "Social Class Versus Income Revisited: An Empirical Investigation," *Journal of Marketing Research* 18 (May 1981): 192–208.
19. Coleman, "The Continuing Significance of Social Class to Marketing."
20. Leonard Beeghley, *Social Stratification in America: A Critical Analysis of Theory and Research* (Santa Monica, Ca.: Goodyear, 1978).
21. August B. Hollingshead and Fredrick C. Redlich, *Social Class and Mental Illness: A Community Study* (New York: John Wiley, 1958).
22. Donald W. Hendon, Emelda L. Williams and Douglas E. Huffman, "Social Class System Revisited," *Journal of Business Research* 17 (November 1988): 259.
23. Coleman, "The Continuing Significance of Social Class to Marketing."
24. Gerhard E. Lenski, "Status Crystallization: A Non-Vertical Dimension of Social Status," *American Sociological Review* 19 (August 1954): 405–12.
25. Richard P. Coleman, "The Significance of Social Stratification in Selling," in *Marketing: A Maturing Discipline, Proceedings of the American Marketing Association 43rd National Conference,* ed. Martin L. Bell (Chicago: American Marketing Association, 1960): 171–84.
26. Melinda Beck and Richard Sandza, "The Lottery Craze: Multimillion-Dollar Prizes Raise New Concerns That the Games Prey on the Poor," *Newsweek* (September 2, 1985): 16; Rhoda E. McKinney, "Has Money Spoiled the Lottery Millionaires," *Ebony* (December 1988): 150.
27. Beeghley, *Social Stratification in America.*
28. R. Vanneman and F. C. Pampel, "The American Perception of Class and Status," *American Sociological Review* 42 (June 1977): 422–37.
29. Turner, "Sociology," 260.
30. See Ronald Paul Hill and Mark Stamey, "The Homeless in America: An Examination of Possessions and Consumption Behaviors," *Journal of Consumer Research* 17 (December 1990): 303–21.

31. Joseph Kahl, "The American Class Structure," (New York: Holt, Rinehart and Winston, 1961).
32. Beeghley, *Social Stratification in America.*
33. E. Barth and W. Watson, "Questionable Assumptions in the Theory of Social Stratification," *Pacific Sociological Review* 7 (Spring 1964): 10–16.
34. Zick Rubin, "Do American Women Marry Up?" *American Sociological Review* 33 (1968): 750–60.
35. Sue Browder, "Don't be Afraid to Marry Down," *Cosmopolitan* (June 1987): 236.
36. K. U. Ritter and L. L. Hargens, "Occupational Positions and Class Identifications of Married Working Women: A Test of the Asymmetry Hypothesis," *American Journal of Sociology* 80 (January 1975): 934–48.
37. Browder, "Don't Be Afraid to Marry Down," 236.
38. J. Michael Munson and W. Austin Spivey, "Product and Brand-User Stereotypes Among Social Classes: Implications for Advertising Strategy," *Journal of Advertising Research* 21 (August 1981): 37–45.
39. Stuart U. Rich and Subhash C. Jain, "Social Class and Life Cycle as Predictors of Shopping Behavior," *Journal of Marketing Research* 5 (February 1968): 41–49.
40. Thomas W. Osborn, "Analytic Techniques for Opportunity Marketing," *Marketing Communications* (September 1987): 49–63.
41. Coleman, "The Continuing Significance of Social Class to Marketing."
42. Jeffrey F. Durgee, "How Consumer Sub-Cultures Code Reality: A Look at Some Code Types," in *Advances in Consumer Research,* ed. Richard J. Lutz (Provo, Utah: Association for Consumer Research, 1986)13: 332–37.
43. David Halle, America's Working Man: Work, Home, and Politics Among Blue-Collar Owners (Chicago: The University of Chicago Press, 1984); David Montgomery, "America's Working Man," *Monthly Review* (1985): 1.
44. Quoted in Coleman and Rainwater, *Standing in America,* 139.
45. Durkheim (1958) quoted in Roger Brown, *Social Psychology* (New York: The Free Press, 1965).
46. Lenore Skenazy, "Affluent, Like Masses, are Flush with Worries," *Advertising Age* (July 10, 1989): 55.
47. Herbert J. Gans, "Popular Culture in America: Social Problem in a Mass Society or Social Asset in a Pluralist Society?" in *Social Problems: A Modern Approach,* ed. Howard S. Becker (New York: Wiley, 1966).
48. Edward O. Laumann and James S. House, "Living Room Styles and Social Attributes: The Patterning of Material Artifacts in a Modern Urban Community," *Sociology and Social Research* 54 (April 1970): 321–42; see also Stephen S. Bell, Morris B. Holbrook, and Michael R. Solomon, "Combining Esthetic and Social Value to Explain Preferences for Product Styles With the Incorporation of Personality and Ensemble Effects," *Journal of Social Behavior and Personality* (1991) 6 (6), 243–274.
49. "Reading the Buyer's Mind," *U.S. News & World Report* (March 16, 1987): 59.
50. Paul Fussell, *Class: A Guide Through the American Status System* (New York: Summit Books, 1983): 29.
51. Elizabeth C. Hirschman, "Secular Immortality and the American Ideology of Affluence," *Journal of Consumer Research* 17 (June 1990): 31–42.
52. Coleman and Rainwater, *Standing in America,* 150.
53. Fussell, *Class,* 30.
54. Bickley Townsend, "What the Rich are Like," *American Demographics* (December 1987): 16.
55. Monica Gonzales, "Bargain Hunters," *American Demographics* (June 1989): 21.
56. Jerry Adler, "For Sale: The Rich Look," *Newsweek* (June 22, 1987): 80.
57. Jason DeParle, "Spy Anxiety; The Smart Magazine That Makes Smart People Nervous About Their Standing," *Washingtonian Monthly* (February 1989): 10.
58. Dennis Rodkin, "Wealthy Attitude Wins Over Healthy Wallet: Consumers Prove Affluence is a State of Mind," *Advertising Age* (July 9, 1990): S-4.
59. James Sterngold, "How Do You Define Status? A New BMW in the Drive. An Old Rock in the Garden," *New York Times* (December 28, 1989): C1.
60. David E. Sanger, "Japan Drinks Up France, with a Beaujolais Chaser," *New York Times* (November 17, 1989): A4.
61. "Japan's Consumer Boom: The Pricey Society," *The Economist* (September 9, 1989): 21.

62. John Brooks, *Showing Off in America* (Boston: Little, Brown, 1981),13.

63. Thorstein Veblen, *The Theory of the Leisure Class* (1899; reprint New York: New American Library, 1953),45.

64. Joan Kron, *Home-Psych: The Social Psychology of Home and Decoration* (New York: Clarkson N. Potter Inc., 1983).

65. Lois W. Banner, *American Beauty* (Chicago, Ill.: University of Chicago Press, 1983).

66. Scott Dawson and Jill Cavell, "Status Recognition in the 1980's: Invidious Distinction Revisited," in *Advances in Consumer Research,* ed. Melanie Wallendorf and Paul Anderson (Provo, Utah: Association for Consumer Research, 1986)14: 487–91; William H. Form and Gregory P. Stone, "Urbanism, Anonymity, and Status Symbolism," *American Journal of Sociology* 62 (1957): 504–14; Erving Goffman, "Symbols of Class Status," *British Journal of Sociology* 2 (December 1951): 294–304; Georg Simmel, "Fashion," *Journal of Sociology* 62 (1904): 120–55.

67. C.R. Snyder and H.L. Fromkin, *Uniqueness: The Human Pursuit of Difference* (New York: Plenum Press, 1980).

68. Dawson and Cavell, "Status Recognition in the 1980's"; Goffman, "Symbols of Class Status."

69. Caroline Rennolds Milbank, "When Your Own Initials Are Not Enough: A Brief History of Status Symbols," *Avenue* (October 1990): 63.

70. Ron Alexander, "In the Mutable World of Chic, Designers' Initials Are Out, Simplicity Is In," *New York Times* (May 21, 1989): 54.

71. Alexander, "In the Mutable World of Chic, Designers' Initials Are Out, Simplicity Is In."

72. Brooks, *Showing Off in America.*

73. Brooks, *Showing Off in America,* 31–32..

Subcultural Segmentation (I): Ethnic and Religious Groups

When Alexandra Inciardi left home at the age of 18, she was the first in her Brooklyn neighborhood to do so in a long time. Alex came from a close-knit family of Italian-Americans, and it was hard to leave. She still missed many things about home, especially her mother's pasta e fasulo, manicotti, calamari e scungilli, and other delicacies. . . .

CHAPTER **13**

Still, Alex had a new "family" now. She was a "Dead Head," part of a cadre of loyal followers who follow the Grateful Dead band around the country—some for almost twenty years. Many Dead Heads have opted for life on the road instead of pursuing more conventional paths, such as going to college and settling down. Dead Heads look as if they just walked out of a 1960s time machine. They wear tie-dyed T-shirts, headbands, and granny dresses, and some live in decommissioned school buses painted in psychedelic colors. Their belongings are covered with stickers sporting Grateful Dead symbols, particularly skulls, tap-dancing skeletons, and roses.[1] Alex had to admit that this life was a lot more exciting than her Catholic high school, but she knew her family was waiting for her to get this fling out of her system and return home to Brooklyn where she belonged.

SUBCULTURES

Citizens of a country have much in common: They observe the same national holidays, their expenditures will be affected by the economic health of their country, and they may join together in rooting for their country's team in the Olympics. Nonetheless, while this broad cultural membership gives us the raw material with which to fashion consumer experiences, the ways we weave this material into the fabric of our own unique versions of reality can vary enormously. The Dead Heads described above, while predominantly American, obviously have little in common with a farmer in the Midwest, a housewife in Boston, or an executive in Los Angeles. Variations in life-styles and priorities, both subtle and blatant, are affected by group memberships *within* the society-at-large. These groups are known as **subcultures,** whose members share beliefs and common experiences that set them apart from other members of a culture.

Just as Alexandra was torn between her allegiance to her old neighborhood and the Dead, every consumer belongs to many subcultures. These include religious groups, age groups, ethnic groups, and even regional groups (e.g., Texans versus New Yorkers). As with Dead Heads, sometimes even leisure activities can evolve into a subculture, if this activity draws the consumer into a unique social situation with enough intensity. Consumers in these subcultures—whether Dead Heads, retired people touring the country in Winnebagos, or members of youth gangs—create their own worlds, complete with their own norms, language, and product insignias (e.g., the skulls and roses used to signify the Grateful Dead subculture).

Major subcultures will be discussed in detail in this chapter and the next. This chapter focuses on ethnic and religious identifications, and Chapter 14 considers consumer subcultures that are defined by people of a common age or area of residence. In some cases, the subcultures to be considered are already widely used by marketers as a segmentation variable (e.g., race), while the potential of others is just beginning to be recognized (e.g., religion).

INTENSITY OF AFFILIATION

Subcultural memberships often have a significant impact on our behavior as consumers. Of course, some of our subcultural identifications are more powerful than others, so as we review the effects of various types of subcultures, it is important to bear in mind that segmentation strategies that take subcultural membership into account must also consider the relative *intensity* of consumers' various affiliations.

For example, the musical tastes or fashion choices of college students around the world, whether they are black, Taiwanese, Protestant, or Southern, in many ways probably have more in common with each other than with older members of their ethnic or religious groups. This global homogeneity within an age subculture is the key to the success of marketing enterprises ranging from Benetton and Esprit clothing to such rock performers as U2 or Madonna. Global marketing campaigns targeted to members of a common subculture can overcome language barriers by emphasizing visual symbols and music that does not require translation.

ETHNIC AND RELIGIOUS SUBCULTURES

Ethnic and religious identity is often a significant component of a consumer's self-concept. An ethnic subculture consists of a self-perpetuating group of consumers who are held together by common cultural ties that is identified both by its members and by others as being a distinguishable category.[2]

In some countries, like Japan, ethnicity is almost synonymous with the dominant culture, since virtually everyone claims the same homogeneous cultural ties. In a heterogeneous society like the United States, however, many different cultures are represented, and consumers may expend great effort to keep their ethnic identification from being submerged into the mainstream of the dominant society. Membership in these groups often is predictive of such consumer variables as level and type of media exposure, food preferences, the wearing of distinctive apparel, political behavior, leisure activities, and even willingness to try new products.

ETHNIC STEREOTYPES

Many of these subcultures have powerful stereotypes associated with them. Members of a subgroup are assumed to possess certain traits, even though these assumptions often are erroneous. The same trait can be cast either positively or negatively, depending upon the communicator's intentions and biases. For example, the Scottish stereotype in the United States is largely positive, so the supposed frugality of this ethnic group is viewed favorably. Scottish imagery has been used by the 3M company to denote value (e.g., Scotch tape) and also by a motel chain that offers inexpensive lodging. However, invoking the Scottish "personality" might carry quite different connotations to consumers in Britain or Ireland—one person's "thrifty" is another's "stingy."

 MARKETING OPPORTUNITY

Ethnic restaurants are a fast-growing segment of the food industry, whether in the United States, Canada, Europe, or Japan. For example, while restaurant patronage in the U.S. increased by 10 percent in a four-year period, this rate increased by 43 percent for Mexican restaurants and 54 percent for Asian restaurants. Ethnic restaurants are a part of the internationalization of lifestyles, where consumers reach out for new experiences. A greater concentration of ethnic restaurants is found in the northeastern and western parts of the United States and in urban areas of Canada, with relatively fewer establishments in the South or the Midwest. Chinese is the most frequently served cuisine, followed closely by Mexican and Italian (these three types account for over 70 percent of all ethnic restaurants). Many other cuisines are underrepresented, or not represented at all, hinting at opportunities for entrepreneurs who wish to carve out a distinctive niche.[3]

MARKETING USES OF ETHNIC STEREOTYPES   Ethnic symbolism has been used in the past by marketers as a shorthand to connote certain product attributes. The subcultures involved often were minorities and the images employed were crude and unflattering. Blacks were depicted as subservient, Mexicans as bandits.[4] As the civil-rights movement gave more power to minority groups and their rising economic status commanded respect from marketers, these negative stereotypes began to disappear. Frito-Lay responded to protests by the Hispanic community and stopped using the Frito Bandito character in 1971. Quaker Foods gave Aunt Jemima a makeover in 1989 to mark her 100th birthday. In the words of a company spokesman, her new image reflects a youthful grandmother who "knows how to cook and enjoy it."

DE-ETHNICITIZATION   Products that are marketed with an ethnic appeal are not necessarily intended for consumption only by the ethnic subculture from which they originate. **De-ethnicitization** refers to the process where a product formerly associated with a specific ethnic group is detached from its roots and marketed to other subcultures. This process is illustrated by the case of bagels, a bread product formerly associated with Jewish culture and now mass-marketed. Recent variations include jalapeno bagels, blueberry bagels, and even a green bagel for St. Patrick's Day. As a novelty item, a California company even markets tiny bagels as "bagel seeds."[5] A similar attempt to assimilate ethnic products into mainstream culture is underway by Goya Foods, a major marketer of Hispanic food products. As one company executive noted, "Several food items such as tacos, spaghetti, pasta, and burritos were once considered the domain of an ethnic group, and now they're mainstream."[6]

NEW ETHNIC GROUPS

The dominant American culture always exerted pressure on immigrants to divest themselves of their origins and become rapidly absorbed into the host culture. As President Theodore Roosevelt put it in the early part of the century, "We welcome the German or the Irishman who becomes an American. We have no use for the German or the Irishman who remains such."[7]

While the bulk of American immigrants historically came from Europe, immigration patterns have shifted dramatically in the latter part of this century. New immigrants are much more likely to be Asian or Hispanic. As these new waves of immigrants settle in the United States, marketers are attempting to track their consumption patterns and adjust their strategies accordingly. Figure 13-1 shows how new waves of immigrants are changing the ethnic composition of major American cities.

AFRICAN-AMERICANS

Blacks, or African-Americans, comprise a significant racial subculture and account for 12 percent of the U.S. population. While black consumers do differ in important ways from whites, the black market is hardly as homogeneous as many marketers seem to believe.

Historically blacks were separated from mainstream society (unfortunately, not by choice). More recently, though, increasing economic success

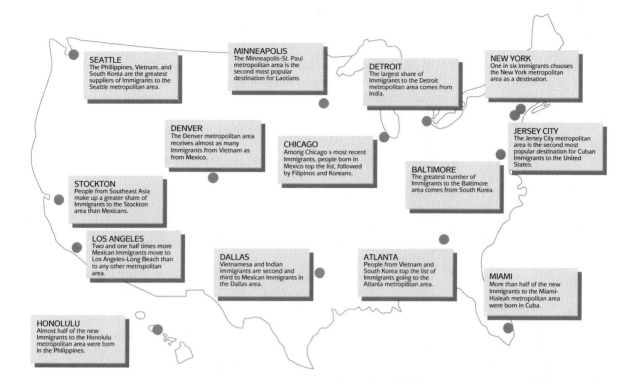

Figure 13-1 America's Newest Markets: Newest Markets *American Demographics,* Sept. 1988, 27.

and the many cultural contributions of this group that have been absorbed by mainstream white culture, have in some instances blurred the lines between American blacks and whites.

Indeed, some commentators have argued that black/white differences are largely illusory. Different consumption behaviors can better be explained by differences in income, the relatively high concentration of African-Americans in urban areas, and other dimensions of social class than by racial differences. With some exceptions the overall spending patterns of blacks and whites *are* roughly similar. Though the average black household income in 1984 was only 63 percent of whites', the *proportions* of monies allocated to different categories do not vary all that much. Both blacks and white spent about ⅔ of their incomes on housing, transportation, and food.[8]

BLACK/WHITE CONSUMPTION DIFFERENCES

Nonetheless, there clearly are some differences in consumption priorities and marketplace behaviors that demand marketers' attention.[9] One reason is the vast market potential of this group: If American blacks were a separate nation, their buying power would rank twelfth of any Western country.[10] Because of the growing economic power of this segment, black consumers often represent a fresh opportunity for otherwise saturated markets. Here are examples of important usage differences in some product categories.[11]

- Blacks account for only 2 percent of all spending on trucks and vans, while they account for almost a quarter of all spending on mass transit. This difference reflects the concentration of blacks in urban areas.
- Blacks purchase 10 percent of televisions, radios, and sound equipment.
- Blacks buy 17 percent of all encyclopedias and reference books sold.
- Blacks spend 28 percent more than other American consumers on baby products.
- Blacks buy 27 percent more cooking ingredients than average.
- Blacks buy more than one-half of all the cognac sold in the United States.
- Blacks comprise 19 percent of the market for toiletries and cosmetics, and 34 percent for haircare products. Black women spend over $500 a year on health and beauty products, three times the rate of white women.

 ## MARKETING OPPORTUNITY

Cosmetics lines developed specifically for black consumers have done well. Black skin can have 35 distinct undertones (as compared to seven for whites), so possibilities for different product formulations are much larger.[12] In a first for a major cosmetics company, Maybelline introduced a line of makeup products for black consumers called Shades of You. Until now, major companies have opted to include shade ranges for darker skin as a part of their regular lines. Maybelline already sells the leading eye makeup brand for black women.[13]

BLACKS AND THE MEDIA

Blacks are heavy media users. Black households watch an average of ten hours of television a day, a rate 39 percent higher than the average American household. This segment tends to prefer established programming and is less likely to experiment with new offerings. As a result, they are more likely to be loyal to major networks, cable networks, and "superstations" such as WTBS, which attracts about 10 percent of the black viewing audience. In addition, readership of local morning daily newspapers (as opposed to major regional papers) is 30 percent higher than with adults overall, and blacks also are more likely to read classified ads and circulars.

BLACK REPRESENTATION IN MAINSTREAM MEDIA Historically, blacks have not been well represented in mainstream advertising, but this situation is changing. Blacks now account for about one-quarter of the people depicted in ads, (a rate even greater than their actual proportion of the overall population), and commercials are increasingly likely to be racially integrated.[14] The more striking and important change, though, is the *way* black people are portrayed on television. Unlike earlier shows that presented blacks in stereotyped roles, such as "Sanford and Son" and "The Jeffersons," most television roles created for blacks now tend to depict them as middle-to-upper class individuals who also happen to be black (e.g., "The Cosby Show").[15]

BLACK-ORIENTED MEDIA   Several major magazines, such as *Jet, Ebony, Essence,* and *Black Enterprise,* target this segment exclusively, and with great success. *Jet,* for example, claims to reach over 90 percent of the black male audience.[16] Black media tend to depict consumers in their natural social

Ebony is targeted to a solely black readership. Reprinted by permission of *EBONY* Magazine and Johnson Publishing Company, Inc.

environment and more positively than in the general media, so it is not surprising that many blacks gravitate to these magazines and newspapers.[17]

Targeted Advertising. Advertising to blacks often is better-executed when it is sensitive to important cues and avoids symbols irrelevant to the black subculture. For this reason, it is not uncommon for companies to commission a specialized agency to develop a separate ad campaign specifically targeted to the black market. Canadian Mist's general advertising campaign featured the motif "Canada at its best" and emphasized picturesque scenery and a rural lifestyle. A separate advertising program for blacks was developed by a black agency, which instead focused on style and an urban environment.[18]

Family Emphasis. A Crest toothpaste ad done by a black agency had a powerful impact on target consumers. It depicted a simple act: A father lovingly showing his son how to knot a tie. The copy reads: "I'm going to be involved with my son as much as I can."[19] This idealized father/son relationship often is taken for granted by whites, but it hits home to many black consumers, 40 percent of whom grow up in fatherless households.[20] Advertising has in general tried to promote a positive image of black men, either stressing family involvement or a sense of style.

The BUPPIE. This change also has been dictated by the growing black middle class, and the emergence of the so-called BUPPIE, or Black YUPPIE.[21] Although some marketers assume that black consumers who have moved up the social ladder forsake their ethnic identities, this does not appear to be the case. Middle-class blacks instead appear to span subcultures, exhibiting the attitudes of the white middle-class while still holding on to their black heritage. Black shoppers respond well to products that appeal to their racial pride.[22] This tact was taken in an ad targeted to blacks by Miller beer featuring a middle-class black man. The copy read "He moved up, but not out."

▼ MARKETING PITFALL

The R. J. Reynolds Tobacco Company ignited a lot of controversy when it announced plans in 1990 to test-market a menthol cigarette, called Uptown, specifically to black consumers. Although the marketing of cigarettes to minorities is not a novel tactic, this was the first time a company explicitly acknowledged the strategy. Many critics immediately attacked the proposal, arguing that the campaign would exploit poor blacks. The publishers of black-oriented newspapers and magazines were caught in the middle, since they stood to receive substantial advertising revenues from the campaign. For example, approximately 10 percent of *Jet's* advertising revenues come from cigarette advertising. For its part, the company claimed that its actions were a natural result of shrinking markets and the need to more finely target increasingly small segments. Unlike other ethnic groups, which do not seem to display marked cigarette preferences, the tastes of black consumers are easy to pinpoint. According to the company, 69 percent of black consumers prefer menthol, more than twice the rate of smokers overall. After market research indicated that blacks tend to open cigarette packs from the bottom, the company decided to pack Uptowns with the filters facing down. Reynolds claimed that the product was not designed specifically for blacks, though it acknowledged that was likely to attract a disproportionate share of black smokers. Following a storm of criticism by both private health groups and Government officials (including the Secretary of Health and Human Services), the company announced that it was canceling its test-marketing plans. It would not comment on the likelihood that the cigarette would ever be introduced.[23]

First date.

Her Mama insisted,
"OK, as long as you stay in the neighborhood."
His Dad suggested,
"Go someplace where you'll feel
welcome and comfortable."
His wallet pleaded, "Take it easy man, easy."
He smoothly stated,
"And after the movie, we'll go
to Mickey D's."

© 1985 McDonald's Corporation

IT'S A GOOD TIME
FOR THE GREAT TASTE

McDonald's

This ad for McDonald's was developed by a black ageny for black markets. *Courtesy of McDonald's Corporation.*

Maximum Care For Beautiful Hair. MoistureMax.

MoistureMax protects all types of hair—relaxed, natural or pressed—from moisture loss caused by combing, brushing, blow drying or hot styling.

MoistureMax's soothing, saturating formula of panthenol, lanolin, and jojoba oil penetrates hair to replenish natural moisture and restore sheen. Dryness, breakage and split ends simply melt away. So hair becomes easier to comb. Unlike other oil moisturizers, our feather-light formula contains no beeswax to weigh your hair down.

Try new MoistureMax Oil Sheen Spray when styling your hair. It gives you MoistureMax protection, while giving lasting sheen.

Keep beautiful hair in the family. With maximum care from MoistureMax.

Lustrasilk

© 1991 Lustrasilk Corporation of America.

Give Your Hair What It Needs Most. MoistureMax.

This ad for MoistureMax hair products promotes the stability of the black family. Courtesy of Lustrasilk Corporation of America, Inc.

Black Celebrities. The use of black celebrities and sports figures is also on the rise. The proliferation of black role models appears to be reducing the racial distinctions formerly made by many.[24] However, this strategy does not guarantee success with black consumers. For example, while Pepsi has used singer Michael Jackson in its ad campaigns, its research showed that he did not appeal to twenty-five to forty-year-old blacks, who interpreted his plastic surgery and eccentric behavior as a desire to distance himself from his black roots.[25] On the other hand, a black version of the popular cartoon character Bart Simpson became extremely popular in the black community in the early 1990s. Bart has been recast in the image of several black celebrities, including Malcolm X, Bob

MULTICULTURAL DIMENSIONS

The recent proliferation of ethnic dolls in America's toy stores reflects society's growing cultural diversity. While non-Caucasian dolls used to appear only in collections of dolls from around the world, all major manufacturers have now introduced ethnic dolls to the mass market. These new entrants include Kira, the Asian fashion doll, and Emmy, the African-American baby doll. Mattel recently introduced a trio of dolls named Shani (which means "marvelous" in Swahili), Asha, and Nichelle that represent the range of African-American facial features and skin tones. And, while Mattel has sold a black version of Barbie for over twenty years, it only recently began to promote the doll in television and print campaigns.[27]

Marley ("Rasta Bart"), and Michael Jordan ("Air Bart"). Bart's popularity in the black subculture has been attributed to his status as an outsider with an "attitude" who battles established society.[26]

HISPANIC-AMERICANS

The Hispanic subculture is a sleeping giant, a segment that was until recently largely ignored by many marketers. The growth and increasing affluence of this group has now made it impossible to overlook, and the Hispanic consumer is now diligently courted by many major corporations. For example, Pepsi sponsors local ethnic festivals in major cities, and the company also signed the music group Miami Sound Machine for its Latin promotions.[28]

Because of this subculture's high birthrate, it is projected that Hispanics will outnumber blacks as the nation's largest minority group by the year 2015. This dramatic growth rate is charted in Figure 13-2. The number of Hispanics in the United States grew by 30 percent between 1980 and 1988, and the birthrate within this subculture is four times that of the population average.[29]

THE HISPANIC MARKET

Demographically, two important characteristics of the Hispanic market are worth noting: (1) It is a young market. The median age of Hispanic-Americans is 23.6, compared with the U.S. average of 32. And (2) the Hispanic family is much larger than the rest of the population's. The average Hispanic household contains 3.5 people, compared to only 2.7 people for other U.S. households. These differences will obviously affect the overall allocation of income to various product categories. For example, Hispanic households spend 15 percent to 20 percent more of their disposable income than the national average on groceries.[30] There are now over 19 million Hispanic consumers in the United States, and a number of factors make this market segment extremely attractive.

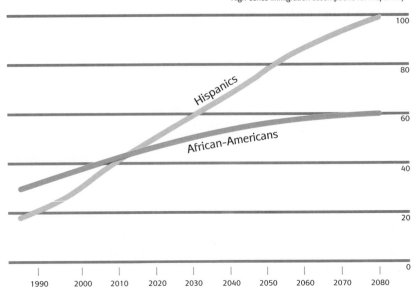

(Number of Hispanics and African-Americans in millions, 1980—2080.
Middle-series fertility and mortality assumptions.
High-series immigration assumptions for Hispanics)

Figure 13-2 The Growth of the Hispanic Market

Source: U.S. Bureau of the Census, Projections of the Hispanic Population: 1983 to 2080, Current Population Reports, Series P-25, No. 995, 1986

- Hispanics tend to be brand-loyal, especially to brands from their country of origin. About 45 percent of Hispanic consumers in one study reported that they always buy their usual brand, while only one in five said they frequently switch brands.[31]
- Hispanics are highly concentrated by national origin, which makes them relatively easy to reach. Over 50 percent of all Hispanics live in the Los Angeles, New York, Miami, San Antonio, San Francisco, and Chicago metropolitan areas. For this reason, 70 percent of Avon's sales representatives in the Los Angeles area are Latino.[32]
- Education levels are increasing dramatically. In the period between 1984 and 1988, the number of Hispanics with four years of college increased by 51 percent. The number of men in managerial and professional jobs increased by 42 percent, and the corresponding increase of 61 percent for women was even more encouraging.[33]

THE ROLE OF THE CHURCH   While Hispanics traditionally have been predominantly Catholic, millions of Hispanics are leaving the Roman Catholic Church. It is estimated that about one in five Hispanics now practices some form of evangelical Protestantism. This change is ascribed to two factors: (1) The evangelical Protestants have adopted sophisticated marketing techniques, such as providing local clergy with profiles of Hispanic communities in a campaign to convert large numbers of Hispanic Catholics, and (2) the style of U.S. Catholicism is alien to many Hispanics. It tends to be more rational and bureaucratic and is not viewed by many as being responsive to the more emotional and mystical Hispanic experience. For example, the belief in miraculous healing that is prevalent in Latin American Catholicism does not tend to be emphasized in American churches.[34]

THE ROLE OF THE FAMILY The importance of the family to Hispanics cannot be overstated. Preferences to spend time with family influence the structure of many consumption activities. As one illustration, the act of going to the movies has a different meaning for many Hispanics, who tend to regard this activity as a family outing. One study found that 42 percent of Hispanic moviegoers attend in groups of three or more, as compared with only 28 percent of Anglo consumers.

Behaviors that underscore one's ability to provide well for the family are reinforced in this subculture. Clothing one's children well is regarded in particular as a matter of pride.[35] In contrast, convenience and a product's ability to save time is not terribly important to the Hispanic homemaker, who is willing to purchase labor-intensive products if it means that her family will benefit. For this reason, a time-saving appeal short-circuited for Quaker Foods, which found that Hispanic women tend to cook Instant Quaker Oats on the stove, refrigerate it, and serve it later as a pudding.[36] This orientation also explains why generic products do not tend to do well in the Hispanic market; these consumers value the quality promised by well-known brand names.

 MARKETING OPPORTUNITY

Ethnic soap operas, shown on American television, are becoming big business. Hispanic Americans are avid consumers of soap operas, called *telenovellas.* Univision, the biggest Spanish-language network, airs ten different ones each day. These shows are produced by Latin American networks, and some viewers complain that they do not address the problems of Hispanic-Americans, such as illegal immigration, getting a job, or speaking the language. The second-largest Spanish-language network, Telemundo, finally aired a *telenovella* about a U.S. Hispanic family in 1989.[37]

The pervasiveness of the family theme can be seen in many marketing contexts. When Johnson Wax decided to enter the Hispanic market with Future floor polish, market research revealed that Hispanic consumers cleaned their floors regularly, but did not wax them. The company's television commercial therefore depicted a housewife standing on her dull floor and asked: "We know your floors are clean, but do they shine?" Traditional gender roles are then reinforced as the husband leaps into the air, shouting "resalta" ("outstanding").[38]

APPEALING TO HISPANIC SUBCULTURES
The behavior profile of the Hispanic consumer includes a need for status and a strong sense of pride. A high value is placed on self-expression

and familial devotion. Some campaigns have played to Hispanics' fear of rejection and apprehension about loss of control and embarrassment in social situations. Conventional wisdom is to create action-oriented advertising and to emphasize a problem-solving atmosphere. Assertive role models who are cast in non-threatening situations appear to be effective.[39]

Procter & Gamble is the biggest advertiser in Hispanic media. The company spent nearly $21 million catering to this segment in 1988. P&G also was one of the first to establish a Hispanic corporate marketing structure that has Hispanic group brand managers. It has focused on introducing products such as diapers, cleansers, and grooming products that capitalize on the youth and large family size prevalent among Hispanics.[40]

MARKETING BLUNDERS Many initial efforts by Americans to market to this subculture were, to say the least, counterproductive. Companies bumbled in their efforts to translate advertising adequately or to compose copy that could capture desired nuances. These mistakes do not occur so much anymore as marketers become more sophisticated in dealing with this market and as Hispanics themselves become involved in advertising production. Some translation mishaps:

- The Perdue slogan "It takes a tough man to make a tender chicken" was translated to read: "It takes a sexually excited man to make a chick affectionate."
- Budweiser was promoted as "the queen of beers."
- A burrito was mistakenly called a "burrada," which means big mistake.
- Braniff, promoting its comfortable leather seats, used the headline: "Sentado en cuero," which was interpreted as "Sit naked."
- Coors beer's slogan "get loose with Coors" appeared in Spanish as "get the runs with Coors."

HISPANIC IDENTITY Native language and culture are important components of Hispanic identity and self-esteem (about three-quarters of Latinos still speak Spanish when at home), and these consumers are very sympathetic to marketing efforts that acknowledge and emphasize the Hispanic cultural heritage.[41] More than 40 percent of Hispanic consumers say they deliberately attempt to buy products that show an interest in the Hispanic consumer, and this jumps to over two-thirds for Cuban-Americans.[42]

Level of Acculturation. A consumer's level of **acculturation** refers to the degree to which he or she has learned the ways of a different culture from the one in which he or she was originally raised. This factor is especially important when considering the Hispanic market, since the degree to which these consumers are integrated into the American way of life varies widely. For instance, about 38 percent of all Hispanics live in barrios, or predominantly Hispanic neighborhoods, which tend to be insulated from mainstream society.[43]

Differences in Cultural Integration. On the one hand, many Cuban-American families with high educational levels fled Castro's regime in the late 1950s and early 1960s, worked hard for many years to establish themselves, and are now firmly entrenched in the Miami political and economic establishment. Because of this affluence, businesses in South Florida now make an effort to target *YUCAs,* young, upwardly mobile Cuban-Americans.[44]

On the other hand, it is estimated that anywhere from 1.8 million to 5.4 million immigrants enter the country illegally each year.[45] The majority of these people have less than a fifth grade education and are concerned with fitting into their new country. Since they are eager to adapt to their new environment, these consumers tend to look for products they perceive to be more American. In some cases, this entails learning about entirely new product categories. One

Who keeps Laura de Oña entertained?

Name: Laura de Oña.
Occupation: Attorney.
Age: 43.
Family: Mother of two.
Car: Mercedes Benz.
Hobbies: Playing tennis.
Last vacation spot: Hawaii
Latest book: *Atlas Shrugged.*
Radio Station: WQBA-FM, for the latest in Latin and American music.

The Super Q/FM listener profile is best represented by people like Laura de Oña. These career oriented, bilingual, educated Latins from 25 to 49 make up the majority of our listening audience. This Latin market in South Florida represents over $8.7 billion in spending power which most companies cannot ignore. You can reach this market by advertising on WQBA-FM.

For information contact Veronica Serra, National Sales Manager: WQBA AM/FM (305) 441-2073.

This trade ad for WQBA-FM, a South Florida radio station, describes its Hispanic listeners, who fit the profile of the YUCA (Young, upwardly mobile Cuban-American). *Courtesy of WQBA-FM Miami.*

example is the air freshener, which is not common in Central America. Many immigrants must be taught what an air freshener is before they can be convinced to buy one brand over another.[46]

Leaving one's culture and family to go to a new place creates many needs that can be partially addressed by products and services. Recent immigrants (both legal and illegal) share the common experience of "going north" to the United States, where they encounter a strange culture and often leave family members behind. This frightening odyssey was incorporated by AT&T in its campaign to boost international calling volume. In a Spanish-language commercial called "Countryside," a young man says goodbye to his mother and promises to keep in touch. The announcer says: "The decision of leaving the family is based on a promise: Keeping it united."

Progressive Learning. The acculturation of Hispanic consumers may be understood in terms of the **progressive learning model.** This perspective assumes that people gradually learn a new culture as they increasingly come in contact with it. Thus, we would expect the consumer behavior of Hispanic-Americans to be a mixture of practices taken from their original culture and those of the new or *host culture.*[47]

Research has generally obtained results that support this pattern when factors such as shopping orientation, the importance placed on various product attributes, media preference, and brand loyalty are examined.[48] When the *intensity* of ethnic identification is taken into account, consumers who retained a strong ethnic identification differed from their more-assimilated counterparts in the following ways:

- They had a more negative attitude toward business in general (probably caused by frustration due to relatively low income levels).
- They were higher users of Spanish language media.
- They were more brand loyal.
- They were more likely to prefer brands with prestige labels.
- They were more likely to buy brands specifically advertised to their ethnic group.[49]

SEGMENTING HISPANIC SUBCULTURES   As with other large subcultural segments, marketers are now beginning to discover that the Hispanic market is not homogeneous. Subcultural identity is not as much with being Hispanic as it is with the particular country of origin. Mexican-Americans, who make up about 62 percent of all Hispanic-Americans, also are the fastest-growing subsegment; their population has grown by 40 percent since 1980. In contrast, Cuban-Americans are by far the wealthiest sub-segment, but they are also the smallest Hispanic ethnic group, and are older on average than other Hispanics.[50] Because of large cultural differences among segments, it is important to address specific wants and needs of Hispanic subgroups. The Winn-Dixie supermarket chain, for example, promotes holidays and dishes native to individual countries and employs the theme: "Winn-Dixie tiene el sabor de mi pais" (Winn-Dixie has the flavor of my country).[51]

While many corporations are just now waking up to the potential of the Hispanic market, others that sell harmful products such as junk food, cigarettes, and alcohol discovered this market long ago. These industries donate over $1 million a year to Hispanic groups, and critics point to a high concentration of liquor stores and related advertising in Hispanic neighborhoods. Available evidence indicates that Mexican-born men stand a greater chance of dying of cirrhosis of the liver and that Hispanic men also are more likely to die of lung cancer than are Anglos. The smoking rate of fourth and fifth grade Hispanic boys is roughly five times that of Anglo boys.[52]

ASIAN-AMERICANS

Though their numbers are still relatively small, Asian-Americans are the fastest-growing minority group in the United States. Marketers are just beginning to recognize their potential as a unique market segment. This subculture is attractive because Asian-Americans typically are hard working and many have above-average incomes. The average household incomes of Asian-Americans are more than $2000 greater than whites and $7000-$9000 higher than blacks and Hispanics.

This subculture places a very high priority on education and sends a large percentage of children to college. Of Asian-Americans over the age of 25, about a third have completed four or more years of college, twice the graduation rate of whites and more than quadruple that of blacks and Hispanics.[53]

ASIAN-AMERICAN SEGMENTATION

Despite its potential, this group is hard to market to, because it is actually composed of subgroups that are culturally diverse and speak many different languages and dialects. The term Asian refers to 12 nationalities, with Chinese being the largest subgroup and Filipino and Japanese second and third, respectively.[54] Also, although their birth rate is increasing at almost four times the rate of most other groups, Asian-Americans still comprise only about 2 percent of the population, so mass marketing techniques often are not viable to reach them.[55] Finally, Asian-Americans save more of their wages and borrow less, preferring to keep large balances in conservative passbook accounts rather than investing their earnings.

On the other hand, as one Asian-American advertising executive noted, "Prosperous Asians tend to be very status-conscious and will spend their money on premium brands, such as BMW and Mercedes-Benz, and the best French cognac and Scotch whiskey."[56] This group also is a good market for technically oriented products. They spend more than average on such products as VCRs, personal computers, and compact disc players.[57]

The problems encountered by American marketers when they first tried to reach the Hispanic market also occurred when targeting Asians and Asian-Americans. Some attempts to translate advertising messages and concepts into Asian media have backfired. Coca-Cola's slogan "Coke Adds Life" was translated as "Coke brings your ancestors back from the dead" in Japanese. Kentucky Fried Chicken ran into a problem when it described its chicken as "finger-licking good" to the Chinese, who don't lick their fingers in appreciation when food is good.[58]

Advertisers often overlook the complex differences among Asian subcultures, and they may be insensitive to cultural practices. It is not unusual, for example, for advertisements targeted to Koreans to use Japanese models. One company ran an ad in Chinese to wish the community a Happy New Year, but the characters were upside down. A recent footwear campaign depicted Japanese women performing footbinding, a practice done exclusively in China.[59]

REACHING THE ASIAN-AMERICAN SEGMENT   Many marketers are discouraged by the lack of media available to reach Asian-Americans.[60] Practitioners generally find that advertising in English works best for broadcast ads, while print ads are more effective when executed in Asian languages.[61] Filipinos are the only Asians who predominantly speak English among themselves; most Asians prefer media in their own languages.[62] The most frequently spoken languages among Asian-Americans are Mandarin Chinese, Korean, Japanese, and Vietnamese.[63]

One Success Story.   One of the first companies to realize the potential of the Asian-American segment was Metropolitan Life. Since these consumers tend to be well educated and place a very high priority on the education and security of their children, they seemed ideal prospects for insurance products. Qualitative research showed marked differences among Asian subsegments in their attitudes toward insurance. These differences paralleled those between Cuban-Americans and Mexican-Americans, in that subsegments' degree of acculturation affect understanding and interest in products and services.

In general, Asians tend to be leery of buying insurance, superstitiously equating its purchase with old age and death. The company found that Chinese consumers emphasize family members' protection and education, so they were more likely to be interested in whole-life policies. On the other hand, Vietnamese consumers, many of whom were recent immigrants, tended to be unfamiliar with the concept of insurance. Still, this group is seen as having potential since they are very survival-oriented.[64] Based upon this research, a Chinese ad campaign stressed the role of insurance in protecting children. A print ad from the campaign is shown here. As a reward for its efforts, Met Life increased its premiums among Asian Americans by 22 percent in one year.[65]

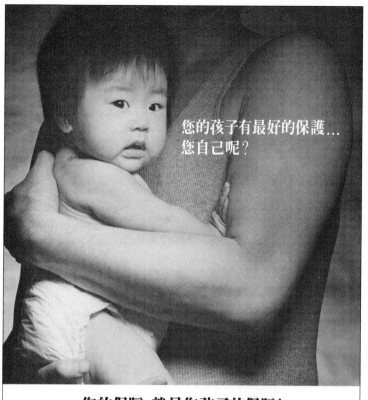

您的孩子有最好的保護…
您自己呢？

您的保障，就是您孩子的保障！

父母對子女的愛，無微不至。
任何父母都會給予自己的孩子最大的關懷和最好的保護。不過，偉大的父母們可千萬別忘記了自己。若您希望您的孩子安定幸福，您必需先爲自己作出

保障，光替您的孩子着想是不足夠的。
大都會保險公司的營業代表經驗豐富，服務態度優良，他們了解您的責任，會爲您選擇一種最適合您的保險計劃。

大都會保險公司，使您高枕無憂
❊ **MetLife**®
汽車 • 房屋 • 健康 • 儲蓄人壽 • 退休金 • 互助基金

Met Life appeals to Asian-Americans' family priorities in this ad. The caption reads: "You protect your baby. Who protects you?" Reprinted with permission of Metropolitan Life Insurance Company.

RELIGION AND CONSUMPTION

Heritage Village, a religiously oriented entertainment center in South Carolina, illustrates the relationship between religion and consumer behavior. Attendance at this 2300 acre complex is exceeded only by the Disney theme parks. It features a church, a passion play, and replicas of Old Jerusalem, along with a bustling shopping mall called "Main Street USA." A central theme of the park is its idealized presentation of America's past and traditional values, the pristine vision of America desired by those who make the Heritage Village pilgrimage.[66]

Religion per se has not been studied extensively in marketing, possibly because it is seen as a "taboo" subject.[67] However, the little evidence that has been accumulated indicates that religious affiliation has the potential to be a valuable predictor of consumer behavior.[68] Religious subcultures in particular may exert a significant impact on such consumer variables as personality, attitudes toward sexuality, birthrates and household formation, income, and political attitudes. One study that examined this issue, for example, found marked differences among Catholic, Protestant, and Jewish college students in preferences for weekend entertainment activities, as well as the criteria used in making these decisions. For example, price was a relatively more important criterion for Protestants, while desire for companionship was highest for Jews. Catholics were most likely to designate dancing as a favored activity than were the other two groups, but much less likely to select sex![69]

THE CATHOLIC SUBCULTURE

Catholic dogmas encompass virtually all of the individual's behavior. The Church is characterized by a rigid organizational structure, and personal interpretations of events are minimized. Some observers have inferred that Catholic consumers as a result tend to be fatalistic and are less likely to be innovators.

Catholics have more children than either Protestants or Jews. Sexuality is seen as instrumental, in the sense that it is performed for the purpose of procreation rather than recreation. There is some evidence that this attitude is changing: As far back as 1975, 50 percent of Catholics endorsed the idea that a husband and wife may engage in sex for pleasure alone, as compared to only 29 percent who said this in 1965.[70]

Members of this religious group traditionally have a lower socioeconomic status than Jews and Protestants. This deficit may stem from a variety of causes, including earlier religious discrimination. Other factors include traditionalism, restricted knowledge-seeking, and an emphasis on collective rather than individual initiative.

MARKETING PITFALL

Australia's largest independent beer brewer announced plans to sponsor the Pope's visit to that country in late 1986. It also announced plans to throw a huge party for 250,000 people after his mass and issue "special edition" beer cans bearing his picture. Needless to say, the nation's aborigines, who have a severe alcoholism problem, were not pleased with this arrangement.[71]

THE PROTESTANT SUBCULTURE

In contrast to Catholics, Protestant dogma stresses the faith of the individual. The Bible is viewed more as descriptive than as evidence of divine control. This tradition encourages the acquisition of scientific knowledge. Protestants tend to be less authoritarian and to value work and personal hardship as an avenue toward upward social mobility.

While not all Protestants are wealthy, they appear in disproportionate numbers in the upper classes. Explanations for this relative affluence include:

- An emphasis on industriousness and hard work.
- A low fertility rate that facilitates the upward mobility of children.
- A U.S. social structure where Protestants were historically part of the *"power-elite."*[72]

Early colonists were overwhelmingly Protestant, which allowed this group to create the foundations of the American social system, and thus create "barriers-to-entry" for other groups. The "Protestant establishment" still dominates leadership positions in the private sector and is also over-represented in science, education, government, and the military.[73] It is only recently that Irish Catholics have reached economic parity with Protestants, while Conservative and Reform Jews have surpassed this level.[74]

THE WASP SUBCULTURE The WASP (White Anglo-Saxon Protestant) subculture may be thought of as the one ethnic group not acknowledged to *be* an ethnic group. After all, no one has yet used the term WASP-American! Despite this "ethnic invisibility," the WASP subculture has been a dominant force in the larger picture of American culture.[75]

THE AMERICAN IDEAL   The WASP in many ways is a symbol of the American ideal. Idealized images of the WASP are frequently employed in advertising to epitomize the "good life" and the amenities associated with "old money" (see Chapter 12). The WASP symbolizes to many immigrants the light at the end of the tunnel: If one desires to assimilate, to "make it" in America, this is the end result.

As a result, the formal eating rituals devised by WASPs and propagated by such etiquette guides as Emily Post are assumed to be the "proper" way to eat and entertain. The leisure activities associated with this subculture (e.g., golfing, yachting, squash), often are seen as socially "correct."[76] Marketers have done more than their share to propagate this ideal. In particular, the success of influential designer Ralph Lauren hinges on his ability to create images of an idealized WASP life-style.

THE JEWISH SUBCULTURE
Jewish ethnicity exerts an exceptionally strong influence on consumers, since it incorporates both cultural and religious dimensions. American Jews tend to be of relatively high socioeconomic status and average family size is relatively low (with the exception of some Orthodox groups).

Judaism reinforces individual responsibility for actions and self-education.[77] Jewish consumers have a personality structure characterized by high product innovation tendencies, need for achievement, anxiousness, emotionality, and individualism.[78] One study of Jewish versus gentile consumers indeed found that the Jewish respondents were more likely to have been exposed to educational materials in childhood, to use more sources in the process of information search, to be product innovators, and to transfer more consumption information to others.[79]

MARKETING AND THE JEWISH SUBCULTURE   Some marketers have specifically employed Jewish symbolism. The Bank Leumi Trust Company of New York, an Israel-based bank, capitalized on its ethnic ties to reach

Jewish and gentile customers with ad copy such as the following used to promote Individual Retirement Accounts: "Some people need a little help getting to the Promised Land. If you dream of retiring to a land of milk and honey, you're going to need plenty of bread."[80] One famous campaign for a bakery company used Chinese, blacks, and other spokesmen to tell consumers "You don't have to be Jewish to love Levy's real Jewish rye."[81]

MARKETING OPPORTUNITY

One of the most significant Jewish-related marketing developments is the increase in demand for kosher food. Each year, about 500 new kosher products appear on the market to satisfy this demand. This trend is being driven by two developments: (1) increased religious observance by young Jews, and (2) the belief among many gentiles that kosher food is of higher quality. In addition to some Jews, Seventh-Day Adventists and Moslems have very similar dietary requirements and are good customers for kosher food.[82] It is estimated that less than a third of the 6 million consumers who buy kosher products are Jewish.[83]

The potential of the kosher market has prompted some of the nation's largest manufacturers to get involved. General Foods distributed 100,000 copies of a children's activity booklet called "Brachos (Prayers) for Breakfast." Wise Potato Chips produces kosher chips, and Eagle Snacks also makes kosher snack foods. Of the 330 products made by Pepperidge Farm, Inc., 255 are now kosher.[84] The ads for Sun-Maid and Delta Airlines provide two other recent examples of this interest.

THE BORN-AGAIN SUBCULTURE

Recent years have seen a dramatic increase in the number of consumers who profess to be born-again Christians, or evangelicals. A recent Gallup Poll indicates that one-third of American adults say they are born-again. While this movement has affected a variety of social classes and consumer types, it is strongest among women, older adults, and Southerners. It is also a relatively downscale phenomenon: The number of adults who describe themselves as "born again" steadily decreases as education and income levels rise.[85] The born-again movement is exerting a significant impact on American marketing as well as on *demarketing,* or discouraging demand for products and services. This community has been influential in altering the content of media programming and advertising that is seen to unduly emphasize sex and violence.

CONSUMPTION CHARACTERISTICS OF THE BORN-AGAIN SEGMENT   The evidence is unclear as to whether the consumption behavior of evangelicals is radically different from that of other subcultures. In general, highly religious Protestants are more likely to endorse traditional sex-role orientations, to be below-average users of credit, and to place relatively low emphasis on purchasing national brands. They also are not as likely as

Photo courtesy of Delta Air Lines, Inc.

Some major companies, such as Sun-Maid raisins and Delta Airlines, attempt to appeal to Jewish consumers by using symbolism and language understood by this consumer subculture. Courtesy of Sun-Diamond Growers of California.

the general public to listen to rock-and-roll music (perhaps due to a perceived emphasis on sex and drugs), preferring gospel and contemporary Christian music. And, while there are no differences in terms of such activities as eating out or attending concerts, born-again Christians do attend movies less frequently than do other groups.[86]

▼ MARKETING PITFALL

Some merchants who cater to the born-again segment have run into trouble for targeting these consumers *too* exclusively. A car dealer in Virginia is representative of attempts to service only true believers. He unveiled a "Christian Members Buying Plan," which would allow some people to purchase their cars at rock-bottom prices. In addition, he proposed to donate part of the profit from every sale to the buyer's church. The American Civil Liberties Union and other groups quickly objected to the plan, arguing that it discriminates against non-Christians. The group had been involved in an earlier dispute, where a Florida gas station owner had posted a sign reading "For Christians Only: 10 percent discount on labor." The car dealer stated he had no intention of dropping his plan and admitted to some economic motivation for conjuring up this kind of promotion during a sluggish sales season. As he noted, "We're in business to make a profit. Your Senator and your Congressman, when they run for election, they go to a church or a Sunday schoolclass because they want the votes of the people there. It's the same principle."[87]

Christian Media. Christian broadcast media have become a powerful cultural force for many consumers. For example, approximately 12 percent of all U.S. radio stations have a religious format. In addition, about 200 local television stations regularly feature religious programming, and television preachers have an estimated audience of over 15 million people. This number represents almost the combined membership of the United Methodist, Presbyterian, and Episcopal churches.[88]

Not surprisingly, some research indicates that born-agains subscribe to religious magazines at a much higher rate than do other Christians, and that they are higher-than-average subscribers to home-oriented magazines. Also of no surprise is the finding that almost 15 percent of these consumers list a televised church service as one of their three favorite television programs.

The Christian publishing industry has also shown phenomenal growth. According to trade figures, 37 million people spend $1.4 billion annually at Christian bookstores. According to one industry official, consumers are now very selective about what they buy, so Christian merchants must adopt "a commitment to a way of life to excel as God's retailer."[89]

Many Christian bookstores have expanded their product mix. In addition to the traditional assortment of inspirational books and records, most carry what one official termed "holy hardware." These stores stock items ranging from "I Am Blessed" jogging suits to watches with pictures of the twelve apostles. Grace, the pro-life doll, was introduced in 1987. When squeezed, the doll delivers the message: "God knew me even before I was born . . . I used to be a little person inside my mother's tummy. . . . My mommy thinks I'm very special. She's so happy she had me." More than 20,000 of these dolls, priced from $40 to $50, were sold in a four-month period.[90]

CHAPTER SUMMARY

Consumers identify with many groups that share common characteristics and identities. These large groups that exist within a society are subcultures, and membership in them often gives marketers a clue about individuals' consumption decisions. A large component of a person's identity is often determined by his or her ethnic origins and religious background.

Recently, several minority groups have caught the attention of marketers as their economic power has grown. Segmenting consumers by their ethnicity can be effective, but care must be taken not to rely on inaccurate (and sometimes offensive) ethnic stereotypes.

Black Americans are a very important market segment. While in some respects the market expenditures of these consumers do not differ that much from whites, blacks are above average consumers in such categories as personal care products. In the past, blacks were either ignored or portrayed negatively in mainstream advertising, but this is changing as more blacks actually work on the development of campaigns and as specialized black media increase in importance.

Hispanic-Americans and Asian-Americans are other ethnic subcultures that are beginning to be actively courted by marketers. The size of both groups is increasing rapidly and in the coming years will dominate some major markets. Asian-Americans on the whole are extremely well educated, and the socioeconomic status of Hispanics is increasing as well. Key issues for reaching the Hispanic market are consumers' degree of acculturation into mainstream American society and the recognition of important cultural differences among Hispanic subgroups (e.g., Puerto Ricans, Cubans, Mexicans). Both Asian- and Hispanic-Americans tend to be extremely family-oriented and are receptive to advertising that understands their heritage and reinforces traditional family values.

While the impact of religious identification on consumer behavior is not clear, some differences among religious subcultures do emerge. In particular, cultural characteristics of Protestants, Catholics, and Jews result in varied preferences for leisure activities and orientations toward consumption. Some of these factors are closely related to social class. White Anglo-Saxon Protestants (WASPs) in particular have played a dominant role in the formation of American cultural values largely due to their cultural emphasis on achievement and early domination of the American power structure. The market power of the growing numbers of evangelical Christians is uncertain at this point, but opportunities exist to cater to the unique needs of this segment.

KEY TERMS

Acculturation	Progressive learning model
De-ethnicitization	Subculture

REVIEW QUESTIONS AND DISCUSSION TOPICS

1. R. J. Reynolds' controversial plan to test-market a cigarette to black consumers raises numerous ethical issues about segmenting subcultures. As one observer noted, "The irony is that if R. J. Reynolds made shoes or shirts and specifically marketed to blacks, they would probably be regarded as progressive and socially positive."[91] Does a company have the right to exploit a subculture's special characteristics, especially to increase sales of a harmful product like cigarettes? What about the argument that virtually every business that follows the marketing concept designs a product to meet the needs and tastes of a preselected segment? For example, the chapter also notes that Maybelline developed a makeup line specifically for black women, yet this did not seem to bother anyone. What do you think?

2. The chapter notes that products can function as socialization agents, citing the example of the air freshener product category. What other examples

can you find that serve this important function? What special problems do these create for marketers?

3. Describe the progressive learning model and discuss why this phenomenon is important when marketing to subcultures.

4. The chapter notes that a beer company tried a marketing tactic using a religious symbol (the Pope). Are some categories more likely to be appropriate than others as candidates for religious segmentation?

5. Evangelical groups have been instrumental in organizing boycotts of products advertised on shows they find objectionable, especially those that, they feel, undermine "family values." Do consumer groups have a right or a responsibility to dictate the advertising a network should carry?

6. An official with a Christian organization defended the Christian Members Buying Plan described in the chapter, arguing that "We are sick and tired of Christians and Christian values being expunged from every area of public life. This isn't separation of church and state; this is a private merchant."[92] Do you agree?

HANDS-ON EXERCISES

1. Can you locate any current examples of marketing stimuli that depend upon an ethnic stereotype to communicate a message? How effective are these appeals?

2. To understand the power of ethnic stereotypes, conduct your own poll. For a set of ethnic groups, ask people to anonymously provide attributes (including personality traits and products) most likely to characterize each group using the technique of free association. How much agreement do you obtain across people? Compare the associations for an ethnic group between actual members of that group and non-members.

NOTES

1. John Skow, "In California: The Dead Live On," *Time* (February 11, 1985): 11.
2. See Frederik Barth, *Ethnic Groups and Boundaries: The Social Organization of Culture Difference* (London: Allen and Unwin, 1969); Michel Laroche, Annamma Joy, Michael Hui, and Chankon Kim, "An Examination of Ethnicity Measures: Convergent Validity and Cross-Cultural Equivalence," in *Advances in Consumer Research,* ed. Rebecca H. Holman and Michael R. Solomon (Provo, Utah: Association for Consumer Research, 1991)18: 150–57; Melanie Wallendorf and Michael Reilly, "Ethnic Migration, Assimilation, and Consumption," *Journal of Consumer Research* 10 (December 1983): 292–302; Milton J. Yinger, "Ethnicity," *Annual Review of Sociology* 11 (1985): 151–80.
3. Wilbur Zelinsky, "You Are Where You Eat," *American Demographics* (July 1987): 6.
4. Marty Westerman, "Death of the Frito Bandito," *American Demographics* (March 1989): 28.
5. Eils Lotozo, "The Jalapeno Bagel and Other Artifacts," *New York Times* (June 26, 1990): C1.
6. Quoted in Cara S. Trager, "Goya Foods Tests Mainstream Market's Waters," *Advertising Age* (February 9, 1987): S-20.
7. Quoted in Peter Schrag, *The Decline of the WASP* (New York: Simon and Schuster, 1971): 20.
8. William O'Hare, "Blacks and Whites: One Market or Two?" *American Demographics* (March 1987): 44–48.
9. For recent studies on racial differences in consumption, see Robert E. Pitts, D. Joel Whalen, Robert O'Keefe, and Vernon Murray, "Black and White Response to Culturally Targeted Television Commercials: A Values-Based Approach," *Psychology &*

Marketing 6 (Winter 1989): 311–28; Melvin T. Stith and Ronald E. Goldsmith, "Race, Sex, and Fashion Innovativeness: A Replication," Psychology & Marketing 6 (Winter 1989): 249–62.

10. Monroe Anderson, "Advertising's Black Magic Helping Corporate America Tap a Lucrative Market," Newsweek (February 10, 1986): 60.

11. Brad Edmonson, "Black Markets," American Demographics (November 1987): 20; O'Hare, "Blacks and Whites"; "Older Products Look to Blacks for Rejuvenated Sales Growth," The Wall Street Journal (February 28, 1985): 1.

12. Nejet Delener, "Cosmetics & HBA's for Black Consumers: A Growing, Profitable—But Ignored—Market," Marketing News (March 15, 1985): 32.

13. Pat Sloan, "New Maybelline Line Targets Blacks," Advertising Age (December 17, 1990): 1.

14. Robert E. Wilkes and Humberto Valencia, "Hispanics and Blacks in Television Commercials," Journal of Advertising 18 (Winter 1989): 19.

15. Alvin P. Sanoff, "TV's Disappearing Color Line," U.S. News & World Report (July 13, 1987): 56.

16. W. Franklyn Joseph, "Blacks' Ambition Enters the Picture," Advertising Age (March 14, 1985): 26.

17. Marie Spadoni, "Marketing to Blacks—How Media Segment the Target Audience," Advertising Age (November 19, 1984): 43.

18. Jeffery L. Kovach, "Minority Sell: Ads Target Blacks, Hispanics, but . . . ," Industry Week (November 11, 1985): 29.

19. Joseph, "Blacks' Ambition Enters the Picture."

20. Anderson, "Advertising's Black Magic: Helping Corporate America Tap a Lucrative Market."

21. Joseph, "Blacks' Ambition Enters the Picture."

22. "'Black Pride' Plays Role in Buying Goods," Marketing News (February 19, 1990): 10; Jerome D. Williams and William J. Qualls, "Middle-Class Black Consumers and Intensity of Ethnic Identification," Psychology & Marketing 6 (Winter 1989): 263–86.

23. "Plans for Testmarketing Cigarette Canceled," The Asbury Park Press (January 1990): 20; Anthony Ramirez, "A Cigarette Campaign Under Fire," New York Times (January 12, 1990): D1.

24. Sanoff, "TV's Disappearing Color Line."

25. Westerman, "Death of the Frito Bandito."

26. Michael Marriott, "I'm Bart, I'm Black, and What About It?" New York Times (September 19, 1990): C1.

27. Kim Foltz, "Mattel's Shift on Barbie Ads," New York Times (July 19, 1990): D17; Lora Sharpe, "Dolls in All the Colors of a Child's Dream," The Boston Globe (February 22, 1991): 42.

28. Brad Edmondson, "Pepsi's Latin Fizz," American Demographics (September 1987): 22.

29. Joe Schwartz, "Hispanics in the Eighties," American Demographics (January 1988): 42.

30. Joe Schwartz, "Hispanic Opportunities," American Demographics (May 1987): 56–59.

31. Schwartz, "Hispanic Opportunities."

32. Howard LaFranchi, "Media and Marketers Discover Hispanic Boom," The Christian Science Monitor (April 20, 1988): 1.

33. Joe Schwartz, "Rising Status," American Demographics (Janaury 10, 1989).

34. Roberto Suro, "Switch by Hispanic Catholics Changes Face of U.S. Religion," New York Times (May 14, 1989): 1.

35. "'Cultural Sensitivity' Required When Advertising to Hispanics," Marketing News (March 19, 1982).

36. Westerman, "Death of the Frito Bandito."

37. Brad Edmondson, "Mexican Soap," American Demographics (January 1989): 18.

38. Kristine Stiven, "Educational Approach Shines," Advertising Age (February 13, 1989): S-10.

39. "'Cultural Sensitivity' Required When Advertising to Hispanics," Marketing News, 45.

40. Richard Edel, "Future Seen in P & G's Well-Oiled Machine," Advertising Age (February 13, 1989): 5–14.

41. "Dispel Myths Before Trying to Penetrate Hispanic Market," Marketing News (April 16, 1982): 1.

42. Schwartz, "Hispanic Opportunities."
43. Sigfredo A. Hernandez and Carol J. Kaufman, "Marketing Research in Hispanic Barrios: A Guide to Survey Research," *Marketing Research* (March 1990): 11–27.
44. David J. Wallace, "How to Sell yucas to YUCAs," *Advertising Age* (February 13, 1989): 5-6.
45. Marcy Magiera, "New Arrivals Find Warm Welcome as Consumers," *Advertising Age* (February 9, 1987): 5–14.
46. Magiera, "New Arrivals Find Warm Welcome as Consumers."
47. Melanie Wallendorf and Michael D. Reilly, "Ethnic Migration, Assimilation, and Consumption," *Journal of Consumer Research* 10 (December 1983): 292–302.
48. Ronald J. Faber, Thomas C. O'Guinn, and John A. McCarty, "Ethnicity, Acculturation and the Importance of Product Attributes," *Psychology & Marketing* 4, (Summer 1987): 121–34; Humberto Valencia, "Developing an Index to Measure Hispanicness," in *Advances in Consumer Research,* ed. Elizabeth C. Hirschman and Morris B. Holbrook (Provo, Utah: Association for Consumer Research, 1985)12: 118–21.
49. Rohit Deshpande, Wayne D. Hoyer, Naveen Donthu, "The Intensity of Ethnic Affiliation: A Study of the Sociology of Hispanic Consumption," *Journal of Consumer Research* 13 (September 1986): 214–20.
50. Schwartz, "Rising Status."
51. David J. Wallace, "How to sell yucas to YUCAs."
52. Fernando Gonzalez, "Study Finds Alcohol, Cigarette Makers Target Hispanics," *The Boston Globe* (November 23, 1989): A11.
53. Richard Kern, "The Asian Market: Too Good to Be True?" *Sales & Marketing Management* (May 1988): 38.
54. Donald Dougherty, "The Orient Express," *The Marketer* (July/August 1990): 14.
55. Kern, "The Asian Market."
56. Quoted in Donald Dougherty, "The Orient Express," *The Marketer.*
57. Doughterty, "The Orient Express."
58. Marty Westerman, "Fare East: Targeting the Asian-American Market," *Prepared Foods* (January 1989): 48–51.
59. Eleanor Yu, "Asian-American Market Often Misunderstood," *Marketing News* (December 4, 1989): 11.
60. Marianne Paskowski, "Trailblazing in Asian America," *Marketing and Media Decisions* (October 1986): 75–80.
61. Ellen Schultz, "Asians in the States," *Madison Avenue* (October 1985): 78.
62. Dougherty, "The Orient Express."
63. Westerman, "Fare East: Targeting the Asian-American Market."
64. Paskowski, "Trailblazing in Asian America."
65. John Schwartz and Dorothy Wang, "Tapping into a Blossoming Asian Market; the Pull of Ethnic Ties," *Newsweek* (September 7, 1987): 47.
66. Thomas C. O'Guinn and Russell W. Belk, "Heaven on Earth: Consumption at Heritage Village, USA," *Journal of Consumer Research* 16 (September 1989): 227–38.
67. Elizabeth C. Hirschman, "Religious Affiliation and Consumption Processes: An Initial Paradigm," *Research in Marketing* (Greenwich, Conn.: JAI Press, 1983): 131-70.
68. See, for example, Nejet Delener, "The Effects of Religious Factors on Perceived Risk in Durable Goods Purchase Decisions," *The Journal of Consumer Marketing* 7 (Summer 1990): 27–38.
69. Hirschman, "Religious Affiliation and Consumption Processes."
70. Andrew M. Greeley, *The American Catholic* (New York: Basic Books, 1977).
71. Stewart Slavin, "Trouble Brewing Over Beer Firm's Plan to Sponsor Pope," *The Bergen Record* (Bergen, N.J.), (October 5, 1986).
72. C. Wright Mills, *The Power Elite* (New York: Oxford University Press, 1956).
73. Kenneth R. Hardy, "Social Origins of American Scientists and Scholars," *Science* (September 9, 1975): 497–506; Hirschman, "Religious Affiliations and Consumption Processes"; Stanley Verba and Norman H. Nie, *Participation in America: Political Democracy and Social Equality* (New York: Harper & Row, 1972).
74. Wade Clark Roof, "Socioeconomic Differentials Among White Socioreligious Groups in the United States," *Social Forces* 58 (September 1979): 280–88.
75. Peter Schrag, *The Decline of the Wasp* (New York: Simon & Schuster, 1971): 14.

76. Elizabeth C. Hirschman, "Upper-Class WASPs as Consumers: A Humanist Inquiry," in *Research in Consumer Behavior,* ed. Jagdish N. Sheth and Elizabeth C. Hirschman (Greenwich, Conn.: JAI Press, 1988)3: 115–48.
77. Elizabeth C. Hirschman, "American Jewish Ethnicity: Its Relationship to Some Selected Aspects of Consumer Behavior," *Journal of Marketing* 45 (Summer 1981): 102–10.
78. Hirschman, "Religious Affiliation and Consumption Processes."
79. Hirschman, "American Jewish Ethnicity."
80. Susan Chira, "Leumi Appeal Not Just Ethnic," *New York Times* (May 14, 1984): D1.
81. Westerman, "Death of the Frito Bandito."
82. Isadore Barmash, "The Drive to Promote Kosher Food," *New York Times* (April 11, 1989): D25.
83. Joan Delaney, "New Kosher Products, from Tacos to Tofu," *New York Times* (December 31, 1989): F13.
84. Delaney, "New Kosher Products, from Tacos to Tofu."
85. Brad Edmondson, "Bringing in the Sheaves," *American Demographics* (August 1988): 28.
86. Priscilla LaBarbera, "Consumer Behavior and Born Again Christianity," in *Research in Consumer Behavior,* ed. Sheth and Hirschman: 193–222..
87. "Auto Dealer's 'Christian Plan' is Called Bias," *New York Times* (May 27, 1990): 23.
88. LaBarbera, "Consumer Behavior and Born Again Christianity"; Robert Ostling, "Power, Glory—and Politics," *Time* (February 17, 1986): 62–69.
89. Quoted in Sandra Blakeslee, "Christian Publishing Industry Does a Hard Sell on Religion," *New York Times* (July 19, 1987).
90. Lenore Skenazy, "Grace Gives Pro-Life Message," *Advertising Age* (January 5, 1987).
91. "A Cigarette Campaign Under Fire," *New York Times* (January 12, 1990): D1.
92. "Auto Dealer's 'Christian Plan' is Called Bias."

Subcultural Segmentation (II): Age and Regional Groups

CHAPTER 14

A wedding in a mall? Mary and Jim Padalino are both "mall walkers," a growing group of elderly people who exercise in shopping malls. By some estimates, as many as 500,000 people in the United States regularly engage in this activity. Many malls open their doors early in the morning to allow older people to begin their workouts before the shopping day begins. These "senior athletes" enjoy this environment, because it allows them to socialize with others of their own age, and to maintain their health in a secure, protected environment. Some malls have taken to etching mileage markers in walls, and the Conta Costa Community College (where else but in California?) even offers a course on mall walking.

Mary and Jim decided to be true to their hobby, so they got married in the mall. A tuxedo store provided the apparel, and other stores pitched in as well. The "lavish" affair was catered by Arby's, Burger King, and Long John Silver's. The couple now jets around the country promoting mall walking to seniors. Their sponsor: Avia, the shoe company. Recognizing a growing market, Avia targeted this niche with a special walking shoe that provides "extra traction for smoother, slicker mall floors."[1]

AGE SUBCULTURES

The era in which a consumer is born creates for that person a cultural bond with the millions of others born during the same time period. People of similar ages undergo similar experiences and share many common memories about cultural heroes (e.g., John Wayne vs. Clint Eastwood, or Frank Sinatra vs. Bruce Springsteen), important historical events (e.g., the 1969 moon flight versus the 1986 Challenger disaster), and so on. As the mall-walking craze attests, consumers tend to feel comfortable with others of their own age (termed an **age cohort**) or background.

THE POWER OF NOSTALGIA

Because consumers within an age-group confront crucial life changes at roughly the same time, the values and symbolism used to appeal to them can evoke powerful feelings of nostalgia (see Chapter 4). Adults over thirty are particularly susceptible to this phenomenon.[2]

PRODUCTS EVOKE SHARED MEMORIES   As noted in Chapter 4, product sales can be dramatically affected by linking the brand to vivid memories and experiences, especially for items that are associated with childhood or adolescence. As observed by the maker of a candy bar called the Big Hunk, which has been on the market since 1950, "Adults turn back into children when they bite into candy. . . . If you remember buying a Big Hunk every Saturday when you went to the movies, you're going to buy the memory every time you buy the product."[3]

Many advertising campaigns have played upon the collective memories of consumers by resuscitating old pop classics. Michelob's "The Night Belongs to Michelob" campaign sponsored such heroes of classic rock as Eric Clapton, Steve Winwood, and Roger Daltrey, and Ford Mercury commercials are produced against a background of classic songs. A campaign developed by The California Raisin Advisory Board featuring Marvin Gaye's "I Heard It Through the Grapevine" breathed new life into the flagging raisin industry. *Memories* magazine, which was founded to exploit the nostalgia boom, goes so far as to offer advertisers discounts if they run old ads next to their current ones.

MARKETING OPPORTUNITY

A reunion is an event based on a shared age cohort. People who were not necessarily fond of each other in high school or college nonetheless get together to celebrate the common experience of being together at the same time and place. It is estimated that more than 50,000 reunions are held in the United States each year.

In addition to the boon this nostalgia provides to caterers and professional reunion organizers, some marketers realize that the people who attend reunions often represent a valuable customer base. They are self-selected to be fairly successful, since the "failures" tend not to show up! Some companies are now using reunion-goers to test new products, and

An extremely successful advertising campaign by the California Raisin Advisory Board used Motown music to appeal to baby boomers' memories of youth.

travel-related businesses interview attendees about their trips or provide special promotional packages for returning consumers.[4]

Common Musical Preferences: Glenn Miller Meets Bonjovi. An interesting demonstration of the power of a common age-group to influence experiences throughout life concerns the relationship between age and musical preferences. One study uncovered evidence that consumers tend to focus on the popular songs they enjoyed during the period in which they first reached maturity—those same musical preferences carry forward into later life.[5]

This study found that the "imprinting" period for musical tastes peaks at around age 24 for most people—the songs that were popular at that age tend to be preferred in later years as well. Consumers who were 24 in, say, 1986, tended to prefer Peter Gabriel's "Sledgehammer," a chart-topper in that year. Similar results were obtained for other hits, such as the Mills Brothers' "Smoke Rings" (1932) and "The Duke of Earl" by Gene Chandler (1962). Using a similar strategy, the Nickelodeon cable network programs its "Nick at Nite" segment, which features reruns, by selecting the shows that were highly rated when its major audience was 12 years old.[6]

THE TEEN MARKET: "GRODY TO THE MAX"

As anyone who has been there knows, the process of puberty and adolescence can be both the best of times and the worst of times. Many exciting changes happen as individuals leave the role of child and prepare to assume the role of adult. These changes create a lot of uncertainty about the self, and the need to belong and to find one's unique identity as a person becomes extremely important.

At this age, choices of activities, friends, and "looks" often are crucial to social acceptance. Teens actively search for cues from their peers and from advertising for the "right" way to look and behave. Advertising geared to teens, as exemplified by the Mountain Dew ad shown here, is typically action-oriented and depicts a group of "in" teens using the product. Teens use products to express their identities, to explore the world and their new-found freedoms in it, and also to rebel against the authority of their parents and other socializing agents. Consumers in this age subculture have a number of needs, including experimentation, belonging, independence, responsibility, and approval from others. Product usage is a significant medium to express these needs.

ATTRACTIVENESS OF THE TEEN MARKET

Because they are so interested in many different products and have the resources to obtain them, the teen market is avidly courted by many marketers. This is done most effectively when this subculture is addressed in language it understands and appreciates. The average teen earns over $60 a week and has no bills to pay. Even younger teens can make $100 a month or more by mowing lawns, baby-sitting, or receiving an allowance. Much of this money goes toward "feel-good" products: cosmetics, posters, and fast food.

With discretionary income of over $50 billion, teens are the prime movers in many categories, though this influence is waning as the number of consumers in this age group decreases relative to older groups. For example, people aged 15 to 25 are the prime market for the movie industry, so movie producers pay close attention to the behavior of this segment. Most teens are preoccupied with their appearance and body-image and are avid consumers of beauty products, clothing, and other appearance-related items.[7]

BRAND LOYALTY   Marketers view teens as "consumers-in-training," since brand loyalty often is developed during this age. This means that a teenager who is committed to a brand may continue to purchase it for many years to come. Such loyalty creates a "barrier-to-entry" for other brands that were not chosen during these pivotal years. Thus advertisers sometimes try to "lock in" consumers to certain brands so that in the future they will buy these brands more or less automatically. As one teen magazine ad director observed: "We . . . always say it's easier to start a habit than stop it."[8]

PURCHASE INFLUENCE   Teens exert a big influence on the purchase decisions of their parents (see Chapter 9).[9] Sixty percent of teens, for instance, say they influence the vacation choices of their families.[10] In addition to providing "helpful" advice to parents, teens are increasingly *buying* products on behalf of the family. The majority of mothers are now employed outside the home and have less time to shop for the family.

Client: PEPSI-COLA COMPANY   Time: 30 SECONDS

Product: MOUNTAIN DEW   Title: "BIKE DANCE"   Comml. No.: PEMX-0873

MUSIC

SINGERS: Give me some fun in the blazin' sun,

Give me a friend or two.

And when my thirst is at its worst,

Give me a Mountain Dew.

Dew it to it, Mountain Dew.

Dew it to it, cool and smooth.

When I got a thirst,

Your undiluted,

Undisputed,

Dew it to it

Mountain Dew!

Pepsi Co. appeals to the teen market by showing popular people in active settings. Courtesy of PEPSI-COLA COMPANY.

In fact, seven out of ten mothers of teens work, and five of those seven are employed full-time.[11]

This fundamental change in family structure has altered the way marketers must conceive of teenage consumers. Though teens still are a good market for discretionary items, in recent years their spending on such "basics" as groceries is even larger than for non-essentials. A market research firm specializing in this segment has gone so far as to label teens "skippies"—school kids with income and purchasing power.[12] One survey of sixteen- to seventeen-year-old girls found that over a three-month period a significant proportion of them had purchased such staple items as cereal, frozen meals, cheese and yogurt, and salad dressing.[13] Marketers are beginning to respond to these changes. The number of pages devoted to food advertising in *Seventeen* magazine increased by 31 percent in one year. A Campbell's ad that ran on MTV reflected this change as well: It depicted a solitary teenager warming up soup in the kitchen.

MARKETING OPPORTUNITY

"Tweens" are an emerging age segment now being targeted by some marketers. This term refers to kids aged 9 to 16, who are in that uneasy period between childhood and adolescence. This group tends to form brand preferences that differ from their parents'. Because working parents have been giving kids in this age group increased responsibility for many purchases, some brand managers refer to tweens as "third parents," and a variety of companies are now trying to win their loyalty.

Polaroid developed the "Cool Cam" for tweens, and Borden's research led to Spirals snacks. Focusing on the tween's potential role as influencer, an Acura dealer in California devised an ad showing three pre-driving age boys drooling over the car. The voice-over: "Number one in customer satisfaction, even among future consumers."

Jordache developed a controversial campaign for this segment when its research showed that customers for its jeans were more likely to be twelve-year olds than twenty-five-year olds. The resulting ads, generated from focus groups with tweens, were eventually pulled, but not before they received a lot of media attention. Each ad had tweens talking about a sensitive subject. In one, a kid asked another, "Have you ever seen your parents naked?" while in another a girl complained, "I hate my mother. She's so much prettier than I am."[14]

TEENS' INFLUENCE ON FASHION AND POPULAR CULTURE

Youth subcultures are often responsible for driving changes in cultural styles and fashions (see Chapter 17). Because resistance to authority and the established way of doing things is a hallmark of adolescence, these subcultures sometimes add a "hard edge" to existing styles. For example, "heavy metal" music is largely directed to younger males. This motif has spawned an entire subculture, which prescribes appropriate dress, jewelry, tattoos, and so on.

The "anti-establishment" bonding of youth over the years—whether they are "teddy boys" or "mods" in the U.K., punks, Rastafarians, beatniks, or hippies—influences developments in fashion, music, and cinema. However, teenage rebellion may be more illusion than fact. The Gallup Youth Survey, which tracks the attitudes of teenagers, reported that 40 percent of respondents aged 13 to 15 want *more* homework, and that over half of all teens in the survey attend church.[15] While teens gravitate to rebellious images, there may be a limit to how much they want to actually live out the deviant fantasies they encounter in the media.

MTV: A CULTURAL FORCE   One important media source is MTV, which has emerged as a major cultural force for teens. Over 30 percent of the

cable channel's viewers are between the ages of 12 and 17. MTV speaks teens' language and does not patronize them. Most important, it is a significant socialization agent, since it allows teens all over the country and even much of the world to keep in touch with the latest developments and symbols that define their youth subculture. There are roughly 1.37 billion people between the ages of 10 and 19 in the world. Companies like Benetton, Levi Strauss, Swatch, and Gillette have found that they can advertise globally to teenagers, but only through television. The Swatch Company is even considering a regularly scheduled global show for teens, to be called "Swatch This."[16]

BIG (WO)MAN ON CAMPUS: THE COLLEGE MARKET   Advertisers   spend more than $100 million a year to influence the purchases of college students, who purchase about $20 billion worth of products a year. After paying for books, board, and tuition, the average student has about $200 per month to spend, so this interest is not surprising. As one marketing executive observed, "This is the time of life where they're willing to try new products. . . . This is the time to get them in your franchise."[17]

Many college students are away from home for the first time, and they must make many buying decisions that used to be made for them by parents, such as the purchase of some routine personal care products or of cleaning supplies. Some marketers are attracted by this lack of experience. As one executive put it, "Advertisers look at the college student as someone who can be more easily influenced than someone who has developed brand preferences."[18]

REACHING THE COLLEGE MARKET

College students pose a special challenge for marketers, since they are hard to reach via conventional media. Students watch less television than other people, and when they do watch they are much more likely to do so after midnight. Students also do not read newspapers as much. AT&T and other large companies have found that the best way to reach students is through their college newspapers; about 90 percent of students read their college paper at least one day a week, which explains why $17 million a year is spent on advertising in college newspapers.[19]

Other strategies to reach students include the widespread distribution of sampler boxes containing a variety of personal care products in student centers and dormitories and the use of posters (termed wall media). Still, word-of-mouth appears to be the most effective determinant of product usage (see Chapter 11).

MARKETING OPPORTUNITY

College students are avid gift givers. Birthdays rank first among gift-giving occasions, followed by major holidays. However, even such holidays as Thanksgiving, St. Patrick's Day, and Halloween appear to stimulate gift purchases. College bookstores report that the dominant theme is romance and sentimentality, especially at Greek-oriented colleges where students give Rush presents as well as Valentine's Day offerings. Students spend an average of $10 to $15 per gift. In addition, greeting cards are the single most popular student purchase at college bookstores.[20]

BABY BOOMERS

People born between the years of 1946 and 1964 are referred to as **baby boomers.** This age segment is the source of many fundamental cultural and economic changes. The reason: Power in numbers. As G.I.'s returned home after World War II, they began to establish families and careers (aided by the G.I. Bill) at a record pace. The children born during this era have dominated consumer culture ever since.

Imagine a large python that has swallowed a mouse; the mouse moves down the length of the python, creating a moving bulge as it goes. So it is with baby boomers, as seen in Figure 14-1. As teenagers in the 60s and 70s, the "Woodstock Generation" created a revolution in style, politics, and consumer attitudes. Now that they are older, they continue to influence popular culture in important ways.

ECONOMIC POWER: HE WHO PAYS THE PIPER, CALLS THE TUNE

Because of the size and buying power of the boomer group over the last twenty years, marketers focused most of their attention on the youth mar-

Figure 14-1 The origins of the Baby Boomer Age Cohort: National Center for Health Services

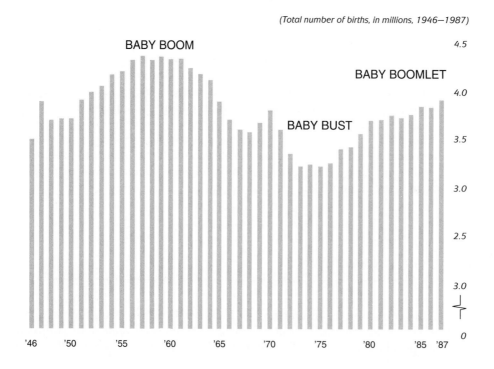

(Total number of births, in millions, 1946—1987)

ket. The popular slogan at the time, "Don't trust anyone over thirty," also meant that people over thirty had trouble finding products appropriate to their age-groups. Times have changed, and again it is the baby boomers who have changed them. This "mouse in the python" has moved into its late twenties to early forties, and this is now the age group that exerts the most impact on consumption patterns. Consumers aged 25 to 34 now head 23 percent of all U.S. households, making them the largest market segment in the United States.[21] Most of the growth in the market will be accounted for by people who are moving into their peak earning years. Households with incomes greater than $50,000 (in 1985 dollars) will constitute 25 percent of the population in the year 2000, a figure almost double the current proportion of affluent households.[22]

As baby boomers grow older, they are moving up to more responsible and lucrative jobs. This means that consumers on the average are becoming older and wealthier. Between now and the year 2000, the number of U.S. households is projected to increase by 16 million. Eleven million of these units will be headed by consumers aged 35 to 50. This movement is echoed in the ad for VH1, the music-video network that caters to those who are a bit too old for MTV. In one case, copy intended to appeal to boomers reads, "The generation that dropped acid to escape reality . . . is the generation that drops antacid to cope with it."

▲ MARKETING OPPORTUNITY

This increase in wealth, and the desire for new and better things that accompanies it, has prompted many marketers to develop new products or reposition old ones. Maxwell House Coffee attempted to counter an image problem: Their consumer research showed that coffee drinkers were perceived by many to be nervous, older, and somewhat downscale. In fact, unit sales of coffee have declined about 1 percent a year since 1962 as a new generation changed its drinking habits. In response, the company introduced its "Private Collection" label to appeal to more upscale baby boomers.[23]

Levi Strauss owes its success to baby boomers, who adopted blue jeans as a symbol of their generation. But sales of blue jeans peaked in 1981, and then fell steadily as these consumers (and their waistlines) outgrew their blue jeans. The company introduced a new line of pants that provide a looser fit, called Dockers, to win back their traditional consumers. The success of Dockers created a new clothing category, "new casuals," as other manufacturers attempt to regear for aging boomers.[24]

BOOMERS' IMPACT ON THE MARKETPLACE Consumers aged 35 to 44 spend the most on housing, cars, and entertainment. In addition, consumers aged 45 to 54 spend the most of any age category on food (30 percent above average), apparel (38 percent above average), and retirement programs (57 percent above average). To appreciate the impact middle-aged consumers have and will have on our economy, consider this: At current spending levels, a 1 percent increase in householders aged 35 to 54 results in an additional $8.9 billion in consumer expenditures.[25]

The Baby Boomlet. In addition to the direct demand for products and services created by this age group, these consumers also are creating a new baby boom of their own to keep marketers busy in the future. Since fertility rates have dropped, this new boom is not as big as the one that created the baby boom generation; the new upsurge in child bearing in comparison can best be described as a *baby boomlet.*

Many couples postponed getting married and having children because of the new emphasis on careers for women. These consumers now are beginning to hear the ticking of the biological "time clock." They are having babies in their late 20s and early 30s, resulting in fewer (but perhaps more pampered) children per family. Couples in the 25 to 34 age group account for 22 percent of all married couples, but for 35 percent of married couples with children. This new emphasis on children and the family has created opportunities for products such as cars (e.g., the success of the "mini-van" concept), services (e.g., the day-care industry, as exemplified by the Kinder-Care chain), and media (e.g., magazines such as *Working Mother,* and localized magazines for parents that exist in more than 70 American cities).[26]

SEGMENTING BOOMERS: THE "NEW-COLLARS"

Many people feel that baby boomers are synonymous with yuppies, as depicted in television shows like "Thirtysomething." So-called yuppies (even including those who abhor the term) in actuality make up only a small fraction of this age group. Although these upscale consumers exert an influence on popular culture and marketing efforts far out of proportion to their size, they by no means speak for all baby boomers.

An important baby boomer segment that is beginning to make its presence felt has been termed **New-Collar Workers.** Others have described them as "would-be's": They *would be* yuppies, but their lower incomes prevent them from attaining more opulent lifestyles. These consumers, primarily 21 to 40 years old, occupy a gray area between professional and blue collar jobs. Many of them hold service jobs vital to the functioning of our services-dominated economy, such as pharmacists, dental hygienists, and computer operators. They make approximately $15,000 to 30,000 a year, so they are neither affluent nor poor, despite the fact that many are college-educated. This group may be thought of as the "non-yuppies" of the baby boomer segment.

As a group, new-collars tend to be highly individualistic, pragmatic, and skeptical of institutions. These traits set them apart from older generations of gray- and pink-collar workers, who largely identified with the more traditional ideals of the working class.

New-collars are a hybrid of traditional values and the liberalizing effects of their experiences growing up in the 1960s. They thus tend to exhibit a strong commitment to the family, but are more flexible in many ways, stylistically, sexually, and so on, than were their parents. These consumers tend to read such publications as *People* magazine, and *TV Guide* and music plays an important role as a bonding experience. Rock singer Bruce Springsteen might be thought of as the "poet laureate" of this new segment.[27]

THE ELDERLY CONSUMER: MARKETING TO THE GRAY MARKET

The old woman sits alone in her dark apartment, while the television blares out a soap opera. Once every couple of days she slowly and painfully opens her triple-locked door with arthritic hands and ventures out to the corner store to buy essentials like tea, milk, and cereal, always being sure to pick the least expensive brand. Most of the time she sits in her rocking chair, thinking sadly of her dead husband and the good times she used to have as a young woman.

Is this the image you have of a typical elderly consumer? Until recently, many marketers did. As a result, they largely neglected the elderly in their feverish pursuit of the baby boomer market. But as our population ages and people are living longer and healthier lives, the game is rapidly changing. A lot of businesses are beginning to replace the old stereotype of the poor recluse. The newer, more accurate image is of an elderly person who is active, interested in what life has to offer, and is an enthusiastic consumer with the means and willingness to buy many goods and services. The popularity of the television sitcom "The Golden Girls," which stars four older women with full social lives reflects the changing views of the elderly in American society.

GRAY POWER: SHATTERING STEREOTYPES   The elderly market consists of approximately 52 million people aged 55 and older, though for many purposes consumers are not classified as "elderly" until they reach the age of sixty-five, when Social Security benefits begin. The Bureau of Labor Statistics estimates that the mature market will grow by 62 percent between 1987 and 2015, compared to a 19 percent rate of growth for the overall U.S. population.[28] This increase makes the mature market the second fastest growing market segment in the United States, lagging only behind the baby-boomers. Such dramatic growth can be explained by a declining birthrate, improved medical diagnoses and treatment, and a resultant increase in life expectancy.

SENIORS' ECONOMIC CLOUT   There is abundant evidence that the economic health of elderly consumers is good and getting better. In the period between 1979 and 1987, householders 65 and over showed an income gain of 16 percent, the largest increase of any age group. And, it is crucial to remember that income alone does not capture the spending power of this group—elderly consumers are finished with many of the financial obligations that siphon off the income of younger consumers. Eighty percent of consumers past age 65 own their own homes, and 80 percent of those homes are mortgage-free. In addition, child-rearing costs are over with. And, as evidenced by the popularity of the bumper sticker that proudly proclaims "We're Spending Our Children's Inheritance," many seniors now feel better about spending money on themselves rather than continuing to skimp for the sake of children and grandchildren. Some of the important areas that stand to benefit from the surging gray market are described in Table 14-1.

MARKETING OPPORTUNITY

A few marketers are beginning to recognize the vast potential of the senior market, and are designing products and services to cater to the specific needs of the elderly.

- A variety of catalogs have sprung up to service the older consumer. "Mature Wisdom," published by Hanover House, sells such items as *The After 50 Cookbook,* magnifying glasses, and even a book entitled *Sex After 60.*
- One company has already targeted the elderly institutional market with a line of cookies, drinks, and puddings marketed under the Appleways logo.[29] These products offer extra calcium, nutrients, and fiber and are designed to alleviate some of the decline in sensory ability older people experience.
- Grand Circle Travel of Boston targets customers over 50 by direct mail; the agency sent out over 7 million catalogs in 1986 to potential travelers.[30] Grandtravel of Chevy Chase, Md. packages vacations specifically for grandparents and grandchildren, including two-week tours to Kenya and Alaska.[31] American Airlines offers a 10 percent discount to passengers over 65, and in 1986 these travelers accounted for 7 percent of the carrier's customers.
- Take Time, Inc., a health club chain, opened fitness centers for people over age 50.[32] In contrast to the "no pain, no gain" philosophy of some younger fitness enthusiasts, these centers emphasize the fun and social aspects of exercise. Instead of aerobics, older people do the Charleston to the accompaniment of big band music and then relax at a juice bar. The company has also developed a line of exercise clothing for this segment, and it released an exercise video starring Pat Boone.
- The Publix grocery chain in Florida, which has many elderly customers, puts benches in front of stores, makes restrooms easily available to patrons, and teaches employees how to make things easier for the stores' older clientele. For example, check-out clerks are instructed to give older customers two light bags to carry instead of one heavy bag.[33]

SELF-CONCEPT: YOU'RE ONLY AS OLD AS YOU FEEL

Market researchers who work with the elderly often comment that people think of themselves as being 10 to 15 years younger than they actually are. In fact, research confirms the popular wisdom that age is more a state of mind than of body. A person's mental outlook and activity level

TABLE 14-1 Growth opportunities in the gray market

Category	Trends	Growth Areas
The Home	emphasis on convenience and leisure time	games, video, cooking, housekeeping aids
Health Care	need for nutritionally correct foods, exercise facilities	nursing homes, pharmaceuticals, health foods
Travel & Leisure	leisure time, disposable income	cruises, tourism
Education	decline in number of college-age students; more positive attitudes toward learning, self-help among older, better-educated consumers	colleges, "how-to" books and videos,
Financial Planning	need for retirement planning, greater assets than in the past	speculative investing, vacation homes
Health & Fitness	desire to recapture youth and retard aging	cosmetic surgery, vitamins, skin treatments, bifocal contact lenses

Source: Adapted from Jeff Ostroff, "An Aging Market," *American Demographics* (May 1989): 26.

has a lot more to do with his or her longevity and quality of life than does *chronological age,* or the actual number of years lived.

PERCEIVED AGE   A better yardstick to categorize the elderly is **perceived age,** or how old a person feels. Perceived age can be measured on several dimensions, including "feel-age" (i.e., how old a person feels) and "look-age" (i.e., how old a person looks).[34] The older the consumers get, the younger they feel relative to actual age. For this reason, it is advisable to emphasize product benefits rather than age-appropriateness in marketing campaigns, since many consumers will not relate to products targeted to their chronological age.[35]

▼ MARKETING PITFALL

Understanding the psychological needs of the elderly is especially acute in the housing industry.[36] Although developers frequently emphasize the term "retirement" in promotions for housing communities, they should be aware that in a 1977 Roper survey only 5 percent of retirees said they would like to live only among people of their own age. These ads also tend to emphasize total leisure and older people's vulnerability, two points that are damaging to the elderly consumer's self-esteem. Promotions emphasizing an active, full life in a secure environment are likely to be more effective.

Repelling Messages. In fact, some marketing efforts targeted to the elderly have backfired because they reminded people of their age, or presented their age group in an unflattering way. One of the more famous blunders was committed by Heinz. A company analyst found that many elderly people were buying baby food because of the small portions and easy chewing consistency, so it introduced a line of "Senior Foods" made especially for denture wearers. Needless to say, the product failed. Consumers did not want to admit that they required strained foods (even to the supermarket cashier). They preferred to purchase baby foods, which they could pretend they were buying for a grandchild.

MARKETING OPPORTUNITY

OLD IS BEAUTIFUL

The aging of America is changing ideals of beauty. As the youth market declines, the standards we use to make judgments about beauty are evolving (see Chapter 7). Slowly but surely, older models are beginning to redefine glamour and beauty. This appeal is exemplified in the Jockey underwear ad. Several of the major modeling agencies have now established separate divisions for older women—what Ford Models, one of the largest agencies, terms "post-ingenue" talent.[37] *Lear's* magazine, launched in 1988, is designed "For the Woman Who Wasn't Born Yesterday." The magazine uses photographs of women aged 40 to 60, and does not retouch the pictures.

SEGMENTING THE SENIOR SUBCULTURE

The senior subculture represents an extremely large market: The number of Americans 65 and older exceeds the entire population of Canada.[38] Because this group is so large, it is helpful to think of the mature market as actually consisting of four subsegments: an "older" group (aged 55–64), an "elderly" group (aged 65–74), an "aged" group (aged 75–84), and finally a "very old" group (85 and up).[39]

The elderly market is well suited for segmentation. Older consumers are easy to identify by age and stage in the family life cycle. Most receive Social Security benefits, and many belong to organizations catering to the elderly. The American Association of Retired Persons has approximately 12 million dues-paying members. Its main publication, *Modern Maturity,* has the largest circulation of any American magazine.

CONFRONTING OLD AGE Several segmentation approaches begin with the premise that a major determinant of elderly marketplace behavior is the way a person deals with being old.[40] Some people become depressed,

"Jockey For Her is the best fitting underwear I've ever worn. It's so comfortable. And now my favorite granddaughters wear Jockey For Girls®. Just Jockey."

Catherine Councell Moll
Grandmother/Banker
Sheboygan, Wisconsin

So Comfortable
JOCKEY
For Her

For Pantyhose That Fit . . . Wear Jockey For Her Pantyhose with Lycra®

Jockey Apparel is one of many advertisers that is increasingly featuring attractive older models in its ads. JOCKEY FOR HER, SO COMFORTABLE and JOCKEY Figure are trademarks of and used with permission of Jockey International, Inc.

withdrawn, and apathetic as they age, some are angry and resist the thought of aging, and some appear to accept the new challenges and opportunities this period of life has to offer. For example, one ad agency devised a segmentation scheme for American women over the age of sixty-five on two dimensions: self-sufficiency and perceived opinion leadership.[41] The study yielded many important differences among the resulting groups. For example, the self-sufficient group was found to be more independent, cosmopolitan, and outgoing. They were more likely to read a book, attend concerts and sporting events, and dine out.

The Innovative Elderly. This finding highlights the stereotype that elderly people are set in their ways, stubborn, and resistant to change. The implication is that mature consumers are exceptionally brand loyal and unwilling to try new products or services. This belief appears to be true only to the extent that the elderly are more experienced and skeptical of product claims and puffery. They don't appear to be as fickle as younger consumers, but will try new things if given a good reason for doing so.[42]

▼ MARKETING PITFALL

Many consumer products will encounter a more sympathetic reception from the elderly if packages are redesigned to be sensitive to physical limitations. While aesthetically appealing, packages are often awkward and difficult to manage, especially for those who are frail or arthritic. Also, many serving sizes are not geared to smaller families, widows, and other people living alone, and coupons tend to be for family-sized products, rather than for single servings.

A few companies are beginning to confront these issues. Procter & Gamble is working on a snap-top lid for Tide detergent, and General Motors is redesigning some Oldsmobiles to include bigger buttons, clearer displays, and simplified operating instructions. A number of apparel manufacturers are replacing buttons with Velcro snaps. Still, many packages are very difficult to use.[43] Seniors in particular have difficulty with pull-tab cans and push-open milk cartons. Ziploc packages and clear plastic wrap also are difficult to handle. Packages need to be easier to read and should be made lighter and smaller. Finally, designers need to pay attention to contrasting colors. A slight yellowing of the lens as one ages makes it harder to see background colors on packages. Discerning between blues, greens, and violets becomes especially difficult. The closer identifying type colors are to the package's or advertisement's background color, the less visibility and attention they will command.

THE ELDERLY AND THE MEDIA

A number of specialty magazines have been introduced in recent years that focus on the active lifestyles of today's elderly, such as *Modern Maturity, 50 Plus,* and *Lear's.* In addition, television is a very important medium, because the elderly often rely on it as a window onto society. The elderly watch 60 percent more television than average households and prefer programs that provide news and current events as a way to keep up. They also watch more golf, baseball, and bowling on television than the average consumer. The elderly tend to listen to radio news at all times of the day and are above the norm in readership of news magazines.

ADVERTISING TO THE ELDERLY In one survey, one-third of consumers over age 55 reported that they deliberately did *not* buy a product because of the way an elderly person was stereotyped in the product's advertising.[44] Most contemporary advertising underrepresents the elderly, and this will have to change as the population ages. For example, more than one-third of Americans over the age of 50 are regular consumers of soft drinks, yet few older consumers are ever seen in soft drink advertising.

Some marketers are beginning to glamorize older people, including DeBeers diamonds, Clairol hair coloring products, and American Express. This appears to be a sound strategy: in a 1989 Gallup Poll, 77 percent of respondents reported that they react positively to advertising featuring older people, and 63 percent believe that advertisers are overly obsessed with youth.[45] A longitudinal (i.e., historical) analysis indicated that the portrayal of the elderly in magazine advertising is in fact increasing and that the people in these ads tend to have prestigious positions.[46]

In general, the elderly have been shown to respond well to ads that provide an abundance of information. Unlike other age groups, these consumers often are not amused, or persuaded, by imagery-oriented advertising. A successful strategy has been to construct advertising depicting the aged as well-integrated, contributing members of society. The copy emphasis should be on them expanding their horizons rather than clinging precariously to life. As noted earlier, the elderly tend to think of themselves as younger than their actual age, and they should be depicted that way in advertising—a point made in the ad for *Modern Maturity* magazine.

Basic Guidelines. Some basic guidelines have been suggested for effective advertising to the elderly. These include the following:

- Keep language simple.
- Use clear, bright pictures.
- Use action to attract attention.
- Speak clearly, and keep the word count low.
- Use a single sales message, and emphasize brand extensions to tap consumers' familiarity.
- Avoid extraneous stimuli (i.e., excessive pictures and graphics can detract from the message).

GEOGRAPHICAL SUBCULTURES: OF "GOOD 'OLE BOYS" AND YANKEES

If you have traveled to or lived in other parts of the country, you may have experienced the feeling of being slightly out of sync with your environment. The people may speak the same language, yet you may have difficulty understanding some things they say. Brands and store names may be confusing; some are familiar and some are not. And, some familiar items may masquerade under different names. One person's "hero" is another's "grinder" is another person's "submarine sandwich" is another person's "hoagie."

Citizens of the United States share the same national identity, yet the consumption patterns of different regions have been shaped by unique climates, cultural influences, and resources. These differences allow us to legitimately talk about "regional personalities" as well as a "national personality." In many cases it is efficient to divide the country up into geographic markets based upon definitions provided by the U.S. Census Bureau. These markets are called **Standard Metropolitan Statistical Areas (SMSAs)**, and are used as a reference by market researchers, manufacturers, and retailers.

Modern Maturity magazine teaches advertisers how to appeal to the senior market. A major theme, as used in this ad, is that these consumers think of themselves as ten to fifteen years younger than they actually are. Courtesy of *Modern Maturity Magazine.*

REGIONAL CONSUMPTION DIFFERENCES

The lifestyles of people in each region differ in a variety of ways, some quite subtle and some quite noticeable, some easy to explain and some not so obvious. The fact that people in the Northeast are better customers for ski equipment than are those in the Southwest is fairly predictable. The reason that new mothers in the West are about 50 percent more likely to breast-feed their babies than their counterparts in the South may be a little harder to fathom.[47]

The beer industry has been particularly active in reinforcing regional identification. The Miller Brewing Company exhibited its own version of regional marketing when it developed a first—an entire campaign targeted only to one state. It seems that Texan consumers buy more Miller Lite than anyone else, so the company threw a beer party in six Texas cities that it billed as the biggest party in history.[48]

Heileman Distilleries is now fifth in sales in the United States largely because of its regional marketing efforts. The company operates ten breweries across the United States, and its position in each of its markets is backed up with sponsorship of major local events and other regional promotions. As the company's marketing vice president explained, "The primary objective of being a regional brand is to make the consumer think that 'this product is mine.' . . . People tend to think positively about their hometowns, and a product strongly identified with this aura is likely to strike a responsive chord. . . ."[49] Some of Heileman's successful regional brands include Old Style, Colt 45, Lone Star, Rainier, and Samuel Adams.

There clearly are regional differences in product and lifestyle preferences. Compared to the national average, those in the West eat more health foods and buy more exercise equipment. They also are more likely to write a letter to a newspaper editor, and they accept new products at a higher rate. For example, 45 percent of consumers in the West own imported cars, compared to only 21 percent of Midwesterners.[50]

On the other hand, residents of New York City live up to the stereotype of the fast-paced urban lifestyle. They lead the nation in per capita consumption of Scotch, gin, and vodka. Men buy 44 percent more clothes than the average, and women are far above average in purchases of panty hose and hair spray.[51]

FOOD PREFERENCES   Realizing these differences, many national marketers regionalize their offerings to appeal to different tastes. Campbell's puts a stronger dose of jalapeno pepper in its nacho cheese soup in the Southwest, and it sells "ranch-style" beans only in Texas.[52] Similarly, some leading brands do significantly better in some parts of the country than others: While Kraft Miracle Whip is the nation's best seller in the mayonnaise category, it only turns in a third place performance in the Northeast.[53]

Denny's Restaurants, a national chain based in California, adapts its menu to the different regions it serves. For example, though chili is served in many outlets, this dish takes a variety of forms. In Texas, it contains no beans and is very spicy, in Cincinnati, "five-way" chili is served with chili sauce, cheese, raw onions, beans, and spaghetti. On the West Coast, the same dish is served with a side order of salsa. Similarly, a Denny's customer can only order a bagel and cream cheese if he or she is in Hawaii, southern Florida, or the region north of Virginia and east of Harrisburg, Pa. Those customers, however, can't take advantage of the catfish special, which is only available in parts of the South and Midwest.[54]

AUTOMOBILE PREFERENCES   The automobile is a key life-style vehicle. One's choice of car says a lot about the image one is trying to convey, whether that image is sleek and sexy, economical and down-to-earth, or rough 'n tough. It's not surprising, then, that car preferences vary on a regional basis. For example, Texans, who comprise only 7 percent of the population, buy 10 percent of all trucks sold. In fact, Texas is the only state where trucks are the majority of *all* new vehicles sold.

More money has been spent over the last five years by car makers on regional and local "spot" advertising than on national advertising in the automobile category.[56] General Motors began to develop a regional marketing system after it was noticed that sales were weak on the West Coast. The company developed special ads for the California market to appeal to this geographic segment. While the Chevrolet Cavalier is sold nationwide as a utility family vehicle, the campaign in California emphasizes the car's sportiness and excitement.

Chrysler has adopted a similar strategy: While spokesman Ricardo Montalban plugs the fancy interior of the LeBaron GTS in the Midwest and elsewhere, the California commercials emphasize acceleration and handling. BMW buyers also are not evenly distributed around the country: Of the top fifty dealerships, eighteen are located in California and seven are in Texas. While Georgia has only three BMW dealerships, all three are in the top ten. This reflects the high concentration of successful young people in Atlanta who fit the car's target market profile.[57]

THE ARTS AND ENTERTAINMENT   The types of entertainment sought by consumers around the country differ markedly as well. A survey performed for the National Endowment for the Arts showed that jazz and classical music are the most popular in the West and Midwest, and that consumers in the West like museums and the theater more than other Americans.[58]

A Gallup poll revealed that Easterners most prefer to watch television, read, and go to the movies, while those in the West most prefer eating out, dancing, and visiting with friends. Consumers in the Midwest were most likely to enjoy parlor games and cards.

MULTICULTURAL DIMENSIONS

The Paris Burger King does more business than any other outlet in the world, and the same is true for the Kentucky Fried Chicken store in Beijing. Despite the almost universal appeal of American fast food, however, adaptations must be made to cater to regional tastes. McDonald's operates in fifty-two countries, but with some variations. The company serves beer in Germany, wine in France, and sugar-cane juice in Malaysia. Japanese customers can buy corn chowder and Teriyaki McBurgers, and McSpahgetti is sold in the Philippines.[55]

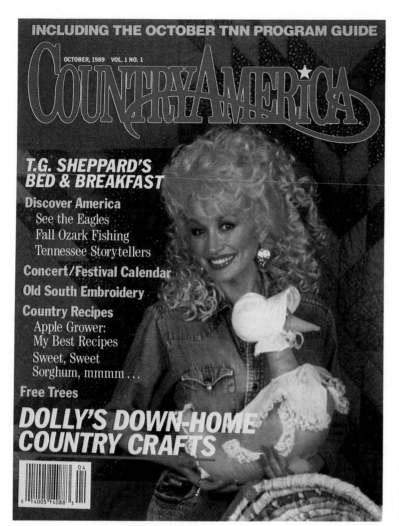

Country America magazine is one of many media vehicles recently developed to appeal to readers' regional identifications. *Courtesy of Country America Magazine.*

The Mystery of the Southern Consumer. In contrast, Southerners expressed a preference for rest and relaxation, preferring to stay at home and work around the house.[59] One overall pattern that emerges is that people in the South are much less likely to take part in organized activities or entertainment of virtually *any* kind. In one study that looked at participation in forty different leisure activities, people in the South were less likely to participate in thirty-seven of them. In particular, this group was far less likely to visit museums, attend concerts, play sports, or take pictures. They were, however, more likely to express a preference for singing and listening to religious or County/Western music.

Does this mean that Southerners are lazy? More likely this pattern reflects the focus in Southern culture on activities that revolve around the home, church, and family, choices that do not tend to show up on surveys. The ad for *Country America* is an example of a magazine specifically targeted to this regional group.

THE NINE NATIONS OF NORTH AMERICA

The Bureau of the Census divides the United States into regions, each of which encompasses a number of states. An alternate conceptualization of the country that specifically considered geographic subcultures was proposed by a journalist named Joel Garreau in 1981.[60] This scheme, called **The Nine Nations of North America,** postulates that "America" does not really exist at all. Garreau claimed that there actually are nine separate "nations" within the geographical boundaries of the United States and Canada, each with its own priorities and customs. This approach drew a lot of attention from marketers who were looking for new ways to divide their markets. The map in Figure 14-2 provides more detail about the eight "nations" within the U.S. (excluding the "nation" of Quebec, which is centered in Canada), as adapted by the Ogilvy & Mather advertising agency for its own analyses.

For example, the "Breadbasket" is home to "Middle America," where people are largely conservative and hard-working. "Ecotopia" in the Northwest United States is environmentally oriented and associated with "New Age" philosophy. "MexAmerica" in the Southwest is largely influenced by its Hispanic roots, and the culture of "The Islands" in southern Florida and the Caribbean also is heavily influenced by interactions with Latin America (including revenues from the illegal drug industry). Other "nations" include Dixie (or the "New South"), The Foundry (sometimes called "The Rust Belt"), The Empty Quarter, New England, and Quebec.

PROBLEMS WITH THE NINE NATIONS   Garreau's insights were quite interesting, and many of his observations make intuitive sense. For example, subsequent work on this categorization scheme verifies that occupants of

Figure 14-2 The Eight Nations of the United States: The Eight Nations of the United States, The Ogilvy & Mather Listening Post, 1983, p. 3

the Ecotopia "nation" are more likely to be employed in executive or professional positions, are more likely to be college-educated and politically liberal, and tend to be highly inner-directed. In contrast, Dixie residents are more likely to be blue-collar, politically conservative, and outer-directed.[61]

However, it is important to remember that the precise borders of The Nine Nations are largely based upon personal observations and guesses about how to divide up the country. Other researchers have noted that the "nations" themselves contain pockets that most likely better belong to other "nations" (e.g., ecologically minded Santa Monica, CA is in Mex-America, not Ecotopia).

More systematic work that explicitly examined the values of people living in each "nation" has not provided overwhelming support for the "Nine Nations" typology *per se*.[62] Nonetheless, Garreau's observations were a valuable impetus to marketers to begin to think of the United States as a mosaic composed of many different geographic subcultures.

GEODEMOGRAPHY

The Western Union Company wanted to improve the cost-effectiveness of its network of offices. The company undertook a market evaluation with the following goals:

- Analyze the number of Western Union agents needed in an area.
- Determine where new agents would be most profitably located.
- Identify new market opportunities.

This project involved several steps. The company constructed a profile of the typical customer for money-wire services, and then attempted to identify areas where these customers were likely to live. It engaged a market research company to identify the geographic distribution of these customers at the zip code level and defined areas as either unserved, partially served, or saturated.

The search for new ways to segment markets more precisely, coupled with the increasing sophistication of data collection and analysis techniques, has enabled companies like Western Union to incorporate geographic variables into their marketing strategies. Marketers have looked at product movement since the 1930s, when A. C. Nielsen tracked changes in actual store inventories at the regional level.[64] Modern **geodemographic** techniques allow companies to go well beyond broad regional differences. Many now segment markets down to the neighborhood block. The provision of this type of analysis to marketers has become a profitable niche for several market research companies.

APPLICATIONS OF GEODEMOGRAPHY Marketers have been successful at adapting sophisticated analytical techniques originally developed for other applications, such as the military and oil and gas exploration. These techniques, which can now employ data at the neighborhood or even household level, are used in a variety of ways:

- A bank examined its penetration of accounts by customer zip codes.
- A direct marketer chose the most economical "drop points" for deliveries.

- A utility company compared demographic data with billing patterns to fine-tune energy conservation campaigns.[65]
- A chain of ice cream stores helped franchisees develop sales promotion programs for local markets by providing them with demographic profiles of actual users and information about the sales potential of untapped customer groups.[66]
- A manufacturer test-marketed a new product to examine differences in product preferences by region of the country.

A basic assumption of geodemography is that "birds of a feather flock together": people who live near one another share similar characteristics. Some companies use U.S. Census data in a statistical technique known as *cluster analysis* to identify census tracts around the country that seem to share the same characteristics. Then, a marketer who wants to reach only those consumers in one or more of these clusters (say, a direct marketer who wants to mail expensive catalogs only to the most likely sales prospects) can target only certain zip codes in an area and ignore others.

PRIZM.   One such clustering technique is the PRIZM system developed by Claritas, Inc. This system classifies every U.S. zip code into one of forty categories, ranging from the most-affluent "Blue-Blood Estates" to the least well-off "Public Assistance."[67] A resident of Southern California might be classified as "Money & Brains" if he or she lives in Encino (zip code 91316), while someone living in Sherman Oaks (zip code 91423) would be a "Young Influential."[68]

SINGLE-SOURCE DATA: BRINGING IT ALL TOGETHER   While an abundance of data exists on American consumption patterns, this information tends to be found in a range of separate data bases difficult to examine simultaneously. This problem is now being surmounted by several projects that employ **single source data.** In these situations, all of the relevant information is collected on a matched basis, so that different aspects of consumption and demographic data can be combined for the same unit of analysis (e.g., a census tract).

This comprehensive strategy was first implemented in the Behavior-Scan project, begun in 1980 by Information Resources, Inc. (IRI). That system combined UPC scanners, household panels, and television to track purchases. A total approach allows marketers to test the impact of changes in advertising, pricing, shelf placement, and promotions on consumer behavior patterns. Similar systems are now available or under development by other organizations, such as Nielsen and SAMI/Burke.[69]

CHAPTER SUMMARY

People have many things in common with others merely because they are about the same age or live in the same part of the country. Consumers who grew up at the same time share many cultural memories, so they may respond to marketers' nostalgia appeals that remind them of these experiences.

Four important age subcultures are teens, college students, baby boomers, and the elderly. Teenagers are making a transition from childhood to adulthood, and their self-concepts tend to be unstable. They are receptive to products that help them to be accepted and enable them to assert their independence. Because many teens earn money but have few financial obligations, they are a particularly important segment for many non-essential or expressive products, ranging from chewing gum to clothing fashions and music. Because of changes in family structure, many teens also are taking more responsibility for their families' day-to-day shopping and routine purchase decisions. College students are an important, but hard to reach market. In many cases, they are living alone for the first time, so they are making important decisions about setting up a household.

Baby boomers are the most powerful age segment because of their size and economic clout. As this group ages, its interests have changed and marketing priorities have changed as well. The needs and desires of baby boomers affect demands for housing, child-care, automobiles, clothing, and so on. While some assume that all baby boomers are yuppies, in fact only a small proportion of boomers fit into this affluent, materialistic category. Other emerging sub–segments, such as new-collars, are probably more representative of future directions this age subculture will take.

As the population ages, the needs of elderly consumers will also become increasingly influential. Many marketers traditionally ignored the elderly because of the stereotype that they are too inactive and spend too little. This stereotype is no longer accurate. Most of the elderly are healthy, vigorous, and interested in new products and experiences—and they have the income to purchase them. Marketing appeals to this age subculture should focus on consumers' self-concepts and perceived ages, which tend to be more youthful than their chronological ages. Marketers also should emphasize concrete benefits of products, since this group tends to be skeptical of vague, image-related promotions. Personalized service is of particular importance to this segment.

Consumption preferences can differ dramatically depending on the region of the country. Tastes and traditions vary from East to West and North to South. Regional marketing rather than a uniform national strategy is beginning to be practiced by many companies, who are learning to tailor their products to local preferences. Sophisticated geodemographic techniques, which assume that people who live together share important characteristics, are being developed to fine-tune advertising and direct-marketing efforts by identifying and targeting consumers with relevant demographics in common.

KEY TERMS

Age cohort
Baby boomers
Geodemographics
New-Collar Workers
Perceived age

Single source data
Standard Metropolitan Statistical Areas (SMSAs)
The Nine Nations of North America

REVIEW QUESTIONS AND DISCUSSION TOPICS

1. What are some possible marketing opportunities present at reunions? What effects might attending such an event have on consumers' self–esteem, body image, affect, and so on?

2. The chapter noted that college students are an especially good market for gifts and greeting cards. Why might this be?

3. Why have "baby boomers" had such an important impact on consumer culture in the second half of this century?
4. How has the "baby boomlet" changed attitudes toward child-rearing and created demand for different products and services?
5. What are some marketing ramifications of the growth of the "new collar" segment?
6. Is it practical to assume that people age 55 and older constitute one large consumer market? What are some approaches to further segmenting this age subculture?
7. Why is television such an important outlet for many elderly consumers?
8. What are some important variables to keep in mind when tailoring marketing strategies to the elderly?
9. Geodemographic techniques assume that people who live in the same neighborhood have other things in common as well. Why is this assumption made, and how accurate is it?
10. Discuss some ways that geodemographic techniques can be applied to refine current marketing strategies. In what types of environments or regions is this less likely to be true?
11. Single source data systems give marketers access to a wide range of information about a consumer, just by knowing his or her address. Do you believe this "knowledge power" presents any ethical problems with regard to consumers' privacy? Should access to such information be regulated by the government or other bodies? Should consumers have the right to limit access to these data?

HANDS-ON EXERCISES

1. Conduct some exploratory market research on friends who are attending college versus those who went to work directly after high school. Can you discern any differences in attitudes and consumer behavior between these two groups?
2. Interview a sample of elderly people about their attitudes toward consumption, media, and leisure activities. To what degree do these different responses correspond to the segmentation variables discussed in the chapter?
3. Find good and bad examples of advertising targeted to elderly consumers. To what degree does advertising stereotype the elderly? What elements of ads or other promotions appear to determine their effectiveness in reaching and persuading this group?
4. Identify some regional differences in product preferences among members of your class. How might a marketing strategy for one of these products be tailored to each regional segment?

NOTES

1. Joseph Pereira, "Pricey Sneakers Worn in Inner City Help Set Nation's Fashion Trend," *The Wall Street Journal* (December 1, 1988): A1.
2. Bickley Townsend, "Ou sont les reiges d'antan? (Where are the snows of yesteryear?" *American Demographics* (October 1988): 2.
3. "Chuckles' Rebirth," *American Demographics* (May 1987): 23.

4. Jeffrey P. Rosenfeld, "Reliving It Up," *American Demographics* (June 1987): 48.
5. Morris B. Holbrook and Robert M. Schindler, "Some Exploratory Findings on the Development of Musical Tastes," *Journal of Consumer Research* 16 (June 1989): 119–24.
6. Randall Rothenberg, "The Past is Now the Latest Craze," *New York Times* (November 29, 1989): D1.
7. Selina S. Guber, "The Teenage Mind," *American Demographics* (August 1987): 42.
8. Ellen Goodman, "The Selling of Teenage Anxiety," *The Washington Post* (November 24, 1979).
9. Ellen R. Foxman, Patriya S. Tansuhaj, and Karim M. Ekstrom, "Family Members' Perceptions of Adolescents' Influence in Family Decision Making," *Journal of Consumer Research* 15 (March 1989): 482–91.
10. Andrew Malcolm, "Teen-Age Shoppers: Desperately Seeking Spinach," *New York Times* (November 29, 1987): 10.
11. Malcolm, "Teen-Age Shoppers."
12. John Blades, "Tracking Skippies: TRU Researches Habits of Elusive Groups—Teens," *The Asbury Park Press* (March 2, 1991): C1.
13. Malcolm, "Teen-Age Shoppers."
14. Alice Cueno, "Targeting 'Tweens': Madison Avenue's Call of the Child," *U.S. News and World Report* (March 20, 1989): 84; Carol Hall, "Tween Power," *Marketing and Media Decisions* 22 (October 1987): 56–62; Kit Mill, "Pre-Teen Buying Power," *Marketing and Media Decisions* (April 1989): 96–98.
15. "Exploding the Myths About Teenagers," *U.S. News & and World Report* (February 10, 1986): 80.
16. Kevin Kelly, "Selling the World: Mouseketeers to Marketers," *Whole Earth Review* (Winter 1989): 36.
17. Quoted in Fannie Weinstein, "Time to Get Them in Your Franchise," *Advertising Age* (February 1, 1988): S-6.
18. Quoted in "Advertisers Target College Market," *Marketing News* (October 23, 1987).
19. Beth Bogart, "Word of Mouth Travels Fastest," *Advertising Age* (February 6, 1989): S6; Janice Steinberg, "Media 101," *Advertising Age* (February 6, 1989): S-4.
20. Liane McAllister, "Campus Clout," *Gifts & Decorative Accessories* (July 1987): 80.
21. "The Big Picture," *American Demographics* (March 1989): 22–27.
22. Fabian Linden, "Middle-Aged Muscle," *American Demographics* (October 1987): 4.
23. Amy Dunkin, "Maxwell House Serves Up a Yuppie Brew," *Business Week* (March 2, 1987): 62.
24. Andrew Pollack, "Jeans Fade but Levi Strauss Glows," *New York Times* (June 26, 1989): D1.
25. Peter Francese, "A Symphony of Demographic Change," *Advertising Age* (November 9, 1988): 130.
26. Albert Scardino, "The New Baby Boom Spurs Local Magazines for Parents," *New York Times* (June 26, 1989): D1.
27. Kenneth I. Walsh and Sharon F. Golden, "The New-Collar Class," *U.S. News & World Report* (September 15, 1985): 59.
28. William Lazer and Eric H. Shaw, "How Older Americans Spend Their Money," *A.D.* (September 1987): 36.
29. Charles D. Schewe, "Marketing to an Aging Population: Responding to Physiological Changes," *Journal of Consumer Marketing* (Summer 1988)5: 61–74.
30. Paul B. Brown, "Last Year It Was Yuppies—This Year It's Their Parents," *Business Week* (March 10, 1986): 68–74.
31. Melinda Beck, "Travels with Grandpa: Seeing the World—and the Grandkids—at Once," *Newsweek* (July 30, 1990): 48; Jeff Ostroff, "An Aging Market," *American Demographics* (May 1989): 26–59.
32. Brad Edmonson, "Take Time for Exercise," *American Demographics* (January 1987): 22.
33. Brown, "Last Year It Was Yuppies."
34. Benny Barak and Leon G. Schiffman, "Cognitive Age: A Nonchronological Age Variable," in *Advances in Consumer Research,* ed. Kent B. Monroe (Provo, Utah: Association for Consumer Research, 1981)8: 602–6.
35. David B. Wolfe, "An Ageless Market," *American Demographics* (July 1987): 27–55.
36. Wolfe, "An Ageless Market."

37. Mary Martin Niepold, "Fabulous and 40-Plus," *Marketing Communications* (September 1988): 17–60.

38. Lenore Skenazy, "These Days, It's Hip to be Old," *Advertising Age* (February 15, 1988).

39. William Lazer and Eric H. Shaw, "How Older Americans Spend Their Money," *American Demographics* (September 1987): 36.

40. Ellen Day, Brian Davis, Rhonda Dove, and Warren A. French, "Reaching the Senior Citizen Market(s)," *Journal of Advertising Research* (December/January 1987/88): 23–30; Warren A. French and Richard Fox, "Segmenting the Senior Citizen Market," *Journal of Consumer Marketing* 2 (1985): 61–74; Jeffrey G. Towle and Claude R. Martin, Jr., "The Elderly Consumer: One Segment or Many?" in *Advances in Consumer Research,* ed. Beverlee B. Anderson (Provo, Utah: Association for Consumer Research, 1976)3: 463.

41. Day, et al., "Reaching the Senior Citizen Market(s)."

42. Many studies have examined elderly consumers' shopping patterns and product choices, see J. Barry Mason and William O. Bearden, "Profiling the Shopping Behavior of Elderly Consumers," *The Gerontologist* 18 (1978)5: 454–61; James R. Lumpkin and Barnett A. Greenberg, "Apparel-Shopping Patterns of the Elderly Consumer," *Journal of Retailing* 58 (Winter 1982): 68–89; Mary C. LaForge, "Learned Helplessness as an Explanation of Elderly Consumer Complaint Behavior," *Journal of Business Ethics* 8 (May 1989): 359–66; Betsy D. Gelb, "Exploring the Gray Market Segment," *MSU Business Topics* 26 (Spring 1978): 41–46; Elaine Sherman, "The Senior Market: Opportunities Abound," *Direct Marketing* 50 (June 1987): 82; Valarie A. Zeithaml and Mary C. Gilly, "Characteristics Affecting the Acceptance of Retailing Technologies: A Comparison of Elderly and Nonelderly Consumers," *Journal of Retailing* 83 (Spring 1987): 49–68; Mary C. Gilly and Valarie A. Zeithaml, "The Elderly Consumer and Adoption of Technologies," *Journal of Consumer Research* 12 (December 1985): 353–57.

43. "Gray Expectations: A New Force in Design," *Business Week* (April 11, 1988): 108; Mary Bender, "Packaging for the Older Consumer," (speech delivered at the Annual Winter Conference of the Gerontology Institute of New Jersey, Princeton, N.J., March 6, 1987).

44. Melinda Beck, "Going for the Gold," *Newsweek* (April 23, 1990): 74.

45. J. Ward, "Marketers Slow to Catch Age Wave," *Advertising Age* (May 22, 1989): S1.

46. Anthony C. Ursic, Michael L. Ursic, and Virginia L. Ursic, "A Longitudinal Study of the Use of the Elderly in Magazine Advertising," *Journal of Consumer Research* 13 (June 1986): 131–33.

47. "States of Stress," *American Demographics* (February, 18, 1987).

48. Dody Tsiantar and Annetta Miller, "Playing to the Home Crowd: 'Regional Advertising' Takes on a New Dimension," *Newsweek* (August 7, 1989): 45.

49. Quoted in George Rathwaite, "Heileman's National Impact with Local Brews," *Marketing Insights* (Premier Issue, 1989): 108.

50. Brad Edmondson, "From Dixie to Detroit," *American Demographics* (January 1987): 27.

51. Edmondson, "From Dixie to Detroit."

52. Edmondson, "From Dixie to Detroit."

53. Brad Edmondson, "America's Hot Spots," *American Demographics* (1988): 24-30.

54. Brad Edmondson, "Chili Recipes," *American Demographics* (April 1987): 22.

55. Calvin Trillin, "Uncivil Liberties: American Fast Food Restaurants Around the World," *The Nation* (April 10, 1989): 473; David Kilburn, "In Japan, It's the Teriyaki McBurger," *Advertising Age* (September 11, 1989): 16.

56. Edmondson, "From Dixie to Detroit."

57. "The 'Beemer' Buyer," *American Demographics* (August 1987): 22.

58. Edmondson, "From Dixie to Detroit."

59. Edmondson, "From Dixie to Detroit."

60. Joel Garreau, *The Nine Nations of North America* (Boston, Mass.: Houghton Mifflin, 1981).

61. *Ogilvy & Mather Listening Post* (New York: Olgilvy & Mather, 1983).

62. Lynn R. Kahle, "The Nine Nations of North America and the Value Basis of Geographic Segmentation," *Journal of Marketing* 50 (April 1986): 37–47.

63. Thomas W. Osborn, "Analytic Techniques for Opportunity Marketing," *Marketing Communications* (September 1987): 49–63.
64. Osborn, "Analytic Techniques for Opportunity Marketing."
65. Osborn, "Analytic Techniques for Opportunity Marketing."
66. Dwight J. Shelton, "Birds of a Geodemographic Feather Flock Together," *Marketing News* (September 28, 1987): 13.
67. Michael J. Weiss, *The Clustering of America* (New York: Harper & Row, 1988).
68. Bob Minzesheimer, "You Are What You Zip," *Los Angeles* (November 1984): 175.
69. Osborn, "Analytic Techniques for Opportunity Marketing."

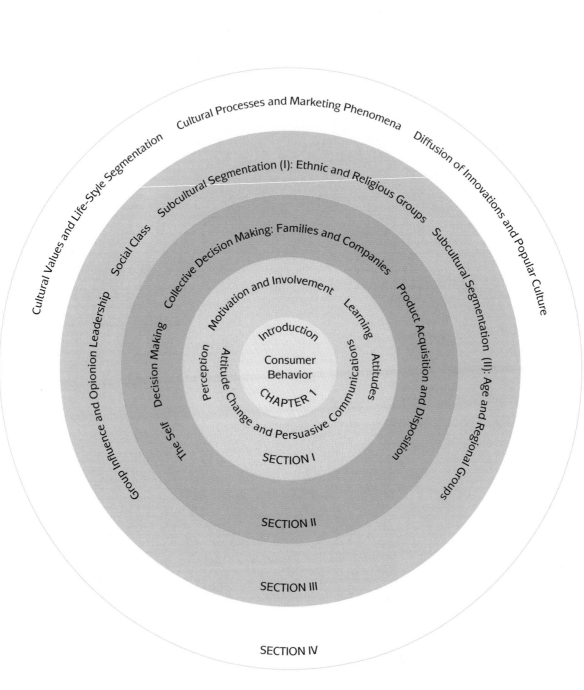

The final Section of this book considers consumers as members of a broad cultural system. Chapter 15 focuses on lifestyles; how we choose categories for ourselves based on similarities in aesthetic taste, leisure activities, and the different social roles we play. This Chapter also examines how underlying values differ among people from cultures around the world, and how these fundamental beliefs about the world translate into variations in consumer behavior. Chapter 16 looks at ways marketing activities are affected by, and contribute to, such undercultural processes as myths and rituals, and at how consumer behaviors, both positive and negative, are influenced by the cultural messages around us. Finally, Chapter 17 considers how ideas, new products, and fashions spread among members of a culture. This Chapter brings us back full circle, to a fundamental point that was made in Chapter 1: Consumers are people too, and marketers must understand how they contribute to and are affected by people's daily lives and popular culture. In the final analysis, marketing is the creation of a lifestyle, and this Section demonstrates just how much our daily lives as consumers are affected by marketing strategy.

The Consumer and Culture

Cultural Values and Life-style Segmentation

On her way home from her job at the ad agency, Jackie pulls her Volvo into the supermarket parking lot. After anxiously checking her Rolex, she figures this is a good opportunity to pick up a few things on her way to her squash game. Once in the market, Jackie reminds herself to stay away from "empty calories," or her figure and heart will pay the price. She quickly grabs some goat cheese, pesto sauce, and sun-dried tomatoes, first making sure that she's selecting biodegradable packages. Jackie is really looking forward to her casual dinner with Hank, which she will try to squeeze in after making an appearance at the meeting protesting plans to put an incinerator near her neighborhood. Hank seems to be fitting into her plans to settle down and raise a family. No more life in the fast lane for her; those wild days are a thing of the past.

Jackie fits the profile of women characterized by advertisers as "green consumers."[1] She has a professional career, is active in the community, is nutrition-conscious, and she checks ingredients and prices carefully. She also feels that environmentalism is here to stay, and it should not be portrayed as hip or trendy in advertising. She also has a bit of the Yuppie in her, as evidenced by her Volvo, Rolex, and passion for squash. She is, however, an updated version, since her values regarding the family, sexual behavior, and materialism have recently changed.

CULTURE

Culture, a concept crucial to the understanding of consumer behavior, may be thought of as a society's personality. It includes both abstract ideas, such as values and ethics, as well as the material objects and services produced or valued by a group of people, such as automobiles, clothing, food, art, and sports. Culture is the accumulation of shared meanings, rituals, norms, and traditions among the members of an organization or society.

Ironically, the effects of culture on consumer behavior are so powerful and far-reaching that this importance is sometimes difficult to grasp or appreciate. Like a fish immersed in water, we do not always appreciate this power until we encounter a different culture. A consumer's culture determines the overall priorities he or she attaches to different activities and products. It also mandates the success or failure of specific products and services. A product that provides benefits consistent with those desired by members of a culture at any point in time has a much better chance of attaining acceptance in the marketplace. For example, the U.S. culture started to emphasize the concept of thinness as an ideal of appearance in the mid-1970s. The premium placed on this goal, which stemmed from underlying values like mobility, wealth, and a focus on the self, greatly contributed to the success of Miller Lite beer at that time. However, when Gablinger introduced a lo-cal beer seven years earlier, in 1968, the product failed. This product was "ahead of its time," since American consumers were not interested in this benefit in the 1960s.

ASPECTS OF CULTURE

Culture is not static. Especially in modern society, it is continually evolving, synthesizing old ideas with new ones. A cultural system consists of three functional areas, all of which are complexly interrelated:[2]

1. *Ecology:* the way a system is adapted to its habitat. This is shaped by the technology used to obtain and distribute resources (e.g., industrialized societies versus Third World countries). The Japanese, for example, greatly value products that are designed for efficient use of space because of the acute lack of space in that island nation.[3]
2. *Social structure:* the way orderly social life is maintained. This includes the domestic and political groups that are dominant within the culture (e.g., the nuclear family versus the extended family).
3. *Ideology:* the mental characteristics of a people and the way they relate to their environment and social groups. The members of a society possess a common **worldview.** They share certain ideas about principles of order and fairness. They also share an **ethos,** or a set of moral, aesthetic, and evaluative principles.

DIMENSIONS OF VARIABILITY   Although every culture is different, four stable dimensions have been identified that appear to account for much of this variability:[4]

1. *Power distance:* the way interpersonal relationships form when differences in power are perceived. Some cultures emphasize strict, vertical

**Show your respect again.
Call Japan.**

She raised you from a little boy to a man of substance. Taught you loyalty, integrity, tradition. So when you left Tokyo, you took your mother's words of wisdom with you. Why not tell her how much they've meant to you?

With AT&T International Long Distance Service, it costs less than you'd think to stay close. So go ahead. **Reach out and touch someone.**

JAPAN, AUSTRALIA	Economy 3am–2pm	Discount 8pm–3am	Standard 2pm–8pm
AVERAGE COST PER MINUTE FOR A 10-MINUTE CALL*	**$ .95**	**$1.20**	**$1.58**

*Average cost per minute varies depending on the length of the call. First minute costs more; additional minutes cost less. All prices are for calls dialed direct from anywhere in the continental U.S. during the hours listed. Add 3% federal excise tax and applicable state surcharges. Call our toll-free number for further information or if you'd like to receive an AT&T international rates brochure **1 800 874-4000.** © 1986 AT&T

AT&T
The right choice.

AT&T uses a cross-cultural appeal to generate more long-distance calling. Courtesy of AT&T INTERNATIONAL COMMUNICATIONS SERVICES.

relationships (e.g., Japan), while others, such as the United States, stress a greater degree of equality and informality.

2. *Uncertainty avoidance:* the degree that people feel threatened by ambiguous situations and have beliefs and institutions that help them to avoid this uncertainty.

3. *Masculinity:* the degree to which sex roles are clearly delineated (see Femininity Chapter 7).

4. *Individualism:* the extent to which the welfare of the individual versus that of the group is valued (see Chapter 11). Cultures differ in their emphasis on **individualism** versus **collectivism.** In collectivist cultures, people subordinate their personal goals to those of a stable in-group. In contrast, consumers in individualist cultures attach more importance to personal goals, and people are more likely to change memberships when a group's demands become too costly (e.g., workplace, churches, etc.). Whereas a collectivist society will stress such

values as self-discipline and accepting one's position in life, people in individualist cultures emphasize personal enjoyment, excitement, equality, and freedom. Some strongly individualistic cultures include those of the United States, Australia, Great Britain, Canada, and the Netherlands. Venezuela, Pakistan, Taiwan, Thailand, Turkey, Greece, and Portugal are some examples of strongly collectivist cultures.[5]

NORMS AND VALUES   Members of a culture share a system of meaning, which means that they have learned to accept a set of beliefs and practices governing their existence. These beliefs are taught to members of a culture by socialization agents, including parents, friends, and teachers. The process of learning the beliefs and behaviors endorsed by one' own culture is termed **enculturation,** while the learning of a new culture (usually a more difficult task), is **acculturation.**

Values.   Every culture has a set of values that it imparts to its members. A value is an enduring belief that some state is preferable to its opposite.[6] For example, people in one culture might feel that being a unique individual is preferable to subordinating one's identity to the group, while another group may emphasize the opposite.

In many cases, values are universal. Who does not desire health, wisdom, or world peace? What sets cultures apart, though, is the *relative importance,* or ranking, of values. This set of rankings constitutes a culture's **value system.**[7] To illustrate a difference in value systems, consider the results of a study by the Dentsu advertising agency. Consumers in New York, Los Angeles, and Tokyo were asked to indicate their preferences regarding the goals an ideal society should aim for. Although the two American cities represent quite different regional subcultures (see Chapter 14), there was a high degree of consensus within the American sample. Both groups (perhaps reflecting an urban influence) said their highest ideal is a "society in which people can live safely." In contrast, Tokyo residents ranked first the goal of a "society with a comprehensive welfare system." While about 45 percent of the Americans endorsed the idea of a "society which is very competitive, but in which everybody has an equal chance of success," only 25 percent of Tokyo residents echoed this sentiment.[8]

Norms.   Values are very general ideas about good and bad goals. From these flow **norms,** rules dictating what is right or wrong, acceptable or unacceptable. Some norms, called *enacted norms,* are explicitly decided upon, such as the amount of foreign material permissible in various food products. Many norms, however, are much more subtle. These *crescive norms* are embedded in a culture and are only discovered through interaction with other members of that culture. Crescive norms include the following.[9]

Custom.   A *custom* is a norm handed down from the past that controls basic behaviors, such as division of labor in a household or the practice of particular ceremonies.

More. A *more* is a custom with a strong moral overtone. A more often involves a taboo, or forbidden behavior, such as incest or cannibalism. Violation of a more often meets with strong punishment from other members of a society.

Convention. *Conventions* are norms regarding the conduct of everyday life. These rules deal with the subtleties of consumer behavior, including the "correct" way to furnish one's house, wear one's clothes, serve at a dinner party, and so on.

All three types of crescive norms may operate to completely define a culturally appropriate behavior. For example, a more may tell us what kind of food is permissible to eat. Note that mores vary across cultures, so a meal of dog may be taboo in the United States, while Hindus would shun a steak and Moslems would avoid pork products. A custom dictates the appropriate hour at which the meal should be served. Conventions tell us how to eat the meal, including such details as the utensils to be used, table etiquette, and even the appropriate apparel to be worn at dinnertime.

Again, we often take these conventions for granted, assuming that they are the "right" things to do. The belief in the superiority of one's own cultural practices and products is termed **ethnocentrism.** The degree to which consumers are ethnocentric can help to predict the likelihood they will accept foreign products.[10] American consumers who score high on a scale designed to measure this belief are more likely to prefer domestic brands to imports, and they also place more emphasis on choosing American-made products when weighing alternatives.

MULTICULTURAL DIMENSIONS

Each culture develops its own aesthetic standards and unique forms of symbolism used to communicate various qualities. The use of these symbols may be quite alien to an observer from another culture. Consider, for example, this script from a recent commercial for the Gekkeikan brand of Japanese sake (rice wine):[11]

Flower, bird, wind, moon.

Flower, bird, wind, moon.

Feelings blossom as a flower, before one knows

Wishes take flight like a bird, even farther it goes.

A dream carried on a breeze relentlessly free

Our fancy attracted by the moon, a tempting mystery

Japan overflows with things to charm the senses

The Japanese sake, "Gekkeikan," satisfies the sensitive mind of the Japanese.

This imagery may seem quite mysterious to a Westerner more accustomed to seeing glamorous men and women or party scenes in beer and wine ads. To the Japanese, though, flowers, birds, the wind, and the moon traditionally symbolize aesthetic pleasure. The goal of the ad is to establish sake as another source of pleasure. This commercial was intended to bolster the sponsor's reputation as a quality sake manufacturer.

MARKETING AND CULTURE

Marketers contribute to culture by creating products and symbols that *signify* cultural ideals. Levi's jeans, Marlboro cigarettes, and Coca-Cola have been successfully linked with such abstract attributes as freedom and individuality and are viewed around the world as symbols of America.

The relationship between marketing and culture is a two-way street. The study of new products and innovations in product design successfully produced by a culture at any point in time provides a window onto the dominant cultural ideals of that period. Consider, for example, some American products that reflect underlying cultural processes:

Univision, a Hispanic-American television network, attempts to associate its logo with some well-known symbols of America. COPYRIGHT UNIVISION, INC., created by Alan Stess & Associates.

AMONG THE SYMBOLS THAT MATTER MOST TO 20 MILLION AMERICANS IS A BRAND NEW ONE.

UNIVISION is Hispanic-America's television network. And we're introducing a brand new logo for the exciting new decade ahead.

UNIVISION

- The TV dinner, which provided convenience and also hinted at changes in family structure.
- Cosmetics made of natural materials and not animal-tested, which tap consumers' apprehensions about pollution, waste, and animal rights.
- Condoms marketed in pastel carrying cases for female buyers, which signal changes in attitudes toward sexual responsibility and frankness.

THINK GLOBALLY, ACT LOCALLY   As corporations increasingly find themselves competing in many markets around the world, the debate has intensified regarding the necessity of developing separate marketing plans for each culture. On one hand, it has been argued that many cultures, especially those of relatively industrialized countries, have become so homogenized that the same approach will work throughout the world. By standardizing marketing strategy, the company can benefit through economies of scale. There is little need to undergo the time and expense of developing a separate strategy for each culture.[12] This viewpoint represents an **etic perspective,** which focuses upon commonalities across cultures.

Europe, Inc.   This approach is considered especially applicable to the European Community, where formerly separate economies are being merged into one market of 325 million consumers, resulting in standardization of prices, brand names, and advertising.[13] Many companies are responding to this dramatic change by consolidating the different brands sold in individual countries into common "Eurobrands." In the U.K. and France, for example, the Marathon candy bar sold by Mars Inc. is becoming the Snickers bar (a somewhat risky move, considering that the British refer to women's underwear as knickers).[14]

NATIONAL CHARACTER   On the other hand, many marketers endorse an **emic perspective,** which focuses on variations within a culture. They feel that each culture is unique, with its own value system, conventions, and regulations. This perspective argues that each country has a **national character,** a distinctive set of behavior and personality characteristics.[15] An effective strategy must be tailored to the sensibilities and needs of each specific culture. The ad for Northwest Airlines is intended to supply some pointers for doing business in the Orient while it establishes the airline as an authority on Asian cultures.

Taste and Stylistic Preferences.   As opposed to Americans, Europeans favor dark chocolate over milk chocolate, which they regard as suitable only for children. Sara Lee sells its pound cake with chocolate chips in the United States, raisins in Australia, and coconut in Hong Kong. Whisky is considered a "classy" drink in France and Italy, but not in England. Crocodile bags are popular in Asia and Europe, but not in the United States. Americans' favorite tie colors are red and blue, while the Japanese prefer olive, brown, and bronze.[16]

Advertising Preferences and Regulations. Consumers in different countries are accustomed to different forms of advertising. In general, ads that focus on universal values, such as love of family, travel fairly well, while those with a specific focus on life-styles do not. In some cases, advertising content is controlled. For example, pricing in Germany is controlled by the government, and special sales can be held only for a particular reason, such as going out of business or the end of the season. Advertising also focuses more on the provision of factual information rather than on the aggressive hard sell. Indeed, it is illegal to mention the name of competitors.[17] A similar emphasis on facts can be found in Spain and Denmark. In contrast, the British and the Japanese regard advertising as a form of entertainment. Compared to the United States, British television commercials contain less information,[18] and Japanese advertising is more likely to feature emotional appeals.[19] As in Germany, comparative advertising is rare in Japan, but for a different reason: The Japanese consider this practice impolite.

Superstitions and Cultural Sensitivities. Marketers must be aware of a culture's norms regarding such sensitive topics as taboos and sexuality. Opals signify bad luck to the British, while hunting dog or pig emblems are offensive to Moslems. The Japanese are superstitious about the number four. *Shi,* the word for four, is also the word for death. For this reason, Tiffany sells glassware and china in sets of five in this country. Also, the Japanese consider pierced ears to be a form of self-mutilation.

Modesty. Cultures vary sharply in the degree to which reference to sex and bodily functions is permitted. Many American consumers pride themselves on their sophistication. However, some would blush at much European advertising, where sexuality is more explicit. This dimension is particularly interesting in Japan, which is a culture of contradictions. On the one hand, the Japanese are publicly shy and polite. On the other hand, sexuality plays a significant role in this society. One half of the films made in Japan are of an erotic nature, and until recently prostitution was legal. Manga, the extremely popular Japanese comic books that comprise a billion dollar industry, stress themes of sex and violence. Advertising is frequently risque, and sex is used to sell many household products. Nudity is quite commonplace in Japanese advertising and general media.[20] Bare-breasted women are routinely featured in newspapers and on television.

The Japanese are also quite cavalier about bodily functions, largely due to the lack of privacy in their society. They often rely on earthy humor to sell products. One advertisement for a hemorrhoid preparation depicts

NORTHWEST ASIA SERIES

U.S. RESERVATIONS 1-800-225-2525, INTERNATIONAL RESERVATIONS 1-800-447-4747
© 1989 Northwest Airlines, Inc.

Northwest Airlines educates readers about cultural differences while promoting its own services. Courtesy of Northwest Airlines.

a man sitting on the toilet, whining about his pain. Another spot featured a famous Japanese actress dressed as a tampon. The Fuji Latex Co., a large condom manufacturer, built a tower at its factory shaped like its product.[21]

DOES GLOBAL MARKETING WORK?   Although the argument for a homogeneous world culture is appealing in principle, in practice it has met with mixed results. One reason for the failure of global marketing is that consumers in different countries have different conventions and customs, so they simply do not use products the same way. Kellogg, for example, discovered that in Brazil big breakfasts are not traditional—cereal is more commonly eaten as a dry snack. Procter & Gamble found that its ads for Camay soap in Japan did not work, because they featured men complimenting women on their appearance. This directness was very jarring to the Japanese, and the campaign had to be discontinued.[22]

Some large corporations, such as Coca-Cola, have been successful in crafting a single, international image. However, as noted earlier, it may be argued that they are really exporting a uniquely American image. Not many companies have such a strong franchise. Even Coca-Cola must make minor modifications to the way it presents itself in a culture. Although Coke commercials are largely standardized, local agencies are permitted to edit them to highlight close-ups of local faces.[23]

Translation Problems.   The language barrier is one problem confronting marketers who wish to break into foreign markets. Chapter 13 noted some gaffes made by U.S. marketers when advertising to ethnic groups in their own country. Imagine how these mistakes are compounded outside of the United States! One technique that is used to avoid this problem is *back-translation,* where a translated ad is retranslated into the original language by a different interpreter to catch errors. Some specific translation obstacles that have been encountered around the world include:[24]

- Fresca (a soft drink) is Mexican slang for lesbian.
- When spelled phonetically, Esso means "stalled car" in Japan.
- Ford had several problems in Spanish markets. The company discovered that a truck model it called "Fiera" means ugly old woman in Spanish. Its Caliente model, sold in Mexico, is slang for a streetwalker. In Brazil, Pinto is a slang term meaning "small male appendage."
- When Rolls Royce introduced its "Silver Mist" model in Germany, it found that the word "mist" is translated as excrement. Similarly, Sunbeam's hair curling iron, called the "Mist-Stick," translated as *manure wand.*
- Vicks is German slang for sexual intercourse, so the company name had to be changed to Wicks in this market.

IDENTIFYING DOMINANT CULTURAL VALUES

Every culture is characterized by its members' endorsement of a value system. These end states may not be equally endorsed by everyone, and in some cases values may even seem to contradict one another (e.g.,

Americans appear to value both conformity and individuality, and seek to find some accommodation between the two). Nonetheless, it is possible to identify a general set of **core values** that seem to define a culture.

Such values as freedom, youthfulness, achievement, materialism, and activity have been claimed to characterize American culture, but even these basic beliefs are subject to change. For example, Americans' emphasis on youth is eroding as the population ages (see Chapter 14). Cultural values are communicated and reinforced through advertising, as is demonstrated in Table 15-1. This table, using a technique known as *content analysis*, identified the dominant values underlying a set of American print ads representing the period from 1900 to 1980. The prevalence of product effectiveness as an underlying advertising theme is obvious.

Despite their importance, values have not been widely applied to direct examinations of consumer behavior. One reason is that such broad-based concepts as freedom, security, or inner harmony are more likely to affect general purchasing patterns than to differentiate between brands within a product category. For this reason some researchers have found it convenient to make distinctions among such broad-based *cultural values* as security or happiness, *consumption-specific values* as convenient shopping or prompt service, and such *product-specific values* such as ease of use or durability.[25]

TABLE 15-1 Cultural values frequently emphasized in advertising

Overall Value	Themes Included	Proportion of Ads Using as Central Theme
Practical	effective, durable, convenient	44
Family	nurturance in family, happy home, getting married	17
New	Modern, improved	14
Cheap	economical, bargain, good value	13
Healthy	fitness, vigorous, athletic	12
Sexy/vain	good appearance, glamorous, erotic	13
Wisdom	knowledge, experience	11
Unique	expensive, valuable, distinctive, rare	10

Source: Adapted from Richard W. Pollay, "The Identification and Distribution of Values Manifest in Print Advertising 1900–1980," in *Personal Values and Consumer Psychology,* ed. Robert E. Pitts, Jr. and Arch G. Woodside (Lexington, Mass.: Lexington Books, 1984), 111–35.

THE ROKEACH VALUE SURVEY The psychologist Milton Rokeach identified a set of **terminal values,** or desired end states, that apply (to various degrees) to many different cultures. The *Rokeach Value Survey,* a scale used to measure these values, also includes a set of **instrumental values,** which are composed of actions needed to achieve these terminal values.[26] These two sets of values appear in Table 15-2.

THE LIST OF VALUES (LOV) Though some evidence indicates that differences on these global values do translate into product-specific preferences and differences in media usage, the Rokeach Value Survey has not been widely applied to consumer behavior issues.[27] As an alternative, the *LOV* (List of Values) *Scale* was developed to isolate values with more direct marketing applications.

This instrument identifies nine consumer segments based on the values they endorse and relates each to differences in consumption behaviors. These segments include consumers who place a priority on such values as sense of belonging, excitement, warm relationships with others, and security. For example, people who endorse the value of sense of belonging are more likely to read *Reader's Digest* and *TV Guide,* drink and entertain more, prefer group activities, and be older than do people who do not endorse this value as highly. In contrast, those who endorse the value of excitement prefer *Rolling Stone* and are younger than those who do not.[28]

THE MEANS-END CHAIN MODEL Another research approach that incorporates values is termed a **means-end chain model.** This approach assumes

TABLE 15-2 Two types of values in the Rokeach value survey

Instrumental Values	Terminal Values
Ambitious	A comfortable life
Broadminded	An exciting life
Capable	A sense of accomplishment
Cheerful	A world at peace
Clean	A world of beauty
Courageous	Equality
Forgiving	Family security
Helpful	Freedom
Honest	Happiness
Imaginative	Inner harmony
Independent	Mature love
Intellectual	National security
Logical	Pleasure
Loving	Salvation
Obedient	Self-respect
Polite	Social recognition
Responsible	True friendship
Self-controlled	Wisdom

Source: Richard W. Pollay, "Measuring the Cultural Values Manifest in Advertising," *Current Issues and Research in Advertising* (1983): 71–92.

that very specific product attributes are linked at levels of increasing abstraction to terminal values. The person has valued end states, and he or she chooses among alternative means to attain these goals. Products are thus valued as the means to an end. Through a technique called *laddering,* consumers' associations between specific attributes and general consequences are uncovered. Consumers are helped to climb up the "ladder" of abstraction that connects functional product attributes with desired end states.[29]

To understand how laddering works, consider a women who expresses a liking for a flavored potato chip. Probing might reveal that this attribute is linked to a strong taste (another attribute). A consequence of a strong taste is that she eats fewer chips. As a result, she won't get fat. This in turn means that she will have a better figure. Finally, a better figure results in greater self-esteem, a terminal value for this person.[30]

MECCAS. The notion that products are consumed because they are instrumental to attaining more abstract values is central to one application of this technique, called the *Means-End Conceptualization of the Components of Advertising Strategy* (MECCAS). In this approach, researchers first generate a map depicting relationships between functional product or service attributes and terminal values. This information is then used to develop advertising strategy by identifying such elements as:[31]

- *Message elements:* the specific attributes or product features to be depicted.
- *Consumer benefit:* the positive consequences of using the product or service.
- *Executional framework:* the overall style and tone of the advertisement.
- *Leverage point:* the way the message will activate the terminal value by linking it with specific product features.
- *Driving force:* the end value upon which the advertising will focus.

This technique was used to develop advertising strategy for Federal Express. The researchers developed a "Hierarchical Value Map" for secretaries, an important group of decision makers in the category of overnight delivery services. As shown in Figure 15-1, concrete attributes of competitive services, such as having a drop box or on-time delivery, were successively related to more abstract benefits, such as "makes me look good" or "save time." These intermediate levels were then linked, or laddered, to reveal their relationship to the terminal values of peace of mind and self-esteem.

Based on these results, an advertisement was created. Its message elements emphasized Federal Express' satellite communications network. The consumer benefit was the reliability of the service, which made work easier. The executional framework was a humorous one. A secretary is trying to track down an overnight delivery. She and her boss are interrupted and taken to view the Federal Express satellite system. As a result, the secretary sees the benefit of using the company. The leverage point is that using this service allows her to be in control, which in turn provides peace of mind, the driving force (terminal value).

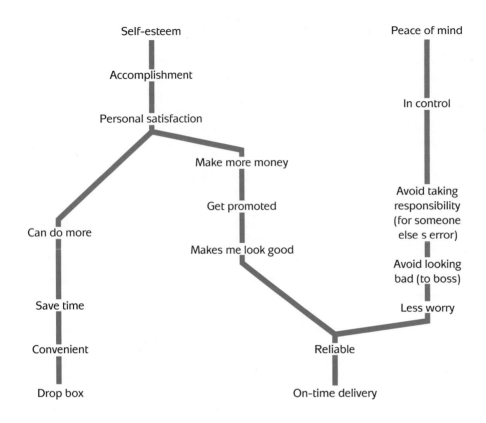

Figure 15-1 Secretaries' Hierarchical Value Map for Overnight Delivery Services   Reynolds and Craddock *Journal of Advertising Research,* April/May 1988, 43-54

THE VALUE OF MATERIALISM

Members of "cargo cults" in the South Pacific literally worshiped cargo that was occasionally salvaged from crashed aircraft or washed ashore from ships. These people believed that these ships and planes were piloted by their ancestors, and they tried to attract them to their villages. During World War II, they went so far as to construct fake planes from straw in hopes of luring real ones.[32]

While not everyone literally worships products this way, things do play a central role in many people's lives. One of the most important values of relevance to the study of consumer behavior is **materialism,** or the importance people attach to worldly possessions. Americans inhabit a highly materialistic society where people often gauge the worth of themselves and others in terms of how much they own.

We sometimes take the existence of an abundance of products and services for granted, until it is remembered how recent many of these developments are. For example, in 1950 two of five American homes did not have a telephone, and in 1940 half of all households still did not possess complete indoor plumbing. In contrast, many Americans now energetically seek "the good life," which abounds in material comforts.

About 40 percent of households have two or more cars, and over $200 billion is spent on vacations in a year.[33] Advertising encourages this emphasis on consumption, and increasingly portrays consumption as an end in itself, rather than as a means to attain well-being.[34]

Of course, not everyone stresses the value of materialism to the same degree. Individual differences have been found among consumers in terms of this emphasis. One approach partitions materialism into three categories: possessiveness, nongenerosity, and envy.[35] Possessiveness is most closely related to the value attached to accumulating objects, but each component taps a different aspect of materialism. The three subscales used to measure these traits are shown in Table 15-3.

Teaching the World to Buy. For better or worse, the value of materialism has been exported around the world. Although a third of the world's countries have a per capita gross national product of less than $500, even poor Third World countries are influenced by images in Western media touting the virtue of elaborate consumption. For example, consider how the material expectations of consumers in the People's Republic

---

TABLE 15-3 A scale to measure materialism

Possessiveness subscale

1. Renting or leasing a car is more appealing to me than owning one
2. I tend to hang on to things I should probably throw out
3. I get very upset if something is stolen from me, even if it has little monetary value
4. I don't get particularly upset when I lose things[*]
5. I am less likely than most people to lock things up[*]
6. I would rather buy something I need than borrow it from someone else
7. I worry about people taking my possessions
8. When I travel I like to take a lot of photographs
9. I never discard old pictures or snapshots

Nongenerosity subscale

1. I enjoy having guests in my home[*]
2. I enjoy sharing what I have[*]
3. I don't like to lend things, even to good friends
4. It makes sense to buy a lawnmower with a neighbor and share it[*]

5. I don't mind giving rides to those who don't have a car[*]
6. I don't like to have anyone in my home when I'm not there
7. I enjoy donating things to charities[*]

Envy subscale

1. I am bothered when I see people who buy anything they want
2. I don't know anyone whose spouse or steady date I would like to have as my own[*]
3. When friends do better than me in competition it usually makes me happy for them[*]
4. People who are very wealthy often feel they are too good to talk to average people
5. There are certain people I would like to trade places with
6. When friends have things I cannot afford it bothers me
7. I don't seem to get what is coming to me
8. When Hollywood stars or prominent politicians have things stolen from them I really feel sorry for them

Note: [*] = reverse scored

Source: Russell W. Belk, "Materialism: Trait Aspects of Living in a Material World," *Journal of Consumer Research* (December 1, 1985): 265–80. Reprinted with permission of The University of Chicago Press.

of China have escalated. Twenty years ago, the Chinese strove to attain what they called the "three bigs": bikes, sewing machines, and wristwatches. This wish list was later modified to become the "new big six," adding refrigerators, washing machines, and televisions. At last count, the ideal is now the "eight new things." This list now includes *color* televisions, cameras, and video recorders.[36]

As countries become more Westernized, marketing and advertising tends to stress hedonistic values and product benefits (i.e., fun, gratification, or pleasure) rather than utilitarian ones (i.e., the product satisfies basic physical needs and delivers satisfactory performance). An analysis advertising of the appeals used in three Asian countries illustrates this point. The People's Republic of China is still the least Westernized nation in the Pacific Rim, and advertising is strictly regulated to encourage utilitarian appeals and the promise of a better life. In contrast, Hong Kong is highly Westernized, and its advertising was indeed found to stress a hedonistic existence, often holding out specific promises of emulating the American life-style. Taiwan, which is currently in the middle of these two extremes, also exhibited a mixture of appeals, though over time these are evolving in the direction of Hong Kong's materialistic emphasis.[37] The "Westernization" of global culture is further discussed in Chapter 17.

LIFE-STYLES

In traditional or collective societies, one's consumption options are largely dictated by class, caste, village, or family. In a modern consumer society, however, people are more free to select the set of products, services, and activities that define themselves, and in turn create a social identity that is communicated to others. One's choice of goods and services indeed makes a statement about who one is and about the types of people with which one desires to identify.

Life-style can be described in terms of shared values or tastes, especially as these are reflected in consumption patterns. Life-style marketing recognizes that people sort themselves into groups on the basis of the things they like to do, how they like to spend their leisure time, and how they choose to spend their disposable income.[38] These choices in turn

MULTICULTURAL DIMENSIONS

Eighty percent of free time in western Europe, Canada, Japan, and the United States is used up by six activities: watching television, seeing friends, playing sports, reading, and going to meetings and cultural events. However, the relative allocation of time to these activities differs widely: The Japanese spend about half of their leisure time watching television, while in Norway this activity accounts for only 19 percent of spare time. The Dutch read for an average of 5.5 hours per week, compared with 2.6 hours weekly for British consumers.[39]

create opportunities for market segmentation strategies that recognize the potency of a consumer's chosen life-style in determining both the types of products purchased and the specific brands more likely to appeal to a designated life-style segment.

THE VALUE OF LIFE-STYLE MARKETING

Consumers often choose products, services, and activities over others *because* they are associated with a certain life-style. For this reason, life-style marketing strategies attempt to position an offering by fitting it into this pattern of consumption. As an example of the power of this approach, take the case of Subaru. When this car manufacturer entered the U.S. market in the early 1970s, it had virtually no name recognition and struggled to compete with other, better-known imports. Subaru became the official car of the U.S. ski team and linked itself to the life-styles of people who enjoy skiing. The company now has the highest market share for imports in several Snow Belt states.[40]

Because a goal of life-style marketing is to allow consumers to pursue their chosen ways to enjoy their lives and express their social identities, a key aspect of this strategy is to focus on product usage in social situations (see Chapter 10). The goal of associating a product with a social situation is a long-standing one for advertisers, whether the product is included in a round of golf, a family barbecue, or a night at a glamorous disco surrounded by "jetsetters."[41] Thus people, products, and settings are combined to express a certain consumption style, as diagramed in Figure 15-2.

LIFE-STYLE AND SELF-DEFINITION

In an economic sense, one's life-style represents the way one has elected to allocate income, both in terms of relative allocations to different products and services and to specific alternatives within these categories.[42] Other somewhat similar distinctions have been made to describe consumers in terms of their broad patterns of consumption, such as those differentiating consumers who devote a high proportion of total expenditures to food, advanced technology, or to such information-intensive goods as entertainment and education.[43]

These economic approaches are useful in tracking changes in broad societal priorities, but they do not begin to embrace the symbolic nuances

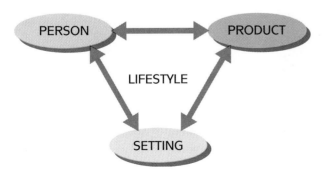

Figure 15-2 Linking Products to Life-styles

that separate life-style groups. Life-style is more than the allocation of discretionary income. It is a statement about who one is in society and who one is not. Group identities, whether of hobbyists, athletes, or drug users, gel around forms of expressive symbolism. The self-definitions of group members are derived from the common symbol system to which the group is dedicated.

Such self-definitions have been described by a number of terms, including *life-style, taste public, consumer group, symbolic community,* and *status culture.*[44] The recreational vehicle ad shown here demonstrates how a market segment is defined by a particular allocation of time and money to a well-defined and exclusive leisure activity. Note the ad's claim that the RV dealer has the product that "says you're you!"

This ad for Jayco motor homes appeals to a specific lifestyle segment. It notes that people who drive RVs have a lot in common with other RV owners. *Courtesy of Jayco, Inc.*

PRODUCT COMPLEMENTARITY

Use of the term life-style implies that we must look at patterns of behavior to understand consumers. In many cases, products do not seem to "make sense" if unaccompanied by companion products (e.g., fast food and paper plates, a suit and tie), or are incongruous in the presence of others (e.g., a Chippendale chair in a high-tech office, or Lucky Strike cigarettes with a solid gold lighter). As one set of researchers noted, ". . . all goods carry meaning, but none by itself. . . . The meaning is in the relations between all the goods, just as music is in the relations marked out by the sounds and not in any one note."[45]

Product complementarity occurs when the symbolic meanings of different products are related to each other.[46] These sets of products, termed **consumption constellations,** are used by consumers to define, communicate, and perform social roles.[47] Table 15-4 shows some constellations that have been identified for a set of occupational roles.

THE CASE OF THE YUPPIE   One social role that serves as an excellent example of the power of a consumption constellation is the Yuppie (young urban professional).[48] Consider the following collection of products: A Rolex watch, Brooks Brothers suit, New Balance running shoes, Sony Walkman, and BMW automobile. While these goods bear no relation to one another via function, form, mutual corporate identification, and so on, many consumers might nonetheless group them as a symbolic whole. The owner of one or two of these items might be predicted to own the rest, and all when taken together may be used to define the role of yuppie. Indeed, as shown on page 497, a popular book in the 1980s even featured an explicitly labeled "blueprint" of a yuppie constellation on its cover.

Yuppies are defined demographically as consumers aged 25 to 34 who live in urban areas and earn at least $30,000 per year.[49] Somewhat similar social roles exist in other countries. The U.K. has its Sloane Rangers and the French have their Bon Chic Bon Genres.[50] Of course, this simple description does not do justice to a social stereotype that had such a profound impact on consumption patterns and marketing strategies over the last decade. Even though people now take pains to avoid being labeled yuppies, these consumers were a prime target for a variety of status-laden products. They have been described as displaying ". . . a whole pattern of elitist consumption."[51] The yuppie social role, it may be argued, had as great an influence on defining cultural values and consumption priorities in the 1980s as did hippies on their generation two decades earlier. For example, hippies popularized psychedelic Volkswagen vans and "head shops," while yuppies did the same for BMWs and the Sharper Image catalog.

MARKETING OPPORTUNITY

A California man recognized the marketing value of the yuppie label and bought the licensing trademark on the word. Nothing can be described with the adjective yuppie unless he approves and is compensated. As of the end of 1986, he had made over $200,000 on the word.

He also sold "Yuppie Chow," a 6 oz. box of popcorn that retailed for up to $9.00 a box. The product facetiously claimed to ". . . meet the high acquisitive demands of yuppies and help to ensure their development into strong, healthy millionaires."[52]

PSYCHOGRAPHICS

Consider a marketer who wishes to target a student population. She identifies her ideal consumer as "a twenty-one-year-old senior marketing major living on a large university campus who has parents making between $20,000 and $50,000 per year." You may know a lot of people who fit this description. Do you think they are all the same? Would they all be

TABLE 15-4 Product constellations associated with occupational roles

Professional	*Attorney*	*Public defender*
Seiko watch	Prince tennis racket	Levi's cords
Burberry raincoat	leather briefcase	Wallaby shoes
Lacoste shirt	Am. Exp. gold card	Calvin Klein glasses
Atlantic magazine	Cadillac El Dorado	Molson beer
Brooks Bros. suit	Michelob beer	L. L. Bean shirts
Bass loafers	Vantage cigarette cigars	RCA VCR
silk tie	Johnston & Murphy shoes	Volkswagen Rabbit
French wine	L. L. Bean catalog	*Esquire*
BMW		
Businessman	*Salesman*	*Suit salesman*
Tiffany jewels	Farrah slacks	Zenith TV
Steuben glass	Budweiser beer	Oldsmobile 98
leather briefcase	Buick Skylark	Whirlpool freezer
Cross pen	Coca-Cola	Gillette shaver
cuff links	McDonald's	Old Spice cologne
Ralph Lauren shirt	M & M's	Miller beer
VCR	Puritan gold shirts	JVC stereo
Lincoln Continental	Fayva shoes	
Wall St. Journal	Samsonite luggage	
	Timex watch	
Blue collar worker	*Unskilled worker*	*Janitor*
Schaefer beer	Chevrolet	Remington shaver
AMF bowling ball	Goldstar TV	Aramis cologne
Ford pick-up truck	*NY Daily News*	Fruit-of-the-Loom
Levi's jeans	Hanes T-Shirts	Dial soap
Marlboro cigarettes	Levi's jeans	Campbell's soup
RCA TV	Coca-cola	Coca-Cola
Field & Stream	Miller beer	Sunkist orange soda
Black & Decker tools	McDonald's	
McDonald's	Camel cigarettes	

Source: Michael R. Solomon and Henry Assael, "The Forest or the Trees: A Gestalt Approach to Symbolic Consumption," in **Semiotics: New Directions in the Study of Signs for Sale**, ed. Jean Umiker-Sebeck (Berlin: Mouton de Gruyter, 1987), 189–218.

THE YUPPIE HANDBOOK

The State-of-the Art Manual for
Young Urban Professionals

Marissa Piesman and Marilee Hartley

Cross Pen
Pin Stripe Suit
Sony Walkman
Rolex Watch
Ralph Lauren Suit
Squash Racquet
Cartier Tank Watch
Burberry Trench Coat
Coach Bag
Fresh Pasta
Gucci Briefcase
Gourmet Shopping Bag
Running Shoes
Co-op Offering Prospectus
L.L. Bean Duck Hunting Boots

The Yuppie Handbook, a popular, satirical treatment of yuppies, provided a map for one consumption constellation prevalent in the 1980s. Note the many categories of products and services included in the yuppie role. *The Yuppie Handbook,* copyright © 1984 by Longshadow Books. Reprinted by permission of Longshadow Books, a division of Simon & Schuster, Inc.

likely to share common interests and buy the same products? Probably not, since their life-styles are likely to differ considerably.

Knowledge of a market's demographics is essential to devising efficient marketing strategies (see Chapter 9). In many cases, however, these objective characteristics are not sufficient to fine-tune strategies. Consumers can share the same demographic characteristics and still be very different people.

To "breathe life" into demographics, marketers turn to **psychographics,** which involves the ". . . use of psychological, sociological, and anthropological factors . . . to determine how the market is segmented by the propensity of groups within the market—and their reasons—to make a particular decision about a product, person, ideology, or otherwise hold an attitude or use a medium."[53]

Psychographic research was developed in the 1960s and 1970s to address the shortcomings of two other types of consumer research: motivational research and quantitative survey research. Motivational research, which involved intensive one-to-one interviews and projective tests, yielded a lot of information about a few people. This information often was idiosyncratic and not very useful or reliable (see Chapter 3). At the other extreme, large-scale demographic surveys yield a little information about a lot of people. As one researcher observed, ". . . The marketing manager who wanted to know why people ate the competitor's cornflakes was told '32 per cent of the respondents said taste, 21 percent said flavor, 15 percent said texture, 10 percent said price, and 22 percent said don't know or no answer.'"[54]

In many applications, the term psychographics is used interchangeably with life-style to denote the separation of consumers into categories based on differences in choices of consumption activities and product usage. Using data from large samples, marketers create profiles of customers who resemble each other in terms of their activities and patterns of product usage.[55] Demographics allow us to describe *who* buys, but psychographics allow us to understand *why* they do.

CONDUCTING A PSYCHOGRAPHIC ANALYSIS

Some early attempts at life-style segmentation "borrowed" standard psychological scales (often used to measure pathology or personality disturbances) and tried to relate scores on these tests to product usage. As might be expected, such efforts were largely disappointing (see Chapter 7). These tests were never intended to be related to everyday consumption activities and yielded little in the way of explanation for purchase behaviors. The technique is more effective when the variables included are more closely related to actual consumer behaviors. If you want to understand purchases of household cleaning products, you are better off asking people about their attitudes toward household cleanliness than testing for personality disorders.

Most contemporary psychographic research attempts to group consumers according to some combination of three categories of variables: Activities, Interests, and Opinions **(AIOs).** Some typical dimensions used to assess life-style are listed in Table 15-5. Typically, people are given a long list of statements and are asked to indicate how much they agree with each one. Lifestyle is thus "boiled down" by discovering how people spend their time, what they find interesting and important, and how they view themselves and the world around them, as well as demographic information.

Typically, the first step in a psychographic analysis is to determine which life-style segments are producing the bulk of customers for a particular product. The researchers will determine who uses the brand and will try to isolate heavy, moderate, and light users. They will also look for patterns of usage and attitudes toward the product. In many cases, just a few life-style segments will account for the majority of brand users.[56] Marketers often target heavy users primarily, even though they may constitute a relatively small number of total users. As a very general rule of thumb, the *20/80* rule tells us that 20 percent of a product's users account for 80 percent of the volume of product sold.

TABLE 15–5 Life-style dimensions

Activities	Interests	Opinions	Demographics
Work	Family	Themselves	Age
Hobbies	Home	Social issues	Education
Social events	Job	Politics	Income
Vacation	Community	Business	Occupation
Entertainment	Recreation	Economics	Family size
Club membership	Fashion	Education	Dwelling
Community	Food	Products	Geography
Shopping	Media	Future	City size
Sports	Achievements	Culture	Stage in life cycle

Source: William D. Wells and Douglas J. Tigert, "Activities, Interests, and Opinions," *Journal of Advertising Research* 11 (August 1971): 27–35.

After the heavy users are identified and understood, the brand's relationship to them must be considered. Not all heavy users are the same. They may have quite different reasons for using the product. For instance, marketers at the beginning of the walking shoe craze assumed that purchasers were basically burned-out joggers. Subsequent psychographic research showed that there were actually several different groups of "walkers," ranging from those who walk to get to work to those who walk for fun. This realization resulted in shoes aimed at different segments, from Footjoy Joy-Walkers to Nike Healthwalkers.

USES OF LIFE-STYLE SEGMENTATION Life-style segmentation can be used in a variety of ways:

- To define the target market. This information allows the marketer to go beyond simple demographic or product usage descriptions (e.g., middle-aged men, or frequent users).
- To create a new view of the market. Sometimes marketers create their strategies with a "typical" customer in mind. This stereotype may not be correct because the actual customer may not match these assumptions. Marketers of a facial cream for women were surprised to find their key market was composed of older, widowed women rather than the younger, more sociable women to whom they were pitching their appeals.
- To position the product. Psychographic information can allow the marketer to emphasize features of the product that fit in with a person's life-style. Products targeted to people whose life-style profiles show a high need to be around other people might focus on the product's ability to help meet this social need.
- To better communicate product attributes. Psychographic information can offer very useful input to advertising creatives who must communicate something about the product. The artist or writer

can have a much richer mental image of the target consumer than that obtained through dry statistics, and this insight will improve his or her ability to "talk" to that consumer. For example, research conducted for Schlitz beer found that heavy beer drinkers tended to feel that life's pleasures were few and far between. Commercials were developed using the theme that told these drinkers: "You only go around once," so "reach for all the gusto you can."[57]

- To develop overall strategy. Understanding how a product fits, or does not fit, into consumers' life-styles allows the marketer to identify new product opportunities, chart media strategies, and create environments most consistent and harmonious with these consumption patterns.

- To market social and political issues. Life-style segmentation can be an important tool in political campaigns and can also be employed to find commonalities among types of consumers who engage in destructive behaviors, such as drug use or excessive gambling.

One recent life-style study looked at drunk driving by young males, who comprise the segment of the general population most likely to be involved in alcohol-related fatalities. This study highlights the value of supplementing simple demographics with a psychographic approach. It allows us to identify subtypes of males aged 18 to 24 who are most likely to have a problem, and to devise strategies to directly reach these segments.

Four distinct segments of young males were identified by the researchers. A brief description of each segment is provided in Table 15-6. Members of one segment, named "good timers" by the researchers, are more likely to believe that it is fun to be drunk, that the chances of an accident while driving drunk are low, and that drinking allows you to do better with girls. These insights could be used in a media campaign directed to this group that would try to change these beliefs.[58]

VALS

The most well-known and widely used segmentation system is **VALS (Values and Life-styles)**, developed at what is now SRI International in California.[59] Based on responses to a lengthy survey administered to about 1600 U.S. households in 1980, a researcher named Arnold Mitchell devised a system to place consumers into one of nine life-style clusters, or "VALS Types." The VALS system has been used by well over 200 corporations and advertising agencies in their marketing efforts. Since this system has recently been updated, both VALS versions will be discussed here.

THE ROOTS OF VALS   The VALS typology was created by splicing together perspectives from two prominent social scientists. The first was the work of psychologist Abraham Maslow, who developed a hierarchy of "needs growth." As described more completely in Chapter 3, these needs range from physical ones, such as food and shelter, up to the attainment of spiritual fulfillment.

The second perspective was drawn from the work of sociologist David Reisman, who made a distinction between people who are *inner-directed* and those who are *outer-directed*. Outer-directeds tend to look to others

TABLE 15–6 Thumbnail sketches of young male drivers

Segment 1: Good Timers (23 Percent)

Heavy partiers, with a macho and sensation-seeking orientation

The highest incidence of reported drinking-driving behaviors

Youngest of all segments (average age 20)
Least likely to be married (13 percent)
About half work full-time (55 percent)
About half attend school (47 percent)

When drinking, the vast majority (92 percent) prefer beer
Heavy and frequent drinkers relative to other segments:
  36 percent claim consuming 5-6 drinks at a time at least weekly
  10 percent claim consuming 1-2 drinks at a time daily

Most likely to drink wile driving or sitting in car (13 percent)
Most likely to drink at rock concerts (40 percent)
Most likely to drink at parties (61 percent)

Most likely to watch MTV (46 percent)
Heavy 7 P.M.-midnight radio listening (64 percent)
High preference for AOR (album oriented rock) radio format (53 percent)

Segment 2: Well Adjusted (27 Percent)

Most content and satisfied with their lives, with no problem behavior and average in partying and macho tendency

Next to the lowest rate of reported drinking-driving

Mid-range in age (average age 21)
Less likely to be married (20 percent)
About half work full-time (54 percent)
About half attend school (41 percent)
When drinking, most (85 percent) prefer beer
Light and infrequent drinkers relative to other segments:
  15 percent claim consuming 5-6 drinks at a time at least weekly
  2 percent claim consuming 1-2 drinks at a time daily
Not likely to drink while driving or sitting in car (3 percent)
Note likely to drink at rock concerts (15 percent)
Less likely to drink at parties (32 percent)

Less likely to watch MTV (35 percent)
Less 7 P.M.-midnight radio listening (51 percent)
Less preference for AOR radio format (42 percent

Segment 3: Nerds (24 Percent)

Generally unhappy, and below average in problem behavior, partying, sensation seeking, and macho orientation

The lowest reported drinking-driving problem

Oldest of segments (average age 22)
Most likely to be married (33 percent)
About half work full-time (56 percent)
About half attend school (45 percent)

When drinking, fewer than other segments (78 percent) prefer beer
Light and infrequent drinkers relative to other segments:
  6 percent claim consuming 5-6 drinks at a time at least weekly
  3 percent claim consuming 1-2 drinks at a time daily

Least likely to drink while driving or sitting in car (1 percent)
Least likely to drink at rock concerts (10 percent)
Least likely to drink at parties (28 percent)

Least likely to watch MTV (27 percent)
Less 7 P.M.-midnight radio listening (51 percent)
Least preference for AOR radio format (34 percent)

Segment 4: Problem Kids (24 Percent)

Above average problem behavior tendency and an average profile on all other factors

Next to the highest level of reported drinking-driving

Mid-range in age (average age 21)
More likely to be married (30 percent)
Most work full-time (67 percent)
Fewest of any segment attend school (25 percent)

When drinking, the vast majority (87 percent) prefer beer
Heavy and frequent drinkers relative to other segments:
  26 percent claim consuming 5-6 drinks at a time at least weekly
  6 percent claim consuming 1-2 drinks at a time daily

Likely to drink while driving or sitting in car (6 percent)
Likely to drink at rock concerts (29 percent)
Likely to drink at parties (48 percent)

Less likely to watch MTV (36 percent)
Heavy 7 P.M.-midnight radio listening (57 percent)
Highest preference for AOR radio format (64 percent)

Source: John L. Lastovicka, John P. Murry, Erich A. Joachimsthalor, Gurav Bhalla, and Jim Schevrich, "A Lifestyle Typology to Model Young Male Drinking and Driving," *Journal of Consumer Research* 14 (September 1987), 257–63. Reprinted with permission of the University of Chicago Press.

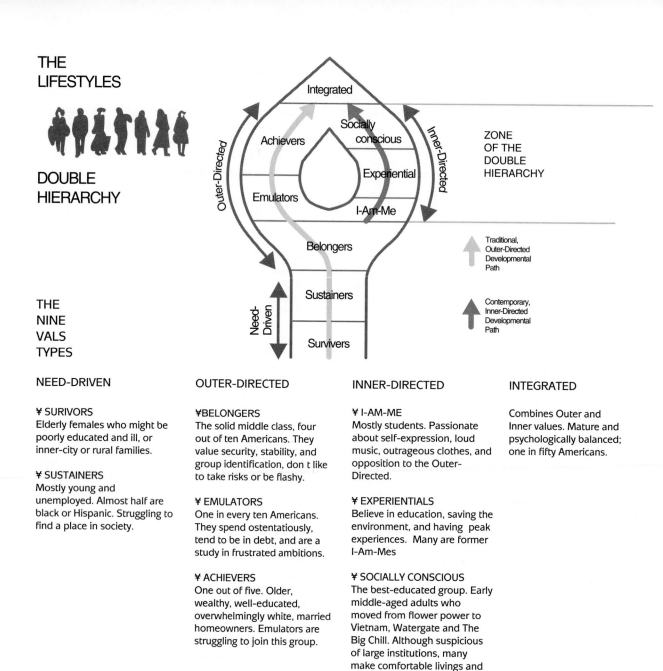

THE
LIFESTYLES

DOUBLE
HIERARCHY

THE
NINE
VALS
TYPES

ZONE
OF THE
DOUBLE
HIERARCHY

Traditional,
Outer-Directed
Developmental
Path

Contemporary,
Inner-Directed
Developmental
Path

Chart from: SRI International

NEED-DRIVEN

¥ SURIVORS
Elderly females who might be poorly educated and ill, or inner-city or rural families.

¥ SUSTAINERS
Mostly young and unemployed. Almost half are black or Hispanic. Struggling to find a place in society.

OUTER-DIRECTED

¥ BELONGERS
The solid middle class, four out of ten Americans. They value security, stability, and group identification, don t like to take risks or be flashy.

¥ EMULATORS
One in every ten Americans. They spend ostentatiously, tend to be in debt, and are a study in frustrated ambitions.

¥ ACHIEVERS
One out of five. Older, wealthy, well-educated, overwhelmingly white, married homeowners. Emulators are struggling to join this group.

INNER-DIRECTED

¥ I-AM-ME
Mostly students. Passionate about self-expression, loud music, outrageous clothes, and opposition to the Outer-Directed.

¥ EXPERIENTIALS
Believe in education, saving the environment, and having peak experiences. Many are former I-Am-Mes

¥ SOCIALLY CONSCIOUS
The best-educated group. Early middle-aged adults who moved from flower power to Vietnam, Watergate and The Big Chill. Although suspicious of large institutions, many make comfortable livings and have influential jobs.

INTEGRATED

Combines Outer and Inner values. Mature and psychologically balanced; one in fifty Americans.

Figure 15-3 The VALS Double Hierarchy

as guides to behavior and values and to see society and its rules as the source of moral authority. They regard possessions as a way to signal to others one's worth as a person. It has been estimated that seven out of ten Americans would be classified as outer-directeds.[60]

Inner-directeds tend to rebel against materialism and the work ethic. Personal expression and individual taste are paramount: These consumers "follow their own drummer." A good example of an appeal directed to these individualistic consumers was an ad for Grape-Nuts cereal. A woman sat alone, outside, dreamily gazing at natural beauty. The copy: "Morning is your time." Inner-directeds also tend to exercise more regularly, since they set their own goals and don't depend on others for encouragement; they aren't governed by "peer pressure."[61]

The VALS typology combines these two approaches, and progresses from those consumers who are forced to focus primarily on satisfying basic survival needs to those who are free to concentrate on spiritual pursuits. Along the way, it makes the distinction between those at the same place in the needs hierarchy who satisfy these needs in an inner- vs. outer-directed fashion. The nine original VALS types are profiled in Figure 15-3. Many marketers have explicitly targeted one or more VALS types. The system has even been used by the United Farm Workers to target direct mail and phone call strategies for a national grape boycott. Can you guess which VALS types they were aiming for?

CONSUMPTION DIFFERENCES AMONG VALS TYPES   One important difference among VALS types is in media usage. For example, survivors, sustainers, and belongers tend to be home alone and watch daytime soap operas, while the societally conscious like dramas and documentaries. Achievers are good prospects for sports and news shows. Magazines such as *Time* and *The New Yorker* tend to be read by achievers, while *Readers' Digest* is appreciated more by belongers.

Belongers also are good customers for domestic family cars, while a "muscle" car like the Chevrolet Camaro appeals to emulators. Achievers will go for such luxury cars as the BMW or Mercedes to display their status. A societally conscious person might also buy a Mercedes, but this will more likely be due to its perceived technical superiority rather than its status.[62]

Throwing the Bull.   A classic example of how VALS was used to modify a successful advertising campaign was in the strategy employed by Merrill Lynch. When the brokerage house shifted agencies in 1978, it had been using the theme "Bullish on America" for 12 years. The ad campaign featured a series of commercials featuring a herd of bulls thundering across a plain. A VALS analysis, however, revealed that this approach appealed primarily to belongers, mass-market consumers who want to fit in rather than stand out. In contrast, the Merrill Lynch target customer was an achiever: affluent business and government leaders who exhibit leadership, self-confidence, and who tend to be heavy investors. The new agency thus shifted instead to a lone bull (symbolizing a strong individualist) and the theme became "A Breed Apart."

 MARKETING OPPORTUNITY

A Texas builder found that different VALS types even display varied preferences for housing design and used the system to segment his models. Achiever women like small kitchens that are easy to clean, but don't mind cleaning big, luxurious bathrooms. Belonger women, on the other hand, like big kitchens that can become the center of family activities. The company designed homes for achievers featuring impressive façades, security systems, and luxurious carpeting. Energy-efficient homes were offered to the societally conscious.[63]

CRITICISMS OF VALS

Despite the widespread use of VALS, it is by no means perfect, and in any case it may eventually become a victim of its own success: If every company used exactly the same segmentation system, competitive advantage would evaporate. Some of the criticisms of VALS have been:[64]

- Consumers are put into only one VALS category. The system assumes that every person can be given one of nine labels (though "secondary" scores are provided to clients). Yet many people probably fall into two or more types; it may be rare to find a "pure" example of a type. Thus individual differences tend to be obscured in the effort to derive a limited number of workable categories.
- The system assumes that a person never changes categories. In reality, people may act like one type for one product category, but like a different type in a different situation. Someone may exhibit achiever characteristics when buying a car, say, and act like an emulator when buying a stereo system (especially if product knowledge for this category is low).
- The system was developed from concepts taken from clinical and developmental psychology. Instead of measuring basic psychological characteristics, it measures values that are supposed to reflect those characteristics. These can change over time. For example, ecological products (the province of the societally conscious) may become status symbols (and hence desired by achievers) as social values change.
- Since the actual measurement system is a trade secret, it is very difficult to test the validity and reliability of the data.
- Many product decisions are not that closely related to personal values. The purchase of low involvement products, for example, may be more affected by simple income levels.
- Some companies believe that this approach is not worth the extra cost (the service costs from $20,000 to over $150,000 per year).
- The system does not deal with the probability that many consumers with the motivation to buy certain products do not have the corresponding incomes required to actually purchase them.

VALS 2   The last concern is being addressed in a revised version of VALS.[65] Responding to some economic and demographic changes, it was decided by the developers that this new psychographic system would *not* be as closely related to values and life-styles. These changes include the evolution of a global economy and the increasing diversity of products and media that result in greater fragmentation of life-styles.

VALS 2 divides people into eight groups that are determined both by psychological characteristics and "resources," which include such factors as income, education, energy levels, and eagerness to buy. VALS 2 appears to be easier to use, but it has abandoned some of the conceptual foundation on which the original VALS was based. In the VALS 2 structure, groups are arrayed vertically by resources and horizontally by self-orientation, as shown in Figure 15-4. The new top group is termed "actualizers," who are successful consumers with many resources. This group is concerned with social issues and is open to change. The next three groups also have sufficient resources but differ in their outlooks on life:

- *Fulfilleds* are satisfied, reflective, and comfortable. They tend to be practical and value functionality.
- *Achievers* are career-oriented and prefer predictability over risk or self-discovery.
- *Experiencers* are impulsive, young, and enjoy offbeat or risky experiences.

The next three groups have fewer resources:

- *Believers* have strong principles, and favor proven brands.

Figure 15-4 VALS 2

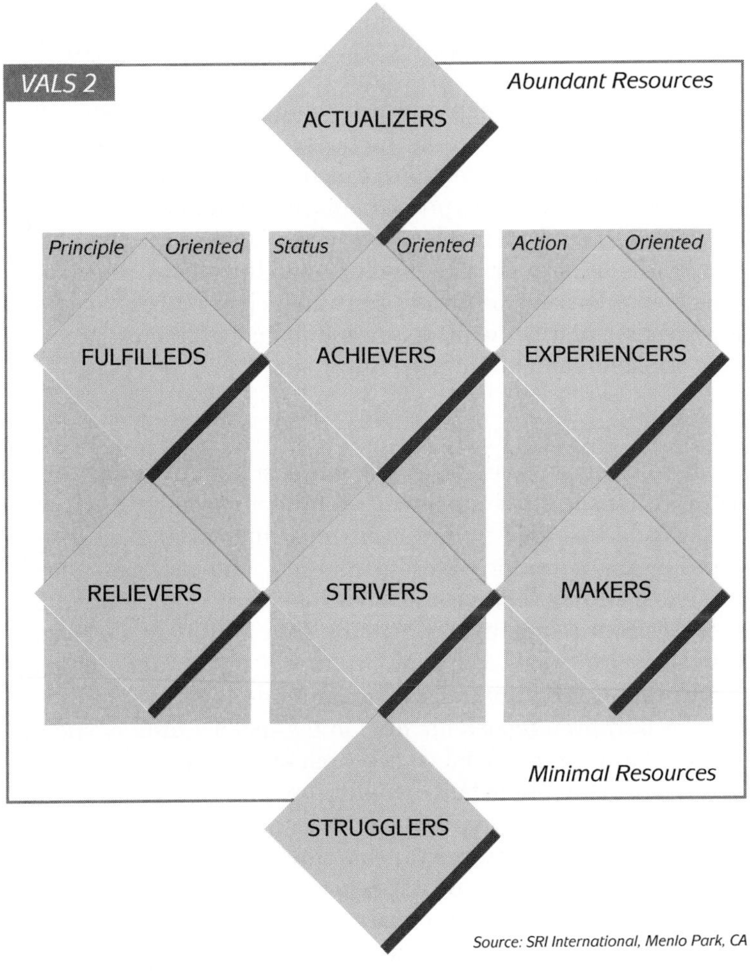

VALS 2

ACTUALIZERS — Abundant Resources

Principle Oriented | Status Oriented | Action Oriented

FULFILLEDS | ACHIEVERS | EXPERIENCERS

RELIEVERS | STRIVERS | MAKERS

Minimal Resources

STRUGGLERS

Source: SRI International, Menlo Park, CA

- *Strivers* are like achievers, but with fewer resources. They are very concerned about the approval of others.
- *Makers* are action-oriented and tend to focus their energies on self-sufficiency. They will often be found working on their cars, canning their own vegetables, or building their own houses.

Finally, *strugglers* are at the bottom of the ladder. They are most concerned with meeting the needs of the moment, and thus strongly resemble the survivor and sustainer groups they replaced.

INTERNATIONAL LIFE-STYLE SEGMENTATION   VALS is by no means the only lifestyle segmentation scheme available. Researchers in a number of countries have developed psychographic strategies to apply to their own populations. One classification scheme, developed by McCann-Erickson London, segments British male and female consumers separately. Lifestyle categories in this system include such segments as Avant Guardians (interested in change), Pontificators (traditionalists, very British), Chameleons (follow the crowd), and Sleepwalkers (contented underachievers).

A very popular Canadian campaign for Molson Export beer based its commercials on psychographic research showing target customers to be like boys who never grew up and who were uncertain about the future and intimidated by women's new-found freedoms. Accordingly, the ads feature a group of men called "Fred and the boys," whose get-togethers emphasize male companionship and protection against change. They repeatedly assure the consumers that the beer "keeps on tasting great."[66]

Consumers in Japan are sometimes called "life designers" to reflect the growing number of people who express themselves autonomously (much like inner-directeds). The equivalent of outer-directed has been termed *hitonami consciousness;* which translates as "aligning oneself with other people." One Japanese segmentation scheme divides consumers into "tribes" and includes among others a crystal tribe (which prefers well-known brands), a my home tribe (family-oriented), and an impulse buyer tribe.[67]

VALUE AND LIFE-STYLE TRENDS

One application of life-style analysis is to forecast **social trends,** or broad directions in which society is moving. Careful demographic analyses can, of course, provide valuable information regarding probable changes in social behavior, potential for different markets and product categories, and so on. For example, changes in birthrates can exert a huge impact on demand for products as diverse as baby food and life insurance. Still, this statistical portrait does not allow us to tap more subtle changes in priorities and values. For this reason, examinations of changes in orientations toward life, preferences for how one's leisure time is spent, and attitudes toward important social issues such as democracy, materialism, and religion can yield important insights on possible changes in consumption patterns. For example, many observers have noted a shift toward *"neo-traditionalism":* conservative values, a renewed commitment to the family, and a tempering of the rampant materialism of the 1970s and 1980s. In the words of one observer, in the 1990s we can expect emphases on "romance, religion, and rattles."[68]

Of course, trend forecasting is a bit like reading one's horoscope in the paper. Sometimes forecasts are so general they can't help but come true, and only some proportion of more specific ones actually do. The problem is, we don't know until after the fact which ones will. The following sections contain some recent predictions of trends we can expect in the 1990s (note that they sometimes contradict each other). Which will be accurate? Take your pick.

VOLUNTARY SIMPLICITY AND ENVIRONMENTALISM   Consumers will forsake their pursuit of status symbols for a life that is ". . . outwardly simple and inwardly rich."[69] Look for a surge in camping and wilderness products. With the introduction of its Origins line of cosmetics, the Estee Lauder Co. was the first major U.S. beauty company to bring natural, non-animal tested products in recyclable containers into department stores.[70] Concern for the environment, or the *green movement,* is also affecting marketing strategies for products ranging from diapers to fast food. The emphasis on conservation and responsible use of resources has even affected the fashion world, which typically encourages consumers to discard the old and embrace the new rather than to use a product until it wears out.[71]

ENHANCEMENT OF SELF-FULFILLMENT   Consumers will value individualistic, unique experiences over conventional status symbols. Look for a boom in unusual vacations and highly segmented cable television stations. This shift is depicted in the IMP (inner motivated person) depicted in the ad for *Harper's Magazine.* Reflecting this change, BMW is slowly changing its emphasis on being a status vehicle (i.e., "the yuppie car"). Newer ads instead emphasize the quality of technology and design.[72] Similarly, Stouffer's emphasizes self-fulfillment with its theme of "Set yourself free."[73]

TIME POVERTY   The increase in working couples leads to greater value placed on convenience products and services that minimize time and effort spent in purchasing (see Chapter 10). Husbands will assume more responsibility for household chores and purchases. Increased reliance on catalogs, professional shoppers, and home automation will occur.[74] The Japanese are leading the way in developing new convenience products. Recent time and money-saving hits in Japan include instant pasta, size-adjustable baby shoes, and tropical fish rentals.[75]

 MARKETING OPPORTUNITY

The increasing desire for convenience is changing the way people shop for groceries, and supermarket chains are trying to adapt to these changes. Although couples where both partners work and couples where only one works both average two weekly trips to the market and spend about the same ($57.00 per trip), working couples spend 15 percent less

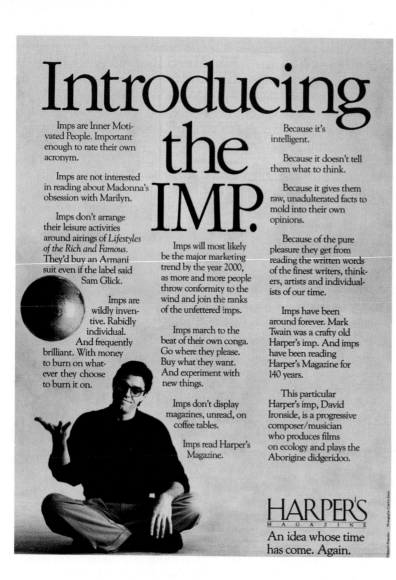

time in the market. To facilitate this "race" through the market, some chains display floor plans at the entrance.[76] Home delivery of food is growing twice as fast as take-out or drive-through.

However, the convenience trend can be overdone. One company wanted to sell sheets in supermarkets, reasoning that working women would welcome this addition. They quickly found that consumers hated this idea. An important benefit of shopping for sheets is looking at a wide range of designs and colors, and fantasizing how one's bedroom would look with them. Consumers felt that a supermarket could not offer this diversity, and that their mood would be too pragmatic while in the supermarket to fantasize. The idea was shelved.[77]

DISILLUSIONMENT OF WORKING WOMEN Women will discover that working outside of the home is not as "liberating" as they thought. A return to traditional husband/wife roles will occur, as women abandon careers and stay home with the children.[78] Women are now more likely than men to say they "work very hard most of the time," and their use of pain relievers is growing dramatically.[79] In 1976, the values most likely to be endorsed by women were security and self-respect. By 1986, this emphasis had shifted to a paramount desire for warm relationships.[80]

DECREASED EMPHASIS ON NUTRITION AND EXERCISE   While Americans still appear to be concerned about their health, the obsession of many with diet and exercise appears to be subsiding. Americans appear to be adopting more of an "okay in moderation" outlook. Fewer consumers are avoiding salty products or foods with additives or report a willingness to pay more for "all-natural" foods.[81] Opposition to the consumption of red meat also appears to have peaked.[82] In addition, fewer Americans are taking exercise classes, jogging, or playing tennis. The only activity to show an increase is walking for exercise.[83]

"COCOONING"   Consumers will insulate themselves from such world problems as pollution and crime by staying home as much as possible: "They're going to go home and pull the covers over their heads, eat comfort food, watch VCRs, have babies, and stay married."[84]

"NON-CONSUMPTION" AS A LIFE-STYLE   In recent years abstention from certain products and practices has become a way of life for many consumers who have adopted "non" as a code-word for a life-style. Membership in support groups that help people to stop various forms of consumption, including alcohol, narcotics, gambling, overeating, and even sex, has doubled in the last decade. Some products have succeeded at positioning themselves in terms of attributes they do *not* possess. These include 7-UP ("The Un-Cola"), Club Med ("The antidote to civilization"), and even Max Factor's "No color mascara."[85] In addition, the concept of "lite" versions of products has permeated everything from wine to ice cream.

CHAPTER SUMMARY

Culture may be thought of as a society's personality. It is composed of a distinct ecology, social structure, and ethos. Members of a culture tend to share a common perspective on what is right or wrong or what end states are particularly desirable to strive for. These priorities constitute a culture's value system. Culture dictates both general consumption priorities, such as whether the individual or the group should take precedence, and very specific desires and practices. One important value that distinguishes modern consumer culture from more traditional societies is materialism, an emphasis on the accumulation of worldly possessions. An etic approach emphasizes commonalities across cultures, and this is reflected in attempts by some global marketers to devise standardized strategies to implement in many markets. An emic approach to culture stresses the unique aspects of each culture and highlights the need to tailor the marketing plan in light of each culture's set of norms and values. While in some cases very abstract messages that have universal appeal can be employed, even these must often be communicated in different ways to be consistent with cultural practices.

Consumer life-styles refer to the ways people choose to spend their time and money. Marketers can employ life-style segmentation by grouping consumers in terms of their activities, interests, and opinions. Life-style research is useful to track societal trends in consumption preferences and also to position specific products and services to different segments. Psychographic techniques attempt to classify consumers in terms of psychological, subjective variables in addition to observable characteristics (demographics). A variety of systems, such as VALS, has been developed to identify consumer types and to differentiate them in terms of their brand or product preferences, media usage, leisure time activities, and attitudes toward such broad issues as politics and religion.

Interrelated sets of products and activities are associated with social roles to form consumption constellations. By understanding the connections between product symbolism and social behavior, marketers can position their products within desired constellations. The priorities assigned to sets of products and services in a culture change over time, and these shifts in values must be monitored by marketers. The chapter concludes by considering some trends in life-style and value changes in the 1990s, including neo-traditionalism, self-fulfillment, and environmentalism.

KEY TERMS

Acculturation
AIOs
Collectivism
Consumption constellations
Core values
Culture
Emic perspective
Enculturation
Ethnocentrism
Ethos
Etic perspective
Individualism
Instrumental values

Life-style
Materialism
Means-end chain model
National character
Norms
Product complementarity
Psychographics
Social trends
Terminal values
Values and Life-styles, (VALS)
Value system
Worldview

REVIEW QUESTIONS AND DISCUSSION TOPICS

1. Culture can be thought of as a society's personality. If your culture were a person, could you describe its personality traits?
2. Marlboro, Coca-Cola, and Levi's are mentioned as brands that have become cultural symbols of America. Can you name some brands that perform the same function for other cultures? What are the strategic advantages of developing such a product?
3. What are the four dimensions that have been used to differentiate among cultures? How would you describe your culture in terms of each of these dimensions?
4. What is the difference between an enacted norm and a crescive norm? Identify the set of crescive norms operating when a man and woman in

your culture go out for dinner on a first date. What products and services are affected by these norms?

5. Organizations such as labor unions and domestic manufacturers attempt to tap American ethnocentrism by promoting "Made in the U.S.A." campaigns that stress the importance of choosing American-made products to protect the economy. Are these campaigns effective? Should products be promoted on the basis of their country of origin rather than in terms of sheer quality? What types of consumers are most likely to be influenced by an ethnocentric campaign?

6. Chapter 6 discusses the evolution of consumers' attitudes toward the wearing of fur. How can these changes be interpreted in terms of shifts in underlying American values?

7. The value of materialism encourages people to direct their efforts toward the accumulation of convenience and luxury goods. Do you agree that this value is dominant in your culture?

8. Due to increased competition and market saturation, marketers in industrialized countries increasingly are trying to develop Third World markets by encouraging people in underdeveloped countries to desire Western products. Should this practice be encouraged, even if the products being marketed may be harmful to consumers' health (e.g., cigarettes) or divert needed money away from the purchase of essentials? If you were a trade or health official in a Third World country, what guidelines, if any, might you suggest to regulate the import of luxury goods from advanced economies?

9. What is the difference between an etic and an emic approach to the study of culture? How would adherence to one or the other perspective influence the development of a marketing plan for a foreign culture?

10. Construct a hypothetical means-end chain model for the purchase of a bouquet of roses. How might a florist use this approach to construct a promotional strategy?

11. Compare and contrast the concepts of life-style and social class.

12. In what situations is demographic information likely to be more useful than psychographic data, and vice versa?

13. Alcohol drinkers vary sharply in terms of the number of drinks they may consume, from those who occasionally have one at a cocktail party to regular imbibers. Explain how the 20/80 rule applies to this product category.

14. Describe the underlying principles used to construct the VALS system. What are some positive and negative aspects of this approach to life-style segmentation?

15. What impact has the return to "neo-traditionalism" had on contemporary marketing strategies?

16. The chapter describes several apparent trends in lifestyles and values, including an emphasis on self-fulfillment, women's disaffection with careers, and a growth in environmentalism. Do you agree with these assessments? What do you believe to be the most important changes in values in the 1990s? Are these changes positive or negative?

HANDS-ON EXERCISES

1. At a library or newsstand, collect a set of advertisements for a product that is sold in many different countries. Analyze the cultural symbolism and values employed in these ads. How similar are the ads to each

other? Is the company using a standardized marketing strategy, or a localized one?

2. Perform a cultural analysis for a country other than the one you live in. Describe the culture in terms of its ecology, social structure, and ideology. If possible, consult members of this culture to determine its dominant values, as well as some specific norms regarding product consumption. How do these norms differ from your own culture? What adaptations would you have to make to market a snack food or personal care product to this culture?

3. Conduct a *content analysis* of print advertising by making a copy of every tenth ad appearing in both a major magazine targeted to men and one targeted to women. Using a panel of three judges, categorize each sampled ad in terms of the dominant theme of the ad (use the categories listed in Table 15-1 as a guide). What conclusions can you draw about the dominant appeals currently employed in national magazine advertising? Do you detect any differences in the messages sent to men versus women?

4. Administer the Materialism Scale in Table 15-3 to a sample of business majors and another group of liberal arts majors. What predictions might you make regarding group differences on this value? For each statement, ask respondents to circle a number on a scale:

   Strongly disagree   1   2   3   4   5   6   7   Strongly agree

   Note: When scoring, be sure to remember that items marked with an asterisk are reverse scored. That is, a response of "7" should be scored as a "1," a "6" as a "2," and so on. Sum each person's score for each subscale, and calculate the average response for each sample. Do the two groups differ in terms of their mean responses?

5. If you were segmenting a consumer group in terms of their relative level of materialism, how might your advertising and promotional strategy take this difference into account? Construct two versions of an ad for a suntan lotion, one to appeal to a high materialism segment, and one to appeal to a low materialism segment.

6. Compile a set of recent ads that attempt to link consumption of a product with a specific life-style. How is this goal usually accomplished?

7. The chapter mentions that psychographic analyses can be used to market politicians. Conduct research on the marketing strategies used in a recent, major election. How were voters segmented in terms of values? Can you find evidence that communications strategies were guided by this information?

8. Construct separate ad campaigns for a cosmetics product targeted to the belonger, achiever, experiential, and societally conscious VALS types. How would the basic appeal differ for each group?

9. Conduct a backward segmentation study among members of your class. Collect brand usage data for several product categories, including soft drinks, cosmetics, magazine readership, leisure activities, and automobile ownership. Can you find similarities across people in terms of their specific patterns of consumption? What are some qualifications or problems associated with this analysis?

10. Using media targeted to this group, construct a consumption constellation for the social role of college student. What set of products, activities, and interests tend to appear in advertisements depicting "typical" college students? How realistic is this constellation? What factors might be operating to distort the correspondence of this constellation to reality?

NOTES

1. Joseph M. Winski, "Green Consumer: Concern for Environment No Fad," *Advertising Age* (September 24, 1990): 24.
2. Clifford Geertz, *The Interpretation of Cultures* (New York: Basic Books, 1973); Marvin Harris, *Culture, People and Nature* (New York: Crowell, 1971); John F. Sherry, Jr., "The Cultural Perspective in Consumer Research," in *Advances in Consumer Research,* ed. Richard J. Lutz (Provo, Utah: Association for Consumer Research, 1985)13: 573-575.
3. William Lazer, Shoji Murata, and Hiroshi Kosaka, "Japanese Marketing: Towards a Better Understanding," *Journal of Marketing* 49 (Spring 1985): 69-81.
4. Geert Hofstede, *Culture's Consequences* (Beverly Hills, Ca.: Sage, 1980).
5. Daniel Goleman, "The Group and the Self: New Focus on a Cultural Rift," *New York Times* (December 25, 1990): 37; Harry C. Triandis, "The Self and Social Behavior in Differing Cultural Contexts," *Psychological Review* 96 (July 1989): 506; Harry C. Triandis, Robert Bontempo, Marcelo J. Villareal, Masaaki Asai and Nydia Lucca, "Individualism and Collectivism: Cross-Cultural Perspectives on Self-Ingroup Relationships," *Journal of Personality and Social Psychology* 54 (February 1988): 323.
6. Richard W. Pollay, "Measuring the Cultural Values Manifest in Advertising," *Current Issues and Research in Advertising* (1983): 71-92.
7. Milton Rokeach, *The Nature of Human Values* (New York: Free Press, 1973).
8. *A New Partnership: New Values and Attitudes of the New Middle Generation in Japan and the U.S.A.* (Tokyo: Dentsu Institute for Human Studies, 1989).
9. George J. McCall and J.L. Simmons, *Social Psychology: A Sociological Approach* (New York: The Free Press, 1982).
10. Terence A. Shimp and Subhash Sharma, "Consumer Ethnocentrism: Construction and Validation of the CETSCALE," *Journal of Marketing Research* 24 (August 1987): 280-90.
11. *The Latest Commercials 1988-1989* (Tokyo: Dentsu Inc.).
12. Theodore Levitt, *The Marketing Imagination* (New York: The Free Press, 1983).
13. Kevin Cote, "The New Shape of Europe," *Advertising Age* (November 9, 1988): 98.
14. Steven Prokesch, "Selling in Europe: Borders Fade," *New York Times* (May 31, 1990): D1.
15. Terry Clark, "International Marketing and National Character: A Review and Proposal for an Integrative Theory," *Journal of Marketing* 54 (October 1990): 66-79.
16. Julie Skur Hill and Joseph M. Winski, "Goodby Global Ads: Global Village is Fantasy Land for Marketers," *Advertising Age* (November 16, 1987): 22.
17. Matthias D. Kindler, Ellen Day, and Mary R. Zimmer, "A Cross-Cultural Comparison of Magazine Advertising in West Germany and the U.S.," (unpublished manuscript, The University of Georgia, 1990).
18. Marc G. Weinberger and Harlan E. Spotts, "A Situational View of Information Content in TV Advertising in the U.S. and U.K.," *Journal of Marketing* 53 (January 1989): 89-94.
19. Jae W. Hong, Aydin Muderrisoglu, and George M. Zinkhan, "Cultural Differences and Advertising Expression: A Comparative Content Analysis of Japanese and U.S. Magazine Advertising," *Journal of Advertising* 16 (1987): 68.
20. Laurel Anderson Hudson and Marsha Wadkins, "Japanese Popular Art as Text: Advertising's Clues to Understanding the Consumer," *International Journal of Research in Marketing* 4 (1988): 259-72.
21. Damon Darlin, "Myth and Marketing in Japan," *The Wall Street Journal* (April 6, 1989): B1.
22. Hill and Winski, "Goodbye Global Ads."
23. Hill and Winski, "Goodbye Global Ads."
24. David A. Ricks, "Products That Crashed Into the Language Barrier," *Business and Society Review* (Spring 1983): 46-50.
25. Donald E. Vinson, Jerome E. Scott, and Lawrence R. Lamont, "The Role of Personal Values in Marketing and Consumer Behavior," *Journal of Marketing* 41 (April 1977): 44-50.
26. Milton Rokeach, *Understanding Human Values* (New York: The Free Press, 1979); see also J. Michael Munson and Edward McQuarrie, "Shortening the Rokeach Value Survey for Use in Consumer Research," in *Advances in Consumer Research,*

ed. Michael J. Houston (Provo, Utah: Association for Consumer Research, 1988)15: 381–86.

27. B. W. Becker and P. E. Conner, "Personal Values of the Heavy User of Mass Media," *Journal of Advertising Research* 21 (1981): 37–43; Vinson, Scott, and Lamont, "The Role of Personal Values in Marketing and Consumer Behavior."

28. Sharon E. Beatty, Lynn R. Kahle, Pamela Homer, and Shekhar Misra, "Alternative Measurement Approaches to Consumer Values: The List of Values and the Rokeach Value Survey," *Psychology & Marketing* 2 (1985): 181–200; Lynn R. Kahle and Patricia Kennedy, "Using the List of Values (LOV) to Understand Consumers," *Journal of Consumer Marketing* 2 (Fall 1988): 49–56; Lynn Kahle, Basil Poulos, and Ajay Sukhdial, "Changes in Social Values in the United States During the Past Decade," *Journal of Advertising Research* 28 (February/March 1988): 35–41.

29. Thomas J. Reynolds and Jonathan Gutman, "Laddering Theory, Method, Analysis, and Interpretation," *Journal of Advertising Research* 28 (February/March 1988): 11–34; Beth Walker, Richard Celsi, and Jerry Olson, "Exploring the Structural Characteristics of Consumers' Knowledge," in *Advances in Consumer Research,* ed. Melanie Wallendorf and Paul Anderson (Provo, Utah: Association for Consumer Research, 1986)14: 17–21.

30. Reynolds and Gutman, "Laddering Theory, Method, Analysis, and Interpretation."

31. Thomas J. Reynolds and Alyce Byrd Craddock, "The Application of the MECCAS Model to the Development and Assessment of Advertising Strategy: A Case Study," *Journal of Advertising Research* (April/May 1988): 43–54.

32. Russell W. Belk, "Possessions and the Extended Self," *Journal of Consumer Research* 15 (September 1988): 139–68; Melanie Wallendorf and Eric J. Arnould, "'My Favorite Things': A Cross-Cultural Inquiry into Object Attachment, Possessiveness, and Social Linkage," Journal of Consumer Research 14 (March 1988): 531–47.

33. Fabian Linden, "Who Has Buying Power?" *American Demographics* (August 1987): 4, 6.

34. Russell W. Belk and Richard W. Pollay, "Images of Ourselves: The Good Life in Twentieth Century Advertising," *Journal of Consumer Research* 11 (March 1985): 887–97.

35. Russell W. Belk, "Materialism: Trait Aspects of Living in the Material World," *Journal of Consumer Research* 12 (December 1985): 265–80.

36. David K. Tse, Russell W. Belk, and Nan Zhou, "Becoming a Consumer Society: A Longitudinal and Cross-Cultural Content Analysis is of Print Ads from Hong Kong, the People's Republic of China, and Taiwan," *Journal of Consumer Research* 15 (March 1989): 457–72; see also Annamma Joy, "Marketing in Modern China: An Evolutionary Perspective," *CJAS* (June 1990): 55-67, for a review of changes in Chinese marketing practices since the economic reforms of 1978.

37. Tse, et al., "Becoming a Consumer Society."

38. Benjamin D. Zablocki and Rosabeth Moss Kanter, "The Differentiation of Life-Styles," *Annual Review of Sociology* (1976) 269–97.

39. Doris Walsh, "Foreign Leisure," *American Demographics* (February 1987): 60.

40. Chester A. Swenson, "How to Sell to a Segmented Market," *Journal of Business Strategy* 9 (January-February 1988): 18.

41. William Leiss, Stephen Kline, and Sut Jhally, *Social Communication in Advertising* (Toronto: Methuen, 1986).

42. Zablocki and Kanter, "The Differentiation of Life-Styles."

43. Mary Twe Douglas and Baron C. Isherwood, *The World of Goods* (New York: Basic Books, 1979).

44. Richard A. Peterson, "Revitalizing the Culture Concept," *Annual Review of Sociology* 5 (1979): 137–66.

45. Douglas and Isherwood, *The World of Goods,* 72–73.

46. Michael R. Solomon, "The Role of Products as Social Stimuli: A Symbolic Interactionism Perspective," *Journal of Consumer Research* 10 (December 1983): 319–29.

47. Michael R. Solomon and Henry Assael, "The Forest or the Trees?: A Gestalt Approach to Symbolic Consumption," in *Marketing and Semiotics: New Directions in the Study of Signs for Sale,* ed. Jean Umiker-Sebeok (Berlin: Mouton de Gruyter, 1988): 189–218; Michael R. Solomon, "Mapping Product Constellations: A Social Categorization Approach to Symbolic Consumption," *Psychology & Marketing* 5 (1988)3: 233–58.

48. Michael R. Solomon and Bruce Buchanan, "A Role-Theoretic Approach to Product Symbolism: Mapping a Consumption Constellation," *Journal of Business Research* 22 (March 1991): 95–110

49. Howard W. Combs and McRae C. Banks, "Marketing to Yuppies," *SAM Advances Management Journal* (Summer 1987): 52.

50. Russell W. Belk, "Yuppies as Arbiters of the Emerging Consumption Style," in *Advances in Consumer Research,* ed. Richard J. Lutz (Provo, Utah: Association for Consumer Research, 1986)13: 514–19.

51. Belk, "Yuppies as Arbiters of the Emerging Consumption Style," 515.

52. Chris Lehmann, "The Y-Word Becomes a Trademark," *Mother Jones* (October 1986): 10.

53. See Lewis Alpert and Ronald Gatty, "Product Positioning by Behavioral Life Styles," *Journal of Marketing* 33 (April 1969): 65–69; Emanuel H. Demby, "Psychographics Revisited: The Birth of a Technique," *Marketing News,* (January 2, 1989): 21; William D. Wells, "Backward Segmentation," in *Insights into Consumer Behavior,* ed. Johan Arndt (Boston: Allyn & Bacon, 1968): 85–100.

54. William D. Wells and Douglas J. Tigert, "Activities, Interests, and Opinions," *Journal of Advertising Research* 11 (August 1971): 27.

55. Alfred S. Boote, "Psychographics: Mind Over Matter," *American Demographics* (April 1980): 26–29; William D. Wells, "Psychographics: A Critical Review," *Journal of Marketing Research* 12 (May 1975): 196–213.

56. Joseph T. Plummer, "The Concept and Application of Life Style Segmentation," *Journal of Marketing* 38 (January 1974): 33–37.

57. Berkeley Rice, "The Selling of Lifestyles," *Psychology Today* (March 1988): 46.

58. John L. Lastovicka, John P. Murry, Erich A. Joachimsthaler, Gurav Bhalla, and Jim Scheurich, "A Lifestyle Typology to Model Young Male Drinking and Driving," *Journal of Consumer Research* 14 (September 1987): 257–63.

59. An example of a consumer typology developed by another company is the CUBE Concept, which stands for Comprehensive Understanding of Buyer Environments (see Wally Wood, "Valentine-Radford's Cube Concept," *Marketing & Media Decisions* 23 (April 1988): 140.

60. Brad Edmondson, "The Inner-Directed Work Out," *American Demographics* (April 1987): 24–25.

61. Edmondson, "The Inner-Directed Work Out."

62. Rice, "The Selling of Lifestyles."

63. Rice, "The Selling of Lifestyles."

64. John Hadley, "J. Walter Thompson on VALS," *On Line* (Spring 1982): 2; Rice, "The Selling of Lifestyles."

65. Martha Farnsworth Riche, "VALS 2", *American Demographics* (July 1989): 25.

66. Ian Pearson, "Social Studies: Psychographics in Advertising," *Canadian Business* (December 1985): 67.

67. Leiss, et al., *"Social Communication in Advertising."*

68. Lenore Skenazy, "Welcome Home: Trend Experts Point to 'Neo-traditional,'" *Advertising Age* (May 16, 1988): 38.

69. Ronald D. Michman, "New Directions for Life-Style Behavior Patterns," *Business Horizons* (July-August 1984): 60.

70. Pat Sloan, "Cosmetics: Color it Green," *Advertising Age* (July 23, 1990): 1.

71. Woody Hochswender, "The Green Movement in the Fashion World," *New York Times* (March 25, 1990).

72. Kim Foltz, "As Baby Boomers Turn 40, Ammirati and BMW Adjust," *New York Times* (January 26, 1990): D17.

73. Kahle, et al., "Changes in Social Values in the United States During the Past Decade."

74. Michman, "New Directions for Life-Style Behavior Patterns."

75. *1989 Hit Products in Japan* (Tokyo: Dentsu Inc, 1989).

76. Timothy Harris, "Fast and Easy: US Supermarkets Market Convenience Foods as Lifestyles," *Marketing* (October 29, 1987): 17.

77. Judith Langer, "Where does the Consumer's Personal Style Fit In?" *American Demographics* (October 1987): 48.

78. Skenazy, "Welcome Home."

79. DDB Needham Worldwide's Life Style Study, reported in *Advertising Age* (September 24, 1990): 25.

80. Kahle, et al., "Changes in Social Values in the United States During the Past Decade."
81. DDB Needham Worldwide's Life Style Study, 25.
82. Burdette Breidenstein, "Changes in Consumers' Attitudes Toward Red Meat and Their Effect on Marketing Strategy," *Food Technology* (January 1988): 112−16.
83. DDB Needham Worldwide's Life Style Study, 25.
84. David Streitfeld, "What's Up, Trendwise?" *The Washington Post* (November 28, 1988): D5.
85. Molly O'Neill, "Words to Survive Life With: None of This, None of That," *New York Times* (May 27, 1990): 1.

Cultural Processes and Marketing Phenomena

C

HAPTER 16

Every morning, Gayla Utley wakes up on Sleighbell Drive in Christmas Lake Village, a subdivision of Santa Claus, Indiana.

Long after most Americans have packed up their Christmas decorations and thrown out their tree, Utley and her neighbors are shopping at Holly Plaza. During the dog days of summer, her son waterskis on Noel Lake. For a night out, the family eats at the North Pole restaurant.

Utley and her friends live in the most exclusive neighborhoods of Santa Claus—neighborhoods called Santa's Fairways and Reindeer, on streets called Blitzen Drive, West Ornament Lane, and Sled Run. . . .

No one here takes Christmas lightly. Status in this wealthy town . . . comes from a year-round commitment to Christmas. Here, families don't impress each other with Porsches, BMWs, or hot tubs. They do it with Christmas lights. . . .

It's not the kids in Santa Claus who can't let the Christmas season end—it's the adults. "I have a curio cabinet in my house filled with my Santa Claus collection," boasts Utley, who has gone to Halloween parties dressed as a Christmas package. "You've just got to love Christmas to live here."[1]

INTRODUCTION

Many people read with amusement about the "quaint" rituals and practices of primitive societies, never realizing how much their own behavior is affected by rituals, myth, and other aspects of their culture. Even social scientists have been slow to recognize that many of the same concepts they use to describe, say, natives of Papua New Guinea or Australian aborigines, can also apply to sophisticated consumers in Tokyo, London, or New York. Although the field is only beginning to acknowledge their importance, the ramifications of such "extraordinary" consumer behaviors are profoundly felt by many industries, ranging from the makers of personal care products and greeting cards to such services as caterers and travel agents.

The description of Santa Claus, Indiana above illustrates that consumers are dramatically influenced by their cultural beliefs and practices. This chapter will explore some of these influences, including the effects of myths and rituals as well as the "sacredness" of many objects, events, and even people in the modern marketplace. In addition, while many marketing textbooks imply that all consumption activities are "good" and should be encouraged, simple observation tells us this is not true. Many consumer behaviors are destructive, personally, socially, and economically. This chapter will also acknowledge the "darker side" of consumer behavior by considering such behaviors as addiction, vandalism, and shoplifting, to expand the scope of what marketers consider as consumer behavior.

MYTHS AND CONSUMER CULTURE

Every society possesses a set of myths that define that culture. A **myth** is a story containing symbolic elements that expresses the shared emotions and ideals of a culture. The story often features some kind of conflict between two opposing forces, and its outcome serves as a moral guide for people. In this way, a myth reduces anxiety because it provides consumers with guidelines about their world.

An understanding of cultural myths is important to marketers, who in some cases (most likely unconsciously) pattern their strategy along a mythic structure. Consider, for example, the way that a company like McDonald's takes on "mythical" qualities.[2] The "golden arches" are a universally recognized symbol, one that is virtually synonymous with American culture. They offer sanctuary to Americans around the world, who know exactly what to expect once they enter. Basic struggles involving good versus evil are played out in the fantasy world created by McDonald's advertising, as when Ronald McDonald confounds the Hamburglar. McDonald's even has a "seminary" (Hamburger University) where inductees go to learn appropriate behaviors.

Myths serve four interrelated functions in a culture:[3]

1. *Metaphysical.* They help to explain the origins of existence.
2. *Cosmological.* They emphasize that all components of the universe are part of a single picture.

3. *Sociological.* They maintain social order by authorizing a social code to be followed by members of a culture.
4. *Psychological.* They provide models for personal conduct.

THE STRUCTURE OF MYTHS: BINARY OPPOSITION

Myths can be analyzed by examining their underlying structures, a technique pioneered by the anthropologist Claude Levi-Strauss (no relation to the blue jeans company). Levi-Strauss noted that many stories involve **binary opposition** (e.g., nature versus technology). Characters, and in some cases, products, are often defined by what they are *not* rather than by what they are (e.g., "This is *not* your father's Oldsmobile," "I can't believe it's *not* butter").

MEDIATING CHARACTERS The conflict between opposing forces is sometimes resolved by a mediating figure who can link the opposites by sharing characteristics of each. For example, many myths contain animals that have human abilities (e.g., a talking snake) to bridge the gap between culture and nature, just as cars (technology) are often given animal names (nature) like Cougar, Cobra, or Mustang.

The Disney organization has used this principle quite effectively.[4] Its cartoon characters are often lovable, but possess exaggerated forms of human imperfections that make these flaws less threatening. Snow White's seven dwarves, for example, can be viewed as a sanitized version of the Seven Deadly Sins.

MODERN MYTHS

While we generally equate myths with the ancient Greeks or Romans, modern myths are embodied in many aspects of modern popular culture, including comic books, movies, holidays, and even commercials.

POW! WHAM! COMIC BOOK HEROES Comic book superheroes demonstrate how a myth is communicated to consumers. Indeed, some of these figures represent a *monomyth,* a myth that is common to many cultures.[5] A hero emerges from the everyday world with supernatural powers and wins a decisive victory over evil forces. He then returns with the power to bestow good things on his fellow men. This basic theme can be seen in such stories as Lancelot, Hercules, and the Greek Odyssey.

These heroes are familiar to most consumers, and are often used to endorse products and sell merchandise. Indeed, they are often viewed as more credible and effective than celebrity endorsers. Not even counting movie spinoffs or licensing deals, comic books today are a $300 million a year industry. The familiar comic book format is sometimes adapted by advertisers as well.

It's a Bird. It's a Plane. It's a Monomyth. The American version of the monomyth is perhaps best epitomized by Superman, a Christ-like figure who renounces worldly temptations and restores harmony to his community. Heroes like Superman are sometimes used to blanket a product, store, or service with desirable attributes.

HOLLYWOOD AS MYTH MACHINE Many "blockbuster" movies draw directly on mythic themes. While dramatic special effects or attractive stars

This ad for Scoresby Scotch borrows the familiar comic book format to communicate with consumers. Courtesy of Glenmore Distilleries Company, Louisville, KY 40202.

certainly don't hurt, a number of these movies perhaps also owe their success to their presentation of characters and plot structures that follow mythic patterns. Some examples of these mythic blockbusters include:[6]

Gone with the Wind. Myths are often set in times of upheaval, such as warfare. In this story, the North (which represents technology and democracy) is pitted again the South (which represents nature and aristocracy). The movie depicts a romantic era (the antebellum South) where love and honor were virtues. This era is replaced by the newer forces of materialism and industrialization (i.e., modern consumer culture). The movie depicts a lost era where man and nature existed in harmony.

Jaws. This movie represents primitive human fears about the untamed forces of nature. The shark challenges the security of the community and thus of civilization. This cosmological lesson teaches that primal forces can still rise up to hurt civilized people, who have grown smug over their power to control nature.

E.T.: The Extraterrestrial. E.T. is a familiar myth involving Messianic visitation. A gentle creature from another world visits Earth and performs miracles (e.g., reviving a dying flower). His "disciples" are neighborhood children, who help him combat the forces of modern technology and an unbelieving secular society. The metaphysical function of myth is served by teaching that the humans chosen by gods are pure and unselfish.

The Star Wars Trilogy. This immensely profitable series of movies is clearly patterned after traditional myths.[7] While set in a modern, futuristic society, the characters wear medieval clothing (e.g., Princess Leia in her gown, and Darth Vader in his helmet and armor). Luke Skywalker epitomizes the pure hero, and Hans Solo

This ad was used in a corporate campaign for McCann-Erickson's Tokyo office. It plays off of the Superman myth by depicting a superhero with light beams radiating from his eyes. The headline reads: "We're ready to rejuvenate your advertising." Courtesy of McCann-Erickson Hakuhodo Inc.

(note that his name literally means alone) is the rogue hero. Darth Vader is a fallen angel, whose lust for power corrupts his nobility. Powerful forces are in conflict, including nature vs. technology (The forest vs. the Death Star) and innocence vs. corruption (Ewoks vs. Jabba the Hutt).

HOLIDAY HEROES Most cultural holidays are based on a myth, and often a real (e.g., Miles Standish on Thanksgiving) or imaginary (e.g., Cupid on Valentine's Day) character is at the center of the story. These holidays persist because their basic elements appeal to consumers' deep-seated needs.[8]

The Santa Claus Myth. As evidenced by the Christmas story at the beginning of the chapter, perhaps the most important holiday myth involves Santa Claus. The Coca-Cola Co. claims credit for inventing the modern image of Santa, which it distributed in its advertising in 1931. Until that time (the company claims), Santa was pictured as a cartoonlike elf.[9]

More likely, our contemporary image of Santa Claus was shaped by the famous nineteenth-century cartoonist Thomas Nast, whose rendering of Santa was related to his other drawings depicting "fat cats" like Boss Tweed and the Robber Barons, greedy capitalists who exploited the poor and lived in useless luxury.

Santa stands in opposition to Christ as a god of materialism. Perhaps it is no coincidence, then, that he appears in stores and shopping malls—*secular* temples of consumption. Whatever his origins, the Santa Claus myth serves the purpose of socializing children by teaching them to expect a reward when they are good and that members of society get what they deserve.

COMMERCIALS AS MYTHS Commercials can be analyzed in terms of the underlying cultural themes they represent. For example, commercials for Pepperidge Farm ask consumers to "remember" the mythical good old days when products were wholesome and natural. The theme of the underdog prevailing over the stronger foe (i.e., David and Goliath) has been used by Chrysler and Avis.[10]

From the Campfire to the "Boob Tube." The television has replaced the tribal storyteller as the transmitter of cultural myths. It is perhaps not a coincidence that the nightly prime time viewing slot is also the traditional story-telling time, when myths were passed from generation to generation huddled around the fire.

These traditional stories allowed people to pass along information about important cultural figures (real and imaginary). Today, many of people's common memories instead are composed of fictional characters created by advertising, such as Mr. Clean, the Jolly Green Giant, Charlie the Tuna, or even the pitiful Mr. Whipple. Consumers respond positively to these product icons because they embody various human characteristics in humorous or understandable ways. These figures thus personify cultural values and in the process create strong bonds between consumers and the products they represent.

MERRY OLD SANTA CLAUS.

This Thomas Nast cartoon, published in 1881, provides some insights into the origins of the modern-day Santa Claus myth. This jolly figure is not Santa, but rather a caricature of a "fat cat" Robber Baron of the period who has accumulated an abundance of worldly possessions. Source: T. Nast, "Merry Old Santa Claus," in Russell W. Belk, *Journal of American Culture* (Spring 1987): 88. NorthWind Picture Archives.

SACRED AND PROFANE CONSUMPTION

Many types of consumer activity involve the demarcation, or binary opposition, of boundaries, such as good versus bad, male versus female, even regular versus lo-cal. One of the most important of these sets of boundaries is the distinction between the sacred and the profane. **Sacred** objects and events are "set apart" from normal and treated with some degree of respect or awe. They may or may not be associated with religion, but most religious items and events tend to be regarded as sacred. **Profane** consumer objects and events are ordinary, everyday objects and events that do not share the "specialness" of sacred ones. (Note that profane does not mean vulgar or obscene in this context.)

Due to social and cultural change in recent times, a variety of consumer activities have moved from one sphere to the other. Some things that were formerly regarded as sacred have now become *desacralized* and profane, and other, everyday phenomena now are regarded as sacred.[11]

DESACRALIZATION **Desacralization** occurs when a sacred item or symbol is removed from its special place, or is duplicated in mass quantities becoming profane as a result. For example, souvenir reproductions of sacred monuments such as the Washington Monument or the Eiffel Tower, such artworks as *The Mona Lisa,* or adaptations of important symbols such as the American flag by clothing designers, eliminate their special aspects by turning them into unauthentic commodities, produced mechanically with relatively little value.[12]

MARKETING THAT GOOD OLD TIME RELIGION Religion has to some extent been desacralized. Religious symbols, such as stylized crosses or New Age crystals, have moved into the mainstream of fashion jewelry.[13] Religious holidays, particularly Christmas, are regarded by many (and

The adaptation of a sacred symbol such as a flag to make a fashion statement, in this case for a $1500 leather jacket by designer Jeff Hamilton, alters the meaning of the symbol (at least temporarily) by moving it into the world of the profane. Source: Pam Gallagher, "Glory Days," *Asbury Park Press* (February 28, 1991): E1. David Dempster/OFFSHOOT STOCK.

For fast, fast, fast relief take two tablets.

In the Episcopal Church, we believe that some of the oldest ideas are still the best.
Like the regular worship of God. Come join us as we celebrate this Sunday.
The Episcopal Church

This is one of several ads created for a Minneapolis church that was helpful in recruiting worshipers. Critics have accused these ads of being "flippant" and "sensational." What do you think? Courtesy of Church Ad Project, 1021 Diffley, Eagan, MN 55123.

criticized by some) as having been transformed into secular, materialistic occasions devoid of their original sacred significance.

Even clergymen are increasingly adopting secular marketing techniques. Televangelists rely upon the power of television, a secular medium, to convey their messages, and the Catholic Church generated a major controversy after it hired a prominent public relations firm to promote its anti-abortion campaign.[14]

Nonetheless, many religious groups have taken the secular route. The Mormons sponsored a $12 million campaign in *Readers Digest,* and *Newsweek: On Campus* featured the comedian Father Guido Sarducci in a humorous ad designed to recruit college students as padres.[15]

SACRALIZATION   The **sacralization** process occurs when ordinary objects, events, and even people, take on sacred meaning to a culture or to specific groups within a culture. For example, pieces of the Berlin Wall, the Super Bowl, and Elvis Presley have become sacralized to some consumers.

OBJECTIFICATION   Sacredness is often concretized in objects. The *objectification* process means that profane products of various kinds take on sacred qualities. One way this can occur is through *contamination,* where objects associated with sacred events or people become sacred in their own right. This explains the desire by many fans for items belonging to, or even touched by, famous people. Even the Smithsonian Institution in Washington, D.C. maintains a display featuring such "sacred items" as the ruby slippers from *The Wizard of Oz,* a phaser from "Star Trek," and Archie Bunker's chair from the television show "All in the Family," all reverently protected behind sturdy display glass.

Collections.   In addition to museum exhibits displaying rare objects or those that have meaning to large numbers of people (such as Dorothy's ruby slippers), even mundane, inexpensive things may be set apart in *collections,* where they are transformed from profane items to sacred ones. An item is sacralized as soon as it enters a collection, and it takes on a special significance to the collector that may be hard to comprehend by the outsider. The contents of collections range from movie memorabilia, rare books, and autographs to G.I. Joe dolls, Elvis memorabilia, and even junk mail.[16]

DOMAINS OF SACRED CONSUMPTION

Sacred consumption events permeate many aspects of the marketing experience. We find ways to "set apart" a variety of places, people, and events. In this section, some of these domains of sacredness will be briefly described.

SACRED PLACES

Sacred places have been "set apart" by a society because they have religious or mystical significance (e.g., Bethlehem, Mecca, Stonehenge) or because they commemorate some aspect of a country's heritage (e.g., the Kremlin, the Emperor's Palace in Tokyo, the Statue of Liberty). Remember that in many cases the sacredness of these places is due to the property of contamination; that is, something sacred happened on that spot, so the place itself takes on sacred qualities.

Still other places are created from the profane world and imbued with sacred qualities. Graumann's Chinese Theater in Hollywood, where movie stars leave their footprints in concrete for posterity, is one such place. Even the modern shopping mall can be regarded as a secular "cathedral of consumption," a special place where community members come to practice shopping rituals.

Theme parks are a form of mass-produced fantasy that take on aspects of sacredness. In particular, Disney World and Disneyland (and their new outposts in Europe and Japan) are destinations for pilgrimages from consumers around the globe. Disney World displays many characteristics of more traditional sacred places. It is even regarded by some as having healing powers. A trip to the park is the most common "last wish" for terminally ill children.[17]

HOME SWEET HOME   In many cultures, the home is a particularly sacred place. It represents a crucial distinction between the harsh, external world and consumers' "inner space." Americans spend more than $50 billion a year on interior decorators and home furnishings, and the home is a central part of consumers' identities.[18] Consumers all over the world go to great lengths to create a special environment that allows them to create the quality of "homeyness." This effect is created by personalizing the home as much as possible, using such devices as door wreaths, mantle arrangements, and a "memory wall" for family photos.[19]

The Modern Hex Sign.   Various products have been used throughout history to protect the sacredness of the home, ranging from fear-inspiring markings, Amish hex signs, lamb's blood, and garlic (to keep away vampires) to homemade signs such as "If caught here tonight you'll be found here in the morning."[20] In modern times, of course, the maintenance of this sacred space is the foundation of the home security industry, which provides both technical devices and ominous signs to ward off invaders.

SACRED PEOPLE

People themselves can be sacred. They are idolized and set apart from the masses. Even mundane items touched or used by sacred people become valuable:

> At $15.95 per head, about 700,000 people annually make the pilgrimage to Graceland, the home of Elvis Presley. True pilgrims surround themselves with Elvis artifacts. One such fan wears an Elvis watch and earrings, has furnished her home with Elvis plates, cups, clocks, statues, and rugs, and even named her daughter Lisa (after Presley's daughter). She claimed, "There can never be too much Elvis."[21]

Many businesses thrive on consumers' desire for artifacts associated with famous people, as exemplified by the thriving market for celebrity autographs. One entrepreneur dug dirt from the lawns of Johnny Carson, Shirley MacLaine, Katharine Hepburn, and forty-three other stars. He sold 20,000 vials of celebrity dirt in three years, at $1.95 a vial. Patrons of Grave Line Tours in Hollywood ride in a silver hearse to eighty infamous sites, such as the home of Sharon Tate (who was killed by Charles Manson) and the hotel where comedian John Belushi overdosed. A store called A Star is Worn sells items donated by celebrities—a black bra autographed by Cher recently went for $575. As one observer commented, "They want something that belonged to the stars, as if the stars have gone into sainthood and the people want their shrouds."[22]

The public's fascination with the images of celebrities, living or dead, endures. The images of dead stars are frequently brought back to life to endorse products. James Dean hawks for Jack Purcells sneakers, and Babe Ruth sells Zenith products. Licensing fees for dead celebrities now average about $100 million per year.[23]

The sacredness of some celebrities has spawned a secondary industry—celebrity look-alikes and sound-alikes. The simulated voice of Louis Armstrong now appears in ads for the Hershey Food Corp., Canada Dry, and Milk Bones.[24] Elvis Presley has imitators around the world. By one estimate, about 100 women make their living impersonating Marilyn Monroe.[25] This type of advertising is so pervasive that several lawsuits have been brought by stars (e.g., Woody Allen) to prevent doubles from using their likenesses.[26] Look-alikes continue to be used, as long as a disclaimer notice appears within the ad.[27]

SACRED EVENTS

Many consumers' activities also have taken on a special status. Public events in particular resemble sacred, religious ceremonies, as exemplified by the recitation of the Pledge of Allegiance before a game or the reverential lighting of matches at the end of a rock concert.[28]

SPORTS   For many people, the world of sports is sacred and almost assumes the status of a religion. The roots of modern sports events can be found in ancient religious rites, such as fertility festivals (e.g., the original Olympics).[29] Indeed, it is not uncommon for teams to join in prayer prior to a game. The sports pages are like the Scriptures (and we describe ardent fans as reading them "religiously"), the stadium is a house of worship, and the fans are members of the congregation. Devotees engage in group activities, such as tailgate parties and the "Wave," where (resembling a revival meeting) participants on cue join the wavelike motion as it makes its way around the stadium.

Sports Heroes.   The athletes that fans come to see are godlike; they are reputed to have almost superhuman powers (especially superstars like Michael Jordan, who is accorded the ability to fly in his Air Nikes). Athletes are central figures in a common cultural myth, the hero-tale. Often the hero must prove him- or herself under strenuous circumstances (e.g., the starter is unexpectedly injured) and victory is achieved only through sheer force of will.

One extremely popular Coke commercial, which featured the football player Mean Joe Greene and an admiring little boy, follows the same plot structure as the fairy tale of the Lion and the Mouse. The injured hero has his confidence restored by the humble mouse/boy, allowing his heroic persona to be rejuvenated. He then shows his gratitude to his benefactor.[30]

TOURISM   Tourism is another example of a sacred, non-ordinary experience of extreme importance to marketers. When people travel on vacation, they occupy sacred time and space. The tourist is continually in search of "authentic" experiences that differ from his or her normal world.[31] The tourism experience involves binary oppositions between work and leisure and being "at home" versus "away." This theme is reflected in Club Med's motto, "The antidote to civilization."

Buying Memories. The desire to capture these sacred experiences in objects forms the bedrock of the souvenir industry. Whether a personalized matchbook from a wedding or New York City salt-and-pepper shakers, souvenirs represent a tangible piece of the consumer's sacred experience.

The importance of these markers is obvious; U.S. gift shops alone sell 23 billion souvenirs a year. This product class provides a form of *tangibilized contamination,* where the sacredness of the experience "rubs off" onto the object.[32] In addition to personal mementos, such as ticket stubs saved from a favorite concert, these are other types of sacred souvenir icons:[33]

- Local products (e.g., wine from California, Scotch from Scotland)
- Pictorial images (e.g., post cards)
- "Piece-of-the rock" (e.g., seashells, pinecones)
- Symbolic shorthand—literal representations of the site (e.g., a miniature Eiffel Tower or Statue of Liberty)
- Markers (e.g., Hard Rock Cafe T-shirts, matchbook covers).

RITUAL

A **ritual** is a set of multiple, symbolic behaviors that occur in a fixed sequence, and that tend to be repeated periodically.[34] Though bizarre tribal ceremonies, perhaps involving animal or virgin sacrifice, may come to mind when people think of rituals, in reality many contemporary consumer activities are ritualistic.

A typical Western birthday party exemplifies such an activity. Prescribed acts such as the playing of certain party games, the opening of gifts and reassuring each guest about how wonderful the gift is (whether one likes it or not), and ending the party with cake and ice cream, complete with the lighting and blowing out of candles (symbolizing an added year) usually follow a ritualistic pattern that guests implicitly understand.

Rituals can occur at a variety of levels, as noted in Table 16-1. Some affirm broad cultural or religious values, while others occur in small groups or in isolation. Market researchers discovered, for example, that for many people the act of late-night ice cream eating has ritualistic overtones, often involving a favorite spoon and bowl.[35]

Many businesses owe their livelihoods to their ability to supply **ritual artifacts,** or items used in the performance of rituals, to consumers. Birthday candles, diplomas, specialized foods and beverages (e.g, wedding cakes, ceremonial wine, or even hot dogs at the ball park), trophies and plaques, band costumes, greeting cards, and retirement watches, are all used in consumer rituals. In addition, consumers often employ a *ritual script,* which identifies artifacts, the sequence in which they are used, and

TABLE 16-1 Types of Ritual Experience

Primary Behavior Source	Ritual Type	Examples
Cosmology	Religious	baptism, meditation, mass
Cultural values	Rites of passage	graduation, marriage
	Cultural	festivals, holidays (Valentine's Day), Super Bowl
Group learning	Civic	parades, elections, trials
	Group	fraternity initiation, business negotiations, office luncheons
	Family	mealtimes, bedtimes, birthdays, Mother's Day and Christmas
Individual aims and emotions	Personal	grooming, household rituals

Source: Dennis W. Rook, "The Ritual Dimension of Consumer Behavior," *Journal of Consumer Research* 12 (December 1985).

who uses them. Examples include graduation programs, fraternity manuals, and etiquette books.

GROOMING RITUALS

Whether brushing one's hair 100 strokes a day or talking to oneself in the mirror, virtually all consumers undergo private grooming rituals. These are sequences of behaviors that aid in the transition from the private self to the public self, or back again. These rituals serve various purposes, ranging from inspiring confidence before confronting the world to cleansing the body of dirt and other profane materials.

Body care rituals also function as ways for parents to pass along cultural notions about cleanliness, pride, modesty, or even ethnic tradition to their children. Compared to Anglos, for example, Mexican-Americans use more hair care products but fewer skin care products or tampons. These differences reflect cultural beliefs about appearance and sexuality.[36]

When consumers talk about their grooming rituals, some of the dominant themes that emerge from these stories reflect the almost mystical qualities attributed to grooming products and behaviors. Many people for instance emphasize a before and after phenomenon, where the person feels magically transformed after using certain products (similar to the Cinderella myth).[37] It should be obvious that the personal care products industry encourages these rituals and constantly seeks to introduce new products that it hopes will be included in such practices.

Two sets of binary oppositions expressed in personal rituals are private/public and work/leisure. Many beauty rituals, for instance, reflect a transformation from a natural state to the social world (as when a woman "puts on her face"), or *vice versa.* In these daily rituals, women reaffirm the value placed by their culture on personal beauty and the quest for eternal youth.[38] This focus is obvious in ads for Oil of Olay Beauty Cleanser, which proclaim " . . . And so your day begins. The Ritual of Oil of Olay." Similarly, the bath is viewed as a sacred, cleansing time, a way to wash away the sins of the profane world. As the copy of an ad for Vitabath, a bathing product, noted: " . . . Bathtime is your time for daydreams and indulgence. The time to lose yourself in a beautiful private world . . ."[39]

GIFT-GIVING

The promotion of appropriate gifts for every conceivable holiday and occasion provides an excellent example of the influence consumer rituals can exert on marketing phenomena. In the **gift-giving ritual,** consumers procure the perfect object (artifact), meticulously remove the price tag (symbolically changing the item from a commodity to a unique good), carefully wrap it, and ritually deliver it to the recipient.[40]

Every culture prescribes certain occasions and ceremonies for giving gifts, whether for personal or professional reasons. The giving of birthday presents alone is a major undertaking. Americans on average buy about six birthday gifts a year, about one billion gifts in total.[41] Business gifts are an important component in defining professional relationships (expenditures on business gifts exceeded $1.5 billion in 1989), and great care is often taken to ensure that the appropriate gifts are purchased. This process is so crucial that some people make a nice living as corporate gift consultants, and a similar service is offered by some retailers.

THE GIFT-GIVING PROCESS   The gift-giving ritual can be broken down into three distinct stages.[42] During *gestation,* the giver is motivated by

ULTICULTURAL DIMENSIONS

The importance of gift-giving rituals is underscored by considering Japanese customs, where the *wrapping* of a gift is as important (if not more so) than the gift itself. The economic value of a gift is secondary to its symbolic meaning.[45] Gifts are viewed as an important aspect of one's duty to others in one's social group. Giving is a moral imperative (known as *giri*). Each Japanese has a well-defined set of relatives and friends with which he or she shares reciprocal gift-giving obligations (*kosai*).[46] In keeping with the Japanese emphasis on saving face, presents are not opened in front of the giver, so that it will not be necessary to hide one's possible disappointment with the present.

Compared to Americans, Japanese consumers view a greater number of occasions as meriting the exchange of gifts. They have two major gift-giving seasons, *ochugen* in mid-summer and *oseibo* at the end of the year, which together account for a quarter of all Japanese retail purchases. Many of these gifts are high-status food and drink items, such as frozen steaks flown in from Kansas, or imported German beer.[47]

an event to procure a gift. This event may be either *structural* (i.e., prescribed by the culture, as when people buy Christmas presents), or *emergent* (i.e., the decision is more personal and idiosyncratic). The second stage is *prestation,* or the process of gift exchange. The recipient responds to the gift (either appropriately or not), and the donor evaluates this response. In the third stage, known as *reformulation,* the bonds between the giver and receiver are adjusted (either looser or tighter) to reflect the new relationship that emerges after the exchange is complete. Negativity can arise if the recipient feels the gift is inappropriate or of inferior quality. The donor may feel the response to the gift was inadequate or insincere or a violation of the *reciprocity norm,* which obliges people to return the gesture of a gift with one of equal value.[43] Both participants may feel resentful for being "forced" to participate in the ritual.[44]

SELF-GIFTS   The ritual of rewarding oneself by giving **self-gifts** is recognized by some marketers. People commonly find (or devise) reasons to give themselves something; they "treat" themselves. Consumers rely on the self-gifting process as a way to regulate their behavior, rewarding themselves for good deeds, consoling themselves after negative events, or as a way of motivating themselves to accomplish some goal.[48] Thus, McDonald's claims "You deserve a break today," and the fur industry encourages women to buy themselves a coat, rather than waiting for somebody else to get the idea.

Figure 16-1 displays a projective stimulus similar to ones used in research on self-gifting (see Chapter 3 for other examples of projective stimuli). Consumers are asked to tell a story based on this picture, and their responses are analyzed to discover the reasons people view as legitimate for rewarding themselves. For example, one recurring story that might emerge would be that Mary, the woman in the figure, had a particularly grueling day at work and needs a "pick-me-up" in the form of a new fragrance. This theme (excitement) could then be incorporated into a promotional campaign for a perfume.

HOLIDAY RITUALS

On holidays consumers step back from their everyday lives and perform ritualistic behaviors unique to those times.[49] Holiday occasions are filled with ritual artifacts and scripts and are increasingly cast as a time for giving gifts by enterprising marketers. Holidays also often mean big business to hotels, restaurants, travel agents, and so on. As the story at the beginning of the chapter illustrates, many people take their holidays seriously, and these ritual times result in many purchases. The marketing of Christmas products is worth about $37 billion a year. Liquor stores alone sell an additional billion dollars worth of merchandise during the holiday season.

Holidays provide a formalized time to reaffirm—and sometimes to redefine—everyday relationships. As one illustration, while Mother's Day is an important holiday in the United States, the U.K., and other countries, the rituals associated with it reflect cross-cultural differences in the nature of the mother/child relationship, as well as the evolving nature of these ties.[50]

Mother's Day is the fourth largest card-buying holiday in the United States overall, but it ranks second among Hispanic-Americans, who also buy cards for their *comadres,* a woman who is close to a child, but not

Figure 16-1 Based upon a Projective to Study the Motivations Underlying the Giving of Self- Gifts Source: David G. Mick, Michelle DeMoss, and Ronald J. Faber, "Latent Motivations and Meanings of Self-Gifts: Implications for Retail Management," (Research Report, Center for Retailing Education and Research, University of Florida, 1990).

necessarily a relative. And, mirroring changes in family structure, of the 145 million Mother's Day cards sold annually, about 10 percent now are designed for somebody who is not the sender's mother. Many of these are instead sent to single fathers (e.g., "Love to Dad on Mother's Day").[51]

◢ MARKETING OPPORTUNITY

In addition to established holidays, new occasions are invented to capitalize on the need for cards and other ritual artifacts that will then need to be acquired. The ritual exchange of greeting cards is widespread; more than 120 million adults buy at least one greeting card in a year.[52]

Companies can emphasize the "sacredness" of their products by promoting their own anniversaries (e.g., the fiftieth anniversary of Spam), and different occasions and relationships can be honored.[53] These cultural events are often invented by the greeting card industry, which conveniently stimulates demand for more of its products. Some recently invented holidays include Secretaries' Day and Grandparents' Day.

VALENTINE'S DAY Valentine's Day is a good example of holiday rituals that translate into big business. Normal standards regarding sex and love are relaxed or altered as people express feelings that may be hidden during the rest of the year through the exchange of cards, gifts, and other gestures. Valentine's Day is second only to Christmas in the number of greeting cards exchanged. The billion cards purchased yield about $280 million yearly for card makers.[54]

In addition to cards, a variety of gifts are exchanged, many of which are touted by marketers to represent aphrodisiacs or other sexually related symbols. For the "Valentine's couple who has everything," the Grand Hyatt in Washington, D.C. offers a Valentine's package including a night's stay in the hotel's best suite, round-the-clock chauffeured limo, bathrobes, a masseur, manicurist, hairstylist, makeup artist, two dozen roses, caviar, champagne, a gourmet breakfast-in-bed, and a romantic message of the guests' choice towed through the sky by an airplane when the lucky couple checks in. Total cost—$10,000.[55]

Some other recent "hot" gifts include:[56]

- A dozen fresh oysters (claimed to possess "magical" sexual powers).
- Designer silk panties, delivered gift wrapped and perfumed.
- A "love bracelet" derived from the old-fashioned chastity belt, which is bolted together on a loved one's wrist.

HALLOWEEN   Like Christmas, Halloween is a holiday that has been converted from a religious observance to a secular event. However, in contrast to Christmas, the rituals of Halloween (e.g., trick-or-treating and costume parties) primarily involve non-family members. In 1989, more than $440 million worth of Halloween products were purchased, excluding candy.[57]

Halloween is an unusual holiday, because its rituals are the *opposite* of many other cultural occasions. In contrast to Christmas, it celebrates evil instead of good and death rather than birth, and it encourages revelers to extort treats with veiled threats of "tricks" rather than rewarding only the good. Because of these oppositions, Halloween has been described as an *anti-festival,* where the symbols associated with other holidays are distorted. For example, the Halloween witch can be viewed as an inverted mother figure. The holiday also parodies the meaning of Easter by stressing the resurrection of ghosts, and of Thanksgiving by transforming the wholesome symbolism of the pumpkin pie into the evil jack-o-lantern.[58]

Bring on the Baby BOOmers.   Halloween observances among adults are booming, changing the character of this holiday. While adults bought only 10 percent of all Halloween costumes sold a decade ago, they now account for about 50 percent of all sales. Halloween is now the second most popular party night for adults (after New Year's Eve), and one in four grown-ups wear a costume.

This shift has been attributed to adult fears aroused by stories of children receiving tampered candy containing poison, razor blades, and so on which encouraged people to plan supervised parties rather than send their children out trick-or-treating.[59] Another factor accounting for the popularity of Halloween among adults is that, unlike other holidays, a family is not required to celebrate it. This permits single people to participate without feeling lonely or left out.[60]

Many businesses have capitalized on this demographic change in Halloween rituals. Hallmark Cards now designs two-thirds of its Halloween cards for adults and has labeled this market "Baby *BOOm*ers." The Spencer Gifts chain has established "Boo Bazaars" and the holiday is now second only to New Year's in sales for the company. As a store executive noted, "These people are serious about their costuming. This is a night to express their creativity. They don't want just masks anymore—they want an image."[61]

Accompanying this new emphasis on Halloween as an adult holiday, the liquor industry has come under fire for attempting to reinforce the idea that Halloween is as much an occasion to drink as St. Patrick's Day or New Year's Eve.[62] The industry's goal is to boost sales during a normally slow period. Miller Brewing Co., Anheuser-Busch, Coors, and Jack Daniels are some companies that have recently launched extensive Halloween promotions. A public advocacy group has complained that ". . . beer companies try to make drinking a part of every celebration . . . these types of promotions are clearly attractive to young consumers."[63]

RITES OF PASSAGE

What does a dance for recently divorced people have in common with a fraternity Hell Week? Both are examples of modern **rites of passage,** or special times marked by a change in social status. Every society, both primitive and modern, sets aside times where such changes occur. Some of these changes may occur as a natural part of consumers' life cycles (e.g., puberty or death), while others are more individual in nature (e.g., getting divorced and reentering the dating market).

Rites of passages involve changes in behaviors, and often these changes can entail a variety of products and services promoted as necessary to mark the status transition. These can range from the need of the newly hired junior executive to shed his or her student uniform and invest in a business wardrobe, to weddings and bar mitzvahs, or to training bras for pubescent girls.[64]

Some marketers attempt to reach consumers on occasions in which their products can enhance a transition from one stage of life to another. For example, a chain of fur stores ran a series of ads positioning a fur coat as a way to celebrate "all of life's moments." Suggested moments included a thirtieth birthday, a raise, a second marriage, becoming a new grandmother, and even a "divorce is final" fur coat—"shed the tears and slip into a fur," reads the ad.[65]

STAGES OF ROLE TRANSITION   Much like the metamorphosis of a caterpillar into a butterfly, consumers' rites of passage consist of three phases.[66] The first stage, *separation,* occurs when the individual is detached from his or her original group or status (e.g., the college freshman leaves home). *Liminality* is the middle stage, where the person is literally in-between statuses (e.g., the new arrival on campus tries to figure out what is happening during orientation week). The last stage, *aggregation,* takes place when the person reenters society after the rite of passage is complete (e.g., the student returns home for Christmas vacation as a college "veteran").

Rites of passage mark many consumer activities, as exemplified by fraternity pledges, recruits at boot camp, or novitiates becoming nuns. A similar transitional state can be observed when people are prepared for certain occupational roles. For example, athletes and fashion models typically undergo a "seasoning" process. They are removed from their normal surroundings (e.g., athletes are taken to training camps, while young models often are moved to Paris), indoctrinated into a new subculture, and then returned to the real world in their new roles.

THE FINAL PASSAGE: MARKETING DEATH.   The rites of passage associated with death support an entire industry. Survivors must make fairly expensive purchase decisions, often on short notice and driven by emotional and superstitious concerns.

Funeral ceremonies help the living to organize their relationships with the deceased, and action tends to be tightly scripted, down to the costumes (e.g., the ritual black attire, black ribbons for mourners, the body in its best suit) and specific behaviors (e.g., sending condolence cards or throwing a wake). Mourners "pay their last respects," and seating during the ceremony is usually dictated by mourners' closeness to the individual. Even the cortege (the funeral motorcade) is accorded special status by other motorists, who recognize its separate, sacred nature by not cutting in as it proceeds to the cemetery. These ceremonial activities are guided and overseen by ritual specialists, such as the coroner, the funeral director, and the clergyman.[67]

MARKETING OPPORTUNITY

A new market segment is being created as more consumers plan for their funerals well in advance. The industry delicately terms this "Pre-Need" versus the more traditional "At Need" situation. About 40 percent of funerals during the 1980s were prearranged, either to spare families from further trauma while in mourning or to take advantage of sizable discounts (the average cost of a prearranged funeral is $2000) and the desirability of reserving prime space in advance.[68]

THE DARKER SIDE OF CONSUMER BEHAVIOR

Consumers are often depicted as rational decision makers calmly doing their best to obtain products and services that will maximize the health and well-being of themselves, their families, and their society. An expanded view of the consumer, as we have seen, also includes a person who often buys things on a whim or simply because they make him/her feel good or look good.

Even though this enlarged picture comes closer to an accurate portrayal, it still falls short of capturing some important aspects of consumer behaviors. These behaviors are not necessarily enlightened or constructive, and they can be quite negative. For example, Halloween is a sacred night where macabre fantasies can be acted out. Hideous figures from popular culture (e.g., Count Dracula, Frankenstein, or more recently Freddie Krueger from *The Nightmare on Elm Street*) are among the most popular costumes. In addition, modern comics increasingly incorporate characters and plots representing the "dark side" of consumer behavior. Catwoman, one of Batman's adversaries, is depicted as a hooker complete with leather whip, and the Joker has evolved into a sadistic killer who beat Robin to a pulp in 1988, after readers voted in favor of Robin being killed off in a telephone poll.[69]

Other darker behaviors can stem from social pressures, such as excessive drinking or cigarette smoking, and the cultural value placed upon money can encourage such activities as shoplifting or insurance fraud. Exposure to unattainable media ideals of beauty, sex, love, success, and happiness can be a source of dissatisfaction with the self (and result in eating disorders, a reliance on plastic surgery, and so on, as discussed in Chapter 7).

While marketers do not necessarily create negative consumer behaviors, they can often be instrumental in encouraging them or at least in providing opportunities for them to develop. Although a careful consideration of complex topics like addiction is well beyond the scope of this book, it is worthwhile to at least briefly acknowledge the "dark side" of consumer behavior.

ADDICTIVE CONSUMPTION

Consumer **addiction** is a physiological and/or psychological dependency on products or services. While most people equate addiction with drugs, virtually any product or service can be seen as relieving some problem or satisfying some need to the point where reliance on it becomes extreme.

In some cases, it is fairly safe to say that the consumer, not unlike a drug addict, has little to no control over consumption. The products control the consumer, whether alcohol, cigarettes, chocolate, or diet colas. Even the act of shopping itself is an addicting experience for some consumers. Much negative or destructive consumer behavior can be characterized by three common elements:[70]

1. The behavior is not done by choice.
2. The gratification derived from the behavior is short-lived.
3. The person experiences strong feelings of regret or guilt afterwards.

GAMBLING Gambling is an example of a consumption addiction that touches every segment of consumer society, whether it takes the form of expensive casino wagering or betting on sports events with friends or through a bookie. While a problem gambler is most likely a black or Hispanic under the age of thirty who makes less than $25,000 a year, many addicts are highly motivated professionals.[71] Excessive gambling can be quite destructive, resulting in lowered self-esteem, debt, divorce, neglected children, and so on. According to one psychologist, gamblers exhibit a classic addictive cycle of experiencing a "high" while in action and depression when stopped, which leads them back to the thrill of the action. Money, however, is the substance they abuse, not drugs.[72]

It has been estimated that there are from 1 to 3 million addicted gamblers in the United States, and for many others who are not addicted, gambling is a steadily growing consumer activity. In 1988, about $240 billion was wagered legally and illegally in the United States, and this amount is growing by 10 percent annually. Americans spend roughly fifteen times as much money on gambling as they do on churches, twice as much as on higher education, and more than one-half of what is spent on food.[73]

"Buy a Ticket to a Dream." Gambling fever spreads beyond the casino industry. Fully 80 percent of the citizens of New York State played Lotto for a $45 million jackpot in 1988. Italians spend about $12 billion per year on wagers of various kinds, amounting to $210 bet for every person in Italy.

Though dependent upon the selection of random numbers, lotteries provide consumers with an illusion of control by encouraging them to pick familiar numbers (e.g., one's license plate, or a combination of children's birthdays). A cottage industry has sprung up to feed this illusion, including sales of dream books, horoscopes, and computer-selected numbers.[74]

COMPULSIVE CONSUMPTION

For some consumers, the expression "born to shop" is taken quite literally. These consumers shop because they are compelled to do so, rather than because shopping is a pleasurable or functional task. **Compulsive consumption** is repetitive shopping, often excessive, as an antidote to tension, anxiety, depression, or boredom. "Shopaholics," as they are called, turn to shopping much the way addicted people turn to drugs or alcohol.[75]

Compulsive consumption is distinctly different from the impulse buying considered in Chapter 10. The impulse to buy a specific item is temporary and centers on a specific product at a particular moment. In contrast, compulsive buying is an enduring behavior that centers on the process of buying, not the purchases themselves. As one woman who spent $20,000 per year on clothing confessed, "I was possessed when I went into a store. I bought clothes that didn't fit, that I didn't like, and that I certainly didn't need."[76]

CONSUMED CONSUMERS

People who are used or exploited, whether willingly or not, for commercial gain in the marketplace can be thought of as **consumed consumers.** The situations in which consumers themselves become commodities can range from traveling road shows that feature dwarfs and midgets to the selling of body parts and babies. The consumers who are consumed as the commodities in these transactions find themselves in roles and events that tend to depersonalize them. Emotional or economic needs are frequently involved, and like addictive consumers, they often have little or no control over the events or their behavior.

PROSTITUTION Prostitution, one of the earliest examples of consumers as commodities, is a source of significant activity in today's marketplace.

Consider that expenditures on prostitution are estimated to be more than $20 billion per year—equivalent to the domestic shoe industry.[77]

The use of women as products is a manifestation of the more general attitude throughout history that has regarded women as property. In many societies, prostitutes are demeaned and are often physically separated from sacred women (wives, mothers, and "nice" girls). These women help to preserve the sanctity of the family and of society by providing men with an outlet for their "impure" impulses.

Many prostitutes make their own boundaries to separate their inner selves from the commoditization of their bodies. They create a new identity when working, which may involve the wearing of a wig and/or taking on a street name. Just as patrons commoditize the prostitute, she in turn does not view them as people.

SELLING THE BODY PIECEMEAL   A new type of business that deals in consumers as commodities relies upon those who are willing to exchange only one or a few pieces at a time. People can either donate or sell body parts, and these transactions can occur either before or after death. Consumers are encouraged to designate their eyes, organs, or whole cadavers to science upon entering the next life, while others sacrifice a kidney to another person while still in this one. Some women serve essentially as hair factories when they sell their tresses to be made into wigs. Well over 11 million people per year are paid to donate their blood in the United States (this figure does not include voluntary donations), creating a $2 billion per year industry.[78]

BABIES FOR SALE   The inability of many couples to have babies has created an industry where babies are products and women are the factories that produce them.[79] There is widespread demand for these services; Americans visit doctors more than 2 million times per year because to infertility problems.[80]

If a woman is unable to conceive a child even with the help of medical procedures, a more controversial measure is available. A *surrogate mother* is a woman who is paid to be impregnated (medically) with the sperm of the father. She then carries the baby to term instead of the mother. While this practice has been denounced by feminists as a form of reproductive slavery, others point to the depersonalizing of the fundamental human relationship that develops between mother and child.[81] Nonetheless, it is estimated that between 600 and 2000 babies have been born via this method.

DEVIANT BEHAVIOR

Many consumer behaviors are not only self-destructive or socially damaging, they are illegal as well. Crimes committed by consumers against businesses have been estimated at more than $40 billion per year. These include shoplifting, employee pilferage, arson, and insurance fraud. Arson alone causes $2 billion per year in damages and is growing by 25 percent annually. Many arson-related insurance frauds committed by consumers occur just prior to the holiday season, when Christmas trees are set afire and surrounded by empty gift boxes to boost insurance claims.[82]

FROM NOW ON, SHOPLIFTING IN THE U.S. IS A VERY, VERY DIRTY BUSINESS.

For the last four years, Colortag has significantly cut losses for European store owners.

The device is a plastic tag that doesn't beep, but sprays permanent ink on the garment when the thief breaks it open. A fifty dollar shirt becomes worthless. The motive to steal it is gone.

No false alarms. No big installations. No guards. No action needed from the store clerks. No expensive prosecutions.

And thefts are down by as much as 90%.

Cut your losses and increase your profits with Colortag. Because it's time shoplifting got even dirtier.

Call Don Barnett at our New York office for the full story. (212) 888-1629.

Colortag

Colortag, Inc., 3 West 57th Street, New York, NY. 10019.

The Colortag system is one technique that has been used in Europe and the United States to deter shop-lifters. A plastic tag squirts ink on a garment when a thief breaks it open, render-ing the item worthless. Courtesy of COLORTAG, INC.

A retail theft, in one form or another, is committed every five seconds. *Inventory shrinkage* due to shoplifting and employee theft is a massive problem for businesses that is passed onto consumers in the form of higher prices (about 40 percent of the losses can be attributed to employees rather than shoppers). A family of four spends about $300 extra per year because of markups to cover shrinkage.[83] The problem is not unique to the United States. For example, shrinkage losses in Great Britain are estimated at more than a million pounds per day.[84]

Shoplifting is America's fastest-growing crime; it increased by a third in a period of only four years. The large majority of shoplifting is not done by professional thieves or by people who genuinely need the stolen items.

About three-quarters of those caught are middle or high income people who shoplift for the thrill of it or as a substitute for affection. An ink-spraying device that covers a would-be shoplifter when an item is taken to permit easy detection is one of the new technological steps being taken by some retailers to reduce shoplifting.[85]

ANTI-CONSUMPTION

One form of destructive consumer behavior can be thought of as **anti-consumption,** whereby products and services are deliberately defaced or mutilated. Anti-consumption can range from graffiti on buildings and the desecration of graves to product tampering, where innocent consumers are hurt or killed. Some recent examples of anti-consumption include:

- In Detroit, sections of abandoned buildings literally disappear as bricks are hauled away by vandals, who then resell them at $50 per brick to dealers.[86]
- About one quarter of British Telecom's call boxes do not work because of vandalism. The company must cope with 500,000 attacks on its public phones in a year's time.[87]
- The Los Angeles bus system placed fifty ads featuring a provocative picture of Madonna in bus shelters to advertise *Interview* magazine. Fans broke the glass panels in about 40 of the shelters to "liberate" the posters. The system also experienced the theft of 125 Batman posters.[88]

As one form of anti-consumption, an underground group called "Truth in Advertising" defaced these posters to make political statements. Gerd Ludwig/Woodfin Camp & Associates.

Motivations for anti-consumption can range from peer pressure to rage against some aspect of society. Whatever the cause, these varied behaviors result in large but unknown costs to society and reflect the overlooked importance of recognizing the darker side of consumer behavior.

CHAPTER SUMMARY

Much of modern consumer behavior goes beyond our typical picture of the rational consumer. Many purchase and consumption activities are influenced by such cultural processes as myths, rituals, and sacred experiences.

This chapter describes some of these "extraordinary" consumption activities. It illustrates some of the ways modern myths are translated into advertising and popular culture, ranging from comic book heroes to the marketing of Christmas. One important principle underlying the structure of many of these myths is that of binary opposition, where events are defined in terms of the conflict between two opposing forces (e.g., Technology versus Nature).

Some sacred aspects of consumer behavior involving places, people, and events are highlighted. They are sacred in the sense that they are somehow removed from profane (ordinary) space or time. Sacred consumption embraces many important marketing activities, from tourism to gift giving. The movement from the sacred to profane (desacralization) and vice versa (sacralization) is also considered, as are consumer rituals involving such phenomena as grooming, gift giving, and holidays.

The chapter also acknowledges the darker side of consumer behavior. Many consumption activities are negative or destructive. This dark side includes addictions and compulsive behaviors (e.g., gambling, drugs, or even compulsive shopping). People themselves may be used (and abused) as products when they are treated as profane commodities (e.g., prostitutes). Other deviant behaviors discussed include shoplifting and vandalism.

KEY TERMS

Addiction	Profane
Anti-consumption	Rites of passage
Binary opposition	Ritual
Compulsive consumption	Ritual artifacts
Consumed consumers	Sacralization
Desacralization	Sacred
Gift-giving ritual	Self-gifts
Myth	

REVIEW QUESTIONS AND DISCUSSION TOPICS

1. Explain the principle of binary opposition, and apply this principle to a modern advertising campaign.
2. Discuss the distinction between sacred and profane consumption. What are some marketing implications of positioning a product as either sacred or profane?
3. How do the consumer decisions involved in gift giving differ from other purchase decisions?
4. The chapter argues that not all gift giving is positive. In what ways can this ritual be unpleasant or negative?

5. What are some of the major motivations for the purchase of self-gifts? Discuss some marketing implications of these.
6. Everyday objects like cars, televisions, and money may be said to have sacred qualities. How do these objects become sacred? Do you agree with this contention?
7. Describe the three stages of the rite of passage associated with graduating from college.
8. How do holiday ceremonies reflect cultural myths?
9. Identify the ritualized aspects of football that are employed in advertising.
10. "People can be marketed just like any other product." Do you agree?

HANDS-ON EXERCISES

1. Select a successful movie and analyze it in terms of its mythic themes (e.g, *Rocky*). What are the underlying messages of the movie? Are the plot and the movie's characters similar to other movies you have seen? Would the underlying message of the movie be easily understood by people from other cultures?
2. Construct a ritual script for a wedding in your culture. How many artifacts can you list that are contained in this script?

NOTES

1. Blayne Cutler, "Here Comes Santa Claus (Again)," *American Demographics* (December 1989): 30–31.
2. Conrad Phillip Kottak, "Anthropological Analysis of Mass Enculturation," *Researching American Culture,* ed. Conrad P. Kottak (Ann Arbor, Mich.: University of Michigan Press, 1982): 40–74.
3. Joseph Campbell, *Myths, Dreams, and Religion* (New York: E. P. Dutton, 1970).
4. Kottak, "Anthropological Analysis of Mass Enculturation."
5. Jeffrey S. Lang and Patrick Trimble, "Whatever Happened to the Man of Tomorrow? An Examination of the American Monomyth and the Comic Book Superhero," *Journal of Popular Culture* 22 (Winter 1988): 157.
6. Elizabeth C. Hirschman, "Movies as Myths: An Interpretation of Motion Picture Mythology," in *Marketing and Semiotics: New Directions in the Study of Signs for Sale,* ed. Jean Umiker-Sebeok (Berlin: Mouton de Guyter, 1987): 335–74.
7. Arthur A. Berger, *Signs in Contemporary Culture: An Introduction to Semiotics* (New York: Longman, 1984); Hirschman, "Movies as Myths"; Koenraad Kuiper, "Star Wars: An Imperial Myth," *Journal of Popular Culture* (Spring 1988): 77–86.
8. Bruno Bettelheim, *The Uses of Enchantment: The Meaning and Importance of Fairy Tales* (New York: Alfred A. Knopf, 1976).
9. Jerry Schwartz, "At Age 104, Coke Congratulates Itself," *New York Times* (August 11, 1990): C3.
10. Bernie Whalen, "Semiotics: An Art or Powerful Marketing Research Tool?" *Marketing News* (May 13, 1983): 8.
11. Russell W. Belk, Melanie Wallendorf, and John F. Sherry, Jr., "The Sacred and the Profane in Consumer Behavior: Theodicy on the Odyssey," *Journal of Consumer Research* 16 (June 1989): 1–38.
12. Belk, et al., "The Sacred and the Profane in Consumer Behavior."
13. Deborah Hofmann, "In Jewelry, Choices Sacred and Profane, Ancient and New," *New York Times* (May 7, 1989).
14. Quoted in "Public Relations Firm to Present Anti-Abortion Effort to Bishops," *New York Times* (August 14, 1990): A12.
15. Martin E. Marty, "Sunday Mass and the Media: There's a Fine Line in Religious Advertising Between Tasteful and Tacky," *Across the Board* 24 (May 1987): 55.

16. For an extensive bibliography on collecting, see Russell W. Belk, Melanie Wallendorf, John F. Sherry, Jr., and Morris B. Holbrook, "Collecting in a Consumer Culture," in *Highways and Buyways,* ed. Russell W. Belk (Provo, Utah: Association for Consumer Research, in press).

17. Kottak, "Anthropological Analysis of Mass Enculturation."

18. Joan Kron, *Home-Psych: The Social Psychology of Home and Decoration* (New York: Clarkson N. Potter, Inc., 1983); Gerry Pratt, "The House as an Expression of Social Worlds," in *Housing and Identity: Cross-Cultural Perspectives,* ed. James S. Duncan (London: Croom Helm, 1981): 135–79; Michael R. Solomon, "The Role of the Surrogate Consumer in Service Delivery," *The Service Industries Journal* 7 (July 1987): 292–307.

19. Grant McCracken, "'Homeyness': A Cultural Account of One Constellation of Goods and Meanings," in *Interpretive Consumer Research,* ed. Elizabeth C. Hirschman (Provo, Utah: Association for Consumer Research, 1989): 168–84.

20. Dennis W. Rook, "Modern Hex Signs and Symbols of Security," in *Marketing and Semiotics: New Directions in the Study of Signs for Sale,* ed. Jean Umiker-Sebeok (Berlin: Mouton de Guyter, 1987): 239–46.

21. Quoted in Peter Applebome, "New Stop for Elvis Fans Who Can't Get Enough," *New York Times* (August 7, 1989): A8.

22. James Hirsch, "Taking Celebrity Worship to New Depths," *New York Times* (November 9, 1988): C1.

23. Mindy Weinstein, "Dead Stars are In," *Advertising Age* (August 14, 1989): 44.

24. Judann Dagnoli, "Ads Trumpet Satchmo's Immortality," *Advertising Age* (April 30, 1990): 26.

25. Bob Greene, "Some Like It Hot," *Esquire* (October 1987): 59.

26. Fred Kirby, "Woody Allen Wins Lawsuit to Stymie National Video Lookalike," *Variety* (May 22, 1985): 84.

27. James P. Forkan, "Send in the Clones; Ads Must ID Celeb Doubles," *Advertising Age* (May 20, 1985): 2.

28. Emile Durkheim, *The Elementary Forms of the Religious Life* (New York: Free Press, 1915).

29. Susan Birrell, "Sports as Ritual: Interpretations from Durkheim to Goffman," *Social Forces* 60 (1981)2: 354–76; Daniel Q. Voigt, "American Sporting Rituals," in *Rites and Ceremonies in Popular Culture,* ed. Ray B. Browne (Bowling Green, Ohio: Bowling Green University Popular Press, 1980): 125–40.

30. Alf Walle, "The Epic Hero," *Marketing Insights* (Spring 1990): 63.

31. Dean MacCannell, *The Tourist: A New Theory of the Leisure Class* (New York: Shocken Books, 1976).

32. Belk, et al., "The Sacred and the Profane in Consumer Behavior."

33. Beverly Gordon, "The Souvenir: Messenger of the Extraordinary," *Journal of Popular Culture* 20 (1986)3: 135–46.

34. See Dennis W. Rook, "The Ritual Dimension of Consumer Behavior," *Journal of Consumer Research* 12 (December 1985): 251–64; Mary A. Stansfield Tetreault and Robert E. Kleine III, "Ritual, Ritualized Behavior, and Habit: Refinements and Extensions of the Consumption Ritual Construct," in *Advances in Consumer Research,* ed. Marvin Goldberg, Gerald Gorn, and Richard W. Pollay (Provo, Utah: Association for Consumer Research, 1990)17: 31–38.

35. Kim Foltz, "New Species for Study: Consumers in Action," *New York Times* (December 18, 1989): A1.

36. Melanie Wallendorf and Daniel Nelson, "An Archaeological Examination of Ethnic Differences in Body Care Rituals," *Psychology & Marketing* 3 (1986)4: 273–89.

37. Dennis W. Rook and Sidney J. Levy, "Psychosocial Themes in Consumer Grooming Rituals," in *Advances in Consumer Research,* ed. Richard P. Bagozzi and Alice M. Tybout (Provo, Utah: Association for Consumer Research, 1983)10: 329–33

38. Diane Barthel, *Putting on Appearances: Gender and Attractiveness* (Philadelphia, Pa.: Temple University Press, 1988).

39. Quoted in Diane Barthel, *Putting on Appearances: Gender and Advertising* (Philadelphia, Pa.: Temple University Press, 1988).

40. Belk, et al., "The Sacred and the Profane in Consumer Behavior."

41. Monica Gonzales, "Before Mourning," *American Demographics* (April 1988): 19.

42. John F. Sherry, Jr., "Gift Giving in Anthropological Perspective," *Journal of Consumer Research* 10 (September 1983): 157–68.

43. Daniel Goleman, "What's Under the Tree? Clues to a Relationship," *New York Times* (December 19, 1989): C1.

44. John F. Sherry, Jr., Mary Ann McGrath, and Sidney J. Levy, "The Dark Side of the Gift," (paper presented at the Winter Marketing Educators' Conference, Orlando, Fla., 1991).

45. Colin Camerer, "Gifts as Economics Signals and Social Symbols," *American Journal of Sociology* 94 (Supplement 1988): 5180–5214.

46. Robert T. Green and Dana L. Alden, "Functional Equivalence in Cross-Cultural Consumer Behavior: Gift Giving in Japan and the United States," *Psychology & Marketing* 5 (Summer 1988): 155–68.

47. "Where Christmas Comes in July," *The Economist* (July 25, 1987): 30.

48. David Glen Mick and Michelle DeMoss, "Self-Gifts: Phenomenological Insights from Four Contexts," *Journal of Consumer Research* 17 (December 1990): 327.

49. See for example Russell W. Belk, "Halloween: An Evolving American Consumption Ritual," in *Advances in Consumer Research,* ed. Richard Pollay, Jerry Gorn, and Marvin Goldberg, (Provo, Utah: Association for Consumer Research, 1990), 508–17; Melanie Wallendorf and Eric J. Arnould, "We Gather Together: The Consumption Rituals of Thanksgiving Day," *Journal of Consumer Research* 18 (June 1991): 13–31.

50. Menkes, "Britain's Mother's Day Promotion: Phone Ordering, Courier Delivery," *Publisher's Weekly* (March 16, 1990): 13.

51. Georgia Dullea, "How do You Spell Mother? Any Old Way," *New York Times* (May 14, 1989): 38.

52. Rick Lyte, "Holidays, Ethnic Themes Provide Built-In F&B Festivals," *Hotel & Motel Management* (December 14, 1987): 56; Megan Rowe, "Holidays and Special Occasions: Restaurants are Fast Replacing 'Grandma's House' as the Site of Choice for Special Meals," *Restaurant Management* (November 1987): 69; Judith Waldrop, "Funny Valentines," *American Demographics* (February 1989): 7.

53. David Finn, "Anniversaries Represent Golden Opportunities for Marketers," *Marketing News* (April 24, 1989): 8.

54. Keith Bradsher, "Valentines are Still 2 Sweet 2 be 4 Gotten," *Los Angeles Times* (February 12, 1988): 1.

55. Sharon Warren Walsh, Paul Fahri, and Lena H. Sun, "Can't Buy Me Love," *The Washington Post* (February 6, 1989): WB3.

56. Lynn Asinof, "Valentine's Day Prompts Offbeat Promotions and Unusual Gifts," *The Wall Street Journal* (February 8, 1990): A1.

57. Stacy Botwinick, "Halloween Conjures Up Bewitching Profits," *Playthings* (March 1990): 48.

58. Theodore Caplow, Howard M. Bahr, Bruce A. Chadwick, Reuben Hill, and Maragaret M. Williams, *Middletown Families: Fifty Years of Change and Continuity* (Minneapolis, Minn.: University of Minnesota Press, 1982).

59. N. R. Kleinfeld, "The Weird, the Bad and the Scary," *New York Times* (October 15, 1989): 4.

60. Georgia Dullea, "It's the Year's No. 2 Night to Howl," *New York Times* (October 30, 1988): 20.

61. Quoted in Matthew Grimm, "Older Revelers Make Halloween an Adult Fair," *Adweek's Marketing Week* (October 23, 1989): 4.

62. Paul Fahri, "Brewing Up More Spirits; Liquor Firms Promoting Halloween for Adults," *The Washington Post* (October 31, 1989): D1.

63. Quoted in Thomas R. King, "Brewer's Hope for Treat from Promotion Tricks," *The Wall Street Journal* (1989): B1.

64. Michael R. Solomon and Punam Anand, "Ritual Costumes and Status Transition: The Female Business Suit as Totemic Emblem," in *Advances in Consumer Research,* ed. Elizabeth C. Hirschman and Morris Holbrook, (Washington, DC: Association for Consumer Research, 1985) 12: 315–18.

65. "Divorce Can be Furry," *American Demographics* (March 1987): 24.

66. Arnold Van Gennep, *The Rites of Passage,* trans. Maika B. Vizedom and Gabrielle L. Caffee (London: Routledge and Kegan Paul, 1960; orig. published 1908); Solomon and Anand, "Ritual Costumes and Status Transition."

67. Walter W. Whitaker III., "The Contemporary American Funeral Ritual," in *Rites and Ceremonies in Popular Culture,* ed. Ray B. Browne (Bowling Green, Ohio: Bowling Green University Popular Press, 1980): 316–25.
68. Gonzales, "Before Mourning"; Michael Specter, "Hot Tombs: The Last Yuppie Status Symbol," *The New Republic* (September 11, 1989): 22.
69. Richard B. Woodward, "Comics as Inspiration: Are We Having Fun Yet?" *New York Times* (April 23, 1989): 1; Joe Queenan, "Drawing on the Dark Side: Today's Comic Books Combine Slick Art and Sadistic Sex," *New York Times Magazine* (April 30, 1989): 32.
70. Georgia Witkin, "The Shopping Fix," *Health* (May 1988): 73; see also Arch G. Woodside and Randolph J. Tyrappey III, "Compulsive Consumption of a Consumer Service: An Exploratory Study of Chronic Horse Race Track Gambling Behavior," (Working Paper # 90-MKTG-04, A.B. Freeman School of Business, Tulane University, 1990).
71. James Barron, "Are We All Really Losers with Gambling, a Spreading Social Addiction?" *New York Times* (May 31, 1989): A18.
72. Quoted in Daniel Goleman, "Biology of Brain May Hold Key for Gamblers," *New York Times* (October 3, 1989): C9.
73. Brad Edmondson, "The Demographics of Gambling," *American Demographics* (July 1986): 38.
74. James Cook, "Lottomania," *Forbes* (March 6, 1989): 92; Clyde Haberman, "The Die is Still Cast, and Italy is Still Betting on It," *New York Times* (February 13, 1990): A4.
75. Thomas C. O'Guinn and Ronald J. Faber, "Compulsive Buying: A Phenomenological Explanation," *Journal of Consumer Research* 16 (September 1989): 154.
76. Quoted in Anastasia Toufexis, "365 Shopping Days Till Christmas," *Time* (December 26, 1988): 82; see also Ronald J. Faber and Thomas C. O'Guinn, "Compulsive Consumption and Credit Abuse," *Journal of Consumer Policy* 11 (1988): 109–21; Mary S. Butler, "Compulsive Buying—It's No Joke," *Consumer's Digest* (September 1986): 55.
77. Helen Reynolds, *The Economics of Prostitution* (Springfield, Ill.: Charles C. Thomas, 1986).
78. "Precious Drops," *The Economist* (October 14, 1989): 28.
79. See Elizabeth Hirschman, "Exploring the Dark Side of Consumer Behavior: Metaphor and Ideology in Prostitution and Pornography," in *Gender and Consumer Behavior,* ed. Janeen A. Costa (Salt Lake City, Utah: University of Utah 1991): 303–14.
80. William D. Mosher, "Infertility: Why Business Is Booming," *American Demographics* (July 1987): 42–43.
81. Barbara Katz Rothman, "Cheap Labor: Sex, Class, Race and 'Surrogacy,'" *Society* 25 (March-April 1988): 21.
82. Paul Bernstein, "Cheating—The New National Pastime?" *Business* (October–December 1985): 24–33.
83. "Shoplifting: Bess Myerson's Arrest Highlights a Multibillion-Dollar Problem that Many Stores Won't Talk About," *Life* (August 1988): 32.
84. Roy Carter, "Whispering Sweet Nothings to the Shop Thief," *Retail & Distribution Management* (January/February 1986): 36.
85. Catherine A. Cole, "Deterrence and Consumer Fraud," *Journal of Retailing* 65 (Spring 1989): 107–20; Stephen J. Grove, Scott J. Vitell, and David Strutton, "Non-Normative Consumer Behavior and the Techniques of Neutralization," in *Marketing Theory and Practice,* ed. Terry Childers, et al., (1989 AMA Winter Educators' Conference; Chicago: American Marketing Association, 1989), 131–35.
86. "Dismantling Detroit," *Time* (April 24, 1989): 25.
87. "Call Box Unobtainable," *The Economist* (March 12, 1988): 57.
88. Bradley Johnson, "Madonna Scores in L.A. Bus Shelters," *Advertising Age* (June 18, 1990): 12.

Diffusion of Innovations and Popular Culture

CHAPTER 17

When Amanda brought home her new $60.00 pair of jeans, her mother was eager to see what was so special about them. As Amanda pulled them out of the bag to proudly show them off, her mother shrieked, "I can't believe the mistake that store made! They gave you a defective pair—these have huge rips in them. Let's hurry up and take them right back, and I'm going to give them a piece of my mind while I'm at it!" Amanda just laughed at her old-fashioned mother for being so out of it. "Mom, get with the program. These are supposed to be ripped. That's the style. Everybody knows that."

In the early 1990s, it was happening all over the place. People were taking perfectly good blue jeans and ripping them to shreds. In another era, consumers would indignantly return ripped clothing. Now they were paying a premium for it. How, then, did the ripped style come to be accepted and desirable, even if only for a while?

A variety of forces combined to create this style. In the mid-1980s, ripped jeans were spotted on the streets of Paris by the designers Marithe and Francois Girbaud, who seemed to sense intuitively that such an innovation would be a hit. They introduced "destroyed jeans" with a few horizontal rips to European consumers in 1985. At the same time in the United States, the 1960s were coming back in style for many teens. Coincidentally, ripped clothes were associated with the political activism and "anti-establishment" feeling of those times. To identify with that rebellious spirit, some kids began to rip their jeans with razor blades.

The trend took off, and a few shrewd manufacturers jumped on the bandwagon. An executive for the Jou Jou line noted, "We started ripping garments that we already had made. We quickly ran out of the inventory."[1] Macy's department stores started to carry this line, giving the ripped look wider distribution. The European and American trends began to merge in the late 1980s. The British singer George Michael helped fuel the fire when he wore jeans with ripped knees in his "Faith" video, which was widely shown on MTV.

Even though more and more kids began to adopt the ripped look, many merchandisers were reluctant to take the risk of carrying them. The look reached the status of mainstream fashion, though, when *Sassy,* a teen magazine, ran a story on ripped jeans in 1989. Now many young teens began to wear the pants, waiting until they were sure that their friends would accept them. The fashion quickly spread as teens who traveled around the country saw the style and brought it back home with them. The gaping holes of the 1990s had come a long way from the small, symmetrical rips of the mid-1980s. As time goes by and styles change yet again, most of these jeans will probably be retired to closets—or cut down to shorts.

THE PRODUCTION AND DIFFUSION OF POPULAR CULTURE

The Rolling Stones. Miniskirts. Wide ties. Fast food. High-tech furniture. Postmodern architecture. Teenage Mutant Ninja Turtles. We inhabit a world brimming with different styles and possibilities. The food we eat, the cars we drive, the clothes we wear, the places we live and work, the music we listen to—all are influenced by the ebb and flow of popular culture and fashion.

Our tastes and product preferences are not formed in a vacuum. Choices are driven by the images presented to us in mass media, our observations of those around us, and even by our desires to live in the fantasy worlds created by marketers. These options are constantly evolving and changing. A clothing style or type of cuisine that is "hot" one year may be "out" the next, as the "obsolete" products in the AT&T ad so painfully remind us.

Amanda's ripped jeans illustrate some of the characteristics of fashion and popular culture:

- Styles often are rooted in and reflect deeper societal trends (e.g., politics and social conditions).

As this AT&T ad demonstrates, many product styles are doomed to become obsolete. Courtesy of AT&T INTERNATIONAL COMMUNICATIONS SERVICES.

- Styles usually originate as an interplay between the deliberate inventions of designers and businesspeople and spontaneous actions by ordinary consumers. Designers, manufacturers, and merchandisers who can anticipate what consumers want will succeed in the marketplace. In the process, they also help to fuel the fire by encouraging mass distribution of the item.
- These trends can travel widely, often between countries and continents. Influential people in the media play a large role in deciding which of these trends will succeed.
- A style begins as a risky or unique statement by a relatively small group of people, then spreads as others increasingly become aware of the style and feel confident about trying it.
- Most styles eventually wear out, as people continually search for new ways to express themselves and marketers scramble to keep up with these desires.

THE PRODUCTION OF CULTURE PERSPECTIVE

Consumers may at times feel overwhelmed by the sheer number of choices in the marketplace. A person trying to decide on something as routine as a necktie has literally hundreds of alternatives to choose from. Despite this seeming abundance, however, the options available to consumers at any point in time actually represent only a small fraction of the total set of possibilities.

The selection of certain alternatives over others, whether automobiles, dresses, computers, recording artists, political candidates, religions or even scientific methodologies, is the culmination of a complex filtration process resembling a funnel, as depicted in Figure 17-1. Many

The Cultural Selection Process

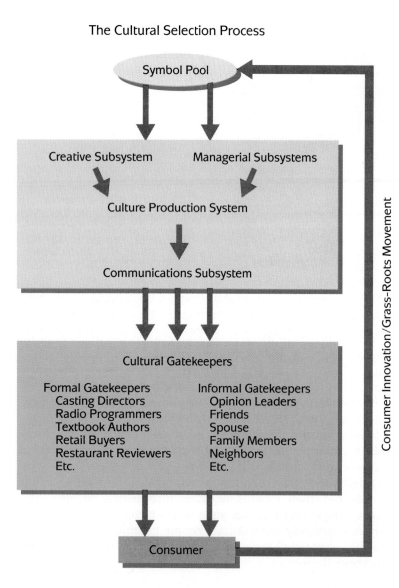

Figure 17-1 The Cultural Selection Process: Adapted from Michael R. Solomon, "Building up and Breaking down: The impact of Cultural Sorting on Symbolic Consumption," in *Research in Consumer Behavior,* ed J. Shath and E. C. Hirschman, Greenwich, CT. JAI Press 1988, 325-351 (cf Endnote 4).

possibilities initially compete for adoption, and these are steadily winnowed down as they make their way down the path from conception to consumption.

CULTURE PRODUCTION SYSTEMS   No single designer, company, or advertising agency is totally responsible for creating popular culture. Every product, whether a hit record, a car, or a new clothing style, requires the input of many different participants. The set of individuals and organizations responsible for creating and marketing a cultural product is termed a **culture production system (CPS)**.[2]

The nature of these systems helps to determine the types of products that eventually emerge from them. Factors such as the number and diversity of competing systems and the amount of innovation versus conformity that is encouraged are important. For example, an analysis of the Country Western music industry has shown that the hit records it produces tend to be similar to one another during time periods when it is dominated by a few large companies, whereas there is more diversity when a greater number of producers are competing within the same market.[3]

The different members of a culture production system may not necessarily be aware of or appreciate the roles played by other members, yet many diverse agents work together to create popular culture.[4] Each member does his or her best to anticipate which particular images will be most attractive to a consumer market. Of course, those who are able to consistently forecast consumers' tastes most accurately will be successful over time. To illustrate these interrelationships, Table 17-1 highlights the many cultural specialists associated with the creation of a hit record.

Components of a CPS.   A culture production system has three major subsystems: (1) a *creative subsystem* responsible for generating new symbols and/or products; (2) a *managerial subsystem* responsible for selecting, making tangible, mass producing and managing the distribution of new symbols and/or products; and (3) a *communications subsystem* responsible for giving meaning to the new product and providing it with a symbolic set of attributes that are communicated to consumers. An example of the three components of a culture production system for a record would be: (1) a singer (e.g., Madonna, a creative subsystem); (2) a company (e.g., Sire Records, which manufactures and distributes Madonna's records, a managerial subsystem); and (3) the advertising and publicity agencies hired to promote the albums (a communications subsystem).

THE DIFFUSION OF INNOVATIONS

New products and styles termed **innovations** constantly enter the market. If they are successful (most are not), they spread through the population. First they are bought and used by only a few people, and then more and more consumers decide to adopt them, until in some cases it seems that everyone has them. Of course, this saturation often is only temporary, as people get tired of products and/or new ones are introduced to take their place. **Diffusion** refers to the process whereby a new product, service, or idea spreads through a population.

TABLE 17-1 Cultural specialists in the music industry

Specialist	Functions
Songwriter(s)	Compose music and lyrics. Must reconcile artistic preferences with estimates of what will succeed in the marketplace
Performer(s)	Interpret music and lyrics. May be formed spontaneously, or may be packaged by an agent to appeal to a predetermined market (e.g., The Monkees, Menudo, New Kids on the Block)
Teachers and Coaches	Develop and refine performers' talents
Agent	Represents performers to record companies
A&R Executive	Artists & Repertoire executives at a record company acquire artists for the label
Publicists, Image consultants, Designers, Stylists	Create an image for the group that is transmitted to the buying public
Recording technicians, Producers	Create a recording to be sold
Marketing Executives	Make strategic decisions regarding performers' appearances, ticket pricing, promotional strategies, and so on.
Video Director	Interpret the song visually to create a music video that will help to promote the record
Music Reviewers	Evaluate the merits of a recording for listeners
Disc Jockeys, Radio Program Directors	Decide which records will be given airplay and/or placed in the radio stations' regular rotations.
Record Store Owner	Decide which of the many records produced will be stocked and/or promoted heavily

▼ MARKETING PITFALL

The issue of what exactly constitutes a "new" product is quite important to many businesses. It is said that "imitation is the sincerest form of flattery," and decisions regarding how much (if at all) one's product should resemble competitors are often a centerpiece of marketing strategy (e.g., packaging of "me-too" or look-alike products). On the other hand, the product cannot be a total duplicate; patent law is concerned with the precise definition of what is a new product and protecting that invention from illegal imitation.

A *knockoff* is a style that has deliberately been copied and modified, often with the intent to sell to a larger or different market. For example, *haute couture* clothing styles presented by top designers in Paris and elsewhere are commonly "knocked off" by other designers and sold to the mass market.

It is difficult to legally protect a design (as opposed to a technological feature), but pressure is building in many industries to do just that. Manufacturers argue that, say, a distinctive curve on a car bumper is as important to the integrity of the car as is a mechanical innovation. Legislation is being considered to protect new designs with a ten-year copyright (clothing would be exempt).[5] This movement highlights the importance of the question: "What exactly is an innovation?"

TYPES OF ADOPTERS   A consumer's decision to adopt an innovation resembles the sequence discussed in Chapter 8. The person moves through the stages of awareness, information search, evaluation, trial, and adoption, though the relative importance of each stage may differ depending upon how much is already known about a product, cultural factors, and so on.[6]

However, not all people adopt an innovation at the same rate. Some do so quite rapidly, and others never do at all. Consumers can be placed into approximate categories based upon their likelihood of adopting an innovation. These categories can be related to phases of the product life cycle concept used widely by marketing strategists. As shown in Figure 17-2, the designation of a person as an innovator, an early adopter, part of the early or late majority, or as a laggard depends upon what stage of the life cycle a product is in when the person decides to use it. A laggard, for example, is quite slow to try something new; by the time he or she gets around to it, the product may well be on its last legs.

The bell curve indicates the approximate percentage of consumers overall who fall under each category. The main point here is that in many cases, roughly one-sixth of the population (innovators and early adopters) is very quick to adopt new products and one-sixth of the people are very

Figure 17-2 Types of Adopters

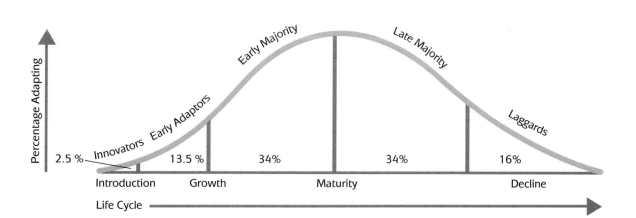

slow. The other two-thirds are somewhere in the middle, and these majority adopters represent the mainstream public. These consumers are interested in new things, but they do not want them to be *too* new. In some cases, people deliberately wait to adopt an innovation because they assume that its technological qualities will be improved, or that the price will fall after it has been on the market awhile.[7]

Innovators. Even though innovators represent only 2.5 percent of the population, marketers are always interested in identifying them. These are the brave souls who are always on the lookout for novel developments and will be the first to try a new offering. Just as generalized opinion leaders do not appear to exist (see Chapter 11), innovators tend to be category-specific as well. A person who is an innovator in one area may even be a laggard in another. For example, a gentleman who prides himself as being on the cutting edge of fashion may have no conception of new developments in recording technology, and may still stubbornly cling to his phonograph albums even while he searches for the latest *avant garde* clothing styles in obscure boutiques.

Despite this qualification, some generalizations can be offered regarding the profile of innovators.[8] Not surprisingly, for example, they tend to be have more favorable attitudes toward taking risks. They also are likely to have higher educational and income levels and to be socially active.

Early Adopters Versus Innovators. Early adopters share many of the same characteristics as innovators, but an important difference is their degree of concern for social acceptance, especially with regard to expressive products such as clothing, cosmetics, and so on. Generally speaking, an early adopter is receptive to new styles because he or she is involved in the product category and also places high value on being *in fashion.* What appears on the surface to be a fairly high-risk adoption (e.g., wearing a skirt 3 inches above the knee when most people are wearing them below the knee) is actually not *that* risky. The style change has already been "field-tested" by innovators, who truly took the fashion risk. Early adopters are likely to be found in "fashion-forward" stores (e.g., Bloomingdale's) featuring the latest "hot" designers. In contrast, true innovators are more likely to be found in small boutiques featuring as-yet unknown designers.

TYPES OF INNOVATIONS Innovations can occur on a symbolic level or a technological level. A *symbolic innovation* communicates a new social meaning (e.g., a new hairstyle or car design), while a *technological innovation* involves some functional change (e.g., central air conditioning or car airbags).[9] Whether symbolic or functional, new products, services, and ideas have characteristics that determine the degree to which they will probably diffuse. As a general rule, innovations that are more novel are *least* likely to diffuse. This is because things that are fairly similar to what is already available require fewer changes in behavior to use. On the other hand, an innovation that radically alters a person's life-style requires the person to modify his or her way of doing things, thus requiring more effort to adapt to the change.

Behavioral Demands of Innovations. Innovations can be categorized in terms of the degree to which they demand changes in behavior from adopters. Three major types of innovations have been identified, though these three categories are not absolutes. They refer in a *relative* sense to the amount of disruption or change they bring to people's lives.

A *continuous innovation* refers to a modification of an existing product, as when Cheerios introduces a Honey Nut version of its cereal, or Levi's promotes shrink-to-fit jeans. This type of change may be used to set one brand apart from its competitors. Most product innovations are of this type. They are *evolutionary* rather than *revolutionary*. Small changes are made to position the product, add line extensions, or merely to alleviate consumer boredom.

Consumers may be lured to the new product, but adoption represents only a minor change in consumption habits, perhaps adding to the product's convenience or to the range of choices available. A typewriter company, for example, many years ago modified the shape of its product to make it more "user-friendly" to secretaries. One simple change was curving the tops of the keys, a convention that is carried over on today's computer keyboards. The reason: Secretaries complained that the flat surfaces were hard to use with long fingernails.

A *dynamically continuous innovation* is a more pronounced change in an existing product, as represented by self-focusing 35mm cameras or touch-tone telephones. These innovations will have a modest impact on the way people do things, creating some behavioral changes. The IBM Selectric typewriter, which uses a typing ball rather than individual keys, permitted secretaries to instantly change the typeface of manuscripts by replacing one Selectric ball with another.

A *discontinuous innovation* creates major changes in the way we live. Major inventions such as the airplane, the car, the computer, and television have radically changed modern lifestyles. The personal computer has in many cases supplanted the typewriter, and it has created the phenomenon of "telecommuters" by allowing many consumers to work out of their homes.

Of course, the cycle continues—new continuous innovations are constantly being made for computers (e.g., new versions of software), dynamically continuous innovations, such as the keyboard "mouse," compete for adoption, and discontinuous innovations like wrist-watch personal computers loom on the horizon.

PREREQUISITES FOR SUCCESSFUL ADOPTION Regardless of how much behavioral change is demanded by an innovation, several factors are desirable for a new product to succeed.[10]

Compatibility. The innovation should be compatible with consumers' life-styles. As one illustration, a manufacturer of personal care products tried unsuccessfully several years ago to introduce a cream hair-remover for men as a substitute for razors and shaving cream. This formulation was similar to that used widely by women to remove hair from their legs. Though the product was simple and convenient to use, it failed because men were not interested in a product they perceived to be too feminine and thus threatening to their self-concepts.

Trialability. The product should have trialability. Since an unknown is accompanied by high perceived risk, people are more likely to adopt an innovation if they can experiment with it prior to making a commitment. To reduce this risk, companies often choose the expensive strategy of distributing free "trial-size" samples of new products.

Degree of Complexity. The product should be low in complexity. A product that is easier to understand and use will be chosen over a competitor. This strategy requires less effort from the consumer, and it also lowers perceived risk. Manufacturers of videocassette recorders, for example, have put a lot of effort into simplifying VCR usage (e.g., on-screen programming) to encourage adoption.

Observability. Innovations that are easily observable are more likely to spread, since this quality makes it more likely that other potential adopters will become aware of its existence. The rapid proliferation of "fanny packs" (pouches worn around the waist in lieu of wallets or purses) was due to their high visibility. It was easy for others to see the convenience offered by this alternative.

Relative advantage. Most importantly, the product should offer relative advantage over other alternatives. The consumer must believe that its use will provide a benefit (either tangible or symbolic) other products cannot offer.

SYMBOLIC DIFFUSION: THE GLOBAL VILLAGE AND CULTURAL HOMOGENIZATION

- In Peru, Indians carry rocks painted to look like transistor radios.
- In addition to their traditional ceremonial wedding costumes, participants in Niger now add cheap quartz watches to their regalia.
- Natives in Papua New Guinea put Chivas Regal wrappers on their traditional drums and wear Pentel pens instead of nosebones.
- When a princess marries a Zulu king in Ethiopia, tribesmen watch "Pluto Tries to Become a Circus Dog" on a Viewmaster while a band plays "The Sound of Music."[11]

As these examples illustrate, it is not unusual for a culture to borrow products and ideas from others. Each culture is an importer and an exporter of symbols. In particular, many cultures incorporate Western objects with their traditional practices. In the process, the meanings of these objects are transformed and adapted to local tastes (at times in seemingly bizarre ways).

MTV AND COCA-COLA: THE WESTERNIZATION OF GLOBAL CULTURE
Since U.S. culture is created by citizens with roots from around the globe, it is natural that American popular culture is affected by these diverse influences. American marketers borrow heavily from other cultures when creating images for their products. In many cases these images are designed to appeal to consumers from certain ethnic and national subcultures, such as Hispanics, Jews, or Irish-Americans (see Chapter 13).

MULTICULTURAL DIMENSIONS

The Japanese are particularly enthusiastic borrowers of Western culture. Western words are used as a shorthand for anything new and exciting, even if consumers do not necessarily understand their meaning. This has created a phenomenon known as "Japlish," where new Western sounding words are merged with Japanese. Cars are given names like Fairlady, Gloria, and Bongo Wagon. Consumers buy *deodoranto* (deodorant) and *appuru pai* (apple pie). Ads urge shoppers to *stoppu rukku* (stop and look), and products are claimed to be *yuniku* (unique).[13] English phrases often are used in puzzling ways. Coca-Cola cans say "I feel Coke & sound special," and a company called Cream Soda sells a range of products with the slogan "Too old to die, too young to happy."[14]

The freedom associated with the United States makes the American life-style particularly desirable to Japanese youth, who widely adopt American fashions, particularly *Amekaji* (American casual clothing). The California surfer look is also popular. In fact, the University of California at Los Angeles sells about $16 million worth of clothing with the UCLA logo to the Japanese every year. Surfer jackets and boards also sell well, as do skateboards and sailboards.[15] Some Japanese teenagers cruise down the main streets of Tokyo with surfboards on the roofs of their cars, even though they are not near the ocean. Also reflecting the Westernization process, some of the favorite foods of Japanese teens are hamburgers, french fries, and ice cream.[16]

In addition, some climactic world events create domestic marketing opportunities, as when Communism declined in Eastern Europe. At that time, such companies as AT&T, Pepsi, and Miller beer used this important development in their advertising. An American ad for Drixoral, a cold medication, proclaimed: "In the New Year, may the only cold war in the world be the one being fought by us."[12]

The West (and especially the United States) is a *net exporter* of popular culture. Western symbols, in the form of images, words, and products, have diffused throughout the world. This influence is eagerly sought by many consumers, who have learned to equate Western life-styles in general and the English language in particular with modernization and sophistication.

Consumers in smaller, developing countries generally prefer products from established foreign producers, and will often pay a premium for these items.[17] Chinese women, for example, are starting to demand Western cosmetics costing up to a quarter of their salaries, ignoring domestically produced competitors. As one Chinese executive noted, "Some women even buy a cosmetic just because it has foreign words on the package."[18]

A negative backlash? Some critics deplore the creeping Americanization of their cultures. Debates continue in Europe on the imposition of quotas limiting American television programming.[19] The French have banned the use of such English terms as *le drugstore, le fast food,* and even *le marketing.*[20] Brazil's most popular performing artist is a blond woman named Xuxa, who is backed by the Paquitas—seven girls with golden hair. Some Brazilians have expressed concern that their national idol is blond, even though the majority of her admirers clearly are not.[21]

Demand for American products also extends to cigarettes, which are widely distributed in Third World and Asian countries. Though some of these countries have stringent regulations regarding cigarette advertising, brand logos appear in many places. These images are not necessarily placed by the cigarette companies, but rather by others who are trying to capitalize on the cachet of American products. Concern is specifically focused on use of these logos for children's products. In Asia, cigarette ads appear on school notebooks, kites, and gum packages. Some children's swimsuits in Thailand are sold with the Marlboro logo on them.[22]

THE FASHION SYSTEM

The **fashion system** consists of all those people and organizations involved in creating symbolic meanings and transferring these meanings to cultural goods. Fashion can be thought of as a *code,* or language, that helps us to decipher these meanings.[23] Unlike a language, however, fashion is context-dependent. The same item can be interpreted differently by different consumers and in different situations.[24] The meaning of many products is *undercoded*—there is no one precise meaning, but rather much room for interpretation among perceivers.

At the outset, it may be helpful to distinguish among some confusing terms. *Fashion* is the process of social diffusion by which a new style is adopted by some group(s) of consumers. *A fashion* (or style) refers to a particular combination of attributes. To be *in fashion* means that this combination is currently positively evaluated by some reference group. Thus the term *Danish modern* refers to particular characteristics of furniture design (i.e., a fashion in interior design). This does not necessarily imply that Danish modern is a fashion that is currently desired by consumers.[25]

CULTURAL CATEGORIES
The meaning that does get imparted to products reflects underlying **cultural categories,** which reflect the basic ways we characterize the world.[26] Our culture makes distinctions between different times, between leisure and work, between genders, and so on. The fashion system provides us with products that signify these categories. For example, the apparel industry gives us clothing to denote certain times (e.g., evening wear, resort wear), it differentiates between leisure clothes and work clothes, and it promotes masculine and feminine styles.

INTERDEPENDENCE AMONG PRODUCT MEANINGS
These cultural categories affect many different products and styles. As a result, it is common to find that dominant aspects of a culture at any point in time tend to be reflected in the design and marketing of very different products. This is a bit hard to grasp, since on the surface a clothing style, say, has little in common with a piece of furniture or with a car. Yet, as seen in the earlier discussion of cultural values in Chapter 15, an

overriding concern with a value such as achievement or environmentalism can determine the types of products likely to be accepted by consumers at any point in time. These underlying or *latent* themes then surface in various aspects of design. A few past examples of this interdependence will help to demonstrate how a dominant fashion motif reverberates across industries:

- Costumes worn by movie and rock stars can affect the fortunes of the apparel and accessory industries. A movie appearance by actor Clark Gable without a hat (unusual at that time) dealt a severe setback to the men's hat industry, while Jackie Kennedy's famous "pillbox hat" prompted a rush for hats by women. Other cross-category effects include the craze for ripped sweatshirts instigated by the movie *Flashdance,* a boost for cowboy boots from the movie *Urban Cowboy,* and the rock star Madonna's legitimation of lingerie as an acceptable outerwear clothing style.

- The Louvre in Paris was recently remodeled to include a controversial glass pyramid at the entrance designed by the architect I. M. Pei. Shortly thereafter, several designers unveiled pyramid-shaped clothing at Paris fashion shows.[27]

- People's postures seem to be affected by dominant clothing fashions, a phenomenon sometimes remarked upon by photographers and historians. Even when posing nude, models in the late-Victorian era tended to protrude the rear portion of their anatomies to resemble bustles, while nudes in the 1920s tended to slouch like the debutantes of the time, and their counterparts in the 1940s stuck out their chests while tucking in their stomachs, producing the period's popular hourglass figure.[28]

- In the 1950s and 1960s, much of America was preoccupied with science and technology. This concern with "space-age" mastery was fueled by the Russians' launching of the Sputnik satellite, which prompted fears that America was falling behind in the technology race. The theme of technical mastery of nature and of futuristic design became a motif that cropped up in many aspects of American popular culture of the time, from car designs with prominent tailfins to high-tech kitchen styles.

A cultural emphasis on science in the late 1950s affected product designs, as seen in this car with large tailfins (to resemble rockets) shown here.   R. Gates/ Frederic Lewis.

COLLECTIVE SELECTION

Fashions tend to "sweep" the country; it seems that all of a sudden "everyone" is doing or wearing the same styles. Some sociologists view fashion as a form of *collective behavior*–a wave of social conformity. How do so many people get "tuned-in" to the same phenomenon at once, as happened with ripped jeans?

Remember that creative subsystems within a culture production system attempt to anticipate the tastes of the buying public. Despite their unique talents, members of this subsystem are also members of mass culture. As such, they are drawing from a common set of ideas and symbols and are influenced by the same cultural phenomena as the eventual consumers of their products. The process by which certain symbolic alternatives are chosen over others has been termed *collective selection.*[29] As with creatives, members of the managerial and communications subsystems also seem to develop a common frame of mind. Although products within each category must compete for acceptance in the marketplace, they can usually be characterized by their adherence to a dominant theme or motif–be it "The Western Look," "New Wave," "Danish Modern," or "Nouvelle Cuisine."

The process of collective selection was observed in a study of *haute couture* (high fashion) by the sociologist Herbert Blumer.[30] He noted that at a typical Paris show, over 100 designs are shown to about 200 buyers. Despite this abundance, insiders can easily identify a range of about thirty designs that will be seriously considered. Of these approximately six to eight designs are actually chosen by buyers.

As members of competing managerial subsystems, these buyers are of course intense rivals, yet their choices tend to converge to a very high degree. As Blumer's observations indicate, the buyers typically are unable to specify their choice criteria. They are merely reacting to their common exposure to the same symbol pool:

> When the buyers were asked why they chose one dress in preference to another–between which my inexperienced eye could see no appreciable difference–the typical, honest, yet largely uninformative answer was that the dress was "stunning."[31]

THE VALUE OF COLLECTIVE SELECTION   Collective selection allows consumers to cope with the rapid pace of change in modern society. By abandoning old styles for new ones, the consumer is able to keep up with changes in his or her culture. When seen in this light, shopping is a future-oriented, adaptive activity: We try to anticipate changes in our lives by keeping up with the latest developments in merchandise (i.e., "So *this* is what everyone will be wearing this year!").

A Designer Conspiracy?   The public must be *ready* to adopt a new style, however.[32] The fashion industry discovered this the hard way when it tried to push the "midi" to women in the early 1970s and the miniskirt to older businesswomen more recently.[33] While many consumers talk of a "fashion conspiracy" where designers try to manipulate their tastes, this argument goes only so far. If designers have not correctly anticipated a need, they cannot force people to adopt their products. Consumers "vote" on new styles with their pocketbooks.

BEHAVIORAL SCIENCE APPROACHES TO FASHION

Fashion is a very complex process that operates on many levels. At one extreme, it is a macro, societal phenomenon affecting many people simultaneously. At the other, it exerts a very personal effect on individual behavior. A consumer's purchase decisions are often motivated by his or her desire to be in fashion. Fashion products also are aesthetic objects, and their origins are rooted in art and history. For this reason, there are many perspectives on the origin and diffusion of fashion. Though these cannot be described in detail here, some major approaches can be briefly summarized.[34]

PSYCHOLOGICAL MODELS OF FASHION

Many psychological factors help to explain why people are motivated to be in fashion. These include conformity, variety-seeking, personal creativity, and sexual attraction. For example, many consumers seem to have a "need for uniqueness": they want to be different, but not *too* different.[35] This helps to explain why people often conform to the basic outlines of a fashion, but try to improvise and make a personal statement within these guidelines.

Fashion and Sexuality. One of the earliest theories of fashion proposed that "shifting erogenous zones" (sexually arousing areas of the body) accounted for fashion changes. Different parts of the female body are the focus of sexual interest, and clothing styles change to highlight or hide these parts. For example, people in the Victorian era found shoulders exciting, a "well-turned ankle" was important in the beginning of this century, while the back was the center of attention in the 1930s. Some contemporary fashions suggest that the midriff is now an erogenous zone. (Note: Until very recently, the study of fashion focused almost exclusively on its impact on women. Hopefully, this concentration will broaden as scholars and practitioners begin to appreciate that men are affected by many of the same fashion influences).

While these shifts may be due to boredom, some have speculated that there are deeper reasons for changes in focus; body areas symbolically reflect social values. In medieval times, for example, a rounded belly was desirable. This preference was most likely a reflection of the high mortality rate when virtually constant pregnancy was necessary to stabilize population growth. Interest in the female leg in the 1920s and 1930s coincided with women's new mobility and independence, while the exposure of breasts in the 1970s signaled a renewed interest in breast-feeding.[36] Breasts were deemphasized in the 1980s as women concentrated on careers, but a larger bust size is now more popular as women try to combine professional activity with child-rearing (see Chapter 7).

Many articles of clothing in particular carry individual sexual symbolism, both for men and women. The wearing of fur, for example, may symbolically impart characteristics of the animal to the consumer. The Russian in his bearskin hat is a Russian Bear, while the girl who wears a mouton coat to her first dance may be seen as a lamb going to market.

Women who wear rabbit are like Playboy Bunnies—sexually eager and somewhat silly. On the other hand, a woman who wears a fox coat is more independent and wily—she is a "foxy lady."

It been suggested that the male tie is a symbol of potency (especially the bright red or yellow "power tie"). It may not be a coincidence that priests, who are celibate, do not wear ties, while the narrow cord ties often worn by older men suggest a withering of passion. The male hat has also been interpreted this way by some historians. High hats tend to be in fashion during periods of male dominance, while squashed or less assertive ones appear at other times.[37]

ECONOMIC MODELS OF FASHION Economists approach fashion in terms of the model of supply and demand. Items that are in limited supply have high value, while those readily available are less desirable. Rare items command respect and prestige.

Conspicuous Consumption. Veblen's classic notion of conspicuous consumption proposed that the wealthy consume to display their prosperity, for example by wearing expensive (and at times impractical) clothing. As noted in Chapter 12, this approach is somewhat outdated, since upscale consumers often engage in parody display, where they deliberately adopt formerly low status or inexpensive products, such as jeeps or ripped jeans. Other factors also influence the demand curve for fashion-related products. These include a *prestige-exclusivity effect,* where high prices still create high demand, and a *"snob" effect,* where lower prices reduce demand.[38]

SOCIOLOGICAL MODELS OF FASHION The collective selection model discussed previously is an example of a sociological approach to fashion. In addition, much attention has been focused on the relationship between product adoption and class structure.

The Trickle-Down Theory. The **trickle-down theory of fashion,** first proposed in 1904 by Georg Simmel, has been one of the most influential approaches to understanding fashion. It states that there are two conflicting forces that drive fashion change. Subordinate groups try to adopt the status symbols of the groups above them as they try to climb up the ladder of social mobility. Dominant styles thus originate with the upper classes and *trickle-down* to those below.

Those people in the superordinate groups are constantly looking below them on the ladder to ensure that they are not imitated. They respond to imitation by adopting new fashions to differentiate them from those below. These two processes create a self-perpetuating cycle of change—the machine that drives fashion.[39]

This process is indeed evident in some instances. For example, "designer jeans," popular in the 1970s and 1980s, were positioned as upscale clothing, and were significantly more expensive than ordinary jeans (the term "designer" implies limited production and individual styling). Once designer jeans diffused to the lower classes and saturated the mass market, the original wearers quickly abandoned them—they had acquired a lower class image.

Modifications to the Trickle-Down Theory. The trickle-down theory was quite useful for understanding the process of fashion changes when applied to a society with a stable class structure which permitted the easy identification of lower- versus upper-class consumers. This is not such an easy task in modern times. It also did not account for middle-class groups who possess *both* motivations: to differentiate themselves from those below them, and to imitate those above them.[40] In modern Western society, then, this approach must be modified to account for new developments in mass culture:

- A perspective based on class structure cannot account for the wide range of styles that are simultaneously made available in our society. Modern consumers have a much greater degree of individualized choice than in the past because of advances in technology and distribution. Elite fashion has been largely replaced by mass fashion, since media exposure permits many groups to become aware of a style at the same time.
- Consumers tend to be more influenced by opinion leaders who are similar to them. As a result each social group has its own fashion innovators who determine fashion trends. It is often more accurate to speak of a *trickle-across effect,* where fashions diffuse horizontally among members of the same social group.[41]
- Finally, current fashions often originate with the lower classes and *trickle-up.* Grassroots innovators typically are people who lack prestige in the dominant culture. Since they are less concerned with maintaining the *status quo,* they are more free to innovate and take risks.[42] Remember, for example, that the ripped jeans phenomenon most likely started with spontaneous slashing by "ordinary" people. Designers often get their inspiration by observing "street life" or obscure trends. Recent examples of the "trickle-up effect" include Cajun cuisine and rap music.

CYCLES OF FASHION ADOPTION

In the early 1980s, Cabbage Patch dolls were all the rage among American children. Faced with a limited supply of the product, some retailers reported near-riots among adults as they tried desperately to buy the dolls for their children. A Milwaukee disc jockey jokingly announced that people should bring catcher's mitts to a local stadium because 2000 dolls were going to be dropped from an airplane. Listeners were instructed to hold up their American Express cards so their numbers could be aerially photographed. More than two dozen anxious parents apparently didn't get the joke; they showed up in subzero weather, mitts in hand.[43] Although the Cabbage Patch craze lasted for a couple of seasons, it eventually died out and consumers moved on to other things, such as Teenage Mutant Ninja Turtles, which grossed more than $600 million in 1989.[44]

Although the longevity of a particular style can range from a month to a century, fashions tend to flow in a predictable sequence. The **fashion life cycle** is quite similar to the more familiar *product life cycle.* An item or idea progresses through basic stages from birth to death, as shown in Figure 17-3.

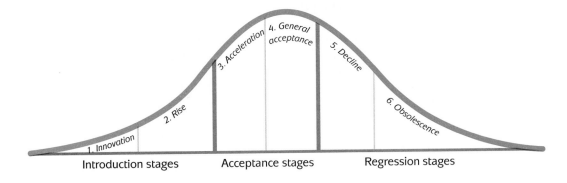

Figure 17-3 A Normal Fashion Cycle

UP THE CHARTS "WITH A BULLET": STAGES OF ACCEPTANCE   The fashion acceptance cycle is evident in the Top 40 music industry. In the *introduction* stages, a song is listened to by a small number of music innovators. It may be played in clubs or on "cutting edge" college radio stations. During the *acceptance* stages, the song enjoys increased social visibility and acceptance by large segments of the population. A record may get wide airplay on Top 40 stations, steadily rising up the charts "like a bullet."

In the *regression* stages, the item reaches a state of social saturation as it becomes overused, and eventually it sinks into decline and obsolescence as new songs rise to take its place. A hit record may be played once an hour on a Top 40 station for several weeks. At some point, though, people tend to get sick of it and focus their attention on newer releases. The former hit record eventually winds up in the discount rack at the local record store.

Figure 17-4 illustrates that fashions are characterized by slow acceptance at the beginning, which (if the fashion is to "make it") rapidly accelerates and then tapers off. Different classes of fashion can be identified by considering the relative *length* of the fashion acceptance cycle. While many fashions exhibit a moderate cycle, taking several years to work their way through the stages of acceptance and decline, others are extremely long-lived or short-lived. These two extreme forms of fashion are classics and fads.

Classics.   A **classic** is a fashion with an extremely long acceptance cycle. It is in a sense "anti-fashion," since it guarantees stability and low risk to the purchaser for a long period of time. Keds sneakers, introduced in 1917, have been successful because they appeal to those who are turned off by the high fashion, trendy appeal of L.A. Gear, Reebok, and others. When consumers in focus groups were asked to project what kind of building Keds would be, a common response was a country house with a white picket fence. In other words, the shoes are seen as a stable, classic product. In contrast, Nikes were often described as steel and glass skyscrapers, reflecting their more modernistic image.[45]

Fads. A **fad** is a very short-lived fashion. Fads are usually adopted by relatively few people. Adopters may all belong to a common subculture, and the fad "trickles across" members but rarely breaks out of that specific group. Some successful fad products include hula hoops, snap bracelets, and "pet rocks." A recent fad that was very profitable for its inventor was the Wacky Wallwalker, a spider-like plastic toy made in Japan that "climbs" down a wall. Over 150 million Wallwalkers were sold in a short period of time.[46]

Streaking was a fad that hit college campuses in the mid-1970s. This term referred to students running naked through classrooms, cafeterias, and dorms. Though the practice quickly spread across many campuses, it was primarily restricted to college settings. Streaking highlights several important characteristics of fads:[47]

- A label of some kind is usually assigned to the fad.
- Participants are similar to one another.
- The behavior is novel (fads have no history).
- The fad is considered somehow odd by existing standards.
- The fad is non-utilitarian—it does not perform any meaningful function.
- It is often adopted on impulse; people do not undergo stages of the rational decision-making process before joining in.
- The fad diffuses rapidly, gains quick acceptance, and is short-lived.

Figure 17-4 A Comparison of the Acceptance Cycles of Fads, Fashions, and Classics: Kaiser *The Social Psychology of Clothing,* MacMillan 1985, p. 347

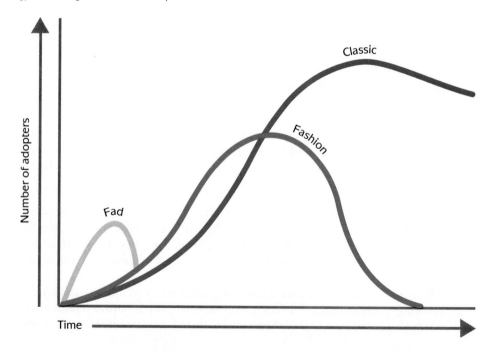

You always come back to the basics.

HIGH CULTURE AND POPULAR CULTURE

Do Beethoven and The New Kids on the Block have anything in common? While both the famous composer and the teenage singing group are associated with music, many would argue that the similarity stops here. Culture production systems create many diverse kinds of products, but some basic distinctions can be offered regarding their characteristics.

ARTS AND CRAFTS

One distinction can be made between arts and crafts.[48] An **art product** is viewed primarily as an object of aesthetic contemplation without any functional value. A **craft product,** in contrast, is admired because of

TABLE 17-2 Cultural formulae in public art forms

Art Form/ Genre	Classic Western	Science Fiction	Hard-Boiled Detective	Family Sitcom
Time	1800s	Future	Present	Anytime
Location	Edge of civilization	Space	City	Suburbs
Protagonist	Cowboy (Lone Indiv.)	Astronaut	Detective	Father (Figure)
Heroine	Schoolmarm	Spacegal	Damsel in distress	Mother (Figure)
Villain	Outlaws Killers	Aliens	Killer	Boss Neighbor
Secondary Characters	Townfolk Indians	Technicians in Spacecraft	Cops Underworld	Kids Dogs
Plot	Restore law and order	Repel aliens	Find killer	Solve problem
Theme	Justice	Triumph of humanity	Pursuit and discovery	Chaos and confusion
Costume	Cowboy hat, boots, etc.	High-tech uniforms	Raincoat	Regular clothes
Locomotion	Horse	Spaceship	Beat-up car	Station wagon
Weaponry	Sixgun Rifle	Rayguns	Pistol Fists	Insults

Source: Arthur A. Berger, *Signs in Contemporary Culture: An Introduction to Semiotics* (New York: Longman, 1984), 86.

the beauty with which it performs some function (e.g., a ceramic ashtray or hand-carved fishing lures). A piece of art is original, subtle, and valuable, and is associated with the elite of society. A craft tends to follow a formula that permits rapid production and makes it easier to understand. According to this framework, elite culture is produced in a purely aesthetic context and is judged by reference to recognized classics. It is high culture—"serious art."[49]

CULTURAL FORMULAE   Mass culture, in contrast, churns out products specifically for a mass market. These products aim to please the average taste of an undifferentiated audience and are predictable because they follow certain patterns. As illustrated in Table 17-2, popular art forms such as detective stories or science fiction, generally follow a **cultural formula** where certain roles and props often occur consistently.[50] Romance novels are an extreme case of a cultural formula. Computer programs allow users to "write" their own romances by systematically varying certain set elements of the story.

HIGH ART VERSUS LOW ART   The distinction between high and low culture is similar to the difference between sacred and profane worlds, as discussed in Chapter 16. However, the line between elite culture and popular culture, or between high art and low art, is not as clear as it may first appear.

In addition to the possible class bias that drives such a distinction (i.e., we assume that the rich have culture while the poor do not), high and low culture are blending together in interesting ways. Popular culture reflects the world around us; these phenomena touch rich and poor.[51] In Europe, advertising is widely appreciated as an art form. Advertising executives are often public figures in Great Britain. For over ten years Europeans have paid up to $30 to watch an all-night program in a movie theater consisting of nothing but television commercials.[52]

In a sense, all cultural products that are transmitted by mass media become a part of popular culture.[53] Classical recordings are marketed in much the same way as Top 40 albums, and museums use mass-marketing techniques to sell their wares. The Metropolitan Museum of Art even runs a satellite gift shop out of Macy's department store.

Art Sells.   The arts are big business. Americans alone spend more than $2 billion per year to attend arts events.[54] Marketers often incorporate high art imagery to promote products. They may sponsor artistic events to build public goodwill or feature works of art on shopping bags.[55] When observers from Toyota watched customers in luxury car showrooms, the company found that these consumers tended to view a car as an art object. This theme was then used in an ad for the Lexus with the caption: "Until now, the only fine arts we supported were sculpture, painting, and music."[56]

Different artistic styles can also be used to convey desired product images. Some ads deliberately employ well-known painting styles or artworks to imbue profane objects (i.e., products) with an aura of sophistication. For example, a French billboard for a brand of bleach manufactured by Colgate-Palmolive borrowed a famous painting by artist Edgar Degas' called "The Ironers;" a bottle of the bleach was substituted for a bottle of wine that appears in the original.

▲ MARKETING OPPORTUNITY

Creators of aesthetic products are increasingly adapting conventional marketing methods to fine-tune their mass market offerings. Market research is used, for example, to test audience reactions to movie concepts. Though testing cannot account for such intangibles as acting quality or cinematography, it can determine if the basic themes of the movie strike a responsive chord in the target audience. This type of research is most appropriate for blockbuster movies, which usually follow one of the formulae described above.

Ad themes were tested for the movie *The Hunt for Red October,* which dealt with a Soviet submarine commander trying to defect to the West. Surveys among the target audience of men over twenty-five showed they were largely uninterested in the political aspect of the movie, but liked the suspense. As a result, no hammers or sickles appeared in the movie ads, which played down the East/West angle.[57]

The content of movies themselves also can be influenced by consumer research. Typically, free invitations to pre-screenings are handed out in malls and movie theaters. Attendees are asked a few basic questions about the movie, then some are selected to participate in focus groups. Though groups' reactions usually result in only minor editing changes, occasionally more drastic effects result. When initial reaction to the ending of the movie *Fatal Attraction* was negative, Paramount Pictures spent an additional $1.3 million to shoot a new one.[58]

Even record companies are starting to get into the act. PolyGram Records has sent tapes of unreleased songs to active record buyers to obtain their input regarding which should be released as singles. Chrysalis Records went one

This French billboard demonstrates the adaptation of famous paintings ("high art") to sell products ("low art"). In this version of Edgar Degas' "The Ironers," a brand of bleach (made by Colgate-Palmolive) replaces a bottle of wine. Courtesy of Colgate Palmolive.

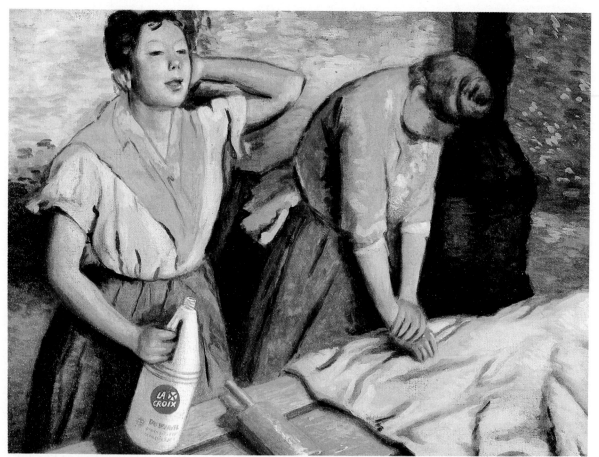

MADAME DEGAS DÉTACHE SON LINGE

1940. 'The Patriot' by the Emerson Radio Corporation.

1946. No longer manufactured.

1947. Out of date.

1953. Garaged.

1980. Garage Sale.

1981. Flea Market.

1983. Antique Show.

1984. Madison Avenue Gallery.

1989. The Metropolitan Museum of Art.

HG
HOUSE & GARDEN

Nothing endures but change.

This *House & Garden* ad illustrates the life cycle of an Emerson radio to illustrate how the value of a cultural product changes over time. The radio evolved from a basic, functional product when it was first manufactured to an outmoded antique and was finally enshrined in the Metropolitan Museum of Art. Reprinted by permission of *HG Magazine* © 1989 CONDE NAST PUBLICATIONS INC.

step further. To pretest Jethro Tull's Crest of a Knave album in 1987, the company advertised for Tull fans in twenty cities. These consumers, most of whom were over thirty, rated the different cuts on the album and recommended the order in which they should appear. One tune was rated as unusually boisterous by these fans. This song became the first single released from the album, but it was deliberately targeted to younger listeners. The album went on to sell more than 500,000 copies.[59]

MARKETING AND REALITY

Television advertisers pay careful attention to the content of shows in which their ads appear. Professional screeners scrutinize programs to be sure that their contents do not conflict with the advertiser's message or product. Objections are made to general themes, such as sexual content, to counteract possible pressure from religious or other groups. In addition to such broad concerns as sexual content, even very subtle messages are monitored. For example, pizza companies do not like to advertise in shows where blood flows, since they feel it will cause viewers to make negative associations with tomato sauce. Similarly, drug companies avoid placing ads on any program where a character commits suicide by overdosing on sleeping pills.[60]

This commercial screening process illustrates that at times the line between marketing creations and reality seems to blur. While advertising, package design, and other aspects of marketing strategy clearly draw upon the influences of popular culture, does this influence work the other way as well?[61] To what degree is the world of popular culture shaped by the efforts of marketers? This book has stressed throughout the importance to consumer behavior of interactions between marketing activities and popular culture. By this point, it is (hopefully) clear that marketing strategies are affected by aspects of consumers' everyday existence. It is appropriate to conclude the book, then, by considering the opposite issue: to what degree are consumers' perceptions of reality affected by marketers?

MARKETING AND CULTURAL PRODUCTS

Marketing sometimes seem to exert a "self-fulfilling prophecy" on popular culture. As commercial influences on popular culture increase, marketer-created symbols make their way into our daily lives to a greater degree. Historical analyses of Broadway plays, bestselling novels, and the lyrics of hit songs, for example, clearly show large increases in the use of brand names over time.[62]

Members of culture production systems create and transmit images of an imaginary world, which then may become reality as consumers scramble to acquire the products that will help them to attain the life-style depicted in that fantasy environment. The nebulous relationship between marketing imagination and reality is clearly illustrated by the designer Ralph Lauren, who provides consumers with a reality of his own invention. Though he was born to a Bronx family of modest means (and originally named Ralph Lifshitz), Lauren brilliantly paints a picture in his advertising of a romantic, moneyed world that can be made available to anyone with sufficient funds—regardless of breeding (see Chapter 12). When Lauren develops ideas for a new line of clothing or home furnishings, he starts by creating a "plan" containing fictional people and life-styles. His creative team then goes about developing "costuming" for this plan.[63]

PRODUCT PLACEMENT   In many cases the appearance of specific products or the use of brand names in scripts is no accident. More than thirty companies in the United States specialize in **product placement.** Their job is to get exposure for a product by inserting it into a movie or a television show. This practice has become so common that 20 percent of consumers report they actively look for brands in movies.[64]

Some critics argue that the practice of product placement has gotten out of hand: shows are created with the purpose of marketing products rather than for their entertainment value. Some children's shows have been berated for essentially being extended commercials for a toy. One major film company recently sent a letter to large consumer products companies to solicit product placements for an upcoming movie production, and even provided a fee scale: $20,000 for the product to be seen in the movie, $40,000 for an actor to mention the product by name, and $60,000 for the actor to actually use the product.[65]

The movie *Rocky IV* clearly showed products by Panasonic, Sony, and Lamborghini, while *Ghostbusters* featured Coca-Cola and *Desperately Seeking Susan* highlighted Polaroid. Perhaps the greatest product placement success story was Reese's Pieces; sales jumped by 65 percent after the candy appeared in the film *E.T.*[66]

Types of Product Placement. There are two basic types of product placement. *On-set placement* is straightforward. The product is incorporated into the actual film set, as when specific brands of food are the focus in a kitchen scene.[67] *Creative placement* involves finding ways to insert the brand into filming, as when it "happens" to appear on outdoor advertising or in a real commercial playing on a television in the background. This strategy also includes the use of "plugs," where brand mentions are made in the context of news shows or other programming. The charts in Figure 17-5 provide further detail about where and when these plugs tend to occur.

SEEING IS BELIEVING (?)

The mass media play a large role in consumer socialization and decision making.[68] People often engage in *para-social interaction* with television, where they actively relate to television characters and vicariously experience and evaluate the different lifestyles portrayed.[69] Children in particular display a strong belief in the reality of contrived photographic images.[70] If anything, confusion between reality and advertising should accelerate as media programming and advertising come to resemble each other more and more. For example, marketers targeting youth have been strongly affected by the techniques used to make music videos, such as quick cuts, and fast-paced musical accompaniment. As one MTV executive commented, "It's almost hard to tell one {video} from the other {commercials}."[71]

The blurring of marketing and reality is the issue behind current debates regarding distinctions between advertising and editorial content in media. "Advertorials," advertisements that are composed in heavy type to look like articles, frequently appear in magazines and can account for up to 10 percent of a magazine's revenues.[72]

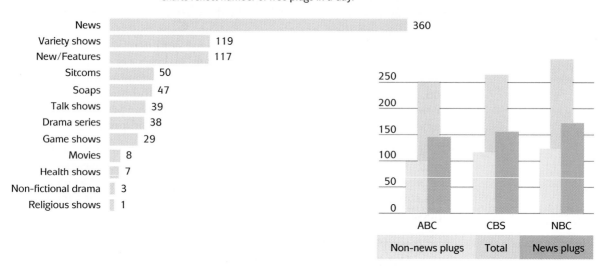

Where plugs occur on TV
There were 360 plugs on news programs during one 24-hour period, accounting for more than 40% of the day s total of 818. Charts reflect number of free plugs in a day.

News	360
Variety shows	119
New/Features	117
Sitcoms	50
Soaps	47
Talk shows	39
Drama series	38
Game shows	29
Movies	8
Health shows	7
Non-fictional drama	3
Religious shows	1

Non-news plugs | Total | News plugs

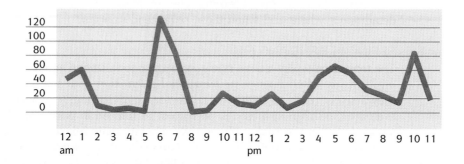

When plugs occur on TV
The greatest number of free advertising mentions of products and brands comes during early-morning news programming. Chart reflects number of free plugs in a day.

Figure 17-5 Product Plugs on TV Reprinted with permission from Advertising Age, Jan. 29, 1990, p. 6.

Some companies have even come under fire for designing highly visible cause-marketing campaigns. When the Quaker Oats Company announced plans to sponsor a series of public service announcements on behalf of the American Medical Association, some broadcasters refused to run the spots because the commercials featured company spokesman Wilford Brimley and their release was tied to Quaker's upcoming media plan.[73]

THE CULTIVATION EFFECT   These images appear to significantly influence consumers' perceptions of reality, affecting viewers' notions about such issues as dating behavior, racial stereotypes, and occupational status.[74] Studies of the **cultivation hypothesis,** which relates to media's ability to distort consumers' perceptions of reality, have shown that heavy television viewers tend to overestimate the degree of affluence in the country, and these effects also extend to such areas as perceptions of the amount of violence in one's culture.[75]

As consumers increasingly rely on mass-produced imagery as a window onto the "real world," they come to accept what they are seeing as real. As the boundaries between marketing and reality continue to blur, we hope future marketers will consider this when they make their own contributions to this ubiquitous consumption imagery.

CHAPTER SUMMARY

This chapter examines dynamics of consumer behavior at the very broad, cultural level. Products are viewed in the context of systems of meaning, produced by a wide variety of cultural specialists. These specialists are components of culture production systems; large-scale enterprises that combine to create, produce, and communicate the many symbolic alternatives available to modern consumers. These alternatives take the form of both tangible products and intangible experiences and aesthetic events. Marketing's role in the creation of elite, high culture and popular culture is considered here as well.

All ideas, products, and aesthetic experiences must circulate through a population to be successful. The diffusion of innovation process is described, including characteristics of innovations that make them more or less likely to be adopted and differences among consumers that affect their likelihood of adopting them.

The chapter examines some instances of cultural diffusion, especially in terms of the Westernization of global culture.

The remainder of the chapter considers the phenomenon of fashion, an important form of symbolic diffusion. Dynamics of the fashion system are discussed, especially as these relate to the production of popular culture. This section also examines the interchange between marketing systems and popular culture. Diverse approaches from the social sciences that affect the spread of fashion are summarized. These perspectives are drawn from sociology (e.g., the trickle-down theory), economics (e.g., demand models and conspicuous consumption) and psychology (e.g., need for uniqueness or sexuality). The chapter considers differences in fashion cycles, as exemplified by fads and classics, and concludes by discussing marketing's role in creating vehicles of popular culture.

KEY TERMS

Art product	Diffusion
Classic	Fad
Craft product	Fashion life cycle
Cultivation hypothesis	Fashion system
Cultural categories	Innovations
Cultural formula	Product placement
Culture production system (CPS)	Trickle-down theory of fashion

1. What is a culture production system, and what are its components? Diagram an example of a CPS for the publishing industry.
2. Innovators are a small minority of consumers, yet marketers are very interested in identifying and reaching them. Why? How might you go about locating innovators?
3. People who shop at trendy department stores often pride themselves on being innovators. Are they really? Why or why not?
4. Provide an example of a discontinuous innovation currently vying for adoption. What are the factors working for and against its eventual success in the marketplace?
5. The chapter argues that the United States is a net exporter of popular culture. Do you agree? What are some of the marketing ramifications of this demand for Western culture by other countries? Do you believe this influence is positive or negative?
6. The book states that fashion is like a language. How is it similar, and how is it different?
7. Define and provide an example of a cultural principle.
8. Some consumers complain that they are "at the mercy" of designers: they are forced to buy whatever styles are in fashion, because nothing else is available. Do you agree that there is such a thing as a "designer conspiracy?"
9. Describe the trickle-down theory of fashion change, and try to locate historical examples of this phenomenon. What are some of the factors that reduce its explanatory power in today's market?
10. What is the basic difference between a fad, a fashion, and a classic? Provide examples of each.
11. What is the difference between an art and a craft? Where would you characterize advertising within this framework?
12. The chapter mentions some instances where market research findings influenced artistic decisions, as when a movie ending was reshot to accommodate consumers' preferences. Many people would most likely oppose this use of consumer research, claiming that books, movies, records, or other artistic endeavors should not be designed to merely conform to what people want to read, see, or hear. What do you think?
13. Commercial messages increasingly are being structured to resemble editorial comments or regular programming. Is this a wise strategy? What, if any, ethical problems do you see arising from this trend?

1. Identify a product or style that was recently introduced into your social environment. Construct a history of the diffusion of this product. What types of people used it first? What types of people do not use it at all? What characteristics of the product or style probably contributed to its eventual success or failure?
2. Obtain some periodicals from Asian or Third World countries, and analyze them in terms of American or European influences. Collect ads for brands also found in the West. Do these ads differ from those used domestically for the same product? To what degree is the brand's Western origins used as a selling point?
3. The chapter notes that dominant cultural principles are manifested in a variety of products. Identify a set of products and/or styles that are cur-

rently considered to be "in" (hint: newspapers often publish lists of "what's hot and what's not" at year's end). Based on this list, can you find any evidence of common cultural principles being reflected in different categories? How might you use these insights to design a product in yet another category?

4. Observe people in the process of watching television. Can you find any evidence of para-social interaction?

NOTES

1. Quoted in Bill Barol, "Anatomy of a Fad," *Newsweek* (Special Issue on Teens) (1990): 41.
2. Richard A. Peterson, "The Production of Culture: A Prolegomenon," in *The Production of Culture,* ed. Richard A. Peterson (Sage Contemporary Social Science Issues (Beverly Hills: Sage 1976)33: 7–22.
3. Richard A. Peterson and D. G. Berger, "Entrepreneurship in Organizations: Evidence from the Popular Music Industry," *Administrative Science Quarterly* 16 (1971): 97–107.
4. Elizabeth C. Hirschman, "Resource Exchange in the Production and Distribution of a Motion Picture," *Empirical Studies of the Arts* 8 (1990)1: 31–51; Michael R. Solomon, "Building Up and Breaking Down: The Impact of Cultural Sorting on Symbolic Consumption," in *Research in Consumer Behavior,* ed. J. Sheth and E. C. Hirschman (Greenwich, Conn.: JAI Press, 1988): 325–51.
5. Edmund L. Andrews, "When Imitation Isn't the Sincerest Form of Flattery," *New York Times* (August 9, 1990): 20.
6. Eric J. Arnould, "Toward a Broadened Theory of Preference Formation and the Diffusion of Innovations: Cases from Zinder Province, Niger Republic," *Journal of Consumer Research* 16 (September 1989): 239–67; Susan B. Kaiser, *The Social Psychology of Clothing* (New York: Macmillan, 1985); Thomas S. Robertson, *Innovative Behavior and Communication* (New York: Holt, Rinehart and Winston, 1971); Everett M. Rogers, *Diffusion of Innovations,* 3rd ed. (New York: The Free Press, 1983).
7. Susan L. Holak, Donald R. Lehmann, and Fareena Sultan, "The Role of Expectations in the Adoption of Innovative Consumer Durables: Some Preliminary Evidence," *Journal of Retailing* 63 (Fall 1987): 243–59.
8. Hubert Gatignon and Thomas S. Robertson, "A Propositional Inventory for New Diffusion Research," *Journal of Consumer Research* 11 (March 1985): 849–67.
9. Elizabeth C. Hirschman, "Symbolism and Technology as Sources of the Generation of Innovations," in *Advances in Consumer Behavior,* ed. Andrew Mitchell (Provo, Utah: Association for Consumer Research, 1981)9: 537–41.
10. Rogers, *Diffusion of Innovations.*
11. Examples adapted from Russell W. Belk, "Third World Consumer Culture," *Research in Marketing* (Greenwich, Conn.: JAI Press, 1988): 103–27.
12. Randall Rothenberg, "Marketing with Images of Glasnost," *New York Times* (December 27, 1989): D15.
13. John F. Sherry, Jr. and Eduardo G. Camargo, "'May Your Life be Marvelous': English Language Labeling and the Semiotics of Japanese Promotion," *Journal of Consumer Research* 14 (September 1987): 174–88.
14. Bill Bryson, "A Taste for Scrambled English," *New York Times* (July 22, 1990): 10.
15. Rose A. Horowitz, "California Beach Culture Rides Wave of Popularity in Japan," *Journal of Commerce* (August 3, 1989): 17; Elaine Lafferty, "American Casual Seizes Japan; Teenagers Go for N.F.L. Hats, Batman and the California Look," *Time* (November 13, 1989): 106.
16. Blayne Cutler, "Move Over, Miso," *American Demographics* (May 1988): 56.
17. Chin Tiong Tan and John U. Farley, "The Impact of Cultural Patterns on Cognition and Intention in Singapore," *Journal of Consumer Research* 13 (March 1987): 540–44.
18. Quoted in Sheryl WuDunn, "Cosmetics from the West Help to Change the Face of China," *New York Times* (May 6, 1990): 16.
19. Steven Greenhouse, "The Television Europeans Love, and Love to Hate," *New York Times* (August 13, 1989): 24.

20. Sherry and Camargo, "'May Your Life Be Marvelous?'"
21. James Brooke, "Brazil's Idol is a Blonde, and Some Ask 'Why?'" *New York Times* (July 31, 1990): A4.
22. Philip J. Hilts, "U.S. Tobacco Ads in Asia Faulted," *New York Times* (May 5, 1990): 35.
23. Umberto Eco, *A Theory of Semiotics* (Bloomington, Ind.: Indiana University Press, 1979).
24. Fred Davis, "Clothing and Fashion as Communication," in *The Psychology of Fashion,* ed. Michael R. Solomon (Lexington, Mass.: Lexington Books, 1985): 15–28.
25. Melanie Wallendorf, "The Formation of Aesthetic Criteria Through Social Structures and Social Institutions," in *Advances in Consumer Research,* ed. Jerry C. Olson (Ann Arbor, Mich.: Association for Consumer Research, 1980)7: 3–6.
26. Grant McCracken, "Culture and Consumption: A Theoretical Account of the Structure and Movement of the Cultural Meaning of Consumer Goods," *Journal of Consumer Research,* 13 (June 1986): 71–84.
27. "The Eternal Triangle," *Art in America* (February 1989): 23.
28. Alison Lurie, *The Language of Clothes* (New York: Random House, 1981).
29. Herbert Blumer, *Symbolic Interactionism: Perspective and Method* (Englewood Cliffs, N.J.: Prentice Hall, 1969); Howard S. Becker, "Art as Collective Action," *American Sociological Review* 39 (December 1973); Richard A. Peterson, "Revitalizing the Culture Concept," *Annual Review of Sociology* 5 (1979): 137–66.
30. Blumer, *Symbolic Interactionism.*
31. Blumer, *Symbolic Interactionism.*
32. Kaiser, *The Social Psychology of Clothing.*
33. Anastasia Toufexis, "A Rousing No to Mini-pulation; American Women Send Designers Back to the Drawing Board," *Time* (April 25, 1988): 91.
34. For more details, see Susan B. Kaiser, *The Social Psychology of Clothing* (New York: Macmillan, 1985); George B. Sproles, "Behavioral Science Theories of Fashion," in *The Psychology of Fashion,* ed. Michael R. Solomon (Lexington, Mass.: Lexington Books, 1985): 55–70.
35. C. R. Snyder and Howard L. Fromkin, *Uniqueness: The Human Pursuit of Difference* (New York: Plenum Press, 1980).
36. Lurie, *The Language of Clothes.*
37. James Laver, *Modesty in Dress: An Inquiry into the Fundamentals of Fashion* (New York: Houghton Mifflin, 1969); Lurie, *The Language of Clothes.*
38. Harvey Leibenstein, *Beyond Economic Man: A New Foundation for Microeconomics* (Cambridge, Mass.: Harvard University Press, 1976).
39. Georg Simmel, "Fashion," *International Quarterly* 10 (1904): 130–55.
40. Grant D. McCracken, "The Trickle-Down Theory Rehabilitated," in *The Psychology of Fashion,* ed. Michael R. Solomon (Lexington, Mass.: Lexington Books, 1985): 39–54.
41. Charles W. King, "Fashion Adoption: A Rebuttal to the 'Trickle-Down' Theory," in *Toward Scientific Marketing,* ed. Stephen A. Greyser (Chicago: American Marketing Association, 1963), 108–25.
42. Alf H. Walle, "Grassroots Innovation," *Marketing Insights* (Summer 1990): 44–51.
43. "Cabbage-Hatched Plot Sucks in 24 Doll Fans," *New York Daily News* (December 1, 1983).
44. "Turtlemania," *The Economist* (April 21, 1990): 32.
45. Anthony Ramirez, "The Pedestrian Sneaker Makes a Comeback," *New York Times* (October 14, 1990): F17.
46. Dennis Hevesi, "Pursuing the Inspired and the Silly at Fad Fair III," *New York Times* (November 13, 1987): B1.
47. B. E. Aguirre, E. L. Quarantelli, and Jorge L. Mendoza, "The Collective Behavior of Fads: The Characteristics, Effects, and Career of Streaking," *American Sociological Review* (August 1989): 569.
48. Howard S. Becker, "Arts and Crafts," *American Journal of Sociology* 83 (January 1987): 862–89.
49. Herbert J. Gans, "Popular Culture in America: Social Problem in a Mass Society or Social Asset in a Pluralist Society?" in *Social Problems: A Modern Approach,* ed. Howard S. Becker (New York: Wiley, 1966).
50. Arthur A. Berger, *Signs in Contemporary Culture: An Introduction to Semiotics* (New York: Longman, 1984).

51. Ray B. Browne, "Popular Culture: The World Around Us," in *The Popular Culture Reader,* ed. Jack Nachbar, Deborah Weiser, and John L. Wright (Bowling Green, Ohio: Bowling Green University Popular Press, 1978): 12–17.
52. Peter S. Green, "Moviegoers Devour Ads," *Advertising Age* (June 26, 1989): 36.
53. Michael R. Real, *Mass-Mediated Culture* (Englewood Cliffs, N.J.: Prentice-Hall, 1977).
54. John P. Robinson, "The Arts in America," *American Demographics* (September 1987): 42.
55. Annetta Miller, "Shopping Bags Imitate Art: Seen the Sacks? Now Visit the Museum Exhibit," *Newsweek* (January 23, 1989): 44.
56. Kim Foltz, "New Species for Study: Consumers in Action," *New York Times* (December 18, 1989): A1.
57. Randall Rothenberg, "Movie Promoters Adopting Modern Marketing Skills," *New York Times* (February 23, 1990): D1.
58. Helene Diamond, "Lights, Camera . . . Research!" *Marketing News* (September 11, 1989): 10.
59. Denise Topolnicki, "Do Marketers Control What We See?" *Psychology Today* (June 1989): 73.
60. Bill Carter, "Screeners Help Advertisers Avoid Prime-Time Trouble," *New York Times* (January 29, 1990): D1.
61. See Morris B. Holbrook, "Mirror, Mirror, on the Wall, What's Unfair About Advertising?" *Journal of Marketing* 51 (July 1987): 95–103; Richard W. Pollay, "The Distorted Mirror: Reflections on the Unintended Consequences of Advertising," *Journal of Marketing* 50 (April 1986): 18–36.
62. Monroe Friedman, "The Changing Language of a Consumer Society: Brand Name Usage in Popular American Novels in the Postwar Era," *Journal of Consumer Research* 11 (March 1985): 927–37; Monroe Friedman, "Commercial Influences in the Lyrics of Popular American Music of the Postwar Era," *Journal of Consumer Affairs* 20 (Winter 1986): 193.
63. "A Dream World Labeled Lauren," *Marketing Insights* (June 1989): 91.
64. Betty Sharkey, "Moviegoer Study Finds 20% Look for Brand Names," *Adweek's Marketing Week* (August 29, 1988): 27.
65. Randall Rothenberg, "Is it a Film? Is it an Ad? Harder to Tell?" *New York Times* (March 13, 1990): D23.
66. Benjamin M. Cole, "Products That Want to Be In Pictures," *Los Angeles Herald Examiner* (March 5, 1985): 36.
67. Brian Oliver, "The Latest Screen Stars," *Marketing* (March 1986): 12.
68. See Russell W. Belk and Richard Pollay, "Images of Ourselves: The Good Life in Twentieth Century Advertising," *Journal of Consumer Research* 11 (1985): 887–98; Irving Janis, "The Influence of Television on Personal Decision Making," in *Television and Social Behavior: Beyond Violence and Children,* ed. S. Whitney and R. Abels (Hillsdale: Lawrence Erlbaum, 1980): 161–89; Roy Moore and George Moschis, "The Effects of Family Communication and Mass Media Use on Adolescents' Consumer Learning," *Journal of Communication* 31 (1981): 42–51; Thomas C. O'Guinn and Ronald J. Faber, "Mass Mediated Consumer Socialization: Non-Utilitarian and Dysfunctional Outcomes," in *Advances in Consumer Research,* ed. Melanie Wallendorf and Paul Anderson (Ann Arbor, Mich.: Association for Consumer Research, 1987)14: 473–77.
69. Donald Horton and R. Richard Wohl, "Mass Communication and Para-Social Interaction," in *Drama in Life: The Uses of Communication in Society,* ed. J. Combs and M. Mansfield (New York: Hasting House, 1956), 212–78.
70. Paul Messaris and Larry Gross, "Interpretations of a Photographic Narrative by Viewers in Four Age Groups," *Studies in the Anthropology of Visual Communication* 4 (1974): 99–111.
71. Quoted in Jennifer Pendleton, "Chalk Up Another Victory for Trend-Setting Rock 'N' Roll," *Advertising Age* (November 9, 1988): 160.
72. Jonathan Alter, "The Era of the Big Blur," *Newsweek* (May 22, 1989): 73.
73. Julie Liesse, "Line Between Public Service, Paid Ads Blurs," *Advertising Age* (October 8, 1990): 28.

74. George Gerbner, Larry Gross, Nancy Signorielli and Michael Morgan, "Aging with Television: Images on Television Drama and Conceptions of Social Reality," *Journal of Communication* 30 (1980): 37–47.

75. Stephen Fox and William Philber, "Television Viewing and the Perception of Affluence," *Sociological Quarterly* 19 (1978): 103–12; W. James Potter, "Three Strategies for Elaborating the Cultivation Hypothesis," *Journalism Quarterly* 65 (Winter 1988): 930–39; Gabriel Weimann, "Images of Life in America: The Impact of American T.V. in Israel," *International Journal of Intercultural Relations* 8 1984): 185–97.

Glossary

Absolute threshold the minimum amount of stimulation that can be detected on a sensory channel.(**43**)

Acculturation the degree to which a consumer has learned the ways of a different culture from the one he or she was originally raised in.(**428**)

Acculturation the process of learning the beliefs and behaviors endorsed by another culture.(**480**)

Activation models of memory approaches to memory stressing that depending upon the nature of the processing task, different levels of processing occur that activate some aspects of memory rather than others.(**115**)

Adaptation occurs when a sensation becomes so familiar that it is no longer the focus of attention.(**50**)

Addiction a physiological and/or psychological dependency on products or services.(**537**)

Advertising clutter occurs when too many messages compete for consumers' attention in the same place or medium.(**48**)

Affect the way a consumer feels about an attitude object.(**134**)

Affinity marketing a strategy that allows a consumer to emphasize his or her identification with some organization (e.g., when organizations issue credit cards with their names on them)(**359**)

Age cohort consumers of the same approximate age who have undergone similar experiences.(**446**)

AIOs Activities, Interests, and Opinions—variables used by researchers in grouping consumers.(**498**)

Androgyny the possession of both masculine and feminine traits.(**217**)

Anti-consumption actions taken by consumers involving the deliberate defacement or mutilation of products.(**541**)

Art product a creation viewed primarily as an object of aesthetic contemplation without any functional value.(**567**)

Atmospherics the use of space and physical features in store design to evoke certain effects in buyers.(**316**)

Attention the assignment of cognitive capacity to selected stimuli.(**50**)

Attitude a lasting, general evaluation of people (including oneself), objects, or issues.(**134**)

Attitude object (A_o) anything toward which one has an attitude.(**134**)

Attitude toward the advertisement (A_{ad}) a predisposition to respond in a favorable or unfavorable manner to a particular advertising stimulus during a particular exposure occasion.(**139**)

Autocratic decisions purchase decisions made almost exclusively by one or the other spouse.(**287**)

Baby boomers people born between the years of 1946 and 1964, a cohort that is the source of many important cultural and economic changes.(**452**)

Balance theory a theory that considers relations among elements a person might perceive as belonging together, and people's tendency to change relations among elements in order to make them consistent or "balanced."(**144**)

Behavior a consumer's actions or intentions with regard to an attitude object.(**134**)

Behavioral influence perspective stresses that consumer decisions are learned responses to environmental cues.(**242**)

Behavioral learning theories perspectives on learning that assume that learning takes place as the result of responses to external events.(**100**)

Binary oppositions sets of converse principles used by a culture to define meanings (e.g., nature versus technology).(**519**)

Body cathexis a person's feelings about aspects of his or her body.(**224**)

Body image a consumer's subjective evaluation of his or her physical self. (**224**)

Brand loyalty a pattern of repeat product purchases, accompanied by an underlying positive attitude toward the brand.(**265**)

Buyclass theory of purchasing a classification scheme that uses three decision-making dimensions to describe the purchasing strategies of an organizational buyer: (1) level of information search needed, (2) the seriousness with which all possible alternatives must be considered, and (3) the degree to which the buyer is familiar with the purchase task.(**278**)

Classic a fashion with an extremely long acceptance cycle.(**565**)

Classical conditioning learning that occurs when a stimulus eliciting a response is paired with another stimulus that initially does not elicit a response on its own. Over time, this stimulus also causes a similar response because of its association with the first stimulus.(**101**)

Closure the gestalt principle that describes a person's tendency to supply missing information in order to perceive a holistic image.(**55**)

Cognition the beliefs a consumer has about an attitude object.(**134**)

Cognitive development the ability to comprehend concepts of increasing complexity as a person ages.(**297**)

Cognitive dissonance a state of tension created when beliefs or behaviors conflict with one another. People are motivated to reduce this inconsistency (or dissonance) and thus eliminate unpleasant tension.(**75**)

Cognitive learning learning that occurs as a result of internal mental processes. This perspective views people as problem solvers who actively use information from the world around them to master their environment.(**105**)

Cognitive structure a set of beliefs about products and the way these beliefs are mentally organized by a consumer.(**255**)

Collectivism a cultural orientation that encourages people to subordinate their personal goals to those of a stable in-group. Values such as self-discipline and group accomplishment are stressed.(**479**)

Communications model this framework specifies that a number of elements are necessary for communication to be achieved, including a source, message, medium, receivers, and feedback.(**167**)

Comparative advertising a strategy where a message compares two or more specifically named or recognizably presented brands and makes a comparison of them in terms of one or more specific attributes.(**178**)

Comparative influence the process whereby a reference group influences decisions about specific brands or activities.(**354**)

Compensatory decision rules information about attributes of competing products is averaged in some way; poor standing on one attribute can potentially be offset by good standing on another.(**259**)

Compulsive consumption repetitive shopping, often excessive, used to relieve tension, anxiety, depression, or boredom.(**538**)

Congruity theory a consistency theory that specifically addresses how attitudes are affected when a person is linked to an object.(**147**)

Conspicuous consumption the purchase and prominent display of luxury goods to provide evidence of a consumer's ability to afford them.**(405)**

Consumed consumers people who are used or exploited, whether willingly or not, for commercial gain in the marketplace.**(538)**

Consumer behavior those processes involved when individuals or groups select, purchase, use, or dispose of products, services, ideas, or experiences to satisfy needs and desires.**(4)**

Consumer satisfaction or dissatisfaction (CS/D) the overall attitude a person has about a product after it has been purchased.**(330)**

Consumer socialization the process by which people acquire skills that enable them to function in the marketplace.**(294)**

Consumption constellations a set of products and activities used by consumers to define, communicate, and perform social roles.**(495)**

Core values a set of important values that seem to define a specific culture.**(487)**

Craft product a creation valued because of the beauty with which it performs some function. This type of product tends to follow a formula that permits rapid production and makes it easier to understand.**(567)**

Cultivation hypothesis relates to media's ability to distort consumers' perceptions of reality.**(575)**

Cultivation theory the media teaches people about a culture's values and myths. The more a consumer is exposed to mass media, the more he or she will accept the images depicted there as accurate portrayals of the real world.**(295)**

Cultural categories groupings that reflect the basic ways members of a society characterize the world (e.g., play versus work).**(558)**

Cultural formula a sequence of media events where certain roles and props tend to occur consistently.**(568)**

Culture production system (CPS) the set of individuals and organizations responsible for creating and marketing a cultural product.**(551)**

Culture the values, ethics, rituals, traditions, material objects, and services produced or valued by the members of a society.**(478)**

De-ethnicitization the process where a product formerly associated with a specific ethnic group is detached from its roots and marketed to other subcultures.**(418)**

Decay structural changes in the brain produced by learning decrease resulting in loss of memory.**(121)**

Decision polarization following group discussion of alternatives, individuals' choices tend to become more extreme (polarized), in either a conservative or risky direction.**(366)**

Deindividuation a process where individual identities get submerged within a group, reducing inhibitions against socially inappropriate behavior.**(365)**

Demographics observable measurements of a population's characteristics (e.g., birth rate, age distribution, income).**(279)**

Desacralization the process that occurs when a sacred item or symbol is removed from its special place, or is duplicated in mass quantities, and becomes profane as a result.**(524)**

Determinant attributes those product features that significantly influence the consumer's choices among alternatives.**(7)**

Differential threshold the ability of a sensory system to detect changes or differences among stimuli.**(44)**

Diffusion the process whereby a new product, service, or idea spreads through a population.**(551)**

Drive the desire to satisfy a biological need in order to reduce physiological arousal.**(66)**

Ego involvement the importance of a product to a consumer's self-concept.**(70)**

Ego the system that mediates between the id and the superego.**(79)**

Elaboration likelihood model (ELM) depending upon the personal relevance of a message, one of two routes to persuasion (central versus peripheral) will be followed. The route taken determines the relative importance of message contents versus other characteristics, such as source attractiveness.(187)

Embeds tiny figures inserted into magazine advertising by use of high-speed photography or airbrushing. These hidden figures, usually of a sexual nature, supposedly exert strong but unconscious influences on innocent readers.(45)

Emic perspective an approach to studying cultures that stresses the unique aspects of each culture.(483)

Encoding information is entered from short-term memory into long-term memory in a recognizable form.(112)

Enculturation the process of learning the beliefs and behaviors endorsed by one's native culture.(480)

Ethnocentrism the belief in the superiority of one's own cultural practices and products.(481)

Ethnography: an in-depth study of a group's behaviors, social rules, and beliefs, as performed in its natural environment.(21)

Ethos a set of moral, aesthetic, and evaluative principles.(478)

Etic perspective an approach to studying cultures that stresses commonalities across cultures.(483)

Evaluative criteria the dimensions used by consumers to compare competing product alternatives.(259)

Evoked set those products already in memory plus those prominent in the retail environment that are actively considered during a consumer's choice process.(254)

Exchange the process whereby two or more organizations or people give and receive something of value.(4)

Expectancy disconfirmation model consumers form beliefs about product performance based upon prior experience with the product and/or communications about the product that imply a certain level of quality. Their actual satisfaction will depend on the degree to which performance is consistent with these expectations.(337)

Expectancy theory theory that suggests behavior is largely "pulled" by expectations of achieving desirable outcomes, or positive incentives, rather than "pushed" from within.(68)

Experience changes that occur as the result of acquiring stimulation.(48)

Experiential paradigm a research perspective that stresses the subjective, non-rational aspects of consumption.(16)

Experiential perspective stresses the **gestalt** or totality of the product or service experience, focusing on consumers' affective responses in the marketplace.(242)

Exposure an initial stage of perception where some sensations come within range of consumers' sensory receptors.(48)

Extended family a traditional family structure where several generations live together.(279)

Extended problem solving an elaborate decision-making process, often initiated by a motive that is fairly central to the self-concept and accompanied by perceived risk. The consumer tries to collect as much information as possible, and carefully weighs product alternatives.(243)

Extended self external objects that are used to define the self.(213)

Fad a very short-lived fashion.(566)

Family household a living unit containing at least two people who are related by blood or marriage.(279)

Family life cycle a classification scheme that segments consumers in terms of changes in income and family composition and the changes in demands placed upon this income.(286)

Fantasy a self-induced shift in consciousness, often focusing on some unattainable or improbable goal. Sometimes fantasy is a way of compensating for a lack of external stimulation or for dissatisfaction with the actual self.(205)

Fashion life cycle similar to a product life cycle, it describes the "career" of a fashion as it progress from introduction to obsolescence.(564)

Fashion system those people and organizations involved in creating symbolic meanings and transferring these meanings to cultural goods.(558)

Figure-ground relationship the gestalt principle whereby one part of a stimulus configuration dominates a situation while other aspects recede into the background.(**56**)

Focus groups a qualitative research technique that gathers information from group interaction that is focused on a series of topics introduced by a discussion leader or moderator.(**83**)

Fraudulent symbols symbols, once associated with a specific social class, that diffuse through society and lose their original meaning and value.(**407**)

Functional theory of attitudes focuses on how attitudes facilitate social behavior. According to this pragmatic approach, attitudes exist because they serve some function for the person.(**166**)

Geodemographic techniques that combine consumer demographic information with geographic consumption patterns to permit precise targeting of consumers with specific characteristics.(**467**)

Gestalt psychology a school of thought that maintains people derive meaning from the totality of a set of stimuli, rather than from any individual stimulus.(**55**)

Gift-giving ritual the events involved in the presentation and acceptance of a gift.(**531**)

Goal a consumer's desired end state.(**66**)

Habitual decision making choices made out of habit, without additional information search or deliberation among products.(**243**)

Heuristics mental rules of thumb that lead to a speedy decision.(**261**)

Hierarchy of effects a fixed sequence of steps that occurs during attitude formation. This sequence varies depending upon such factors as the consumer's level of involvement with the attitude object.(**135**)

Homeostasis state of being where the body is in physiological balance. Goal-oriented behavior attempts to reduce or eliminate an unpleasant motivational state and return to a balanced one.(**68**)

Id the system oriented toward immediate gratification.(**79**)

Ideal of beauty a model, or exemplar, of appearance valued by a culture.(**224**)

Impulse buying occurs when the consumer experiences a sudden urge to purchase an item that he or she cannot resist.(**317**)

Individualism a cultural orientation that encourages peoples to attach more importance to personal goals than to group goals. Values such as personal enjoyment and freedom are stressed.(**479**)

Inertia consumption at the low end of involvement, where decisions are made out of habit because the consumer lacks the motivation to consider alternatives.(**69, 265**)

Information search a consumer searches for appropriate information to make a reasonable decision.(**247**)

Information-processing paradigm a research perspective that views consumers as rational decision-makers.(**15**)

Informational social influence conformity that occurs because the group's behavior is taken as evidence about reality.(**363**)

Innovation a product or style perceived as new by consumers.(**551**)

Instrumental values goals that are endorsed because they are needed to achieve desired end states (terminal values).(**488**)

Interference as additional information is learned, it displaces the earlier information, resulting in memory loss for the item learned previously.(**122**)

Interpretation the process whereby meanings are assigned to stimuli.(**54**)

Interpretivism: a research perspective that produces a "thick description" of consumers' subjective experiences and stresses the importance of the individual's social construction of reality.(**16**)

Involvement the motivation to process product-related information.(**68**)

JND (just noticeable difference) the minimum change in a stimulus that can be detected by a perceiver.(**44**)

Lateral cycling a process where already-purchased objects are sold to others or exchanged for other items.**(338)**

Learning a relatively permanent change in a behavior caused by experience.**(100)**

Life-style a set of shared values or tastes exhibited by a group of consumers, especially as these are reflected in consumption patterns.**(492)**

Limited problem solving consumers are not motivated to search for information or to rigorously evaluate each alternative. They instead use simple decision rules to arrive at a purchase decision.**(243)**

Long-term memory the system that allows us to retain information for a long period of time.**(115)**

Market beliefs specific beliefs or decision rules pertaining to marketplace phenomena.**(262)**

Marketing mix the combination of variables over which marketers have control. These factors are often known as the "Four P's"—product, place, price, and promotion.**(7)**

Materialism the importance consumers attach to worldly possessions.**(490)**

Means-end chain model an approach to studying values, this technique assumes that very specific product attributes are linked at levels of increasing abstraction to terminal values.**(488)**

Memory a process of acquiring information and storing it over time so that it will be available when needed.**(112)**

Motivation an internal state that activates goal-oriented behavior.**(66)**

Motivational research a qualitative research approach, based on psychoanalytic (Freudian) interpretations, with a heavy emphasis on unconscious motives for consumption.**(81)**

Multi-attribute attitude models an attitude model that assumes that a consumer's attitude (evaluation) of an attitude object will depend on the beliefs he or she has about several or many attributes of the object. The use of a multi-attribute model implies that an attitude toward a product or brand can be predicted by identifying these specific beliefs and combining them to derive a measure of the consumer's overall attitude.**(150)**

Myth a story containing symbolic elements that expresses the shared emotions and ideals of a culture.**(518)**

National character a distinctive set of behavior and personality characteristics that describe a country's people or culture.**(483)**

Negative reinforcement the environment weakens responses to stimuli so that inappropriate behavior is avoided.**(104)**

New-collar workers a segment of consumers, primarily twenty-one to forty years old, who occupy a gray area between professional and blue collar jobs. These people tend to hold many traditional values but are also receptive to new values and lifestyles.**(454)**

Noncompensatory decision rules simple rules used to evaluate competing alternatives; a brand with a low standing on one relevant attribute is eliminated from the consumer's choice set.**(259)**

Normative influence when a reference group helps to set and enforce fundamental standards of conduct.**(354)**

Normative social influence conformity that occurs when a person alters his or her behavior to meet the expectations of a person or group.**(363)**

Norms rules dictating what is right or wrong.**(362, 480)**

Nuclear family A contemporary living arrangement composed of a married couple and their children.**(279)**

Observational learning occurs when people watch the actions of others and note the reinforcements they receive for their behaviors.**(106)**

Operant conditioning occurs as the individual learns to perform behaviors that produce positive outcomes and to avoid those that yield negative outcomes.**(102)**

Opinion leaders people who are knowledgeable about products, and who are frequently able to influence others' attitudes or behaviors with regard to a product category.**(371)**

Parental yielding occurs when a parental decision maker is influenced by a child's product request.**(290)**

Parody display the deliberate avoidance of widely used status symbols; to seek status by mocking it.**(407)**

Perceived age how old a person feels rather than his or her chronological age.**(457)**

Perceived risk the belief that use of a product has potentially negative consequences, either physical or social.**(253)**

Perception the process by which stimuli are selected, organized, and interpreted.**(33)**

Personality a person's unique psychological makeup, which consistently influences the way a person responds to his or her environment.**(203)**

Persuasion an active attempt to change attitudes.**(165)**

Physical evidence the tangible cues associated with a service, used by consumers to infer service quality.**(323)**

Pleasure principle behavior is guided by the desire to maximize pleasure and avoid pain.**(79)**

Point of purchase stimuli (POP) promotional materials deployed in stores or other outlets to influence consumers' decisions at the time products are purchased.**(319)**

Positive reinforcement reward provided by the environment that strengthens responses to stimuli.**(104)**

Positivism: a research perspective that relies on principles of the"scientific method," and assumes that a single reality exists. Events in the world can be objectively measured, and the causes of behavior can be identified, manipulated, and predicted.**(16)**

Principle of cognitive consistency states that consumers value harmony among their thoughts, feelings, and behaviors, and they are motivated to maintain uniformity among these elements.**(141)**

Principle of similarity the Gestalt principle that describes how consumers tend to group objects that share similar physical characteristics.**(56)**

Problem recognition this occurs whenever the consumer sees a significant difference between his or her current state of affairs and some desired or ideal state. This recognition initiates the decision-making process.**(245)**

Product complementarity the symbolic meanings of products in different functional categories are related to one another.**(495)**

Product placement the process of obtaining exposure for a product by arranging for it to be inserted into a movie, television show, or some other medium.**(572)**

Profane objects and events that are ordinary or of the everyday world.**(523)**

Progressive learning model this perspective assumes that people gradually learn a new culture as they increasingly come in contact with it. Consumers who are assimilating into a new culture, mix practices from their old and new environments to create a hybrid culture.**(430)**

Projective techniques the presentation of an ambiguous, unstructured object, activity, or person to which the consumer responds in some way (e.g., explaining the object, telling a story about it, drawing a picture of it, etc.). Projectives are used when it is believed that a consumer will not or cannot respond meaningfully to direct questioning.**(85)**

Psychographics the use of psychological, sociological, and anthropological factors to construct market segments.**(497)**

Psychophysics the science that focuses on how the physical environment is integrated into the consumer's subjective experience.**(43)**

Rational perspective stresses the consumer as a careful, analytical decision maker who tries to maximize utility in purchase decisions.**(240)**

Reactance a"boomerang effect" that sometimes occurs when consumers are threatened with a loss of freedom of choice. They respond by doing the opposite of the behavior advocated in a persuasive message.**(368)**

Reality principle the ego seeks ways to gratify the id that will be acceptable to society.**(79)**

Reference group an actual or imaginary individual or group who has a significant effect upon an individual's evaluations, aspirations, or behavior.**(354)**

Relational marketing the strategic perspective that stresses the long-term, human side of buyer/seller interactions.**(322)**

Retrieval desired information is accessed from long-term memory.**(112)**

Rites of passage sacred times marked by a change in social status.**(535)**

Ritual artifacts items (e.g., consumer goods) used in the performance of rituals.**(529)**

Ritual a set of multiple, symbolic behaviors that occur in a fixed sequence and that tend to be repeated periodically.**(529)**

Sacralization a process that occurs when ordinary objects, events, or people take on sacred meaning to a culture or to specific groups within a culture.**(526)**

Sacred objects and events that are set apart from normal life and treated with some degree of respect or awe.**(523)**

Schema organized collections of beliefs and feelings represented in a cognitive category.**(33)**

Self-concept the attitude a person holds toward him- or herself.**(202)**

Self-gifts products or services bought by consumers for their own use as a reward or consolation.**(532)**

Self-image congruence models these models predict that products will be chosen when their attributes match some aspect of the self.**(212)**

Self-perception theory an alternative explanation of dissonance effects, it assumes that people use observations of their own behavior to infer their attitudes toward some object.**(143)**

Semiotics a field of study that examines the correspondence between a sign and the meaning or meanings it conveys.**(59)**

Sensation the immediate response of sensory receptors (i.e., eyes, ears, nose, mouth, fingers) to such basic stimuli as light, color, and sound.**(33)**

Sensory memory temporary storage of information received from the senses.**(114)**

Sex-typed traits characteristics that are stereotypically associated with one sex or the other.**(216)**

Shopping orientation a consumer's general attitudes and motivations regarding the act of shopping.**(313)**

Short-term memory the system that allows us to retain information for a short period of time.**(114)**

Single source data data including different aspects of consumption and demographic data for a common consumer segment.**(468)**

Sleeper effect refers to some instances where differences in attitude change caused by positive versus less positive sources seem to get erased over time.**(168)**

Social class the overall rank of people in a society. People who are grouped within the same social class are approximately equal in terms of their social standing, occupations, and lifestyles.**(386)**

Social comparison theory asserts that people compare their outcomes with others' as a way to increase the stability of their own self-evaluation, especially when physical evidence is unavailable.**(364)**

Social judgment theory assumes that people assimilate new information about attitude objects in light of what they already know or feel. The initial attitude acts as a frame of reference, and new information is categorized in terms of this standard.**(143)**

Social marketing the promotion of causes and ideas (social products), such as energy conservation, museums, and population control.**(190)**

Social mobility the movement of individuals from one social class to another.**(396)**

Social power the capacity of one person to alter the actions of another.**(359)**

Social stratification the process in a social system by which scarce and valuable resources are distributed unequally to status positions that become more or less permanently ranked in terms of the share of valuable resources each receives.**(389)**

Social trends broad directions in which a society is moving.**(506)**

Source credibility a communications source's perceived expertise, objectivity, or trustworthiness.**(169)**

Standard Metropolitan Statistical Area (SMSA) a major market area as defined by the U.S. Census, used as a reference by market researchers, manufacturers, and retailers.**(461)**

Starch Test a widely used commercial measure of advertising recall for magazines.**(125)**

Status crystallization the extent to which different indicators of a person's status (e.g., income, ethnicity, occupation) are consistent with one another.**(393)**

Status hierarchy a ranking of social desirability in terms of consumers' access to such resources as money, education, and luxury goods.**(389)**

Status symbols products that are purchased and displayed to signal membership in a desirable social class.**(404)**

Stimulus ambiguity a condition occurring when the meanings conveyed by an ad are unclear. Ambiguous stimuli will usually be interpreted in a way that is consistent with the consumer's own set of needs and motives.**(55)**

Stimulus discrimination occurs when behavior caused by two stimuli is different, as when consumers learn to differentiate a brand from its competitors.**(102)**

Stimulus generalization occurs when the behavior caused by a reaction to one stimulus occurs in the presence of other, similar stimuli.**(102)**

Storage knowledge entered in long-term memory is integrated with what is already in memory and "warehoused" until needed.**(112)**

Store image a store's "personality," composed of such attributes as location, merchandise suitability, and the knowledge and congeniality of the sales staff.**(316)**

Store loyal a pattern of consistent patronage and positive attitudes toward a store.**(314)**

Subculture a group whose members share beliefs and common experiences that set them apart from other members of a culture.**(416)**

Subliminal perception the processing of information presented below the level of the consumer's awareness.**(45)**

Superego the system that internalizes society's rules and that works to prevent the id from seeking selfish gratification.**(79)**

Symbolic interactionism a sociological approach which stresses that relationships with other people play a large part in forming the self. People live in a symbolic environment, and the meaning attached to any situation or object is determined by a person's interpretation of these symbols.**(208)**

Symbolic self-completion theory this theory predicts that people who have an incomplete self-definition in some context will compensate by acquiring symbols associated with a desired social identity.**(211)**

Syncratic decisions purchase decisions made jointly by both spouses.**(287)**

Synoptic ideal a model of spousal decision making where the husband and wife take a common view and act as joint decision makers, assigning each other well-defined roles and making mutually beneficial decisions to maximize the couple's joint utility.**(288)**

Targeted marketing strategy defines both a market and the tactics used by the organization to satisfy that market.**(7)**

Taste cultures a group of consumers who share aesthetic and intellectual preferences.**(398)**

Terminal values end states desired by members of a culture.**(488)**

The Nine Nations of North America a geographical classification scheme that divides America into separate "nations" within the geographical boundaries of the United States and Canada, each with its own priorities, customs, and consumption patterns.**(466)**

Theory of reasoned action an updated version of the Fishbein multi-attribute attitude theory that considers such factors as social pressure and A_{act} (the attitude toward the act of buying a product, rather than on just the product itself).**(155)**

Trickle-down theory of fashion
states that fashions spread as the result of status symbols associated with the upper classes "trickling down" to other social classes as these consumers try to emulate those with greater status.**(563)**

Two-factor theory proposes that two separate psychological processes are operating when a person is repeatedly exposed to an ad. Repetition increases familiarity and thus reduces uncertainty about the product but over time boredom increases with each exposure. At some point the amount of boredom incurred begins to exceed the amount of uncertainty reduced, resulting in wear-out.**(176)**

Value system a culture's ranking of the relative importance of values.**(480)**

Values and Lifestyles (VALS) a psychographic segmentation system used to categorize consumers into clusters, or "VALS Types."**(500)**

Want the particular form of consumption chosen to satisfy a need.**(67)**

Weber's Law the stronger the initial stimulus, the greater its change must be for it to be noticed.**(44)**

Word-of-mouth communication information transmitted by individual consumers on an informal basis.**(368)**

Worldview ideas shared by members of a culture about principles of order and fairness.**(478)**

Company & Product Index

THIS INDEX IS DIVIDED INTO three sections: a company and product index, a name index (of people, organizations, books, magazines, movies and television shows), and a general subject index. Glossary terms are in **boldface** type. Page numbers in *italics* reference the Instructor's Annotated Edition.

Rosie the Riveter, 217–218

Salem cigarettes, 56
Sara Lee, 205
Saran Wrap, 85
Schick, 22
Schlitz beer, 500
Scoresby Scotch, 520
Shades of You, 420
Shoppers' Video, 321
Simpson, Bart, 424–425
Skoal Bandit tobacco, 173
Smith & Wesson, 217
Smith & Wollensky restaurant, 137
Smithsonian Institution, 526
Snickers candy, 4, 483
Snuggle fabric softener, 22
Soft Sheen Products, 425
Sony Walkman, 208, 209
Spiegel Co., 228, 314, 315
Sprite, 422
SRI International, *459*, 500
Stouffer's foods, 507
Subaru automobiles, 493
Subliminal Perception Company, 45
Sun-Maid raisins, 436, 437
Sunkist, 257
Sunlight dishwashing liquid, 35–36
Sunsweet prunes, 183
Superman, 519, 521
Swatch, 451

Take Time, Inc., 456
Teddy Grahams, 37
Teenage Mutant Ninja Turtles, 564
Telemundo, 427
Tesco food store, 319

Tide detergent, 258
Toro snow thrower, 55
Total cereal, 152–153
Tower Records, 319
Toyota, 180–181, 427, 568
Trifari, 319
Triumph cigarettes, 179
Trivial Pursuit, 118–119
Tropicana Premium Pack orange juice, 179
Tupperware, 314, 366

UndercoverWear company, 366
United Farm Workers, 503
University of California at Los Angeles (UCLA), 557
Univision, 427, 482
Uptown cigarettes, 422–423

Values and Lifestyles (VALS), *459*, 500,
    502–   506, 591
Victoria's Secret, 201
Virginia Slims cigarettes, 1, 3, 205, 266
Vitabath, 531
Vivarin, 80
Volkswagen, 178, 326, 327

Wacky Wallwackers, 566
Wendy's restaurants, 332
Western Union Company, 467, 468
Weyerhauser lumber, 323–324
Whittle Communications, 9, 124, 125, 280
Winn-Dixie supermarkets, 430
WQBA-FM radio, 429

Young & Rubican, *22*
Young American's Bank, 298

Name Index

Subject Index

cartoon characters, 109–110, 173
case study, research, 21–22
catalog sales, 313–314, 456, 468
categorization,
        cultural, 558–560
        of family members, 282
        primitive, 35, *255*
        product, 255–259
        See also market segmentation
cathexis, body, 224, 582
Catholic subcultures, 124, 426–427, 434,
        525, *538*
celebrities, 168, 169, 354, 424–425
        artifacts of, 527–528, 541
        as communication sources, 171–174, 573
        emulation of, 112
        involvement with, 69–70
        product identification with, 124
        Q ratings of, 174
        unit relation with, 146, 207
        See also endorsements, celebrity;
                personality (product or brand)
censorship, 368, 484–485
census, national, 279–280
Central Americans. *See* Hispanic-Americans
central route to persuasion, 187–188
ceremonies. *See* **rituals**
chain model, means-end, 488–490, 586
chain stores, 463, 467, 468
change,
        agents of, 5, 158, 292, 403–404, 553–
                554, 561, 563–564
        awareness of product, 44
character, national, 483–486, 486–492, 524
characters, advertising,
        cartoon, 109–110, 173
        imaginary human, 168, 184, 218, 519,
                522, 537, 572
        product icon, 12, 58, 110, 190, 522
characters, television, 168, 184, 190–191, 279,
        284
charity and donations, 83, 143, 360, 402, 539
child-care services, 281, 286, 454
children, 79
        baby, 454, 539
        cognitive development of, 296–297
        in the family, 280–282, 434
children as consumers, 117, 281–282, 286–287,
        293, 438, 454, 458
        advertising to, 300–304, 375, 425, 448,
                450, 571, 573
        brand consciousness of, *87*, 297–298, 448,
                558
        influence of, 290–291, 448–451
        purchasing by, *294*, 297–298, 311–312,
                449
        teaching negative behavior to, 111–112
        toys for, 295–303, 424, 425, 438, 534–
                535, 564, 573
        training of, 111–112, 294–300, 558, 573
China, People's Republic of, 58, 322, 389–391,
        491–492, 557
Chinese-Americans, 431–432
chocolate and memory, *39*
choice, freedom of, 47–48, 91, 91–94, 141–142,
        156, 561

See also decision making, consumer;
        purchasing, consumer
Christian subcultures, 426–427, 434–435,
        436–438, 517
Christmas industry, 517
chunking, information, 114, 175
churches, roles of the, 426–427
cigarettes,
        advertising of, 53, 55, 58–59, 431, 558
        consumption of, 1–3, 7–8, 10–11, 13–14,
                18–19, 21, 22, 91, 94, 142,
                191, 422–423, 431
        See also smokers
class, social. *See* **social class**
classic fashions, 565–566, 582
classical conditioning, 101–102, 107–110, 582
classification (product). *See* products
cleaning products (household), 35–36, 142,
        180, 245, 258, 427, 570
clinical psychology, 13–14
closure, principle of, 55–56, 57, 582
clothing products, 65–66, 163–164, 166, 169–
        170, 201–202, 228, 229, 285, *294*,
        366, 427, 557
        anticonformist, 367, 407–408, 415, 450
        career apparel, 323, 496, 562–563
        fashion innovations in, 373, 559–560,
                561–567
        shoes, 375–376, 406, 565–566
        wardrobe consultants on, 267–268
clubs and membership groups, 353–354, 357,
        378
        consumers, 111, 300, 303, 359, 456, 458
        fan, 69–70
        men's, 353–354, 452
        women's, 378, 451
clues. *See* cues, perceptual
cluster analysis,
        statistical, 468–469
        VALS system, *459*, 500, 502–506, 591
        VALS2 system, 504–506
clusters of possessions, 166, 398, 400, 495–496,
        497
        AIOs, 498–500, 581
clutter, advertising, 48, 49, 52, 461, 581
co-consumers, 327–329
cocooning, 509
codes, class, 398–401
        See also **norms**; **social class**
codes, product (bar), 19
coercion, power from, 361–362
cognition, 134–135, 582
        categorization and, 254–259
        independence of affect and, 137–138
        memory and, 112–127
        principle of consistent, 141–148, 588
        See also **attitudes**; beliefs
cognitive development, 296–297, 301, 582
        See also **learning**, human
cognitive dissonance, 75, 142, 582
cognitive learning, 105–107, 111–112, 177–179,
        186, 582
cognitive psychology, 16
cognitive responses to advertising, 41
cognitive structure, 255, 582
cohabitating couples, 282–283
cohesiveness, group, 357

and cultural selection, 550–551, 563–564
family, 288–294
heuristic, 261–268, 290–291, 585
individual and group, 84–85, 276–279
memory and, 112
multi-attribute model of, 150–152
noncompensatory rules of, 259–260, 587
organizational vs., 276–279
rational, 15–16, 180–181, 240–241, 251, 588
reference group influences on, 354–362, 563
sex roles and, 288–290
theories of, 15–16, 240–247, 259–260, 365–366, 536–537
types of group influence on, 355
See also purchasing, consumer
decision polarization, 366, 583
declassification, product, 38
defacement, product, 541–542
deindividuation, 365, 366, 583
delivery services, 489–490
demand, building, 246–247, 339–340, 563
demarketing, 436
demography, 2, 8, 13–14, 19–20, *226*, 496–499, 534, *538*, 584
statistics, 279, 418, 419, 425–426, 429, 430, 431, 453, 455
See also geodemographics; statistics
density *vs.* crowding, 328–329
depersonalization, 538–539
desacralization, 524–525, 584
design styles, 553, 558–560
designated drivers campaign, 191
designer products, 171, 563, 572
destruction, product, 541–542
detective stories, 568
determinant attributes, 7, 584
deviance, social,
consumer crime and, 539–541, 568
fear of, 363, 450
diet and exercise, 227–229, 509
differential threshold, 44, 584
differentiation, brand, 174–175
diffusion,
of innovations, 551–556, 584
of responsibility, 365
direct mail marketing, 48, 110, 284–285, 313–314
disasters, environmental, 337
disclaimers, advertising, 301
disconfirmation model, expectancy, 337, 584
discontinuous innovation, 555
discounts, price, 263
discrimination, stimulus, 51, 102, 110, 590
display,
conspicuous consumption, 211, 359, 403, 405–407, 491–492, *537*, 563, 583
parody, 407–408, 563, 587
store, 316–317, 334
disposition, product, 338–340
dissatisfaction, consumer, 337–338
dissonance, cognitive, 75, 142, 582
distortion of information, 370, 371
distraction, advertising as, *126*, 183
distribution, retail, *553*

divorce rates, 281
Dixie, region of, 465, 466–467
do-it-yourself products and services, 323–324, 329
donations and charity, 83, 143, 360, 402, 539
donors, blood or organ, 539
door-in-the-face technique, *143*, 365
double standard, the, 539
See also sex roles
downscaling, 407, 436
drama, marketing message, 184–186
dramaturgical perspective. See role theory
drawings, projective, 86–89, *91*, 302, 318, 333, 371, 532–533
dreams, 81
drive, 66–67, 101, 584
drive theory, 68
drunk driving, 500, 501
duration, stimulus, 51

early purchasers, 373–374, 375
eating disorders, 228–229
Ec (European Community). *See* Europe
ecology, human, 13–14, 478
economic time, 329–331
economics, 14, *22*, 83, 562, 563
of information, 93–94, 250–251
Ecotopia, 466–467
education, 457
of consumers, 409, 429–430
income and, 391–392, 394
levels, 394, 426, 431
effect, the von Restorff, 120
effects, hierarchy of, 135–136, 143, 585
effort,
problem-solving, 243–244
search, 247–248, 251–253
See also **involvement**, consumer
ego, 79, 85–86, 166, 584
ego involvement, 70, 584
800 numbers, 111
elaborated codes, 399–401
elaboration, 69, 114–115
elaboration likelihood model (ELM), 187–190, 584
elderly consumers, 445, 455–461, *459*, 462
electronic technologies, 19, 36, 314, 320–321
electronics industry products, 259–260, 374, 431
elimination by aspects rule, 260
elite culture, 567–566
ELM, 69, 187–190, 584
embeds (magazine advertising), 45–46, 584
emergent design (research), *21*
emic perspective, 483–486, 584
emotional appeal (message), 76, 180–181, 334–335, 484
fear motivations and, 183–184, 363, 370, *478*, 479
irritating, 140
empty nest families, 287
Empty Quarter, The, 466
enacted norms, 480
encoding of information, 112–115, 584
enculturation, 480–481, 584
endorsements, celebrity, 171–174, 360, 375–376, 519

mavens, marketing, 373–374, *374*
MC, 155
meaning,
    memory and, 113–117
    of signs (semiotics), 14–15, 59, 398–401,
        589
    stimulus, 57–59, 558–560
means-end chain model, 488–490, 586
Means-End Conceptualization of the
        Components of Advertising
        Strategy (MECCAS), 489–490
measurement. *See* testing and measurement
MECCAS, 489–490
media, mass, 11–12, 70, 295, 503
    African-Americans and the, 420–425
    Christian, 438
    communications, 167, 551–552, 569
mediation, 519
memorabilia, 121, 529
    See also souvenirs industry
memory, human, 522, 586
    activation models, 115–117, 581
    interference, 121–122, 586
    interference and decay of, 121–122
    internal, 112–115, 248
    long-term, 113–115, 118–121
    odor and, *39*
    process, 112–113
    retrieval, 118–127, 248, 252
    selectivity of, *120*, 168
    sensory, 113–114, 120–121, 589
    sleeper effect and, 168
    storage, 115–118, 249
    systems, 113–115
    tests and measurements, 120, 124–127
    types of, 113
    See also information processing, human;
        learning human
men, 463, 500
    body changes by, 230–231
    clothing for, 6, 496, 563, 567
    fatherhood roles of, 222–224, 281, 282,
        284, 422, 533
    masculinity concepts of, 22, 83, 166,
        216, 479
    stereotypes of, 418, 496, 500, 501, 555,
        562, 563
    See also sex roles
mentions, product, 571–572
message-response involvement, 70
messages, marketing, 167, 571–575
    argument presentation in, 177–179
    as art form, 184–186
    characteristics of, 174–186
    emotional *vs.* rational appeals in, 180–181
    ignored, 48, *50*
    options for, 174–175
    positive and negative elements of, 175, 458
    repetition and duration of, 176–177
    sources of, 167–174, 522
    subliminal, 44–48
    three basic components of, 58–59
    verbal *vs.* visual, 175–177
metaphors, marketing message, 184–186
methodologies, research,
    qualitative, 83–91
    See also consumer behavior research

MexAmerica region, 466–467
Mexican-Americans, 430, 530
microeconomics, 13–14
Middle America region, 466
middle class Americans, 390–391, 395, 422,
    564
middle-aged consumers, 452–455
mindlessness, 106
minority groups. *See* names of sub-cultures
mnemonic qualities, 122
mobility, social, 395–396
modeling, behavior, 106–107, 111–112, 295,
    357
    See also celebrities
models, real (non-celebrity), 173, 356, 358,
    375–376
modesty, norms of, 485–486
monetary issues, 253
money, 527, 537–538
    social class and, 391–393, 401–403, 454,
        468–469
monomyths, 519
mood congruence effect, 119
mood management theory, *137*
moods, consumer, 334–335
moral lesson messages, 183–184
mores, societal, 481
Moslem subculture, 370
motherhood. *See under* women
Mother's Day, 533
motifs, dominant fashion, 558–560
motivation, 249, 587
    cognitive consistency and, 141–148, 588
    conflicting, 74–76
    Dichter's interpretations of, 81–82
    direction of, 73–78
    Freudian interpretations of, 79–81
    hidden, 79–91
    major areas of, 82
    the process of, 66–67, 106
    strength of, 67–73
motivation to comply (MC), 155
motivational research, 81–83, 498, 587
movies, 369, 426, 427, 448, 464, 537, 559, 568
    blockbuster, 519–522, 569–570
    product placement in, *37*, 45, 47, 123, 571
    See also names of movies in the NAME
        INDEX
multi-attribute attitude models, 150–155, 587
multicultural dimensions, 4, 78, 219, 280, 284,
    291
    of American endorsers abroad, 174
    of bargaining, 322
    country-of-origin information, 262
    cross-cultural and, 479–480, 556–557
    of ethnic dolls, 425
    of food preferences, 43, 74, 370, 464, 481
    of fragrance preferences, 39
    of gift giving, 531, 534
    of modern myths, 519–522
    of product counterfeiting, 102
    reasoned action theory and, 156
    of social hierarchies, 389–391
    of spousal purchasing decisions, 289
    of time conceptions, 333
    See also cultural values; international
        marketing

multiple selves, 208–209
multiplicative rule, triad, *145*
MUM Effect, 370
museums, *20*, 526, 529, 560, 567, 569, 571
music, 56–57, 113, 138, 316, 565, 569
    age cohort, 447
    functional (environmental), 39–40
    industry specialists, 551, 552
    product jingles, 56, 102, 103, 108, 120–121
    rock, 47, 138, 174, 180, 220, 415, 416,
        447, 454–455, 551, 552,
        564–565, 570–571
mythology, product, 12, 94
    See also characters, advertising
myths, cultural, 518–523, 587

names, product, 55, 113
    attitude elicited by, *140*, 262
    capitalizing on well-known, 102, *108*, 552–
        553, 569
    changing, 4
    choosing, 89
    conditioning and, 107–110
    licensing of, 102, 109–110, 146–147, 407–
        408, 495–496
    made-up, 107
    public domain, 110
    puns in, *108*
    television show, 122
names of subcultures,
    baby boomers, 280, 452–455, 534, 582
    born-again Christian, 426, 436–438
    BUPPIEs, 422
    Dead Heads, 415
    gay, 282–283
    green consumers, 477
    hippies, 415, 450
    skippies, 449–450
    tweens, 450
    WASPs, 435
    YUCAs, 429
    yuppies, 422, 453–454, 477, 495–496,
        497
    See also ethnic groups; *names of religious*
        groups
national character, 483–486, 524, 587
Nations, Nine. *See* **Nine Nations of North**
        America, The
Native Americans, 230–231, 405–406
NB, 155–156
need recognition, 245–246
needs,
    artificial, 91–92, 93
    biological vs. learned, 67–68
    channeling of unacceptable, 80–81
    classifications of, 76–78, 500, 502–503
    concerns about manipulation of, 91–94
    conflicting, 74–76
    new sets of, 246–247
    wants *vs.*, 73–74, 92
negative elements of advertisements, 175
negative messages in advertising, 139–140,
    190, 362
negative reinforcement, 104–105, *118,*
    369–370, 587
negative self-image, *205*, 226, 228–229
negotiation of outcomes, *21*

networks,
    associative, 115–118
    referral, 377–379
New Age, 466
new attributes (product), 153
new breed, 480
New England, 19–20, 466
New Grown-Ups, the, 403–404
new needs (consumer), 246–247
new products,
    adoption prerequisites, 555–556
    diffusion of, 551–556, 563–565
    failure of, 7–8, 94, 110, 254–255, 337–
        338, 458
    marketing of, 7, 10–11, 108–110, 179,
        246–247, 369–370, 372, 487,
        551–552
    See also **innovation**; products
new task purchasing, 293–294
New York City, 463
new-collar workers, 454–455, 587
newlyweds, 280, 286
newspapers, 175, 451
Nine Nations of North America, The, 466–
    467, 590
nodes, memory, 115–117, 122
nomothetic research, 17
non-celebrities, endorsements by, 173, 356,
    358, 375–376
non-consumption as a life-style, 509
non-store shopping, 313–314
noncompensatory decision rules, 259–260,
    587
normative beliefs (NB), 155–156
normative influence, 354, 355, 587
normative social influence, 363, 587
norms, 155–156, 362, *372,* 480–481, 484–
    486, 532, 587
nostalgia, 121, 123–124, 446–447
notes, fragrance, *40*
nouveau riches, 403
novelty, pattern unpredictability, 52–53, 120,
    362, 566
    See also **innovation**
nuclear family, 279, 587
nudity, 485
numbers. *See* statistics

obedience and compliance, 364–366
obituary, product, 90
object, attitude. *See* **attitude object (Ao)**
object, the marketing message, 58–59
objectification, 526, 527
objective self-awareness theory (OSA), 204
objectivity,
    of consumers, 20, 253
    of data, *20*
    of researchers, 18
observability, new product, 556
observational learning, 106–107, 587
obsolescence, 549, 571
occupation, prestige by, 90, 392, 394, 496, 536
odor, perception, 39–40, *120*, 319
oil industry, 92, 325
old money, 401–403
on-set product placement, 573
ongoing search, 249

plots, formula, 567, 568
plugs, product, 572–574
point of purchase stimuli (POP), 318–319, 588
point-of-sale, *255*
polarization, attitude, 147–148
polarization, decision, 366, 583
political statements, 541
polling, consumer, 157, 171–172
polychronicity, 331
POP, 318–319, 588
popular culture. *See* culture, popular
popularity, endorser. *See under* celebrities
population figures. *See* **demography**; statistics
positioning. *See* product positioning
positive reinforcement, 104–105, 361, 532–533, 588
positivism, *15*, 16, 17–20, 588
possessions, worldly,
    accumulation of, 490–492, *566*
    clusters of, 398, 400, 495–496, 497, 498–500, 581
    materialistic emphasis on, 210, 490–492, 522, 523, 586
    memory and, 122–124
    women as, 405, 538–539
    See also **gift-giving rituals**
POSSLQ, 282
post-positivism, *15*
post-purchase dissonance, 142–143
posters (wall media), 451, 541
postpurchasing, issues, 5
posture, body, 560
potlatch, the, 405–406
poverty, time, 330–331
power,
    brand, 264–265
    family, 288–290, 293
    need for, 76
    perceptions of, 478–479
    social bases of, 359–362, 435, 478–479, 589
pre-school children, 281
preconsciousness, processing and, *107*
predicting consumer behavior, research on, 17–20, 204
prepurchasing, 5, 249
pressure, social, 155, 331–332, 537
    See also **norms**
prestige products. *See* **status symbols**
prices,
    price-quality relationship, 263–264, 487, 527
    product, 7, 102, 540, 562
    product placement, 573
primary demand, 246–247
priming, category, *259*
priming, interpretation, 55
principle of cognitive consistency, 141–148, 588
principle of least interest, 363
principle of similarity, the, 56, 590
principle-oriented consumers, 505–506
principles, gestalt perception, 55–57
print media, 89, *124*, 175, 219, 248, 283, 360, 371, 420, 485
    comics and books, 109–110, 485, 519

high-involvement by, 70, 73, 373, 492, 573
newspapers, 175, 451
positioning of, 51, *124*, 327, 399, 421–422, 432, 438, 451, 454, 458, 460, 465
value emphasis in, 438, 461, 487, 488, 525, 567
See also magazines
priorities,
    cultural, 480–481, 487
    needs and, 77
privacy, consumer, information sales and, 19–20
private-label brands, 110
pro-bono advertising, 190–191
proactive interference, 122
problem recognition, 243–247, 588
procedural time, 333
product complementarity, 495–496, 588
product form, 7, 44
product icons. *See under* characters, advertising
product life-cycle, 171, 180, 246, 564, 567
    availability, 142
    family life cycle and, 286–287
    innovation and diffusion, 551–556
    obsolescence, 549, 571
    recycling, 338–340
    trials or testing of, 157, 264, 300–301, 556
    usage, 20, 332, 334, 423
    See also life-cycle
product line extensions, 109–110, 299, 420
Product, Place, Price, Promotion (Four P's), 7, 586
product placement, 7, 125, 284–285, 572–574, 588
    See also placement, advertising
product positioning, 3, 7, 110, 115–116
    categorization and, 257–259, 498–500, 499
    maps, 10–11, *91*, 497
    strategies, 256–259, *316*, 329, 389, 404, 418, 422–423, 438, 458
    See also **targeted marketing strategy**
production, means of, 386
productivity, music and, 41
products,
    anti-consumption of, 509, 541–542
    categorization of, 38, 255–259
    category prototype, 257–258
    for children, *294*, 297–303
    complementarity of, 495–496, 588
    ethnic group usage of, 420
    evaluative criteria for, 259–261, 316, 584
    evoked set of, 115–116, 254, 584
    fake, 102
    generic, *3*, 102, 110, 427
    gray market, 456–457
    health concerns and, 7–8, 184, 188, 190, *211*, 247, 398, 431, 509
    information search about, 244, 247–253, 263, 278, 278–279, 292, 322, 329, 586
    level of satisfaction with, 335–338
    major motives linked to types of, 82, 488–490
    market beliefs about, 263–264
    materialistic value of, 490–492, 571

responses (consumer),
    barriers to, 87
    baseline or matrix, *87*
    dissatisfaction, 337–338
    eliciting, 143, 393–394
    focus group, 22, 42–43, 83–85, 375,
        570, 585
    problem-solving, 243–244
    projective, 85–91, 302, 318, 333, 371,
        532–533, 588
    reactance, 142, 368, 458, 588
    See also multicultural dimensions;
        testing and measurement
restaurant industry, 74, 123, 137, 325, 388,
    417, 463
restricted codes, 399–401
retailing. *See* stores
retention, behavior, 106
retirement, attitudes toward, 457–458
retrieval, information, 112–113, 118–127, 588
retro ads, 123
retroactive interference, 122
reunion-goers, 446–447
reward, reinforcement, 104–105, 361,
    532–533, 588
risk, 277, 293
    perception, 251, 253, 372, 587
    social, 70, 168, 253, 366
    tolerance of, 84–85, 554, 564
risky shift, 365–366
rites of passage, 248, 535–536, 588
ritual artifacts, 529–530, 533–534, 556, 588
rituals, 2, 288, 362, 405–406, 528, 529–538,
    588
    gift-giving, 20, 35, 334, 451–452, 529,
        531–534, 585
    levels of, 529–530
    product consumption, 2, 87
    wedding and marriage, 248, 280, 406,
        556
    See also **behavior**
rock music industry, 47, 138, 174, 180, 220,
    415, 416, 447, 454–455, 551, 552,
    564–565, 570–571
    See also celebrities
role theory, 5–6, 208, 210–211, 325
roles,
    reversal, 220–221
    transition, 535–536
    See also sex roles; theater
Roman Catholic subcultures, 124, 426–427,
    434, 525, *538*
romance novels, 568
room uses. *See under* household
routes to persuasion, 187–190
routines, behavior, *530*
rules,
    compensatory decision, 259, 261
    of informal behavior (norms), 362, *372*,
        480–481, 484–486, 532, 587
    noncompensatory decision, 259–260
rumors, costly, 369–370
RV's, 494

sacralization, 526, 528–529, 589
sacred, the, 490, 523, 526, 589
sales promotion. *See* promotion strategies

salespersons, roles of service personnel and,
        315, 319, 321–322, 323–325, 496
salience, 290
    of beliefs, 150
    brand, 120, 122
sampling,
    in-store, 319
    product, 157, 264, 300–301, 451, 556
sandwich generation, 282
Santa Claus myth, the, 517, 522, 523, 526
Satanism, 47
satisfaction levels, consumer, 335–338
saturation, market, 313–314, 564–565
scales. *See* testing and measurement
scanning, product code, 19
schedule, reinforcement, 104–105
schema, 33, 55, 117, 589
science, designs from, 560
science fiction, 521–522, 568
scientific method, 17–19, *21*
    See also consumer behavior research
scripts, behavior, 117, 529–530, 533
search, information. *See* **information search**
seasons, colors analysis by, *39*
secondary demand, 246–247, 339–340
secret shoppers, 104–105
sectors, culture production system, 550–551
security needs, 166, 527
segmentation, market. *See* market segmentation
selection,
    collective, 561–562
    cultural, 550–551
    perceptual, 48–54
self-completion, symbolic, 211, 590
self-concept, 70, 202–203, 395–396, 457–458,
        462, 589
    consumption and, 210–213, 267–268, 355,
            428, 456–458, 493–494, 539
    ego and, 70, 79, 85–86, 166, 584
self-congruity theory, 212
self-consciousness, 204–205
self-esteem, 205–208, 457–458
    body image and, 224–232, 485–486,
            489, 560, 562–563, 582
self-gifts, 532–533, 537–538, 589
self-help tapes, subliminal, 46–47
self-identity, 376–377, *558*
    age and, 457–460, 462
    class and, 395
    ethnicity and, 421–422, 430
    extended, 204, 213, 585
    female, *211*
    life-style and, 493–496, 539
    secret, 87, 534
self-image congruence models, 212, 326, 589
self-perception theory, 143, 589
    See also **perception**
self-service, 325
selves, multiple, 208–209
semantic-differential scale, 149
semantics, 14
semiotics, 14–15, 59, 398–401, 589
senior consumers, 445, 455–461, *459*, 462
sensation, 33, 589
sensory memory, 113–114, 120–121, 589
sensory systems (human), 33, 41-42, 113–
            114, 120–121, 589

product, 3, 58, 80–81, 388–389, 400,
    495–496, 554, 570–573
sacred, 523, 526–529
status, 74, 404–409, 496, 497, 504, 507,
    531, 535, 563, 590
    See also **consumption constellations;**
        fashion; signs
symbols, sex. *See* celebrities; sex
symbols of status. *See* **status symbols**
syncratic decisions, 287, 590
syndicated services (consumer data), 18–19,
    125–126, 157, 279
synoptic ideal, 288–289, 590
system, value. *See* **value systems**
systems, color analysis, 38–39
systems, high tech. *See* electronic technologies

taboos, cultural, 484–486
tactfulness, 484–486, 531
Taiwan, 492
tampering, product, 541–542
targeted marketing strategy, 3, 7, 450, 497,
    590
    to African-Americans, 420–425
    to children, 298–304, 375, 425, 448,
        450, 571, 573
    to the elderly, 445, *459*, 460–461
    See also marketing opportunity
task definition, 334
taste cultures, 364, 398–400, 483, 492–496,
    561, 590
taste perception. *See* **perception**, taste
TAT, 87
tattoos, 231–232
techniques, research. *See* consumer behavior
    research
technology, innovations in, 19, 320–321,
    554–555, 560
    See also electronic technologies
teenagers, *47*, 205, 447–452, 557
telenovellas, 427
telephone industry, 111, 114, *430*, 479, 541
    See also COMPANY & PRODUCT
        INDEX
television, 420, 438, 451, 460, 464, 525
    children's, 295, 301–304, 571, 573
    informercials, 169, 301–302
    involvement by, 70, 492, 537, 557, 569,
        571–572
    news, 120, 574
    product placement on, 572–575
    role models on, 190–191, 279, 295, 427,
        454, 455, 557, 568
    show titles, 122
    targeted cable, 427, 450–451, 453, 482
    See also names of shows in the NAME
        INDEX
television advertising, 50, 319
    informercials, 169, 301–302
    positive and negative elements in, 175,
        460–461
    and programming, 54, 334–335, 526,
        572–574
    See also advertising
temporal factors, 329–334
    See also time

tension,
    cognitive dissonance, 75, 142, 582
    reduction motivation, 67–68, *478*, 479
terminal values, 488–490, 590
terror management theory, *478*
testing and measurement, 19
    attitude, 148–149, 156–157, 302
    behavior prediction, 156–157, 204
    consumer involvement scale, 71–73
    eye-movement, 51–52, 120
    of incorrect inferences, 117–118
    Information Display Board (IDB), 251
    marital power relations, 289
    memory, 120, 124–127
    opinion leadership, 376–379
    projective, 85–91, 302, 318, 333, 371,
        532–533, 588
    sexual identity, *216*
    of social class, 392–395
    Starch Test, 125–126, 589
    taste, 42–43, *43*
    thematic apperception test (TAT), 87
    See also responses (consumer)
testing products. See trials, product
Texas, 463, 464
textures, product, 41–42
The Nine Nations of North America,
    466–467, 590
theater, retailing and services as, 314–316,
    319–320, 324–325
theft and fraud, 47, 539–541, 568
Thematic Apperception Test (TAT), 87
theme parks, 332, 334, 433, 526–527
theory,
    of attitude functions, 166, 585
    balance, 144–147, 582
    behavioral learning, 100–105, 135, 582
    buyclass purchasing, 278, 292–293, 582
    cognitive learning, 105–107, 111–112,
        177–179, 186, 582
    congruity, 147–148, 212, 583
    cultivation, 295, 304, 583
    drive, 68
    expectancy, 68, 337, 584
    role, 5–6, 208, 210–211, 325, 334,
        538–539
    self-perception, 143, 589
    social comparison, 364, 589
    social judgment, 143–144, 589
    symbolic self-completion, 211, 590
    trickle-down fashion, 563–564, 591
    two-factor, 176–177, 591
    See also consumer behavior research
theory of reasoned action, 155–156, 591
thinness, ideal of, 478
Third World, the, 556–558
    See also names of countries
thresholds, sensory, 43–44, 47–48
through-put sector, *551*
throw-away society, 338
tie relationships, 377–378
tie-ins, multi-media, 73
time,
    allocation of, 329–330, 492, 507–508
    changing attitudes over, 157–158, 264–
        265, 482–483, 487, 571
    compression by speech, 41, 120–121